Exploring Marriage and the Family

Critical Readers

William Arkin
San Jose State University

Carlfred Broderick
University of Southern California

Larry Bumpass
University of Wisconsin

Mark Canfield
Howard Community College

Carole Carroll
Middle Tennessee State University

Louis Clunk
Golden West College

Harold Cooper
Randolph-Macon College

Kenneth Davidson
University of Wisconsin at Eau Claire

Ben Dickerson
Stephen F. Austin State University

Jacquie Eddleman
Southern Illinois University

Carol Ehrlich
University of Maryland Baltimore County

Cynthia F. Epstein
Bureau of Applied Social Research

Harold Feldman
Cornell University

Charles Figley
Purdue University

Jerome Folkman
Ohio State University

Fay Greckel
Indiana University Southeast

Loretta Greenleaf
West Virginia University

Rudolph Harris
Des Moines Area Community College

Joan Huber
University of Illinois

Martha L. Ice
College of DuPage

William Kenkel
University of Kentucky

Carolynne Kieffer
University of Missouri–Columbia

Marvin R. Koller
Kent State University

E. E. LeMasters
University of Wisconsin

Roger W. Libby
University of Massachusetts

Eleanor Macklin
State University of New York at Oswego

Lonny Myers
Midwest Population Center, Chicago

Sarah Pappas
Hillsborough Community College

LaVada Pepper
Richland College

Olgert Pocs
Illinois State University

Ira Reiss
University of Minnesota

Carl Ridley
University of Arizona

Christa Reiser
East Carolina University

Constantina Safilios-Rothschild
University of California at Santa Barbara

Gene Starbuck
Mesa College

Marvin Sussman
Wake Forest University

Patricia Thompson
Herbert Lehman College, CUNY

James Thompson
Tennessee Wesleyan College

Charlotte Twombly
Essex Community College

J. Richard Udry
University of North Carolina

Robert Walsh
Illinois State University

James Walters
University of Georgia

Melvin J. Williams
East Carolina University

Exploring Marriage and the Family

David Knox
East Carolina University

Scott, Foresman and Company   Glenview, Illinois
Dallas, Tex.   Oakland, N.J.   Palo Alto, Cal.   Tucker, Ga.   London, England

To Frances, Lisa, and David III

Knox, David, 1943–
    Exploring marriage and the family.
    Includes bibliographies and index.
    1. Marriage.   2. Family.   I. Title.
HQ734.K663   301.42   78-10937
ISBN 0-673-15046-1

The author and publisher would like to thank all sources for the use of their material. The credit lines for copyrighted materials appearing in this work may be found in the Acknowledgments section beginning on page 562. The Acknowledgments section is an extension of this copyright page.

12345678910–MUR–8584838281807978

Preface

My years of teaching courses in marriage and the family have convinced me that students learn more if a course builds on their personal insights and natural interest in the subject. This premise has shaped *Exploring Marriage and the Family*. The text has evolved through many stages of planning, research, writing, and refinement. But at each stage I have worked with two primary goals in mind: to develop a carefully researched and up-to-date text, and to keep it readable and interesting to students.

The basic material that forms the core of any marriage and family course is presented here in a straightforward, developmental framework. As the table of contents reveals, there is ample discussion of sex roles, love relationships, sexuality, dating, marriage, and the rearing of a family. But the text also moves beyond these basics to discuss important topics of current interest. Singlehood, cohabitation, sexual and economic fulfillment, dual-career marriages, childfree marriages, and the years beyond middle age all receive in-depth treatment. And, to stimulate thinking about directions of change, I have concluded each chapter with comments on current and future trends in marriage and family life.

In addition to having a broad base of well-researched material, the text is easy to read and geared to students. Each chapter is clearly and carefully organized so that it is easy to follow. Plentiful examples reinforce key points and consistently relate abstract concepts back to human experience. Lively quotations sprinkled throughout the text add another perspective, while photographs and cartoons both illustrate and amplify the basic material.

The text is self-contained pedagogically, with the important features of a study guide built right in to make each student's initial reading and later study more effective. Chapter outlines provide a preview, and chapter summaries and study questions provide a review for every chapter. In addition, each chapter closes with an up-to-date bibliography that will help students research term papers and provide sources for further reading and study. A glossary at the end of the book defines important terms, supplying the page numbers on which they are presented, and appendixes cover basic material on sexual anatomy, reproduction, and venereal disease. A final appendix listing resources and organizations will aid students who research special topics and prove useful as a guide to reliable counseling and consumer services.

Exploring Marriage and the Family was written to be read by students, but it was planned as a flexible tool for teachers to teach from. The accompanying Instructor's Manual provides teaching aids as well as about nine hundred test items. Since these are keyed to text pages and topics, instructors may select the items that will best test students on the material covered in their course. And the numerous test items for each chapter also enable teachers to vary exams from term to term, or in the case of multiple sections, from class to class.

As the manuscript goes to press, I would like to thank those who have participated in its development. I am grateful to my editors at Scott, Foresman—Walter Dinteman, for his guidance since its inception, and Christine Bowman, for her attention to detail in managing the text into the production stages. The critical readers, whose names appear opposite the title page, made many useful suggestions for improving the text, although they are in no way responsible for any shortcomings. I would also like to thank Barbara Von Hofe, for ensuring the appropriate use of the English language, and Cynthia Wease, who typed the manuscript through numerous drafts.

David Knox

Overview

Contents

PART 1 Perspectives

Chapter **1**

Exploring Marriage and the Family— An Introduction

Call it a clan, call it a network, call it a tribe, call it a family.
Whatever you call it, whoever you are, you need one.
                                                                    Jane Howard

A sophomore was looking over her university catalog to select courses for the next term. A course on marriage and the family caught her eye. Her immediate reaction was that "everybody knows about marriage and the family" and that a course in the area "seems unnecessary." But she and her boyfriend had been having trouble lately, her parents were unhappy in their marriage, and her sister was getting divorced. Perhaps there were some issues worth exploring.

In this introductory chapter we will consider several reasons for studying marriage and the family, define some terms, review the historical background of contemporary marriage and family patterns, examine the question of whether marriage is "obsolete," and consider some of the limitations of social science research. This last goal is important since current research in the field of marriage and the family needs to be interpreted with some cautions in mind.

WHY STUDY MARRIAGE AND THE FAMILY?

In beginning to study any new subject—and especially one which, on the surface, it seems "everybody knows about"—it may be helpful to consider the potential benefits of doing so. Here are some of the benefits you might derive from systematically studying marriage and the family.

Develop a More Rational Perspective of Marriage and Family Relationships

Sex roles, love, and sex are issues we generally respond to on an emotional level. Believing that there are radical differences between women and men, experiencing feelings of love, and managing sexual desires all involve emotions. Part 1 of this text, *Perspectives*, examines these issues from a less personal and more rational viewpoint. Regarding sex roles, while there are biological, psychological, and sociological differences between the sexes, it is interesting to explore to what extent this is true and why the differences exist. In looking at love, we are concerned with what factors create love and with the various styles of loving. In reference to sex, we examine what people value and what they do. In short, we will use social science research to enlarge our perspective on sex roles, love, and sexuality.

Make More Informed Relationship Decisions

We can use the broader perspective on marriage and the family as a basis for making decisions in our own relationships. In Part 2, *Decisions,* we will explore the advantages and disadvantages of marriage, singlehood, living together, contract cohabitation, and communes. We will see that just as the pros and cons for each life-style change, people are continually reevaluating them and making new decisions. Even deciding to marry is not necessarily a permanent decision since about one third of America's spouses return to singlehood.

Learn More About Marriage Relationships

In addition to developing a more rational perspective and making informed decisions, systematically studying marriage relationships may help to move us beyond stereotypes. While there is a tendency to think of all marriage relationships as being similar to those of our parents or friends, there are about 50 million married couples in America.[1] These couples represent different social classes, generations, races, religions, and ethnic backgrounds. In Part 3, *Involvements,* we will look at some of the variety in marriage relationships, including interracial, interreligious, college, military, and group marriages. And since an increasing number of women are pursuing careers outside the home, a separate chapter is devoted to dual-career marriages. But regardless of the type of marriage relationship, intimate involvement necessitates adjustment and compromise. Two areas of adjustment are given special attention—money and sex.

Plan for Successful Family Living

Although fewer married couples are choosing to have children, most do. Not only are the number and spacing of children important, but effective child-rearing procedures are essential. In Part 4, *Families,* planning, having, and rearing children are our major concerns. Families are not always two parents and two children. A family may consist of one parent rather than two and of one child or many children instead of the traditional two. And families don't just consist of small offspring in bassinets and playpens. Young children become teenagers who want rooms, cars, and educations of their own.

Prepare for Transitions

As the children in the family grow up, they leave home. As a result, their parents are alone once again. Unless these spouses have prepared for the later years of life, they may face loneliness, boredom, and financial problems. Part 5, *Transitions,* focuses not only on the "empty nest" stage of the family life cycle, but examines divorce and widowhood as terminal points of the marriage relationship. We will consider the societal and individual reasons for divorce, and we will examine the bereavement process and ways to minimize the trauma of this life crisis.

THE MEANING OF MARRIAGE

Just as we tend to assume that marriage is something with which we are all famil-iar, we may also assume that everyone agrees on what marriage is. Let's define marriage as used in this text and review the major types.

Definition of Marriage

Marriage in America is a relationship in which two adults of the opposite sex make an emotional and legal commitment to live together. Most marriages involve a public announcement and are undertaken with the hope of permanence. Sub-sequent children of the union are socially and legally recognized as legitimate. Let's explore the several aspects of this definition more fully.

An emotional commitment. Most people say they want to get married be-cause they are "in love." This motivation reflects that marriage is a relationship sought by two people who care a great deal for each other, who are happy, and who want to share their lives together. A twenty-seven-year-old single person said, "Marriage is one way of helping to ensure that in the future someone will be caring about me, and I will be caring in return. I want to be involved in a relation-ship that provides a stable feeling of belonging." At its basis, American marriage is an emotional commitment to share time and space with another.

Marriage is that relation between man and woman in which the independence is equal, the dependence mutual, and the obligation reciprocal.

Louis Kaufman Anspacher

A legal commitment. Marriage also involves a legal contract. Unlike the con-tract one signs in purchasing a car or renting an apartment, the marriage contract is between the couple and the state. And the contract can be dissolved only by legal action of the state. The marriage contract is unique in several ways. Its pro-visions are unwritten, its penalties are unspecified, and the terms of the contract are typically unknown to the bride and groom at the time of the wedding (Weitzman, 1975, p. 531). It is interesting to note that no couple is ever given an overview of the terms of their marriage contract. They are never asked if they are willing to assume the duties, rights, and obligations it specifies (Weitzman, 1975, p. 531).

But what do the spouses agree to when they sign the marriage certificate?[2] Although the legal responsibilities vary from state to state, the typical obligations assumed by the wife include: (1) Live where her husband decides (Carlson vs.

Marriage is a legal relationship carrying with it legal responsibilities. This nineteenth-century marriage certificate reminds the partners of their obligations to each other.

Carlson, 1953, p. 256); (2) perform household and domestic duties with no compensation[3] (Rucci vs. Rucci, 1962, p. 221); (3) have sexual relations with her husband (Brown et al., 1971); and (4) assume almost total responsibility for child care (Geduldig vs. Aiello, 1974, p. 41).

In exchange, the husband must provide his wife and children with food, clothing, and shelter[4] and as many of the amenities of life as he can manage by working for wages or a salary[5] (Clark, 1968, p. 181). All states, even those with community property systems, place responsibility of family support on the husband (Kay, 1974).

Public announcement. In addition to the emotional and legal aspects of marriage, most couples publicly announce their intentions before the wedding (Stephens, 1963). "The fact that Diana and I were actually getting married was not real to me until I saw her picture in the paper and read the sentence that we were to be married on June 3," recalled an art major. The newspaper is not the only means of publicly announcing the private commitment. Telling parents, siblings, and friends about wedding plans helps to verify for the partners that they are serious about each other and also helps to marshal the social and economic support to launch the couple into the marital orbit.

Hope of permanence.   "Till death do us part" is included in the traditional marriage ceremony. The phrase reminds the bride and groom that marriage is the most binding commitment they have ever made. Unlike a car payment that stops, or a living-together relationship they can walk away from at any time, marriage represents a point after which there is no easy turning back. Emotional, legal, and economic consequences await the spouse who regards marriage as a lark. And while about one third of all first marriages end in divorce, each marriage is begun with the hope that it will last.

Legitimacy of children.   Our society gives complete social approval for sexual intercourse between individuals who are legally married. Such a relatively stable unit helps to ensure that subsequent children will have adequate care and protection, will be socialized for productive roles in society, and will not become the burden of those who did not conceive them. Marriage grants couples not only the right to have children but authority over them. Where children will live, the personal values they will be taught, and the roles they are to adopt are left to the parents' discretion.[6]

Types of Marriage

While we will explore the range of marriage relationships in Chapter 10, there are two major types of marriage: monogamy (one man and one woman) and polygamy (more than one man and/or more than one woman). Monogamy is the only legal type of marriage in America. While people in group and homosexual relationships may regard themselves as married, legally they are not. Polygamy may involve polygyny (one man and several women) or polyandry (one woman and several men). But how common are these types of marriage? Of the 238 societies studied by anthropologist George P. Murdock, about 20 percent were strictly monogamous and 80 percent permitted polygyny. Only about 1 percent were polyandrous (Murdock, 1949, p. 28).[7] The American view that the vast number of polygynous societies are motivated by the desire on the part of men for sexual variety is erroneous. Men in all societies who seek sexual variety usually do so in extramarital relationships, not by taking extra wives. The major motivation for several wives is economic: Many wives are sought to help care for possessions and to produce heirs. Usually only wealthy men can afford more than one wife (Reiss, 1976, p. 8).

Although there are many varieties of families in the United States, the most prevalent is the nuclear family consisting of a married couple and their children.

THE MEANING OF FAMILY

Although frequently used together, the terms *marriage* and *family* have very different meanings. Let's define family and examine the various types.

Definition of Family

The U.S. Census Bureau defines a family as a group of two or more persons who are related by blood, marriage, or adoption. While two spouses or two siblings may constitute their own family, the term usually implies the presence of children ("We want to begin a family after we've been married a few years").

As already noted, marriage provides the context in which a couple may have legitimate offspring. "Who are your parents?" is a question every lost child in a large department store is supposed to be able to answer. And, by doing so, the child confirms society's success in placing children in supportive family units.

Regardless of whether a family includes one or two parents (18 percent of all children under the age of eighteen are in single-parent homes according to a 1977

Census report), the care, protection, and socialization of children is a central focus. The human infant is dependent on adult care for its survival. And, unlike many lower animals who can survive without their parents within a relatively short time after birth, human parenthood in industrial societies involves being available and receptive to offspring for sixteen or more years. Much of this time is spent in socialization. "Socialization is the process by which the young human being acquires the values and knowledge of his/her group and learns the social roles appropriate to his/her position in it" (Goode, 1964, p. 10).

Types of Family

Just as there are various types of marriages, there are corresponding family types. From monogamous marriages, the nuclear family consisting of husband, wife, and their children has emerged. It is the most prevalent family form in America. A nuclear family may be the family of orientation (the family into which one is born or adopted), or the family of procreation (the family which one begins through marriage and having one's own children). Polygamous families result from polygamous marriages. These families (polygynous and polyandrous) consist of more than one husband or wife and their children. And finally, the extended family (which may be either monogamous or polygamous) includes additional generations. In an extended family, the nuclear couple's parents, siblings, or other relatives live with them as well as their children.

To express the various marriage and family types in more personal terms, you live in a society which insists that you be married to only one other person at a time. Hence, should you choose to marry, you will have a monogamous marriage. Should you and your partner have children, your family will be a nuclear family. And should all of you move in with your parents (or they with you), you will be living in an extended family.

MARRIAGE AND THE FAMILY: DIFFERENCES AND SIMILARITIES

The definitions and types of marriage and the family just described do not emphasize the differences. Yet there are five elements which suggest that marriage and the family are different concepts. Table 1.1 outlines these differences.

Children are the basic difference between the concepts of marriage and the family. All the items listed in the column under "marriage" are in reference to adults, and all the items listed in the column under "family" relate to both adults and children.

On the other hand, both marriage and the family are said to be primary groups,[8] or groups which are characterized by "intimate face-to-face association and cooperation" (Cooley, 1929, p. 23). Primary group members care about each other and have a durable relationship. Your parents and siblings represent your

TABLE 1.1   Some Differences Between the Concepts of Marriage and the Family.

Marriage	Family
1. Usually initiated by a public ceremony	1. Public ceremony not essential
2. Usually involves two people	2. Usually involves three or more people
3. Ages of the individuals tend to be similar	3. The individuals are of varying ages, more than one generation
4. Individuals usually choose each other	4. Children do not choose a family but are born or adopted into unit
5. Ends when one spouse dies	5. Continues when one spouse dies

SOURCE: Adapted from Axelson, 1977.

primary group if you are unmarried. If you are married, your spouse is another member of your primary group. You can most likely "see" a primary group by looking at those seated with you for Thanksgiving dinner. Or, go to the emergency entrance of your local hospital and observe those in the waiting room who brought patients in. More often than not, they will be members of the patients' primary groups.

In general, you can count on primary group members to be interested in responding to your needs. A close friend or <u>fiancé</u> may also be a primary group member depending on how closely he or she responds as would other primary group members. Your parents and spouse will probably give you ten dollars without pressing you to return it. Will your closest friend? Will your fiancé? yes

MARRIAGE AND THE FAMILY IN COLONIAL AMERICA

We have considered the reasons for and potential benefits of studying marriage and the family, defined the major terms, and examined the differences between them. Now we turn to the historical development of contemporary marriage and family patterns. By learning about families in colonial America, we may be able to understand contemporary family patterns better and see what has remained constant and what has changed in family life.

To begin with, we must recognize that life in general was radically different several hundred years ago. Today's easy four-hour flight from England to America on the Concorde supersonic jet was hardly the experience of the early settlers in the seventeenth and eighteenth centuries. The one- to two-month voyage involved rough seas, cramped quarters, insufficient food, and inadequate sanitation. Many died before reaching the new land.

Those who survived the hazardous and demanding voyage had no Holiday Inns in which to rest and enjoy good food. Rather, their first houses were "huts and hovels . . . digging themselves into caves and pits on hillsides and river banks, or pitching tents which they covered with ship's canvas" (Larkin, 1966, p. 12).[9] And instead of buffet dinners and a house doctor, food was scarce and medical care was unavailable or inadequate. In the beginning, men came alone and faced such hardships without wives or families. After the establishment of the first settlement in Jamestown, Virginia, in 1607, the colonists kept coming.

Because settlers came to America from different cultures, at different times, and to different places, it is erroneous to talk about "the" colonial family. The early colonies were divided into three geographical regions: New England (Maine to New York); Middle (New York to Maryland); and the South (Maryland to Georgia) (Calhoun, 1960). Communication between the three regions was very limited, and there was a "tendency of the individuals in one colony to view individuals in other colonies as culturally different and as 'foreign' in their behavior patterns, even though all were settlers in the New World" (Bell, 1975, p. 26). Because of the regional differences, we will examine each group separately.

The Puritans of New England

Puritans (radical Protestants who had seceded from the Church of England) and their descendants were the primary leaders of the emerging American society during the colonial period (Miller, 1956, p. ix). The men were predominantly middle-class merchants and businessmen, and they brought their wives and children with them to America.[10] Unlike Jamestown, an all-male settlement, the Massachusetts Bay Settlement (1630) began as a family settlement. This meant that every person who lived in the settlement was expected to belong to a family. Single women were described as a dismal spectacle and single men were treated as criminal suspects (Queen & Habenstein, 1974, p. 296). In Hartford, Connecticut, single men were taxed twenty shillings a week "for the selfish luxury of solitary living" (p. 296). It was also felt that if a bachelor had his own house, he might turn it into a brothel (Turner, 1955, p. 70).

Marriage.   The Puritans wanted their members to get married and stay married. Religious values (avoiding temptation), social values (belonging to a family settlement), and economic values helped to emphasize the importance of the marital relationship. The Puritan woman had little choice for an adult role other than wife and mother. Only in marriage could she achieve adult status. And men were taught that their best chance for survival was to find "a wife to satisfy imperative needs—clothing, food, medical care, companionship, sex, and . . . status" (Hunt, 1959, p. 238).

But the man and woman who wanted to get married had to follow a pre-

Just as the ritual of getting married varied from one colonial region to the next, wedding ceremonies have also differed from one historical period to the next. This quilt portrays a traditional New England church wedding in 1876.

scribed pattern: (1) The parents of the couple had to give their consent; (2) the town clerk had to be informed of such consent; (3) banns (public notice of intent to wed) had to be posted several days prior to the marriage; and (4) the marriage had to be registered (Kephart, 1977, p. 82). As involvement by the town clerk indicates, marriage was a civil contract. Ministers and priests were not only unnecessary, they were forbidden to officiate at weddings (Murstein, 1974, p. 315). Marriages were performed by a justice of the peace or other civil magistrate. There was no standard ceremony, and weddings usually took place in the bride's home.

Couples who did not go through the proper steps described above (parental consent, town clerk, etc.) were harassed with fines and social criticism. Nevertheless, their marriages were regarded as valid. These common-law marriages required one basic element—the mutual consent of the two parties involved. As long as each partner wanted to be the spouse of the other and was willing to act out the role, the marriage was valid.

Whether partners were married by clerk or common law, the marriages stuck. Divorce in colonial New England was almost nonexistent. Although there were specific grounds for divorce—adultery, bigamy, desertion, and impotence (Blake, 1963)—from 1639 to 1760, New England had an average of fewer than one divorce or annulment per year (Howard, 1904, p. 225).

Sex. The Puritans approved of sex only within marriage. Both men and women were expected to come to the marital bed as virgins. Being unable to delay sexual pleasure until marriage was denounced as succumbing to the temptations of the flesh and marked the individuals as not being among God's "chosen." Even kissing in public was viewed as lacking constraint. A Captain Kemble had returned from a long sea voyage and kissed his lady as he stepped on shore. As a result, he "was promptly lodged in the stocks" (Train, 1931, p. 347).

The consequences for engaging in premarital intercourse were more severe. Once discovered, the culprits had to make a public confession of their immorality. Additional punishment may have included fines or "stripes" (lashes). And, some violators got more than lashes:

> In Hartford, Connecticut, in 1739, not only was Aaron Starke pilloried, whipped, and branded on the cheek for seducing Mary Holt, and ordered to pay ten shillings to her father, but he was ordered to marry her when both should be "fit for the condition." (Turner, 1955, p. 74)

One way to catch those who jumped the gun before marriage was the "seven months rule." If a couple had a baby within seven months after their marriage, they were required to humble themselves before the congregation by confessing that they had had intercourse before marriage. If the parents were unwilling to make the public confession, their child was refused baptism which meant eternal damnation (Martinson, 1970, p. 28).

Bundling. Any discussion of sex among the Puritans would not be complete without reference to bundling, also called tarrying. Although not unique to the Puritans, bundling was a courtship custom which involved the would-be groom's sleeping in the girl's bed in her parents' home.[11] But there were rules to restrict sexual contact. Both partners had to be fully clothed, and a wooden bar was placed between them. In addition, the young girl might be encased in a type of long laundry bag up to her armpits, her clothes might be sewn together at strategic points, and her parents might be sleeping in the same room (Murstein, 1974, p. 317).

The justifications for bundling were convenience and economics. Aside from church, bundling was one of the few opportunities a couple had to get together to talk and learn about each other. Since daylight hours were consumed by heavy work demands, night became the time for courtship. But how did bed become the place? New England winters were cold. Firewood, oil for lamps, and candles were in short supply. By talking in bed, the young couple came to know each other without wasting valuable sources of energy (Howard, 1904, p. 182).

Although bundling flourished in the middle of the eighteenth century, it provoked a great deal of controversy. "Jonathan Edwards attacked it on the pulpit, and other ministers, who had allowed it to go unnoticed, joined in its suppression" (Calhoun, 1960, p. 71). By about 1800, the custom had virtually disappeared.

The Puritan woman. Puritan New England was a man's world. As one historian writes: "The proper conduct of a wife was submission to her husband's instructions and commands. He was her superior, the head of the family, and she owed him an obedience founded on reverence" (Morgan, 1966, p. 43). A wife's subordinate relationship to her husband was based on the Biblical teaching, "Wives, be subject to your husband as unto your God." Anyone who questioned this position was, in essence, questioning God's will.

The Puritan woman spent her day working in the home weaving cloth for garments, washing clothes, making candles, cooking, preserving food, and tending children—about eight of them in 1700.[12] Her social life was limited to church on Sunday and attending a religious "lecture" on Thursday (Goodsell, 1919, p. 352).

In addition to being restricted to the home, the Puritan woman was not expected to be an intellectual companion to her husband. Formal education was mainly for boys, and girls were permitted to attend school only in the summer. But their "education" rarely went further than the three R's and social graces. The negative effect of "book learning" by women was supposedly illustrated in the case of the wife of Connecticut's Governor Hopkins. It was said that she went crazy by straining her brain too much with reading and writing (Morgan, 1966, p. 16).

Children. Life was not carefree for Puritan children. The Puritans viewed children as sinful creatures whose spirit had to be broken. To them, a mischievous two-year-old was displaying the desire to rebel against God and man (Demos, 1970).

Children were to be seen and not heard. They had no legal rights. The father was in complete control of their education, religion, preparation for life work, and marriage (Goodsell, 1919, p. 346). And, as already mentioned, children worked. Since it was assumed that "idleness was the devil's workshop," they were expected to keep busy.

The Southern Colonies

While similar in some ways to Puritan New England, the colonial South was also very different. In contrast to the Puritans who had broken ties with the Church of England, lived in small villages, and came to the new land as families seeking homes, the Southern colonists kept their ties with the Anglican faith, lived on isolated farms, and came to the new land as unattached men seeking fortunes (Queen & Habenstein, 1974, p. 315).

The bachelors soon became restless and wanted female companionship. As a result, Southern businessmen arranged for shipments of women to come to the new land to become wives of the adventurers. The price for a woman was her passage and 120 pounds of tobacco (Queen & Habenstein, 1974, p. 320).

As the availability of women increased, all adults were expected to be married. And since the Anglican faith was dominant in the South, marriage was a religious affair which could be performed only by a minister.[13] Since a minister was not always available, common-law marriages were recognized also.

Although marriage between white men and black or Indian women was forbidden, sex between them was not. As long as a white husband was discreet, his wife was expected to accept his extramarital activities even though no socially approved extramarital encounter was permitted wives. If a wife became jealous of her husband's "left-handed connections" (often with black slaves on the plantation), she was "warned against jealousy and advised to conceal knowledge of her husband's infidelity" (Queen & Habenstein, 1974, p. 319).[14]

The Middle Colonies

Between the New England and Southern were the Middle Colonies. The attitudes of these colonists toward marriage, sex, women, and children represented a blend of the Puritans and Southerners.

Historically, the best remembered of the middle colonists are the Quakers. Referred to as the Society of Friends, the Quakers stressed inner spirituality and outward cooperativeness. Their marriage ceremony was neither civil like that of the Puritans nor religious like that of the Southerners but personal. "The couple to be married would rise, take each other by the hand, and declare their commitment to each other before God and company" (Trueblood, 1966, p. 102). No minister or justice of the peace was necessary because "it is God who makes them man and wife" (p. 102).

1607–1776 in Perspective

In summary, the colonial families, whether Quaker, Southern, or Puritan, were very different from families today. Between 70 and 90 percent of the families lived on farms where the colonists built homes, made furniture and clothing, and raised food. Although there were trade centers where individuals could take their surplus goods and exchange them for what they lacked, for the most part the family was an economically self-sufficient unit (Adams, 1974, p. 63).

Recreational, religious, and educational processes were also based in the home. With no amusement parks, movies, or concerts, family members did whatever playing they did at home. And while the church offered a place for worship on Sundays, the parents were responsible for the souls of their offspring. Bible reading by the father, who was the undisputed head of the household, is part of colonial history. Although children were obligated to respect their parents—with damnation as the threat for not doing so—not all were obligated to attend school. In some cases, schools were not available. In other cases, the children were needed to work. As a result, children received a major portion of their education at home.

It is difficult to pinpoint specific influences of colonial America on today's family. Events before and after the period make the origins of various beliefs and practices almost impossible to determine. An exception, however, is our body of laws relating to sex between unmarried men and women. These laws, which punish such intimacy, are a definite reflection of Puritanism (DeBeaumont, 1958).

TRANSITION FROM COLONIAL TO CONTEMPORARY AMERICA

Social, technological, and economic influences of the nineteenth and twentieth centuries reshaped colonial marriage and family patterns into those we recognize today. The social influences included a rapidly expanding population and the shift from rural to urban living. While there were only 4 million colonists, today there are over 215 million Americans. Immigration accounted for a major boost in population growth between 1820 and World War i. During that period over 30 million immigrants—Italians, Jews, Germans, Chinese, Mexicans, Puerto Ricans, and many others—came to America. They brought with them their own ethnic versions of family rules and rituals. In many respects ethnic group values and family patterns have blended together in the American "melting pot"; other differences have survived intact so that there remain today many variations in family patterns.

In addition to rapid population growth, there was a movement from rural to urban centers. While most Americans once lived in rural areas, today over 75 percent live in urban areas. The shift from the farms to the cities was linked to the Industrial Revolution. More efficient farming technology and machinery improved productivity, and fewer were needed to produce food for the growing population (DeFleur, D'Antonio, & DeFleur, 1976, p. 341). They moved their families to the urban centers which were also benefiting from technology. The creation of the cotton gin and steam-powered loom contributed to the success of an increasing number of new factories and meant more jobs. Many of these jobs were filled by women who were working outside their homes for the first time.

As a result of these social, technological, and economic changes, marriage and family patterns changed. These may be described in reference to family ties, family functions, marriage, women, and children. Let's explore each of these in more detail.

Family Ties

The importance of family ties has diminished since colonial times. In colonial America, the term "family" usually referred to the married couple, their children, and extended kin (parents, grandparents, siblings, uncles, aunts, etc.). While they may not have shared the same house, they lived close together and their lives "connected" with each other. However, during America's agricultural phase, which was characterized by the availability of cheap land on the frontier, young married couples who "went West" developed their own family patterns without the constraints (or supports) of their elders (Lantz et al., 1977). Since extended kin were often left behind, the nuclear family became the norm.

In modern America, occupational mobility and educational pursuits have made it common for young married couples to live several states away from their original homes, quite withdrawn from their parents and extended kin. "My son got a job in Los Angeles," a mother from Georgia explained, "and I haven't seen him in three years."

Although career commitments may create a geographical distance between an individual and his or her parents, educational differences may create an intellectual/emotional distance. "It's not that I live too far away from my folks to visit them," observed Melissa, a graduating senior. "It's just that we don't have anything in common anymore. I'm not interested in which of my mother's nieces had a baby, and my parents aren't interested in who Chaucer was. The topics we can discuss are safe and boring, and the result is I see them very little."

Family Functions

In addition to there being more physical, intellectual, and emotional distance between family members, the modern family no longer fulfills all the functions it did in colonial times. Today the economically self-sufficient family is almost non-existent. Processed and packaged foods come from the supermarket freezer rather than from the family vegetable garden. Mom's homemade soup has been replaced for the most part by Campbell's and Heinz. And the clothes the family wears are now mass-produced and bought from large department stores. As a result, family members may produce very little. The family is now a consumer unit rather than a producing unit.

With the demise of the farm-based family,[15] the educational, religious, and protective functions of the family have also become less important. Schools and religious institutions now provide the bulk of formal learning experiences about life and the life beyond. Law enforcement agencies have virtually taken over the protective function of the family. Police and military forces help protect us from criminal and foreign assault.

This farm-based extended family has at least one critical function in common with the more typical urban or suburban nuclear family—providing close ties of affection and caring for its members. Historically, many rural families have additionally fulfilled other social, economic, educational, and religious functions.

But no other institution has taken over the basic function of the family—emotional bonding. Providing love and care for its members is its specialty. We can buy lunch at a restaurant and pay a counselor to listen to our problems, but neither the waitress nor the counselor really cares about us to the point of earning a living to help support us, providing us a place to live, or helping us prepare for the future. Our parents and marriage partners are expected to care, and this function survives today.

Criteria for a Marriage Partner

Since colonial times, the criteria for a good mate have changed. The "good wife" in the colonial period was valued for her domestic aptitude—her ability to spin yarn, make clothes, cook meals, preserve food, and care for children. The "good husband" was evaluated primarily in terms of being an economic provider. While these issues may still be important, contemporary mates are more likely to be sought after on the basis of personal qualities, particularly for love and companionship, than for either utilitarian or economic reasons.

Marriage Roles

Individuals expect their role relationships in marriage to be more equalitarian today than previously. Over 90 percent of 252 white and black high-school students agreed that they should have an equal voice with their future marriage partner in making decisions which affect the family as a whole (Moore & Knox, 1978). Such an expectation is in stark contrast to the rigid traditional roles of the colonial era. The Depression of the 1930s was a basic cause of the trend toward more equalitarian marriage roles. In families during this era, the father's authority declined because he was no longer the primary breadwinner. In some cases only mothers and children could find work (Farber, 1973).

The Status of Women

As late as 1850, a woman's personal property legally belonged to her husband, she could not vote, and she had little access to formal education (Kephart, 1977, p. 83). With few exceptions, her role was to manage her household and her

Although many of the women's rights goals set forth at Seneca Falls in 1848 have been achieved, the movement has always encountered considerable opposition. This cartoon from 1859 mocks a feminist speaker and her audience at Seneca Falls.

Yᴇ MAY SESSION OF Yᴇ WOMAN'S RIGHTS CONVENTION—Yᴇ ORATOR OF Yᴇ DAY
DENOUNCING Yᴇ LORDS OF CREATION.

children.[16] But the women's rights movement had begun in 1848 with a convention in Seneca Falls, New York. The convention resulted in a declaration of these objectives for women: to gain legal control of their personal property, to gain the right to vote, and to be admitted to academic institutions. These specific goals have largely been achieved: Women may now own their own businesses, be active politically as voters or as elected officials, and attend prestigious women's and coeducational schools.

The Status of Children

The status of children has also changed. During the colonial period, children were economic assets, not liabilities. They provided an invaluable work force for the economically self-sufficient family. Today, children are an economic drain and must be wanted and loved for reasons other than for the work they can perform. Modern-day parents are psychologically rewarded by their children and see life as more fulfilling with them (Whelan, 1976, p. 92).

In summary, the transition of marriage and the family from colonial to contemporary America can be described as a weakening of family ties, fewer family functions, new criteria for a good mate, and more equalitarian relationships between spouses. While the causes of transition are numerous and diffuse, changing from an agricultural to an industrial economy and from a rural to an urban society predominates.

IS MARRIAGE OBSOLETE?

Although the transition from the colonial to the contemporary family resulted in a number of positive changes, some people have been concerned that these changes will eventually bring about the end of marriage. With more individuals delaying marriage,[17] more couples divorcing,[18] and widespread infidelity,[19] marriage has been called "a wretched institution" (Cadwallader, 1966), "obsolete" (Roy, 1972), and "Hell" (Perutz, 1973). But what is the basis for these accusations?

Attack and Counterattack

The attack against marriage has come on two fronts—historical and personal (Mace & Mace, 1977). The historical argument says that the institution of marriage was established to fulfill societal needs which are no longer significant. Marriage was primarily needed to ensure that children were born and socialized so that society itself would survive. In addition, marriage was essential to provide children for labor in an agricultural economy, to carry on family traditions (names, businesses), and to provide economic security for women and children (dependents). But, the argument continues, since our society has changed (we are in little danger of becoming extinct, few children have farms to work on, few people are concerned about family traditions, women can be economically independent, etc.), we don't need marriage or families any more.

The rebuttal to this argument emphasizes that marriage has changed to meet new needs. Rather than meeting institutional needs, contemporary marriage fulfills individual needs—primarily companionship needs (Burgess & Locke, 1945). No other institution in American society provides such a stable source of emotional support for its members as does the family.

Traditional marriage role relationships have also been attacked on personal grounds—they restrict freedom. The spouses in a traditional marriage are expected to forsake personal growth and fulfillment for the sake of the partner and the marriage. "I'd like to go back to school," expressed one spouse, "but I'm afraid it will change my outlook too much. Since my husband never went to college, I think it would be dangerous for our marriage for me to go now."

The question raised by those who reject the criticism that traditional marriage restricts personal freedom is, "Freedom from what?" While traditional marriage does restrict one's choices, marriage also offers an intense involvement with and commitment to another person. In a society characterized by many transitory and less intense relationships, someone who "really cares" often becomes very precious. "This need for a one-to-one relationship in which we give ourselves, and find ourselves, through total sharing with another seems to be a widespread and fundamental need" (Mace & Mace, 1974, p. 25). For this reason, it seems safe to say that marriage and the family are here to stay.

Optimism for Successful Marriage

In general, university students are very optimistic about marriage. Of three hundred undergraduates, fewer than 7 percent felt that there was "too little freedom" in marriage, and over 96 percent felt that they were personally capable of developing a good marriage (Whitehurst, 1977, pp. 295–98). "I can't imagine not being married someday, and not being happily married," said a university junior.

In a larger nationwide study, over twenty thousand high-school graduates were asked about their goals in life. Finding the right person to marry and having a happy family headed the list (Eckland & Bailey, 1976, p. 18). Those who are married evidently agree about the importance of a happy marriage. Over fifteen thousand husbands and wives listed "being in love" and "marriage" as two primary sources of their happiness (Shaver & Freedman, 1976, p. 28). In another study, 85 percent of over 200,000 spouses reported that their "expectations of happiness in marriage were being fulfilled" *(Better Homes and Gardens,* 1978, p. 17).

A couple in their forty-third year of marriage wrote, "Like Winston Churchill, we consider that getting married was the best thing we ever did. As we look back together across the years we see that marriage has contributed enormously to our personal growth, our enjoyment of life, our understanding of other people, our willingness to be adventurous and take risks, and our sense of fulfillment" (Mace & Mace, 1977, p. 390).

SOME CAUTIONS ABOUT RESEARCH

The material in this book is based on a comprehensive review of current research in marriage and the family. The chapters attempt to focus on what is, rather than on what we believe or want to be true. For instance, while we may believe that equality for women has been achieved, the data show that women typically earn two thirds of what men do for the same job; they are awarded fewer than 20 percent of the medical and legal degrees; and they represent fewer than 2 percent of the politicians in Congress. But while attempting to be value free, the "facts" provided by social scientists aren't necessarily reliable. In reflecting on the various studies referred to in this book, it is important to be aware of various research limitations.

Sampling

While the data in the above paragraph reflect actual counting and tabulation (you can tabulate the percentage of medical and legal degrees, the percentage of women in Congress, etc.), most information about marriage and the family is based on samples—studying a relatively small number of individuals and assuming that those studied are similar to a larger group encompassing many people not studied. For example, suppose you want to know what percentage of sophomore women (SW) on your campus are living with their boyfriends. While the most accurate way to get this information is to get an anonymous "yes" or "no" response from every sophomore woman, doing so is not practical. In order to save yourself some time, you could ask a few SWs to complete your questionnaire and assume that the rest of the SWs who did not complete your questionnaire would say "yes" or "no" in the same proportion as those you did ask. In order to decide who those few SWs would be, you could put the names of every SW on your campus on separate note cards, stir these cards in your bathtub, put on a blindfold, and draw one hundred cards. Since each SW would have an equal chance of having her card drawn from the tub, you would have what is known as a random sample. And after adding up the yes's and no's from the questionnaires you would ask each SW to complete, you would have a fairly accurate idea of the percentage of sophomore women on your campus who were living with their boyfriends.

Because of the trouble and expense of obtaining random samples, most researchers study those to whom they have convenient access.[20] This often means students in their classes. The result is an abundance of research on "convenience" samples who are white, Protestant, middle-class college students. And the responses of this group cannot be assumed to be similar to a non-college population which includes different races, religions, age groups, and social classes. Of over fifty studies on cohabitation (living together), fewer than 5 percent have focused on non-college students.

Terminology

In addition to being alert to potential sampling shortcomings, consider how the phenomenon being researched is defined. For example, what is *living together?* How many people, of what sex, spending what amount of time, in what place, engaging in what behaviors will constitute your definition? Researchers of living together have used over twenty definitions (Cole, 1977). "To share a bedroom for at least four nights per week for at least three consecutive months with someone of the opposite sex" is one definition used by many researchers (Macklin, 1972, p. 463).

And what about other terms? What is meant by *marital happiness, adjustment, satisfaction,* or *success?* Before accepting that most people are happily married or unhappily married, be alert to the definition used by the researcher in the hypothetical study. Exactly what is it that the researcher tried to measure?

Researcher Bias

Even when the sample is random and the terms are carefully defined, two researchers can examine the same data and arrive at different conclusions. In your hypothetical study of sophomore women who are living together with boyfriends, suppose you find that a quarter of your respondents report that they are living together. In discussing your study, would you also state that the majority of the students (75 percent) were not living together? In effect, you can focus on either aspect of the data to make the point you want to make. Many researchers tend to focus on selected aspects of the data they are reporting.

Time Lag

There is typically a two-year lag between the time a research study is completed and its appearance in a professional journal. Since textbooks are based on these journals and take from three to five years of writing and development, by the time you read the results of a study, other studies may have been conducted which reveal different findings. In 1965, 1970, and 1975, unmarried women students at a large, Southern, state-supported university were asked if they had experienced intercourse. Between the first and second studies the reported rate of intercourse increased 9.6 percent. Between the second and third studies, the rate increased 18 percent (King et al., 1977, p. 456). Hence, the research you read this year may not reflect current reality.

In view of the research problems of sampling, terminology, investigator bias, and time, why bother to report the findings? The research picture is not as bleak as it may seem at first. A number of studies have been conducted on random samples which give us, as accurately as is possible, a picture of what is currently happening. In addition, even though the bulk of studies are not based on national random samples, some information is better than no information. When enough nonrandom studies are conducted in one area, a consistency in the findings may give us information that approximates the information we would get from a large random sample. The alternative to gathering data is guessing, and this is unacceptable.

TRENDS

Each chapter of this book will end with a discussion of specific trends in different aspects of marriage and the family. In general, the future of marriage and family relationships includes increased governmental interest and the accumulation of more sophisticated data. President Jimmy Carter expressed in his 1977 inaugural address the hope that his administration would be instrumental in "strengthening the American family." Carter called for a White House Conference on Families in order to explore the impact of federal policies on the stability of American families. This could serve as a precedent for continuing and growing interest in the family on the part of government.

One result of increased interest in marriage and the family is the proliferation of more sophisticated data. The National Opinion Research Center in Chicago collects annual data from a random sample of noninstitutionalized adults eighteen years old and over in the United States. In addition, since the quality of research improves as competition for journal space increases, editors of journals dealing with marriage and the family are able to select from a number of submitted manuscripts only those that reflect higher quality research. A review of articles published in *The Journal of Marriage and the Family* will verify this trend.

SUMMARY

This introductory chapter has been concerned with developing a justification for studying marriage and the family, defining terms, reviewing historical antecedents of contemporary marriage and family patterns, questioning the idea that marriage and the family are obsolete, and reviewing various research limitations. Potential benefits to be derived from the systematic study of marriage and family relationships include developing a more rational perspective, making more informed decisions, and preparing for inevitable transitions.

While the terms *marriage* and *family* are often linked together, they are different. More often than not, the term *family* implies the presence of children and concern for their socialization. The term *marriage* focuses on the emotional and legal relationship between spouses.

Contemporary marriage and family patterns are quite different from those of the colonial period. Among the Puritans, single men were taxed and single women were pitied. Intercourse among the unmarried was severely punished. For those who married, the approval of their parents was essential. A "good" husband was defined as a capable worker and provider, whereas a "good" wife was valued for her domestic skills. There was an average of less than one divorce per year for 120 years in colonial New England.

In the over two hundred years since the colonial period, kinship ties have weakened, family functions (except emotional bonding) have been taken over by other institutions, single people have achieved more approval, husbands and wives have come to see each other mainly as companions, and having children has become a matter of choice rather than of economic necessity.

But there is some concern that marriage is obsolete. Some say that marriage no longer serves the functions it once did and should be replaced by other life-styles such as communal living, cohabitation, or singlehood. But marriage still serves the basic function of creating the intimacy of a one-to-one relationship. While an increasing number of people will opt for other alternatives, there is little chance that marriage will disappear from our society.

The remaining chapters reflect current research on marriage and family relationships. But research has its limitations. Sampling, terminology, researcher bias, and time lag are issues which should be kept in mind when evaluating the usefulness and validity of a research study.

Trends in marriage and the family include increased governmental interest and more sophisticated research. The recognition that much of government policy ultimately has an impact on the American family has led to increased concern that this impact be positive. More sophisticated data have resulted from more individuals entering the field of marriage and the family and competing for journal space by improving the quality of the research.

STUDY QUESTIONS

1. Discuss several potential benefits which can result from studying marriage and the family.
2. About how many married couples are there in America?
3. Define *marriage*.
4. Is marriage regulated by state or federal law?
5. What are the legal obligations of the wife? Of the husband?
6. Why does our society encourage individuals to marry before they have children?
7. Discuss the major types of marriage. What form of marriage do most societies have?
8. Define *family*.
9. Distinguish between the family of orientation and the family of procreation.
10. A major goal of the family is to socialize its offspring. What does this mean?
11. What are the various types of family?

12. What are several differences between marriage and the family?
13. What is a primary group?
14. Why is it not possible to talk about "the" colonial family?
15. How did the Puritans feel about unmarried people?
16. What was the Puritan procedure for getting married?
17. How frequent was divorce among the Puritans?
18. What were the consequences for engaging in premarital sexual intercourse in Puritan New England?
19. What was the seven months rule?
20. Discuss the nature of and reasons for bundling.
21. Discuss the role of the Puritan woman.
22. What was it like to be a child in Puritan New England?
23. In what ways were the Southern and New England colonies different?
24. What was unique about the Quaker marriage ceremony?
25. Discuss the social, technological, and economic influences of the nineteenth and twentieth centuries which reshaped marriage and family patterns into those we recognize today.
26. What role did immigration play in expanding the population and in adding new dimensions to American family life?
27. How do some family ties today differ from those in colonial America? Why the change?
28. How have the functions of the family changed since the colonial era? What basic family function remains?
29. How have the critieria for a "good husband" and "good wife" changed since colonial times?
30. Contrast the status of women and children in colonial and contemporary America.
31. Discuss the arguments (pro and con) that marriage is obsolete.
32. What is the justification for feeling optimistic about marriage?
33. List and discuss several issues which should be considered in evaluating research.
34. Discuss the trends referred to in this chapter.

NOTES

1. In March 1977, there were 48,002,000 married couples in the U.S. (U.S. Bureau of the Census, 1978).

2. The legal relationship between husband and wife has its basis in English common law. Such a law provided that the husband and wife merged into a single legal identity—that of the husband. In essence, the wife became a legal nonperson referred to as "femme couverte" (Blackstone, 1765). Her property and earnings belonged to her husband and her personal conduct was subject to his control. Of course, subsequent laws in the United States have increased economic and personal independence for the wife (Cavan, 1974, p. 230).

3. It has been estimated that the average housewife's yearly services are worth $13,364 (Galbraith, 1973, p. 78). Feminists have suggested that housewives should be paid for their work to lessen their dependent status.

4. Until recently, the wife was affected by the husband's legal responsibility to support the family in that she had to apply for and obtain credit in his name, not her own, and must have had his explicit permission to do so (NOW, 1973).

5. The courts are reluctant to define "support" and interfere in the marital relationship. In the case of McGuire vs. McGuire (1953), the wife of a wealthy man complained that her husband had not given her any money and had not provided her with clothes for the past three years. Beyond buying groceries, he had refused to buy other household necessities. The court refused

to consider the wife's complaint because "The living standards of a family are a matter of concern to the household, and not for the courts to determine . . ." (McGuire vs. McGuire, 1953, p. 342). Without the court's help in obtaining support, the wife has little recourse. The Citizens' Advisory Council on the Status of Women (1972) aptly describes the present situation: "A married woman living with her husband can, in practice, get only what he chooses to give her" (p. 38).

Should the couple divorce, the wife can expect even less financial support. Although most states hold the husband theoretically liable for alimony, it is actually awarded in fewer than 15 percent of all divorce cases (Nagel & Weitzman, 1971). Regarding child support, 62 percent of divorced fathers fail to comply fully with the court-ordered payment (Eckhardt, 1968).

6. In recent years the rights of children have been asserted with increasing frequency (see Bennett & McDonald, 1977).

7. Group marriage consisting of many males and many females is the least common of polygamous marriages (Murdock, 1949, p. 28).

8. Primary groups are often described in contrast to secondary groups. The latter consist of individuals who have no personal long-term interest in caring for your needs. Examples might be a bridge club or bowling team.

9. Log cabins were introduced later by the Swedes and Finns who had been accustomed to living in heavily forested areas (Lynes, 1963).

10. Wives were a stabilizing influence in the early colonies. Although the Virginia climate was relatively mild, the Jamestown settlers became restless and discontented, which threatened the settlement with disintegration. Not until women sailed from England to become wives did conditions in Virginia stabilize (Kephart, 1977, p. 123).

11. Bundling was also used to accommodate a visitor. Since space was limited, he or she might be offered "half a bed" (Calhoun, 1960, p. 129).

12. Researchers do not all agree on how large (or small) the families of colonial New England were (Seward, 1973).

13. Among Catholic colonists in Maryland, however, civil marriages were recognized (Queen & Habenstein, 1974, p. 323).

14. If the husband became emotionally involved with his mistress, his wife might seek revenge by selling the slave to another plantation (Queen & Habenstein, 1974, p. 320).

15. Less than 5 percent of the United States population is actively engaged in farming (DeFleur, D'Antonio, & DeFleur, 1976, p. 368).

16. Some eighteenth century women were involved in roles that took them outside the home. They were teachers, newspaper publishers, and merchants of groceries, wines, and musical instruments (Queen & Habenstein, 1974, p. 298).

17. In 1960, 28 percent of the women between the ages of twenty and twenty-four were single (never married). But in 1977, 45 percent of the women in this age category were single (U.S. Bureau of the Census, 1978).

18. In 1960 there were thirty-five divorced people for every one thousand married people. In 1977, there were eighty-four divorced people for every one thousand married people (over twice as high) (U.S. Bureau of the Census, 1978, Table E).

19. About 60 percent of all husbands and 45–50 percent of all wives have intercourse with someone other than their spouse by age forty (Libby, 1977).

20. There are commendable exceptions—for instance, the researchers Zelnik and Kantner (1977) used random samples as the basis for their writings on sexual behavior.

BIBLIOGRAPHY

Adams, B. N. *The family: A sociological interpretation.* Chicago: Rand McNally, 1974.

Axelson, L. Department of Housing Management and Family Development, Virginia Polytechnic Institute and State University, Blacksburg, Virginia. Personal communication, 1977.

Bell, R. R. *Marriage and family interaction.* Homewood, Ill.: Dorsey Press, 1975.

Bennett, W. M., and McDonald, L. Rights of children. *The Family Coordinator,* 1977, *26,* 4, 333–37.

Better Homes and Gardens (eds.). *Report on the American family.* Des Moines, Iowa: Meredith Corporation, 1978.

Blackstone, W. *Commentaries* (Vol. 1). 1765.

Blake, N. M. *The road to Reno: A history of divorce in the United States.* New York: Macmillan, 1963.

Brown, B. et al. The equal rights amendment. *Yale Law Journal,* 1971, *80,* 940.

Burgess, E. W., and Locke, H. J. *The family: From institution to companionship.* New York: D. Van Nostrand, 1945.

Cadwallader, M. Marriage as a wretched institution. *Atlantic Monthly,* November 1966, 62–8.

Calhoun, A. *A social history of the American family.* New York: Barnes and Noble, 1960.

Carlson vs. Carlson. 75 Arizona 308 256 P 2d 249 (1953).

Cavan, R. S. Legal regulation of marriage. In *Marriage and family in the modern world readings* (4th ed.), R. S. Cavan (ed.). New York: Thomas Y. Crowell, 1974, 229–52.

Citizens Advisory Council on the Status of Women. *The equal rights amendment and child support laws.* Washington, D.C.: U.S. Government Printing Office, 1972.

Clark, H. *The law of domestic relations.* St. Paul: West Publishing, 1968.

Cole, C. L. Cohabitation in social context. In *Marriage and alternatives: Exploring intimate relationships,* R. Libby and R. Whitehurst (eds.). Glenview, Ill.: Scott, Foresman, 1977, 62–79.

Cooley, C. H. *Social organization.* New York: Charles Scribner's Sons, 1929 (Originally published in 1907).

DeBeaumont, G. *Marie, Or slavery in the United States: A novel of Jacksonian America.* Stanford, Calif.: Stanford University Press, 1958.

DeFleur, M., D'Antonio, W., and DeFleur, L. *Sociology: Human society.* Glenview, Ill.: Scott, Foresman, 1976.

Demos, J. *A little commonwealth: Family life in Plymouth colony.* New York: Oxford University Press, 1970.

Eckhardt, K. Deviance, visibility and legal action: The duty to support. *Social Problems,* 1968, *15,* 470.

Eckland, B. K., and Bailey, J. P., Jr. National longitudinal study of the high school class of 1972 (second follow-up). Research Triangle Park, N.C.: Research Triangle Institute, 1976.

Farber, B. *Family and kinship in modern society.* Glenview, Ill.: Scott, Foresman, 1973.

Galbraith, J. K. The economics of the American housewife. *The Atlantic,* August 1973, 78.

Geduldig vs. Aiello. 94 S. Ct. 2485 (1974).

Goode, W. J. *The family.* Englewood Cliffs, N. J.: Prentice-Hall, 1964.

Goodsell, W. *A history of the family as a social and educational institution.* New York: Macmillan, 1919.

Gordon, M. (ed.) *The American family in social–historical perspective* (2nd ed.). New York: St. Martin's Press, 1978.

Howard, G. E. *A history of matrimonial institutions* (Vol. 2). Chicago: University of Chicago Press, 1904.

Hunt, M. M. *The natural history of love.* New York: Alfred A. Knopf, 1959.

Kay, H. H. *Sex-based discrimination in family law.* St. Paul: West Publishing, 1974.

Kephart, W. M. *The family, society, and the individual.* New York: Houghton Mifflin, 1977.

King, K., Balswick, J. O., and Robinson, I. E. The continuing premarital sexual revolution among college females. *Journal of Marriage and the Family,* 1977, *39,* 3, 455–59.

Lantz, H., Schultz, M., and O'Hara, M. The changing American family from the preindustrial to the industrial period: A final report. *American Sociological Review,* 1977, *42,* 3, 406–21.

Larkin, O. *Art and life in America.* New York: Holt, Rinehart and Winston, 1966.

Libby, R. W. Extramarital and comarital sex: A critique of the literature. In *Marriage and alternatives: Exploring intimate relationships,* R. Libby and R. Whitehurst (eds.). Glenview, Ill.: Scott, Foresman, 1977, 80–111.

Lynes, R. *The domesticated Americans.* New York: Harper and Row, 1963.

Mace, D., and Mace, V. *We can have better marriages—If we really want them.* Nashville: Abingdon Press, 1974.

_____. Counter-epilogue. In *Marriage and alternatives: Exploring intimate relationships,* R. Libby and R. Whitehurst (eds.). Glenview, Ill.: Scott, Foresman, 1977, 390–96.

Macklin, E. D. Heterosexual cohabitation among unmarried college students. *The Family Coordinator,* 1972, *21,* 4, 463–72.

Martinson, F. M. *Family in society.* New York: Dodd, Mead, 1970.

McGuire vs. McGuire, 175 Neb. 226, 59 N. W. 2d, P. 336, 352 (1953).

Miller, P., (ed.). *The American Puritans: Their prose and poetry.* Garden City, N. Y.: Doubleday (Anchor), 1956.

Moore, K., and Knox, D. White and black marriage role expectations. *Family Perspective,* 1978, in press.

Morgan, E. *The Puritan family.* New York: Harper and Row, 1966.

Murdock, G. P. *Social structure.* New York: Macmillan, 1949.

Murstein, B. I. *Love, sex, and marriage through the ages.* New York: Springer, 1974.

Nagel, S., and Weitzman, L. Women as litigants. *Hastings Law Journal,* 1971, *23,* 189–91.

The National Organization for Women. *Women and credit.* Chicago: NOW, 1973.

Perutz, K. *Marriage is hell.* New York: William Morrow, 1973.

Queen, S. A., and Habenstein, R. W. *The family in various cultures.* Philadelphia: J. B. Lippincott, 1974.

Reiss, I. L. *Family systems in America.* Hinsdale, Ill.: Dryden Press, 1976.

Roy, R. Marriage: For and against. In *Marriage: For and against.* New York: Hart Publishing, 1972, 61–72.

Rucci vs. Rucci. 23 Conn. Sup. 221, 181 A. 2d 125 Super. Ct. (1962).

Seward, R. R. The colonial family in America: Toward a socio-historical restoration of its structure. *Journal of Marriage and the Family,* 1973, *35,* 1, 58–70.

Shaver, P., and Freedman, J. Your pursuit of happiness. *Psychology Today,* August 1976, 26, et passim.

Stephens, W. N. *The family in cross-cultural perspective.* New York: Holt, Rinehart and Winston, 1963.

Train, A. *Puritan's progress.* New York: Charles Scribner's Sons, 1931.

Trueblood, E. E. *The people called Quakers.* New York: Harper and Row, 1966.

Turner, E. S. *A history of courtship.* New York: E. P. Dutton, 1955.

U.S. Bureau of the Census. Marital status and living arrangements, March, 1977. *Current Population Reports,* Series P-20, No. 323. Washington, D.C.: U.S. Government Printing Office, 1978.

Weitzman, L. J. To love, honor, and obey? Traditional legal marriage and alternative family forms. *The Family Coordinator,* 1975, *24,* 4, 531–48.

Whelan, E. M. *A baby . . . maybe?* Indianapolis, Ind.: Bobbs-Merrill, 1976.

Whitehurst, R. N. Youth views marriage: Awareness of present and future potentials in relationships. In *Marriage and alternatives: Exploring intimate relationships,* R. Libby and R. Whitehurst (eds.). Glenview, Ill.: Scott, Foresman, 1977, 294–301.

Zelnik, M., and Kantner, J. Sexual and contraceptive experience of young unmarried women in the United States, 1976 and 1971. *Family Planning Perspectives,* 1977, *9,* 2, 55–71.

Chapter 2

Sex Roles

Helmer: First and foremost, you are a wife and mother.
Nora: That I don't believe any more. I believe that
first and foremost I am an individual.

Henrik Ibsen, in A DOLL'S HOUSE

American men are self-reliant and strong; they rarely, if ever, cry; they have full-time careers and support their families; and they are not especially interested in changing diapers, planning a meal, or buying clothes for their children. In contrast, American women need husbands to protect and support them; they are emotional and they cry when they are unhappy; they have a special knack that men lack for nurturing babies, preparing gourmet meals, and finding good buys on food, clothes, and household items.

Do these descriptions sound familiar? If they do, it is not necessarily because the people we know fit the descriptions. Instead, we recognize the stereotypes because we have all learned what the traditional roles of men and women are supposed to be in our society. In this chapter we will explore the origins of these traditional roles, how we learn roles, their consequences, and trends. We begin by defining some basic terms.

TERMINOLOGY

Sociologists, psychologists, anthropologists, and psychiatrists often have different definitions and connotations for the terms *sex, gender identity,* and *sex role*. We will use these terms in the following way.

Sex

This term refers to the biological distinction of being female or male. Such a distinction includes external genitalia (vulva/penis), internal genitalia (ovaries/testes), chromosomes (XX/XY), hormones (estrogen/androgen), and secondary sex characteristics (high voice/deep voice). While we tend to think of females and males as having only those characteristics appropriate to their sex, there may be considerable variation. Some individuals may have the genitalia of one sex but the hormonal and chromosomal makeup of the other (Money & Ehrhardt, 1972).

Gender Identity

In contrast to the biological distinction between being female or male, gender identity is the psychological state of viewing one's self as a girl or a boy and later as a woman or a man. Such an identity is usually formed by about age three. While one's gender identity and biological sex are usually the same, they may be different. For example, some individuals have been reared as one sex while anatomically being the other (Money & Ehrhardt, 1973).

Sex Role

Also known as gender role, sex role refers to the socially accepted characteristics and behaviors typically associated with one's gender identity. In our society females are believed to be emotional, dependent, and home-oriented, while males are expected to hide their emotions, be independent, and be career-oriented.

ORIGINS: HOW SEX ROLES DEVELOPED

The australopithecines who lived in southeastern Africa about two million years ago are regarded as the first ancestors of modern humans.[1] These prehistoric ancestors were gatherers and hunters—that is, they survived by gathering fruits, vegetables, grasses, etc. that grew naturally in the environment and by hunting a variety of animals. In order for this group and those who followed to continue to exist, provisions had to be made for infant care, food, and defense. Which sex took care of which responsibility formed the basis for a division of labor which continues in modified form today.

Care of Dependent Young

Unlike most animals, which must get their own food when they are weaned, human offspring are dependent on adults for food as well as protection and security for many years. Women became the primary caretakers of the dependent young for biological and practical reasons. They alone could nurse their infants to ensure a good start in life. And nursing meant being available to their infants every few hours. Going away on an extended hunting venture was incompatible with a hungry infant.

Hunting

Although women could gather berries and fish local waters, they could not be depended on to secure meat. Suppose they were pregnant or the infant were sick? Hence, encumbered by neither pregnancy nor child care, males were free to be away as necessary to return with sufficient meat. Since they caught the meat, a highly valued resource, they controlled its distribution throughout the group. And because they controlled something of value, they became the more powerful, dominant group (Friedl, 1975).

Defense

Similarly, the woman who was pregnant or responsible for caring for a small infant could not defend the existing territory. In addition, males were more suited for physical combat in that they are bigger and stronger than females (Harris, 1975).[2] As we move toward the possibility of pushbutton warfare, the physical prowess issue is minimized as evidenced by the expanding role of women in the military.

SOCIALIZATION: HOW WE LEARN OUR ROLES

Although we live in a highly advanced technological society, females and males are still socialized for different roles. Let's examine how this is done.

Significance of the Environment

The vast majority of psychological and social characteristics designated as feminine or masculine in any given culture are not innate. Rather, they are learned from the environment in which the individual grows up. Sex-role prescriptions in America not only signal the color of the blanket in which an infant is to be wrapped,

Sex roles are largely dependent on cultural definitions, but they are not immune to change. Many aspects of traditional sex roles have been challenged in recent years, including the assumption that only boys should have paper routes.

they dictate appropriate toys for children (doll or football), clothes (dress or pants), work roles (babysitter or paperboy), and curriculum (home economics or shop). Sex roles also tell an individual whether to be aggressive or passive in sexual interaction.

But different cultures prescribe different behaviors for their females and males. When Margaret Mead visited three New Guinea tribes in the early 1930s, she observed that the Arapesh socialized both sexes to be feminine by Western standards. In essence, the Arapesh person was taught to be cooperative and responsive to the needs of others. In contrast, the Tchambuli were known for dominant women and submissive men—just the opposite of our society. And both of these societies were unlike the Mundugumor, which socialized only ruthless, aggressive, masculine personalities. The Mundugumor tribesman or tribeswoman was typically incapable of experiencing or expressing emotion that was not grounded in hostility (Mead, 1935).[3] The inescapable conclusion of a cross-cultural perspective of human behavior is that human beings are what they are taught to be.

Perhaps the clearest illustration of how the environment influences the development of sex-appropriate behaviors is the case in which an infant born as a biologically normal male was reared as a female. Due to surgical mishap during circumcision, the male no longer had a penis and his parents were encouraged to rear him as a girl. The infant's name, clothing, and hairstyle were changed when he was seventeen months old and genital reconstruction as a female was begun. Since this child had a twin brother, it was possible to observe the effects of each child's respective socialization.

> The mother reported: "I started dressing her not in dresses but, you know, in little pink slacks and frilly blouses . . . and letting her hair grow." A year and six months later, the mother wrote that she had made a special effort at keeping her girl in dresses, almost exclusively, changing any item of clothes into something that was clearly feminine. "I even made all her nightwear into granny gowns and she wears bracelets and hair ribbons." The effects of emphasizing feminine clothing became clearly noticeable in the girl's attitude towards clothes and hairdo another year later, when she was observed to have a clear preference for dresses over slacks and to take pride in her long hair. (Money & Ehrhardt, 1972, p. 119)

Theories of Sex-Role Learning

Although most theorists agree that the environment has a profound effect on the development of sex-role behavior, they do not agree on the specific processes. Let's explore the alternative explanations of how female and male sex roles are acquired.

Social learning. Derived from the school of behavioral psychology, the social-learning perspective emphasizes that when sex-appropriate behaviors are rewarded and sex-inappropriate behaviors are punished, a child learns the behaviors appropriate to his or her sex. For example, when two brothers were quite young, they enjoyed playing "lady." Each of them would put on a dress, wear high-heeled shoes, and carry a pocketbook. Their father came home early one day and angrily demanded that they "take those clothes off and never put them on again. Those things are for women." In essence, the boys were punished for playing "lady," but rewarded with their father's approval for playing "cowboys," complete with guns and "Bang! You're dead!" dialogue.

While the systematic rewarding and punishing of appropriate and inappropriate sex-role behavior is influential in socializing an individual to become female or male, some social scientists feel other factors are involved. "It is too simplistic to account, by itself, for children's learning of sex roles. The rate at which these roles are learned, and the scope of their content, require additional processes" (Williams, 1977, p. 160).

Cognitive-developmental. The cognitive-developmental theory suggests that one of these processes involves developing the mental maturity to understand the concept of gender—femaleness or maleness (Kohlberg, 1966, 1969). Although two-year-olds can label themselves and each other as "girl" or "boy," they have superficial criteria for doing so. People who wear long hair are girls and those who never wear dresses are boys. Two-year-olds believe that they can change their gender by altering their hair or changing clothes.

Not until age six or seven does the child view gender as permanent (Kohlberg, 1969). In Kohlberg's view, this cognitive understanding is not a result of rewards and punishments for appropriate sex-role behaviors, but it involves the development of a specific mental ability to grasp the idea that certain basic characteristics of people do not change even though their hairstyle might. And once children learn that gender is permanent, they seek to become a competent and proper member of their gender group. For example, a child standing on the edge of a school playground may observe one group of children jumping rope while another group is playing football. His or her self-concept ("I am a boy" or "I am a girl") connects with the observed sex-appropriate behavior and he or she joins one of the two groups. Once in the group, the individual tries to develop the behaviors appropriate to his or her sex.

Modeling. In addition to the social-learning and cognitive-developmental perspectives of acquiring sex roles, the concept of modeling is important. Modeling involves the observation of another's behavior and the imitation of that behavior. Bill, an eight-year-old neighbor, recently helped his younger sister repair her tricycle. But the Saturday before this event, Bill had observed his dad putting new spark plugs in their Oldsmobile. His dad is the "fix-it man" in their home, and Bill, modeling after his dad, is the "fix-it man" in his dad's absence.

But the importance of modeling in the development of sex-role behavior is controversial. While a modeling perspective implies that children will tend to imitate the parent of the same sex, research demonstrates that they show no systematic preference for modeling after either sex (Maccoby & Jacklin, 1974a). In the example given above, Bill's older sister may be as interested in working with her father on the Oldsmobile as Bill. But the opportunity for her to do so may be limited if her mother insists that she come inside and set the table, make the beds, and vacuum the house.

In reviewing the social-learning, cognitive-developmental, and modeling perspectives of how individuals become typical women and men, it is clear that no one explanation is adequate. Rather, depending on the situation, the age of the child, and his or her parents, each process is influential at different times and in differing degrees.

Consider, for example, the four-year-old girl who gets "dressed up" for a brief appearance at her parents' party. She is willing to do this because of a history of reinforcement with praise, approval, and warm compliments from adults when she "looks pretty," a harbinger of things to come. She wears a long skirt like her mother's and helps to pass the hors d'oeuvres, modeling from her mother the appropriate ways that a female behaves as a hostess. At the same time, she can see that all the other women are dressed similarly, and she can observe their tone of voice, their gestures, and the kinds of things they talk about. From this experience and numerous others like it she forms generalizations about the state of being female in her world. All three kinds of learning are occurring, each facilitating the other, to organize the child's sex-role concepts and sex-typed behavior. (Williams, 1977, pp. 164–65)

One way of learning sex roles is to observe and imitate the behavior of role models. As these children reinact a prototypical "screen kiss," their body positions reflect the traditional sex roles of male aggressiveness and female passivity.

Sources of Socialization

Implied in the preceding discussion of various theories on socialization is the idea that different social environments are created for females and males. Since parents, teachers, and the mass media are influential agents in shaping a child's environment, what are the effects of each? Researchers have provided the following answers to this question.

Parents.   Depending on the sex of their children, parents tend to describe even newborn children differently. Thirty first-time parents, fifteen parents of girls and fifteen parents of boys, were asked within twenty-four hours of their child's birth to "describe your baby as you would to a close friend or relative." Although hospital records listing the weight, length, and Apgar scores[4] of the babies showed no significant differences, the parents described their daughters as little, beautiful, delicate, and weak, and sons as firmer, more alert, stronger, and better coordinated (Rubin et al., 1974).

Such differential perceptions in the hospital are carried forward to the nursery. Eleven mothers, all of whom had young children of both sexes, were observed as they played with a six-month-old boy in a nursery. Five of them saw the baby dressed in blue pants and were told that his name was Adam. The other six saw the same baby, introduced as Beth, dressed in pink. Three toys—a fish, a doll, and a train—were placed on a table in front of the baby and mothers. Though unaware of their differential treatment, those women who thought the baby was a boy gave him the train more frequently. If they thought the baby was a girl, a doll was offered more frequently. Likewise, the mothers smiled at the baby they thought was a girl more often than the mothers who thought the baby was a boy (Will et al., 1974).

But beyond these differential reactions in hospital and nursery settings, there are few differences in the way parents treat their daughters and sons (Maccoby & Jacklin, 1974a). Those differences which do exist seem to be specific to toys, "chaperonage," and discipline. Parents tend to give their daughters dolls (their sons, footballs), to be more protective of their daughters (so as to avoid sexual molestation), and to administer more physical punishment to their sons than daughters (Newson & Newson, 1968; Maccoby & Jacklin, 1974a).

Teachers.   While parents get the child first and provide the most pervasive influence, teachers represent a major source of influence outside the home. In a study of how and when preschool teachers spoke to the children in their classroom, the researchers observed that the teachers rewarded boys for being aggressive (by showing attention when they were rowdy), rewarded girls for being dependent (by showing attention when they were near), and gave more individual instruction to boys (Serbin & O'Leary, 1975). And all of the fifteen teachers who were being observed were unaware that they were treating the sexes differently.

Media. In addition to parents and teachers, books and television play a large part in socialization. They convey attitudes about the two sexes as well as providing role models. In a review of 2,750 stories from 134 children's readers (Women on Words and Images, 1972), the following ratios were discovered:[5]

Boy-centered to girl-centered stories	5:2
Adult male to adult female main characters	3:1
Male biographies to female biographies	6:1
Male animal stories to female animal stories	2:1
Male folk or fantasy stories to female folk or fantasy stories	4:1

But aside from the ratios, which imply the greater importance of males, various stories pictured males as brave, persevering, achieving, and ingenious whereas females were portrayed as incompetent and fearful except when baking cookies or sewing.

Television, of course, has its input, too. It has been estimated that the typical teenager has spent more time in front of the television than in school (Gerbner & Gross, 1976). And the characters on the screen are usually stereotyped in traditional roles.

Recently Wonder Woman, Police Woman, and the Bionic Woman have helped shift the statistics, but it is interesting that Wonder Woman, when she isn't saving the world, works as a secretary, and the Bionic Woman teaches elementary school. Heroines such as Charlie's Angels usually take their orders from an authoritative man instead of figuring who dunnit. Even Angie Dickinson's competent police woman is often bailed out of a jam by her male partner. Heroines typically unmask the villain by accident or by luck. When women succeed, these programs seem to be saying, it is not by virtue of their own talents. (Real women attribute success to luck more often than skill, too . . . .) To land the job of TV heroine, a woman must be slender, beautiful, and young. A male adventurer may be fat (Cannon), bald (Kojak), old (Barnaby Jones), or paralyzed (Ironside). (Tavris & Offir, 1977, p. 181)

Is Socialization Everything?

Many of the differences between women and men are only reflections of different socializations. But does this mean that there are no fundamental differences between the sexes—that socialization is the sole cause of the differences we can observe? No it does not. While men and women are basically more alike than different, there are some biological differences worth noting. Women and men have different chromosomes, hormones, and anatomies.

Chromosomes. Women and men have different genetic makeups. Every normal human ovum (egg) contains twenty-two "regular" chromosomes and one X chromosome. Every normal human sperm contains twenty-two "regular" chromosomes and one X *or* Y chromosome. While the regular chromosomes contain various genes which determine the individual's eye color, hair color, body type, etc., the extra chromosome determines sex. And since the sex chromosome in the ovum is *always* X (the female chromosome), the sex chromosome in the male determines the sex of the child. If the sperm contains an X chromosome, the match with the female chromosome will be XX, and a female will result. If the sperm contains a Y chromosome, the male chromosome, the match with the female chromosome will be XY, and a male will result. Hence, the normal female has forty-four regular chromosomes (twenty-two from each parent) plus an X chromosome from her mother and an X chromosome from her father. The normal male also has forty-four regular chromosomes and an X chromosome from his mother but a Y chromosome from his father.

Hormones. The chromosomal differences between the sexes result in hormonal differences. The XX or XY sex chromosomes of an embryo determine whether ovaries or testes will develop. These gonads become important in the manufacture of sex hormones. And while both sexes produce hormones found in the other, androgen is the dominant male hormone and estrogen is the dominant female hormone.

But what does the presence of more androgen in the man and more estrogen in the woman have to do with behavioral differences between the sexes? Aggression is a possibility:

> The fact that sex hormones seem to have a direct effect in aggression in all species and that they have an early and pervasive influence on the nervous system seems to be a strong factor in explaining the pervasive sex differences in human aggression. Castrated males of all species are more docile and tractable, and the effect must come from loss of most of their male hormone. Human females treated with androgen for certain clinical disorders (such as breast cancer) become more active and aggressive and more openly sexual. Aggression in male animals seems to increase at the time of maturation of the gonads when hormonal systems are fully functional. Estrogen derivatives have been used to quiet aggressive behavior in humans. (Weitz, 1977, p. 18)

While some evidence of a hormonal basis for aggression is present, the issue is not that clear-cut. Among animal species, females may become violently aggressive in the defense of their young. And, among humans, it is difficult to know how much aggression among men is socially induced. War and violent crime are considered appropriate for men but not for women. Even in suicide, men choose the blazing gun, women the sleeping pill (Tavris & Offir, 1977).

Anatomy/physiology. In addition to chromosomal and hormonal differences, a number of physical characteristics differentiate the sexes. These differences begin before birth since the male fetus is two to four times more likely to be stillborn during the first four months than the female fetus (Lerner, 1968). In the

United States, during the first year of life, 33 percent more males than females die (Garai & Scheinfeld, 1968). And the pattern continues throughout life. Not only is the woman less likely to die each year, she will live about ten years longer than the man. In 1977, the life expectancy for women was eighty-one years in contrast to seventy-two years for men.

Although men have higher mortality rates at younger ages than women, they are taller, heavier, and stronger than women. The average height for the adult man is five feet, eight inches. For women it is five feet, three inches. But regardless of height or frame, men weigh about ten pounds more than women. And while men evidence more physical strength than women, it is not clear how much of this difference is innate and how much is cultural. "The physically inferior are not women but any human being who does not develop the body's potential—exactly what women have been taught not to do for centuries" (Scott, 1974).[6] What they have been encouraged to do is type, sew, and work on assembly lines—those jobs which require superiority in manual dexterity. (When women and men are compared on fine muscle coordination, women are superior.)

The anatomical and physiological differences just described help to ensure different life experiences for the respective sexes. Only women have the capacity to experience menstruation, pregnancy, childbirth, and the nursing of infants. In contrast, only men will experience erection, ejaculation, impregnating a woman, and daily beard growth.

CONSEQUENCES OF SEX-ROLE SOCIALIZATION

While some differences between women and men are the result of biology and specifically male or female life experiences, it is clear that other differences are consequences of being socialized into the male or female sex role. We now explore these consequences for both sexes.

Individual Consequences of Sex-Role Socialization

Socialization as a woman or man has many implications for individuals. Because males and females learn different sex roles, they tend to differ in many ways including self-concept, self-confidence, competitiveness, and emotional expression.

Self-concept. While a review of self-esteem studies reveals that women feel no worse about themselves than men do generally (Maccoby & Jacklin, 1974a), women may envy men more than men envy women (Tavris & Offir, 1977). When kindergarten children were asked if they would rather be a girl or boy, six of the twenty-nine girls in contrast to one of twenty-nine boys expressed a desire to be

One factor that may interfere with a woman's self-acceptance is the expectation that she should conform to the society's ideal image of youthfulness, physical beauty, and sexual attractiveness.

the other sex (Ollison, 1977). This preference for being male has been demonstrated in other age groups extending into adulthood. While between 2.5 and 4 percent of adult men recall a conscious desire to be the other sex, between 20 and 31 percent of adult women recall having wished that they were male (Sherman, 1971).

Disenchantment with being a woman may be related to *sexism*—the systematic persecution, domination, and degradation of women based on the supposed inferiority of women and supposed superiority of men—or to traditional sex roles (Seidenberg, 1974). It has also been found that women's self-acceptance is in part tied to their physical attractiveness. "The demand to be fashionable, to alter one's body or face, takes its toll on women who constantly feel the need to keep up this front and never to appear as their real, perhaps unacceptable selves" (Whitehurst, 1977, p. 7).

Self-confidence.   In addition to a tendency to prefer being the other sex, women tend to be less self-confident than men. When college students are asked to predict the grades they will make in the upcoming semester, women usually predict that they will make lower grades than men predict they will make (Crandall, 1969). And while it might be assumed that this prediction reflects female modesty (and male bravado), women tend to believe that things which happen to them are outside their control rather than under their control. Technically referred to as external versus internal locus of control, the former is characteristic of females and the latter is characteristic of males (Simon & Feather, 1973). As an example, women at the state fair more often choose to play a game of luck (did your color win?) than skill (throwing darts at balloons) (Deaux et al., 1975). The game of luck assumes that winning is a result of something other than personal skill—external factors—while the game of skill assumes a personal-internal sense of control.

Expectations to fit stereotypes.   A range of other male-female differences probably results from the expectation that men and women should fit the stereotypes for their own sex. Males experience considerable pressure to fit the culturally defined image of masculinity—competitive, aggressive, independent, emotionless. One man had the following recollection of his first awareness that he was supposed to compete.

Men are expected to fit the tough, strong, masculine mold—and one of the obvious rewards for doing so is peer group approval.

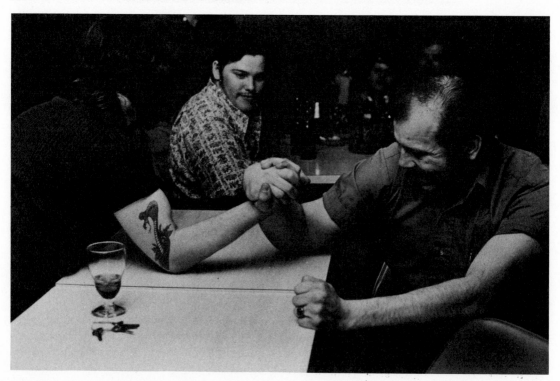

Each morning during the summer, as I cuddled up in the quiet of a corner with a book, my mother would push me out the back door and into the yard. And throughout the day, as my blood was let as if I were a patient of seventeenth century medicine, I thought of the girls sitting in the shade of porches playing with their dolls, toy refrigerators, and stoves. There was the life, I thought! No constant pressure to prove oneself. No necessity always to be competing. (Lester, 1973, p. 112)

Aggressiveness in the competitive struggle is another facet of the male mirage. But some males don't feel like being aggressive. "I didn't want to be dominant and pushy because I learned at an early age that domineering people may get their way on a superficial level but they don't get love or acceptance on any deep level," observed one male (Keith, 1971).

The competitive/aggressive themes are played to the hilt in baseball and football. But not all males are interested in these sports. A banker reflected on his earlier sandlot years:

During the game I always played the outfield. Right field. Far right field. And there I would stand in the hot sun wishing I was anyplace else in the world. Every so often a ball looked like it was coming in my direction and I prayed to God that it wouldn't happen. If it did come, I promised God to be good for the next thirty-seven years if He let me catch it—especially if it was a flyball. (*Unbecoming Men,* 1971)

Along with being competitive and aggressive, males are expected to be independent and self-sufficient. One executive said, "It's difficult for me to express dependence. Feelings of dependence are identified with weakness or 'untoughness' and our culture doesn't accept these things in men" (Bartolome, 1972, p. 75). Real males (whoever and wherever they are) are supposed to know what is best in all situations for all problems.

Knowing what is best in all situations implies being in control which also implies not showing emotion. In the novel and film of *Love Story,* Phil said to Oliver just outside the hospital room where his daughter had died, "I wish I hadn't promised Jenny I'd be strong for you." Both men were straining to control their emotions. They were determined to remain true to the male stereotype.

Relationship Consequences of Sex-Role Socialization

In addition to affecting individuals, sex-role socialization has a strong influence on our marriage and family roles and relationships. Most little girls grow up expecting to be wives and mothers and most boys learn that as men they will have careers and be "breadwinners."

Marriage: A personal trap?   Most women feel enormous pressure to get married. The role of wife is often revered as the way to adult feminine identity in our society. But the consequences of socializing women for marriage (to the exclusion of other options) may be negative. There is abundant evidence that although marriage is often "good" for men, it is more often "bad" for women (Bernard, 1972). About their marriage, more wives than husbands report frustration, dissatisfaction, problems, unhappiness, and a desire to divorce. About their mental health, more married women than married men have felt they were about to have a nervous breakdown, have experienced more psychological and physical anxiety, and more often blame themselves for their own lack of adjustment (Bernard, 1972; Gurin, Veroff, & Feld, 1960; HEW, 1970; Campbell, 1975).

A changed relationship with her husband and the role of the housewife are key aspects contributing to the poorer mental health of wives than husbands. Prior to marriage, the woman is catered to by the man. He tells her how nice she looks, takes her to dinner, movies, and concerts, and gives her his undivided attention. She is led to believe that his world revolves around her. After marriage, she discovers that his world revolves around his work. And, she becomes the caterer. In her classic article, "Why I Want a Wife" *(See Box)*, Judy Syfers brings home just how exhausting a wife's work can be and underscores the convenience of having a hard-working wife around the house.

Some wives also find themselves unprepared to cope with the responsibility for their husbands' psychic needs. "Wives learn with a shock that their husbands are not truly such sturdy oaks. They can no longer take it for granted that their husbands are stronger than they. . . . For some it becomes a full-time career to keep the self-image of [their] husbands intact" (Bernard, 1972, p. 41).

In addition to the problem of propping their husbands up (physically and emotionally), some housewives find their role to be lonely, monotonous, and exhausting. Regarding loneliness, Bernard (1972) wrote, "Her only significant relationships tend to be with her husband who, however, is absent most of the day. Most of her social and emotional needs must be satisfied by her children who are hardly adequate to the task" (p. 50). And monotony creeps in. In a sample of forty housewives, three fourths reported that they were bored (Oakley, 1974, p. 81). And the amount of time spent in the monotonous routine of housework is mindboggling. The average number of hours per week reported by the forty housewives just mentioned was seventy-seven (Oakley, 1974, p. 93). "The worst thing is," reported one wife, "you're never finished. I always go to bed knowing that there's something I should have done" (p. 95).

But increasingly, wives are leaving the home and entering the work force. And doing so results in an identity outside the home. In a *Psychology Today* survey, employed wives reported feeling less anxious than housewives (28 percent compared to 46 percent) and less lonely (26 percent compared to 44 percent) (Shaver & Freedman, 1976).

Marriage: An achievement barrier?   Part of the stifling effect of marriage on women is its capacity to limit their achievement in other areas (e.g., education). This is particularly true of wives who drop out of school to support their husbands. The "Boy Wolf Story" describes this pattern which was especially common in the 1960s:

I Want a Wife

I want a wife who will take care of **my** physical needs. I want a wife who will keep my house clean. A wife who will pick up after me. I want a wife who will keep my clothes clean, ironed, mended, replaced when need be, and who will see to it that my personal things are kept in their proper place so that I can find what I need the minute I need it. I want a wife who cooks the meals, a wife who is a **good** cook. I want a wife who will plan the menus, do the necessary grocery shopping, prepare the meals, serve them pleasantly, and then do the cleaning up while I do my studying. I want a wife who will care for me when I am sick and sympathize with my pain and loss of time from school. I want a wife to go along when our family takes a vacation so that someone can continue to care for me and my children when I need a rest and change of scene.

SOURCE: Excerpted from "Why I Want a Wife" by Judy Syfers, THE FIRST MS. READER. New York: Warner Paperback Library, 1973, p. 24.

Once upon a time there was a pretty young wolfess who was happy and carefree. She liked to flirt with all the young wolves, go to rabbit runs, and sleep till noon. She enjoyed all the nice things that young, carefree wolfesses do.

Then she met a handsome young wolf who had strong legs and big plans. Her heart went flutter when he told her about all the great things he was going to be and do—just as soon as he graduated from wolf school. She was going out of her head with anticipation of the day when they could mate and have their own lair. Then the wolf-boy said: "But we could have a lair now, if you would do all the hunting while I finish wolf school." She agreed. So now, she arose early in the morning to hunt while wolf-boy went to class, played intramural wolf-polo, hung around the wolf-pub, and chewed on loco weed.

Then some little wolves came along and the young mama wolf had to get up early and take the little wolves to the day wolf care center before she went hunting. Hunting was hard for the young wolfess because she was not as strong or old as the mature hunters and only brought back small rabbits. But, no matter, when wolf-boy graduated she could sit back and enjoy her litter of pups and all would be well. Occasionally she noted her fur was not as soft and shiny as it once was, and she was too tired from getting up early to take the cubs to the wolf-sitters and hunting all day to go out with wolf-boy as she had done before. Sometimes he would stay out all night howling with the other student wolves at the wolf-pub.

Finally wolf-boy graduated and was the leader in his pack. He was making more kills and was looked up to by all the other wolves. Other young wolfesses liked him and hung around him. One day, he left with a younger, sleeker wolfess, never to return.

MORAL: The name of this trick is: "Let's me and you work *my* way through wolf school." (Wright, 1978)

Motherhood: A short venture?   While most women are employed during the first years of their marriage, the majority are socialized to leave work and retreat into the home at least until their children are in school. A woman who marries at age twenty-one will have her last child at thirty and can anticipate attending that child's wedding at fifty-two (Glick, 1977, pp. 7–8). Since she can expect to live to be eighty or more, she will have over a quarter of a century in which she is not in the role of mother. "This period can be especially difficult if the women has no other pursuits except those of providing for her family. It is even more difficult if her financial position is insecure and she has no means of supporting herself should she find herself without a spouse" (Whitehurst, 1977, p. 21).

Marriage and motherhood: The best of everything?   For many women, the traditional sex roles of wife and mother offer more in the way of rewards than drawbacks. Of 120,000 women responding to a survey of *Redbook* magazine readers, three fourths said they were "at least relatively satisfied with the traditional division of labor, in which the wife is primarily responsible for homemaking" (Tavris & Jayaratne, 1973, p. 128). In contrast to many working mothers, full-time homemakers can more freely control and plan their own work and be their own bosses. They are more likely than employed women to see their children's first steps and hear their first words instead of getting a report from a babysitter or child-care worker. Women who enjoy the homemaker role find greater fulfillment in caring for those they most love than in working in a more impersonal setting toward more impersonal goals. They do not see the traditional role as an achievement barrier because they define achievement as providing a good home life for their families and rearing their children successfully.

Man's obligation to work.   The role of men in our society has its own difficulties and rewards. A recent career advertisement in a national magazine showed a young wife looking at her husband while leaning on his shoulder. The man-to-man caption read, "One day, it suddenly strikes home that we're going to be working for a living the rest of our lives." Just as the female is channeled into the role of housewife and mother, the male is tracked into the world of gainful employment to support a wife and children. He has little choice. He must work—his wife, children, parents, in-laws, and peers expect it. A college senior who heard this in a lecture said, "Baloney! I'm not getting caught in the work trap. I'm going to paint houses now and then—just enough to keep me going—and enjoy life." Three years after graduation he called and said, "I'm married now and stuck in a crummy job. I want to get into graduate school so I can get a good job." Notice his focus had changed from "if a job" to "which job."

The man's responsibility to earn an income has implications for his health and self-esteem. Regarding health, nearly half of all male workers are in manual trades—factory work, construction industries, and semi-skilled crafts. Their labor is "physical rather than mental, hazardous rather than safe. . ." (Walum,

1977, p. 178). Each year over two million U.S. workers are injured on the job (Richardson et al., 1975, p. 343).

While the health of the male workers is jeopardized, their self-esteem may take a greater beating. "Rather than leaving their home and entering a world in which they are in control, they perform monotonous, routine, and unimportant tasks. There are few intrinsic or extrinsic rewards" (Walum, 1977, p. 178). Regarding the extrinsic rewards, somehow our society assumes that the man who makes $50,000 annually is more of a man than the one who makes $5,000 annually. Ultimately a man must turn his brain into gold. Otherwise, it's assumed that "he doesn't have what it takes."

A man's identity equals his job.   Ask a man who he is and he will tell you what he does. His identity is in reference to his job. It is the principal means by which he confirms his masculinity. In two classic studies of unemployment during the Great Depression, job loss was regarded as a greater shock to men than to women, although the loss of income would affect both. The unemployed man lacked anything to be involved in either physically or psychologically (Lynd, 1937; Komarovsky, 1950).

The identification of self with job becomes problematic when it forces human concerns into a low priority (Miller, 1971). In a study of forty young business executives, one researcher observed how "work not only took most of their time, but also most of their energy. So when they returned home, they felt 'drained' and able to communicate very little with their wives and children" (Bartolome, 1972).

The over-involvement with work and the subsequent lack of concern for human values often backfires. One researcher said, "The more occupational success they [men] attain, the more conflict ridden are their marriages . . ." (Walum, 1977, p. 179). And in reference to children, one father told his five-year-old daughter who had asked him to play with her, "Don't bother Daddy. I'm busy. Please leave the study." Later that afternoon when he came into his little girl's room to play with her, she said, "Don't bother me. I'm busy. Please leave my room."

Society-Wide Consequences of Sex-Role Socialization

Socialization into male and female sex roles has also had society-wide consequences, including inequality of the sexes economically, politically, and educationally. Let's look at these areas more closely.

Economics.   In spite of laws forbidding discrimination, women earn considerably less than men. While the differences vary with the type of work, in no job classification of the Department of Labor do women earn more than two thirds of what men in the same category earn. Even in the clerical category, women earn 61 percent of what men do (U.S. Bureau of Labor Statistics, 1975). And the wage gap exists even when the sexes are matched for age, education, experience, skill, tenure on the job, and being employed full time (Treiman & Terrell, 1975; Suter & Miller, 1973).

Despite all the figures demonstrating lower salaries for women, the myth continues that women own most of the wealth in America. But after analyzing Census Bureau data, a researcher concluded, "A study of the facts thoroughly discredits the cliches about women and their wealth. Not only are poor women poorer than poor men, but rich men are richer than rich women. . . . Men, not women, earn, own, and control most of the wealth of this country" (Bernard, 1975, p. 241).

Politics. Although women represent over half of all persons of voting age in the United States, their absence in political offices is conspicuous. "Not only has there never been a woman U.S. President, Vice-President, or Supreme Court Justice, there has never been more than one or two female Senators at a time. . . . Women usually represent only about 2 percent of Congress" (Whitehurst, 1977, p. 84).

Prior to the election of 1974, there had been only three female governors in the history of the United States. And these three succeeded their husbands who either died in office or were not qualified to run for another term. A first happened in 1974 when Ella Grasso was elected governor of Connecticut in her own right. However, despite some gains, "women are still, by and large, excluded from major power centers and women as a group lack any resources other than sheer numbers to trade in for political influence" (Whitehurst, 1977, p. 85).

Education. In addition to economic and political differences between the sexes, women earn fewer educational degrees at every level than men. Table 2.1 reflects the percentage of degrees conferred on men and women in the United States for the 1975–1976 academic year. Whether women seek husbands rather than degrees, or the school system discourages them away from career (not job)

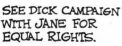

SEE DICK CAMPAIGN WITH JANE FOR EQUAL RIGHTS.

B.C.

3-30

LOOK, LOOK, SEE DICK AND JANE GET A JOB AT THE MINES.

SEE DICK GET AN OFFICE JOB.

SEE JANE GET THE SHAFT.

TABLE 2.1   Earned Academic Degrees 1975—1976.

Type of Degree	Percentage Granted to Men	Percentage Granted to Women
Bachelor's	54	46
Master's	54	46
Doctor of Philosophy	77	23
Medicine	84	16
Law	81	19
Dentistry	95	5

SOURCE: Adapted from Education Division of Department of Health, Education, and Welfare, 1978.[7]

preparation, or the society does not provide enough educated female models for professional attainment, the result is the same—women tend to have other priorities than earning academic degrees. The more advanced the degree, the less likely a woman is to earn it.

SEX ROLES TODAY

Traditional sex roles have clearly had a strong influence on individuals, family relationships, and the society as a whole. But individuals and families today may or may not fit the traditional sex-role patterns or have traditional values. Let's look at the contemporary family and at current ideas about the "ideal" man or woman.

The Contemporary Family

Not a great deal has changed regarding the division of labor in the family since the prehistoric hunting and gathering days. Both sexes typically regard the woman's employment role as secondary to her familial role. In a national probability sample of 1,230 households with children under age thirteen, 82 percent of the 1,230 adults who were interviewed agreed strongly or partially that "a woman with small children should go to work only if the money is really needed" (Yankelovich et al., 1977, p. 69). And 74 percent agreed strongly or partially that "It's up to the man to be the main provider in the family" (p. 68). While male australopithecines left their families to search for meat, modern males leave home to search for money (which is used to buy meat).

TABLE 2.2 The Ideal Woman.

Characteristics	Percent saying trait is essential to being "ideal" woman	
	Women	Men
Able to love	97	92
Stand up for beliefs	90	82
Warm	88	83
Self-confident	87	76
Gentle	86	79

SOURCE: Adapted from Tavris, 1977, p. 37.

But sex roles are changing the family in at least two major ways: Women are having fewer children and are entering the labor force in increasing numbers. And since roles basically develop in conformity with the kind of work people do, women will continue to move their influence beyond the home into the public arena (Scanzoni, 1976; Huber, 1977).

Today's Ideal Woman

The contemporary woman is expected to be loving, assertive, warm, self-confident, and gentle. As Table 2.2 indicates, these are the top five of twenty characteristics of the "ideal woman" as identified by 28,000 relatively young, educated Americans.[8] Notice that two of these characteristics (assertiveness and self-confidence) are usually associated with masculinity. That the ideal woman is expected to be more assertive and self-confident suggests that fewer young people being socialized in today's society will tend to be exclusively feminine or masculine. Rather, their personalities will be androgynous, that is, they will reflect characteristics of both genders. Research by Bem suggests that androgynous people may feel freer to explore their environment than those who have exclusively male or female characteristics (Bem, 1977).

Today's Ideal Man

The same is true of today's "ideal man"—that is, he has some traditionally masculine traits but also some traditionally feminine traits. The strong, brave, aggressive image of the "Marlboro man" is fading. Today, the ideal man combines self-confidence and assertiveness (not aggression) with the ability to love and to be warm. Table 2.3 reflects the top five of twenty characteristics of the ideal man

TABLE 2.3 The Ideal Man.

Characteristics	Percent saying trait is essential to be "ideal" man	
	Men	Women
Able to love	88	96
Stand up for beliefs	87	92
Self-confident	86	86
Fights to protect family	77	72
Warm	68	89

SOURCE: Adapted from Tavris, 1977, p. 37.

identified by the same 28,000 people mentioned above. In analyzing the survey the researcher observed:

> The macho male who is tough, strong, aggressive, and has many sexual conquests is not admired by either sex. Men want to be more warm and loving than they feel they are. Masculinity today is a set of admirable qualities, appropriate for women too, rather than a set of merit badges that must be earned and rewon. Most people don't think men have to prove their manhood any more in daring feats of faucet-fixing or hand-to-hand combat. (Tavris, 1977, p. 35)

TRENDS

Sex-role trends include fewer barriers to women, fewer workaholic men, and more androgynous people. In the past ten years, a number of barriers to women have been removed. Opportunities now exist for women to become judges, business executives, doctors, and generals where recently there was little if any chance of doing so. And, little girls have now joined the boys on the Little League field. While inequities still exist in the economic and political arenas, advances are being made on both fronts.

In addition to women gaining greater access to the positions in society they desire, more men are beginning to question the value of devoting their lives to chasing the buck. Personnel managers in private industry now speak of a "new breed" who are less willing to take a promotion if it would mean moving their families or greater personal stress (Filene, 1976, p. 393).

As pressures to perform traditional female or male roles are lessened, an increasing number of people will be regarded as androgynous—they will have both

feminine and masculine characteristics. In a study of two thousand under-graduates, one third were classified as androgynous (Bem, 1977, p. 209). Such androgynous individuals feel more free to follow their own interests independent of the sex-role implications (Bem & Lenney, 1976).

SUMMARY

The term *sex* refers to the biological distinction of being male or female. In contrast, a person's *gender identity* is his or her self-concept of being a girl and later a woman, or a boy and later a man. *Sex roles,* also known as gender roles, are the socially accepted characteristics and behaviors associated with one's gender identity. In our society, the traditional role of women is to be emotional, dependent, and home-oriented whereas the male role is to be unemotional, independent, and career-oriented. Traditional sex roles have their roots in the prehistoric pattern of men hunting and fighting while women, of necessity, cared for the young who needed their mother's milk.

Although modern societies are much more complex, females and males are still socialized to fill different roles. The social learning theory suggests that children learn their roles by being rewarded for gender-appropriate behaviors and punished for inappropriate (opposite sex) behaviors. The cognitive-developmental view of sex-role learning is that children must first reach the stage where they understand that their gender is permanent, and then they can actively seek to acquire masculine or feminine characteristics. A third theory of sex-role learning involves modeling, or learning either male or female behaviors by observing and imitating those who have already learned their sex roles. While biology may provide a disposition to behave in certain ways, it is the society (represented by parents, teachers, and mass media) which guides the individual's behavior patterns into culturally approved sets—girls are "supposed" to play with dolls, and boys are "supposed" to play with footballs. A combination of the major theories provides the best explanation of sex-role learning.

Sex-role socialization has many consequences for individuals, family relationships, and the society as a whole. While sex roles are changing, women's self-esteem and self-confidence are less than men's on the average and men find themselves needing to fit the aggressive, independent, emotionless male stereotype. Sex-role socialization pushes most women toward the wife and mother role (instead of into careers) and requires that men devote themselves to careers sometimes at the expense of their families. Male and female socialization has also contributed to economic, political, and educational inequality of the sexes. The future of sex roles includes fewer barriers to women, fewer workaholic men, and more androgynous people.

STUDY QUESTIONS

1. Distinguish between the terms *sex, gender identity,* and *sex role.*
2. Describe the traditional sex roles for women and men.
3. Describe the prehistoric roots of the traditional roles.
4. How do the research by Mead on the three New Guinea tribes and the case history reported by Money emphasize the importance of the environment in socializing females and males?
5. List and describe in detail three perspectives which help to explain how sex roles are learned.
6. How do parents treat their daughters and sons differently?
7. How do teachers respond differently to female and male students in preschool?
8. Discuss the influence of books and television in perpetuating sex-role stereotypes.
9. How do females differ from males in reference to chromosomes, hormones, and physical make-up?
10. Compare the self-concept and self-confidence of females and males.
11. Give examples of several ways males may try to live up to their sex-role stereotype.
12. Why is marriage sometimes described as a personal trap for females? As an achievement barrier?
13. What do some women who are full-time homemakers and mothers say about the positive aspects of their role?
14. Discuss the implications of the obligation of men in our society to work.
15. What are the economic, political, and educational differences between women and men in our society?
16. Describe the ideal woman in contemporary American society.
17. Describe the ideal man in contemporary American society.
18. Explain what is meant by an androgynous person.
19. What are several emerging trends in sex roles?

NOTES

1. Appreciation is expressed to Drs. Robert Bunger and Greysolynne Fox, Department of Sociology and Anthropology, East Carolina University, for their assistance in the development of this section.

2. Anthropologists are divided on this issue. Reed (1975) asserts that the heavy domestic burdens carried out by women made them as strong as males.

3. Fortune (1939) made another visit to these societies, and his finding did not agree with Mead's. For example, in the Arapesh society, he observed that males held the ultimate power and were responsible for waging war.

4. A physician's rating of the infant's color, muscle tonicity, reflex irritability, heart and respiratory functioning.

5. In a recent update using books published after 1972, when the first survey was published, WWI found that the ratio for biographies had improved markedly (to 2:1), but the ratio of boy-centered to girl-centered stories had worsened (to 7:2). Some individual books had changed, but the overall picture was not much altered (Tavris & Offir, 1977).

6. The Supreme Court ruling that females may play Little League baseball and the increasing number of professional women athletes may signal a new trend toward encouraging females to develop their bodies.

7. Appreciation is expressed to Dianna Morris, Institutional Research, East Carolina University, for providing this information.

8. These data are based on questionnaires returned by readers of *Psychology Today*.

BIBLIOGRAPHY

Bartolome, F. Executives as human beings. *Harvard Business Review,* November–December 1972, 62–9.

Bem, S. L. Beyond androgyny: Some presumptuous prescriptions for a liberated sexual identity. In *Family in Transition,* A. S. Skolnick and J. H. Skolnick (eds.). Boston: Little, Brown, 1977, 204–21.

Bem, S. L., and Lenney, E. Sex typing and the avoidance of cross-sex behavior. *Journal of Personality and Social Psychology,* 1976, *33,* 1, 48–54.

Bernard, J. *The future of marriage.* New York: Bantam Books, 1972.

Bernard, S. Women's economic status: Some cliches and some facts. In *Women: A feminist perspective,* J. Freeman (ed.). Palo Alto, Calif.: Mayfield, 1975, 238–41.

Campbell, A. The American way of mating: marriage si, children only maybe. *Psychology Today,* May 1975, 37–43.

Crandall, V. J. Sex differences in expectancy of intellectual and academic reinforcement. In *Achievement-related motives in children,* C. P. Smith (ed.). New York: Russell Sage Foundation, 1969, 11–45.

Deaux, K., White, L., and Farris, E. Skill versus luck: Field and laboratory studies of male and female preferences. *Journal of Personality and Social Psychology,* 1975, *32,* 629–36.

Filene, P. Him/her/self. In *Scenes from life: Family, marriage, and intimacy,* J. Blankenship (ed.). Boston: Little, Brown, 1976, 389–410.

Fortune, W. F. Arapesh warfare. *American Anthropologist,* 1939, *41,* 22–41.

Friedl, E. *Women and men: An anthropologist's view.* New York: Holt, Rinehart and Winston, 1975.

Garai, J. E., and Scheinfeld, A. Sex differences in mental and behavioral traits. *Genetic Psychology Monographs,* 1968, *77,* 162–299.

Gerbner, G., and Gross, L. The scary world of TV's heavy viewer. *Psychology Today,* April 1976, 41–5ff.

Glick, P. C. Updating the life cycle of the family. *Journal of Marriage and the Family,* 1977, *39,* 1, 5–13.

Gurin, G., Veroff, J., and Feld, S. *Americans view their mental health.* New York: Basic Books, 1960.

Harris, M. Male supremacy is on the way out. It was just a phase in the evolution of culture. A conversation with Marvin Harris, by Carol Tavris. *Psychology Today,* January 1975, 61–9.

Huber, J. Department of Sociology, University of Illinois at Urbana–Champaign. Personal communication, 1977.

Keith, J. My own men's liberation. *WIN Magazine,* September 1971, 22–6.

Kohlberg, L. A cognitive-development analysis of children's sex-role concepts and attitudes. In *The development of sex differences,* E. E. Maccoby (ed.). Stanford, Calif.: Stanford University Press, 1966.

_____. Stage and sequence: The cognitive-developmental approach to socialization. In *Handbook of socialization theory and research,* D. A. Goslin (ed.). Chicago: Rand McNally, 1969, 347–480.

Komarovsky, M. Functional analysis of sex roles. *American Sociological Review,* 1950, *15,* 508–16.

Lerner, I. M. *Heredity, evolution, and society.* San Francisco: W. H. Freeman, 1968.

Lester, J. Being a boy. *Ms. Magazine.* July 1973, 112–13.

Lynd, R. S., and Lynd, H. M. *Middle town in transition.* New York: Harcourt, Brace and Co., 1937.

Maccoby, E., and Jacklin, C. N. *The psychology of sex differences.* Stanford, Calif.: Stanford University Press, 1974. (a)

_____. Myth, reality and shades of gray: What we know and don't know about sex differences. *Psychology Today,* December 1974, 109–12. (b).

Mead, M. *Sex and temperament in three primitive societies.* New York: William Morrow, 1935.

Miller, S. M. The making of a confused, middle-aged husband. *Social Policy,* 1971, *2,* 2, 33–9.

Money, J., and Ehrhardt, A. A. *Man and woman, boy and girl.* Baltimore: Johns Hopkins University Press, 1972.

Newson, J., and Newson, E. *Four years old in an urban community.* Harmondsworth, England: Pelican Books, 1968.

Oakley, A. *The sociology of housework.* New York: Pantheon Books, 1974.

Ollison, L. Study referred to in *The Longest War,* by C. Tavris and C. Offir. New York: Harcourt Brace Jovanovich, 1977.

Reed, E. *Women's evolution.* New York: Pathfinder, 1975.

Richardson, C. E. *Living: Health, behavior, environment.* Glenview, Ill.: Scott, Foresman, 1975.

Rubin, J. Z., Provenzano, F. J., and Luria, Z. The eye of the beholder: Parents' views on sex of newborns. *American Journal of Orthopsychiatry,* 1974, *44,* 4, 512–19.

Scanzoni, J. Sex role change and influences on birth intentions. *Journal of Marriage and the Family,* 1976, *38,* 1, 43–58.

Scott, A. C. Closing the muscle gap. *Ms. Magazine,* September 1974, 49.

Seidenberg, R. Is sex without sexism possible? In *Sexual behavior: Current issues,* L. Gross (ed.). Flushing, N.Y.: Spectrum Publications, 1974, 59–72.

Serbin, L. A., and O'Leary, K. D. How nursery schools teach girls to shut up. *Psychology Today,* December 1975, 56–8ff.

Shaver, P., and Freedman, J. Your pursuit of happiness. *Psychology Today,* August 1976, 26–32.

Sherman, J. *On the psychology of women.* Springfield, Ill.: Charles C. Thomas, 1971.

Simon, J. G., and Feather, N. T. Causal attributions for success and failure at university examinations. *Journal of Educational Psychology,* 1973, *64,* 46–56.

Suter, L. E., and Miller, H. P. Income difference between men and career women. *American Journal of Sociology,* 1973, *78,* 962–75.

Syfers, J. Why I want a wife. *The First Ms. Reader.* New York: Warner, 1973, 23–5.

Tavris, C. Masculinity. *Psychology Today,* January 1977, 35 et passim.

Tavris, C., and Jayaratne, T. What 120,000 young women can tell you about sex, motherhood, menstruation, housework—and men. *Redbook,* January 1973, 67–69, 127–29.

Tavris, C., and Offir, C. *The longest war: Sex differences in perspective.* New York: Harcourt Brace Jovanovich, 1977.

Treiman, D. J., and Terrell, K. Sex and the process of status attainment: A comparison of working women and men. *American Sociological Review,* 1975, *40,* 174–200.

U.S., Bureau of Labor Statistics. *U.S. working women: A chartbook, Bulletin 1880* (1975).

U.S., Education Division of Department of Health, Education, and Welfare. Degrees and other formal awards conferred between July 1, 1975 and June 30, 1976. Higher Education General Information Survey (HEGIS XI). Washington, D.C.: U.S. Government Printing Office, May 1978.

U.S., Public Health Service. Selected symptoms of psychological distress. National Center for Health Statistics, Series 11, #37. Vital and Health Statistics, August, 1970.

Unbecoming men: A men's consciousness-raising group writes on oppression and themselves. New York: Times Change Press, 1971.

Walum, L. R. *The dynamics of sex and gender: A sociological perspective.* Chicago: Rand McNally, 1977.

Weitz, S. *Sex roles.* New York: Oxford University Press, 1977.

Whitehurst, C. A. *Women in America: The oppressed majority.* Santa Monica, Calif.: Goodyear Publishing, 1977.

Will, J., Self, P., and Datan, N. Nursery stereotypes. Paper presented at the meeting of the American Psychological Association, New Orleans, 1974.

Williams, J. H. *Psychology of women: Behavior in a biosocial context.* New York: W. W. Norton, 1977.

Women on Words and Images. *Dick and Jane as victims: Sex stereotyping in children's readers.* Princeton, N.J., 1972.

Wright, J. *The boy wolf story.* Unpublished paper, Loyola University, New Orleans, Louisiana.

————. Director of Criminal Justice Program, Loyola University, New Orleans, Louisiana. Personal communication, 1978.

Yankelovich, Skelly, and White. *The General Mills American Family Report 1976–1977.* Minneapolis, Minn.: General Mills, Inc.

Love Relationships

Love doesn't make the world go 'round. Love is what makes the ride worthwhile.

Franklin P. Jones

"Because we're in love" is the reason most Americans give for wanting to get married. Love is the element which is regarded as giving meaning to human relationships. Although parent-child, sibling-sibling, and friend-friend relationships often involve love, woman-man love relationships are the focus of this chapter. We will examine the significance of love, the conditions under which love develops, the range of love feelings, the styles of loving, the effects of love, and trends in love relationships. Let's begin by reviewing several definitions of love.

DEFINITIONS OF LOVE

Because feelings of love are private and the individual alone has access to what he or she experiences, the definitions of love are varied. Some classic definitions of love include:

> When the satisfaction or the security of another person becomes as significant to one as is one's own security, then the state of love exists. (Sullivan, 1947)

> Love is an active power in man; a power which breaks through the walls which separate man from his fellow men. . . . In love the paradox occurs that two beings become one yet remain two. (Fromm, 1956)

> Love is the passionate and abiding desire on the part of two or more people to produce together the conditions under which each can be and spontaneously express his real self; to produce together an intellectual soil and an emotional climate in which each can flourish, far superior to what either could achieve alone. (Magoun, 1948)

> Love is that intense feeling of two people for each other which involves bodily, emotional, and intellectual identification; which is of such a nature as to cause each willingly to forego his personality demands and aspirations in favor of the other; which gains its satisfaction through creating a personal and social identity in those involved. (Koos, 1953)

College students also vary in their definitions of love. Table 3.1 provides some examples from students in a marriage and family class in 1978. Looking at the array of these definitions gives us the feeling of Cherubino in Mozart's *Marriage of Figaro* when he asked, "What is this thing, love?"

> Cherubino was still a beardless adolescent and did not know the answer, but he took it for granted that there was one. So have most other people, and many of them have tried to give it, but the most noteworthy feature about all their answers is how thoroughly they disagree. Sometimes, it seems, they cannot be referring to the same

society. One sociologist observed, ". . . it serves to motivate individuals to do what must be done so that the total social system can maintain itself as a going concern. In short, romantic love induces Americans to fill positions . . . husband-father and wife-mother and form nuclear families that are essential . . . for reproduction and socialization. . ." (Greenfield, 1975, p. 168).

CONDITIONS FOR ESTABLISHING A LOVE RELATIONSHIP

As we have seen, love is significant for personal, marital, and societal reasons. It also occurs under predictable social and psychological conditions. This implies that while our society may set the stage for love feelings to develop, individuals need to have certain characteristics which will enable them to experience these love feelings.

Social Conditions

"Do your own thing," a theme which became popular in America in the late sixties, continues. The idea emphasizes the right (or obligation) of people to find their own meaning in life and to pursue it. "My dad owns a business which recaps steel radial tires, but I'm not getting sucked into that system or lining up for an ulcer like him," remarked a philosophy major. "I'm going to paint houses in the winter and grow vegetables in the summer."

This college student's feelings reflect a spirit of individualism—a need to find one's own way. The making of decisions based on what one wants to do rather than on what one must do for "the family" provides the context for the development of love feelings in our society. Where mate selection is characterized by bargaining between the parents, individual feelings are of little importance (McCall, 1971). What is right and proper according to tradition takes precedence over such feelings.

Psychological Conditions

Psychologically, the potential lover must have a positive self-concept, the ability to self-disclose, and an array of social skills.

Positive self-concept. The way you feel about yourself is your self-concept. A positive self-concept is one in which you like yourself and enjoy being who you are. A person who has achieved genuine self-acceptance can say:

> This is all that I am; I am no more and no less. I am sometimes wise and sometimes foolish. I am sometimes brave and sometimes cowardly. I am caring and uncaring; selfish and unselfish. I am moral and immoral. I am sometimes the best and sometimes the worst. I am all these things. I do not approve of everything I am, but that

doesn't prevent me from recognizing and accepting myself for what I am. (Coutts, 1973, p. 169)

A positive self-concept is important since once you accept yourself, you can believe that others are capable of doing so too. In contrast, a negative self-concept has devastating consequences for the individual and those persons with whom he or she becomes involved. Individuals who cannot accept themselves tend to reject others. They make the assumption, "If he/she wants me, there must be something wrong with him/her" (Miller & Seigel, 1972, p. 63).

The way we feel about ourselves and our ability to relate intimately to others are both learned. Our first potential love relationships were with our parents or the person who cared for us in infancy. As babies, we were literally helpless. When we were hungry, cold, or wet, we cried until someone came to take care of us. Our parents became associated with reducing our discomfort (Miller & Seigel, 1972, p. 42). When we saw them, we knew that everything would be okay.

Being well cared for as infants helps establish a good self-concept by teaching us two things: (1) we are somebody that someone else cares about; and (2) other people are good because they do things (feed, get blanket, change diapers) which make us feel good. Once we learn as young children to love and trust the people we live with, then we can generalize this lesson to others and eventually establish adult love relationships.

Self-Disclosure.   People must be willing to disclose their feelings to others if they want to love and be loved.

> One who does not disclose himself [herself] truthfully and fully can never love another person nor can he [she] be loved by the other person. Effective loving calls for knowledge of the object. How can I love a person whom I do not know? How can the person love me if he [she] does not know me? (Jourard, 1964, p. 25)

It is not easy for people to let others know who they are, what they feel, or what goes on inside their heads. People often fear that, if others really knew what they were thinking, they might be less admired or respected or thought of as crazy. They might be dropped as a friend or lover. Since such withdrawal would be painful, they protect themselves and their relationships by allowing others to know only certain facets of who they are.

Trust is the condition under which people are willing to disclose themselves. In order to feel comfortable about letting someone else inside their heads, they must feel that whatever feelings or information they share will not be judged and will be kept safe with that person. This implies that self-disclosure occurs in relationships with people who are protective of us (not destructive), and with people who are deeply concerned (not resentful or rejecting) (Coutts, 1973). If a trust is betrayed, a person may become bitterly resentful and vow never to disclose themselves again. One sophomore at a large eastern university said, "After I told my boyfriend that I had had a homosexual experience, he told me that he was

shocked and didn't know that I was 'one of those.' He refused to see me again."
This woman will be hesitant to disclose this information about herself again.

Social skills.   In addition to a positive self-concept and the ability to self-disclose, those who develop love relationships with ease often have an array of social skills. They have good eye contact, they smile, they initiate conversations and express an interest in the other person. They also go to the places where there are other people. "I enjoy dancing at the university pubs and that's where you meet a lot of people," remarked a music major. "My roommate doesn't enjoy dancing or being around a lot of people so he stays in our room and watches TV."

DEVELOPMENT OF A LOVE RELATIONSHIP

Having considered various conditions which contribute to the development of love relationships, we now examine the process of "falling in love." Since researchers disagree on how love develops, we will consider several points of view.

Self-disclosure involves letting down barriers and becoming more vulnerable emotionally. If we choose a protective and caring person to disclose our thoughts and feelings to, a positive, intimate relationship can be established or enriched by it.

A Learning Theory View of Love

One explanation for how love develops is based on learning theory. This perspective says that one individual loves another to the degree that the other becomes a source of many different kinds of rewards. "We enjoy parties, diving, surfing, hiking, and movies," remarked one sophomore. "When I want to do something, Robin's the one I want to share it with."

But an array of shared activities is not enough to create the feeling of love. The individual must be physiologically aroused and interpret this stirred-up state in emotional terms (Schachter, 1964). For example, Carol was beginning her first year at a midwestern university. Being three states away from her home, she felt lonely and bored in the impersonal university environment. During registration she met a good-looking junior and they exchanged pleasant glances and small talk, and planned to go out together that night around 8:00. Carol became anxious when Brad had not shown up by 8:45. When he did arrive around 9:00, they went to a concert, drank some beer, and played the pinball machines at a local pub. Carol had a terrific time.

Two days went by before Carol heard from Brad again. He called to ask if she wanted to go home with him for the weekend. By the end of that weekend, Carol felt she was in love. Her loneliness (away from home), fun when they were together, frustration (she never knew when Brad was to call or come by), and sexual arousal (Brad was good-looking but hadn't "tried anything") were enough to induce an agitated, stirred-up state. Since both her roommates were "in love," Carol began to see herself the same way.

The Wheel of Love Model

The wheel of love model offers another explanation of how love develops (Reiss, 1960). In the first stage, the rapport stage, each partner has the feeling that he or she has known the other before, feels comfortable with the other, and is desirous of deepening the relationship.

This desire leads to the stage of self-revelation, or self-disclosure. Intimate thoughts are revealed when talking about each other and their relationship. Such revelations deepen the relationship because it is assumed that confidences of this nature are shared only with special people. And each partner feels special when listening to a confidence from the partner.

Within the safe, intimate relationship, disclosure begets disclosure. A home economics major revealed to her partner that her father was involved in an affair with his secretary and, as a result, the girl had begun to hate her father and mistrust men in general. Her boyfriend disclosed that his mom was an alcoholic and that his home life had been a nightmare. One researcher observed that when partners do not share some of the intimate details of their lives, it is difficult for a love relationship to develop (Gouldner, 1959).

FIGURE 3.1   The Wheel of Love Model.

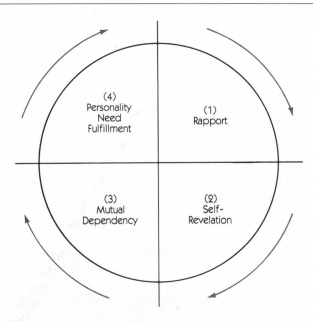

SOURCE: From "Toward a Sociology of the Heterosexual Love Relationship" by I. L. Reiss, MARRIAGE AND FAMILY LIVING, May 1960, 22, 43.

As the level of self-disclosure becomes more intimate, a feeling of mutual dependency develops. Each partner is happiest in the presence of the other and begins to depend on the other for euphoric feelings. Watching television, attending concerts, and cheering at football games is more enjoyable with the partner. "But I won't last a day without you," is the theme of this stage in the development of love.

The feeling of mutual dependency involves the fulfillment of personality needs. The desires to love and to be loved, to trust and to be trusted, to support and to be supported are met in the developing love relationship. Reiss suggested that the initial rapport between the two people may really have been a vague feeling or hope that this other person could fulfill these personality needs. Thus, the circle is completed:

> These four processes are in a sense really one process for when one feels rapport, he [she] reveals himself [herself] and becomes dependent, thereby fulfilling his [her] personality needs. The circularity is most clearly seen in that the needs being fulfilled were the original reason for feeling rapport. (Reiss, 1960, p. 143)

The Clock Spring Alternative

Modifying Reiss's wheel of love model, Borland (1975) suggested viewing the development of love as a clock spring.

> As these four processes occur and lead one into the other, they wind themselves toward a closer and more intimate relationship with an understanding of the real inner self of the other person. As this occurs, the individuals form an increasingly tighter bond to one another in much the same way as a clock spring tightens as it is wound. (Borland, 1975, p. 291)

The "real self" refers to the thoughts and values behind the social scripts that all people read. Shakespeare wrote, "The false face must hide what the false heart doth know." In a developing love relationship, as described by the clock spring model, the individuals would drop their "false faces" and reveal their true feelings to each other more and more.

In a developing love relationship, the partners not only choose to do many things together, but they fulfill each other's need to love and be loved, to trust and be trusted, and to support and be supported emotionally.

FIGURE 3.2   The Clock Spring Alternative

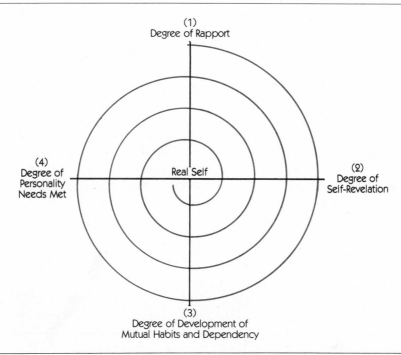

SOURCE: From "An Alternative Model of the Wheel Theory" by D. M. Borland, THE FAMILY COORDINATOR, 1975, 24, 289–92.

In describing the development of love, the clock spring model has several advantages over the wheel model. First, it helps to illustrate the length of time required to wind up a relationship and the difficulty of unwinding it. "The tighter or closer the relationship has progressed around the person's 'real self,' the more difficult it is and the longer it takes to 'unwind' the relationship" (Borland, 1975, p. 291). Second, it depicts the relationship which becomes so tightly overwound that the individuals cannot grow. "I felt that I was being sucked into my partner's world. I was losing sight of my own goals in life," remarked a sociology major. Third, the clock spring model emphasizes the dynamic, fluctuating nature of a love relationship. Like the winding of a clock, the relationship can indefinitely wind and unwind and then wind again at a different level. "This is our fourth year together and we've been through lack of money, living together, and an abortion. Our relationship is strong or weak depending on when we talk about it," remarked one man.

RANGE OF LOVE FEELINGS

The development of love often involves a range of different types of love feelings. These include liking, loving, and what is referred to as romantic love.

Liking

"I never met a man I didn't like," humorist Will Rogers once said. We understand and use the word *like* as he did to imply affection and respect (Rubin, 1973). We have feelings of affection toward those who relate to us in a friendly way. "From the day my roommate asked me if I would like to go shopping with her, we hit it off," a first-semester freshman recalled. Her feelings emphasize the affectionate element of liking. In addition to affection, liking implies respect that is based on a person's admirable characteristics or actions in spheres other than personal relations. Our respect for another person's courage, integrity, or skill may predispose us to like them.

Loving

While affection and respect comprise the basic elements of liking, attachment, caring, and intimacy help to describe the phenomenon of loving (Rubin, 1973, p. 217). Attachment refers to a compelling desire to be with another, to make physical contact with, and, in general, to experience the feeling of being emotionally involved with another person.

In addition to attachment, loving includes caring. An infant may be attached to its mother, but it is incapable of caring, which implies a more mature form of love. Caring means being concerned about what happens to another. When Rhett Butler said to Scarlett O'Hara in *Gone with the Wind,* "Frankly, my dear, I don't give a damn," she knew that she had lost an essential element of Rhett's love—his caring.

Beyond attachment and caring, loving implies intimacy. As has already been suggested, intimacy is both a basic reason for our seeking the love experience and a condition for it. As an element of love, intimacy involves the feeling of relating to another, soul to soul. "My partner is the only one who really knows who I am and what I think. The feelings of closeness, of belonging, of sharing make me feel euphoric," said one engaged person.

Romantic and Realistic Love

Romantic love is different from both liking and loving. It is characterized by such beliefs as love at first sight, there is only one true love, and love is the most important criterion for getting married.

Romantic love is usually described in contrast to realistic love or conjugal love—the love between settled, domestic people (Goode, 1959). Partners who know all about each other, yet still love each other, are said to have a realistic type of love.

The Love Attitude Inventory (LAI) (see Table 3.2) measures the tendency to be romantic or realistic. Agreeing with each of the items (circling 1 or 2) indicates a romantic attitude toward love, while disagreeing with each item (circling 4 or 5) indicates a realistic attitude toward love.

Using the Love Attitude Inventory, several studies have been conducted to find out the degree to which various categories of people are romantic or realistic. When one hundred unmarried men and one hundred unmarried women college students completed the Love Attitude Inventory, the results revealed that men were more romantic than women and that freshmen were more romantic than seniors (Knox & Sporakowski, 1968). Since, traditionally, marriage has been more important to women than to men, the women's more realistic attitude toward love was not surprising. The higher realism scores for seniors were expected because they are older and theoretically had been exposed more to the reality of love relationships.

The man who painted, "Mary Shiminski I Love You!" would very likely agree with most of the Love Attitude Inventory statements. His romantic and persistent pursuit of Mary Shiminski received national media attention—as did their marriage.

TABLE 3.2 Love Attitude Inventory.

Directions: Please read each sentence carefully and circle the number which you believe best represents your opinion. Be sure to repond to all statements.

1. Strongly agree (definitely yes)
2. Mildly agree (I believe so)
3. Undecided (not sure)

4. Mildly disagree (probably not)
5. Strongly disagree (definitely not)

	SA	MA	U	MD	SD
1. Love doesn't make sense. It just is.	1	②	3	4	5
2. When you fall head-over-heels-in-love, it's sure to be the real thing.	1	2	3	④	5
3. To be in love with someone you would like to marry but can't, is a tragedy.	1	2	③	4	5
4. When love hits, you know it.	1	②	3	4	5
5. Common interests are really unimportant; as long as each of you is truly in love, you will adjust.	1	2	③	4	5
6. It doesn't matter if you marry after you have known your partner for only a short time as long as you know you are in love.	1	②	3	4	5
7. If you are going to love a person, you will "know" after a short time.	1	2	3	④	5
8. As long as two people love each other, the religious differences they have really do not matter.	1	②	3	4	5
9. You can love someone even though you do not like any of that person's friends.	1	②	3	4	5
10. When you are in love, you are usually in a daze.	1	2	3	④	5
11. Love at first sight is often the deepest and most enduring type of love.	1	2	3	4	⑤
12. When you are in love, it really does not matter what your partner does since you will love him [or her] anyway.	1	2	3	④	5
13. As long as you really love a person, you will be able to solve the problems you have with that person.	1	②	3	4	5
14. Usually there are only one or two people in the world whom you could really love and be happy with.	1	2	3	④	5

	SA	MA	U	MD	SD
15. Regardless of other factors, if you truly love another person, that is enough to marry that person.	1	2	3ˣ	④	5
16. It is necessary to be in love with the one you marry to be happy.	①ˣ	2	3	4	5
17. Love is more of a feeling than a relationship.	1ˣ	②	3	4	5
18. People should not get married unless they are in love.	1ˣ	2	③	4	5
19. Most people love truly only once during their lives.	1	2ˣ	3	④	5
20. Somewhere there is an ideal mate for most people.	①ˣ	2	3	4	5
21. In most cases, you will "know it" when you meet the right one.	1ˣ	②	3	4	5
22. Jealousy usually varies directly with love; that is, the more you are in love, the greater your tendency to become jealous.	1ˣ	②	3	4	5
23. When you are in love, you do things because of what you feel rather than what you think.	1	2	3	④	5
24. Love is best described as an exciting, rather than a calm thing.	1ˣ	②	3	4	5
25. Most divorces probably result from falling out of love rather than failing to adjust.	1ˣ	②	3	4	5
26. When you are in love, your judgment is usually not too clear.	1	2ˣ	3	④	5
27. Love often comes but once in a lifetime.	1	2ˣ	3	④	5
28. Love is often a violent and uncontrollable emotion.	1	2ˣ	3	④	5
29. Differences in social class and religion are of small importance as compared with love in selecting a marriage partner.	1ˣ	②	3	4	5
30. No matter what anyone says, love cannot be understood.	1	②	3	4	5

SOURCE: DISCUSSION GUIDE TO ACCOMPANY A LOVE ATTITUDE INVENTORY, by D. Knox. Saluda, N.C.: Family Life Publications, Inc., 1971.

Another study compared the love attitudes of fifty men and fifty women high-school seniors with fifty husbands and fifty wives who had been married over twenty years. Both groups revealed a romantic attitude toward love (Knox, 1970). These findings had been expected for the high-school seniors, but not for the older marrieds. One explanation of the findings suggests that those who have been married for twenty years may be expected to adopt attitudes consistent with such a long-term investment of their time and energy. The belief that there is only one person with whom an individual can really fall in love and marry provides cognitive consonance for those who have done so. When these high-school seniors and older marrieds were compared with one hundred young couples (married less than five years), the latter proved very realistic in their attitudes (Knox, 1970). For them, moonlight and roses had become daylight and dishes. They had been married too long to believe that, "As long as you really love a person, you will be able to solve the problems you have with that person," but not long enough to experience the feeling that, "You only really love once."

All of the above studies were conducted on white subjects. When 327 black high-school and college students completed the Love Attitude Inventory, the results revealed that black students had more romantic attitudes toward love than white students (Mirchandani, 1973). One explanation suggests that because black students are more likely to come from broken and economically disadvantaged homes, they may seek romantic love relationships as a means of compensating for their disadvantage (Larson et al., 1976).

LOVE: A SOUND BASIS FOR MARRIAGE?

Researchers do not agree as to whether love provides an adequate basis for marriage. Even though Baum (1971) found that sixty-five engaged men and women defined love as companionship, understanding, sharing, and giving of mutual support, she suggested that marrying for love would be conducive to marital *un*happiness. "People would become dissatisfied with marriage because it does not provide the close companionship that they married for." In essence, Baum felt that these students were asking more of marriage than it could deliver. Her conclusion is significant because her subjects tended to have a realistic attitude toward love. And a realistic view of love has traditionally been thought of as a good preparation for marriage.

When romantic love is considered, most writers and researchers issue glaring indictments against it as a basis for marriage:

> Romance is poor preparation for marriage and is not to be trusted to provide more than a few thrills. It is not enough to marry. (Duvall, 1960, p. 26)

> Of all the possible motives for marriage such as equal social level or education, suitability of temperament, background, religious preference, age, etc., love is the most unstable and ephemeral and yet, is heralded as the most important motive. (DeRougemont, 1948, p. 10)

One marriage and family counselor notes that the qualities that make a man or woman comforting and fulfilling as a marriage partner have little direct connection with the qualities that usually arouse feelings of romance. For example, an attractive, glamorous man or woman may or may not also be a dependable, growing, caring person (Albert, 1973).

In contrast to this negative view of romantic love, Spanier (1972) studied 218 married college students and found no indication that romantic love, as opposed to realistic love, was harmful to marital adjustment. He concluded, ". . . among married couples in a college community, romanticism is not generally excessive, and . . . in cases where there is unusually high romanticism, marital adjustment is not likely to be any lower. In fact, a slight positive correlation (between romanticism and marital adjustment) was found" (p. 486).

What about romantic love and happiness in your marriage? If the love you have for your partner is based on physical attraction, little time together, and few shared experiences, marrying on this basis may be taking an unnecessary risk. To marry someone without spending a great deal of time with him or her (minimum of one year) in a variety of situations (your home, your partner's home, four- or five-day camping trips, etc.) is like buying a Christmas package without knowing what's in it. We need to spend time analyzing our partner.

Many people flinch when they hear the word *analyze* in reference to their love partner. Senator William Proxmire is one of those who has taken this view. In a much publicized statement in 1976, Senator Proxmire identified a study of romantic love sponsored by the National Science Foundation as "my choice for the biggest waste of the taxpayer's money for the month of March. I believe that 200 million Americans want to leave some things in life a mystery, and right at the top of the things we don't want to know is why a man falls in love with a woman and vice versa" (Rubin, 1977, p. 59).

But individuals who get divorced spend a great deal of time analyzing the love relationship with their partner and trying to discover what went wrong. It is better to study our partner and our love relationships before considering marriage.

There is some evidence that the love myth (love is all we need for a successful marriage) is dying and is being replaced by a nonjealous, nonpossessive love (Kilpatrick, 1974). One explanation seems to be that because more people are living together, they are learning more about the opposite sex. Having to deal with grocery shopping, meal preparation, dirty dishes, laundry, and clothes on the floor provides a more realistic setting in which to explore each other.

STYLES OF LOVING

Just as there is a range of feeling from liking to loving and from romanticism to realism, there are different styles of loving. While one researcher (Lee, 1973; 1974) identified six such styles of loving, two others (Hatkoff & Lasswell, 1976) revealed which styles were characteristic of 554 men and women. The six types to be presented are ". . . ideal constructs. Rarely is anyone a 'pure' type. Rather, persons have varying degrees of each quality" (Lasswell & Lasswell, 1976, p. 219).

Eros (Romantic)

The eros style of loving is similar to romantic love already described. Eros individuals seek a lover who is the perfection of physical beauty. They hold an ideal image in their thoughts and try to find the person in real life. The image involves the details of the lover's skin, eyes, hair, body proportions, and fragrance. When the person is "spotted," there is the feeling of having known that person for a long time. "The first time I saw him was several weeks before we met," remarked one of Lee's (1974) 112 respondents. Individuals who fall in love often or who have been in love several times are likely to view love through a romantic set of lenses (Hatkoff & Lasswell, 1977).

Erotic lovers usually experience a chemical or gut reaction on first meeting each other and go to bed soon afterwards. "This is the first test of whether the affair will continue, since erotic love demands that the partner live up to the lover's concept of bodily perfection" (Lee, 1974). However, the erotic relationship also involves psychological intimacy. Each wants to know everything about the beloved, to become part of him or her. "Erotic lovers like to wear matching T-shirts, identical bracelets, matching colors, order the same foods when dining out, etc." (Hatkoff & Lasswell, 1976, p. 7).

Love is an irresistible desire to be irresistibly desired.
Robert Frost

Erotic love is the most transient of the various styles of loving. Because the real must match the ideal in terms of physical beauty and psychological fit, the erotic lover is often disappointed. Although erotic lovers may eventually settle for less, they never forget the compromise and rarely lose hope of realizing the dream. Lee (1974) states, "The purer the erotic qualities of the respondent's love experience, the less his/her chances of a mutual, lasting relationship."

The eros style of loving is more characteristic of men than of women. As noted earlier, men are more romantic in their conception of love than women (Knox & Sporakowski, 1968). Since male socialization includes an emphasis on female beauty and transient relationships, this finding is not surprising.

Ludus (Self-Centered)

In contrast to the erotic lover, the ludic lover views love as a game, refuses to become dependent on any one person, and does not encourage another's intimacy. Like a cat teasing a mouse, the ludic lover keeps the partner at a distance. And, while the ludic lover is criticized by the erotic lover because of his or her lack of commitment, moralists condemn the ludic's implicit promiscuity or hedonism (Lee, 1974). But the ludic lover explains that to make a game of love does not diminish its value. Skill in playing the game is the issue.

Two skills of every ludic are to juggle several people at the same time and to manage each relationship so that no one is seen too often. These strategies help to ensure that the relationship does not deepen into an all-consuming love. The ludic lover may keep two, three, or even four lovers "on the string" at one time. Sex is self-centered and exploitative rather than symbolic of a relationship (Hatkoff & Lasswell, 1976, p. 6).

Don Juan represented the classic ludic lover. To him, the pleasure of the game was in the chase, not in capturing the prize. "Once I am sure that a girl has fallen in love with me, I gradually begin to lose interest in her," is a statement that characterizes the ludic lover.

The ludic lover also tends to be a man.

> Because women are viewed as objects, men relate to them as to objects and their actions, options, and lives are restricted by rules and limitations applicable to objects. Too many men are preoccupied with the accumulation of many sexual conquests rather than with the development of a warm and deep love relationship with another human being. (Israel & Eliasson, 1971)

Storge (Life-Long Friends)

Storge (pronounced *stor-gay*) characterizes the love of friendship, companionship, and affection. "Storgic lovers are essentially good friends who have grown in intimacy through close association, with an unquestioned assumption that their relationship will be permanent (Hatkoff & Lasswell, 1976, p. 6). Without either partner experiencing feelings of ecstasy, storge lovers have a deep caring for each other. Storge love has a subtle beginning. It is as if the partners remember no specific point when they felt love for each other. Yet there is a deep feeling of intimacy which binds each to the other.

The storge lover is practical and predictable. The emotional component of love is low-key. Storge lovers plan their relationship—what they will do together every night. Spontaneity is lacking. To the ludic or erotic lover, storge is a bore (Lee, 1974). But storge love has its advantages.

> Storgic lovers build up a reservoir of stability that will see them through difficulties that would kill a ludic relationship and greatly strain an erotic one. The physical ab-

sence of the beloved, for instance, is much less distressing to them than to erotic lovers; they can survive long separations. . . . Also, in the ludic relationship, something
is happening all the time (a game is being played) . . . and inactivity leads to boredom
. . . . In storge, there are fewer campaigns to fight and fewer wounds to heal. (Lee,
1974)

Women are more likely to be storge lovers than men (Hatkoff & Lasswell,
1976, p. 10), perhaps because female socialization emphasizes caring, companionship, and affection. Previous research has also revealed that women tend to be
more rational about love (Knox & Sporakowski, 1968).

Agape ("Thou"-Centered)

The agapic lover has only the best interests of his or her partner at heart. Such a
lover "would be more likely to help his or her love-object to get medical attention
for a venereal disease contracted from someone else than to be angry or punitive
toward the love-object for having a sexual relationship with another" (Hatkoff &
Lasswell, 1976, p. 4). "Whatever I can do to make your life happy" is the motif of
the agapic lover, even if this means giving up the beloved to someone else.

Neither men nor women are more likely to have an agapic style of love than
the other sex. At least this is true of Americans who live on the mainland. But
among Hawaiians, women are more likely to demonstrate agapic qualities than
men. In observing this phenomenon, the researchers remarked,

The Hawaiian sample which showed women to score significantly higher than men on
the agapic scale, contained a substantial proportion of Orientals. If one looks at the
traditions and norms surrounding sex differences in Oriental cultures this is not at all
surprising. Traditionally, women in Oriental cultures were taught to put their husbands before themselves, an agapic quality. (Hatkoff & Lasswell, 1976, p. 14)

Mania (Intense Dependency)

The manic lover has difficulty functioning without his or her partner. He or she is
obsessed with the beloved. Jealousy and inability to sleep, eat, or think logically
characterize the manic lover. And while the manic lover has peaks of excitement,
he or she also experiences the depths of depression.

Women are more likely to be manic lovers than men (Hatkoff & Lasswell,
1976, p. 5). Traditionally, women were socialized to be dependent. "Even in this
country women in the very recent past needed a husband's signature and consent
to travel abroad, to own property, to borrow money, or even to work" (Safilios-
Rothschild, 1977, p. 32).

Pragma (Logical-Sensible)

Women are more likely to be pragmatic in their love relationships than men.

Pragmatic lovers are inclined to look realistically at their own assets, decide on their
"market value" and set off to get the best possible "deal" in their partners. The prag-

matic lover remains loyal and faithful and defines his/her status as "in love" as long as the loved one is perceived as a "good bargain." (Hatkoff & Lasswell, 1976, p. 5)

Such rationality is similar to that of the storgic lover who also tends to be a woman.

While and because women have not been socialized traditionally to become skilled in the economic and occupational spheres, they have been allowed to develop skills in the emotional sphere, especially in love (Hochschild, 1975). These skills have not only safeguarded women from falling in love with the "wrong" man but have also allowed them to make believe that they love the man who possesses the desirable social and economic characteristics for marriage. (Safilios-Rothschild, 1977, p. 23)

In other words, women traditionally have been taught to seek husbands who are

One of the most obvious changes that comes with a love relationship is an increase in physical contact. Where there is no love or affection, there is little touching.

"good providers" since women themselves have not been reared to become economically self-sufficient.

Lovers who represent the pure forms of eros, ludus, storge, agape, mania, and pragma are difficult to find. Most people have some elements of each.

EFFECTS OF LOVE

Regardless of an individual's style of loving, being involved in a love relationship has predictable consequences on behavior. For instance, people are more likely to touch and enjoy bodily contact with someone they love. In his report on love in self-actualizing people, Maslow (1970) observed, "There is a tendency to want to get closer, to come into more intimate contact, to touch and embrace the loved person." One need only go to the student union on a university campus to observe couples sitting on couches, arm-in-arm and leg-to-leg to sense the effect of love on physical contact.

Love also affects how two people look into each other's eyes. Rubin (1973) observed from his experiment on eye-gazing behavior that the more a couple reported they were in love, the longer they stared into each other's eyes. "Eye contact serves as a mutually understood signal that the communication channel between two people is open. While eye contact is sustained, the actions of either partner are automatically defined as relevant to both of them" (p. 222). Shakespeare suggested that the eyes are the window to the soul. Lovers who look intently into the window seek both to express and to increase the level of intimacy they feel.

Being in love with each other also encourages doing things *for* each other. The property lines of "mine" and "yours" fade as the love relationship deepens. Stereos, portable televisions, and cars are often exchanged. In addition, love cards, candles, and posters are given as random surprises.

TRENDS

The future of love relationships is likely to include less romanticism and the development of new definitions of love. A central element of romantic love is the belief that there is only one person with whom one can "truly" fall in love. This belief has its basis in the past. "Men and women most often loved only once in their lives partly because their life expectancy was much shorter and partly because in most cases their lifestyle did not allow them to meet a great variety of people" (Safilios-Rothschild, 1977, p. 9). But girls born in 1977 have a life expectancy of eighty-one, and boys can expect to live until seventy-two. During this span, each sex will doubtless encounter an array of love relationships and will probably not maintain the belief that there is "only one true love."

One researcher observed that the trend toward a decline in romantic love has already begun. Such a decline is related to greater sexual permissiveness, the diminution of the double standard, and the increasing popularity of living together (Wilkinson, 1978). In essence, as the blockades to spending more time together in intimate interaction are removed, the reality of the woman-man relationship will replace the romantic notions of what it is thought to be.

In addition to less acceptance of the romantic tradition, the "rational" woman and the "romantic" man may acquire new definitions of love. As sex-role stereotypes subside, both sexes will tend to view love as involving "a combination of personal freedom, continuous growth, exclusivity, and sexual satisfaction" (Safilios-Rothschild, 1977, p. 78). This reconceptualization of love will seemingly encourage the development of relationships in which each person can relate freely and openly with the other while avoiding the ". . . domination, power, and indifference games" (Safilios-Rothschild, 1977, p. 78).

SUMMARY

Since love is a personal experience, the definitions of love are as varied as these experiences. But while there is disagreement over the meaning of love, there is agreement on its significance. Love in America is regarded as essential for personal happiness and many consider it a prerequisite for marriage.

Love occurs under certain social and psychological conditions. A society which promotes a spirit of individualism sets the stage for love if the individual in this society has a positive self-concept, the ability to self-disclose, and various social skills.

Once the necessary conditions have been met, love develops as a result of two people sharing a range of mutually enjoyable activities over time. Even when frustrated, the partners can experience increased love for each other because they can interpret their stirred-up physiological state as love feelings.

The development of love may also be viewed as a wheel which involves rapport, self-disclosure, mutual dependency, and personality-need fulfillment. Considering love as a clock spring, the love relationship becomes one of dynamic interaction that winds up and winds down.

The intensity of love varies from liking to loving. Between these extremes is romantic love, which is characteristic of blacks, men, high-school seniors, college freshmen, and people who have been married over twenty years. Whites, women, college seniors, and people who have been married under five years seem to have the most realistic attitude toward love. While most family life educators feel that romantic love is not a sound basis for marriage, others disagree.

Styles of loving include eros (romantic), ludus (self-centered), agape ("thou"-centered), storge (life-long friends), mania (intense dependency), and pragma (logical-sensible). While agape is characteristic of either sex, the last three styles of loving tend to be characteristic of women and the first two styles tend to be characteristic of men.

All styles of loving have their effect on behavior. In general, we want to touch, look into the eyes of, be with, and do things for those we love.

Trends in love relationships include less romanticism and the development of new perspectives on love. Both sexes will tend to view love as providing the potential for human growth rather than a paralyzing emotion or a feeling to be manipulated so as to control the partner.

STUDY QUESTIONS

1. Why are there many definitions of love?
2. Discuss the significance of love in our society.
3. What social and psychological conditions encourage love to develop?
4. What does being well cared for by our parents or others when we are infants teach us?
5. How does self-disclosure relate to love? Under what conditions are we willing to disclose ourselves?
6. Explain the learning theory perspective of how love develops.
7. Describe the wheel and clock spring views of love. What advantages does the latter view have in explaining the developing love relationship?
8. Describe the basic elements of liking and loving.
9. What is romantic love in contrast to realistic love? Are high-school seniors, young marrieds (married under five years), older marrieds (married over twenty years), black people, college men, college women, and college seniors more likely to view love realistically or romantically?
10. Discuss the degree to which romantic love is (or is not) a sound basis for marriage.
11. Describe in detail six styles of loving.
12. How does love affect behavior?
13. Discuss two trends in love relationships.

BIBLIOGRAPHY

Albert, G. Needed: A rebellion against romance. *Journal of Family Counseling,* 1973, *1,* 29–33.

Baum, M. Love, marriage, and the division of labor. *Sociological Inquiry,* 1971, *41,* 107–17.

Borland, D. M. An alternative model of the wheel theory. *The Family Coordinator,* 1975, *24,* 3, 289–92.

Coutts, R. L. *Love and intimacy: A psychological approach.* San Ramon, Calif.: Consensus Publishers, 1973.

DeRougemont, D. The romantic route to divorce. *Saturday Review of Literature,* 1948, *31,* 9–10.

Duvall, E. M. *Being married*. New York: Association Press, 1960.

Fromm, E. *The art of loving*. New York: Harper and Row, 1956.

Goode, W. J. The theoretical importance of love. *American Sociological Review*, 1959, *24*, 38–41.

Gouldner, A. W. Reciprocity and autonomy in functional theory. In *Symposium on sociological theory*, L. Gross (ed.). Evanston: Row, Peterson, and Company, 1959, 241–70.

Greenfield, S. M. Love and marriage in modern America: A functional analysis. In *Confronting the issues*. K. C. W. Kammeyer (ed.). Boston: Allyn and Bacon, 1975, 153–68.

Hatkoff, T. S., and Lasswell, T. E. Male/female similarities and differences in conceptualizing love. Paper presented at the annual meeting of the National Council on Family Relations, October 1976.

―――――. Love and age, sex and life course experiences. Paper presented at the meeting of the National Council on Family Relations, San Diego, 1977.

Hochschild, A. R. Attending to, codifying and managing feelings: Sex differences in love. Paper presented at the meeting of the American Sociological Association, San Francisco, August 1975.

Hunt, M. M. *The natural history of love*. New York: Alfred A. Knopf, 1959.

Israel, J., and Eliasson, R. Consumption society, roles and sexual behavior. *Acta Sociologica*, 1971, *14, 1,* 2, 68–82.

Jourard, S. M. *The transparent self*. Princeton: D. Van Nostrand, 1964.

Kanin, E. J., Davidson, K. R., and Scheck, S. R. A research note on male-female differences in the experience of heterosexual love. *The Journal of Sex Research*, 1970, *6*, 1, 64–72.

Kilpatrick, W. The demythologizing of love. *Adolescence*, 1974, *9*, 33, 24–9.

Knox, D. Conceptions of love at three developmental levels. *The Family Coordinator*, 1970, *19*, 151–7.

―――――. Discussion guide to accompany a love attitude inventory. Saluda, N.C.: Family Life Publications, 1971.

Knox, D., and Sporakowski, M. J. Attitudes of college students toward love. *Journal of Marriage and the Family*, 1968, *30*, 638–42.

Koos, E. L. *Marriage*. New York: Henry Holt, 1953.

Larson, D. L., Spreitzer, E. A., and Snyder, E. E. Social factors in the frequency of romantic involvement among adolescents. *Adolescence*, 1976, *11*, 41, 7–12.

Lasswell, T. E., and Lasswell, M. I love you but I'm not in love with you. *Journal of Marriage and Family Counseling*, 1976, *2*, 3, 211–24.

Lee, J. A. *The colours of love*. Toronto: New Press, 1973.

―――――. The styles of loving. *Psychology Today*, October 1974, 44–50.

Linton, R. *The study of man*. New York: Appleton-Century-Crofts, 1936.

Lynch, J. J. *The broken heart: The medical consequences of loneliness in America*. New York: Basic Books, 1977.

Magoun, F. A. *Love and marriage*. New York: Harper and Row, 1956.

Maslow, A. H. Love in self-actualizing people. In *Motivation and personality*. New York: Harper and Row, 1970, 181–202.

McCall, M. M. Courtship as social exchange: Some historical comparisons. In *People as partners*, J. P. Wiseman (ed.). New York: Canfield Press, 1971, 36–51.

Miller, H. L., and Seigel, P. S. *Loving: A psychological approach*. New York: John Wiley and Sons, 1972.

Mirchandani, V. K. Attitudes toward love among blacks. Unpublished Master's thesis, East Carolina University, Greenville, N.C., 1973.

Reiss, I. L. Toward a sociology of the heterosexual love relationship. *Journal of Marriage and Family Living*, 1960, *22*, 139–45.

Rubin, Z. *Liking and loving: An invitation to social psychology*. New York: Holt, Rinehart and Winston, 1973.

_____. The love search. *Human Behavior,* February 1977, 56–9.

Safilios-Rothschild, C. *Love, sex, and sex roles.* Englewood Cliffs, N.J.: Prentice-Hall, 1977.

Schachter, S. The interaction of cognitive and physiological determinants of emotional state. In *Advances in experimental social psychology,* Berkowitz (ed.). New York: Academic Press, 1964, 49–80.

Spanier, G. B. Romanticism and marital adjustment. *Journal of Marriage and the Family,* 1972, *34,* 481–7.

Stora-Sandor, J. *Alexandra Kollontai: Marxisme et revolution sexuelle.* Paris: François Maspéro, 1973.

Sullivan, H. S. *Conceptions of modern psychiatry.* Washington, D.C.: Alanson White Psychiatric Foundation, 1947.

Walster, E., and Walster, G. W. A new look at love. Reading, Mass.: Addison-Wesley, 1978.

Wilkinson, M. L. Romantic love and sexual expression. *The Family Coordinator,* 1978, *27,* 2, 141–8.

Chapter 4

Sexual Values

T here may be some things better than sex, and some things worse, but there is nothing exactly like it.

W. C. Fields

Is it wrong to have intercourse with someone I've known for only a short time? Why does society look down on a woman who is as sexually active as men are? What does *promiscuous* mean amid today's standards? Questions about sexual values are common among university students. In this chapter we explore the nature of sexual values, how they have changed, and why they have changed. In addition, we examine the motivations for and consequences of sexual intercourse.

DEFINITION OF SEXUAL VALUES

Values may be defined as standards of desirability from which behavioral choices are made (Maiolo, 1978). Sexual values refer to those standards of desirability in reference to sexual behavior. These values may be reflected emotionally ("I would not feel good about having intercourse with someone I did not care about"), intellectually ("I think having nonmarital intercourse without contraception is irresponsible"), or behaviorally ("I had intercourse last night"). Our concern in this chapter is with "values as observable variables in human conduct" (Williams, 1970, p. 439). Who does what with whom, where, and for what reason depends partly on sexual values that are learned from peers, parents, and the media (books, television, movies). Sexual values vary from one person to the next, but the factors of race, sex, decade of birth, rural or urban background, age, education, and perception of being in love have a lot to do with determining a person's values.[1]

ALTERNATIVE SEXUAL VALUES

Reiss (1976) identified four nonmarital sexual-value positions: belief in abstinence; acceptance of the double standard; acceptance of permissiveness with affection; and acceptance of permissiveness without affection. The latter two categories should be viewed as two ends of the same continuum. Sexual encounters occur in the context of different degrees of affection.

Abstinence

Abstinence is based on the belief that sexual intercourse for unmarried men and women is wrong (although other forms of sex may be seen as appropriate). College students who believe in abstinence are more likely to be religiously devout, white, female, freshmen, and uninvolved in a love relationship. A devout student whose religion stressed sexual abstinence commented on his values as follows: "I like having a strong religious faith. I don't feel confused about what my values are or what I will or will not do sexually."

College students are also more likely to hold conservative sexual values during the freshman year since the liberalizing environment of college tends to erode such values. One researcher followed the sexual attitudes of Stanford undergraduates from the fall of their freshman year until the fall of their senior year. About 75 percent of the freshman men and women agreed with the statement, "It is all right for a man/woman to have sexual intercourse with someone he/she loves but is not married to." By the senior year 85 percent of the men and 90 percent of the women agreed with the statement (Miller & Bowker, 1974).

Another characteristic associated with abstinence is race. White men and women are less likely to have intercourse outside of marriage than black men and women. Looking at lower-class students of both races in five universities, one researcher found that whereas 86 percent of the black men and 42 percent of the black women approved of nonmarital intercourse, only 56 percent of the white men and 17 percent of the white women approved (Reiss, 1968). And in a national sample of all never-married women (fifteen through nineteen years old), 31 percent of the whites and 63 percent of the blacks reported having had intercourse by age nineteen (Zelnik & Kantner, 1977, p. 56).

In addition, those who value abstinence tend to be uninvolved in a love relationship (Laner et al., 1977). If you're not going with someone that you *want* to have intercourse with, it's easier to believe intercourse outside of marriage is wrong. Emphasizing the importance of a partner on sexual values, one researcher concluded, ". . . the development of a love relationship, exposure to a new value system in the university or among a group of peers, a partner who is willing to advance or who insists on advancing to greater levels of intimacy, or the prospect of marriage, will take precedence over or negate all other past sexualizing influences" (Spanier, 1975, p. 39).

Not drinking and not smoking marijuana are also associated with abstinence. In a four-year study of high-school and college students, 21 percent of the women who said they were virgins had not smoked marijuana more than once. But 67 percent of those who were not virgins had used marijuana more than once (Jessor & Jessor, 1975).

Double Standard

A double standard[2] of sexuality means that there is one set of standards or principles for men and another for women. The double standard means that it is more acceptable for men to engage in all types of sexual behavior (including intercourse) than for women to do so. One rationale of the double standard has been the belief that men have had uncontrollable appetites for sex. Release through ejaculation is necessary (so the rationale goes) because of the accumulation of regularly produced sperm. Although no deaths have ever been attributable to a lack of sexual release, some women who accept the double standard are willing to look the other way when their boyfriends "relieve themselves" with other women.

Although the double standard allows men to confirm their masculinity by having intercourse, women have traditionally been taught that there is little difference between a "promiscuous" woman and a whore. Promiscuity, which is never clearly defined but might mean any nonmarital sexual behavior, is usually discussed in reference to women, not men. Most women have been socialized to avoid behaviors resulting in this label and to exercise care and restraint in their expression of sexuality and in their choice of sexual partners.

The double standard is a source of irritation for many college women and increasingly for men. The editor for a university newspaper remarked, "Anyone who criticizes my morals just because I go to bed with a guy is unfair. Guys sleep around all the time and no one seems to notice or care." Another student in the same office said, "I've had it with what people think. If you don't sleep with anyone, they think you're a religious freak or you're frigid. If you do, they look the other way but imply that you're making a mistake."

The double standard has long dictated that a woman should guard her reputation and avoid being labeled "promiscuous" or "loose." But among those who subscribe to the permissiveness-with-affection ethic, such so-called "fooling around" may be acceptable for a man or a woman, so long as it occurs within the context of an affectionate relationship.

TABLE 4.1 Gender, Year in School, and Sexual Status.

	Nonvirgin Sexual Status			
	Male		Female	
Year in College	Percent	Number of Respondents	Percent	Number of Respondents
Freshman	36	(151)	19	(138)
Sophomore	63	(145)	30	(151)
Junior	60	(150)	37	(147)
Senior	68	(147)	44	(148)
Total	56	(593)	32	(584)

SOURCE: Adapted from Simon, Berger, and Gagnon, 1972, p. 208.

Although many people may not like the double standard, its influence is very widespread. Table 4.1 reflects the effect of the double standard on college students in twelve different universities. At every grade level, more male than female students reported having had intercourse. Other researchers have similarly documented the double standard among college students (Kaats & Davis, 1970).

Permissiveness with Affection

"I see nothing wrong with having sex with someone you love. When you care about the person, sex is a great experience to share; if you don't, it can be cheap and degrading." This statement by a naval cadet at Annapolis represents the most pervasive sexual standard among college students—permissiveness with affection. This sexual value can also be divided " . . . into two subtypes, the first being that subtype which requires love and/or formal engagement to be present before coitus is justified. The second subtype allows coitus to occur under lesser amounts of affection, such as merely 'strong affection' " (Reiss, 1976, p. 151). In general, women are more likely to demand love and men to settle for strong affection (p. 151). Increasing sexual intimacy is regarded as appropriate with increasing levels of involvement as Table 4.2 reveals. The table is based on the responses of 472 male and female students at Macquarie University in Australia. Heterosexual relationships in Australian society are similar to those found in other Western societies (Collins, Kennedy, & Francis, 1976, p. 373).

The individual who adopts the permissiveness-with-affection value must exercise a level of intellectual sophistication that is not required by those who

TABLE 4.2   Percentage of Respondents Indicating Their Expectation of Opposite Sex Dating Behavior by Intimacy Level, Sex and Courtship Stages.

Level of Intimacy	Expectation of Males	Females	Expectation of Males	Females	Expectation of Males	Females	Expectation of Males	Females
	On First Date		After Several Dates		When Going Steady		When Marriage Is Considered	
At Age 17–19 Years[1]								
Kissing	81.0	94.4	100.0	99.6	100.0	100.0	100.0	100.0
Necking	57.0	33.8	92.0	55.1	99.0	57.2	100.0	57.3
Light Petting	28.0	18.4	80.0	48.7	95.0	58.8	100.0	57.3
Heavy Petting	6.0	4.3	50.0	29.5	88.0	53.0	99.0	57.3
Petting to Orgasm	1.0	2.9	27.0	17.5	73.0	48.2	98.0	57.3
Intercourse	0.0	1.3	12.0	9.4	58.0	35.9	97.0	56.8
At Age 20–24 Years[2]								
Kissing	92.0	88.9	100.0	100.0	100.0	100.0	100.0	100.0
Necking	46.0	59.3	92.0	96.3	100.0	100.0	100.0	100.0
Light Petting	18.0	25.9	84.0	88.9	100.0	100.0	100.0	100.0
Heavy Petting	8.0	7.4	50.0	51.8	94.0	92.6	100.0	100.0
Petting to Orgasm	4.0	3.7	22.0	40.7	92.0	85.2	96.0	100.0
Intercourse	6.0	3.7	20.0	25.9	58.0	74.1	96.0	100.0
At Age 25–30 Years[3]								
Kissing	88.0	86.7	96.8	100.0	100.0	100.0	100.0	100.0
Necking	45.2	46.7	93.6	90.0	96.8	96.7	96.8	100.0
Light Petting	16.7	33.3	74.2	80.0	93.6	96.7	96.8	100.0
Heavy Petting	9.7	13.3	51.6	50.0	90.3	93.3	96.8	100.0
Petting to Orgasm	9.7	10.0	25.8	33.3	77.4	80.0	96.8	100.0
Intercourse	6.5	10.0	25.8	33.3	58.1	63.3	96.8	93.3

[1]N = 100 males, 234 females.
[2]N = 50 males, 27 females.
[3]N = 31 males, 30 females.
SOURCE: Adapted from Collins, Kennedy, and Francis, 1976, p. 375.

choose abstinence (Jurich & Jurich, 1974, p. 740). While the abstinence value is inflexible and stems from an external source (usually religion), intercourse in the context of a love relationship requires an internal examination without the fixed notions of "right" and "wrong." This involves an ability to evaluate personal feelings, feelings of the partner, and the nature of the relationship. For example, Diane and John have been going together for two and one-half years and plan to marry after graduating. Each feels confident that his or her desire for sex with the other springs from a willingness to share the experience rather than from a wish to exploit the other for personal pleasure. They also feel that their sexual sharing will encourage a stronger, deeper commitment to their relationship rather than splinter the relationship because of unwanted guilt. Obviously, examining these elements of self, partner, and relationship before intercourse is more complicated than categorically deciding never to have intercourse outside of marriage.

One of the consequences of adopting the permissiveness-with-affection value is the difficulty of evaluating one's feelings and situation. Knowing when you are "in love" and knowing whether this feeling is likely to last past Saturday night may be difficult. One woman remarked, "Once you get into the permissiveness-with-affection bit, it is easy to fall in love quite often."

To eliminate the potential for this pattern to develop, some students who want sexual experience only with their marriage partner decide to have intercourse during *late* engagement but not before. "My roommate and her boyfriend had intercourse after they had discussed marriage. But they kept having intercourse and nothing was happening about the wedding. Before I have intercourse, my partner and I will have set a date, told my mother, and announced it in the paper." Many other students who have intercourse in the context of a love relationship do not insist that marriage follow (Whitehurst, 1973). A dorm counselor remarked, "Most students know that girlfriends will sleep with their boyfriends when the relationship gets heavy—when they care about each other. But sleeping with a guy doesn't mean you will marry him. The time has passed when people get married just because they have sex."

Permissiveness Without Affection

"Sex is enjoyable and shouldn't have to be justified by being 'in love.' I can have sex with whomever I like and whenever, with no apologies to society for the choices I make." This attitude typifies the sexual value of permissiveness without affection. Dr. Albert Ellis, who supports this position, has said, "Sex that is engaged in without love (or even friendship) can certainly be, and in innumerable cases is, one of the most satisfying human pursuits" (Ellis, 1963, p. 30).

Permissiveness without affection is the least accepted sexual value among college students. As few as 8 to 10 percent of university students surveyed in Iowa, Virginia, and North Dakota indicated approval of intercourse when no particular affection was present (Reiss, 1967, p. 29; Mirande & Hammer, 1974, p. 357).[3] Feelings of emptiness appear to account for the lack of support for this sexual value. Based on their various studies of sexual behavior among college students, Kirkendall and Anderson concluded, "The most intimate and meaningful experience comes when it is as an integral part of a relationship in which people are trying to express care and love for one another. Sex is not simply an end, but is a part of a more encompassing relationship" (Kirkendall & Anderson, 1973, p. 420). Non-college adults also have a negative view of permissiveness without affection. In a study of nearly twenty-five hundred adults in forty-eight states two thirds rejected the idea that "sex is primarily for fun" (Wilson, 1975, p. 62).

While more permissive attitudes about sex may be healthier than the repressive attitudes of earlier eras, it has been suggested that those who favor the most sexual permissiveness risk a psychic cost to themselves. One researcher gave a sexual permissiveness scale test and four personality inventories (psychoticism, neuroticism, extraversion, tendency to lie) to 427 male and 436 female subjects between the ages of twenty and fifty (Eysenck, 1974). He found that those who had the highest scores on the psychoticism scale were also the most permissive sexually (p. 49). But other researchers disagree. One researcher on sexual liberality and personality found no relationship between permissive attitudes and psychotic or neurotic symptoms (Twitchell, 1974). And, in a study which compared couples who were living together and having intercourse with those who were not, the researchers observed that living together was associated with more positive self-attitudes and heterosexual relationships (Peterman et al., 1974, p. 354). Finally, in a Canadian study, respondents with high self-esteem were more likely to report more coital partners than those with low self-esteem (Perlman, 1974, p. 470).

In summary, of the four nonmarital sexual values—abstinence, double standard, permissiveness with affection, and permissiveness without affection, most students begin college with abstinence and/or the double standard as their sexual values. Exposure to the value system of the college community, which is typically more liberal, and the development of a love relationship usually result in the adoption of the permissiveness-with-affection value.

CHANGES IN SEXUAL VALUES

Are we experiencing a sexual revolution? Yes, if reference is made to the changes in sexual values that have occurred in the last twenty years. No, if these changes are interpreted as radical and total, which the term *revolution* implies. That we are becoming more permissive and liberal sexually is a more accurate way to describe the change in our sexual values. Permissiveness implies tolerant attitudes toward sexual ideas and acts, particularly toward those of others (Hunt, 1974, p. 20). Sexual liberalism, in contrast, implies a willingness to engage in certain formerly forbidden acts ourselves (Hunt, 1974, p. 20). "I once thought that intercourse outside of marriage was inappropriate. But that was before I was emotionally involved with anyone."

If we are not experiencing a sexual "revolution" but are becoming more permissive and liberal about sex, what specific changes are occurring in our society? Five of these changes include more open discussion of sex, new meanings for sex, less emphasis on virginity, the gradual demise of the double standard, and shifting moral concerns.

I'm a practicing heterosexual . . . but bisexuality immediately doubles your chances for a date on Saturday night.

Woody Allen

Open Discussion of Sex

Sex is "in." We are saturated with stimuli from magazines, books, music, television, and movies which bring sex to our attention. Regularly televised programs increasingly discuss sexual themes openly and frankly. In the entertainment section of a recent newspaper, a list of the local movies included *1001 Danish Delights, Angel on Fire,* and *Saturday Night at the Baths.* Campus movies do not hesitate to feature R-rated films such as *The Last Picture Show.* With adolescent sexuality as a major theme, this film includes a naked swimming party, first intercourse in a truck-stop motel room, and the dialogue of seven high-school seniors sitting on the running board of a '48 Ford discussing how they could find a female for intercourse. Explicit sexual content of this type was very rare in movies before the mid-1960s.

In addition to the popular media influences, colleges and universities contribute to the open discussion of sex. Increasingly, college health services are offering the "pill" to students whose medical histories allow it. Universities frequently sponsor lectures and seminars on sexuality, contraception, and venereal disease. These occasional talks supplement university course offerings in human sexuality, human sexual dysfunctions, the psychology of sex, and the courtship and marriage courses in sociology and home economics. As a result of the more systematic examination of sex, there is also more open and honest dialogue about sex. To some extent, the days of sharing sexual misinformation on the street corner and in the locker room are over.

As sexual values have changed in recent years, sex as recreation has become increasingly accepted in our society. In addition, the public has been exposed to more explicit sexual stimuli than ever before—through movies and television, books and magazines, as well as in live entertainment.

New Meanings for Sex

Sex for the sole purpose of having children has been replaced largely by an emphasis on sex as recreation and as a unique interpersonal experience. As one sociologist explains it,

> One new value is the very notion that sexual pleasure is right pleasure—that it can be widely enjoyed in a variety of circumstances and perhaps with a variety of partners. Even for the many who still believe that sexual contact should be restricted to the married, marital sex now represents a delight instead of a duty, and even a form of play. This new attitude is consistent with a world in which pleasure in this life has become at least as important as salvation after death. (Gagnon, 1975, p. 45)

A study conducted in 1968 and 1972 showed an increased willingness on the part of college students to experience a variety of sexual activities, including French kissing, breast fondling, genital manipulation, and mutual simultaneous oral-genital contact. Over 250 students from four universities indicated the degree to which they felt it was appropriate to engage in each of the thirteen behaviors within different levels of commitment (casual acquaintance, exclusively dating one person, engaged, etc.). When the responses from 1968 and 1972 were compared, the authors concluded that while women were more conservative than men, both sexes expressed greater approval for engaging in each of the thirteen sexual behaviors in 1972 than in 1968 (Croake & James, 1973).

For most, the desire to experience sexual pleasure is not independent of the relationship in which it occurs. As noted earlier, preference for sex within a love relationship suggests another contemporary view of sex—that it is intrinsically rewarding. Analyzing the important place of sex in our impersonal society, one author observed, "Sexuality represents one form of the search for intrinsic meanings and gratifications—one aspect of an ideology of seeking out non-materialistic goals and rewards" (Petras, 1978, p. 30). Sexual sharing, in this view, allows a person to retreat from the impersonal and often alienating material world and to find nonmaterial rewards with another person. Sex can be a condition which creates ". . . a greater concern for building trust, sincerity, integrity, and a capacity for communication between partners" (Kirkendall & Anderson, 1973, p. 420). It is this dimension of sexual behavior which overshadows sex only for procreation or physical pleasure.

Less Emphasis on Virginity

Of the sexual attitudes in nineteenth-century Victorian England, one author wrote, "Virginity was seldom directly extolled by name since even to mention it was to border on the indelicate. It was assumed that a woman entered marriage as a virgin because any other state would have been unthinkable in respectable circles" (Chesser, 1960, p. 36). While some college students remain virgins until they marry, most do not. As one researcher observed, "Virginity among college students is no longer a big deal; it is no longer an important criterion for social approval. Sincerity and loyalty are given higher social ratings" (Dunlap, 1971, p. 10).

Virginity has decreased in importance among college students in recent years. In 1965, 70 percent of the undergraduate women in one study stated that they felt that nonmarital sexual intercourse was immoral. Five years later, only 34 percent of the women in the same university agreed it was immoral (Robinson, King, & Balswick, 1972, p. 191). While some college students do not consider virginity important as freshmen, many more seem not to value it as seniors. While 71 percent of the freshman women respondents at Stanford approved of intercourse with someone they loved, 90 percent of the senior women respondents had come to approve it (Miller & Bowker, 1974).

Despite these statistical trends, there are some college students for whom virginity is an important consideration. Students in a marriage class were asked to write how they felt about intercourse and why. One student wrote, "I have been taught that sex outside marriage is wrong and I feel that it is. The fact that most of my friends have intercourse doesn't bother me. I can't say if it's wrong for them. But I know it's wrong for me."

Demise of the Double Standard

You recall that according to the double standard there are two standards for sexual behavior—one for men and another for women. Researchers at the University of Georgia have observed over a ten-year period signs of the demise of the double standard (King et al., 1977). As one researcher has observed:

> The basic change . . . during the past centuries has been from an orthodox double standard ethic of premarital sexuality which allowed males to copulate but which condemned their partners as "bad" women, to a more modified version of the double standard wherein women are allowed to have premarital coitus but not with quite the abandon that men are. Of course, this is an oversimplification, and with over 220 million Americans there are many variations in standards. There are those who are fully equalitarian in a permissive direction and also those who are equalitarian in a restrictive direction and there still are those who are orthodox double standard. But the overall shift is toward less dominance of the sexual scene by males. (Reiss, 1976, pp. 190–91)

This by no means indicates full equality of the sexes but rather a lessening of inequality (Libby, 1966).

While the double standard may be weakening, it has not disappeared. "There are double standards everywhere," observed a music major. "It's very hard to ask a guy to go with me to a concert because of the expectation that I should be waiting to be asked out." And when sex is involved it may be even harder to overcome the expectations of the double standard—that men should be aggressive and initiate sex, while women should be passive and wait for the men to take charge of the situation. Women and men often find themselves following a script (doing what they are "supposed" to do) based on a double standard.

Shifting Moral Concerns

Along with the demise of the double standard there has been a shift in the focus of concerns about sexual morality.

> Many influential people are moving away from the view that sexual morality is defined by abstinence from nonmarital intercourse toward one in which morality is expressed through responsible sexual behavior and a sincere regard for the rights of others. While these people do not advocate nonmarital sexual relations, this possibility is clearly seen as more acceptable if entered in a responsible manner, and contained within a relationship characterized by integrity and mutual concern. In other words, the shift is from emphasis upon an act to emphasis upon the quality of interpersonal relationships. (Kirkendall & Libby, 1966, pp. 290–91)

As Kirkendall and Libby (1966, pp. 45–59) point out, a striking illustration of this shift is found in the writings of liberal religious leaders. The comments of Douglas Rhymes, Canon Librarian of Southwark Cathedral, provide one example:

We are told that all sexual experience outside marriage is wrong, but we are given no particular rulings about sexual experience within marriage. Yet a person may just as easily be treated as a means to satisfy desire and be exploited for the gratification of another within marriage as outside it. It is strange that we concern ourselves so much with the morality of pre-marital and extramarital sex, but seldom raise seriously the question of sexual morality within marriage. . . . (Rhymes, 1964, p. 25)

In summary, America's sexual values have greatly changed: sexual intercourse has become a more acceptable topic for discussion, it implies recreation as well as procreation, and it is regarded as one of the few remaining uniquely rewarding experiences in an impersonal and materialistic world. Also, with the erosion of the double standard, virginity has become less important, and concern has focused more on the relationship in which sexual behavior occurs rather than on the act itself.

REASONS FOR CHANGES IN SEXUAL VALUES

The women's movement, the youth movement, perception of adult permissiveness, affluence, contraception, and the declining influence of religion are among the possible reasons for more permissive or liberal sexual values among American youth. Let's look at each of these reasons more closely.

The Women's Movement

A basic theme of the women's liberation movement has been the equalization of rights and privileges for women and men. One result has been an attack on the double standard which allows men the privilege of enjoying sex outside marriage without being especially stigmatized. What men do sexually has been less regulated traditionally than what women do because men's chances for marriage were not diminished or their reputations ruined by having nonmarital intercourse. Traditionally, women have had to carefully monitor their sexual behavior in order to marry and have a secure future. The women's liberation movement has challenged the double standard assumption that to be acceptable a bride should be a virgin. Increasingly, more women are finding that the decision to have nonmarital intercourse does not affect their chances for marriage. Eighty-three percent of 658 male students in twenty-one colleges and universities indicated that they would marry a woman who had had intercourse in a previous relationship (Luckey & Nass, 1969, p. 364). The women's movement has also encouraged women to become economically independent. Consequently, those women who do not marry or who marry later (by chance or choice) will be better able to support themselves than in years past.

However, "*full* equality in the sexual sphere is not possible today given the different priorities of family and occupational roles that males and females have . . . If females think that getting married and starting a family is their first priority in life and place occupational ambitions secondary to this, they will view sex in terms of these goals" (Reiss, 1972, p. 170). In other words, men and women are likely to have somewhat different sexual values and behaviors so long as their career and child-rearing goals differ.

Other Social Movements

While the women's movement has been the most visible social movement in the past few years, the youth movement has helped move our society toward more permissive or liberal sexual values. By questioning adult values, the youth movement sought release from adult controls. Specific targets in the late sixties and early seventies were the right of eighteen-year-olds to vote and the end of the Vietnam War. But as the slogan "make love, not war" reveals, the questioning of adult judgment in the political arena seems to have encouraged the questioning of adult values in other areas, specifically sexual values.

Whereas sexual values were not the central target of the youth movement, the gay liberation movement has focused on sexual values. With banners which read, "Out of the closet" and "Better blatant than latent," male homosexuals and lesbians marched in New York City's Greenwich Village seeking an end to discrimination and brutalization (Gagnon, 1975, p. 48). In addition to public demonstrations, over six hundred homosexual organizations and publications in America (Hunt, 1974, p. 11) have influenced our society's sexual values. Although homosexuals still receive little social support and often encounter hostility from heterosexuals, public awareness of the homosexual's social world, values, and difficulties has encouraged some rethinking of both homosexual and heterosexual values.

Perception of Adult Permissiveness

"My parents have been divorced since I was seven," remarked a high-school junior. "Since then my dad has been involved with numerous women, another marriage, and another divorce. Now he's 'dating' again. My mom doesn't live with her boyfriend, but she might as well. He stays at our house late at night on weekends, and I'm sure they're having sex."

In some families permissive attitudes about sex will be learned from parents. Even children from strictly traditional homes, though, are likely to be exposed to the permissive sexual attitudes of other adults, of friends, and of the media. They need only go to the nearest drugstore or newsstand to see *Playboy, Penthouse, Playgirl,* and *Viva* magazines featuring adult sexual behavior in close-up color photography. The basic value suggested by these sexually oriented magazines is that sex is available and to be enjoyed. Many popular magazines, books, and movies suggest that there are few limits to sexual behavior, and they encourage a permissive attitude toward sex (Davis, 1974, p. 201).

Affluence

More college students have cars than in previous years. A car means instant privacy as well as mobility for seeking food, alcohol, and entertainment (movies, concerts, beaches, mountains). The van provides still more privacy, space, and luxury. One used-van owner said, "In addition to red carpeting and matching curtains, I installed a tape deck in my van. My fiancée and I would rather drink and view the Atlantic from the back of my van than anything else in the world. It's the one place we can be on our own and do our own thing." To some extent, then, the affluence that brings with it cars and other luxuries also brings a degree of freedom and privacy that removes young people from the influence of traditional values.

Related to economic affluence is the law of supply and demand. The power to buy what you want when you want it encourages a devaluation of those things you

Affluent teenagers with cars or vans have the mobility to escape parental watchfulness and control. Removed from their parents, they may establish their own sexual values or be guided by those of the teenaged peer group.

already have. If you can replace something easily when it becomes old or broken, your attachment to it will be less than if you could not replace it. Your awareness that objects and things are replaceable may encourage a feeling that people, too, are replaceable, and so, less precious.

Regarding sexual values, someone who comes to believe that people, like things, can be tossed aside and then easily replaced need not be concerned about the effect of sexual behavior on a relationship with another person. As one student expressed it, "There are so many women on this campus, I don't need to spend six weeks, holding their hands, taking them out to eat, seeing movies, and all that. I make it clear in the beginning that I think sex is a natural part of an affectionate relationship. If the girl doesn't feel that way, I never bother to see her again." The attitude that people can be treated as replaceable is also a by-product of a mass society characterized by impersonal, bureaucratic, secondary-group relationships.

Contraception

Couples may now conveniently separate their sexual values and behavior from their desire to become or avoid becoming parents. The almost 100 percent effective pill permits couples to include sex in their relationship without worrying about pregnancy or the necessity of dealing with an abortion. Although the controversy regarding the potential hazards of birth control pills continues, most college students prefer the pill to other methods of contraception (Miller & Bowker, 1974). If a woman is unable to take the pill because of a family history of blood clots or other relevant health problems, the couple may opt for other methods (e.g., intrauterine device, diaphragm, condom, etc.). But regardless of the contraceptive chosen, the result is the same—lovemaking can be separated from baby making.

The availability of contraception has not, by itself, encouraged permissive sexual attitudes. Rather, the increasing acceptance of permissiveness with affection as a sexual value includes a concern for one's partner and the relationship. The use of contraception is consistent with that value and contributes to its acceptance.

Religious Influences Versus Science

Organized religion has always been concerned about sexual behavior in terms of procreation and the channeling of sexual urges. The central mission of religion as it relates to sexual behavior has been to subordinate the urges of the individual to society's goals. Rather than encouraging casual sexual relationships, Judeo-Christian religion has conveyed that a man and woman should "become one" (marry) and should "be fruitful and multiply."

To help control sexual behavior, many religions set up a dichotomy between body and mind. As traditionally interpreted, while the mind housed the spirit, the body was the place of physical desire (Petras, 1978, p. 72). It became the job of the mind to monitor and control sexual impulses. By implication, the body was corrupt. Unlike lower animals who copulate instinctively, humans were expected to think and act on the basis of "higher" values and ideals. Religion has played a dominant role in defining these values.

Science has provided an alternative way to evaluate sexual behavior and has contributed to a change in sexual values. Scientists who have made landmark contributions to scientific thought about sex include Sigmund Freud, Havelock Ellis, Hendrik van de Velde, Alfred Kinsey, and the team of William Masters and Virginia Johnson.

1. Sigmund Freud (1856–1939) suggested that human sexuality evolves through predictable developmental stages (oral, anal, phallic, latency, genital) with each psychological stage being linked to a change in the body. For example, the phallic stage is characterized by focusing on one's genitals as a source of pleasure. Freud suggested that the phallic stage occurs between the ages of four and six and ushers in the Oedipal period during which the male child hates his father because they are competing for the same woman (his mother).

In addition to the various stages of sexual development, Freud emphasized the need to control, repress, and redirect sexual energy for the benefit of society. Although influential, Freud's work is suspect among many contemporary social scientists. They not only see little data to support Freud's theories but feel that his ideas were colored by the repressive era in which he lived.

2. Havelock Ellis (1859–1939) emphasized that sexual behavior was learned social behavior, that "deviant" sexual behavior was merely that which society labeled as abnormal, and that an enjoyable sex life (a desirable goal) was not something that just happened but had to be perfected. Regarding the sex education of children he wrote, " . . . no doubt is any longer possible as to the absolute necessity of taking a deliberate and active part in this sexual initiation, instead of leaving it to chance revelation of ignorant and perhaps vicious companions or servants" (Ellis, 1931, p. 43).

3. Hendrik van de Velde (1873–1937) was a Dutch gynecologist who in 1926 published a best-seller sex book, *Ideal Marriage*. Like Ellis, van de Velde believed that sexual response was not automatic. He prescribed in detail specific sexual techniques whereby his patients could translate their emotional commitments into delightful orgasms. He also emphasized that sex is a joint affair and considered frigidity or impotence a couple's problem rather than the wife's or husband's problem.

4. Alfred Kinsey (1894–1956) is known as the giant among sex researchers. The publications of *Sexual Behavior in the Human Male* (1948) and *Sexual Behavior in the Human Female* (1953) are notable for the number of respondents —over five thousand for each volume. Unlike his predecessors, Kinsey provided specific statistical evidence about the sexual behavior of ordinary men and women, not of those seeking help for a problem. Instead of guessing about the proportion of women who have orgasms, he collected data and stated that nine out of ten

women reported having experienced an orgasm by age thirty-five.

Since what a person does is one index of what a person values, Kinsey helped to reveal some private sexual values. Ninety-two percent of the men and 62 percent of the women in Kinsey's sample reported having masturbated (Kinsey, 1948, pp. 499–500; Kinsey, 1953, p. 142). Although Kinsey's methodology has been criticized because his subjects were not representative of the whole population and because they were telling what they remembered they had done (which may be different from what they actually did), the Kinsey volumes brought into focus the fact that people value sexual expression.

5. William Masters and Virginia Johnson are co-directors of the Reproductive Biology Research Foundation in St. Louis, Missouri, and the world's leading contemporary sex researchers. Their publications of *Human Sexual Response* (1966) and *Human Sexual Inadequacy* (1970) were on the nonfiction best-seller list of *The New York Times* within four weeks after their respective releases. The first book was a result of twelve years of research in which 694 participants experienced over ten thousand orgasms under laboratory conditions. The sequel focused on the treatment of sexual problems such as frigidity, impotence, and premature ejaculation. In response to *Human Sexual Inadequacy,* the editor of the *Journal of the American Medical Association* commented:

> Today, many people sincerely feel that the present atmosphere of frankness and public concern over sexual matters is basically amoral and destructive. Nevertheless, even the most critical should admit that, if we are able to free some individuals from neurotic guilt feelings about sex and if we can utilize scientific research to stabilize even a few apparently unsuccessful marriages, some good has been served. None of these admirable designs is achieved through ignorance. (Belliveau & Richter, 1970, p. 62)

One effect of scientific inquiry into human sexuality has been to dilute the impact of religion. In addition, the scientific study of sexual behavior has made the examination of sexuality a common aspect of everyday life in our society. *Redbook, McCall's,* and *Cosmopolitan* magazines often feature lead articles on sexual expression which are based on scientific studies. Such articles implicitly encourage the reader to look toward science rather than religion for more relevant, accurate information.

INTERCOURSE: A PERSONAL DECISION

Regardless of the reasons that our society is becoming more sexually permissive, each partner in each new relationship usually considers if, when, and under what conditions intercourse will be included in the relationship. Let's explore the various motives for and consequences of the decision to have intercourse.

Motives for Intercourse

The motive or motives each partner brings to an intercourse experience may differ. Let's examine some of them.

Intimacy.   In our relatively impersonal society, sexual intercourse may provide the experience of being emotionally connected to another human being. The physical closeness of intercourse may signify a more general closeness between the people sharing a relationship. "Though the rim of the penis or the head of the clitoris may provide the most intense stimulation because they are such sensitive nerve packages, these organs are connected to bodies which belong to persons. The skin, for example, is not merely a sausage casing, it is itself a sensual organ which responds to touching, rubbing, and caressing" (Mazur, 1973, pp. 45–46). In the book, *Touching: The Human Significance of Skin,* Montagu wrote that "in the Western world it is highly probable that sexual activity, indeed the frenetic preoccupation with sex that characterizes Western culture, is in many cases not the expression of a sexual interest at all, but rather a search for the satisfaction of the need for contact" (Montagu, 1971, p. 61).

Love.   Related to feelings of intimacy are feelings of love, trust, and caring which may be expressed through sexual intercourse. Rollo May suggested that love was "the capacity for surrender, for giving one's self up" (1969, p. 103). But love also implies giving to another and this includes the giving of intense physical pleasure. "Putting my partner into a world of orgasmic ecstasy is a fantastic experience for me," expressed one member of a sexual awareness group. "It's a time when I feel a deep sense of love."

Fun.   But intercourse may or may not involve love feelings. It may be regarded solely as a pleasurable, sensual experience. A noted marriage counselor described this motive: "Sex is play, sport. Nothing is at stake but spending time together in producing pleasant sensations for each other. Deep feelings may not be present and one may see one's self as a kind of instrument of pleasure and a pleasure seeker" (Neubeck, 1974, p. 92).

Ego enhancement.   Although a couple may engage in intercourse primarily for fun, one (or both) of the partners may be attempting to boost his or her own ego at the expense of the partner. Men traditionally have been socialized to take pride in seducing women and in discussing their conquests with their peers. In one study, 30 percent of the men told a friend that they had had intercourse within a few hours after it occurred. This contrasted with 14 percent of the women who did so (Carns, 1973). Men tend to talk about how much sex they "got," and women talk about the emotional involvement of themselves and their partner (Gagnon & Simon, 1973, p. 70). Hence, men are more motivated than women to have intercourse to enhance their status among their peers.

While some have intercourse to impress friends, others do so for personal reasons. Those who feel inadequate in other areas may seek to compensate for this feeling through intercourse. Finding that someone is interested in having intercourse with them may supply an insecure person with confirmation of his or her own worth.

Having intercourse for our ego enhancement is perhaps the ultimate form of exploitation. The partner is used to prove something rather than being cared for.

Momentum.   It sometimes happens that one or both partners feel that intercourse is simply the next logical step in their developing relationship. "We've done about all there is to do but have intercourse. Since we're so involved already what's the point of stopping here and feeling frustrated?" Although a stage in a relationship may have been reached in which intercourse seems to be the next logical event, there may be other issues to consider. What "seems" right one night does not always seem right the next and vice versa.

Improve relationship.   Some couples have intercourse in hopes that it will improve their relationship. It is impossible to predict the specific effect having intercourse will have on your relationship (Glassberg, 1965; Shope & Broderick, 1967; Miller & Wilson, 1968; Kantner & Zelnik, 1973). One partner reported, "Intercourse for us was the best thing that ever happened. Since we began having sex over a year ago we have felt more emotionally involved with each other. It's really magic." But another said, "It was a mistake for us to have intercourse. I thought it would draw us closer together but it hasn't. My partner has been avoiding me lately and things are not the same. I'm sorry it happened."

Pressure from partner.   Sometimes only one partner is interested in moving the relationship toward intercourse. "I put pressure on her by telling her how frustrated I was. We joked about it a lot, but I believe it did influence her to have intercourse with me. She felt sorry for me."

Please the partner.   Sometimes the influence from the partner is so subtle it is not perceived as pressure. Rather, one partner may feel the need to please the other. "I knew it would make him happy so I made love with him," expressed one woman.

Ensure marriage.   Related to pleasing the partner and putting pressure on the partner is the tactic of using intercourse as a means to get pregnant in order to force the issue of marriage on an undecided or unenthusiastic partner. "Some men need a little nudge to get married," a senior commented. "I saw it happen with my roommate and her boyfriend. They had been dating for five years, but they didn't talk seriously of marriage until she got pregnant."

Rebellion.　When marriage is not the goal, some college students have intercourse to rebel against religion, their parents, or a previous partner. Regarding religion, a sociology major said, "After I took sociology of religion, I felt angry. I had been protecting my virginity because of religious scruples. It turns out that every culture feels differently about sex and uses religion to control sexual behavior. I'm tired of being made to feel guilty about something I have wanted to do for a long time."

Other students rebel against parents. "I'm tired of being told 'no.' It's all I've heard since I was twelve. I'm a college sophomore and I'm on my own now. If I want to have intercourse, my parents can't stop me."

Still other students may rebel against a previous partner as a motive for intercourse. "After Steve dropped me I felt terrible. I felt truly alone for the first

A current and future trend is toward more sexual experimentation at earlier ages. Many of the same motivations that propel adults toward intercourse—momentum, peer or partner pressure, ego enhancement, and rebellion, for instance—are equally strong influences on teenage sexual activity.

time in my life. When Gary came along, we had intercourse the first time we went out. I was on the rebound and I guess I thought it was a way of getting back at Steve for having hurt me."

Rebellion is a questionable motive for having intercourse because the "real" reason is in reference to something else (religion) or someone else (parents, a previous partner). Such external motivations suggest that the sexual partner is being used to help settle a previous issue. The only valid issue is the current intercourse experience and its various implications and consequences.

Revenge.   While intercourse for rebellious reasons uses the sex partner to direct hostility toward others, intercourse for revenge is a direct attack against the partner. "When I found out that she had gone to the drive-in with her old boyfriend, I decided to break off with her. But I wanted to pay her back so I came on real strong about marriage and we had intercourse. When I left her that evening, I left her for good." Clearly, in a case like this sex is used to vent anger. Deception, hostility, and exploitation are all involved.

Style.   Some people include intercourse in heterosexual relationships because it is their style to do so. As one psychology major explained, "For me, intercourse is as natural as breathing—it's got to happen." This motivation may not present problems as long as both partners share a similar perspective. But when they do not, one partner is likely to misinterpret the other's behavior. It would be easy to assume that intercourse implies that the other partner is becoming more emotionally committed, but this may not necessarily be the case. A misunderstanding about the level of mutual commitment would almost certainly bring strain into a relationship and be painful for one or both partners.

Accident.   "We smoked a little dope, drank a lot of wine, and lost our heads. I didn't know what I was doing." While some have a specific motive for having intercourse, others have no reason not to. They drift into a situation and seem to just "let it happen." In reality, intercourse doesn't "just happen." Not to decide against intercourse is in one sense a decision to drift toward intercourse (and vice versa).

The motives for intercourse just discussed are not exhaustive. Others include passion, relief from tension or boredom, duty, and reconciliation. And motives are often mixed. Rarely is an intercourse experience just for love, or passion, or fun, but it stems from a combination of motives.

Consequences of Intercourse

After considering possible motives for having intercourse, you may want to examine the consequences of deciding to have or not to have intercourse in a new relationship.

Personal consequences.   Your personal reaction to intercourse will depend on your motivations (as well as your partner's), your religious devoutness, and the level of involvement with your partner. For example, regarding motivation, expecting the relationship to automatically improve following intercourse may be unrealistic. In reference to religion, if you are strongly influenced by such values, your reaction to violating religious teaching may be intense (Cannon & Long, 1971, p. 46; Christensen, 1969, p. 158).

The level of commitment you perceive from your partner will affect your reaction to intercourse. In a study of college women, 36 percent of those who had a casual "dating" relationship with their boyfriends reported they felt that they had gone too far in having intercourse. In contrast, only 20 percent of the engaged women felt they had exceeded self-imposed limits (Bell & Chaskes, 1970).

Partner consequences.   Since a basic moral principle of life is to do no harm to others, it is important also to consider the effect of intercourse on your partner. While intercourse may be a pleasurable experience with positive consequences for you, your partner may react quite differently. You should make a judgment about your partner's feelings about intercourse and ability to handle the experience. If you suspect that he or she will not feel good about it or be able psychologically to handle it, then you should reconsider whether intercourse would be appropriate.

Relationship consequences.   Regarding the specific effect of intercourse on the relationship of unmarried couples, eighty-one men and seventy-four women who reported having had nonmarital intercourse were asked if they felt the experience had strengthened or weakened their relationship. Over 90 percent of both sexes attributed a strengthening effect to intercourse. In contrast, 1.2 percent of the men and 5.4 percent of the women reported that intercourse had a weakening effect (Burgess & Wallin, 1953, p. 371). But these percentages should be kept in perspective. Although 90 percent felt that having intercourse improved their relationship, there is no comparable study which reveals how couples feel who don't have intercourse. It is possible that 90 percent might also say that not having intercourse improved their relationship.

Regardless of what couples say about the effect of intercourse on their relationship, the experience seems unrelated to breaking up. This finding is based on a random sampling of five thousand sophomores and juniors at four colleges in Boston who were "going with" someone (Hill et al., 1976). In a two-year follow-up, those who had had intercourse were no more likely to have broken up than those who had not had intercourse.

Contraception.   Another potential consequence of intercourse to consider is pregnancy. Once a couple decide to have intercourse, a separate decision must be made as to whether intercourse should lead to becoming parents. If the couple wants to avoid a pregnancy, they must choose and effectively use a contraceptive method. However, in a national probability sample of never-married women ages fifteen through nineteen, only 30 percent of those who were sexually experienced reported that they always used contraceptives, and 25 percent said they never did[4] (Zelnik & Kantner, 1977, p. 62). And pregnancy scares are not uncommon. In a random sample of 875 Michigan State University never-married undergraduates, 44 percent of the women who had had intercourse and 30 percent of the men who had had intercourse reported that the woman had a delayed menstrual period which was interpreted as a pregnancy (Stephenson et al., 1977). About 30 percent of those who have intercourse before marriage become pregnant (Jaffe & Dryfoos, 1976).

One researcher examined four events which must occur before contraception can take place: (1) The individuals must know that intercourse is likely to occur; (2) The contraceptive device (pill, IUD, diaphragm, condom, etc.) must be procured; (3) The sexual partners need to communicate about each other's contraceptive plans to ensure that somebody has done something; and (4) The contraceptive must actually be used (Byrne, 1977, p. 68).

The individuals most likely to progress through these four steps in using contraceptives have positive views about sex, are not anxious discussing it, and feel sex is natural. In contrast, "negative feelings about sex are rarely strong enough to inhibit sexual behavior completely, but they do inhibit the use of contraceptives by affecting each of the four steps needed for contraception" (Byrne, 1977, p. 68).

TRENDS

As sexual values become more liberalized, more unmarried individuals are likely to be engaging in sexual intercourse at earlier ages. Between 1971 and 1976 the prevalence of sexual activity among never-married United States women (ages 15–19) increased 30 percent. And the median age for their first intercourse experience declined about four months during this period (Zelnik & Kantner, 1977, pp. 55, 61). The median ages for 1971 and 1976 were, respectively 16.5 and 16.2 (p. 61).

Today's unmarried young, by and large, are not indiscriminate, they do not practice kinky sex, and while they want sex to be physically intense, they also want it to be emotionally meaningful.

Morton Hunt

In addition to continued sexual permissiveness, it will be more accepted and more common for women to initiate sexual behavior. The trend is for women to feel increasingly more comfortable about expressing their sexuality and preferences by assuming an active sexual role, as well as by initiating sexual relations within the context of all kinds of relationships (Bell, 1975). "But when it comes to pursuing men, women still have a long way to go before they can feel comfortable to do so. . . . A woman's discomfort in pursuing a man to whom she is attracted may be surpassed only by the pursued man's discomfort and fear" (Safilios-Rothschild, 1977, p. 119). In a recent study of fifty-nine college women, over forty participants reported that they did not feel comfortable initiating sexual behavior or letting their partner know exactly what turned them on (Burstein, 1975).

In the future, sex will also be viewed more often beyond its implications for marriage. "Probably the most fundamental change to take place will be a freeing of sexuality of its instrumentality, for both men and women. . . . Sexuality will no longer be the primary resource to be used in the negotiations toward commitment and marriage, but rather an expression of emotions to be enjoyed" (Safilios-Rothschild, 1977, p. 117).

But confusion about sexual values will continue. *Time* magazine commissioned Yankelovich and his associates to assess American opinion about sexual morality. In a nationwide sample of 1,044 persons, 61 percent said that it was getting more difficult to know what's right and wrong in the sexual sphere (*Time,* 1977, p. 112).

SUMMARY

Our sexual values affect the nature of our sexual behavior. Alternative nonmarital sexual values include abstinence, the double standard, permissiveness with affection, and permissiveness without affection. Most college students approve of sex within the context of a love relationship where few approve of sex without concern for the partner.

Sexual values are changing. As a society, we are becoming more open in our discussions about sex, and more people are willing to consider sexual intercourse as a pleasurable event rather than an opportunity to conceive children or as something that should be "saved" until marriage. There is also less emphasis on virginity, and the double standard is declining.

Among the forces bringing change in our sexual values are the women's movement, the youth movement, and gay liberation. These movements seek sexual equality, release from adult controls and values, and the right to pursue any sexual inclinations without harassment or embarrassment. The visibility of adult permissiveness in magazines, books, and movies also influences youth to regard such sexual behavior as appropriate.

Permissive values are also encouraged by greater affluence and the availability of the birth control pill. These economic and technological changes have come at a time when religious influence has waned in favor of a scientific and psychological world view.

The motivations for and consequences of intercourse in each new relationship might be considered in making a decision to have intercourse in that relationship. Some motivations for intercourse are intimacy, love, recreation, rebellion, and revenge. Consequences of intercourse include those for yourself, your partner, and your relationship. Sexual values for the future include a continuation of the liberal trend toward permissiveness, increased acceptance of an active sexual role for women, and a view of sex for its own sake separate from marriage. In the next chapter we will look at how sexual values are translated into actual sexual behavior.

STUDY QUESTIONS

1. Describe the four basic sexual-value positions.
2. What are some background characteristics of the college student who is likely to be a virgin?
3. What is the current status of the double standard?
4. How is the double standard reflected in interaction between men and women?
5. What is the most accepted sexual value among college students?
6. What sexual value has the least support among college students?
7. Describe and explain the typical shift in sexual values that students experience when they are in college.
8. Are we experiencing a sexual revolution in values? Explain.
9. What is the difference between permissiveness and sexual liberalism?
10. In what ways is there a more open attitude toward the discussion of sex today?
11. What are two important meanings of sex that have emerged as part of "the sexual revolution"?
12. What evidence do we have that virginity has become less important among college students?
13. How has the women's movement affected sexual values?
14. How have the youth and gay liberation movements affected heterosexual values?
15. Explain how the attitude that people are easily replaced evolves.
16. How has the availability of effective contraceptives influenced sexual values?
17. What are the central mission and main concerns of organized religion regarding sexual behavior?
18. Summarize the contributions of some influential scientists who have studied sex.
19. Discuss several motives for having intercourse.
20. What are some potential personal, partner, and relationship consequences for having nonmarital intercourse?

21. Discuss the events that must occur before a couple will use contraceptives.
22. How do feelings about sex affect the use of contraceptives?
23. What are several trends in sexual values?

NOTES

1. In general, a higher percentage of those who are black, male, born in the present decade, urban, older, less educated, and who perceive themselves as being in love have liberal sexual values. In contrast, those who are white, female, born in each decade prior to the present one, rural, young, educated, and do not perceive themselves as being in love are more likely to have conservative sexual values.

2. Double standards are pervasive in our society and apply not only to men versus women, but also to singles versus marrieds, blacks versus whites, rich versus poor, educated versus uneducated, etc.

3. Table 4.2 also reflects the lack of support for permissiveness without affection.

4. The pill and condom were used most frequently. Fifty-nine percent reported use of the pill, and 39 percent reported use of the condom. Only the condom offers protection against venereal disease.

BIBLIOGRAPHY

Bell, R. R. Sexuality and sex roles. Paper prepared for the Working Conference to Develop Teaching Materials on Family and Sex Roles, Detroit, November 1975.

Bell, R. R., and Chaskes, J. B. Premarital sexual experience among coeds, 1958 and 1968. *Journal of Marriage and the Family,* 1970, *32,* 81–4.

Belliveau, F., and Richter, L. *Understanding human sexual inadequacy.* New York: Bantam Books, 1970.

Burgess, E. W., and Wallin, P. *Engagement and marriage.* Philadelphia: J. B. Lippincott, 1953.

Burstein, B. Life history and current values as predictors of sexual behaviors and satisfaction in college women. Paper presented at the meeting of the Western Psychological Association, Sacramento, April 1975.

Byrne, D. A pregnant pause in the sexual revolution. *Psychology Today,* July 1977, 67–8.

Cannon, D. L., and Long, R. Premarital sexual behavior in the sixties. *Journal of Marriage and the Family,* 1961, *33,* 36–49.

Carns, D. E. Talking about sex: Notes on first coitus and the double sexual standard. *Journal of Marriage and the Family,* 1973, *35,* 677–88.

Chesser, E. *Is chastity outmoded?* Toronto: W. Heineman, 1960.

Christensen, H. T. The impact of culture and values. In *The individual, sex, and society,* C. B. Broderick and J. Bernard. Baltimore: Johns Hopkins University Press, 1969, 155–66.

Collins, J. K., Kennedy, J. R., and Francis, R. D. Insights into a dating partner's expectations of how behavior should ensue during the courtship process. *Journal of Marriage and the Family,* 1976, *38,* 2, 373–8.

Croake, J. W., and James, B. A four year comparison of premarital sexual attitudes. *Journal of Sex Research,* 1973, *9,* 2, 91–6.

Davis, P. Contextual sex-saliency and sexual activity: The relative effects of family and peer group in the sexual socialization process. *Journal of Marriage and the Family,* 1974, *36,* 1, 196–202.

Dunlap, B. Social and psychological aspects of a contraceptive service for teenagers. *California School Health,* 1971, *6,* 8–13.

Ellis, A. *Sex and the single man.* New York: Lyle Stuart, 1963.

Ellis, H. *Sex in relation to society,* vol. 6 of *Studies in the psychology of sex* (orig. pub. 1910). Philadelphia: F. A. Davis, 1931.

Eysenck, H. J. Personality, premarital sexual permissiveness and assortive mating. *The Journal of Sex Research,* 1974, *10,* 1, 47–51.

Gagnon, J. (issue ed.) *Human sexuality: An age of ambiguity,* written by Bruce Henderson. Boston: Educational Associates, 1975.

Gagnon, J., and Simon, W. *Sexual conduct. The social sources of human sexuality.* Chicago: Aldine, 1973.

Glassberg, B. Y. Sexual behavior patterns in contemporary youth culture: Implications for later marriage. *Journal of Marriage and the Family,* 1965, *27,* 190–2.

Hill, C. T., Rubin, Z., and Peplau, L. Breakups before marriage: The end of 103 affairs. *The Journal of Social Issues,* 1976, 32, 1, 147–68.

Hunt, M. *Sexual behavior in the 1970's.* New York: Dell, 1974.

Jaffe, F. S., and Dryfoos, J. G. Fertility control services for adolescents: Access and utilization. *Family Planning Perspectives,* 1976, *8,* 4, 167–75.

Jedlicka, D. Sequential analysis of perceived commitment to partners in premarital coitus. *Journal of Marriage and the Family,* 1975, *37,* 2, 385–90.

Jessor, S. L., and Jessor, R. Transition from virginity to nonvirginity among youth: A social-psychological study over time. *Developmental Psychology,* 1975, *11,* 4, 473–83.

Jurich, A. P., and Jurich, J. A. The effect of cognitive moral development upon the selection of premarital sexual standards. *Journal of Marriage and the Family,* 1974, *36,* 4, 736–41.

Kaats, G. R., and Davis, K. E. The dynamics of sexual behavior of college students. *Journal of Marriage and the Family,* 1970, *32,* 390–9.

Kantner, J. F., and Zelnik, M. Sexual experience of young unmarried women in the United States. *Family Planning Perspectives,* 1972, *4,* 9–17.

————. Contraception and pregnancy: Experience of young unmarried women in the United States. *Family Planning Perspectives,* 1973, *5,* 21–5.

King, K., Balswick, J., and Robinson, I. The continuing premarital sexual revolution among college females. *Journal of Marriage and the Family,* 1977, *39,* 3, 455–9.

Kinsey, A., Pomeroy, W. B., and Martin, C. E. *Sexual behavior in the human male.* Philadelphia: W. B. Saunders, 1948.

Kinsey, A., Pomeroy, W. B., Martin, C. E., and Gebhard, P. H. *Sexual behavior in the human female.* Philadelphia: W. B. Saunders, 1953.

Kirkendall, L. A. *Premarital intercourse and interpersonal relationships.* New York: Julian Press, 1961.

Kirkendall, L. A., and Anderson, P. B. Authentic selfhood: Basis for tomorrow's morality. In *Human sexuality: Contemporary perspectives,* E. S. Morrison and V. Borosage (eds.). Palo Alto, Calif.: National Press Books, 1973, 413–27.

Kirkendall, L. A., and Libby, R. W. Interpersonal relationships: crux of the sexual revolution. *Journal of Social Issues,* 22, 2, 1966, 45–59.

Laner, M. R., Laner, R. H., and Palmer, C. E. Sexual conservatism and the college student. Paper presented at the meeting of the National Council on Family Relations, 1977.

Libby, R. W. Changing sexual mores today. In *Handbook of sexology,* J. Money and H. Muspah (eds.). Amsterdam: Excerpta Medica Press, 1976.

Luckey, E. B., and Nass, G. D. A comparison of sexual attitudes and behavior in an international sample. *Journal of Marriage and the Family,* 1969, *31,* 2, 364–79.

May, Rollo. *Love and will.* New York: W. W. Norton, 1969.

Maiolo, J. Department of Sociology and Anthropology, East Carolina University, Greenville, N.C. Personal communication, 1978.

Mazur, R. *The new intimacy.* Boston: Beacon Press, 1973.

Miller, H., and Wilson, W. Relation of sexual behaviors, values and conflict to avowed happiness and personal adjustment. *Psychological Report,* 1968, *23,* 1075–86.

Miller, W. B., and Bowker, C. Summary of longitudinal study of Stanford undergraduate sexual behavior. Department of Psychiatry, School of Medicine, Stanford University, 1974.

Mirande, A. M., and Hammer, E. L. Premarital sexual permissiveness: A research note. *Journal of Marriage and the Family,* 1974, *36,* 2, 356–7.

Montagu, A. *Touching: The human significance of skin.* New York: Columbia University Press, 1971.

Neubeck, G. The myriad motives for sex. In *Sexual behavior,* L. Gross (ed.). Flushing, N.Y.: Spectrum Publications, 1974, 89–100.

The New Morality. *Time,* 21 November 1977, 111 ff.

Perlman, D. Self-esteem and sexual permissiveness. *Journal of Marriage and the Family,* 1974, *36,* 3, 470–73.

Peterman, D. J., Ridley, C. A., and Anderson, S. M. A comparison of cohabiting and non-cohabiting college students. *Journal of Marriage and the Family,* 1974, *36,* 344–54.

Petras, J. W. *Sexuality in society.* Boston: Allyn and Bacon, 1978.

Reiss, I. L. *The social context of premarital sexual permissiveness.* New York: Holt, Rinehart and Winston, 1967.

_____. How and why America's sex standards are changing. *Trans-Action,* 1968, *5,* 26–32.

_____. Premarital sexuality: Past, present, and future. In *Readings on the family system,* I. L. Reiss (ed.). New York: Holt, Rinehart and Winston, 1972, 167–89.

_____. The effect of changing trends, attitudes, and values on premarital sexual behavior in the United States. In *Sexuality today and tomorrow.* S. Gordon and R. Libby (eds.). North Scituate, Mass.: Duxbury, 1976, 190–203. (a)

_____. *Family systems in America.* Hinsdale, Ill.: Dryden Press, 1976. (b)

Rhymes, D. *No new morality.* Indianapolis: Bobbs-Merrill, 1964.

Robinson, I. E., King, K., and Balswick, J. L. The premarital sexual revolution among college females. *The Family Coordinator,* 1972, *21,* 189–94.

Safilios-Rothschild, C. *Love, sex, and sex roles.* Englewood Cliffs, N.J.: Prentice-Hall, 1977.

Shope, D. E., and Broderick, C. Level of sexual experience and predicted adjustment in marriage. *Journal of Marriage and the Family,* 1967, *29,* 424–7.

Simon, W., Berger, A., and Gagnon, J. Beyond anxiety and fantasy: The coital experiences of college youth. *Journal of Youth and Adolescence,* 1972, *1,* 208.

Spanier, G. B. Sexualization and premarital sexual behavior. *The Family Coordinator,* 1975, *24,* 1, 33–42.

Stephenson, J. J., Kallen, D. J., Darling, C. A., Tanas, R. S., and Dossey, J. The sexual and contraceptive behavior of never-married college students: Some preliminary remarks. Paper presented at the meeting of the National Council on Family Relations, San Diego, 1977.

Twitchell, J. Sexual liberality and personality: A pilot study. In *Beyond monogamy,* J. R. Smith and L. G. Smith (eds.). Baltimore: Johns Hopkins University Press, 1974, 230–59.

Whitehurst, R. H. Losing virginity: Some contemporary trends. *Medical Aspects of Human Sexuality,* 1973, *1,* 335–41.

Williams, R. *American society: A sociological interpretation.* New York: Alfred A. Knopf, 1970.

Wilson, W. C. The distribution of selected sexual attitudes and behaviors among the adult population of the United States. *The Journal of Sex Research,* 1975, *11,* 1, 46–64.

Zelnik, M., and Kantner, J. F. Sexual and contraceptive experience of young unmarried women in the United States 1976 and 1971. *Family Planning Perspectives,* 1977, *9,* 2, 55–71.

Chapter **5**

Sexual Behavior

ACQUIRING SEXUAL BEHAVIOR: A PSYCHOSEXUAL VIEW

RESEARCH ON SEXUAL BEHAVIOR

The Kinsey Studies—1948 and 1953 • The Hunt Study—1972 • The Zelnik and Kantner Studies—1971 and 1976 • The Hite Study—1976 • Other Studies

TYPES OF SEXUAL BEHAVIOR

Masturbation • Petting • Intercourse

DIFFERENCES IN SEXUAL BEHAVIOR

Female-Male Differences • Social Class Differences • Differences in Other Societies • Parent-Offspring Differences

SEX EDUCATION

What Parents Want • What the Schools Provide

TRENDS

SUMMARY

Whoever named it necking was a poor judge of anatomy.
Groucho Marx

A university professor remarked, "If you could look inside the head of an average college student you would see seven parts sex, two parts booze, and one part grass. They're really into sex." While this professor's assessment may reflect his own fantasies more than reality, sex does loom as a major interest among college students. The university environment is particularly conducive to sexual behavior—young unmarried adults of the opposite sex, maximum freedom to be alone, access to alcohol and/or marijuana, and peers who support liberal sexual values.

In the previous chapter we were concerned with sexual values as guidelines for behavior. In this chapter, we examine sexual behavior—that is, what people actually do. Before exploring who engages in what types of sexual behavior and how often, we will review how sexual behavior is learned. We will also consider how sexual expression differs between the sexes and among the respective social classes. We will look at parent-offspring differences and, finally, we will discuss sex-education programs.

ACQUIRING SEXUAL BEHAVIOR: A PSYCHOSEXUAL VIEW

There are numerous theories about how sexual behavior is acquired. There are biological theories (sexual behavior is instinctive) and hormonal explanations (sexual behavior is biochemically determined). But these theories do not account for environmental influence; consequently, we will focus on the psychosexual explanation. According to this view, individuals learn from their culture and society how to behave sexually. Gagnon and Simon (1973) have emphasized a sociocultural basis for sexual behavior, and they argue that what people do sexually is not the result of a gradual unfolding of biological drives. "Biology equips us with legs. But there's nothing in biology that tells us where we're going to run, or why we should want to. And there's nothing in our biology that tells us why or when we should have sex. Those directions come from our cultural environments" (Gagnon, 1975, p. 63). For example, feeling the "need for sex" is not a blocked biological drive seeking orgasmic release but a result of having learned to define an internal state in sexual ways.

This psychosexual view of sexual behavior also suggests that the most erogenous zone of the body is the mind. It is the mind that selects from the environment those cues which stimulate sexual thoughts and behavior. For example, two adults in an isolated room may or may not interact sexually depending on the social script (shared interpretations and expected behaviors of a social situation) each brings into the room. An individual coming into an empty classroom to catch up on some evening studying will not usually consider the presence of an opposite sex person as creating a potential sexual situation. However, that person might engage in a series of behaviors (look up from studying, smile, move closer, and initiate touching) which would help to define the situation in sexual terms. In the absence of such cues, both assume that their script is to study quietly, and they act accordingly.

Learned social scripts are central to the understanding of sexual behavior from the psychosexual perspective. Social scripts define situations, name actors, and plot behaviors (Gagnon & Simon, 1973, p. 19). In the above example, had the person's fiancée entered the room, the situation would have been defined as a meeting of two lovers thereby making appropriate some form of sexual expression.

Scripts have two dimensions—external and internal. The external portion

Sociosexual scripts provide us with guidelines as to where sexual behavior is or is not to take place. Kissing in the hallway at school is or is not acceptable depending on what group's sexual script governs the individuals' actions. In this case, peer-group norms probably condone, or at least tolerate, kissing in the school halls.

refers to shared meanings or sexual understanding of two actors, as in the example of the couple in an empty classroom. Their words and gestures cue each other as to the appropriate and expected behaviors. Two people making love progress through an elaborate sequence of learned behaviors that is, for them, an essential part of the sexual experience. Saying particular words, petting in an expected sequence, removing each other's clothing—these behaviors are some of the elements our culture agrees are part of sexual expression.

The internal dimension of sexual scripts refers to physiological changes occurring within an individual as a result of attaching sexual meanings to environmental stimuli. Viewing a centerfold or watching a love scene or feeling the touch of another's lips may trigger physiological arousal (erection for the man and vaginal lubrication for the woman). These reactions are in response to items or events in the culture that the individual has learned to regard as sexual.[1]

Children who are being socialized in a particular society are dependent on adults for definitions of what is sexual. As they grow up, they gradually learn about their society's sexual scripts and definitions. Prior to learning this, though, children do not automatically interpret cues as sexual in the same way that adults do.

To assess how two children regard what adults may refer to as sex play, a researcher (Hedges, 1971) put the microphone of a cassette tape recorder near the bathtub where his son and daughter (ages four and six) were taking a bubble bath together. After listening to the tape, he remarked that their dialogue was not sexual but was concerned with who had the most bubbles at his or her end of the tub. For these children, nudity, which adult society generally interprets in sexual terms, meant little. They had not yet developed scripts which would give a sexual meaning to their being naked in the bathtub together.

Unlike children, adults have developed sexual scripts which provide a skeleton of the whos, whats, whens, wheres, and why for given types of sexual activity (See Box, The Sexual Script).

RESEARCH ON SEXUAL BEHAVIOR

Before exploring the various types of sexual behavior people engage in, let's review several of the studies on which this information is based. These studies reflect reported frequencies of various sexual behaviors rather than clinical assessments of sexual functioning (e.g., Masters and Johnson).

The Kinsey Studies—1948 and 1953

As noted in the last chapter, the most comprehensive study of reported sexual behavior was conducted by Alfred C. Kinsey and his associates. They conducted personal interviews with more than sixteen thousand people. And while no study has duplicated the scope of the material presented in *Sexual Behavior in the*

The Sexual Script:
Who, What, When, Where, and Why?

What . . . are the components of a sexual script?

Who one does sex with is defined. The range of "whos" emerges from the social order itself. Most people do sexual things with a restricted number and kinds of other people, usually members of the opposite sex who are about the same age. There are limits set by blood relation, by marital status, and more distantly but nevertheless powerfully by race, ethnicity, religion, and social class. There are certain categories of people with whom sex is or is not allowable. And there are people one fantasizes doing sexual things with, some of whom are on the "approved list" and some who are not.

What one does sexually is also important. Of the whole range of sexual acts that people can perform, most are classified as right or wrong, appropriate or inappropriate. The thought of hugging and kissing is fairly comfortable to most people, if they can specify with whom. Vaginal intercourse seems all right to most experienced heterosexuals, and it is part of the usual marital sexual script. Oral sex and anal sex fit into a script in more complex ways, requiring careful specification of when they occur and with whom, and requiring a complex set of reasons. What is to be done and the order of doing it are learned in fragmentary ways from a variety of social sources.

When is sex appropriate? In the United States, among married couples with children, it is usually after the children have gone to bed or are out of the house. That is, sex is for private times, when no one is likely to knock on the door, and when others do not have to be cared for. In societies whose members generally believe in sexual privacy, but where there is no privacy, people may have intercourse in irregular places (automobiles) and at irregular times (two in the afternoon).

"When" can be construed in a number of ways—the day, the week, the year, or a person's age. Most societies tend to see sex as more or less appropriate at one age, one phase of the human life cycle (e.g., reproductive adulthood), than at another. . . .

Where does the society approve of doing sexual things? As with "when," the notion of privacy is very important here, at least in U.S. society and the societies, present and past, most closely linked to it. These are societies where the bedroom door is closed. When Sigmund Freud concluded that it would be terrible for a child to see his parents having intercourse, he was quite possibly making the mistake of thinking that all of history had been like middle class, nineteenth-century Vienna: a door on every bedroom and no more than two people to a room. For most of human history, however, most families have slept in the same room, hut, cave, or tent, and when there were beds, in the same bed. . . . Notions about the importance—even the necessity—of privacy represent a cultural adaptation that is relatively recent.

Why, finally, do people have sex? That is, not "why" do human beings have the ability to reproduce or put organs together, but what are the culturally appropriate explanations for doing sexual things that people learn? How do individuals explain, both to themselves and others, why they do approved and disapproved sexual things?

The why of sex is its rhetoric. Sex is for: having children; pleasure; lust; fun; passion; love; variety; intimacy; rebellion; degradation; expressing human potential/nature/instincts/needs; exploitation; relaxation; reducing tension; achievement; service. Whatever reasons people offer for doing anything else they use for sex. Some reasons are approved, some disapproved; some we

share with others, some we conceal; we may tell others one thing, and tell ourselves another. We acquire the whys in the same ways we acquire our sexual techniques and sexual preferences. They fit into our scripts, they are substitutable and revisable. "I do it because I love her/him." "I was carried away by passion." "I was being used." "I was just horny at the time." "I feel emotionally closer to the people I have sex with."

"Why" raises the most complicated and perplexing questions of all: questions about which societies and individuals are the most ambivalent; questions that carry with them the greatest potential for confusion, detachment, and alienation as well as clarity, attachment, and innovation.

SOURCE: From HUMAN SEXUALITIES by J. H. Gagnon. Glenview, Il.: Scott, Foresman and Company, 1977, 7–9.

Human Male (1948) and *Sexual Behavior in the Human Female* (1953), some reservations should be kept in mind about the data. These concerns include the subjects, the reliance on recall, and the focus of Kinsey's studies.

Kinsey only studied those individuals who were willing to talk about the intimate details of their sexual lives. The use of volunteer subjects raises the question, "Do those people who did not volunteer to participate in the study have different frequencies and types of sexual behaviors from those who did volunteer for the study?" We don't know and we can't assume either way. Kinsey was aware of this limitation and made no claim to the contrary: "This is a study of sexual behavior in certain groups of the human species . . . not a study of the sexual behavior of all cultures and of all races of man" (Kinsey et al., 1953, p. 4).

In addition to studying only selected groups,[2] Kinsey focused on the biological aspects of sexual behavior without giving equal attention to the emotional factors. Although we know how often the subjects reported having had intercourse, we don't know the meanings they attributed to that sexual experience. A recent sex survey respondent observed, "How often I have intercourse with my partner is very much related to how I am feeling about our relationship." Since emotional variables of this type were not studied, the Kinsey data told us next to nothing about why certain patterns were observed or why one subject's behavior differed from another's.

Another weak point of the Kinsey studies was their reliance on the accurate recall of respondents. The question, "How many persons have you had intercourse with?" requires that people accurately remember events which occurred up to forty years earlier. And for some of those people who can't recall exactly the number of partners they've had, there may be a need to exaggerate or understate the number so as to appear "normal."

The Hunt Study—1972

The Kinsey data are old. To provide an update of the Kinsey studies, Morton Hunt wrote *Sexual Behavior in the 1970's,* which was based on data collected by the Research Guild, Inc., of Chicago. In 1972 the Guild gathered 2026 questionnaires which had been completed in twenty-four American cities. While providing some indication of current trends in sexual behavior, ". . . this study is not, strictly speaking, a replication of the Kinsey surveys, for it is much less detailed, it used a different sampling procedure and a self-administered questionnaire, and these questions were worded differently from Kinsey's" (Hunt, 1974, p. 18).

Commenting on the inadequacies of the Hunt research, Reiss observed that

> The sampling procedure in this study was the poorest of the major studies of the 1970s . . . . The research organization that was hired used the telephone to approach a selected sample of people eighteen and over in twenty-four cities around the country. The telephone approach for a study on sexual attitudes and behavior is probably a very poor choice. Many people do not know if such a call is authentic; others who might be persuaded by a face-to-face contact with an interviewer will not be so persuaded by a phone call. On such a sensitive topic it makes sense to use more personal approaches. The refusal rate was over 80 percent. (Reiss, 1976; p. 177)

The Zelnik and Kantner Studies—1971 and 1976

While the Kinsey and Hunt studies focused on both male and female sexuality, the Zelnik and Kantner research concerned itself only with female sexuality. In 1971 and 1976, Zelnik and Kantner studied a national probability sample of women fifteen through nineteen years of age living in households and in college dormitories in the continental United States. Their sampled population includes women of all marital statuses and races. Their data were collected through personal interviews and are among the best available.

The Hite Study—1976

In contrast to the sophistication of the Zelnik and Kantner studies, *The Hite Report,* presented in 1976 as "a nationwide study of female sexuality," was based on only 3019 of an initial one hundred thousand questionnaires (Hite, 1976, p. 22). This 3 percent return rate is hardly sufficient to provide any meaningful generalizations. But despite methodological shortcomings, the Hite study did make a contribution to sex research literature. Many of the women who completed questionnaires also provided a wealth of anecdotal information and personal insights into their sex lives which was not available from earlier studies.

Other Studies

Information about human sexual behavior is not limited to the research just mentioned. Other studies on this topic include Ehrmann (1959), Christensen (1962, 1966), Reiss (1960, 1967), Simon, Berger, and Gagnon (1972), and Sorensen (1973). A basic problem of all sex research is that we know only what people say they do, not what they actually do. With this caution in mind, let's explore various types of sexual behavior.

TYPES OF SEXUAL BEHAVIOR

While it is not possible to talk about what the "average" person does sexually, we can indicate certain trends among college students regarding masturbation, petting, and intercourse. Since unmarried college students are the most readily available subjects for the academician, there is no scarcity of information about their sex lives.

Masturbation

Also referred to as autoeroticism, masturbation may be defined as any erotic activity that involves voluntary self-stimulation (Katchadourian & Lunde, 1975, p. 268). Masturbation usually occurs in private but may involve two or more people who stimulate themselves, not each other. Mutual stimulation is not masturbation but either petting or homosexual play.

Masturbation remains a relatively taboo subject in our society. Few people feel comfortable discussing it except with close peers. Social disapproval of masturbation is widespread, and while sexual intercourse between a married woman and man is assumed to be right and normal, all nonheterosexual behavior is seen as wrong, unnatural, or incomplete. In addition, it has been assumed in our society that masturbation produces a sexual craving that cannot satisfy itself and, hence, will stimulate desires for intercourse that would not have arisen otherwise (Petras, 1978, p. 180). Society's disapproval of masturbation was so strong at one time that aluminum mitts were used to confine children's hands at bedtime (Malfetti & Eidlitz, 1972, p. 33).

First masturbatory experiences. While boys tend to learn about masturbation from each other, girls are likely to learn from their boyfriends. "After my boyfriend and I petted, I came home and did the same things myself. I've enjoyed masturbating ever since."

Other women discover masturbation themselves or learn about it through the media. As one woman remarked, "I've never talked with any woman about masturbation, and, to my knowledge, women don't talk about it. Although I had heard about it somewhere, I didn't know anything about it until I ordered a sex book for women from an ad in a magazine. I did what it said and now I feel I have come alive sexually."[3] Increasingly, women are receiving permission, instruction, and support in learning about their own bodies (Laws & Schwartz, 1977, p. 62).

Regardless of the source of learning about masturbation, both sexes are beginning to masturbate at earlier ages than reported by Kinsey. By age thirteen, 65 percent of the men and 33 percent of women in the Hunt (1974) study had begun to masturbate (p. 77). These percentages are in contrast to 45 percent and 15 percent reported earlier by Kinsey (1948, p. 500; 1953, p. 141). Some people begin masturbating in infancy and early childhood. "I can't remember when I started masturbating. I just know that I always have," wrote a university freshman.

Masturbation has different meanings for the two sexes. It plunges boys into the sexual world around puberty and teaches them to see girls or women as potential objects for sexual release (Gagnon & Simon, 1973). Boys tend to talk with each other about how they would like to "get inside the pants" of the girl on the playground. But since too many barriers (lack of social skills, girl watched by parents too closely, etc.) make intercourse unlikely in grammar school, the male fantasizes (while he masturbates) "doing to her" what his peers have talked about. Hence, unlike women, men are less likely to believe that a love relationship is necessary for enjoying sex—most of their early sexual experiences have been without females except through fantasy.

Motives. "Because I'm horny," is the most frequent reason given by male and female college students for masturbating (Arafat & Cotton, 1974, p. 303). Being horny implies a condition in which the body calls out for a sexual experience which culminates in orgasm. "I enjoy the pleasurable feelings I get through masturbation," is the second most frequently mentioned motivation for masturbation among college students. "It just feels good. What else can I say?" one student wrote. Other reasons include relieving loneliness, reducing tension, and avoiding intercourse. Regarding the latter, one person said, "I've decided not to have intercourse until I marry. That means I'll have to take care of myself between now and then." A final motivation for masturbating is the time advantage. Because no partner is needed, a person can masturbate whenever she or he wants to, without delays or mutual planning.

Frequency. Regardless of motives, 90 percent of male college students and 60 percent of female college students in one study reported that they currently masturbated (Arafat & Cotton, 1974, p. 299). In another study, single males in their late teens and early twenties masturbated once a week or fifty-two times a year, while females of the same age category averaged about thirty-seven times a year (Hunt, 1974, p. 85).

Gagnon identified a number of factors which affect rates of masturbation:

1. Rates of masturbation go down with age, as do nearly all other forms of sexual activity. Male rates seem to go down further than female rates, perhaps because they start higher.

2. Persons who are conventionally religious (as measured by church attendance) are less likely to masturbate, or masturbate less frequently, than those who are not religious. These differences are not very large, but they are noticeable.

3. When persons marry or begin regular socio-sexual relationships, frequencies and incidence of masturbation drop.

4. It appears that more men who have attended college masturbate (and do so more often) than men who have attended only high school. This appears only among males, and is reflected primarily in increased frequencies of masturbation and in continued patterns of masturbation after marriage. (Gagnon, 1977, p. 156)

Women's sexual fantasies tend to be linked to romantic possibilities, marriage, and social attachments. This comic book is clearly designed to feed the romantic, love-oriented fantasies of young women.

Fantasy.   A rich fantasy colors the masturbatory experience for most men (89 percent always or sometimes) and women (64 percent always or sometimes) (Kinsey, 1948; 1953). Fantasies include intercourse with a loved partner (the most frequent fantasy), sex with strangers, sex with several people at the same time, sex with force, and sex with someone of the same sex (Hunt, 1974). While women's sexual fantasies more typically relate to those ". . . sexual acts which emphasize love, marriage, and social attachment" (Gagnon & Simon, 1973, p. 64), men are less constrained in their fantasy life.

Petting

Petting (while the term may sound dated, no new term has replaced it) may be defined as heterosexual physical stimulation that does not involve intercourse. While petting is thought of most commonly as deep kissing and breast manipulation, it may include mutual stimulation of the genitals and oral sex. Petting is different from foreplay since the word *foreplay* implies that intercourse will follow.

In the absence of contraceptives, petting permits heterosexual expression while minimizing the possibility of a subsequent pregnancy.[4] In addition, petting allows one to think of oneself as a virgin while still experiencing considerable sexual involvement.

The average age for the first petting experience of over six hundred college men was 16.3 years. College women were somewhat older (17.3) when they experienced petting for the first time (Luckey & Nass, 1969, p. 375). Frequency of going out is directly related to petting involvement. "Increased dating frequency results in increased sexual intimacy, since sexual opportunity, desire, and pressure to advance are all likely to increase" (Spanier, 1975, p. 39).

Petting is part of a predictable progression. It moves the couple toward intercourse. One student said, "Once you start heavy petting, it's hard to go back to just kissing and hugging." These feelings reflect the appetitional theory of sexual motivation: an elementary form of sexual involvement once experienced leads to more advanced forms of sexual involvement in a stepwise progression (Hardy, 1964). The name of the theory refers to appetite in that once an individual is satisfied with a given food, the demand for variety increases. In the case of sexual behavior, once it begins in a given relationship, there develops a desire for more and varied forms of sexual involvement.

Researchers have also found that those reporting extensive petting experiences were more likely to drink alcohol, more likely to hold socially and politically liberal views, and less likely to participate in organized religion (Curran, Neff, & Lippold, 1973).

Petting behaviors.   What are the actual petting behaviors of college students? Table 5.1 summarizes the types of petting experiences reported by 195 male and 161 female college students from a large midwestern university (Curran, Neff, &

TABLE 5.1 Percent of Male and Female College Students Reporting Having Experienced Various Petting Behaviors.

Type of Petting Behavior	Males	Females
One minute continuous lip kissing	91.8	90.1
Manual manipulation of female breasts, over clothes	80.0	76.4
Manual manipulation of female breasts, under clothes	78.5	69.6
Manual manipulation of female genitals over clothes	76.4	64.0
Kissing nipples of female breast	71.3	57.1
Manual manipulation of female genitals, under clothes, by male	67.7	52.8
Manual manipulation of male genitals, over clothes, by female	63.1	47.8
Mutual manipulation of genitals	59.0	48.4
Manual manipulation of male genitals, under clothes, by female	55.9	47.2
Manual manipulation of female genitals to massive secretions	54.4	36.6
Manual manipulation of male genitals to ejaculation, by female	46.2	36.6
Oral contact with female genitals, by male	36.9	34.8
Oral contact with male genitals, by female	36.4	27.3
Mutual manual manipulation of genitals to mutual orgasm	36.9	18.0
Oral manipulation of male genitals, by female	32.3	24.8
Oral manipulation of female genitals, by male	32.3	34.2
Mutual oral-genital manipulation	22.6	22.4
Oral manipulation of male genitals to ejaculation	21.5	18.0
Mutual oral manipulation of genitals to mutual orgasm	10.3	8.1
(N)	(195)	(161)

SOURCE: Adapted from Curran, Neff, and Lippold, 1973, p. 127.

Lippold, 1973, p. 127). As an interesting aside, these researchers found that good-looking men reported more involved petting experiences than any of the other respondents. The researchers concluded that " . . . it is advantageous for males to be good-looking and adept interpersonally in order to succeed in obtaining sexual experience, whereas it is not as important for a female to be attractive and have good social skills in order to obtain sexual experience" (Curran, Neff, & Lippold, 1973, p. 130).

Effects of petting.   According to one study, petting resulted in orgasm for two thirds of the single men under age twenty-five surveyed and for half of the single women, ages eighteen to twenty-four (Hunt, 1974, p. 136). In addition, other research has indicated that women who experience orgasm from petting before marriage are more likely to be orgasmic in their first year of marriage. Among the women in the Kinsey sample, 90 percent of those who had experienced an orgasm during premarital petting also reported experiencing a climax during their first year of marriage. If no orgasmic experiences prior to marriage had occurred, only 35 percent reported having had a climax the first year of marriage (Kinsey, 1953). This suggests that premarital petting may contribute to later enjoyment of marital sex.

But petting may also result in guilt feelings. One man in the Hunt study recalled,

> When I started going steady with Amy, we began to pet, and after a while it would get quite heavy, and then we'd both get frightened and guilty and make a pact to see each other but not touch each other. But that would collapse and we'd go further than ever. We'd even stay in bed all night, and masturbate each other to orgasm—and still we had some kind of conviction that it would be wrong to have real intercourse. At times we'd be ready to do it—and, at the very point of trying it, suddenly the vision of what we were doing would come down on us, and we'd stop and feel all torn up. (Hunt, 1974, p. 141)

Intercourse

How many unmarried college students are having intercourse, at what age, with how many partners, and where? Let's examine these issues more closely.

Percent having intercourse.   It is impossible to state the precise percentage of unmarried male and female college students who have intercourse. Each study presents a percentage that is somewhat different from other studies, reflecting different research methods as well as the variability of experiences from campus to campus and year to year. At the University of North Carolina at Chapel Hill, 73 percent of the men and women in a random sample reported having had intercourse (Bauman & Wilson, 1974, p. 329). In summarizing nine studies on the sexual behavior of college students, the author concluded, ". . . about 65 percent of today's male college students engage in coitus and about 50 percent of today's college women [do so]" (Hettlinger, 1974, p. 33).

Researchers have also studied the incidence of intercourse among unmarried teenage women. In a national random sample of white unmarried women between the ages of fifteen and nineteen, 55 percent reported having had intercourse by age nineteen (Zelnik & Kantner, 1977, p. 56). This finding is particularly significant when compared with the findings of a similar study by the same authors in 1971. In that year, 47 percent of the unmarried women between the ages of fifteen and nineteen reported having had intercourse by age nineteen.

We may conclude that while there are doubtless exceptions, in general, more unmarried college men than unmarried college women have intercourse and more unmarried college students have intercourse than do not have intercourse.

Age at first intercourse. Just as unmarried men are more likely than unmarried women to have sexual intercourse, they are likely to have done so about a year earlier than women. In a study in which over six hundred male and female college students reported their age at first intercourse, the average age for the men was 16.3 and for the women 17.3 (Luckey & Nass, 1969, p. 375). These ages are similar to those reported in other studies (Wilson, 1975; Levin, 1975).

Number of partners. Fifty-three percent of the female respondents in the Zelnik and Kantner study who had had intercourse had done so with only one partner (1977, p. 61). While half the women in the Hunt study reported intercourse with an average of only one partner, half the men reported having had an average of six partners (Hunt, 1974, p. 151). Men in the Kinsey sample also averaged six premarital coital partners (Kinsey, 1948). While men have always reported higher rates of premarital coitus, it is interesting to note that men have not increased their average number of premarital partners over the past thirty years.

Place of intercourse. Women in the Zelnik and Kantner study reported their first intercourse experience occurred in their partner's home (44 percent), a friend's home (20 percent), or their own home (15 percent). When asked to identify the most "recent" place they had had intercourse, the partner's home was mentioned by 50 percent of the respondents. While the automobile and motel room may also provide opportunities for intercourse, only 6 percent of the young women reported that their most recent intercourse experience had occurred in a car. A similar percentage reported that their most recent intercourse experience had occurred in a motel room (Zelnik & Kantner, 1977, p. 60).

DIFFERENCES IN SEXUAL BEHAVIOR

Sexual preferences and behaviors are different depending on which sex, social class, and society are being considered. In this section, we examine how women and men view sexual behavior differently, how social class influences its expression, and how other societies differ from our own in the incidence of various sexual practices. As we will see in looking at these variables, the tremendous differences in sexual behavior stem primarily from environmental rather than biological origins.

Female-Male Differences

Due to biological makeup, sex-role socialization, and the learning of different social and sexual scripts, there are dramatic differences in the sexuality of women and men.

Female sexuality. Different orgasmic capacity, different reproductive capability, and concern for the relationship context of sexual intercourse are key phrases which point to the unique features of female sexuality. Regarding orgasm, more women have difficulty achieving orgasm during intercourse than men. Thirty percent of the women Kinsey studied reported that they failed to achieve orgasm during intercourse at least some of the time and 8 percent never experienced a climax (Kinsey et al., 1953). A primary reason for the infrequency of orgasm in women is the failure of their male partners to provide the sexual experience and emotional context often necessary for women to achieve orgasm. In one study, women in committed relationships were found to be much more likely to experience a climax (or climaxes) than those who were not involved in a committed relationship (Burstein, 1975).

In addition, most women are more likely to experience an orgasm by masturbating rather than by having intercourse. One reason women climax more frequently during masturbation than intercourse is that, during masturbation, the woman can provide her own intense rhythmic pressure on and around her clitoris. Such intense stimulation in the clitoral area does not occur during intercourse when the penis is inside the vagina. Since the walls of the vagina do not have nerve endings, a fully penetrated penis is less likely to produce a climax than more direct clitoral contact.

Whereas many women do not easily or regularly reach orgasm during intercourse, women do have a capacity for multiple orgasms which men do not have. A man must wait at least several minutes after experiencing an orgasm before it is possible to achieve another, but a woman can experience several orgasms in rapid succession (Masters & Johnson, 1966).

Not all women experience multiple orgasms, or any orgasms. And, for some women not doing so is a frustrating experience. A reader of *Psychology Today* remarked when responding to a questionnaire,

> I cannot help feeling that I am only half a woman, an empty shell without feelings, because of my inability to reach orgasm. I keep telling myself that I am placing too much importance on this part of life, that I should relax and stop worrying about it. . . . I

cannot help but feel that our society with its sexual preoccupation breeds many problems exactly like mine. There is such a fear of being abnormal—but what is normal in this topsy-turvy chaotic world? (Athanasiou, Shaver, & Tavris, 1970, p. 44)

Regardless of the number of orgasms experienced, women report tremendous variations in the quality and type of orgasm. While Masters and Johnson (1966) established that there are no physiological distinctions between a "clitoral" and a "vaginal" orgasm, 46 percent of the women in Clifford's (1973) study noted a difference in subjective sensations. There was no consistent tendency to prefer one type over the other. Other authors have also explored subjective sensations during orgasm (see Fisher, 1973; Hite, 1976).

In addition to the differences in reference to orgasm between men and women, the reproductive capability of women signals another difference. While men provide the sperm to fertilize the ovum produced by the woman, the man's involvement in reproduction stops there. The female body is a potential baby machine complete with uterus for nurture of the fetus, vagina for its entry into the world, and breasts for its sustenance after birth. No man will ever experience menstruation, giving birth, or nursing an infant. These experiences are unique and result in men and women living in different experiential worlds.

As already noted, women have a stronger tendency than men to limit their experience of intercourse to those partners who provide an emotional context. In general, the more love the woman feels for her partner, the more willing she is to engage in sexual behavior. This tendency holds true even among women who consider themselves to be relatively sexually liberated (Hunt, 1974).

Male sexuality. Relative to female sexuality, male sexuality is more goal oriented, homosocial, and in one sense vulnerable. Regarding goal orientation, one sociologist observed, "Male patterns are characterized by a capacity to treat sexuality as an end in itself, whereas female patterns are less directly sexual and more typically an outgrowth or expression of some more encompassing emotional or social commitment" (Walshok, 1973). In addition, as noted earlier, the man's early and regular experience with masturbation teaches him to dissociate sex and love (Simon & Gagnon, 1969). When masturbating, a man tends to focus on his own sexual pleasure. Orgasmic release is the goal and relationship concerns are peripheral.

Male sexuality also tends to be homosocial (not to be confused with homosexual or heterosexual). This suggests that men (particularly adolescents) engage in sexual behavior with women in reference to their male friends; the emotional involvement with the woman may be incidental (Gagnon & Simon, 1973). For example, one junior intentionally had intercourse with a girl while his roommate was within earshot in the next room. He was having intercourse mainly in reference to his friend, not the girl.

In addition to separating love and sex more than women and being oriented to homosocial values, men are, in one sense, more vulnerable during sexual performance than women. Since intercourse depends on an erection, should the man fail to get or sustain an erection, his self-concept may suffer a tremendous blow. Such loss of self-esteem results from a belief encouraged in all-male peer groups that real masculinity is tied to an erect penis. When the penis goes down, so does the man's ego. "When I couldn't get an erection," wrote one man, "I panicked . . . the whole experience was the most miserable in my life."

Social Class Differences

A person's social class also influences his or her sexual behavior. While individuals differ, each social class has its own view of human sexuality.

Lower class.   The social status referred to here as lower class includes people with low incomes, less than high-school educations, and menial jobs, at best. Kinsey (1948) observed that lower-class men were less likely to masturbate than higher social class men. Around 10 percent of men who had only grade-school educations reported never having masturbated in contrast to 4 percent of college-educated men. Lower-class men are more likely to view masturbation as unnatural and an admission of an inability to seduce a woman. "If you have to do it yourself, you're no good with a woman," wrote one man. And the fact that men designated as being in the lower class have intercourse much earlier and more frequently than those in higher social classes (Kinsey, 1948) may suggest that a masturbatory pattern never develops.

While social class does not seem to affect the frequency of female masturbation, lower-class women were found in one study to view intercourse as ". . . a man's pleasure and a woman's duty. Sexual relations exist for the pleasure of the man; enjoyment for the woman is either optional or disapproved. Women are believed either not to have sexual desires at all or to have much weaker sexual needs" (Rainwater, 1972, p. 189).

Several factors which work against full sexual enjoyment by less educated and low-income women are poor health, inadequate nutrition, and fatigue (Bell, 1974). But fear of pregnancy and greater difficulty in finding, purchasing, and understanding the means of controlling family size are perhaps the greatest hurdles to overcome. While women of low social class are not expected to enjoy sexual relations, they typically assume that their husbands cannot be happy without it, and that they will look elsewhere if they are not satisfied (Rainwater, 1972, p. 189). And, although the sexual desires of men in the lower class may be intense, they are expected to do little to ensure their partners' satisfaction. In general, there is little foreplay except that which is necessary to seduce a woman. What foreplay does exist tends to be mechanical and involves minimal emotional communication (Pierson & D'Antonio, 1974, p. 263).

Middle class.   In contrast to those in the lower class, a common experience of middle-class people is exposure to a college or university environment (Ferdinand, 1970, p. 171). And such exposure sometimes has implications for one's sexual relationships. Eighty-two percent of the college-educated men in Masters and Johnson's study expressed a concern for the coital satisfactions of their partners. Only 14 percent of those men whose formal education did not include college expressed the slightest concern with any responsibility for the sexual satisfaction of their partner (Masters & Johnson, 1966).

Middle-class wives are more likely to view intercourse as enjoyable than lower-class wives. In one study of sixty-six college-educated wives, about one third reported that intercourse was "too infrequent" (Bell, 1974, p. 9). "I have as much right to get off on sex as my husband does," remarked a wife.

Lower- and middle-class women also differ in their views of how to improve their sex lives. While high-school-educated wives suggest "more frequent sex," "more sexual variations," and "more foreplay" as ways of improving the sexual relationships with their husbands, the college-educated wives suggest "more time and privacy" and "that each partner be better able to relate to the other" (Bell, 1974, p. 8). These latter suggestions focus more on the relationship than on sexual technique or frequency.

Upper class.   Prestigious occupations, high incomes, and stability in the community are some of the indices of upper-class membership. And because this group is less accessible than middle- and lower-class respondents, little is known about their sexual behavior. However, in general, as social class level increases, aggressiveness in sexual behavior becomes modified and more care in the sexual relationship is evident (Petras, 1978, p. 109). Such care implies that an upper-class man would rarely consider using force with his female partner. Such force is more common in the lower class.

And, since upper-class youth are often schooled in private single-sex institutions, they may have little access to members of the opposite sex. More frequent masturbation is one result for both women and men (Kinsey et al., 1953, p. 180; 1948, p. 340). Upper-class women who cannot find men of equal social status to marry also have higher rates of masturbation and homosexuality (Kinsey et al., 1953, pp. 180, 490).

Differences in Other Societies

There are tremendous variations in sexual preferences and practices in other societies. Such variation suggests that expressions of human sexuality are learned rather than biological and innate. For example, while having intercourse with one's brother or sister is likely to induce feelings of shame or disgust in our contemporary society, the Dahomey of West Africa and the Inca of Peru have viewed such a relationship as natural and desirable (Stephens, 1963, p. 260). Also, the people of

Mangaia, an island in the South Pacific, are confused at the American man's preoccupation with the female breast. The Mangaian feels that only a hungry baby "should be" interested in this organ (Marshall, 1972, p. 110).

Sexual behavior that is punished in one society may be tolerated in a second and rewarded in a third. In the Gilbert Islands (also in the South Pacific), virginity until marriage is an exalted sexual value and violations are not tolerated. Premarital couples who are discovered to have had intercourse before the wedding are put to death. In contrast, the Lepcha people of India believe that intercourse helps young girls to mature. By the age of twelve, most Lepcha young women are engaging in regular intercourse (Gagnon, 1975, p. 14).

In general, preliterate societies have a tolerant attitude toward premarital sexual behavior. Around two fifths to one half of these societies accept intercourse before marriage for women with few negative sanctions (Ford, 1945; Westermarck, 1922, p. 157). If those preliterate societies that publicly condemn but secretly tolerate premarital intercourse are considered, the proportion is 70 percent (Murdock, 1949, p. 165).

Regarding sex in marriage, Ford and Beach (1951) surveyed 190 societies and found that heterosexual intercourse is the major form of sexual behavior which occurs primarily at night, before sleep, and in a private residence. Men

From one society to the next there are variations in sexual preferences and psychosexual scripts. While black lace undergarments may be part of some erotic scripts in some societies, they would be absurd or offensive in societies with other preferences and other scripts.

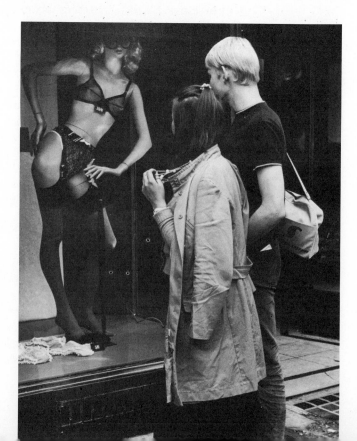

most frequently initiate intercourse, with women being the more passive partners. Most societies prohibit intercourse during menstruation, periods of pregnancy, and the postpartum period (Gebhard, 1972, p. 212).

There are also variations in the frequency of intercourse. While most couples throughout the world have intercourse between two and five times per week (Gebhard, 1972, p. 211), the Basongye in the Kasai province of the former Belgian Congo, even in their fifties and sixties, have intercourse every night (Merriam, 1972, p. 90). In contrast, a Cayapa man may go for several years without having intercourse. Their term for intercourse, *medio trabajo,* means "a little like work" (Altschuler, 1972, p. 55).

Referring to places with which we are more familiar, sexual behavior among the Danes is more permissive than among Americans. In Denmark, sexual intercourse during engagement is traditional. It is a socially accepted and expected behavior. However, the greater sexual permissiveness of Denmark and all of Scandinavia does not necessarily imply promiscuity. Rather, complete sexual intimacy is made a part of the courtship-marriage process (Christensen, 1969, pp. 159–60).

Parent-Offspring Differences

Sexual attitudes also vary from one generation to the next. Thirty-five percent of 217 women students expressed the belief that sexual intercourse during engagement was "very wrong" in contrast to 85 percent of their mothers who expressed the same feeling (Bell & Buerkle, 1962, p. 391). In another study, when mothers and daughters were compared on the way they saw each other's sexual values, the mothers saw their daughters as less accepting of petting and intercourse than the daughters actually were (LoPiccolo, 1973, p. 174).

Why parents worry. A major source of parents' concern is potential pregnancy. Parents do not want to deal with a premarital pregnancy. For a daughter, it may mean a shattered family image ("The Jones girl got pregnant and the guy ran off"), a threatened reputation ("She had an abortion last year"), and a questionable beginning for a marriage ("He married her because she was pregnant"). The consequences of an unwanted pregnancy for the son tend to be less dramatic because he does not carry the baby. However, a major concern is that he could be trapped into a marriage that would not have occurred had it not been for a pregnancy.

Such worries often cause parents considerable anxiety and unhappiness. They may feel frustrated in their inability to control their children's sexual behavior. In general, parents do not know how to communicate effectively with their offspring about sex (Bell, 1972). While some use fear tactics which emphasize the dangers of venereal disease and an unwanted pregnancy, their usual pattern is to give only vague expectations regarding sexual behavior (Libby & Nass, 1971; Bell, 1966). These expectations are usually in the form of "Don't be out too late,"

Parents today tend to worry a great deal when their offspring share campuses, coed dormitories, travel arrangements, or camping trips with members of the opposite sex. While such arrangements today may or may not imply a sexual situation, in earlier generations they were considered to be clear proof of impropriety.

"Who else will be there?" or "What time will you be back?" And, parents usually take great care not to discover what they don't want to see. Although the home of the young woman or man is the most common place for premarital coitus to occur, only six out of each one hundred thousand intercourse events are discovered (Kinsey et al., 1953, p. 326).

Most parents assume that their children, particularly their daughters, will not have intercourse before marriage (Bell, 1972). They assume that "immorality" and "permissiveness" are behaviors of other college youth. An engaged woman said, "I have been having intercourse with my boyfriend since we met three years ago. Mother *must* know because she is aware of our having spent some time at the family's beach house when she and Daddy were on vacation. But, when we went to pick out my wedding dress last week there was never a discussion of whether or not it would be white. I think she is incapable of thinking that I would have intercourse before I was married."

Parental inconsistency.   The premarital sexual behavior of parents and the sexual values they encourage for their children are not necessarily the same. While 30 percent of seventy-eight mothers in one study reported that they had had intercourse in their youth, 97 percent of these same mothers encouraged virginity as the sexual value for their daughters. Among fathers, 51 percent reported having had premarital intercourse themselves while 90 percent wanted their sons to be abstinent until marriage (Wake, 1969).

Discrepancies between what parents have done sexually and the sexual values they want for their children have several explanations. (1) Context. Parents may fear that their indicating a liberal attitude toward sex will be misunderstood and misused by their children. "Sex is OK if you are in love with the person" may be interpreted by a son or daughter as "Sex is OK with anybody I meet as long as I really like him or her." (2) Resentment toward own parents. Some parents feel that their own parents were too lenient and permissive. "My mother let us do what we wanted," expressed a forty-five-year-old mother of two college students, "but she was *too* permissive. I needed some limits on what I did and some guidelines about sexual values." Parents reared in a permissive home often become restrictive in their own homes (Vincent, 1972, p. 148). (3) Unconscious regret. Although parents may check on a questionnaire that they have no regrets about having had intercourse before marriage, they might actually have such feelings. It is easier to check "no regret" than to check "regret." Checking the latter may involve the parent's having to open some old emotional sores (Festinger, 1962). (4) Modeling. Parents tend to duplicate in their own family the parenting behaviors they observed in the family in which they were reared. While there may be effort on the part of some parents to rear their children differently, it is often easy to fall back on the familiar—the way they were reared.

Rather than confront parents about their own premarital sexual behavior, most college youth conceal sexual information they feel would incite parental disapproval. Sixty-three percent of 217 women students said that they would not give their mothers accurate information about their sexual values (Bell & Buerkle, 1962, p. 27).

In summary, parents and their college offspring hold different sexual values. College students are likely to adopt the sexual values of their close friends while parents look the other way. Neither is open and honest with the other about sexual behavior and values. However, parents often foster a permissive value system by defending their children's right to select their own mate, as opposed to an arranged marriage (Reiss, 1969, p. 114). Our free courtship system encourages permissiveness by allowing dating to occur in the absence of parental supervision. This often translates into wine, music, and intercourse in someone's dorm room, apartment, or home.

SEX EDUCATION

Parents are often ambivalent about sex education for their offspring. Whether sex education should be provided, who should provide it (parents or schools), and what content should be covered are some primary concerns.

What Parents Want

While most parents want their children to acquire their sex education and values from the home, they know that they themselves have avoided the issue, much like their own parents. In a study of 250 parents, slightly over 25 percent reported receiving any specific sex education from their mothers and less than 10 percent reported any sex education from their fathers (Libby et al., 1974). One graduate student in family relations remarked, "My folks never told me *anything* about sex. I had to write away for a pamphlet on sex."

On the other hand, parents tend to fear that their talking about sex with their offspring will lead to sexual experimentation. One study showed that this was not true. When parents were the major source of sex education, their maturing children were less likely to engage in intercourse than when parents were not the major source of sex education. As the author concluded, "Rather than stimulate coital experience, parents who were the main source of sex education for their children appeared to have been very effective deterrents, particularly as agents of socialization for female children" (Lewis, 1963, pp. 164–65).

Ideally, parents want both the school and church to support the conservative values of the home (Libby et al., 1974). They hope that teachers in schools and churches will help them perform their tasks of imparting essential sexual information and controlling sexual behavior (Libby, 1970). It is ironic that even though parents prefer the home-school and home-church combinations for sex education, only 6 percent of the 250 parents in the study mentioned above received their own sex education from these two combinations of sources. For most people, close friends are the major source of information about sex (Thornburg, 1974; 1972).

What the Schools Provide

Since 1960, in an effort to reduce sexual ignorance, over five prestigious national panels[5] have recommended that the federal government take a leadership role in encouraging sex education in the secondary-school curriculum (Ambrose, 1976, p. 1). Yet, because education is financed and administered almost entirely through

"We had that in school last week."

state and local school boards, only limited initiatives are possible on the federal level. Throughout the U.S., only 20 percent of the states require sex education in their school systems (Planned Parenthood Federation, 1976).

Sex education programs differ widely in content and presentation. There are four basic types of programs: (1) Plumbing. Anatomy and physiology of men and women are the major concerns of this model. Emphasis is placed on physical maturation, menstruation, puberty, and early adolescence. One student who had been exposed to this model observed, "The course tells you what you've got and how to make babies with it." (2) Consequences. Venereal disease, unwanted pregnancy, shattered educational goals, and potential medical complications are investigated as potential consequences of unprotected intercourse. The economic strain on a marriage forced by a premarital pregnancy is also emphasized (Gordon, 1973). (3) Morality. This model emphasizes responsible sexual behavior involving the use of contraception and avoiding the exploitation of one's partner. While alternative value systems are explored, a basic theme suggests that the best sex is that which enhances the relationship and the self-concepts of the partners. (4) Student-oriented. This model involves the active participation of students in the development and execution of "sex seminars" on campus. It probably has the greatest influence on participants because peers lead the discussions.

TRENDS

Trends in sexual behavior include experimentation with a wider variety of sexual activities, an increased use of contraception, and increased acceptance of sex education in public schools. More people are being socialized to regard intercourse as appropriate for nonmarital relationships, and taboos regarding oral or manual stimulation are also weakening.

Besides including more sexual variety in petting and foreplay, unmarried couples will increase their use of contraception if trends continue. Zelnik and Kantner observed in their 1976 study that individuals of all ages and races were dramatically increasing their regular use of the most effective contraceptives (p. 55).

In addition, our society will increasingly recognize that sexual behavior among youth is already occurring, that parents do not provide adequate sex education, and that the school system must. The Supreme Court ruling defending the right of minors to have access to contraceptives[6] reflects the trend away from pretending that what the young don't know can't hurt them. Instead, the trend will be toward ensuring that individuals in our society have accurate information about their own bodies, reproduction, and the place of sexual behavior in human relationships.

SUMMARY

While sexual behavior involves anatomy and physiology, the pattern of its expression is acquired through learning. The psychosexual view of human sexuality emphasizes the learning of scripts which give sexual meaning to environmental stimuli and which provide guidelines for sexual behavior.

Our information about sexual behavior is limited for the most part to what people say they do. While the studies by Kinsey, Hunt, Zelnik and Kantner, Hite, and others provide some indication of the sexual behavior of Americans, we actually know very little.

Masturbation, petting, and intercourse are reported as being the most frequent types of nonmarital sexual behavior. While boys and men tend to learn about masturbation from peers, and girls and women learn through self-discovery, the predominant motive is sexual pleasure. Although men masturbate more frequently than women, both sexes use an array of techniques and fantasy.

Petting permits a couple to experience sexual pleasure while avoiding pregnancy. Petting ranges from holding hands to mutual oral manipulation of the genitals. According to the appetitional theory of sexual motivation, petting behaviors become progressively more involved as a relationship continues, and there is a trend toward moving from petting to foreplay. Some couples may experience guilt and anxiety over their initial petting experiences.

Most unmarried college students have intercourse. First intercourse occurs around age sixteen for men and at a slightly later age for women. The place of first intercourse is usually in the home of either partner.

Differences in sexual behavior and attitudes are evident in male-female, social class, and cross-cultural comparisons. Women have more difficulty achieving orgasm during intercourse and are more concerned about the relationship context of intercourse than men. Men (particularly adolescents) tend to use their early intercourse experiences to confirm their masculinity among their friends (homosocial behavior).

Social class also affects sexual behavior. While people of higher status tend to view intercourse as a pleasurable event to share, lower-status people more often regard intercourse as a pleasure men have a right to and a duty wives must perform.

Cross-cultural comparisons also emphasize the variability of human sexuality. Sexual behavior that is punished in one society may be tolerated in a second and rewarded in a third. Premarital couples in the Gilbert Islands are put to death if it is discovered that they have had intercourse.

Differences in sexual attitudes also exist between parents and their offspring. Although parents may have been sexually active in their courtship, they want their children to be sexually conservative. The sex education they provide for their children is minimal, but they fear the influence of outside sex educators.

The future of sexual behavior is likely to include a wider variety of sexual behavior, increased use of contraception, and increased acceptance of sex education in public schools. This latter trend will be the last to be realized. Sex remains a subject some parents want to hide from their children. And these parents will be reluctant to permit the school system to provide the sex education they themselves are too uncomfortable to provide.

STUDY QUESTIONS

1. Explain sexual behavior from a psychosexual perspective. Include in your discussion the meaning, types, and functions of scripts.
2. What are some shortcomings of the Kinsey surveys? Why do we regard the Kinsey data as significant?
3. What were the weaknesses and the contributions of the studies by Hunt, Zelnik and Kantner, and Hite?
4. How does masturbation differ from mutual stimulation?
5. How do men and women typically learn about masturbation?
6. Explain how masturbation might influence the way some men view women.
7. Discuss four factors which affect the rates of masturbation.
8. Why do men and women masturbate and what kinds of fantasies often accompany masturbation?
9. Define petting. How does it differ from foreplay and what are the various "functions" of petting?

10. What is the appetitional theory of sexual motivation?
11. What are the most frequent petting behaviors of college men and women?
12. At about what age do male and female college students begin having intercourse?
13. Discuss how female sexuality differs from male sexuality regarding orgasmic capacity, reproduction, and the relationship context of intercourse.
14. What class differences have been found regarding masturbation and in how intercourse is viewed?
15. Compare lower and higher status women in reference to their knowledge about and access to contraception and its subsequent impact on their feelings about intercourse.
16. Describe some societies that have different views regarding incest, the female breast, premarital intercourse, and marital intercourse.
17. What is one major concern of parents who worry about the sexual behavior of their children?
18. Give four explanations of why parents are inconsistent in their sexual values for themselves and their children.
19. What is the major source of sex education for most people?
20. What are four types of sex education programs?
21. About what percent of the states currently require sex education in the school system?
22. What are some basic trends in sexual behavior?

NOTES

1. From another perspective (symbolic interaction), two researchers emphasized that "physical sensations which constitute sexual experience are not merely interpreted by our symbolic systems into sexual phenomena, but even more important, the sexual symbolism also creates sexual experience. . . . We not only respond in terms of our symbols, but the symbols themselves give rise to experience and response" (Gecas and Libby, 1976, p. 34). For example, if you define kissing someone as sexual, it becomes sexual.

2. Examples of the groups sampled by Kinsey included church congregations, clinical groups, college classes, sororities, fraternities, PTA groups, prisoners, women's clubs, etc. Most of these groups represented white, urban, Protestant, college-educated people from the northeastern quarter of the country. Kinsey's findings are most likely to be valid for this type person (Reiss, 1976, p. 131).

3. The twenty-four-page book she referred to is *My Playbook for Women About Sex* by Joan Blank (available from Multi Media Resource Center, 1523 Franklin Street, San Francisco, California 94109). A similar book is *Liberating Masturbation* by Betty Dodson (121 Madison Avenue, New York, N.Y. 10016).

4. There are occasional exceptions to this. One form of petting is for the female to rub her partner's penis inside her vaginal lips without inserting it inside her vagina. While technically the female who does this may be a "virgin," she may also get pregnant since the seminal fluid may leak from the penis and "swim" up the vagina to fertilize the ovum. See "The case of pregnant virgins" (Stout, 1977).

5. The 1960 and 1970 White House Conference on Children, the 1971 White House Conference on Youth, the 1972 Report of the Commission on Population Growth and the American Future, and the 1976 Commission on the Observance of International Women's Year.

6. On June 9, 1977, the United States Supreme Court ruled that states may not bar the sale of contraceptives to children or restrict where adults can buy contraceptives.

BIBLIOGRAPHY

Altschuler, M. Cayapa personality and sexual motivation. In *Human sexual behavior,* D. S. Marshall and R. C. Suggs (eds.). Englewood Cliffs, N.J.: Prentice-Hall, 1972, 38–58.

Ambrose, L. Sex education in the public school: The need for official leadership. *Family Planning/Population Reporter,* 1976, *5,* 5.

Arafat, I. S., and Cotton, W. L. Masturbation practices of males and females. *Journal of Sex Research,* 1974, *10,* 4, 293–307.

Arnstein, R. L. Virgin men. *Medical Aspects of Human Sexuality,* January 1974, 113–27.

Athanasiou, R., Shaver, P., and Tavris, C. Sex. *Psychology Today,* July 1970, 39–52.

Bauman, K. E., and Wilson, R. R. Sexual behavior of unmarried university students in 1968 and 1972. *The Journal of Sex Research,* 1974, *10,* 4, 327–33.

Bell, R. R. *Premarital sex in a changing society.* Englewood Cliffs, N.J.: Prentice-Hall, 1966.

_____. Parent-child conflict in sexual values. In *The social dimension of human sexuality,* R. Bell and M. Gordon (eds.). Boston: Little, Brown, 1972, 21–31.

_____. Female sexual satisfaction and levels of education. In *Sexual behavior: Current issues,* L. Gross (ed.). Flushing, N.Y.: Spectrum Publications, 1974, 3–11.

Bell, R. R., and Buerkle, J. V. Mother and daughter attitudes to premarital sexual behavior. *Marriage and Family Living,* 1961, *23,* 4, 390–2.

_____. Mother-daughter conflict during the launching stage. *Marriage and Family Living,* 1962, *24,* 384–8.

Blank, J. *My playbook for women about sex.* Burlingame, Calif.

Burstein, B. Life history and current values as predictors of sexual behaviors and satisfaction in college women. Paper presented at the meeting of the Western Psychological Association, Sacramento, April 1975.

Christensen, H. T. The impact of culture and values. *The individual, sex, and society,* C. B. Broderick and J. Bernard. Baltimore: Johns Hopkins University Press, 1969, 155–69.

_____. Value behavior discrepancies regarding premarital coitus in three western cultures. *American Sociological Review,* 1962, *27,* 66–74.

_____. Scandinavian and American sex norms: Some comparisons with sociological implications. *Journal of Social Issues,* 1966, *22,* 60–75.

Clifford, R. Female masturbation in sexual development and clinical application. Doctoral dissertation. Department of Psychology, State University of New York at Stony Brook, 1973.

Curran, J. P., Neff, S., and Lippold, S. Correlates of sexual experience among university students. *Journal of Sex Research,* 1973, *9,* 2, 124–31.

Dodson, B. *Liberating masturbation.* New York: Bodysex Designs, 1974.

Ehrmann, W. W. *Premarital dating behavior.* New York: Holt, Rinehart and Winston, 1959.

Ferdinand, T. N. Sex behavior and the American class structure: A mosaic. In *Studies in human sexual behavior: The American scene,* A. Shiloh. Springfield, Ill.: Charles C Thomas, 1970, 166–75.

Festinger, L. A. *A theory of cognitive dissonance.* Stanford: Stanford University Press, 1962.

Fisher, S. *The female orgasm.* New York: Basic Books, 1973.

Ford, C. S. *A comparative study of human reproduction.* New Haven: Yale University Press, 1945.

Ford, C. S., and Beach, F. A. *Patterns of sexual behavior.* New York: Harper and Row, 1951.

Gagnon, J. *Human sexualities.* Glenview, Ill.: Scott, Foresman, 1977.

_____, (ed.). Human sexuality: An age of ambiguity. Boston: Educational Associates, 1975.

Gagnon, J. H., and Simon, W. *Sexual conduct: The social sources of human sexuality.* Chicago: Aldine, 1973.

Gebhard, P. H. Human sexual behavior: A summary statement. In *Human sexual behavior,* D. S. Marshall and R. C. Suggs. Englewood Cliffs, N.J.: Prentice-Hall, 1972, 206–17.

Gecas, V., and Libby, R. Sexual behavior as symbolic interaction. *The Journal of Sex Research,* 1976, *12,* 1, 33–49.

Gordon, S. *The sexual adolescent.* Belmont, Calif.: Duxbury Press, 1973.

Hardy, K. R. An appetitional theory of sexual motivation. *Psychological Review,* 1964, *71,* 1–18.

Hedges, R. Department of Family Development, Western Kentucky University. Personal communication, 1971.

Hettlinger, R. *Sex isn't that simple: The new sexuality on campus.* New York: Seabury Press, 1974.

Hite, S. *The Hite report.* New York: Dell, 1976.

———. *Sexual honesty: By women for women.* New York: Warner Books, 1974.

Hunt, M. *Sexual behavior in the 1970's.* New York: Dell, 1974.

Kantner, J. F., and Zelnik, M. Sexual experience of young unmarried women in the United States. *Family Planning Perspectives,* 1972, *4,* 9–17.

Katchadourian, H. A., and Lunde, D. T. *Fundamentals of human sexuality.* New York: Holt, Rinehart and Winston, 1975.

Kinsey, A. C., Pomeroy, W. B., Martin, C. E. *Sexual behavior in the human male.* Philadelphia: W. B. Saunders, 1948.

———. *Sexual behavior in the human female.* Philadelphia: W. B. Saunders, 1953.

Laws, J. L., and Schwartz, P. *Sexual scripts: The social construction of female sexuality.* Hinsdale, Ill.: Dryden Press, 1977.

Levin, R. J. The end of the double standard? *Redbook,* October 1975, 38.

Lewis, R. A. Parents and peers: Socialization agents in the coital behavior of young adults. *The Journal of Sex Research,* 1963, *9,* 156–69.

Libby, R. W. Parental attitudes toward high school sex education programs. *The Family Coordinator,* 1970, *3,* 234–53.

Libby, R. W., Acock, A. C., and Payne, D. C. Configuration of parental preferences concerning sources of sex education for adolescents. *Adolescence,* 1974, *9,* 3, 73–80.

Libby, R. W., and Nass, G. A. Parental views on teenage sexual behavior. *The Journal of Sex Research,* 1971, *7,* 226–36.

LoPiccolo, J. Mothers and daughters: Perceived and real differences in sexual values. *The Journal of Sex Research,* 1973, *9,* 171–7.

Luckey, E. B., and Nass, G. D. A comparison of sexual attitudes and behavior in an international sample. *Journal of Marriage and the Family,* 1969, *31,* 2, 364–79.

Malfetti, J., and Eidlitz, E. *Perspectives on sexuality.* New York: Holt, Rinehart and Winston, 1972.

Marshall, D. S. Sexual behavior on Mangaia. In *Human sexual behavior,* D. S. Marshall and R. C. Suggs. Englewood Cliffs, N.J.: Prentice-Hall, 1972, 103–62.

Masters, W. H., and Johnson, V. E. *Human sexual response.* Boston: Little, Brown, 1966.

Merriam, A. P. Aspects of sexual behavior among the Bala (Basongye). In *Human sexual behavior,* D. S. Marshall and R. C. Suggs. Englewood Cliffs, N.J.: Prentice-Hall, 1972, 71–102.

Murdock, G. P. *Social structure.* New York: Macmillan, 1949.

Petras, J. W. *Sexuality in society.* Boston: Allyn and Bacon, 1978.

Pierson, E. C., and D'Antonio, W. V. *Female and male: Dimensions of human sexuality.* Philadelphia: J. B. Lippincott, 1974.

Planned Parenthood Federation. *11 million teenagers.* New York: Planned Parenthood Federation of America, 1976.

Rainwater, L. Marital sexuality in four "cultures of poverty." In *Human sexual behavior,* D. S. Marshall and R. C. Suggs. Englewood Cliffs, N.J.: Prentice-Hall, 1972, 187–205.

Reiss, I. L. *Premarital sexual standards in America.* New York: Free Press, 1960.

———. *The social context of sexual permissiveness.* New York: Holt, Rinehart and Winston, 1967.

———. Premarital sexual standards. In *The individual, sex, and society,* C. B. Broderick and J. Bernard. Baltimore: Johns Hopkins University Press, 1969, 109–18.

———. *Family systems in America.* Hinsdale, Ill.: Dryden Press, 1976.

Simon, W., and Gagnon, J. *The sexual scene.* New Brunswick, N.J.: Transaction, 1969.

_____. Psychosexual development. In *Human sexuality: Contemporary perspectives,* E. S. Morrison and V. Borosage (eds.). Palo Alto, Calif.: National Press Books, 1973, 3–17.

Simon, W., Berger, A., and Gagnon, J. Beyond anxiety and fantasy: The coital experiences of college youth. *Journal of Youth and Adolescence,* 1972, *1,* 203–22.

Sorensen, R. *Adolescent sexuality in contemporary America.* New York: World Publishing, 1973.

Spanier, G. B. Sexualization and premarital sexual behavior. *The Family Coordinator,* 1975, *24,* 1, 33–42.

Stephens, W. N. *The family in cross-cultural perspective.* New York: Holt, Rinehart and Winston, 1963.

Stout, R. J. The case of pregnant virgins. *Journal of Sex Education and Therapy,* 1977, *3,* 1, 3–4.

Thornburg, H. D. A comparative study of sex information sources. *Journal of School Health,* 1972, *42,* 88–91.

_____. Educating the preadolescent about sex. *The Family Coordinator,* 1974, *23,* 1, 35–40.

Vincent, C. E. An open letter to the caught generation. *The Family Coordinator,* 1972, *21,* 2, 143–50.

Wake, F. Attitudes of parents toward premarital sexual behavior of children and themselves. *Journal of Sex Research,* 1969, *5,* 3.

Walshok, M. L. Sex role typing and feminine sexuality. Paper presented at the meeting of the American Sociological Association, New York, August 1973.

Westermarck, E. *The history of human marriage.* New York: Allterton, 1922.

Wilson, W. C. The distribution of selected sexual attitudes and behaviors among the adult population of the United States. *The Journal of Sex Research,* 1975, *11,* 1, 46–64.

Zelnik, M., and Kantner, J. Sexual and contraceptive experience of young unmarried women in the United States, 1976 and 1971. *Family Planning Perspectives,* 1977, *9,* 2, 55–71.

Chapter 6

Marriage and Its Alternatives

I would be married, but I'd have no wife,
I would be married to a single life.
                              Richard Crashaw

While this text is about marriage and the family, not all people marry, nor do they have children. In this chapter we explore the reasons for and alternatives to marriage. These alternatives include singlehood, cohabitation (heterosexual or homosexual), contract cohabitation, and communal living. As we shall see throughout this chapter, individuals are continually in the process of reevaluating marriage and its alternatives.

MARRIAGE

In March 1977, there were 48 million married couples in America (U.S. Bureau of the Census, 1978, p. 3), and every year about two million more marriages occur in the United States.[1] While the median age of marriage for women is 21.6 and for men it is 24, by middle age almost 95 percent of both sexes have married (U.S. Bureau of the Census, 1978). Social pressure and individual motivations account for the overwhelming majority of Americans tying the marital knot. But what are these social and personal reasons for marriage?

Society and Marriage

Marriage and the family have traditionally served various functions in our society. But increasingly people are questioning these waning functions.

Traditional functions.   Traditionally, our society has depended on marriage to replace socialized members, to regulate sexual behavior, and to stabilize adult personalities. The very survival of our society depended on the institution of marriage to bind together a man and woman who would bear and socialize new members for society. The necessity of ensuring that new members of a society are socialized to replace the dying is best illustrated by the Shakers. This nineteenth-century religious sect had several thousand members in fifty communities. But because they did not allow their members to have children, the Shakers have virtually disappeared (Murstein, 1974, p. 339).

Related to the replacement function, our society has encouraged marriage as a means of regulating sexual behavior. Unrestricted sexual behavior might make paternity difficult to establish and might result in the burdening of society with the financial cost of rearing children. But marriage, by assigning both a man and a woman to the care of the children, helps to cushion the rest of society from the economic responsibility. Neither government programs nor private charities could accommodate the three million babies born each year.

Marriage has been encouraged to help stabilize adult personalities by providing each adult with a built-in companion. Handling job stress or personal or family crises can be easier if there is a companion to share the problem. Our society cannot provide a counselor for every adult who needs a companion to discuss troubles with. So spouses assume much of society's emotional load.

This companionship function of marriage is relatively new. Unlike the old institutional marriage which was formal and authoritarian and had rigid discipline and elaborate rituals, the new companionship pattern is delineated in terms of interpersonal relationships, mutual affection, sympathetic understanding, and comradeship (Mace & Mace, 1977, p. 391). The shift in these forms of marriage was foreseen over a generation ago by Burgess and Locke (1945) in their book, *The Family: From Institution to Companionship.*

Traditional functions questioned. Recently, the traditional justifications for marriage have been questioned. There is little concern now that our society will "disappear" if people stop marrying. Children would continue to be born. And there is no evidence that monogamous marriage is the best context for rearing a child (McMurtry, 1977, p. 6).

The argument that marriage tends to regulate sexual behavior is true in that most spouses have intercourse with each other most of the time. But, again, the issue is children, and the development of contraceptive technology has made it possible for individuals to make love without making babies. It is the use of contraceptives, not marriage, which now prevents unwanted children.

The emotional support each spouse derives from the marital relationship remains one of the basic functions of marriage. In our society, which consists mainly of impersonal secondary relationships, a sense of belonging may be particularly important. But proponents of singlehood are quick to point out that soaring divorce rates suggest that marriage does not offer much emotional support for some people and that an array of intimate friendships may be superior to the one-to-one marital relationship (Ramey, 1976).

The Individual and Marriage

Although the social justifications for marriage may be waning, individuals continue to be motivated to get married for a variety of reasons, including personal fulfillment, companionship, commitment, and parenthood. We are socialized as children to believe that getting married is what adult men and women do. Even if our parents are divorced, we learn that being married is what they wanted, but it didn't work out. Marriage often becomes a goal to achieve, and achieving that goal is assumed to provide a sense of personal fulfillment.

Others marry for companionship. Although marriage does not ensure it, companionship is the greatest need marriage is expected to provide. Companionship needs are met through dialogue and the sharing of experiences. "Marriage is for growth, for life. It's a place to call home. . . ." (Jourard, 1975, p. 200).

People also marry for the emotional and legal commitment marriage can provide. A thirty-two-year-old single person remarked, "I've been through three relationships in the past year, and it's getting old. I want commitment. I want to get in a relationship where my partner and I will let ourselves completely go and commit ourselves to each other for the full trip."

Some people marry to have children. Only in marriage may couples conceive children with complete social approval. "Having a family has always been part of my life's goals," remarked an accounting major, "and, unlike my sister, I want to be married before I have kids."

Is Marriage for You?

But are these reasons sufficient for you to decide to marry? Such a decision might be based on the consequences (positive or negative) of the respective life-styles. When examining the basic alternatives of marriage and singlehood, it is helpful to keep in mind that these are not discrete categories. Rather, there are many types of marriage relationships (see Chapter 10) and styles of singlehood (discussed in the next section). Hence, the question becomes which style of life appeals to you and is this style within the marriage or singlehood category?

And the decision is not a one-time decision. Most people make the basic decision of marriage versus singlehood numerous times throughout their lives. While the single decide whether or not to marry, the married decide whether or not to stay married. And for the divorced, the question is whether to remain single or to remarry.

Most people eventually decide to marry and to marry again if they become divorced or widowed. One author suggested some reasons why marriage remains the dominant choice for American adults:

> Monogamy persists in part because we have no other strongly held norms that can take its place. It is so security-inducing (like a pill that doesn't cure the disease, but only lessens the pain) that we do not know how to get along without it. If we ever raise a generation of youth secure in themselves and detached from institutions that provide the forms of security with which we are familiar, monogamy might be replaced with another dominant form or set of forms of marriage. That time is not yet with us. . . . (Whitehurst, 1977, p. 19)

SINGLEHOOD

Singlehood is the basic alternative to marriage. Law separates people into "marrieds" and "singles." No matter how married a couple feel they are, if they are not legally married by ceremony or common law, they are two single individuals. And regardless of how single a married person may view himself or herself, unless the marriage has been dissolved by law or death of the spouse, the person is still married. While some people regard being single as "what you are before you get married," others view it as a permanent style of life. Let's review the stereotypes, identities, and meanings of singlehood.

Stereotypes of Singles

Because the vast majority of people marry, those who remain single are sometimes considered strange or even deviant. The swinger and the lonely loser are two stereotypes that are often used to describe adult unmarrieds.

> Singles are swingers—the beautiful people who are constantly going to parties, who have uncommitted lives—and a lot of uncommitted sex. . . . They frolic on clean, sun-drenched beaches and ski the French Alps. They drink Pepsi-Cola. They shop at Lord and Taylor or Neiman Marcus. They vacation in the Hamptons or Rehobeth Beach or with the Club Méditerranée. During the winter, they go to the Caribbean or to Mexico. They have clear complexions and blonde hair, and they look like self-assured winners. They are never ill, never poor, and *never* overweight. (Stein, 1976, pp. 2–3)

Those who do not fit the stereotype of the swinger are sometimes regarded as lonely losers. They are unhappy, depressed, and in therapy. They wish they were married.

The fact that most people do marry at one time or another adds to the pressure felt by some singles to get out and meet potential marriage partners. Singles' bars provide some people with a place to do this, but many others reject such an impersonal and sexually oriented situation and rely instead on friends and family for introductions to other single people.

TABLE 6.1 Change in Men and Women Remaining Single (1960–1977).

	1960	1977
Women Remaining Single (Age 20–24)	28.4%	45.3%
Men Remaining Single (Age 20–24)	53.1%	63.7%

SOURCE: U.S. Bureau of the Census, CURRENT POPULATION REPORTS, Series P-20, No. 323, "Marital Status and Living Arrangements: March 1977," U.S. Government Printing Office, Washington, D.C., 1978, p. 1 (Table A).

They live by themselves and consume great quantities of frozen TV dinners and diet sodas. The women in the group are in constant communication with their mothers, who periodically send them clippings from the local paper announcing yet another engagement of a former high-school classmate. The men in this group visit their mothers every other Sunday. They live by themselves and drink a lot. (Stein, 1976, p. 3)

These stereotypes distort reality. There are tremendous variations among people who are single. Some never go to parties, and while others may be alone some of the time, they may not be lonely.

Identities of Singles

When being single is defined as being unmarried, at any one time about one third or more of American adults are single (Libby, 1977, p. 38). But who are these 51 million singles?

Never-married singles. The largest proportion of singles in American are those who have never married. In 1977 there were over 15 million men and 12 million women (age eighteen and over) in this category (U.S. Census, 1978, p. 7). Table 6.1 illustrates that during the years from 1960 to 1977 there was a dramatic increase in the percentage of men and women between the ages of twenty and twenty-four who remained single.

There are several reasons for a larger percentage of single people at these ages in 1977 than in 1960; they include a greater number of women in college, increased employment opportunities for women, more social support for singlehood (women's movement, peers), availability of effective contraceptives, and the "marriage squeeze" (Glick, 1975). The latter reason refers to an excess of young women at the currently most "marriageable" age. Women tend to marry at age

TABLE 6.2   Life Goals of 2,289 Men and Women Ages Fourteen Through Twenty-five.

	1974	1976
Most important:		
The opportunity to develop as an individual	45%	51%
A happy family life	42%	32%
A fulfilling career	9%	10%
Making a lot of money	5%	7%

SOURCE: From American Council of Life Insurance, 1976, p. 49.

twenty-one and men at age twenty-three. There are more women turning twenty-one than men turning twenty-three in any given year, so these women must compete for the smaller number of males. As a result, more are left without partners. Observing the trend in Table 6.1, Glick remarked,

> It is too early to predict with confidence that the increase in singleness among the young will lead to an eventual decline in life-time marriage, [but] just as cohorts of young women who have postponed childbearing for an unusually long time seldom make up for the child deficit as they grow older, so also young people who are delaying marriage may never make up for the marriage deficit later on. They may try alternatives and like them. (Glick, 1975, p. 4)

Other data suggest that American youth view marriage and family as less important than the opportunity to develop as an individual. A national probability sample of 2,289 young people ages fourteen through twenty-five were asked to indicate those life goals they regarded as most important. Table 6.2 indicates a continued focus on self-development which takes precedence over concerns for a happy family life.

Separated and divorced singles.   There is a tendency to think of single people as only those who have never married. But in 1977 there were about 12 million separated or divorced men and women who were "single again" (U.S. Bureau of the Census, 1978, p. 7).[2]

The divorced man (median age, twenty-nine) and divorced woman (median age, twenty-seven) had been married about seven years. Approximately 80 percent will remarry but will be single for about three years before doing so (U.S. Bureau of the Census, 1976a). And for some, singlehood is the life-style they seek. Having tried marriage, they find the rewards of singlehood greater and its problems less than those of marriage.

Widowed singles.   While some separated and divorced singles opted for singlehood (in contrast to remaining in an unhappy marriage), the widowed are forced into singlehood. In 1977, there were about twelve million widowed singles in this country (U.S. Bureau of the Census, 1978, p. 7, Table 1). Only about half will remarry (U.S. Bureau of the Census, 1976, p. 3).

To the never married, separated, divorced, or widowed, singlehood has different meanings. But there are two basic ways of viewing it—as a life-style or as a stage leading to marriage or remarriage.

Singlehood as a Life-Style Choice

Singlehood is beginning to emerge as a positive alternative to marriage rather than "a residual category for the unchosen and lonely" (Libby, 1977, p. 38). Dr. Roger Libby has identified several social and cultural factors which form the basis for more people choosing singlehood as a life-style:

> 1. There is an eternal, erotic, emotional attraction between people, and a permanent availability of people to each other for emotional and sexual expression regardless of marital or living arrangements or sex. Bernard Farber (1964) predicted a trend away from the orderly replacement of marriage partners (lifetime monogamy) toward a more free-floating permanent availability. He stated: "Permanent availability implies that the basic needs of the individual may change . . . and that meeting personality needs at an early age may not suffice to maintain the marriage" (1964, p. 168).
> 2. There is an emerging autonomy of sexual expression apart from marriage, the family, and reproduction, so that the individual, not the couple or a larger entity, is the lowest common denominator when considering the meaning of sexual conduct (Jetse Sprey, 1969).
> 3. There is increasing visibility and viability of sexual life-styles (called the legitimacy of sexual choice by Ira Reiss, 1973); the full range of choices is receiving increased social support so that realistic options are increased.
> 4. We live in a secretive society where people can do as they wish without negative social sanctions if they are relatively discreet (open opportunity structure).
> 5. Change in one aspect of a culture or in one stage of a sexual career (such as increased sexual intercourse before marriage) affects change in other institutional arrangements or stages (such as the ground rules of sexual behavior for married partners.) New definitions of coupling (such as sexual friendships outside a primary relationship as in sexually open marriage) force a new look at singlehood.
> 6. Sexual behavior cannot be isolated or compartmentalized from the rest of a relationship. Nonsexual motives for sexual behavior and sexual motives for nonsexual behavior make compartmentalization of sex from various emotions, desires, expectations, and fantasies impossible. (Libby, 1977, pp. 41–2)

Given the cultural readiness for increasing numbers of Americans to seriously consider singlehood as an alternative to marriage, what are the motivations to seek singlehood? One researcher interviewed twenty men and twenty women

TABLE 6.3 Motivations To Avoid Marriage and Seek Singlehood.

Avoid Marriage	Seek Singlehood
Restrictions Within Relationship:	Freedom
Suffocating One-to-One Relationship	Career Opportunities
Obstacles to Self-Development	Variety of Experiences and Plurality of Roles
Boredom, Unhappiness, and Anger	Self-Sufficiency
Trapped in Spouse Role	Sexual Availability
Poor Communication with Mate	Spontaneity
Sexual Frustration	Exciting Life-style
Isolation, Lack of Friends, Loneliness	Freedom to Change and Mobility
Limited Mobility and Availability of New	Sustaining Friendships
Experiences	Psychological and Social Autonomy
Marriage Is Unnecessary	

SOURCE: Adapted from Stein, 1976, p. 65.

who represented the never married, separated, divorced, and widowed. Each of the respondents was committed, at least for the time being, to the single life-style.[3] Table 6.3 summarizes the factors these respondents regarded as influential in causing them to want to remain single.

The disadvantages of marriage. As Table 6.3 indicates, those who opt for singlehood may view marriage as restricting their potential for personal growth, as trapping them in an undesirable role as spouse, or as isolating them. A single journalist wrote,

> I have never been a domestic animal. I have never seen myself locked up in the small cosmos of the family. The profession of wife has always filled me with horror. I did not want to play wife. I wanted to write, to travel, to know the world, to use the miracle of having been born. (Fallaci, 1974, p. 56)

The theme of marriage as an obstacle to human growth was the most frequent motivation to avoid marriage mentioned by the forty respondents who were committed to the single life-style. The respondents felt that if you wanted to atrophy and waste away, you should be married (Stein, 1975).

Related to the feeling that one rarely maximizes his or her potential inside the marital relationship is the conviction that the specific roles of wife and husband are roles to be avoided. The single career woman referred to above said that a husband doesn't ask you to be his companion:

He asks you to be his nurse, his secretary, his servant . . . and even if you work twice as hard as he does, even if you have responsibilities far larger than his, he expects you to prepare his coffee, his food, to take his underwear to the laundry or to wash it, and to take care of the house. (Fallaci, 1974, p. 57)

Some men feel that their role is a greater trap than the wife's. One middle-aged man remarked, "As a husband, I am expected to be economically responsible for everything, eat breakfast and dinner with my wife, stay in the house from six at night until morning, have sex only with my wife, and enjoy weekends with a two-year-old."

The spouse role can also isolate a person from other people. In a traditional marriage the partners may carefully control the level of each new relationship for the sake of their marriage. Such control may result in feelings of isolation and loneliness. One woman remarked that she had been more lonely since she had married than when she was single. "My single friends don't call me any more because they assume that I have a built-in companion. I live in the same house with Rex, but companion isn't the word I would use to describe him. I'm terribly lonely."

Even those who have good marital relationships often feel that it is unrealistic to expect their partner to satisfy all their emotional, social, physical, and sexual needs. "To be all things to one person is impossible," one married man concluded. "My wife and I love and care for each other, but we feel that we've got to find some way to take the heavy responsibility off each of us to be everything to the other. We haven't found an answer."

Some people also feel that marriage is no longer necessary. While society has encouraged marriage for the care and protection of children, individuals have married for different reasons. Men have traditionally married for sex and women for economic security. In today's society, the sexual value of permissiveness with affection permits ample opportunity for sex without marriage, and the increasing economic independence of women removes their necessity to get married (Bird, 1972). A divorced woman who recently received her Ph.D. remarked, "For the past eleven years I needed my husband for food and shelter. Now I am economically self-sufficient. For the first time, getting married can be a choice for me. And although I may change, I doubt I'll choose to remarry." Indeed, two researchers observed that occupational achievement among women is associated with remaining single (Mueller & Campbell, 1977).

The benefits of the single life-style. But those who choose singlehood are not just avoiding marriage. They are attracted by the benefits of the single life-style. As noted in Table 6.3, these include freedom, autonomy, and spontaneity. "Being single allows me to do what I want to do, when I want to do it, and with the person or persons I choose," said a twenty-seven-year-old computer programmer. "There are no fences around what I want to do, and a spouse is the thickest, tallest fence I know of."

Freedom for the single person means freedom to change values, have sex with different people, travel more, and have no responsibility for others. The single person enjoys the freedom to change philosophies or life-styles without considering its effect on another. "In the past two years since I've gotten into transcendental meditation, I've made almost all new friends," a graduate student said. "Just as I have changed friends, I think I would have needed to change spouses if my partner had not gotten into the same trip."

The single person may also change sexual partners at will. The freedom to have a variety of sexual relationships is regarded as a major advantage of being single. "When you're married," remarked a divorced university teacher, "you have to act like you aren't sexually attracted to others and you dare not put your thoughts into action. Although the sex life of the single person isn't what married people fantasize it is, it has its advantages."

Freedom from responsibility and freedom to travel are other advantages of the single life-style. Mates are responsible to each other and for any children they

Many people who choose not to marry feel a sense of pride and satisfaction in their social and psychological autonomy. With no responsibilities to a spouse or children, they are free to enjoy either peace and quiet alone or a varied and active social life, depending on their needs at any particular time.

may have; the single person is responsible only to those he or she chooses. A recent graduate living alone remarked, "I don't have to use my paycheck to buy anything except what I want, nor do I need to spend my time cooking or running other people's errands." The single person will also have more money to spend on travel. Plane tickets and hotel rooms for two, three, or more are much harder to afford than for one.

In addition to freedom (the major advantage of singlehood), single people often feel a sense of pride in their psychological and social autonomy. A twice-divorced man who had been single for five years noted:

> I am having an experience I never had before since I was always answerable to someone—my family or wife. I never had the experience of being completely self-motivated. . . . It makes me feel very potent . . . and very responsible for what I do. Productive, capable of dealing with life's exigencies, and capable even of seeking friendly help when I need it. Whether you are self-realized or not cannot be blamed or credited to someone else. (Stein, 1975, p. 495)

People who choose singlehood may be attracted by the spontaneity which the life-style provides. The married person is probably better able to predict when he or she will be doing what than the single person, and some single people abhor regimentation. A friend may call, a new person may be met at work, or someone may drop by, and this will affect the activities for that evening or weekend. "I live not knowing what's going to happen next," observed a thirty-two-year-old accountant, "and I like it that way."

In tomorrow's world being single will be no crime.
Alvin Toffler

The choice to remain single results from factors which motivate the individual to avoid marriage and to seek singlehood. While most people remain single for a combination of the reasons we have discussed, some do so because of responsibility for an ill or aging parent, physical disability, or homosexuality. Some people also have a fear of marriage. "My mom has been divorced three times. Marriage to me means nothing but arguments, misery, and grief. Why would anyone want to get married?" asked a senior art student.

Whatever the reason, marriage does not attract everyone. Among those who have remained single throughout their lives are Plato, Newton, Leonardo da Vinci, Jonathan Swift, Henry David Thoreau, Emily Dickinson, and Florence Nightingale. More contemporary people who have never married (at the time of this writing) include Dixie Lee Ray, Ralph Nader, Barbara Jordan, Joe Namath, and Jerry Brown.

Singlehood as a Stage

Instead of being a permanent choice, singlehood may for some be considered a stage between various life-style choices that are made throughout one's life. In this context, "marriage may be seen as an interim stage, with divorce and singlehood emerging as choices at later stages. . . . Yesterday's choice could be today's stage in transition to tomorrow's new choice" (Libby, 1977, p. 39).

While the choices include singlehood, cohabitation, or marriage, the decision to opt for any one of these at any given time is a complex issue. Contributing to the selection of one alternative is the perception of the positive and negative consequences of doing so when compared with the other alternatives. The single person may be free but lonely and perceive marriage as worth the cost of lost freedom to gain companionship. The married person may be secure but bored and view singlehood, with its variety, as worth the cost of security. The cohabitant may enjoy the spontaneity of "a relationship based on love, not law" but not like the social disapproval generated by the relationship. Legitimizing the relationship with marriage may be worth the risk of losing some spontaneity.

Decisions to end or maintain a specific relationship can be explained in terms of exchange theory. "People enter and remain in relationships (or life-styles) only as long as the relationships and life-styles are evaluated by the interactants to be profitable (profit in exchange terms is rewards minus costs)" (Libby, 1977, p. 52). In addition, "inner feelings, motives, and other less tangible but extremely important emotional and cognitive states" are also influential in making a life-style and partner decision (Libby & Carlson, 1976). "I know it sounds crazy," said one thirty-six-year-old bachelor, "but I feel that it's time for me to be married."

Is Singlehood for You?

Singlehood should not be considered a unidimensional concept. There is an array of styles of singlehood from which to choose. As a single person you may devote your time and energy to career, travel, privacy, heterosexual or homosexual relationships, cohabitation, communal living, or a combination of these experiences over time. The essential difference between traditional marriage and singlehood is the personal and legal freedom to do as you wish.

But while singlehood offers freedom, the issues of loneliness, money, and identity need to be dealt with. Of loneliness, Colette in *The Vagabond* said,

> There are days when solitude for someone my age is a heady wine that intoxicates me with freedom, others when it is a bitter tonic, and still others when it is a poison that makes me beat my head against the wall. . . . This evening I would much prefer not to say which it is; all I want is to remain undecided, and not to be able to say whether the shiver that will seize me when I slip between the cold sheets comes from fear or contentment. (Colette, 1974)

Some singles minimize loneliness by living with someone, becoming involved in work, or developing a capacity for and enjoyment of solitude. A single-by-choice woman artist remarked, "Marriage would interfere with what I enjoy most, my work. I am most creative when I am alone. Fixing supper for someone else or changing a baby's diapers would be dreadful chores."

Henry David Thoreau, who never married, spent two years (1845–47) alone on fourteen acres bordering Walden Pond. He said of the experience, "I love to be alone. I never found the companion that was so companionable as solitude" (1961, p. 111).

Being single also necessitates being economically self-sufficient. Money is less likely to be a problem for a man who has been socialized to expect to work all of his life and who will probably earn more than a woman. A woman who decides not to marry is giving up the potentially larger income her husband might earn. And both men and women who decide not to marry give up the possibility of a two-income family.

The single person must establish an identity—a role. *Role* is a concept which helps to define who one is and what one does. The traditional wife role is one in which the woman lives with one man and takes primary responsibility for his social, emotional, and sexual needs. On the basis of her role, we can predict what she does most of the time. For example, on Saturday at noon she is most likely having lunch with her husband. Not only can we predict what she will be doing, her role tells *her* what she will be doing—interacting with a specific man. One could make similar predictions about the husband role.

While marriage provides an identity in terms of who one is and what one does, the single person must find other roles. A meaningful career is the avenue most singles pursue. A career provides structure, relationships with others, and a strong sense of identity ("I am an interior decorator"). To the degree that singles become meaningfully involved in their work, they tend to be successful in establishing autonomous identities that are independent of the marital state (Baker, 1968; Stein, 1976).

COHABITATION

While the single person may choose to live alone, he or she may also choose to live with someone of the opposite or same sex some or all of the time. In this section, we examine the various issues to consider in heterosexual and homosexual cohabitation.

Heterosexual Cohabitation

In Chapter 8 we will look at heterosexual cohabitation as it exists on college and university campuses. Such cohabitation is rarely regarded as a permanent alternative to marriage. In this chapter, we focus on cohabitation *instead* of marriage.

An alternative to marriage? People who cohabit as an alternative to marriage seek the advantages of traditional monogamy without being legally bonded together.

Love and money are among the motivations for living together instead of getting married. Some couples feel that the legal contract of marriage makes people stay together even though they may no longer love each other. Older people often live together because of the economic advantages. "If we got married," expressed a sixty-seven-year-old man, "they would take her social security benefits away from her. We know a lot of couples who are doing what we do."

Legal implications of heterosexual cohabitation. But there are legal consequences for living together as a permanent alternative to marriage. These include general, child custody, and inheritance problems.

1. General problems. Unmarried couples who live together are sometimes refused apartments or homes by landlords, refused automobile or home coverage by insurance companies or charged higher rates. They may also be refused employee's family health care or group insurance coverage and denied United States citizenship, food stamps, or Social Security survivor's benefits (Weisberg, 1975).

2. Child custody problems. When an unmarried couple has a child or children, the custody issue may arise if the parents decide to separate. The case of *Stanley* v. *Illinois* illustrates the legal consequences of having children without converting the living-together relationship into a legal marriage. Joan Stanley lived intermittently with Peter Stanley for eighteen years. Although they were never married, they had three children. When Joan died, Peter lost custody of his three children. Under Illinois law, the children of unwed fathers become wards of the state upon the mother's death. There is no hearing to determine the father's fitness as a parent, since the presumption under Illinois law is that all unwed fathers are "unfit" to raise their children (Weisberg, 1975, p. 552).

3. Community property and inheritance problems. The couple who live together will probably accumulate considerable property in the form of furniture, a car, a house, etc. But it is no longer clear what belongs to whom if they separate. In the case of Michelle Triola and actor Lee Marvin who lived together for six years, the California Supreme Court held that "the mere fact that a couple have not participated in a valid marriage ceremony cannot serve as a basis for a court's inference that the couple intended to keep their earnings and property separate and independent." In essence, this case states that "cohabitation without marriage gives both parties the right to share property if they separate" (Bernstein, 1977, p. 365).

Regarding inheritance, if an individual fails to make proper provision for the distribution of his or her estate (property) after death, the law of the state in which the death occurs will dictate the disposition of the property. In such cases, a legal spouse is usually automatically entitled to inherit between one half and one third of the mate's estate. But a living-together partner may get nothing. Rather, the next of kin to the partner may be the benefactor of the estate (Weisberg, 1975, p. 553).

Homosexual Cohabitation

In addition to living with someone of the opposite sex, the single person may live with someone of the same sex. Living with a same-sex partner may or may not imply a homosexual relationship. Homosexuals are men and women who have a preference for or engage in sexual activity with members of their own sex. Kinsey found that 4 percent of the men and 2 or 3 percent of the women in his studies reported that they were homosexual throughout their lives (Kinsey, 1948; 1953). No recent study has hinted at an increase in homosexuality since Kinsey's time (Karlan, 1971, pp. 452–53).

Researchers of homosexuality do not agree on its cause. Explanatory theories that have been suggested include biological determinism, early experiences, family environment, and self-labeling. Biological determinists point to studies of twins which show that if one twin is homosexual, the chances are significantly greater than average that the other will be homosexual. Since twins are usually reared in similar environments, it is difficult to separate the biological and environmental influences. Other theorists say that early childhood homosexual experiences cause an individual to become homosexual in later life. But these

Whereas legal sanctions contribute to the stability of heterosexual marital relationships and guarantee married persons certain rights, the absence of legal support for homosexual relationships may have a destabilizing effect and leave the way clear for discrimination against cohabiting homosexual couples.

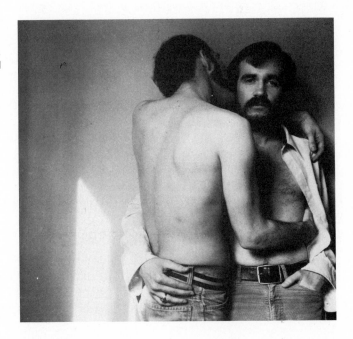

theorists do not explain why the great majority of early homosexual experiences do not lead to a homosexual life-style.

Dr. Irving Bieber focused on the family environment as the basic explanation for homosexuality. He concluded that homosexuals tended to have cold, domineering mothers and ineffectual or hostile fathers (Bieber, 1972). But Bieber focused only on homosexuals receiving psychiatric care. It is possible that heterosexuals receiving psychiatric care would have similar background characteristics. Another researcher compared the parental backgrounds of homosexuals and heterosexuals and concluded that their home environments were very similar (Hooker, 1969).

A more plausible theory, which is attracting increased attention, is that homosexuals adopt their sexual orientation as a result of an early definition, often unconscious and involuntary, of themselves as homosexual (McKee & Robertson, 1975, p. 530). These persons tend to regard people as either strictly heterosexual or homosexual without realizing that males and females may be attracted to either sex. As a result, during exploratory homosexual play, they define themselves as homosexual and become tied to their own definition.

Despite the lack of agreement about the causes of homosexuality, in our society it is not legal for two people of the same sex to marry. Instead, many homosexual couples live together and some may have a "ceremony" and regard themselves as married. Del Martin and Paul Mariah question the basic meaning society has given to marriage and ask,

> Is it polarity, the joining of male-female and penis-vagina that makes a "marriage" whole and therefore "holy"? Isn't it rather the mutual respect and the mutual love for one another, each to and for the other as a human being, that makes the difference? And isn't love "socially desirable"? (Martin & Mariah, 1972, p. 126)

Lacking the legal support for a homosexual marriage, homosexuals who cohabit face innumerable difficulties. The most disturbing aspect of a homosexual love relationship is the social ridicule and disapproval it engenders. Lovers in homosexual relationships must constantly contend with the lack of social approval of their choice.

Homosexual lovers may also be discriminated against in housing, employment, inheritance, and hospital insurance. The issue of civil rights for homosexuals became a widely discussed national issue in June 1977 following singer Anita Bryant's campaign against a Dade County, Florida, law guaranteeing homosexuals equal rights in jobs and housing (*Newsweek*, 1977a).

Contract Cohabitation

Some people want to remain single and to live with someone of the opposite sex, but they do not want to become involved in an emotional, living together relationship. For these people contract cohabitation is a possibility. Under this arrangement, the individual simply hires someone as a companion. Edmund Van Deusen

(1974), a California chemist, did so and recalled of his decision, "My principal need was for someone to talk to. . . . Second, I needed a warm body to go to bed with" (p. 22). He placed the following advertisement in The Free Press, interviewed several applicants, and selected the woman who best fit his job description:

> Free-lance writer looking for woman who would be interested in room, board, and $500 a month. Send name, phone number, and photo to Tom Smith, Box 1251, Laguna Beach, Ca. 92652. (Van Deusen, 1974, p. 25)

Contract cohabitation includes the following elements: (1) It is an eating, sleeping, and living arrangement between employer and employee, based on a written or unwritten employment contract; (2) All contract items, including salary, are defined by the employer and accepted in advance by the employee; (3) Free hours, annual vacations, and social or work activities outside the relationship are guaranteed by the terms of the contract, and (4) The employment contract can be cancelled at any time by either party without reason or explanation (p. i).

An example of a job description for a contract cohabitation relationship follows:

> Specific Tasks—Light housekeeping, meal preparation, household shopping, estimated time per day: two hours.
> Companionship—Weekdays: 6:00 to 8:00 p.m.; Saturday: 3:00 p.m. on; Sunday: All day; Bedtime: Normally 11:00 p.m.; Night off: Wednesday; Vacation: One week with pay per year; Client entertaining: Optional; Social entertaining: Required. (Van Deusen, 1974, p. 111)

While the woman is most often the employee, she may be the employer. This will primarily depend on her financial strength. Although either a woman or a man may be the employer or employee, sex is usually not a major focus of the arrangement. Companionship is the central issue.

The person who becomes involved in contract cohabitation as an employer must have sufficient money to pay his or her employee a salary, and usually he or she has little access to people of the opposite sex who would be willing to live together for free. Neither of these characteristics is typical of most university students. They cannot afford to pay another person for companionship and don't need to.

For the older person with a stable income, contract cohabitation is a greater possibility. For them, living in a large city with little opportunity to meet and to establish meaningful relationships with others may increase the attractiveness of contract cohabitation. Van Deusen, who originated the idea, was fifty when he did so.

Becoming involved in contract cohabitation implies more than money and lack of opportunity to meet others. It is a philosophy of life which says that the best way to get what one wants from an interpersonal relationship is to specify those expectations and pay for their performance. But beyond the specified exchange of money and services is the capacity for a very caring relationship which is not encumbered by the roles of husband and wife. Van Deusen writes,

> This leaves me free to cherish Elaine, whom I have no need or desire to change. Why should I? In thirty days I may never see her again. I can enjoy her for who she is, and she can enjoy me in return. Neither of us is trying to force the other into a preconceived fantasy image. Neither of us feels possessive or possessed. Neither of us is depending on the other for self-image or identity. (Van Deusen, 1974, p. 99)

Is Cohabitation for You?

Since single people are legally free to move in and out of a variety of relationships, cohabiting with someone of the opposite or same sex (or several people in succession) is an alternative. But because existing laws and attitudes discriminate against cohabitants (homosexual more than heterosexual), discrimination must necessarily be considered as a likely part of the price of cohabiting.

For some, the precarious legal position of cohabitation may also be its advantage. While emotional trauma may still result when a cohabiting relationship is terminated, the adversary legal process of a divorce (for heterosexuals) may be avoided. "When the courts get through with your marriage," remarked a divorcee, "you feel humiliated." Other issues to consider in deciding to cohabit are discussed in Chapter 8.

COMMUNES

Remaining single does not mean that an individual must live alone or with only one member of the same or opposite sex. He or she may want to become involved in an array of interpersonal relationships and join a commune. Also referred to as an intentional community, a commune is a group of people who voluntarily associate for the purpose of establishing a whole way of life (Zablocki, 1972). The group consists of three or more people who share their lives out of choice rather than because of blood or legal ties (Fairfield, 1972). About 250,000 individuals, mostly single men and women, live in communes in the United States (Zablocki, 1977).

Types of Communes

Communes are either rural or urban (Berger, Hackett, & Millar, 1972), and urban communes often cluster around university districts. Boston, for example, had over sixty communes in 1972 (Hershberger, 1973). Membership in urban communes tends to be more fluid than in rural communes, which call for greater commitment. A commune member in Boston can move into an apartment at any time, whereas moving out is harder for the communard of rural Twin Oaks, in Louisa, Virginia.

In addition to the urban-rural dichotomy, there are a variety of other types of communes. Religious communes include such groups as the Amish, The Oregon Family, The Lama Foundation, and the Hutterites. Individuals join religious communes to share a spiritual experience with others. Ideological communes (Twin Oaks, Cold Mountain Farm) are committed to secular themes, such as Marxism or behavioral psychology. Those who join an ideological commune wish to participate in planning and implementing a miniature society consistent with specific ideological principles. Hip communes (Drop City, Morning Star Ranch) have received their impetus from the use of drugs such as LSD, mescaline, and peyote. They have a more experiential and mystical quality in contrast to the rational and intellectual quality of the ideological commune. Youth communes, which do not fall into the hip or ideological categories, are usually composed of young people who simply want to share the advantages of group living (for instance, economic and social support and friends). Group marriage communes (The Family, Harrad West) have the primary goal of working out new styles of interpersonal and family relationships (Fairfield, 1972, pp. 2–3).

Motivations for Joining a Commune

Interpersonal and economic motivations are primary in joining a commune. One author observed that sharing lives and experiencing connectedness with others who have the same values is the primary interpersonal motivation for living in a commune (Heckman, 1973).

Writing about The Family, a group marriage commune in Detroit consisting of between forty and fifty adults and six to ten children, Hollenbach observed,

> The group offers, above all else, complete emotional security. . . . Every family member should be able to count on every other one to help him with his needs, to work cooperatively, for the good of the group, and to provide support in a crisis. As long as a person is there . . . he can count on every other person to relate to him, not necessarily positively but as a complete human being. (Hollenbach, 1973, p. 435)

In an effort to ensure warm feelings of intimacy among all group members, some communes try to minimize the importance of married partners to each other and to encourage their allegiance to the group. Dropping last names and referring to each other by first names only, encouraging erotic and emotional relationships among all members, investing the power to make decisions in the group rather than in the husband or wife, and stripping the couple of property are all means of spreading the love bond between the husband and wife among other group members (Kanter, 1973, pp. 288–92).

Group living is also cheaper. Economics was the primary motivation of slightly fewer than seven hundred men and women in sixty urban communes (Zablocki, 1972). Most communes (urban and rural) have central dining facilities and large houses or dorms for inexpensive sleeping quarters.

Women often have another incentive for joining a commune. Some communes offer equality. Child rearing and providing emotional support may be considered community tasks, assignable to men as well as women. Men and women also often work in the same place—a husband doesn't leave for the office but stays at home and does his share of the work. Finally, the rewards for work are equal. Men and women usually earn about the same amount for their work for the collective (Kanter, 1973).

Problems of Communal Living

In spite of the potential benefits of communes, their very survival is difficult. Most last less than two years (Zablocki, 1977; Hershberger, 1973). Among the problems common to commune life are a lack of organization and structure, uncontrolled membership, division of labor, definitions of ownership, economic maintenance, and interpersonal conflicts.

No matter how many communes anybody invents, the family always creeps back.

Margaret Mead

Lack of organization and structure. "There is a real difference among communes over the degree of organization they want. Those that fail to organize their work and their decision-making process tend to find that work stays undone, some decisions never get made, and group feelings develop only with difficulty" (Kanter, 1972a, p. 406). While earlier communes (Oneida, Shakers) were autocratically governed by church elders, many contemporary communes are less structured. Government and laws are rejected as are leaders and rulers (Gardner, 1973).

Anarchism is the prevailing philosophy of some communes (Zablocki, 1972). This view suggests that individuals are better off without any external authorities regulating them. Anarchists do not believe in outside authority since it, by definition, is subversive.

Membership. Regardless of the organizational framework a commune develops for itself, it must deal with the issue of who can be a member. While some communes have an open door policy, most have membership requirements. A member of a commune in Chicago observed, "At first, anybody could join, and we soon found out that everybody (including drunks, addicts, and criminal fugitives) did join. Our rules now include no hard drugs, no couples, no minors, and no children. Membership is still dependent on a unanimous vote of every member which we take after the person has been here six months."

Division of Labor. "Doing your own thing" rarely works in a commune because, for most people, peeling potatoes, washing dishes, and taking out the garbage isn't "their thing." In a study comparing nine long-lived communes of the nineteenth century with twenty-one short-lived communes, Kanter (1972a) observed that one way of ensuring commitment was to share the work. Twin Oaks commune has a labor credit system whereby each member is expected to work forty hours during a seven day week with labor credits assigned to each chore. The more undesirable the work, the greater the point value assigned. Those who choose not to do their share of the work are allowed to goof off a few days in hopes of "being able to get it together again." One communal member wanted to play his drums all day and avoid basic chores. After a "warning," he continued to play his drums and was asked to leave.

Ownership. Commune property is usually held in common. Land, houses, and, in some cases, clothes belong to everyone. Problems occur when individual members try to claim as their own that which belongs to the commune. In one group, a couple became upset with other members of the commune and took a bench they had made with them when they left the commune (Zablocki, 1972).

Lack of organization and structure is sometimes a major problem for communes. While town-meeting-like discussions and group decision making are typical of many communes, these methods tend to be inefficient and fraught with difficulties.

Economic maintenance. A commune must have economic resources to survive, and these are often somewhat unreliable. Some typical resources include a large garden, welfare, windfalls (inheritance, birthday checks, gifts), animals (chickens for eggs, goats for milk), barter (exchange of vegetables and goat milk for grain, hardware, or clothes), gathering (blackberries, plums, blueberries, strawberries), and scavenging (looking for discarded food in alleys behind grocery stores) (Berger, Hackett, & Millar, 1973). Whereas these sustenance sources are more characteristic of rural communes, urban communes survive through members who have "straight" jobs, deal dope, play in bands, or offer a service such as auto repair. In some cases, one or two members will support the entire group. A university teacher who gave his check to the commune each month was asked, "How do you feel about being the entire economic base for your commune?" He replied, "I don't mind giving all my money to the commune. My only regret is that I can't be here with them during the day to help them build our house." But two months after this individual left the commune, it folded.

The problem in communal living most frequently mentioned by respondents from sixty-three communes in the Boston area was personality clashes (Hershberger, 1973). Whereas the marriage relationship requires a person to accommodate his or her needs to one other person, a commune necessitates an adjustment to several people. Matthew Israel (1973) lived in two communes and watched both of them die. His notes on the interpersonal conflicts among the respective members included the following:

> a. Betty believed that one should show beautifying behaviors in a house. For example, one should open or close the window curtains in the living room, straighten up the furniture as needed, and so forth. Sally did not show these behaviors.
>
> b. In Rutland Square House, dinners often did not start until 8:00, 9:00, or 10:00 p.m. I was sometimes irritated by not being able to eat at 6:00 p.m. so as to be able to get out of the house during the evening.
>
> c. Jim and Elaine, poorer than the others, wanted to spend little on food; Randy, Alice, and I didn't mind spending a little more to get variety and quality. Jim and Elaine were vegetarians; the rest of us all enjoyed meat.
>
> d. Since dinner was a communal affair every evening, I found myself unable to entertain a date alone for dinner.
>
> e. Should we have music at mealtime? If so, who chooses the record? How loud?
>
> f. Betty, brought up in Holland, liked the temperature in the house to be 68°. I preferred 71° or 72°. Betty and I sometimes played little games with the thermostat. (Israel, 1973, pp. 397–98)

The future plans of people leaving communes often include travel, living in another group, living alone, moving away to school, and moving out of the area (Hershberger, 1973). Kanter (1972b) makes the point that some communards don't intend for their commune to last. They feel that nothing is forever and that change is a part of life.

Is Communal Living for You?

Decisions about life-styles might be based on the predicted consequences of those decisions. Some predictable positive consequences of joining a commune in contemporary American society might be: (1) The exploration of a life-style different from the convention of marrying, moving to suburbia, and having two children; (2) The opportunity to share work and play with several people at the same time on an intimate basis; and (3) An opportunity to fill your time with a new experience.

Some potential negative consequences of communal living include: (1) If your parents disapprove of your living in a commune, you may weaken or destroy your relationship with them; (2) If you have a stable relationship with someone who disapproves of communal living, your communal involvement could cost you that relationship; and (3) If you want to pursue traditional goals such as getting a master's or doctorate degree, the commune experience will delay and possibly sidetrack you from eventually achieving that goal.

TRENDS

Marriage will continue to be the dominant choice of life-style for most Americans. Over 92 percent will choose this option (Glick, 1978, p. 6). And, while there has been a steady decline since 1973[4] in the marriage rate (the proportion of those married per 1,000 population), "there are reasons to expect the proportion of young adults who marry to level off or to rise moderately for a few years and then to rise still more after that time" (Glick, 1978, p. 7). Reasons for this stabilization or slight rise in the next few years are related to little further change in delaying marriage[5] and an increase in the number of late first marriages of those who have been putting it off (Glick, 1978, p. 7).

Heterosexual cohabitation accounts for only about 1 percent of all adults (U.S. Bureau of the Census, 1977). Although some will regard cohabitation as a permanent alternative to marriage, most will continue to view it as a stage before or between marriages.

Homosexual cohabitation and the gay life-style will continue to meet resistance (e.g., Anita Bryant's Save Our Children Crusade). But attitudes are changing. For example, until 1973, the American Psychiatric Association listed homosexuality as a mental illness. After extensive debate, members of the association agreed to regard homosexuality as a "sexual-orientation disturbance" which stems not from homosexuality itself, but from the reactions of society to it (McKee & Robertson, 1975, p. 526).

Contract cohabitation, a relatively new alternative life-style, has not attracted a large following and will probably continue to be a rare form of singlehood. Unlike contract cohabitation, communal living has historical precedents (Shakers, 1941; Oneida, 1940; Kibbutz, 1921) and is the life-style of choice for about half a million people. This figure has not varied much since 1973 (Zablocki, 1972; 1977) and probably will not.

SUMMARY

Traditionally, marriage has existed to replenish society with socialized members, to regulate sexual behavior, and to stabilize adult personalities. But the problem of overpopulation and the availability of convenient, effective contraceptives have undermined the first two functions. Emotional support remains the primary function of marriage.

The decision to marry involves an assessment of the advantages and disadvantages. Marriage offers a potentially intense primary relationship over time and avoids the stigma and potential loneliness associated with singlehood. But singlehood offers freedom to do as one wishes and avoids the obstacles to personal fulfillment associated with marriage. For many Americans the decision to marry or be single is not permanent. While many singles contemplate marriage, many marrieds ponder whether or not they should stay married.

And the decision is never clear-cut. There are styles of marriage and styles of singlehood. When cohabitation is chosen as a permanent life-style, there are various legal implications. For heterosexuals, discrimination from landlords and insurance companies, child custody, and community property and inheritance problems must be confronted. For homosexuals, marriage is illegal and social ridicule can be a problem.

Older individuals who have the economic resources sometimes become involved in contract cohabitation. This arrangement involves an employer-employee relationship in which behavioral expectations are specified, agreed to, and paid for.

Communal living is another style of singlehood. There are thousands of communes to select from, some of which emphasize religion, various ideologies (Marxism, behavioral psychology), or group marriage. The advantages of communal involvement include living with several people in an intimate environment and sharing expenses.

Although marriage will continue to be the dominant choice for most Americans, the future will involve fewer marriages at later ages with more people experimenting with the various styles of singlehood.

STUDY QUESTIONS

1. About how many marriages occur in the United States each year?
2. What are the traditional functions of marriage in our society and how are these functions being questioned?
3. What is now the most important function of marriage?

4. Discuss various reasons for getting married.
5. Describe two stereotypes of single people. How are these stereotypes inaccurate?
6. Identify three categories of single people.
7. Give several reasons for the increasing numbers of never-married singles.
8. What are two basic ways of viewing singlehood?
9. Discuss the social and cultural factors which form a basis for singlehood.
10. Discuss several motivations and benefits of remaining single.
11. What are the legal implications of heterosexual and homosexual cohabitation?
12. Discuss four explanatory theories of the causes of homosexuality.
13. Discuss the legal status of homosexual marriage.
14. Describe contract cohabitation.
15. Discuss several issues involved in a decision to cohabit.
16. What is a basic element of all communes and what are five types?
17. List several potential problems of life in a commune.
18. What has been happening to the marriage rate in recent years?
19. Describe some other trends in the prevalence of marriage and its alternatives.

NOTES

1. The estimated number of marriages for 1976 was 2,133,000 (*CBS News Almanac,* 1978, p. 227).

2. Specifically, there were 10,458,000 separated or divorced people in March 1977. Of these, men accounted for 1,353,000 separated and 1,887,000 divorced people. Women made up 2,355,000 of the separated and 4,863,000 divorced people (U.S. Bureau of the Census, 1978, p. 7).

3. Each respondent answered negatively to the following questions: (1) Is there one person of the opposite or same sex that you now see exclusively? (2) Do you plan to marry in the near future? (3) Do you plan to live with one person in an exclusive relationship in the near future? (Stein, 1975, p. 23)

4. In 1973, there were 2,277,000 marriages; in 1974, 2,223,000; in 1975, 2,126,000. The marriage rate for the respective years was 10.9, 10.5, and 10.0 (*U.S.A. Statistics in Brief,* 1976).

5. In 1977, the median age at marriage for men was 24.0 and for women, 21.6 in contrast to 22.8 and 20.3 respectively in 1960 (U.S. Bureau of the Census, 1978, p. 2).

BIBLIOGRAPHY

American Council of Life Insurance. *Youth 1976: Finance related attitudes.* New York: The Council, 1976.

Baker, L. G. The personal and social adjustment of the never-married woman. *Journal of Marriage and the Family,* 1968, *30,* 473–9.

Berger, B. M., Hackett, B. M., and Millar, R. R. The communal family. *The Family Coordinator,* 1972, *21,* 4, 419–27.

—————. Supporting the communal family. In *Communes: Creating and managing the collective life,* R. M. Kanter (ed.). New York: Harper and Row, 1973, 345–8.

Bernstein, B. E. Legal problems of cohabitation. *The Family Coordinator,* 1977, *26,* 4, 361–6.

Bieber, I. et al. *Homosexuality: A psychoanalytic study.* New York: Basic Books, 1972.

Bird, C. The case against marriage. In *The future of the family,* L. K. Howe (ed.). New York: Simon and Schuster, 1972, 341–8.

Burgess, E. W., and Locke, H. J. *The family: From institution to companionship.* New York: American Book Company, 1945.

CBS News Almanac. Maplewood, N.J.: Hammond Almanac, 1978.

Colette, *The Vagabond,* E. McLeod (trans.). New York: Farrar, Straus & Giroux, 1974.

Fairfield, R. *Communes U.S.A.: A personal tour.* Baltimore: Penguin Books, 1972.

Fallaci, O. Why I never married. *Ms. Magazine,* December 1974, 56–7.

Farber, B. *Family: Organization and interaction.* San Francisco: Chandler Publishing, 1964.

Gardner, H. Crises and politics in rural communes. In *Communes: Creating and managing the collective life,* R. M. Kanter (ed.). New York: Harper and Row, 1973, 150–66.

Glick, P. C. The future of the American family. Statement before The Select Committee on Population, U.S. House of Representatives, May 23, 1978.

──────. Some recent changes in American families. *Current Population Reports,* Series P-23, No. 52. U.S. Bureau of the Census, 1975.

Greenwald, M., and Danziger, C. Transadulthood: An emerging stage of life. Unpublished manuscript, 1975.

Heckman, J. Cambridge commune: The cat is everyone's. In *Communes: Creating and managing the collective life,* R. M. Kanter. New York: Harper and Row, 1973, pp. 76–79.

Hershberger, A. The transiency of urban communes. In *Communes: Creating and managing the collective life,* R. M. Kanter (ed.). New York: Harper and Row, 1973, 485–91.

Hollenbach, M. Relationships and regulations in the Family of Taos, New Mexico. In *Communes: Creating and managing the collective life,* R. M. Kanter (ed.). New York: Harper and Row, 1973, 430–41.

Hooker, E. Parental relations and male homosexuality in patient and non-patient samples. *Journal of Consulting and Clinical Psychology,* 1969, *33,* 2, 140–42.

Israel, M. L. Irritations and jealousies. In *Communes: Creating and managing the collective life,* R. M. Kanter (ed.). New York: Harper and Row, 1973, 397–9.
[Originally published as "Two Communal Houses and Why I Think They Failed," in *Journal of Behavior Technology, 1,* (Summer 1971).]

Jourard, S. M. Marriage is for life. *Journal of Marriage and Family Counseling,* 1975, *1,* 3, 199–208.

Kanter, R. M. *Commitment and community: Communes and utopias in sociological perspective.* Cambridge, Mass.: Harvard University Press, 1972.(a)

──────. Getting it all together: Group issues in contemporary communes. *American Journal of Orthopsychiatry,* 1972, *42,* 632–43.(b)

──────. Family organization and sex roles in American communes. In *Communes: Creating and managing the collective life,* R. M. Kanter (ed.). New York: Harper and Row, 1973, 287–307.

Karlan, A. *Sexuality and homosexuality.* New York: W. W. Norton, 1971.

Kerr, C. *Sex for women who want to have fun and loving relationships with equals.* New York: Grove Press, 1977.

Kinsey, A. C. et al. *Sexual behavior in the human male.* Philadelphia: W. B. Saunders, 1948.

──────. *Sexual behavior in the human female.* Philadelphia: W. B. Saunders, 1953.

Libby, R. W. Creative singlehood as a sexual lifestyle. In *Marriage and alternatives: Exploring intimate relationships,* R. W. Libby and R. N. Whitehurst (eds.). Glenview, Ill.: Scott, Foresman, 1977, 37–61.

Libby, R. W., and Carlson, J. Sexual behavior as symbolic exchange: An integration of theory. Unpublished manuscript, 1976.

Mace, D., and Mace, V. Counter-epilogue. In *Marriage and alternatives: Exploring intimate relationships,* R. W. Libby and R. N. Whitehurst (eds.). Glenview, Ill.: Scott, Foresman, 1977, 390–96.

Martin, D., and Mariah, P. Homosexual love—woman to woman, man to man. In *Love today,* H. Otto (ed.). New York: Association Press, 1972, 120–34.

McKee, M., and Robertson, I. *Social problems.* New York: Random House, 1975.

McMurtry, J. Monogamy: A critique. In *Marriage and alternatives: Exploring intimate relationships,* R. W. Libby and R. N. Whitehurst (eds.). Glenview, Ill.: Scott, Foresman, 1977, 3–13.

Mueller, C. W., and Campbell, B. G. Female occupational achievement and marital status: A research note. *Journal of Marriage and the Family,* 1977, *39,* 3, 587–93.

Murstein, B. I. *Love, sex, and marriage through the ages.* New York: Springer, 1974.

Newsweek. Battle over gay rights, 6 June 1977, 16 et passim.(a)

——————. Living together, 1 August 1977, 46–50.(b)

Ramey, J. *Intimate friendships.* Englewood Cliffs, N.J.: Prentice-Hall, 1976.

Sprey, J. On the institutionalization of sexuality. *Journal of Marriage and the Family,* 1969, *31,* 432–41.

Stein, P. J. Singlehood: An alternative to marriage. *The Family Coordinator,* 1975, *24,* 4, 489–503.

——————. *Single.* Englewood Cliffs, N.J.: Prentice-Hall, 1976.

Thoreau, H. D. *Walden or life in the woods.* New York: Holt, Rinehart and Winston, 1961.

Toffler, A. *Future shock.* New York: Random House, 1970.

U.S., Bureau of the Census. Marital status and living arrangements. *Current Population Reports,* Series P-20, No. 271. Washington, D.C.: U.S. Government Printing Office, 1974.

——————. Marital status and living arrangements, March, 1975. *Current Population Reports,* Series P-20, No. 287. Washington, D.C.: U.S. Government Printing Office, 1975.

——————. *U.S.A. statistics in brief 1975.* Washington, D.C.: U.S. Government Printing Office, 1975.

——————. Number, timing, and duration of marriages and divorces in the United States: June 1976. *Current Population Reports,* Series P-20, No. 297. Washington, D.C.: U.S. Government Printing Office, 1976.(a)

——————. *U.S.A. statistics in brief 1976.* Washington, D.C.: U.S. Government Printing Office, 1976.(b)

——————. Marital status and living arrangements, March, 1976. *Current Population Reports,* Series P-20, No. 306. Washington, D.C.: U.S. Government Printing Office, 1977.

——————. Marital status and living arrangements, March, 1977. *Current Population Reports,* Series P-20, Number 323. Washington, D.C.: U.S. Government Printing Office, 1978.

Van Deusen, E. L. *Contract cohabitation.* New York: Grove Press, 1974.

Weisberg, D. K. Alternative family structures and the law. *The Family Coordinator,* 1975, *24,* 4, 549–59.

Whitehurst, R. N. The monogamous ideal and sexual realities. In *Marriage and alternatives: Exploring intimate relationships,* R. W. Libby and R. N. Whitehurst (eds.). Glenview, Ill.: Scott, Foresman, 1977, 14–21.

Zablocki, B. *The joyful community.* New York: Penguin Books, 1972.

——————. *Alienation and investment in the urban commune.* New York: Center for Policy Research, 1977.

Chapter 7

Pairing Off

I married for love and got a little money along with it.
Rose Kennedy

You recall from the last chapter that a central goal of marriage from the viewpoint of society is to bond two people together who will produce, protect, nurture, and socialize children to be productive members of society. To ensure that this goal is accomplished, society must make some institutional provision for sexually mature females and males to meet, interact, and pair off in permanent unions for eventual parenthood. The dating institution serves this function and guides man-woman interaction through an orderly process toward mate selection.

After reviewing early dating practices in America, we will explore how dating patterns have changed and the various problems people experience in dating. And since dating is the normal preliminary to mate selection, we will examine the various cultural, sociological, and psychological aspects of why one person chooses another.

DATING IN HISTORICAL PERSPECTIVE

While sitting in one of your classes, you may glance across the room and spot someone who is particularly attractive to you. You may envision a developing relationship with this person, including a number of dating events—eating together, going to parties, seeing movies, attending concerts. The only obstacle to initiating the relationship is your instructor's lecture, which will be over in another twenty minutes. You may plan to approach the person after the class ends and ask if you can borrow yesterday's class notes. If that person is not involved in another relationship and views you as a potential partner, your dating relationship will have begun.

In contrast to the ease of becoming involved in a heterosexual relationship on today's university campus, overwhelming obstacles faced young adults in the early eighteenth century. Not only were coeducational opportunities nonexistent, but an introduction of the boy to the girl's parents had to precede any conversation between the partners. If her parents decided that the boy was not suitable, no relationship would develop. And even if her parents approved of the suitor, the time the couple could be together was limited. Both the girl and the boy were involved in chores or studies, and the little leisure time that was available to them was usually spent with other family members.

When the partners did get together with their parents' approval, they were usually not alone. If they went out, the girl was often accompanied by a chaperone who would arrange the time, place, and events of the meetings between the partners. If they stayed inside, the boy would visit the girl's house. They were expected to stay in the same room (usually the kitchen) with her parents. Private conversations were further limited because there were no telephones and no cars to escape adult monitors.

The transition from a tightly controlled courtship system to the relative freedom experienced by today's youth occurred in response to certain changes in our society. The most basic change was the Industrial Revolution, which began in England in the middle of the eighteenth century. It took women out of the home and placed them in frequent interaction with male workers. No longer were women needed exclusively in the home to spin yarn, make clothes, and process food from garden to table. Commercial industries had developed to provide these services.

Female involvement in factory work decreased parental control, since parents were unable to dictate the extent to which their offspring could interact with those they met at work. Hence, values in mate selection shifted from the parents to the individual. In the past, parents had approved or disapproved of a potential mate on the basis of their own values: Was the person from "good stock"? Did the man have property or a respectable trade? Did the woman have basic domestic skills? In contrast to these parental concerns, individual values emerged which focused more on love feelings between the partners.

As a result of the Industrial Revolution and the subsequent loss of parental control, the Flapper, the "ideal girl" of the Roaring Twenties, became acquainted with young men outside the family circle and felt free to go out with them. With the development of the automobile, couples could escape from their respective parents to do as they wished. Movies provided an additional dark place to share an

Parental supervision of dating and mate selection had decreased significantly by the 1920's. Straitlaced parents may have disapproved of new dating patterns and modern dance steps, but they no longer had the necessary control to enforce older courtship patterns.

evening away from parents. And other commercial establishments arose to meet the entertainment needs of these courtship couples. Within one generation, the age-old rituals of courtship had been abandoned (Saxton, 1977, p. 189).

From the 1920s into the 1960s, the traditional dating script had several specific characteristics: (1) The boy asked the girl several days in advance to attend a specific event; (2) The boy called on the girl and escorted her to their destination; (3) The boy paid any expenses for food or entertainment; (4) After several dates with each other the boy asked the girl if they could go steady.

While the traditional dating script still exists, beginning in the late 1960s an alternative script became more common. Particularly in college, students report "hanging out" or going where they meet members of the opposite sex in informal ways without an introduction. Rather than "dating," they use the term "getting together," which may include the female's initiating relationships, providing transportation, and paying her share for food and entertainment.

FUNCTIONS OF DATING

Since college students take for granted dating, or "getting together," as a natural part of college life, the reasons for dating are rarely examined. Various researchers have suggested that recreation, companionship, socialization, and mate selection are among the basic motivations (Winch, 1963; Skipper & Nass, 1966; Landis & Landis, 1977).

Recreation

Dating, hanging around, or getting together is fun. It occurs with one's peers, away from one's parents, and involves activities selected by the partners because they enjoy them.[1] "I get tired of studying and being a student all day," a straight-A major in journalism said. "Going out at night with my friends to meet guys really clears my head. It's an exciting contrast to the drudgery of writing term papers."

Companionship

In addition to recreation, some students date for companionship. The impersonal environment of a large university may make a secure dating relationship very appealing. "My last two years have been the happiest ever," remarked a senior in interior design. "But it's because of the involvement with my fiancée. During my freshman and sophomore years I felt alone. Now I feel loved, needed, and secure with my partner."

Some students prefer an exclusive relationship to one of casual dating. A study of women at one university revealed that in 1970 almost twice as many were involved in exclusive dating relationships as in 1960 (Bell & Chaskes, 1970, p. 83).

One student remarked, "I've had it with trying to get all the dates I can. They turn out to be like a revolving door; I have to tell the same stories, act the same superficial way, and read the same script for the first several dates. With one person, I can relate in a more open, relaxed way."

Socialization

Prior to puberty, boys and girls interact primarily with their own sex. Each may be laughed at if he or she shows an interest in someone of the opposite sex. And even when boy-girl interaction becomes the norm at puberty, neither sex may know what to do. Dating provides the experience of learning how to initiate conversation and the opportunity to develop an array of skills in human relationships (e.g., listening, empathy, etc.). It also permits an individual to try out different role patterns (e.g., dominance vs. submission) and to assess the "feel" and comfort level of each. Discomfort is not unusual. Three fourths of 3,189 college students reported that they felt less than "very confident" in their relationships with the opposite sex (Landis & Landis, 1977, p. 36).

Considerable dating experience may also be associated with how one views love. In a study assessing the effects of dating on one's tendency to be romantic or realistic about love, the results showed that college seniors have a more realistic attitude toward love than juniors, sophomores, or freshmen. One factor which may contribute to this increase in realism is the greater dating experience of seniors (Knox & Sporakowski, 1968).

Mate Selection

Whether a person dates for recreation, companionship, or learning about the opposite sex, in the process he or she is often looking for a mate. As college students reach their senior year, they sometimes experience increased pressure to single one partner out, raise the level of emotional involvement, and get married. When both partners have mate selection in mind, they tend to have similar values about the desirable characteristics of a mate. Table 7.1 shows how black and white college students ranked the traits of the person they would choose to marry. Both groups considered understanding, affection, maturity, and considerateness to be extremely important.

DATING GAMES

Dating games may be characterized as traditional or contemporary. In the traditional script, initial dating relationships are with several people. Later, when two partners become involved in an exclusive relationship, they are regarded as

TABLE 7.1   Rank of 22 Traits Desired in a Mate by College Students.

Black Students N = 86		White Students N = 86	
1	Understanding	2	Understanding
2	Mutual affection	1	Mutual affection
3	Emotional maturity	3	Emotional maturity
4	Kind and considerate	4	Kind and considerate
5	Dependability	5	Dependability
6	Work and save	7	Work and save
7	Paying bills	10	Paying bills
8	Good health	9	Good health
9	Desire children	12	Desire children
10	"Move ahead"	19	"Move ahead"
11	Liking for people	8	Liking for people
12	Own a home	14	Own a home
13	Sense of humor	6	Sense of humor
14	Political philosophy	18	Political philosophy
15	Sexual attraction	13	Sexual attraction
16	Kind of job	15	Kind of job
17	Plan size of family	11	Plan size of family
18	Good cook	17	Good cook
19	College degree	16	College degree
20	Household repairs	20	Household repairs
21	Similar religion	21	Similar religion
22	Ability to dance	22	Ability to dance

SOURCE: Adapted from Melton and Thomas, 1976, p. 516.

going steady. When they have made a marital commitment, they are regarded as being pinned or engaged (McDaniel, 1969).

Unlike the traditional dating script, the contemporary script involves no specific movement toward marriage. Women and men float in and out of interpersonal relationships which may or may not be exclusive (Libby, 1977).

But these dating scripts represent stereotypes. The dating patterns of many college students reveal elements of both patterns. Dating in an exclusive relationship may be both preceded and followed by the "less restrictive" dating pattern. Recognizing that these patterns may blend, let's explore these dating games in more general terms—when they begin, who can play, where and how they are played. And since every game involves referees and casualties, we will discuss parents and problems.

First Meeting

The places for meeting a potential date vary. Two hundred university students specified how they each met the person they were currently dating.[2] While the most frequently mentioned ways were "through a friend," "in class," or "at a party," others listed "singles' bar," "work," and "church."

Regarding the first date, women were asked, "How would you go about getting a guy to date you?" The majority (59 percent) reported that the best way was to engage him in conversation or ask a friend to introduce him. Others mentioned that "being friendly," "smiling at him," and "being where he'll be" were effective ways of encouraging a man to ask for a date.

Desired Partner

Just as college students seem to know where and how to recruit a dating partner, they seem to know what they are looking for. But men and women tend to look for different qualities. The quality men sought most in their dates was physical attractiveness (69 percent). The conclusions of two studies suggest why men emphasize physical appearance in their dating choices:

1. Men feel that their peers (males and females) will think most highly of them if they are seen with an attractive woman (Sigall and Landy, 1973). "Being with a good-looking woman always makes me feel good," said a second-string quarterback. "I guess it's because I think others think I must be sharp if I can get a real looker to go out with me."

2. Men want in a woman what they think other men want—beauty (Walster et al., 1973). One student recalled that even in grade school he had always enjoyed looking at the more attractive girls and that these were the same girls his peers were looking at.

In addition to an attractive woman, men seek an intelligent date who has a good personality. Other qualities mentioned were self-confidence, understanding, and maturity. The qualities mentioned least frequently were patience, imagination, and success. But college women may be suspicious of what college men say they look for in a date. In a study at Southern Illinois University, a researcher observed, "More than men admit, women say that men look for dates who have money, smoke pot, and have promiscuous relations" (Hendrix, 1978, p. 49).

Women listed honesty (26 percent) as the most desirable quality in the men they dated. Other qualities they looked for were physical attractiveness, consideration, respect, and a good personality. These qualities were consistent with those sought by women reported in earlier studies (Wakil, 1973; McGinnis, 1958).

Although women do not value physical attractiveness in their dates as much as men do, they are aware of the value men attach to it. In one study 396 women listed the items that most concerned them about dating. At the top of the list was "making herself as attractive as possible to attract the boy of her choice" (McDaniel, 1969, p. 103).

Activities

There is considerable variation in the places college students go on dates, the topics they discuss, and the degree to which their activities include sex and drugs.

Places. Going out to eat, seeing a movie, or attending a party are the most frequent dating activities reported by students in the study on university dating mentioned above. Other dates take place at "her place" or "his place"[3] and depending on which of the dating games (traditional or contemporary) the partners approximate, the woman will pay nothing, half, or all the cost of a dating event.

Conversation. The topics college students discuss on their dates are varied. While students report that their dating conversations focus on "ourselves" and "our relationship," other topics include school, future careers, and how much sex is appropriate for the relationship. When the two hundred university students were asked, "How comfortable do you feel about letting your date know what's happening inside your head?" 51 percent reported "very comfortable always." While others said that they were "pretty comfortable" (14 percent) or that it depended on the person and the level of the relationship (16 percent), only 4 percent said that they were uncomfortable revealing their inner thoughts. Both sexes reported that they felt openness was essential to the establishment of a good relationship.

Sex. Both partners in the dating relationship must deal with the issue of "How much sex, how soon?" In general, men try to move the relationship toward sex while women try to move the relationship toward an exclusive commitment (Eshleman, 1978, p. 352). The exchange of sex for commitment and vice versa is sometimes complicated by the fact that men and women may have different timetables for the trading. The two hundred university students were asked, "How many dates do you feel you should have with a person before it is appropriate to kiss, pet, and have intercourse?" Sixty percent of the women and 87 percent of the men felt that a kiss on the first date was appropriate. Forty-five percent of the men expected women to pet by the third date, while only 13 percent of the women felt that petting was appropriate by then. Most women responded that the appropriate time for petting could not be pinned down to a certain number of dates but always depended on the people involved and the nature of the relationship.

The most common response to the question of when intercourse would be appropriate was also that it depended on the couple and their feelings for each other. However, 23 percent of the men felt it appropriate to have intercourse by the third date, in contrast to only 7 percent of the women.

When asked, "What do you say or do to encourage your date to become more sexually intimate?" men offered an array of answers. These included: "be complimentary," "rub her neck," "lie on a waterbed," "become quiet," "make meaningful glances," "act normal," "indicate desire through body language," "say things with sexual overtones," "encourage her to have one more drink," "ask her to spend the night," "tell her I care for her," "start kissing and petting," and "tell her what I expect."

In contrast to the men, women reported the following patterns for encouraging sexual intimacy on dates. "Move closer to him, make eye contact, and kiss him" was the most frequently reported sequence. Other behaviors included: "tell him I like him," "hold his hand," "talk about sex," "talk softly," "stroke his hair," "hug him," "smile a lot," "dress nicely," and "wear perfume." Females reported that they discouraged sexual aggressiveness by asking their date to stop or by moving away from him. Other ways of dealing with pressure for sex included "making small talk," "ignoring his advances," or "pretending to be sick."

Drugs.   Alcohol appears to remain the prevailing drug on the college campus. Of the 200 college students, 72 percent of the men and 66 percent of the women reported some use of alcohol on dates. Apparently, liquor was used more for pleasure than as a means of getting the partner drunk for easier sexual access. In the same study 17 percent of the men and 27 percent of the women reported using marijuana on dates. Because marijuana is illegal, there may be considerable hesitancy in reporting its use. In a confidential questionnaire completed by 345 students at eight major universities, 81 percent of the female respondents reported using the drug occasionally (Koff, 1974, p. 195). In explaining the more frequent use of marijuana among women, the researcher concluded, "The woman has been taught the sex-evil, sex-dirty, sex-forbidden notions more than the sex-fun, sex-enjoyable ones. The lessening of tensions and of inhibitions allows the woman to overcome these concepts and to express her desires" (Koff, 1974, p. 198).

Parents

While love is private, marriage is public. And since dating often leads to marriage, parents are concerned about their sons' and daughters' dating partners. Although college students perceive that their parents have very little or no control over whom they date, parental influence on dating may be both direct and indirect.[4] Parents who have resources (car, money) that their offspring want may make them available in exchange for compliance from their offspring or withhold them for noncompliance (Scanzoni, 1976, p. 112). Such withholding of resources is at considerable cost to the parent-child relationship since college students regard it as a threat to their independence (Edwards, 1973, p. 105). They also resent parental involvement in their dating relationships and regard it as a serious violation of their right to choose their own date and mate.

Indirect parental influences are more subtle and more effective. When possible, parents often choose to live in neighborhoods and enroll their children in schools and social activities (church, dancing lessons, Scouts) which they feel will reinforce their own values. While peers will have the most influence on an individual during the college years, parental influence is often exerted indirectly in that the offspring are likely to select peers whose socialization has been similar to their own.

Meeting potential dates is the biggest dating problem for most people. In the 1960s, such innovations as computer dating, singles bars, and singles apartment complexes emerged to help single people overcome the difficulty of meeting eligible partners.

Problems

While parents are not a major problem for college youth so far as dating is concerned, getting dates, having negative experiences on dates, being exploited, and idealizing the dating partner may all cause difficulties.

Getting dates.   Finding someone to date is the most difficult of all dating problems.[5] Computer dating has emerged as one way to meet a compatible partner. Campus bulletin boards and newspapers often feature advertisements for computer-matched dates. Titles such as "Pick A Date," "Computer Match," and "Why Be Lonely?" are followed by the promise to find the "right" date for the person who completes a questionnaire. The information requested is designed to help the computer match respondents on the basis of social background, personal attitudes, and complementary needs. The individual's profile is matched with similar profiles in the computer and he or she is given a list of several names, usually three.

The suitability of the partners for each other will depend on how accurately they completed their questionnaires. Individuals may tend to indicate that they are more physically attractive than they actually are for fear that otherwise they will be matched with the son or daughter of Frankenstein's monster.

To assess the computer's effectiveness in matching people, a computer dating service gave each participating male three names: one selected on the basis of similar backgrounds and interests, one selected on these factors plus complementary needs (e.g., a need to be submissive, if the male needs to dominate), and one selected at random. Forty-three males dated each of the three women whose names they were given and completed a questionnaire about their experiences. They reported that they felt much more compatible with the first and second date than with the third date. Hence, computer dates, matched on either basis, were more successful than random dates (Strong, Wallace, & Wilson, 1969, p. 170). The females who were dated also completed a questionnaire and stated that they enjoyed the compatible dates (e.g., those based on shared similar interests and values) more than the dates based in part on complementary needs (p. 170).

Another study concluded that computer dating is "at least as efficient as blind dating, chance meetings on campus, and other avenues that are commonly used" (Strong & Wilson, 1969, p. 259). Ninety-four percent of the males and 84 percent of the females indicated that they found at least one satisfactory date among the three choices they were given (p. 259).

An alternative to computer dating used by some older adults is placing an advertisement in publications addressed primarily to single people. In a study of ads placed in the *Singles News Register,* the researchers observed that those seeking partners presented a positive self-image, emphasized "sex appropriate" characteristics (appearance for women, status for men) and specified greater height, age, intelligence, and status for men than for female partners (Cameron et al., 1977, p. 30).

Negative dating experiences.   Finding a partner is not the only difficult aspect of dating. In a study of "dates that failed" the author specified a number of behaviors that contributed to the failure. These behaviors included: either party drank too much, one partner could not dance, and one partner was neglected or was not introduced to others (Albrecht, 1972).

The negative behavior that spoils dates raises a difficult problem for the person who finds it offensive. For example, when one's date talks about himself or herself to the point of boredom, does the partner say something about it, ignore it, or refuse to date the person again? Since it is not normative to give honest feedback on the first date, a likely choice is the last. There is no second date, and the person who engaged in the negative behavior may never know what went wrong. Without such feedback, the person is likely to repeat the negative behavior on subsequent dates, only to be rejected again.[6]

Exploitation.   Men and women may exploit each other sexually and economically in the dating game. Often the man's goal is to have fun rather than to find a marriage partner. In contrast, the woman may be more concerned about developing a lasting relationship. As noted in the chapter on sexual values, there is a direct relationship between a woman's willingness to engage in sexual behavior and her perception that her partner is in love with her. The result is a tendency for the man to pretend that he is more committed to the woman than he actually is, so as to influence her toward greater sexual intimacy. If he terminates the relationship after she permits intercourse, she may feel exploited.

Some sexual exploitation involves force. Eighty-seven percent of 381 randomly selected undergraduate men reported that they had made at least one forceful attempt at intercourse with a girl who tried to fend them off with tears, pleading, and screams (Kanin, 1968).

Exploitation on dates is not limited to sex. A woman without a car reported that she occasionally dated one man because he lived in her hometown and she needed a ride there on alternate weeks. Another said, "He likes to take me out to eat and to a movie every Saturday evening. On my budget, I can't afford to eat out and pay for a movie."

While males tend to be exploited economically, and females tend to be exploited sexually, these are stereotypes. A female art major said that she was dating her partner because he was a good lover but that she wanted no emotional relationship with him. A male history major confessed that he was dating one woman only because she was willing to type his term papers for him.

Idealization. When partners are dating for mate selection rather than recreation, idealization may interfere with their ability to assess the potential mate accurately. Idealization may be defined as (1) attributing desirable qualities to a person who lacks them (the partner never gets depressed or moody), (2) exaggerating the magnitude of the desirable qualities that are present (the partner is "always" happy), and (3) denying the existence of unfavorable qualities (the partner doesn't really drink too much) (Burgess & Wallin, 1953, p. 15). One recently married woman remarked, "I must have been blind when we were dating. I didn't see the kind of person he was until after we were married: stubborn, quick-tempered, and selfish. He's not the guy I thought I was marrying."

But this type of "looking without seeing" is not characteristic of all dating couples. One researcher found that the closer couples got to actually getting married, or the more involved their relationship became, the less likely they were to idealize the partner. This was particularly true for men (Pollis, 1969).

MATE SELECTION

Regardless of the problems of dating, most people date and select a mate in the process. The mutual selection of Rosalynn and Jimmy Carter, Carly Simon and James Taylor, and June Carter and Johnny Cash did not occur by chance. Various cultural, sociological, and psychological factors combined to influence their meeting and marriage.

Cultural Aspects of Mate Selection

Cultural norms for mate selection vary. The degree of freedom an individual has in choosing a marriage partner depends on the culture in which he or she lives. In some cultures arranged marriages predominate; in others, including our own, free choice is the rule. But some "arranging" takes place in all cultures. No culture permits absolute free choice. In this section, we explore arranged marriages and the cultural pressures that operate within a system of free choice.

Arranged marriages. If your marriage were arranged, several people might participate in the selection of your mate. Depending on whether you lived in Ashanti (West Africa), Tepostlán (Mexico), or Japan, your father, both your parents, or your parents with the help of a matchmaker would select your life's companion for you (Stephens, 1963, p. 192).

Their criteria for selecting a mate for you would include bride price, social status, and family custom (Stephens, 1963, p. 197). If you are a girl, your father would arrange your marriage with the boy whose family would pay him the most. The bride price would be your father's compensation for taking care of you until marriage. When you married, you would no longer be around to cook, tend children, or help with the crops. Your marriage would mean the loss of valuable services, and he would expect to be well paid. If you are a man, your wife would be your father's expense.

Social status is another consideration in arranging a marriage. A Kwakiutl man (from Vancouver Island) whose wife had been selected for him said, "The one I wanted was prettier than the one they chose for me, but she was in a lower position than me, so they wouldn't let me marry her" (Ford, 1941, p. 149).

In addition to bride price and social status, your marriage might be arranged because your family adhered to the sororate or levirate custom. In the sororate arrangement, a sister replaces a deceased wife. For example, assume that you, a female, had a sister whose marriage had included an expensive bride price. After your sister moved in with her new husband, her health deteriorated and she died. Since your father received so much money for your sister, he feels he cheated the young husband by giving him a sick woman. You would replace your sister to fulfill your father's promise of a good wife for a good price.

The levirate system implies the inheritance of a dead man's wife by his brother or other male kin. For example, if you are a male, your brother's wife would become yours when he died. Among the Murngin in Australia, taking a brother's wife is not only a privilege but a duty. "Frequently wives thus acquired, being past the age of bearing children or gathering food, are really an economic liability to their heir; but he must take and look after them" (Warner, 1937, p. 62).

Arranged marriages usually occur in societies that have strong kinship groups. In such societies, family ties are more important than such considerations as physical appearance or love. However, for those individuals who have strong personal preferences, it is not unusual for a society that promotes arranged marriages to provide an alternative—elopement. In essence, individuals can disobey their elders, choose their own mates, run away with them, and then wait and hope that the marriage will finally be approved. Among the Iban in Borneo, one anthropologist observed:

> When a young woman is in love with a man who is not acceptable to her parents, there is an old custom called *nunghop bui,* which permits him to carry her off to his own village. She will meet him by arrangement at the waterside, and step into his boat with a paddle in her hand, and both will pull away as fast as they can. If pursued he will stop every now and then to deposit some article of value on the bank, such as a gun, a jar, or a favor for the acceptance of her family, and when he has exhausted his resources he will leave his own sword. When the pursuers observe this they cease to follow, knowing he is cleaned out. As soon as he reaches his own village he tidies up the house and spreads the mats, and when his pursuers arrive he gives them food to eat and toddy to drink, and sends them home satisfied. In the meanwhile he is left in possession of his wife. (Roth, 1891, p. 131)

Although arranged marriages are usually thought of as being characteristic of preliterate and Eastern societies, they have also been part of Western society. The novel and movie *The Godfather* depicted an arranged marriage in the 1940s between a young Sicilian woman and the son of a powerful New York Mafia figure. A great many American marriages have been arranged, up to modern times, both in rural areas and in high society (e.g., the marriage of Consuelo Vanderbilt to the Duke of Marlborough in the 1900s).

Endogamous-exogamous pressures. While some societies exert specific pressure on individuals to marry predetermined mates, other societies are more subtle. America has a system of free choice that is not exactly free. Social approval and disapproval restrict your choices so that you don't marry just *anybody.* Endogamous pressures encourage you to marry those within your own social group (economic, educational, ethnic, religious, racial), and exogamous pressures encourage you to marry outside your family group (avoid marriage to sibling, first cousins).

The pressure towards an endogamous mate choice is especially strong where race is concerned. The following comments from a young black woman illustrate this point:

> No black girls that I know of have ever been dated by a white guy. There are some that wish they could. In fact, I know some white guys, myself, I wouldn't mind going out with, but the black girls are mostly afraid. Even if a white guy asked them out, they wouldn't go out with them. Black boys don't like for black girls to date white guys. Sometimes I see white guys who look nice, and I stop and talk to them. The black boys get upset. They are real screwy. They can date white girls, but we can't date white guys. (Petroni, 1973, p. 146)

This woman's experience illustrates that social pressure is a potential consequence of selecting a dating partner outside one's own racial group. The word "potential" is significant in that there is little social pressure against interracial dating or marriage in some parts of America (e.g., Hawaii).

While social pressures for racial endogamy are sometimes severe, pressures for religious endogamy are milder. Only 14 percent of 5,407 college students expressed strong disapproval toward a hypothetical marriage of a brother or sister to someone "out of the faith" (Gordon, 1964, p. 14). However, most—perhaps 50 to 70 percent—of those marrying in our society still marry within their own religion (Barlow, 1977, p. 149).

In contrast to endogamous marriage pressures, exogamous pressures are mainly designed to ensure that individuals who are perceived to have a close biological relationship do not marry each other. Incest taboos are universal. In no society are children permitted to marry their parent of the opposite sex (Kenkel, 1977, p. 25). In America, siblings and first cousins are also prohibited from marrying each other.

In summary, cultural influences on mate selection range from the selection of a mate by one's parents to the more subtle endogamous-exogamous pressures of friends and parents. Mate selection in America is "free" only to the extent that the individual is willing to marry as the laws of his or her state permit and is capable of withstanding the social pressures for a choice that is not culturally approved. The wife of an interracial couple remarked, "I married Reid because I love him. I still do. But the cost has been high. My father has disowned me. My mother is heartbroken. My friends approve of my marriage, but there is more grief than I thought."

The effect of the cultural influences just described is to narrow your choice of a mate from anybody to those outside your immediate family and to those of the same race, religion, and social class. And while many do marry across racial, religious, and class lines, the endogamous pressures must still be dealt with.

Sociological Aspects of Mate Selection

In addition to various endogamous and exogamous pressures, other sociological factors are at work in selecting a mate. Various theories of mate selection have been generated to explain these influences.

Propinquity (nearness).   An American man married a woman who was born in Vienna, Austria, but she had spent her senior year of high school in his parents' home as a foreign exchange student. Their marriage illustrates the theory of "residential propinquity," which states that the probability that A and B will marry each other decreases as the distance between their residences increases (Bossard, 1932). Half the adults who were married in Columbus, Ohio, had actually lived within sixteen blocks of each other at the time of their first date (Clarke, 1952).

That we can only marry those with whom we interact is obvious, but there is a more subtle meaning to the propinquity theory of mate selection. We tend to date and marry those with whom it is *convenient* to interact (Katz and Hill, 1958, p. 31). Being in the same class, or working at the same job, or living a few blocks from each other permits convenient interaction. Referring to his former fiancée, an English major observed, "When I first transferred to State, I would drive the three hundred miles each way to see her on weekends. I did that three times. Then I noticed a girl in my English literature class; we began studying together, and I stopped the five hours of driving each Friday and Sunday. It took me seven minutes to get to her apartment."

Homogamy. In addition to endogamous-exogamous pressures which restrict your marital choices to certain groups and propinquity factors which influence you to choose those with whom it is convenient to interact, homogamous factors also operate. The homogamy theory of mate selection states that you are attracted to and become involved with those who are similar to you in age, physical appearance, education, social class, and marital status.

We tend to interact socially with those with whom it is convenient to interact. Endogamous pressures and convenience factors have probably influenced these teenagers to date their classmates and neighbors—a relatively homogeneous group socially and culturally.

1.   Age. The median age at which American men first marry is 24.0; for females, it is 21.6 (U.S. Bureau of the Census, 1978, p. 2). When someone gets you a blind date, it is assumed that the person will be of an age similar to yours. Your peers are not likely to approve of your becoming involved with someone twice your age. A student who was dating one of her former teachers said, "He always comes over to my place and I prepare dinner for us. I don't want to be seen in public with him. Although I love him, it doesn't feel right being with someone who is old enough to be my father."

The tendency for males to marry down and females to marry up in age, social class, and education is referred to as the mating gradient (Leslie, 1976, p. 506). Such pairing results in some high-status women and low-status men remaining single. As a function of the mating gradient, the upper-class girl will receive approval from her parents and peers only if she marries someone of equal status. On the other hand, approval is usually not withheld from the male who marries below himself in age and status.

Women express preferences for older men and men for younger women (Jedlicka, 1978). If you are a sophomore female on your campus, you probably experience some social pressure to date males who are sophomores, juniors, or seniors and to avoid dating freshmen. When you are a senior, your peers will approve of your dating other seniors; and there will be less approval for your dating a freshman or sophomore. However, the senior male will receive approval from his peers for dating not only senior females but also juniors, sophomores, and freshmen.

2.   Physical Appearance. Having further narrowed your potential marital partners to those of similar age, you will be influenced by the way they look. Two studies indicate that people tend to become involved with those who are similar in physical attractiveness (Berscheid et al., 1971; Burgess & Wallin, 1953). And, while one researcher found no evidence that college students dated those of similar physical attractiveness, he did find that an individual's evaluation of his or her own physical attractiveness was related to that person's estimate of his or her chances of being accepted by a potential partner (Huston, 1973). One acne-scarred female wrote, "I've got a face full of pimples and I know that the guys I want are not available to me. They take one look at my skin and that's it."

3.   Education. In addition to age and physical appearance, the level of education you attain will influence your selection of a mate. As a college student, you are likely to marry someone who has also been to college. Table 7.2 illustrates the likelihood of selecting a marriage partner with a similar level of education. In general, there is a strong tendency among both men and women to marry someone who is within one educational level (up or down) (Rockwell, 1976, p. 83).

One reason parents send their daughters to college has been the hope that they will marry a college-educated man (Scott, 1965). Not only does college provide an opportunity to meet, date, and marry another college student; it increases the chance that only a college-educated person will seem good enough. A sophomore who worked in a large urban department store during the Christmas

TABLE 7.2   Marriages by Levels of Education.

In 1970, Out of Every 100 Married Couples (All Races Combined):

39 husbands and wives were at the same educational level;*

19 husbands were one level* higher than their wives;

18 wives were one level* higher than their husbands;

12 husbands were two or more levels* higher than their wives;

12 wives were two or more levels* higher than their husbands.

*Educational levels:

0–4 years elementary school	4 years high school
5–7 years elementary school	1–3 years college
8 years elementary school	4 years college
1–3 years high school	5 or more years college

SOURCE: Based on data from the 1970 census. U.S. Bureau of the Census, 1972, PC (2)—4C, p. 269.

holidays remarked, "The two weeks Todd and I spent selling record albums and tapes were great. But our relationship never gathered momentum. I was looking forward to my last two years of school, but Todd said college was a waste of time. I don't want to get too tied to someone who thinks that way."

4.   Social Class. Just as similarity in education affects marital choice, so does social class (Reiss, 1965). Social class reflects not only occupation, income, and education but residence, language, and values. In extensive personal interviews of married students at Western Michigan University, two researchers found that men and women from high-status homes where the father was a professional or a marginal professional were most likely to marry those who had fathers in the same occupational stratum. The same was true of the middle grouping of business, secretarial, and minor government occupations, as well as for the lowest grouping of skilled, unskilled, or farming occupations (Eshleman & Hunt, 1965, p. 32). And, in a related study, a team of researchers observed that college students in prestigious Greek organizations tended to select dates who were members of a sorority or fraternity of equal prestige (Krain et al., 1977).

But there is more to being attracted to those with whom we share something and those we enjoy. The approval of others affects our initiating and continuing a relationship. One researcher studied 316 couples over a ten-week period to assess the effect of the reaction of friends and family on the relationship (Lewis, 1973). To verify the social reaction of others, the partners completed a questionnaire which included such questions as: "How often do your friends make comments to the effect that you both are 'made for each other'?" "How often do members of your family make comments about how nice a pair you two make together?" "How often are you given invitations to a social function by friends who assume that you would just bring along the other person?" The results showed that those 220 couples who continued to date throughout the ten-week period received more positive reactions from friends and family about their involvement than those 96 couples who had broken up by the end of the ten-week period (p. 416).

5.   Previous Marital Status. There is a tendency for the divorced to marry the divorced, the widowed to marry the widowed, and the never married to marry the never married (Bernard, 1956). A divorced mother of two children remarked, "The only person who really understands me is a divorced father. He knows what a lonely experience divorce is and how important children are."

In summary, marriages are most likely to occur between people of similar age, physical appearance, education, social class, and marital status. But researchers do not agree on the extent to which people select as marital partners others with similar personal and social characteristics (Prince & Baggaley, 1963; Trost, 1967; Curran, 1973). However, the researchers do tend to agree that similarity of values is the most important of the homogamous variables.

Values.   In addition to propinquity and homogamy of personal and social characteristics, whether or not two people become involved with each other may be a function of perceived similarity of values. "We are less drawn toward people who look like us, sound like us, or share our mannerisms than we are toward people who *agree* with us" (Rubin, 1973, p. 140). In a series of "phantom-other" experiments, subjects were shown a questionnaire supposedly completed by another person. The responses were fabricated so as to be similar to or different from the way the subject would have completed the questionnaire. The subjects were then asked to indicate how much they thought they would like the other person. The consistent result of the experiments demonstrated the subjects' liking for those who shared their own values and beliefs (Byrne, 1971).

Someone who agrees with us validates our self-confidence. When the person we date shares our values, it confirms that they approve of us and enjoy being with us. We feel like congratulating them on their ability to know quality when they see it. But, while couples who share values may enjoy each other, it is not clear whether their shared values are the cause or the result of their interaction (Snyder, 1964). An engaged woman remarked, "We started dating just for fun, but our values have grown together."

Role compatibility.   Before increasing your commitment to someone who shares your values, you are likely to become concerned about role compatibility. Both you and your partner will take two sets of role expectations into marriage: those you will act out and those you will expect your partner to act out. Whether or not you expect to cook, do laundry, change the oil in the car, or sleep late on

Sunday mornings (or expect your mate to) will depend in large part on your observation of other husbands and wives. While your primary models have been your parents, the role behaviors of your married siblings and friends will also influence the roles in your marriage. A driver for the campus bus remarked, "Mom always waited on Dad hand and foot. While that may have been okay in their marriage, roles are changing. My sister and her husband cooperate in almost everything." In a study of 152 high-school students, females and whites were more equalitarian than males and blacks in their marriage role expectations (Moore & Knox, 1978).

Who does what in any given marriage is not important. Agreement on role responsibilities is important. One researcher studied ninety-nine couples who were either engaged or "going steady" and concluded that the partners chose each other on the basis of role compatibility (Murstein, 1967, p. 695). In another study of ninety-four "seriously attached" couples, the authors concluded that perceived marital role compatibility was related to continuing the relationship (Kerckhoff & Davis, 1962).

In summary, various sociological factors help to account for your attraction to and involvement with potential marital partners. While propinquity implies that you will only become involved with those with whom it is convenient to be involved, homogamous factors involve an element of choice. But social pressures tend to limit choices to those of similar age, physical appearance, education, social class, and previous marital status. After these influences have been felt, you will tend to focus on the values and role expectations of your potential partner. But initiating and continuing your relationship will also depend on psychological factors. We now review these.

Psychological Aspects of Mate Selection

While cultural pressures limit your marital choice to those within certain groups and sociological factors guide your selection within those groups, various psychological factors are also operating. Psychological theories of mate selection include the complementary needs theory, the exchange theory, the ideal mate theory, and the parental image theory. All these are concerned with the way the individual, independent of his or her society, views the mate selection process.

Complementary needs. "In spite of women's liberation and a lot of assertive friends, I am a shy and dependent person," remarked a transfer student. "My need for dependency is met by Warren, who is the dominant, protective type." The tendency for a submissive person to become involved with a person who likes to control the behavior of others (a dominant person) is an example of attraction based on complementary needs. Partners can also be drawn to each other on the basis of nurturance and receptivity. These complementary needs suggest that one person likes to give and do while the other likes to be the benefactor of such care.

That partners select each other on the basis of complementary needs was suggested by Dr. Robert Winch (1955). He emphasized that needs could be complementary if they were different (dominant vs. submissive; nurturant vs. receptive) or if the partners had the same need but at different levels of intensity. As an example of the latter, two individuals may be involved in a complementary relationship when both want to do advanced graduate study. But both need not get Ph.D.'s. The partners will complement each other in the sense that one is comfortable with his or her level of aspiration, represented by a master's degree, but still approves of the other's commitment to earning a Ph.D.

The theory of complementary needs, based on the observation of twenty-five undergraduate married couples at Northwestern University, has been heavily criticized (Bowerman & Day, 1956; Schellenberg & Bee, 1960; Blazer, 1963; Heiss & Gordon, 1964; Tharp, 1963; Murstein, 1961; Roscow, 1957; Trost, 1967). Questions raised about Dr. Winch's theory include the following: (1) Are people aware of their attraction to others who complement their psychological needs or is the process unconscious? (2) Couldn't personality needs be met just as easily outside the couple relationship without selecting a spouse on that basis? For example, a person who has the need to be dominant could get such fulfillment in a job which involved an authoritative role, such as head of a corporation or an academic department. (3) When does a need become complementary as opposed to a similar value? For example, is the desire to achieve at different levels a complementary need or a shared value?

Whether selection of a mate will involve the complementary meshing of one person's needs with those of another is difficult to assess. Two researchers studied ninety-four seriously involved couples in October and again in May to discover what factors were associated with deepening their relationship (Kerckhoff & Davis, 1962). They concluded that value consensus *and* need complementarity were positively related with staying together. But other researchers have found no support for the idea that people are even attracted to each other on the basis of complementary needs (Murstein, 1967; Trost, 1967).

Exchange theory.   You may have already considered the qualities of the person you want to marry and what qualities you have to exchange. Since your parents will not be haggling with your partner's parents as they might be in an arranged marriage, you are your own broker. And your selection will involve various exchanges.

Exchange theorists suggest that you will marry the person who offers you the greatest rewards at the lowest cost of all the people who are available to you (Homans, 1961; Blau, 1964; Gouldner, 1960). Four concepts help to explain the exchange process involved in mate selection: (1) Rewards are behaviors (looking at you with the "look of love"), words ("I love you"), resources (beauty, money), and services (drive you home, type for you) your partner provides which you enjoy and which influence you to continue the relationship; (2) Costs are unpleasant consequences associated with being involved with a partner. One male remarked, "I have to drive across town to pick her up, listen to her nagging mother before we can leave, and be back at her house by 11:30 p.m."; (3) Profit is the excess reward when the costs are subtracted from the rewards; (4) Loss occurs when the costs exceed the rewards. Partners continue their involvement in a relationship as long as they derive more profit from that relationship than from any other relationship available to them. They discontinue relationships where the costs exceed the rewards unless they have no alternative relationship. In this case, they may choose to suffer in an unhappy relationship rather than be alone.

Exchange concepts operate at three levels of the dating relationship—who can date whom, the conditions of the continued dating relationship, and the decision to marry (Waller, 1938). Regarding whom you date, you are attracted to those who have something to exchange. If you are an attractive, self-confident, female college student with the social skills of Princess Grace, you will expect a lot in exchange from the partner you date. An unattractive, inept high-school student has little hope of becoming involved in a dating relationship with you. He has little to exchange for your looks, status, and skills.

Once you identify a person who can offer the equivalent of what you have to exchange, other bargains are made regarding the conditions of your continued relationship. In general, the person who has the least interest in continuing the relationship can dictate the conditions of the relationship (Waller & Hill, 1951, p. 190). "He wanted to date me more than I wanted to date him," said one woman, " so we went where I wanted to go and did what I wanted to do."

Additional exchanges must precede a commitment to marriage. Such a commitment occurs when each partner in the relationship feels that he or she is getting the partner who offers the most rewards of all those currently available. A graduating senior and groom-to-be remarked, "It's easy. I've decided to marry Maria because sharing life with her is more fun than being with anyone else. And marriage is one way to help ensure that we will be together to share our lives across the years."

Parental image.   While the complementary and exchange theories of mate selection are relatively recent, Freud (1927) suggested that the choice of a love object in adulthood represents a shift of libidinal energy from the first love objects, the parents. This means that a man looks for a wife like his mother and a woman looks for a husband like her father. But in a study which compared how seventy-two persons who were getting their marriage licenses viewed their parents and their future mates, the researchers concluded that "both men and women seek to repeat in marriage the relationship they had with their mother" (Aron et al., 1974, p. 17).

In summary, the predominant psychological theories of mate selection involve complementary needs, exchange of rewards, and parents. While the theory of complementary needs suggests that we select another on the basis of needs that complement our own, exchange theory suggests that we seek another on the basis of what he or she has to trade. Neither of these theories focuses on the early parent-child relationship.

TRENDS

The future of dating relationships will include more people spending more time in a number of such relationships, a gradual shift away from traditional dating practices, increased interracial, interreligious, and interethnic dating, and increased confusion about what roles each partner will fill in marriage. As noted in the last chapter, both women and men are marrying later than in previous years. The result of such delay is that each person will have more time to become involved with a variety of people. More time spent dating also has implications for how dating is perceived—more for recreation than for mate selection.

And since dating will be more for recreation than mate selection, the traditional dating pattern which is geared toward early marriage will become less functional. The contemporary pattern of "hanging out" and "getting together," whereby individuals go where they can meet members of the opposite sex in informal ways without an introduction, will grow. The women's movement has been instrumental in increasing the acceptance of women going to singles' bars and initiating relationships (Kerr, 1977).

The future of dating relationships will also include increased interracial, interreligious, and interethnic dating. As desegregation continues, both the probability of interracial dating and the tolerance for it will increase. Endogamous pressures against dating someone of a different religious or ethnic background will also subside.

In addition to a longer period of dating, less traditional dating, and more interracial/religious/ethnic dating, differences in role expectations will become more of an issue. While the women's movement has sensitized women to seek equalitarian relationships with men, socialization of men to perceive women in other than traditional roles has been less extensive. As a result, there may be more confusion during first encounters when the new woman and the traditional man meet. And, since the women's movement has not influenced all women and since some men are nontraditional, the man seeking a woman who wants an equalitarian relationship may be surprised to find a traditional woman and vice versa.

It seems likely that traditional couple-dating will become less common in the future and "hanging out" and "getting together" informally will be more common. With a longer period of dating, it is also likely that recreation, and not mate selection, will be the primary purpose of most dating.

SUMMARY

The institution of dating serves a valuable function for society by guiding man-woman interaction through an orderly process toward mate selection. Dating scripts may be both traditional and contemporary. In the former the male dominates the courtship relationship, which is oriented toward marriage. The latter involves considerable role flexibility that is less directed toward marriage.

In college, dating partners enjoy eating out, seeing movies, and attending parties together. Their conversations are varied but often focus on their developing relationship. While parental interference is not a major dating problem, getting dates, bad experiences on dates, exploitation, and idealization sometimes are.

As dating moves toward mate selection, the partners are influenced by various cultural, sociological, and psychological factors. While marriages in some cultures are arranged by parents or other relatives, our culture relies mainly on endogamous and exogamous pressures to guide mate choice.

Sociological aspects of dating include propinquity, homogamy, values, and role compatibility. While people tend to marry those with whom it is convenient to interact, they also select a partner who is similar in age, physical appearance, education, social class, and marital status. Values represent a special case of homogamy: We are attracted to those who agree with us. But regardless of value similarity, partners look for role compatibility. Who prepares the meals, or washes the dishes, or does the laundry may become major issues when the partners disagree.

Psychological aspects of mate selection are concerned with complementary needs, exchange, and parental image. Complementary needs theory suggests that a dominant person seeks a submissive person and vice versa. They may also seek each other if they both have the same need but at different levels of intensity. Whether couples actually select each other on the basis of complementary needs is difficult to determine. Researchers who have tried to replicate Winch's work have been unsuccessful.

Exchange theory offers a more easily understood alternative. In essence, one individual selects another on the basis of rewards and costs. As long as an individual derives more profit from a relationship with one partner than with any other partner, the relationship will continue. Exchange concepts influence who can date whom, the conditions of the dating relationship, and the decision to marry.

The parental image theory of mate selection says that both men and women tend to select a marriage partner who is similar to their mother. This recent research finding is in contrast to Freud's theory that a man looks for a wife like his mother and a woman looks for a husband like her father.

Trends in dating relationships include a longer period of dating, a gradual shift from the traditional dating pattern to the "getting together" pattern, increased interracial/religious/ethnic dating, and increased concern about role consensus.

Role consensus is increasing as a problem because women are being socialized to seek equalitarian relationships while men typically are not.

Study Questions

1. What valuable societal function does the institution of dating serve?
2. Discuss dating patterns that existed when America was primarily rural.
3. Discuss the impact of the Industrial Revolution on the institution of dating.
4. Discuss four motivations for dating.
5. What characteristics do college students look for in the person they will marry?
6. Contrast two dating games.
7. Where do college students meet their dating partners?
8. Why do men tend to emphasize physical appearance?
9. Where do college students go when they date?
10. How much sexual interaction do college students think is appropriate on the first few dates?
11. How is sexual intimacy encouraged and discouraged by men and women on dates?
12. To what extent are alcohol and marijuana used on dates?
13. To what degree do parents interfere in the dating relationships of their college offspring?
14. Discuss four potential problems of dating.
15. Evaluate the statement, "The freedom to choose your marriage partner depends on the culture in which you live."
16. Where are marriages "arranged"? Who arranges them?
17. Discuss several criteria which are considered when a marriage is arranged.
18. What are the sororate and levirate systems?
19. Discuss elopement in reference to an arranged marriage.
20. Explain the statement, "America has a system of free choice which is not exactly free."
21. What is meant by endogamous and exogamous pressures in mate selection? Give examples.
22. Discuss how propinquity influences mate selection and include in your discussion the issue of convenience.
23. What is the mating gradient and what groups of people are less likely to marry as a function of it?
24. Illustrate how homogamy affects marital choice by citing the results of research on age, physical appearance, education, social class, and previous marital status.
25. Why are people of similar values attracted to each other?
26. How does role compatibility affect marital choice?
27. Illustrate how mates may select each other on the basis of complementary needs. What are two ways in which needs may be complementary?
28. How has Winch's theory of complementary needs been criticized?
29. Discuss mate selection from the perspective of exchange theory. Explain the four basic concepts of exchange theory in your discussion.
30. Discuss how more recent research on parental image and mate choice is inconsistent with Freud's original theory.
31. Discuss four trends in dating relationships.

NOTES

1. Couples with children tend to select activities designed to maximize the enjoyment of their children. Such a selection shifts the focus from adult interests.

2. The information in this and the following three sections is based on an unpublished study (Knox, 1977).

3. High-school students, who do not have easy access to apartments or dorm rooms, end up "driving around" on 25 percent of their dates (Dickinson, 1975, p. 605).

4. One researcher found that mothers, particularly nonworking mothers, exert considerable influence on their daughters' selection of a mate (Bruce, 1976).

5. Finding mates may also be a problem. In Australia a male may pay from $25 to $1000 to a marriage broker to help him find a mate. In 1976 it was estimated that 300,000 wives were needed in Australia (UPI, 1976).

6. Three researchers at the University of Oregon in Eugene devised a program for assisting students in overcoming their fears about dating (Christensen et al., 1975).

BIBLIOGRAPHY

Albrecht, R. A study of dates that failed. In *Encounter: Love, marriage, and the family.* Boston: Holbrook Press, 1972, 57–63.

Aron, A., et al. Relationships with opposite-sexed parents and mate choice. *Human Relations,* 1974, *27,* 17–24.

Barlow, B. A. Notes on Mormon Interfaith Marriages. *The Family Coordinator, 26,* 2, 143–50.

Bell, R. R., and Chaskes, J. B. Premarital sexual experience among coeds. *Journal of Marriage and the Family,* 1970, *32,* 1, 81–4.

Bernard, J. *Remarriage.* New York: Dryden Press, 1956.

Berscheid, E. et al. Physical attractiveness and dating choice: Tests of the matching hypothesis. *Journal of Experimental Social Psychology,* 1971, *7,* 173–89.

Blau, P. M. *Exchange and power in social life.* New York: John Wiley and Sons, 1964.

Blazer, J. A. Complementary needs in martial happiness. *Marriage and Family Living,* 1963, *25,* 89–95.

Bossard, J. H. Residential propinquity as a factor in marriage selection. *American Journal of Sociology,* 1932, *38,* 219–24.

Bowerman, C., and Day, B. A test of the theory of complementary needs as applied to couples during courtship. *American Sociological Review,* 1956, *21,* 602–5.

Bruce, J. A. Intergenerational solidarity versus progress for women? *Journal of Marriage and the Family,* 1976, *38,* 519–24.

Burgess, E. W., and Wallin, P. *Engagement and marriage.* Philadelphia: J. B. Lippincott, 1953.

Byrne, D. *The attraction paradigm.* New York: Academic Press, 1971.

Cameron, C., Askamp, S., and Sparks, W. Courtship American style: Newspaper ads. *The Family Coordinator,* 1977, *21,* 27–30.

Christensen, A., Arkowitz, H., and Anderson, J. Practice dating as treatment for college dating inhibitions. *Behavior Research and Therapy,* 1975, *13,* 321–31.

Clarke, A. C. An examination of the operation of residential propinquity as a factor in mate selection. *American Sociological Review,* 1952, *17,* 17–22.

Curran, J. P. Examination of various interpersonal attraction principles in the dating dyad. *Journal of Experimental Research in Personality,* 1973, *6,* 347–54.

Dickinson, G. E. Dating behavior of black and white adolescents before and after desegregation. *Journal of Marriage and the Family,* 1975, *37,* 602–8.

Edwards, J. N., and Brauburger, M. B. Exchange and parent-youth conflict. *Journal of Marriage and the Family,* 1973, *35,* 101–7.

Eshleman, J. R. *The family: An introduction.* Boston: Allyn and Bacon, 1978.

Eshleman, J. R., and Hunt, C. L. *Social class factors in the college adjustment of married students.* Kalamazoo, Mich.: Western Michigan University, 1965.

Ford, C. S. *Smoke from their fires.* New Haven: Yale University Press, 1941.

Freud, S. Some psychological consequences of anatomical distinction between the sexes. *International Journal of Psychoanalysis,* 1927, *8,* 133–42.

Gordon, A. I. *Intermarriage: Interfaith, interracial, interethnic.* Boston: Beacon Press, 1964.

Gouldner, A. W. The norm of reciprocity. *American Sociological Review,* 1960, *25,* 961-78.

Heiss, J. S., and Gordon, M. Need patterns and mutual satisfaction of dating and engaged couples. *Journal of Marriage and the Family,* 1964, *26,* 337–9.

Hendrix, L. Studying ourselves: The questionnaire as a teaching tool. *The Family Coordinator,* 1978, *27,* 47–54.

Homans, G. C. *Social behavior: Its elementary forms.* New York: Harcourt Brace Jovanovich, 1961.

Huston, T. L. Ambiguity of acceptance, social desirability and dating choice. *Journal of Experimental Social Psychology,* 1973, *9,* 32–42.

Jedlicka, D. Sex inequality, aging, and innovation in preferential mate selection. *The Family Coordinator,* 1978, *27,* 2, 137–40.

Kanin, E. J. Roundup of current research. *Trans-Action,* 1968, *5,* 4.

Katz, A. M., and Hill, R. Residential propinquity and marital selection: A review of theory, method, and fact. *Marriage and Family Living,* 1958, *20,* 27–34.

Kenkel, W. F. *The family in perspective.* Santa Monica, Calif.: Goodyear Publishing, 1977.

Kerckhoff, A. C., and Davis, K. E. Value consensus and need complementarity in mate selection. *American Sociological Review,* 1962, *27,* 295–303.

Kerr, C. *Sex for women who want to have fun and loving relationships with equals.* New York: Grove Press, 1977.

Knox, D. Dating behaviors of university students. Unpublished study, 1977.

Knox, D. H., Jr., and Sporakowski, M. J. Attitudes of college students toward love. *Journal of Marriage and the Family,* 1968, *30,* 638–42.

Koff, W. C. Marijuana and sexual activity. *Journal of Sex Research,* 1974, *10,* 3, 194–204.

Krain, M., Cannon, D., and Bagford, J. Rating-dating or simply prestige homogamy? Data on dating in the Greek system on a midwestern campus. *Journal of Marriage and the Family,* 1977, *39,* 663–74.

Landis, J. T., and Landis, M. G. *Building a successful marriage.* Englewood Cliffs, N.J.: Prentice-Hall, 1977.

Leslie, G. R. *The family in the social context.* New York: Oxford University Press, 1976.

Lewis, R. A. Social reaction and the formation of dyads: An interactionist approach to mate selection. *Sociometry,* 1973, *36,* 409–18.

Libby, R. W. Creative singlehood as a sexual life-style: Beyond marriage as a rite of passage. In *Marriage and alternatives: Exploring intimate relationships,* R. W. Libby and R. N. Whitehurst (eds.). Glenview, Ill.: Scott, Foresman, 1977, 37–61.

McDaniel, C. O., Jr. Dating roles and reasons for dating. *Journal of Marriage and the Family,* 1969, *31,* 97–107.

McGinnis, R. Campus values in mate selection: A repeat study. *Social Forces,* May 1958, 368–73.

Melton, W., and Thomas, D. L. Instrumental and expressive values in mate selection of black and white college students. *Journal of Marrige and the Family,* 1976, *38,* 509–17.

Moore, K., and Knox, D. White and black marriage role expectations. *Family Perspective,* Summer 1978.

Murstein, B. I. The complementary need hypothesis in newlyweds and middle-aged couples. *Journal of Abnormal and Social Psychology,* 1961, *63,* 194–7.

_____. Empirical tests of role, complementary needs, and homogamy theories of marital choice. *Journal of Marriage and the Family,* 1967, *29,* 689–96.

Petroni, F. A. Teenage interracial dating. In *Love, marriage, family: A developmental approach,* M. E. Lasswell and T. E. Lasswell (eds.). Glenview, Ill.: Scott, Foresman, 1973, 144–50.

Pollis, C. A. Dating involvement and patterns of idealization: A test of Waller's hypothesis. *Journal of Marriage and the Family,* 1969, *31,* 765–71.

Prince, A. J., and Baggaley, A. R. Personality variables and the ideal mate, *The Family Coordinator,* 1963, *12,* 93–6.

Reiss, I. L. *Premarital sexual standards in America.* New York: Free Press, 1960.
_____. Social class and campus dating. *Social Problems,* 1965, *13,* 193–205.
Rockwell, R. C. Historical trends and variations in educational homogamy. *Journal of Marriage and the Family,* 1976, *38,* 83–95.
Roscow, I. Issues in the concept of need complementarity. *Sociometry,* 1957, *20,* 216–33.
Roth, H. L. The natives of Borneo. *Journal of the Royal Anthropological Institute of Great Britain and Ireland,* 1891, *21,* 110–37.
Rubin, Z. *Liking and loving: An invitation to social psychology.* New York: Holt, Rinehart and Winston, 1973.
Saxton, L. *The individual, marriage, and the family.* Belmont, Calif.: Wadsworth, 1977.
Scanzoni, L., and Scanzoni, J. *Men, women, and change.* New York: McGraw-Hill, 1976.
Schellenberg, J. A., and Bee, L. S. A re-examination of the theory of complementary needs in mate selection. *Marriage and Family Living,* 1960, *22,* 227–32.
Scott, J. F. Sororities and the husband game. *Trans-Action,* 1965, *2,* 26–32.
Sigall, H., and Landy, D. Radiating beauty: Effects of having a physically attractive partner on person perception. *Journal of Personality and Social Psychology,* 1973, *23,* 2, 218–24.
Skipper, J. K, Jr., and Nass, G. Dating behavior: A framework for analysis and an illustration. *Journal of Marriage and the Family,* 1966, *28,* 412–20.
Snyder, E. C. Attitudes: A study of homogamy and marital selectivity. *Journal of Marriage and the Family,* 1964, *26,* 332–36.
Stephens, W. N. *The family in cross-cultural perspective.* New York: Holt, Rinehart and Winston, 1963.
Strong, E., Wallace, W., and Wilson, W. Three-filter date selection by computer. *The Family Coordinator,* 1969, *18,* 166–71.
Strong, E., and Wilson, W. Three-filter date selection by computer—Phase II. *The Family Coordinator,* 1969, *18,* 256–9.
Tharp, R. G. Psychological patterns in marriage. *Psychological Bulletin,* 1963, *60,* 97–117.
Trost, J. Some data on mate selection: Homogamy and perceived homogamy. *Journal of Marriage and the Family,* 1967, *29,* 739–55.
UPI. Broker Recruits Brides, *Raleigh News and Observer,* 17 January 1976, p. 3, col. 2.
U.S., Bureau of the Census. Marital status and living arrangements: March 1977. *Current Population Reports,* Series P–20, No. 323. Washington, D.C.: U.S. Government Printing Office, 1978.
_____. *Current Population Reports,* Series P–23, No. 48. Washington, D.C.: U.S. Government Printing Office 1974, 77.
_____. PC (2)—4C, 1972, 269.
Wakil, S. P. Campus mate selection preferences: A cross-national comparison. *Social Forces,* 1973, *51,* 271–76.
Waller, W. *The family: A dynamic institution.* New York: The Cordon Company, 1938.
Waller, W., and Hill, R. *The family: A dynamic interpretation.* New York: Holt, Rinehart and Winston, 1951.
Walster, E., Piliavin, J. A., and Walster, G. W. Playing hard to get: Understanding an elusive phenomenon. *Journal of Personality and Social Psychology,* 1973, *26,* 113–21.
Warner, L. W. *A black civilization.* New York: Harper and Row, 1937.
Winch, R. F. The theory of complementary needs in mate selection: Final results on the test of the general hypothesis. *American Sociological Review,* 1955, *20,* 552–55.
_____. Dating, courtship, and engagement. *The modern family.* New York: Holt, Rinehart and Winston, 1963, 638–41.
Wolf, R. Self-image of the white member of an interracial couple. In *People as partners,* J. P. Wiseman (ed.). San Francisco: Canfield Press, 1971, 58–63.
Wright, J., Jr. Director of Graduate Studies and Criminology, Loyola University, New Orleans. Personal communication, 1978.

Chapter 8

Cohabitation

It's cool with our friends, it's cool with our neighbors—our biggest inconvenience is that we don't know what to call each other.

Ron Nagle (quoted in *Newsweek*)

About 25 percent of undergraduate college students have had the experience of living with someone of the opposite sex to whom they were not legally married (Macklin, 1978). For some, living together, or cohabitation as it is called, has become a logical next step in their developing relationship. For others, it is a more satisfactory arrangement than living with a roommate of the same sex or living alone. For a few, it is a permanent alternative to marriage.

In this chapter, we explore the characteristics of college students who cohabit, their motivations for doing so, and the extent of cohabitation on various college and university campuses. In addition, we will examine the process of becoming involved in a cohabiting relationship, the nature of the day-to-day relationship, and the consequences of cohabitation.

WHAT IS COHABITATION?

Although most students have a general understanding of what living together means, over twenty definitions of cohabitation have been suggested by various researchers (Cole, 1977).[1] The central elements of these definitions include:

1. There are two adults of the opposite sex (although children or other couples may live with the adults).
2. The adults are not related.
3. The adults are not legally married to each other by ceremony or by common law.
4. The adults sleep in the same bed or share a bedroom.
5. The couple have met the above criteria fairly consistently for a period of time.

How long does a couple need to live together before they can be regarded as "cohabitors"? This question has generated the most debate in efforts to define cohabitation. The range is from a long weekend to six months (Peterman et al., 1974; Clayton & Voss, 1977). The time frame Macklin (1972) suggested "three or four nights per week for at least three consecutive months" (p. 463), has been used by several researchers. But other researchers feel that the important issue is the couple's perception of the relationship rather than its duration. These researchers contend that the partners are living together if that is how they define their situation (Peterman et al., 1974). There are also several different types of cohabitors: those who are living together because

"Oh, Penny, will you, like, live with me for a little while?"

they are friends or it is convenient to do so; those who are emotionally involved but not committed to marriage to one another; those committed to marry but waiting to do so; and those for whom cohabitation is a permanent alternative to marriage.

Most student cohabitants (probably 50 to 60 percent) regard themselves as having a strong affectionate relationship with their partners, but they are not yet committed to marriage to one another (Macklin, 1975, p. 22). In traditional terms, they are "going steady" except that they have moved in together. This "involved but not committed to marriage" pattern of cohabitation was expressed by one student who said, "The only thing I know about is today. And today I'm happy with my partner. Tomorrow? Who knows? While we both intend to get married someday, we're not sure that it will be to each other."

Some other couples (possibly 10 to 20 percent) are committed to marriage and are living together until it is appropriate or convenient to marry. A number of these people regard their cohabitation as a "trial marriage" (Macklin, 1975, p. 22). Although they may not be officially engaged (engagement ring, newspaper announcement), they plan to be married and are consciously assessing their compatibility. "The idea of agreeing to spend the rest of your life with someone you've never lived with is nonsense," said one cohabitant. "We love each other very much and feel very secure with each other. But we want to see if we can pull it off on a day-to-day basis."

About 10 percent of cohabiting relationships consist of opposite sex friends who enjoy the convenience and economy of living together but who are not involved in a love relationship (Macklin, 1975, p. 22). Although they live together, they have maximum independence and freedom from each other.

Very few college students cohabit as a permanent alternative to marriage (Macklin, 1975, p. 22). Only 1 percent of a random sample of the undergraduate population at the University of Delaware reported that they never wanted to marry (McCauley, 1975). Most students seem to feel that someday they will get married. "Living together is great now," observed a woman who had been living with her partner for six months, "but I wouldn't want to do this forever. I want kids and I wouldn't have them unless I were married."

COHABITATION IS INCREASING

The percentage of students who cohabit on any campus will depend on the definition of cohabitation, the male/female ratio, the housing policy, and how the students are selected for the survey. In other words the number of cohabitors reported in various studies depends not only on the kind of students and the type of setting they are in, but also on the methods and definition of the researchers.

The percentage of students who reported living together in ten studies is presented in Table 8.1. Reviewing all the research on the incidence of living together, Macklin (1978) commented, "Therefore it seems safe to conclude that about one quarter of present U.S. undergraduate students, taking the country as a whole, have had a cohabitation experience."[2] And cohabitation percentages do not seem to vary greatly by region (Bower & Christopherson, 1977).

Although the idea of trial marriages was suggested in the 1920s (Lindsey, 1926, 1927; Russell, 1929), it did not catch on until the mid-1960s (*Newsweek*, 1966; *Time*, 1968). The convergence of social, psychological, and technological changes resulted in more tolerance for and an increased incidence of cohabitation. These changes included new sex norms, skepticism about traditional values, availability of effective contraception, off-campus apartments, and peer support.

New Sex Norms

Social criticism and the fear of it have often functioned to control people's actions, and until recently, any woman who lived with a man she was not married to was said to be a "slut" who was just "shacking up."

Such an expression reflected the double standard—the idea that nonmarital sexual satisfaction was appropriate for men but not for women. Because of the double standard, many women felt that they had to withhold sex until they could get a commitment for marriage. But the double standard is no longer so widely adhered to in American society. This is due, in part, to the women's movement which encouraged women to stop regarding marriage as the ultimate experience, to stop bargaining with sex, and to enjoy it.

The double standard is being replaced by permissiveness with affection. By

TABLE 8.1 Prevalence of Cohabitation on American College Campuses Based Upon Selected Cohabitation Surveys.

Researcher(s)	Time of Study	Region of Country and Campus Type	Percentage of Cohabitation
Arafat and Yorburg (1973)	1971	Northeast Large Urban Univ.	20%
Clatworthy (1975)	1973	Mideast Large State Univ. (Urban Area)	22%
Cole (1973a)	1973	Mideast Small Liberal Arts College (Rural Area)	17%
Huang (1971)	1971	Midwest Large State Univ. (Urban Area)	12%
Henze and Hudson (1974)	1972	Southwest Large State Univ. (Urban Area)	23%
Lautenschlager (1972)	1972	West Coast Large State Univ. (Urban Area)	25%
Macklin (1974)	1972	Northeast Large State Univ. (Small City)	31%
Peterman, Ridley and Anderson (1974)	1972	Northeast Large State Univ. (Small City)	33%
Shuttlesworth and Thorman (1974)		Southwest Large State Univ. (Urban Area)	36%

SOURCE: Adapted from Cole, 1977, p. 68.

this standard, intercourse is justified if a person feels affection for his or her partner and has some indication that the partner returns this affection. "When you're living with someone," said one woman, "everybody knows you're having sex. But you don't live with a guy unless you care about each other—and that's what makes living together okay."

Skepticism Regarding Traditional Values

The questioning of sexual values in the sixties was part of a larger skepticism about adult values, which was in part a reaction to American involvement in Vietnam. Youth began to question the validity of the traditional attitudes that adults were expressing about courtship and marriage. The traditional attitude toward premarital sex, "Don't wear the shoe until you've bought it," was challenged by young people with, "Why not try the shoe before deciding to buy it?"

Young people also disagreed with adults who implied that staying married was the ultimate goal of getting married. Youth felt that personal growth and being happy with your partner took precedence over the legal relationship.

Availability of Effective Contraception

These challenges to traditional values were made easier by new technology—specifically, the separation of lovemaking and babymaking made possible by the availability of safe and effective birth control. One researcher studied the effect of the pill on student cohabitation and concluded:

> Rates of premarital coitus among college students do appear to have increased significantly since the hormonal birth control pill became available in 1960, especially among college women. Cohabitation does appear to have emerged since about the mid-sixties, and willingness of students to cohabit appears to be influenced by changes in birth control and abortion availability in much the same way as is their willingness to have premarital coitus. (Makepeace, 1975)

Off-Campus Apartments

A reevaluation of traditional sexual values and the availability of the pill were necessary but not sufficient conditions to initiate a wave of student cohabitation. A place to cohabit had to be available. University officials made living together more convenient by rejecting the *in loco parentis* philosophy, the belief that administrators had an obligation to "stand in the place of parents" and to monitor the moral behavior of students. An increasing number of officials have relaxed various restrictions which were designed to keep the sexes in separate beds. Twenty-four-hour visitation rights, dorms with no curfew, coed dormitories, and allowing students to live off campus in private apartments have virtually eliminated the structural barriers to cohabitation. Although most universities do not officially allow cohabitation, they do not prevent it.

Peer Support

Most college students have a tolerant or supportive attitude toward living together. Such peer support makes living together easier. Seventy-nine percent of 762 students at a large city college indicated that they would live with a member of the opposite sex if they had the opportunity to do so (Arafat & Yorburg, 1973). And, in a national survey of sixteen state universities, 42 percent of those who had not cohabited would "consider cohabiting to test out the relationship" (Bower & Christopherson, 1975).

These studies indicate that there is considerable peer support for living together. Such attitudinal support when combined with the knowledge of specific friends who live together may, in fact, be influential in encouraging others to

As college administrators moved away from the **in loco parentis** philosophy, relaxed housing policies eliminated many barriers to cohabiting. The student housing scene of the '70's included coed dormitories, more off-campus apartments, and unrestricted dormitory visiting hours on many campuses.

live together. "While I had never considered living together before coming to college, a lot of my friends are doing so," observed one freshman. "That makes it easier for me to consider moving in with my partner."

Cohabitation on college campuses will probably increase. "Cohabitation as a stage in the courtship process is fast becoming a part of the dominant culture —at least among college-educated persons—and may be a natural, to-be-expected outcome when two persons care about one another and enjoy being together" (Macklin, 1975, p. 43).

WHO COHABITS?

Although the social climate on the college campus is conducive to cohabitation, only one fourth of the students have actually done so. What are the differences between those who live together and those who do not?

Characteristics of Cohabitants

While the similarities between cohabitants and noncohabitants are more dramatic than the differences, there are several characteristics which students who cohabit tend to have.

Noninvolvement in organized religion. Cohabitants are much less likely than noncohabitants to attend church or to express a religious preference (Strong & Nass, 1976). But when asked to evaluate their own "religious-mindedness," 45 percent of 126 cohabitants reported that they were "somewhat" or "fairly" religious-minded (Bower, 1975, p. 94). Hence, while cohabitants are not likely to be in church or synagogue, they regard themselves as having a system of values they define as religious.

Liberal life-style. Cohabitants are more liberal about sex, life-style, and drugs than noncohabitants. Of 126 cohabitants, 75 percent of the women and 90 percent of the men believed that "love enhances sex but is not necessary for its enjoyment" (Bower, 1975, p. 40). These percentages are in contrast to a study of noncohabitants in which 71 percent of the women and 83 percent of the men (of twenty thousand respondents) agreed with the statement (Athanasiou et al., 1970, p. 42). While these percentage differences do not appear dramatic, they may indicate less guilt about sex among cohabitants. All of the cohabitants in one study reported having had intercourse before they began living with their partners (Clatworthy, 1975, p. 77). And, another researcher found "low sex guilt" among those who were attracted to various marriage alternatives (Mosher, 1975). A graduate student in history remarked, "Living together and having sex are part of getting to know someone you care about."

Those who live together also regard themselves as more liberal than those who don't. In one study, three times as many cohabitants as noncohabitants characterized their life-style as liberal (Henze & Hudson, 1974, p. 725). Their life-style also tends to include more involvement with drugs. Almost twice as many cohabitants as noncohabitants currently use marijuana and/or hard drugs.[3]

Friends of cohabitants. Who you are and what you think will be mirrored by those whom you regard as close friends. If you define yourself as a religious person, you will seek the companionship of others who share your values. And, if you are living with your partner, you probably have friends who are doing likewise (Macklin, 1974a). Regarding her friends, one cohabitant said, "I didn't 'look' for friends who were living together. It just happened that those people who are my friends are into the same thing I am."

High quality interpersonal relationships. Cohabitants also report higher quality interpersonal relationships than noncohabitants. Eleven hundred students at Pennsylvania State University completed a questionnaire which included items on perceived closeness to ideal partner, openness of communication, need satisfaction, sexual attractiveness, and sexual satisfaction. A score on the "quality index" could range from five to twenty-five with a high score indicating a high quality relationship. Quality scores for each student's most important heterosexual relationship (not necessarily the present relationship) were compared. Those students who were living together rated significantly higher on all items than those who had not lived together (Peterman, Ridley & Anderson, 1974, p. 350). It is not known whether the cohabiting experience leads to higher quality interpersonal relationships or students capable of high quality relationships seek similar companions to live with (p. 351).

In summary, students who live together tend to attend church or express a religious preference less frequently; they have had intercourse before deciding to live together; they are more likely to smoke marijuana and to have close friends who have lived together; they may have been formerly engaged or married; and, finally, they tend to be involved in very high quality relationships. Research has not found any significant difference between cohabitants and noncohabitants regarding grade point average, how happily married they perceive their parents to be, the educational or occupational status of their parents, or the size of the town in which they (the students) were reared (Peterman, Ridley, & Anderson, 1974, p. 349; Macklin, 1976, pp. 119–20).

Predicting Cohabitation

In the previous section we have seen some of the traits that research has found to be more characteristic of cohabitants than of noncohabitants. But what factors affect whether or not any individual is more or less likely to move in with someone of the opposite sex.

Factors affecting opportunity. The following factors enhance the probability that an individual will establish a living-together relationship:

1. Environmental opportunity (e.g., availability of potential partners; permissive housing regulations).
2. Sociocultural norms within the immediate environment (e.g., awareness of others cohabiting; perception of reference group support).
3. Isolation from conventional social control agents (e.g., geographic distance from parents; predictability of parental visits). The significance of this factor is probably influenced by the degree of financial and emotional independence from the parents.
4. Interpersonal attractiveness (e.g., interpersonal competence, personality, physical attractiveness). (Macklin, 1974b, pp. 2–3)

In summary, opportunity to cohabit is dependent on someone to cohabit with, peer support, parents who either don't know or cohabitants who don't care if they know, and the social skills to initiate a living-together experience.

Factors affecting desire. Although an individual has the opportunity to cohabit, he or she may not take advantage of the opportunity. Those factors entering into the decision to cohabit include:

1. Religiosity (e.g., degree to which one identifies with religious groups or beliefs which are consistent with cohabitation).
2. Personality variables (e.g., degree of need for autonomy, capacity for intimacy, acceptance of nontraditional values and sex roles, value placed on self-actualization, comfort with ambiguity and change).
3. Previous sexual or dating experience.
4. Affection for partner and perceived happiness when with the partner. (Macklin, 1974b, pp. 2–3)

In general, those who take the opportunity to live together have no religious reasons not to, are comfortable engaging in nontraditional behavior, have had considerable interpersonal experience, and want to increase the amount of time spent with the partner because they feel happier when with the partner.

LIVING TOGETHER: WHAT IT'S LIKE

Having identified the characteristics of cohabitants and the factors conducive to cohabitation, let's examine what it's like on a day-to-day basis. In this section, we explore such issues as the decision to live together, the understanding regarding commitment, the division of labor, and the problems experienced by cohabitors.

Deciding to Move in Together

Couples rarely make a conscious decision to live together. Almost three fourths of 126 cohabitants said that they "just gradually drifted into sleeping more frequently together" (Bower, 1975, p. 59). When cohabitants in one study were asked, "Who made the first suggestion that you live together?" they were unable to remember a specific time when one of them made the suggestion. In retrospect, both felt that it had been a mutual decision (Keiser, 1975, p. 13). "We were at his place fooling around," recalled one cohabitant, "when I said how nice it would be to have my stereo to listen to. We decided to go to my dorm and get it. Doing so was symbolic because in the next few days we had moved my other stuff in. We never talked about living together, only 'getting my stuff.' "

Most college students who live together do so in the man's apartment. But it is not unusual for the woman to maintain a separate residence. As Macklin observed in her study,

[Most women] also maintained a room in the dormitory or sorority or in an apartment with other girls. Most went back once a day for a few hours to visit, get messages or mail, exchange clothes, shower, or study. Maintaining a separate residence precludes having to explain to parents, insures a place to live if the relationship is not working well, helps maintain contact with female friends, serves as a convenient place to study, and provides often necessary storage space (the boy's room being too small to hold both sets of belongings)" (Macklin, 1972, p. 465).

As already noted, when most college students begin living together, they regard their doing so as neither an alternative nor a prelude to marriage. Rather, they enjoy each other's company and have a "let's see" attitude about the future of their relationship (Macklin, 1972, p. 467). And, most do not begin living together until their relationship has developed considerable momentum. Although there are exceptions, most cohabitants knew their partners for six months to two years (Keiser, 1975, p. 12; Macklin, 1972, p. 465) and regarded their relationship as "strong, affectionate, and monogamous" before they began living together (Bower, 1975, p. 60).

Commitment

How committed are cohabiting relationships? Since marriage is regarded as the ultimate commitment between a woman and a man, those who live together are often thought of as "not really" being committed to each other. One researcher asked nineteen married and nineteen cohabiting couples, "How long do you expect to stay with your partner?" While all the married respondents expressed that they

Before moving in together, most student cohabitants have known each other for half a year or longer. Sharing a dorm room or apartment is not done impulsively in most cases, but begins gradually with a "let's see how it goes" attitude.

felt "fairly strongly" about wanting to stay with their partners at least five years, only two thirds of the cohabiting couples felt the same way (Johnson, 1973).

In the same study, social commitment was defined as the number of people who knew about the relationship and would disapprove if it broke up. As might be expected, married couples named more people who knew about their relationship and would disapprove if they broke up than couples who were living together (Johnson, 1973).

When partners who were engaged, cohabiting, or married were compared on their commitment to each other (pair commitment), the cohabitants were personally as committed to each other as were the engaged partners. But neither the cohabiting nor engaged couples expressed as much commitment to each other as the married partners. As might be expected, when the cohabitants and engaged couples were compared on their commitment to marriage, the cohabitants were less committed to marriage than were the engaged couples (Lewis et al., 1975).

While both sexes in a cohabiting relationship are as personally committed to each other as the partners in an engagement (Lewis et al., 1975, p. 7), it is not clear whether the woman or man is more committed to marriage. While one study emphasized that women were more marriage oriented (Lyness, Lipetz, & Davis, 1972), another concluded just the opposite (Milardo, 1975).

One index of commitment is the amount of time the cohabitants have been living together. In a study of 126 cohabitants (both college and noncollege), the average time that women reported having lived with their current partner was slightly over one year. The men reported slightly over fifteen months (Bower, 1975, p. 56). The conclusion that living-together relationships are not casual encounters is supported by another study in which the researchers found that (on the average) cohabiting couples had been living together for about a year and had known each other eight months before that (Danziger & Greenwald, 1974, pp. 15–16).

In summary, cohabitants feel as personally committed to each other as do engaged couples. But cohabitants are less likely to anticipate marriage as the outcome of their relationship than engaged couples. Cohabitation relationships are not one-night stands. Once two students begin to cohabit, they tend to continue for several months or longer.

Division of Labor

Regardless of their level of commitment, how do cohabitors divide up household jobs? In one study, the division of labor reported by sixty-two cohabiting men and sixty-four cohabiting women was, in general, along traditional lines. Men more often took care of the car, made repairs, and emptied the garbage; women more often shopped for food, washed dishes, and picked up around the house (Bower, 1975, p. 72).

Three researchers compared the division of labor among cohabiting and married couples (Stafford, Backman, & Di Bona, 1977). They concluded, "the couples of the 'now' generation whether cohabiting or married are still dividing the work along traditional lines with the woman bearing the brunt of the labor" (p. 54). The authors suggested that such a traditional division of labor is the unconscious replication of the role relationships the respective partners observed in their parents' marriages. One female cohabitant who cooks, cleans, and does the laundry said, "I really don't mind. I'd rather be taking care of things around the apartment than just sitting around." One might predict that her mother also takes care of her father in a similar manner and feels guilty "just sitting around."

Problems

In addition to the decision to live together, the understanding regarding commitment, and the division of labor, cohabitors sometimes face problems unique to their situation. These problems include disapproving parents, interpersonal concerns such as overdependence on the relationships and lack of space and money.

Parents. Most parents of college students are neither aware nor would approve of their son's or daughter's involvement in a cohabiting relationship. One researcher interviewed seventy cohabiting students regarding their parents' awareness of their cohabitation. None had informed their parents when they first moved in (Huang, 1974). In another study, 80 percent of a group of ninety-two cohabiting students had tried to hide the fact from their parents at some time (Macklin, 1974a).[4]

Hiding such information from parents seems to be based on a prediction by the cohabitants that their parents would not approve. Eighty-eight percent of the mothers of 109 college women disapproved of living together (Sillerud, 1975).[5] The parents most likely to have negative feelings about cohabitation are those who have not attended college, have annual incomes of less than $30,000, have strong religious affiliations, are Catholic, and know few or no other people who have cohabited (Macklin, 1974c, p. 33). Most mothers and fathers disapprove on moral grounds although some feel that cohabitation is likely to be too emotionally stressful or will bind their son or daughter into a relationship too early (p. 16).

Students who do not tell their parents they are cohabiting may feel guilty because of the deception and anxious about possible exposure. In addition, 60 percent of fifty-two cohabiting students expressed sorrow at not being able to share their relationship with their parents (Macklin, 1974a). "I've never been happier than since I moved into Carl's apartment. But the fact that my folks don't know and would be disappointed if they did bothers me. Carl is a very important part of my life, and I feel sad that I can't share him with my parents," said one cohabitant.

Interpersonal concerns. In addition to sometimes experiencing guilt, fear, and sorrow when deceiving their parents, cohabitants may also have feelings of jealousy, overinvolvement, and being trapped with each other. Sixty-one percent of 126 cohabitants said that they had felt jealous of their partner's involvement in other relationships or activities (Bower, 1975, p. 66). Some cohabitants have sex with others outside the cohabiting relationship. In a study of 126 cohabitants, 31 percent of the men and 19 percent of the women reported that they had had sex with one or more partners other than their cohabiting partner since they began living together (Bower, 1975, p. 76). Feelings of overinvolvement seem to produce as much stress in cohabiting partners as jealousy (Bower, 1975; Macklin, 1974a). Overinvolvement may result in a loss of identity or a lack of opportunity to participate in other activities with friends (Macklin, 1974a, p. 29). "I feel like I'm married," is a common expression. "We spend most of our time in the apartment and aren't involved in campus activities. It seems like we're shutting ourselves off from others and from doing whatever they do on campus."

In addition to having experienced feelings of jealousy and overinvolvement, almost half the cohabitants in two studies had felt trapped at some point in the relationship (Bower, 1975, p. 66; Macklin, 1974a, p. 29). "I'm into this thing deeper than I thought," expressed a frustrated cohabitant. "For the past few months our relationship has deteriorated; yet I don't feel easy about breaking up. Living together has cut me off from other people."

Cohabiting couples may also experience sexual problems similar to those experienced by married couples, including differential interest in sex, lack of female

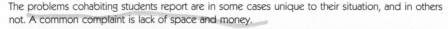

The problems cohabiting students report are in some cases unique to their situation, and in others not. A common complaint is lack of space and money.

orgasm, fear of pregnancy,[6] pain during intercourse, and impotence (Macklin, 1972, p. 468; Bower, 1975, p. 77). A female cohabitant remarked how living together had changed her sex life with her partner. "Before we started living together, we had intercourse less frequently because we weren't as available to each other. But when we were sleeping together every night, intercourse was always a possibility. It became a hassle because I wanted it more often, and he felt that only the male should be the aggressor."

Lack of space or money.   In addition to parental and interpersonal problems, cohabitants complain about lack of space (Bower, 1975, p. 66; Macklin, 1974, p. 29a). "And when you try to get my art equipment into the same quarters with his aquariums, it's close. We've been looking for a larger place but simply can't afford what we need."

Money is another common problem for couples who live together. Since most couples agree that financial obligations should be divided on a fifty-fifty basis (Keiser, 1975), their problem with money is lack of it. Sixty-seven percent of 126 cohabitants regarded this as their most difficult problem (Bower, 1975, p. 66).

In summary, the anxiety associated with their parents not knowing about their living-together relationship is a major concern among college cohabitants. In addition, feelings of jealousy, overinvolvement, and being trapped are problems cohabitants experience with each other. These concerns may be aggravated by the lack of space and money.

COHABITATION AND MARRIAGE

We have looked at several aspects of living together and at some of the problems that may be involved. But an important question remains: How does living together compare to marriage and what effect does it have on marriage?

A Comparison

Since cohabiting couples often indicate that their relationship is bonded by affectionate feelings rather than law, one might predict that they feel stronger about each other and are more satisfied with their relationship than married couples. But intensive interviews with twenty-five cohabiting couples and twenty-six married couples revealed no significant differences between the groups in affective support, interpersonal knowledge, and relationship satisfaction (Martin et al., 1975).

In another study which compared the happiness and problem-solving behavior of twenty cohabiting and twenty married couples, the researchers found no significant differences between the groups (Cole & Vincent, 1975). "Evolving a happy relationship is more likely a factor of the actual patterns of interaction and definition of roles between partners, rather than the legal status of the relationship," the researchers concluded (p. 10).

Partner interaction can be evaluated partly in terms of the frequency and ratio of pleasing and displeasing behaviors. When the behaviors of cohabiting and married couples were compared, there were few differences. Both sets of couples reported "sexual and other affectional behaviors as most pleasing while displeasing behaviors involved self-care and maintenance activities such as not cleaning up after oneself, not taking out the trash, leaving the bathroom dirty, and so on" (p. 11).

But in spite of the similarities between cohabiting and married couples, there are differences. For example, territoriality (having an identified place within the home for one's things) is more characteristic of married than cohabiting couples. When seventy married and twenty cohabiting individuals responded to such questions as, "Do you have a certain and separate portion of the bathroom to place such items as your toothbrush?" and "Do you have a certain and separate chair to sit in at the dinner table?" those who were married were much more likely to answer "Yes" (Rosenblatt & Budd, 1975). In contrast, the cohabiting couples were more likely than married couples to have places within the residence for being alone. The researchers suggested that when you are unmarried it is acceptable to have a private world. But marital norms often convey that each partner's life is now with the other, and feelings of privacy should diminish.

Another difference between cohabiting and married couples is the greater likelihood that cohabiting partners will disagree on the future of the relationship (Lyness, Lipetz, & Davis, 1972). Whether or not to get married is a potential disagreement of cohabitants which married couples have already settled. "I thought all along that we would be married, but I found out my partner had never assumed so," is not an uncommon expression.

And getting out of a relationship is perceived as being easier when cohabiting than when married (although these perceptions may be somewhat naive). "Given similar circumstances (such as arrival of children, shared material items, family/community stigma), individuals in living-together unmarried relationships were less likely to define these issues as potential barriers to termination" (Cole & Vincent, 1975, p. 12). One cohabitant who had recently terminated a relationship said, "If you're married, you've got the courts to contend with when you split. But if you're just living with someone, you can get your socks together and move out before lunch."

Other cohabitants say that termination is not that easy. While the legal ties may not be as great a barrier as in marriage (see *Trends* section in this chapter), the emotional ties are often very strong. "When you've lived with someone, loved them, and cared about them, it's not a simple thing to say good-bye," recalled one cohabitant. "You have to adjust as though you were getting a divorce." Cohabitants are also more fearful of the woman getting pregnant than marrieds. In a comparison of 193 respondents (both cohabiting and married), Williams (1975) observed this phenomenon. And, if the woman became pregnant, cohabitors were much more in favor of an abortion than marrieds (Markowski et al., 1978).

In general, then, the day-to-day relationships of cohabiting and married couples are very similar. Sharing living facilities, eating, and sleeping together are experiences common to both sets of couples. The differences are in terms of greater territoriality among married couples, potentially different ideas about the future in cohabiting couples, the perception of fewer legal barriers to ending a cohabiting relationship, and greater concern over pregnancy among cohabitants than among married people. And, of course, there is greater social support, particularly from parents, for being married than for living together unmarried.

Cohabitation as Preparation for Marriage?

Does cohabitation result in happier marriages? While it is not known what percentage of all cohabitants eventually marry each other (Macklin, 1976, p. 52), some research has been conducted to ascertain how married couples who cohabited before marriage differ from those who did not live together before marriage. One researcher asked spouses in both groups to describe how they felt about their marriage on a seven-point continuum. Those who had lived together before they were married were no more likely to describe their relationship as emotionally close than were those who had not lived together (Olday, 1976).

Marital conflict was also unrelated to cohabitation before marriage. The couples who had cohabited were no less likely to have disagreements over money, sex, recreation, and housekeeping chores than were those who had not lived together (Olday, 1976).

Another researcher interviewed twenty-one couples who had cohabited before they married. She concluded that for most of the couples, the quality of their relationship after marriage was very similar to the quality of the relationship they had prior to marriage. Marriage did not result in any dramatic change—either improvement or deterioration (Berger, 1974).

Further support for the idea that cohabitation doesn't make a great deal of difference was found by Lyness (1978) who compared eleven married couples who had cohabited before marriage with thirteen married couples who had not. The criteria for comparison were sixteen variables related to "open marriage." She found very few differences between the two groups.

In another study at Ohio State University, the researchers concluded, "The data do not support the theory that couples who engage in premarital cohabitation will have better marriages than those who did not engage in premarital cohabitation. The data did not show that premarital cohabitants selected better or more compatible mates" (Clatworthy & Scheid, 1976, p. 3).

EVALUATION: THE CONSEQUENCES OF COHABITATION

Since about a quarter of today's college students cohabit, it is fair to ask, "What are the consequences of doing so?" A disgruntled parent said, "I don't want my kids shacking up. Not only is it immoral, it's not good for them." But is it "not good for them"? Let's explore the positive and negative consequences of living together before marriage.

Positive Consequences

The overwhelming majority of cohabitants evaluate living together in positive terms. When college cohabitants were asked to indicate the degree to which their living-together experience was successful, pleasurable, and maturing, 78 percent indicated that it was successful or very successful (10 percent unsuccessful); 93 percent rated it pleasurable or very pleasurable (1 percent unpleasurable); and 91 percent rated it as maturing or very maturing (no one rated it as "not maturing at all") (Macklin, 1974a).

Table 8.2 reflects the specific cohabitation benefits rated by 126 cohabitants (Bower, 1975, p. 68). "Understanding what is involved in a relationship" was the cohabitation benefit given the highest rating (3.6 out of a possible 5) by the highest percentage (89) of respondents. "It's an experimental stage where you get to know each other," expressed a cohabitant at Southern Illinois University. "I can't imagine how anybody could marry somebody else without knowing any of his/her personal habits. Like even brushing your teeth, or you know, the little things that you don't know about each other that can really bug the hell out of you" (Keiser, 1975, p. 39).

In addition to developing increased understanding of what it's like to live with another, cohabitants often point to personal growth and maturity as benefits of the cohabiting experience. "I've changed since we began living together. Life isn't like it happens in the movies," expressed one cohabitant who had been living with his partner for three years.

Cohabitation as a new step in the courtship process will mean that some couples delay marriage for a longer period of time than if they did not live together (Lyness, 1978). And the longer a couple delays marriage the more opportunity they will have to find out about each other before marrying.

For some, cohabitation may provide some partners with a clear indication that they are not suited for each other. "I love him, but I know that we are incapable of living in the same house," said one sophomore woman. Finding out such information before tying the legal knot may eliminate some unnecessary grief. A team of researchers studied the termination of various premarital relationships and concluded, "The best divorce you get is the one you get before you get married" (Hill, Rubin, & Peplau, 1976, p. 165).

TABLE 8.2   Ratings by 126 cohabitants of positively valued effects of cohabitation.

Benefits of Cohabitation Receiving Positive Rating	Mean Rating of Benefit*	Percent Rating Positively		
		Male	Female	Total
Understanding what is involved in a relationship	3.6	91	87	89
Companionship	3.4	84	84	84
Sexual satisfaction	3.4	86	78	82
Emotional maturity	3.3	77	81	79
Emotional security	3.2	70	75	73
Insight into self	3.1	81	71	76
Insight into the opposite sex	3.1	74	74	74
Self-confidence	3.0	66	67	67
Ability to relate to others	3.0	74	66	70
Physical living conditions	2.8	55	64	60

*Five equals most positive rating possible, one equals most negative rating possible.

SOURCE: Adapted from Bower, 1975, p. 68.

Negative Consequences

While living together may increase self- and partner-understanding, in other cases it may have negative consequences. Living together is dysfunctional when an individual emerges from a relationship severely questioning his or her worth as a person, is unable to form and maintain relationships, refuses to start new relationships, is hostile toward the opposite sex, or becomes incapacitated in other aspects of his or her life.

A team of researchers sought to identify those cohabitation relationships which may have negative consequences for the participants (Ridley et al., 1978). They have suggested that one's level of self-confidence, the degree of prior dating experience, one's reason for living with someone, and the extent to which the cohabitant cuts off herself or himself from other friends will have a lot to do with whether the relationship results in greater interpersonal competence. They have specifically said that the following types of cohabitation relationships are *not* likely to lead to such growth:

1.   The "Linus Blanket" relationship. In this pattern, cohabitation is sought by the person who has an overwhelming need to be involved with someone, anyone. Fear of breaking up causes the individual to acquiesce to his or her partner on

every issue. Such clinging to the relationship at any cost results in no practice in problem solving, hiding oneself from the partner, and reducing the likelihood of benefiting or learning from the experience.

2. Emancipation relationship. Often one partner cohabits as a symbol of independence from parents and rebellion against tradition. But she or he feels guilty about cohabiting and soon withdraws. Unless the individual works out this ambivalence toward the cohabiting relationship, the positive consequences may be minimal.

3. Convenience relationship. While some cohabiting relationships involve mutual convenience, others do not. In the latter pattern, the one partner manipulates the other to continue sexual, domestic, or other favors while withholding any semblance of commitment. Since there is little reciprocity, the relationship becomes one of exploitation (Ridley et al., 1978). Table 8.3 outlines some "good signs" and "concern signs" for couples contemplating living together. The former are predictive of a positive outcome and the latter of a negative outcome.

In summary, cohabitants who enter the living-together relationship for security, rebellion, or exploitation (or a combination of these motivations) may not experience the personal growth of those who live together either to test their relationship or for companionship reasons. The conclusions of Ridley et al. (1978) provide a good summary: "It would be unfortunate to conclude that cohabitation is inherently good or bad preparation for marriage, but rather it should be viewed as having the potential for both, with the characteristics of the individuals and the relationship being of critical importance in determining the long-range effects of cohabitation."

TRENDS

In the future, an increasing number of individuals will cohabit. While cohabitation will continue to be practiced by a minority, an increasing number will regard it as a predictable stage in the courtship process. Particularly among the older, previously engaged, and formerly married, living together may be viewed as a prerequisite to marriage.

Cohabitation will also become more prevalent among those over sixty years of age. One researcher observed that "social structural factors, in this case social security laws which prohibit widowers from remarrying and continuing survivors' benefits, can affect the rate at which individuals opt for a nontraditional lifestyle" (Yllo, 1978, p. 43).

Whether young or old, cohabitants will increasingly consider the legal ramifications of cohabitation (wills, estates, insurance, and property). In essence, the

TABLE 8.3   Questions for consideration by couples contemplating living together.

Questions	"Good" signs and "Concern" signs
1. Could you talk a little bit about how each of you came to the decision to live together?	**Good signs:** Each partner has given considerable thought to the decision, including the advantages and disadvantages of living together. **Concern signs:** One or both partners have given little thought to the advantages and disadvantages of living together.
2. Perhaps each of you could discuss for a minute what you think you will get out of living together?	**Good signs:** Each individual is concerned about learning more about self and partner through intimate daily living. Both wish to obtain further information about each other's commitment to the relationship. **Concern signs:** One or both partners desire to live together for convenience only. They want to live together to show independence from parents or peers.
3. Could each of you discuss what you see as your role and your partner's role in the relationship (e.g., responsibilities, expectations)?	**Good signs:** Each individual's expectations of self and partner are compatible with those of partner. **Concern signs:** One or both individuals have given little thought to the roles or expectations of self and/or partner. Individuals disagree in terms of their expectations.
4. Could each of you identify your partner's primary physical and emotional needs and the degree to which you believe that you are able to fulfill them?	**Good signs:** Each individual has a clear understanding of partner's needs and is motivated and able to meet most of them. **Concern signs:** One or both individuals are not fully aware of partner's needs. Individuals are not motivated or able to meet needs of partner.
5. Would each of you identify your primary physical and emotional needs in your relationship with your partner? To what degree have these needs been met in the past? To what extent are these needs likely to be met if two of you were to live together?	**Good signs:** Each partner clearly understands his or her needs. Most of these needs are presently being met and are likely to continue to be met in a cohabiting relationship. **Concern signs:** One or both partners are not fully aware of their needs. Needs are not being met in the present relationship and/or are not likely to be met if the individuals live together.
6. Could each of you discuss what makes this relationship important to you? What are your feelings toward your partner?	**Good signs:** Partners care deeply for each other and view the relationship as a highly significant one. **Concern signs:** One or both individuals do not care deeply for their partner or do not view the relationship as a highly significant one. Partners have an emotional imbalance with one partner more involved in the relationship than the other.
7. Could each of you explore briefly your previous dating experiences and what you have learned from them?	**Good signs:** Both individuals have had a rich dating history. Individuals have positive perceptions of self and opposite sex and are aware of what they learned from previous relationships. **Concern signs:** One or both partners have had minimal dating experience. Individuals have negative perceptions of self and/or of the opposite sex and do not seem aware of having learned from their prior relationships.

Table continued on next page

TABLE 8.3   Cont.

Questions	"Good" signs and "Concern" signs
8. Perhaps each of you could talk for a minute about how your family and friends might react to the two of you living together?	**Good signs:** Each individual is aware of the potential repercussions of family and friends should they learn of the cohabiting relationship. Family and friends are supportive of the cohabiting relationship, or couple has considered how they will deal with opposition. **Concern signs:** One or both individuals are not fully aware of possible family and friends' reaction to their living together. Family and friends are not supportive of the cohabiting relationship.
9. Could each of you discuss your ability to openly and honestly share your feelings with your partner?	**Good signs:** Each individual is usually able to express feelings to partner without difficulty. **Concern signs:** One or both individuals have difficulty expressing feelings to partner or do not believe expressing feelings is important.
10. Could each of you discuss your partner's strengths and weaknesses? To what extent would you like to change your partner, relative to their strengths or weaknesses?	**Good signs:** Each individual is usually able to accept feelings of partner. Individuals are able to accept partner's strengths and weaknesses. **Concern signs:** One or both individuals are not able to understand and accept partner. Individuals have difficulty in accepting partner's strengths and weaknesses.
11. How do each of you handle relationship problems when they occur? Can you give some examples of difficult problems you have had and how you have dealt with them?	**Good signs:** Both individuals express feelings openly and are able to understand and accept partner's point of view. Individuals are able to mutually solve problems. **Concern signs:** One or both partners have difficulty expressing feelings openly or in accepting partner's point of view. Couple frequently avoids problems or fails to solve them mutually.

SOURCE: Adapted from Ridley et al., 1978, pp. 135–36, Table 1.

legal status of couples who live together is becoming more like that of married couples. On December 26, 1976, the California Supreme Court ruled that expressed or implied agreements between cohabitants are enforceable. In effect, equal division of property and payment of alimony may result from cohabitation as well as marriage. While it is not likely that short-term cohabitation relationships involve enforceable expectations, the longer the relationships remain intact, the greater the mutual understandings, and hence, the greater the probability of having them enforced by the courts if either partner wishes it (Bernstein, 1977).

SUMMARY

About 25 percent of undergraduate college students in America report that they have lived with someone of the opposite sex to whom they were not married. While most college cohabiting relationships consist of partners who live together simply because they are emotionally involved with each other and enjoy being together, some cohabiting couples are committed to eventually marrying one another and are living together until that is possible. Only a few live together solely for the convenience of doing so.

Various social, psychological, and technological factors have led to the increased acceptance of living together. These factors include the sexual norm of permissiveness with affection, the questioning of traditional courtship and marriage values, the availability of the pill, the removal of *in loco parentis,* the existence of off-campus apartments, and increased peer support.

In general, couples who live together are similar (grade point average, perceived happiness of parents, etc.) to those who don't. But cohabitants are also different: They are less involved in organized religion and more liberal about sex and drugs; they tend to have cohabitants as close friends; and they have higher quality interpersonal relationships than noncohabitants. Whether or not a specific individual will cohabit is related to various opportunity and desire factors.

Living-together partners are as committed to each other as engaged partners but less committed than spouses. Most divide household tasks along traditional lines with the woman cooking and cleaning and the man taking out the garbage.

Parents are a problem for most college students who cohabit. Anxiety over not telling them, fear that they will find out, and sorrow at not being able to be open with them about the cohabitation relationship are the central concerns. In addition to parental problems, cohabitants struggle with feelings of jealousy, over-involvement, and feeling trapped in the relationship.

When cohabiting couples marry, they are not very different from married couples who did not live together. Both groups describe their marriage in similar terms and experience similar disagreements. Cohabitation per se doesn't seem to have positive or negative consequences for subsequent marriage.

When asked to evaluate their living-together experience, the majority of cohabitants say that the experience was successful, pleasurable, and maturing. Understanding what it is like to be involved in a relationship and learning about one's self are the primary benefits. Students who live together for reasons of security, rebellion, and exploitation are less likely to benefit from the experience.

The future of cohabitation will involve an increasing number of cohabitants (including those over sixty) and more legal protection (or problems, depending on your point of view) for cohabitants. In essence, the sustained cohabitation relationship which involves mutual expectations and understandings will be similar to marriage relationships in terms of division of property and alimony when the relationship ends.

STUDY QUESTIONS

1. What five characteristics help to define cohabitors?
2. What length of time did couples have to live together before Macklin considered them to be "cohabitors"?

3. What are four types of cohabitation relationships, and approximately what percent of cohabiting relationships are of each type?
4. Discuss five factors which have influenced an increased incidence of cohabitation.
5. In general, are cohabitants more alike or more unlike noncohabitants?
6. Discuss five traits that research has found to be characteristic of college cohabitants.
7. Mention four ways in which college cohabitants are similar to noncohabitants.
8. Specify four factors affecting the opportunity and desire to cohabit.
9. Discuss the typical steps leading up to moving in together. How long do cohabitants usually know each other before moving in? Who usually first suggests living together? Where do they most often live together?
10. When compared to married couples, how committed are cohabiting couples?
11. When compared to engaged couples, how committed are cohabiting couples?
12. How do couples who live together divide household chores? Why?
13. How do most parents feel about their son or daughter cohabiting?
14. In general, how do cohabitants feel about letting their parents know they are living together?
15. What are the characteristics of parents who approve of cohabitation?
16. Why do parents object to their son's or daughter's cohabitation?
17. Discuss four interpersonal problems cohabitants experience.
18. How are space and money a problem for cohabitants?
19. How do cohabitants compare with spouses in terms of being satisfied with their relationships?
20. What behaviors do cohabitants and spouses report as pleasing and displeasing in their relationships?
21. Discuss three ways in which couples who live together are different from married couples.
22. How do married couples who lived together before marriage differ from those who did not live together before marriage?
23. How do cohabitants evaluate the living-together experience? What are the specific benefits they mention?
24. What types of cohabiting relationships are less likely to result in positive consequences for the cohabitants?
25. What are the negative consequences of living together?
26. Discuss future trends in cohabitation.

NOTES

1. While the term *cohabitation* has been used most frequently by researchers, other terms include *trial marriage, quasi-marriage, nonmarital living arrangement, consensual union, unmarried liaison, paramarriage,* and *nonmarital units.* Terms used in the popular media include *unwed couples, unmarried marrieds,* and *the arrangement.* The more traditional and pejorative terms are *shacking up* and *living in sin.*

Research on cohabitation is also limited. Most of the studies consist of small nonrandom samples restricted to white college students. As compared to college student cohabitants, noncollege cohabitants are more likely to have their own source of income, and their parents are more likely to be aware of the arrangement.

2. Regarding cohabitants who are not college students, in 1976 less than 4 percent of the adult population (fourteen years of age or older) reported that they were living with someone of the opposite sex to whom they were not legally married (U.S. Bureau of the Census, 1977). One researcher estimates that, "at the very minimum there are between one and three-quarters and two million people currently living together unmarried in the United States" (Yllo, 1978, p. 42). And college students may represent only a small proportion of these cohabitants (Clayton & Voss, 1977).

3. Of the cohabitants, 57.7 percent of the men and 43.8 percent of the women reported that they "still use marijuana." And 11.5 percent of the men versus 7.1 percent of the women reported that they "still use hard drugs." These percentages are in contrast to noncohabitants—29.0 percent of the men and 23.7 percent of the women "still use marijuana"; 2.6 percent of the men versus 3.3 percent of the women "still use hard drugs" (Henze & Hudson, 1974, p. 725).

4. In a more recent study by Macklin, thirty women college cohabitants reported on their parents' knowledge of their cohabiting. "30 percent of the cohabitants indicated that they had consistently tried to hide their cohabitation from their parents, 16 percent had done so often and 27 percent sometimes. Only 27 percent had never tried to do so. When parents did know, in almost two-thirds of the cases it was because the students had told them; about 10 percent of the time others had told them; and 25 percent of the time the parents had deduced the fact for themselves (Macklin, 1974, p. 28).

5. Where cohabitants sleep when they visit their parents is often a concern to both cohabitants and parents. A writer for a popular magazine observed, "Most parents tell their children, 'You can do what you want in your house, but in ours you live by our standard' . . . and then make up the beds in separate rooms" (Miller, 1976, p. 48).

6. Of 126 cohabitants in Bower's study, 96 percent reported using some type of contraception. The five types of contraception used most often were the pill (87 percent), condom (37 percent), withdrawal (33 percent), foams or jellies (19 percent), and rhythm (17 percent). Twenty percent claimed a contraceptive was used the first time they had intercourse (Bower, 1975, p. 73).

BIBLIOGRAPHY

Arafat, I., and Yorburg, B. On living together without marriage. *Journal of Sex Research,* 1973, *9,* 21–9.

Athanasiou, R., Shaver, P., and Tavris, C. Sex. *Psychology Today,* July 1970, 39–52.

Berger, M. E. Trial marriage follow-up. Unpublished manuscript, 1974.

Bernstein, B. E. Legal problems of cohabitation. *The Family Coordinator,* 1977, *26,* 4, 361–6.

Bower, D. W. A description and analysis of a cohabiting sample in America. Master's thesis, University of Arizona, 1975.

Bower, D. W., and Christopherson, V. A. University student cohabitation: A regional comparison of selected attitudes and behavior. Unpublished manuscript, 1975.

Bower, D. W., and Christopherson, V. A. University student cohabitation: A regional comparison of selected attitudes and behavior. *Journal of Marriage and the Family,* 1977, *39,* 3, 447–54.

Clatworthy, N. M. Living together. In *Old family/new family: Interpersonal relationships,* N. Glazer-Malbin (ed.). New York: D. Van Nostrand, 1975, 67–89.

Clatworthy, N. M., and Scheid, L. A comparison of married couples: Premarital cohabitants with non-premarital cohabitants. Unpublished paper, 1976.

Clayton, R. R., and Voss, H. L. Shacking up: Cohabitation in the 1970's. *Journal of Marriage and the Family,* 1977, *39,* 2, 273–84.

Cole, C. L. Cohabitation in social context. In *Marriage and alternatives: Exploring intimate relationships,* R. Libby and R. Whitehurst (eds.). Glenview, Ill.: Scott, Foresman, 1977, 62–79.

Cole, C. L., and Vincent, J. P. Patterns in cohabitive and marital dyads. Unpublished manuscript, 1975.

Danziger, C., and Greenwald, M. *Alternatives: A look at unmarried couples and communes.* New York: Institute of Life Insurance (Research Services Pamphlet), 1974.

Henze, L. F., and Hudson, J. W. Personal and family characteristics of cohabiting and non-cohabiting college students. *Journal of Marriage and the Family,* 1974, *36,* 4, 722–6.

Hill, C. T., Rubin, Z., and Peplau, L. A. Breakups before marriage: The end of 103 affairs. *Journal of Social Issues,* 1976, *32,* 1, 147–68.

Huang, L. J. Research with unmarried cohabiting couples: Including non-exclusive sexual relations. Paper presented at the meeting of National Council on Family Relations, St. Louis, Missouri, 1974.

Johnson, M. P. Commitment: A conceptual structure and empirical application. *Sociological Quarterly,* 1973, *14,* 395–406.

Keiser, S. D. Cohabitation: A preliminary analysis. Unpublished manuscript, 1975.

Lewis, R. A., Spanier, G. B., Storm, V. L., and LeHecka, C. F. Commitment in married and unmarried cohabitation. Paper presented at the meeting of the American Sociological Association, San Francisco, 1975.

Lindsey, B. B. The companionate marriage. *Redbook,* October 1926.

——————. *The companionate marriage.* Garden City, N.Y.: Garden City Publishers (Doubleday), 1927.

Lyness, J. L. Happily ever after? Following-up living together couples. *Alternative Lifestyles,* 1978, *1,* 1, 55–69.

Lyness, J. L., Lipetz, M. E., and Davis, K. E. Living together: An alternative to marriage. *Journal of Marriage and the Family,* 1972, *34,* 305–11.

Macklin, E. D. Heterosexual cohabitation among unmarried college students. *The Family Coordinator,* 1972, *4,* 463–72.

——————. Unmarried cohabitation on the university campus. Unpublished manuscript, 1974. (a)

——————. *Cohabitation Research Newsletter,* 4, June 1974. (b)

——————. Comparison of parent and student attitudes toward nonmarital cohabitation. Paper presented at the meeting of the National Council on Family Relations, St. Louis, 1974. (c)

——————. Review of research on nonmarital cohabitation in the United States. Paper presented at the Symposium on Current and Future Intimate Life Styles, Connecticut College, New London, Connecticut, 1975.

——————. Assorted notes. *Cohabitation Research Newsletter,* 5, April 1976, 52.

——————. Unmarried heterosexual cohabitation on the university campus. In *The social psychology of sex,* J. Wiseman (ed.). New York: Harper and Row, 1976, 108–142.

——————. Review of research on nonmarital cohabitation in the United States. In *Exploring intimate lifestyles,* B. I. Murstein (ed.). New York: Springer, 1978.

Makepeace, J. M. The birth control revolution: Consequences for college student life-styles. Doctoral dissertation, Washington State University, 1975.

Markowski, E. M., Croake, J. W., and Keller, J. F. Sexual history and present sexual behavior for cohabiting and married couples. *The Journal of Sex Research,* 1978, *14,* 1, 27–39.

Martin, J. K., Polansky, L., Johnson, W., and McDonald, G. A comparison of marriage and heterosexual cohabitation with respect to the variables of interpersonal knowledge, affective support, and satisfaction. Unpublished paper, 1975.

McCauley, B. Unpublished study in preparation for Master's Thesis in Individual and Family Studies, University of Delaware, 1975.

Milardo, R. The implication of exchange orientation on the dyadic formation of heterosexual cohabitors. Unpublished manuscript, 1975.

Miller, M. S. Living together: How parents cope with their sons' and daughters' roommates. *Ladies Home Journal,* May 1976, 44 et passim.

Mosher, J. B. Deviance, growth motivation, and attraction to marital alternatives. Doctoral dissertation, University of Connecticut, 1975.

Newsweek. Unstructured relationship: Students living together. 4 July 1966, 78.

Olday, D. E. Unpublished study comparing persons who cohabited with present spouse before marriage with persons who did not, 1976.

Peterman, D. J., Ridley, C. A., and Anderson, S. M. A comparison of cohabiting and non-cohabiting college students. *Journal of Marriage and the Family,* 1974, *36,* 344–54.

Ridley, C. A., Peterman, D. J., and Avery, A. W. Cohabitation: Does it make for a better marriage? *The Family Coordinator,* 1978, *27,* 129–36.

Rosenblatt, P. C., and Budd, L. G. Territoriality and privacy in married and unmarried cohabiting couples. *The Journal of Social Psychology,* 1975, *97,* 67–76.

Russell, B. *Marriage and morals.* New York: Liveright, 1929.

Sillerud, D. S. Nonmarital cohabitation and marriage: Questionnaire responses of college women and their mothers. Master's thesis, North Dakota State University, 1975.

Stafford, R., Backman, E., and Di Bona, P. The division of labor among cohabiting and married couples. *Journal of Marriage and the Family,* 1977, *39,* 1, 43–57.

Strong, L., and Nass, G. Correlates of willingness among college students to participate in prolonged cohabitation. Unpublished paper, 1976.

Time. Linda: The light housekeeper. 26 April, 1968, 51.

U.S., Bureau of the Census. Marital status and living arrangements: March 1976. *Current Population Reports,* Series P-20, No. 306. Washington, D.C.: U.S. Government Printing Office, 1977.

Williams, M. J. Cohabitation attitudes of East Carolina University students. Unpublished study, 1975.

Yllo, K. A. Nonmarital cohabitation beyond the college campus. *Alternative Lifestyles,* 1978, *1,* 1, 37–54.

Chapter 9

Commitment to Marriage

MARRIAGE AS A COMMITMENT
Individual • Social • Legal

COMMITMENT TO WHOM?
Philosophical Compatibility • Recreational Compatibility • Sexual
Compatibility • Body-Clock Compatibility • Marital Role
Compatibility • Adaptability • Communication • Power Compatibility

PREDICTING MARITAL HAPPINESS
Illusion of the Perfect Mate • Deception During Premarital Period • Confinement
of Marriage • Balancing Work and Relationship Demands • Inevitability of Change

COMMITMENT TIMING
Age • Education

TERMINATION BEFORE ENGAGEMENT
Reasons • Timing of Terminations • Who Terminates the Relationship? • Recovery

ENGAGEMENT
Implications of Engagement • Using the Engagement Period

PERSONAL MARRIAGE CONTRACTS

TRENDS

SUMMARY

Keep your eyes wide open
before marriage, half shut afterwards.
Benjamin Franklin

After a period of dating or casual friendships with various people, most individuals pair off with a partner, perhaps cohabit, and eventually make a commitment to marriage. Whereas the period preceding a marital commitment may involve many relationships over a period of several years, when the decision to marry is made, the individual has just one person in mind.

This chapter is about making a commitment to marriage. Its central concern is how to maximize the chances for a successful marriage by selecting a compatible companion and by timing the commitment correctly. In addition, we will examine the conditions under which a marital commitment occurs, the dynamics of engagement, and the termination of relationships before and after engagement.

MARRIAGE AS A COMMITMENT

The decision to marry represents a multilevel commitment—person to person (individual), family to family (social), and couple to state (legal).

Individual

From the perspective of the individual, commitment to marriage refers to a stated or implied intent to maintain a relationship (Rosenblatt, 1975). Such a desire to establish a permanent commitment may be for reasons of personal fulfillment ("I've always looked forward to getting married"), social approval ("My parents would worry less about me if I got married"), and/or parenthood ("I love children and want to begin a family"). Other people are drawn to marriage as an escape from an unhappy home ("My folks have been drinking since I was twelve, and I'm getting away from home as soon as I can find somebody who will marry me"), a cure for loneliness ("My sister is a glamorous airline stewardess, but she's single and lonely. I don't want that to happen to me"), or a solution to a premarital pregnancy ("Abortion is out of the question; we're going to get married").

Social

In addition to an individual commitment, marriage involves commitments by each of the marriage partners to the family of the spouse. Young married couples are often expected to split their holiday visits between both sets of parents. In essence, each spouse becomes committed to visit his or her in-laws, to help them when appropriate, and to regard the family ties as part of the marital ties.

Legal

In addition to personal commitments to each other and each other's families, a couple that marries makes a legal commitment. State rather than federal laws control marriage. The legal requirements focus on family relationships, mental competence, age, and waiting periods. Regarding family relationships, all states prohibit marriage with one's son or daughter, mother or father, grandmother or grandfather, sister or brother, aunt or uncle, and niece or nephew. And over half the states prohibit the marriage of first cousins. A state may also prohibit the marriage of people if one or both are judged mentally deficient or insane and unable to meet the economic and social responsibilities of marriage.

Table 9.1 summarizes the marriage laws in the various states. Couples who do not meet the age requirements of their state but are intent on getting married sometimes misrepresent their ages or get married in a state where they meet the age requirement. A marriage that is legal in one state becomes valid in all states.

Most states require a waiting period between the time the license is applied for and when the ceremony can be legally performed. It has been estimated that as high as 20 percent of those who apply for a license never return to pick it up, or, if they do pick it up, never use it (Bell, 1975, p. 245). To obtain a license when no waiting period is required, a couple need only present documents certifying that each has taken a blood test and that neither has venereal disease (or that it is not

Drawing by Ed Fisher; © 1973 The New Yorker Magazine, Inc.

"Well, he didn't come right out and ask me to marry him, but he sure talked a lot about preserving America's one-family-farm system."

TABLE 9.1 United States Marriage Laws in 1976.

| State | Age at Which Marriage Can Be Contracted with Parental Consent | | Age below Which Parental Consent is Required | | Physical Examination and Blood Test for Male and Female | | Waiting Period | |
	Male	Female	Male	Female	Period between Examination and Issuance of License	Scope of Medical Examination	Before Issuance of License	After Issuance of License
Alabama	17(a)	14(a)	18	18	30 da.	(b)	—	—
Alaska	16(e)	16(e)	18	18	30 da.	(b)	3 da.	—
Arizona	16(e)	16(e)	18	18	30 da.	(b)	(d)	—
Arkansas	17(e)	16(e)	18	18	30 da.	(b)	3 da.	—
California	18(a, e)	16(a, e)	18	18	30 da.	(b, f, g, h)	—	—
Colorado	16(e)	16(e)	18	18	30 da.	(b, g, i)	—	—
Connecticut	16(e)	16(e)	18	18	35 da.	(b)	4 da.	—
Delaware	18(e)	16(e)	18	18	30 da.	(b)	—	(j)
Florida	18(a, e)	16(a, e)	18	18	30 da.	(b)	3 da.	—
Georgia	18(e)	16(e)	18	18	30 da.	(b, f)	3 da.(k)	—
Hawaii	16	16	18	18	30 da.	(b)	—	—
Idaho	16(e)	16(e)	18	18	30 da.	(b)	3 da.(l)	—
Illinois	16(e)	16(e)	18	18	15 da.	(b, f, g)	—	—
Indiana	18(e)	16(e)	18	18	30 da.	(b, f)	3 da.	—
Iowa	16	16	18	18	20 da.	(b)	3 da.	—
Kansas	18(e)	18(e)	18	18	30 da.	(b)	3 da.	—
Kentucky	18(a, e)	16(a, e)	18	18	15 da.	(b, f)	3 da.	—
Louisiana	18(e)	16(e)	18	18	10 da.	(b)	—	72 hrs.
Maine	16(e)	16(e)	18	18	60 da.	(b)	5 da.	—
Maryland	16(e)	16(e)	18	18	—	—	48 hrs.	—
Massachusetts	18(e)	16(e)	18	18	30 da.	(b)	3 da.	—
Michigan	(m)	16(e)	18	18	30 da.	(b)	3 da.	—
Minnesota	18(a)	16(n)	18	18	—	—	5 da.	—
Mississippi	17(e)	15(e)	21	21	30 da.	(b)	3 da.	—
Missouri	15(e)	15(e)	18	18	15 da.	(b)	3 da.	—
Montana	18(e)	18(e)	18	18	20 da.	(b)	5 da.	3 da.
Nebraska	18	16	19	19	30 da.	(b)	2 da.	—
Nevada	16(a, e)	16(a, e)	18	18	—	—	—	—
New Hampshire	14(n)	13(n)	18	18	30 da.	(b)	5 da.	—
New Jersey	18(e)	16(e)	18	18	30 da.	(b)	72 hrs.	—
New Mexico	16(e)	16(e)	18	18	30 da.	(b)	72 hrs.	—
New York	16	14(p)	18	18	30 da.	(b, f)	—	24 hrs.
North Carolina	16	16(e)	18	18	30 da.	(b, r, s)	(t)	—
North Dakota	16	16	18	18	30 da.	(b, v)	—	—

Continued on next page

TABLE 9.1   Cont.

State	Age at Which Marriage Can Be Contracted with Parental Consent		Age below Which Parental Consent is Required		Physical Examination and Blood Test for Male and Female		Waiting Period	
	Male	Female	Male	Female	Period between Examination and Issuance of License	Scope of Medical Examination	Before Issuance of License	After Issuance of License
Ohio	18(e)	16(e)	18(w)	18(w)	30 da.	(b)	5 da.	—
Oklahoma	16(e)	16(e)	18	18	30 da.	(b)	(x)	—
Oregon	17	17	18	18	30 da.(y)	(b)	7 da.	—
Pennsylvania	16(e)	16(e)	18	18	30 da.	(b, v)	3 da.	—
Rhode Island	18(e)	16(e)	18	18	40 da.	(b, g, s)	—	(aa)
South Carolina	16(e)	16(e)	18	18	—	—	24 hrs.	—
South Dakota	16(e)	16(e)	18	18	20 da.	(b)	—	—
Tennessee	16(e)	16(e)	18	18	30 da.	(b)	3 da.(l)	—
Texas	14(e)	14(e)	18	18	21 da.	(b)	—	—
Utah	16(z)	14(a)	18	18	30 da.	(b)	—	—
Vermont	16(e)	16(e)	18	18	30 da.	(b)	—	—
Virginia	16(a, e)	16(a, e)	18	18	30 da.	(b)	—	—
Washington	17(e)	17(e)	18	18	—	(b, s, v)	3 da.	—
West Virginia	(c)	(c)	18	18	30 da.	(b)	3 da.	—
Wisconsin	16	16	18	18	20 da.	(b)	5 da.	—
Wyoming	17(e)	16(e)	19	19	30 da.	(b)	—	—
Dist. of Columbia	18(a)	16(a)	21	18	30 da.	(b)	3 da.	—

Note: Common-law marriage is recognized in Alabama, Colorado, Georgia, Idaho, Iowa, Kansas, Montana, Ohio, Oklahoma, Pennsylvania, Rhode Island, South Carolina, Texas, and the District of Columbia. (a) Parental consent not required if minor was previously married. (b) Venereal diseases. (c) The state of West Virginia no longer has a minimum age for marriage with parental consent. (d) Blood test must be on record for at least 48 hours before issuance of license. (e) Procedure established whereby younger parties may obtain license in special circumstances. (f) Sickle cell anemia. (g) Rubella immunity. (h) Tay-Sachs disease. (i) Rh factor. (j) Residents, 24 hours; nonresidents, 96 hours. (k) Unless parties are 18 years of age or over, or female is pregnant, or applicants are the parents of a living child born out of wedlock. (l) Unless parties are 18 years of age or over. (m) Has provision in law for parental consent for males. (n) Permission of judge also required. (o) Below age of consent and above minimum age, permission of judge, which is given only for special cause, also required. (p) If under 16 years of age, consent of a family court judge also required. (q) Marriage may not be solemnized within 3 days from date on which specimen for serological test was taken. (r) Mental incompetence. (s) Tuberculosis. (t) Forty-eight hours if both are nonresidents of the State. (u) Any unmarried male of the age of 18 years or upwards, and any unmarried female of the age of 15 years or upwards, and not otherwise disqualified, are capable of consenting to and consummating a marriage. If the male or the female is under the age of 18 years, a marriage license shall not be issued without the consent of the parents or guardian, if there are any. (v) Feeblemindedness, imbecility, insanity, chronic alcoholism. (w) Change from 21 became effective January 1, 1974. (x) Seventy-two hours if one or both parties are below the age for marriage without parental consent. (y) Maximum period between examination and expiration of marriage license. (z) Feeblemindedness, mental illness, drug addiction, and chronic alcoholism. (aa) If female is nonresident, must complete and sign license 5 days prior to marriage. (ab) Male under 18 years may not marry.

SOURCE: CBS NEWS ALMANAC 1978, p. 230.

in the communicable stage). Several states do not require a blood test. The couple may then take their license to a justice of the peace or a clergyman, who is responsible for verifying that they meet the requirements of that state. In over one third of the states a couple can marry the same day they meet.

COMMITMENT TO WHOM?

Although the state in which you reside prohibits you from marrying someone who is blood related, mentally incompetent, or under age, it does not provide guidelines for selecting a compatible partner. A basic element of compatibility is the sharing of similar interests and values.

Compatibility is important because it reduces conflict. Whatever your interests, they are shared by the people you choose as close friends. Consider the difficulty of being *married* to someone who doesn't like what you like. A father wrote to his sons about choosing a compatible partner:

> Choose a woman who, by temperament and essential being, loves what you love—broiled swordfish and roast young duck, coffee, Alfred Noyes' "The Highwayman," the watercolors of Winslow Homer in the Chicago Art Institute, the little crescent moon flung like a child's boomerang across Heaven, dogs and cats, guns, "The Song of Solomon," the great prose-epics of J.R.R. Tolkien. Of course, you will differ about details; you will fancy your coffee sweetened, she will prefer it unsweetened—to each his own! —*but you both will like coffee.* (Root, 1975, p. 139)

As this father observed, it is not necessary (nor is it possible) that you and your partner feel the same way about everything. It is necessary that you feel the same way about issues that you and your partner regard as important. Achieving a compatible relationship necessitates your identifying those issues that are important to you and selecting a partner who shares your attitude. "The phrase to remember in choosing a mate," emphasizes a marriage and family teacher at Loyola University in New Orleans, "is 'Know yourself and marry yourself.'" As a means of increasing your self-understanding and identifying a compatible partner, consider each of the following issues and the degree to which you want your spouse to feel about it as you do.

Philosophical Compatibility

The values that determine your philosophy of life are reflected in your interests and activities. For example, a person with an intellectual philosophy of life is likely to read extensively, attend lectures, and pursue graduate study. Consider the degree to which each of the following orientations and their behavioral expressions characterize you and the degree to which you want them to characterize the person you marry.

Religion.   How important is religion to you? How important "should" it be to your partner? Will your marital happiness be increased if you marry within your faith? Will your marriage be more likely to end in divorce if you marry outside your faith? Research on same-faith and mixed-faith marriages provides inconclusive answers (see discussion, Chapter 10). If religion is important in your life, it may also have an important influence on your marriage.

Introspection.   As a student, you may not identify with a particular organized religion but may instead be involved in the movement towards increased introspection. Transcendental meditation, yoga, and "seeking inner peace" emphasize the value of getting in touch with one's feelings and increasing self-awareness. How much importance do you attach to these experiences, and how important is it to you that your partner share them with you?

Political views.   Women's liberation, abortion legislation, environmental protection, national defense, gun control, censorship, and the rights of "gays" all represent various political concerns. While some individuals regard these issues as worthy of thought, discussion, financial support, and organized effort, others are oblivious to their existence as problems, and some feel that politics generally is a colossal bore. To what degree do you and your partner share similar political orientations and to what degree does the similarity or dissimilarity of your attitudes matter?

Recreational Compatibility

In addition to choosing a partner with a philosophy of life compatible with yours, consider the degree to which your recreational interests are compatible. When asked what he saw in his fiancée, an engaged male replied, "She's incredibly fun to be with." Since the sharing of enjoyable experiences is a major reason for commitment, most people feel cheated if the "fun" fails to continue after marriage. One way to evaluate recreational compatibility with your partner is to examine the degree to which each enjoys being with other people and the various recreational interests you share.

Sociability.   Two aspects of sociability are the need for and the liking of other people (Whipple & Whittle, 1976, p. 15). The person who says "I can't stand to be alone" usually feels anxious unless he or she is with someone else. The presence of others is necessary for a sense of psychic balance. A second-term freshman who lived off-campus said, "Eating alone drives me crazy. I have to read the newspaper or turn on the television to distract me from feeling alone. My roommate graduated last semester and left me in this empty apartment. I'm not coping with solitude very well."

The implication of marrying someone who has difficulty tolerating being alone is a restriction of your own "free time." A husband complained, "I was sitting in a cafe eating a cheeseburger with a friend late last Saturday afternoon. When I got home, my wife implied that she had been miserable until I got there. She wasn't vindictive, she just doesn't like being alone."

In addition to needing people, sociability means liking people and seeking frequent interaction with them. Some people view a "good time" as a room full of people, drinking cocktails, eating pimento cheese on celery, laughing at mildly funny jokes, and swapping stories of the week's events. Other people detest such parties and prefer either to be alone with the partner for a candlelight dinner, to share a quiet evening with one other couple, or to work alone in the workshop while the spouse reads a book. Spouses who view a "good time" differently must either delight in their differences, arrive at a compromise, or endure the conflict.

Recreational interests.   To what degree do you share the recreational interests of your partner? What are your respective feelings about attending cultural events (opera, ballet, symphony, the theater), watching sports (football, golf, racing), participating in sports (jogging, skiing, bowling, fishing, hunting, playing tennis), or more sedentary activities (watching TV, going to movies, reading). And how do you feel about going to parties and/or getting high (alcohol or marijuana)?

Early studies of the relationship between the number of shared recreational activities and marital happiness reached different conclusions. Some researchers found that spouses who shared similar recreational interests were happier than couples who did not (Locke, 1951; Benson, 1952), but other researchers disagreed (Hawkins & Walters, 1952; Gerson, 1960).

A more recent study reflected the leisure-time patterns of 216 husbands and 226 wives and how their activities were related to marital satisfaction (Orthner,

Assessing compatibility is a central problem of mate selection. The personal life-styles, values, and interests of two partners must blend together well if the couple is to have a low-conflict and long-lasting relationship.

1975). As might be expected, sharing joint leisure activities was associated with increased marital satisfaction (Orthner, 1975, p. 97).

This study suggests the positive consequences of selecting a partner who enjoys the same recreational activities as you do. But the type of shared interest may be important. Playing cards together encourages interpersonal communication in a way that watching television together may not. One husband reflected, "If you don't share what you're watching, the fact that you're watching television together won't help your marriage." One researcher observed that the more TV couples watch, the less happy they rate their marriages (Reiser, 1972).

Sexual Compatibility

Joint leisure activities are not limited to playing tennis. ". . . making love is the greatest, most beautiful form of play we know. In its purest most wholesome form it is the uninhibited and enthusiastic sharing by husband and wife in the entrancing, fascinating, aesthetic games of sexual relations" (Miller & Robinson, 1963, p. 264).

Identifying a compatible sexual partner is essential for achieving a happy marriage. Sexual compatibility most often refers to *mutually satisfying* sexual activity including similar feelings about the frequency of intercourse and experimentation. Commenting on the conflict that results when there are considerable discrepancies in desire for intercourse, a marriage counselor and physician observed, "If one of very high drive is mated to one of very low drive, a disaster is predictable from the onset" (Trainer, 1975, p. 124). And a wife mused, "If a woman is loved and satisfied sexually she will do anything for her man—but if she isn't she will do anything to him. It is that simple and that uncomplicated" (Athanasiou et al. 1970, p. 45).

How sexually compatible are spouses? In a study of 2,372 well-educated working wives, over two thirds said that their frequency of intercourse was "about right" (Bell & Lobsenz, 1974, p. 176). The wives averaged age thirty-four and reported having intercourse about nine times per month. While 4 percent said that intercourse occurred too frequently, almost one third felt that it did not occur frequently enough. An earlier study that focused exclusively on college-educated wives reported that 25 percent felt that intercourse was "too infrequent" (Bell, 1972, p. 161).

Among the factors affecting the desire for intercourse are age, health, and childhood training. Spouses of similar age who are in good physical and emotional health and who have positive attitudes about sex are more likely to be sexually compatible than partners who are dissimilar in age and health and who feel that sex is "dirty."

In addition to similar desires for frequency of intercourse, sexual compatibility involves similar feelings about experimentation. Most of the 2,372 wives referred to above blamed their husbands for resisting sexual variety. The authors concluded, "What might be called the 'environment' of sex—where and when one has it, what one wears or doesn't wear, what one says or does to provoke a

TABLE 9.2   Characteristics of Morning and Night People.

Factor	Morning People	Night People
Arising early	Easily	With difficulty
Staying up late	With difficulty	Easily
Efficiency/Energy peak	Peaks early in the day	Peaks late in the evening
Activities	Physical; outdoor	Nightlife or quiet
Energy level	High?	Low?
Values	Beginnings, sunrise, breakfast	?

SOURCE: Adams and Cromwell, 1978, p. 8.

sexual response, what erotic aids one uses—is an increasingly important part of sexual satisfaction for today's young wives."

Assessing sexual compatibility may be difficult. Although two partners may be completely satisfied with their sexual relationship prior to marriage, the realities of marriage may alter their sexual relationship. Satiation (they may tire of having sexual intercourse with each other), ill health, job stress, and children may alter their sexual relationship after marriage.

On the other hand, marriage may improve a couple's sexual compatibility. A person who feels guilty about having intercourse while unmarried may be impotent or unable to experience an orgasm and therefore unenthusiastic about sex. But after marriage, the person no longer feels guilty and becomes more relaxed, sexually aggressive, and positive about sex.

Body-Clock Compatibility

Some of us are "morning people," some of us are "night people." Characteristics which differentiate the two are reflected in Table 9.2. Based on these characteristics, there are four combinations: both husband and wife are morning persons, both are night persons, the wife is a morning person while the husband is a night person, and the husband is a morning person and the wife is a night person (Adams and Cromwell, 1978).

But does it matter if the spouses are matched or mismatched in terms of body clocks? Several researchers who studied twenty-eight married graduate students observed that some out-of-phase couples have less serious conversation, fewer shared activities, less sex, poorer marital adjustment, and more unmanaged conflict (Cromwell et al., 1976; Adams & Cromwell, 1978).

Related to the body-clock issue is that of different energy levels. What is your energy level, and how does it compare with the energy level of your partner? If these levels are not similar, each of you must be able to tolerate the differences, or define the differences as unimportant. Otherwise, negative consequences may be in the offing. Two psychologists offer an extreme example:

> You want to sleep late on a weekend morning and he insists on getting up at some ungodly hour. . . . After you have had a hard day and are ready for a quiet evening with a book or TV and early to bed, he wants to go dancing. (Whipple & Whittle, 1976, p. 64)

Marital Role Compatibility

As a potential husband or wife, what do you expect to do in each of these areas and what do you want your spouse to do? Who "should" pay the bills? "Should" the wife have a job or career? If the wife has an opportunity for a better job if she moves to a new location, "should" the husband go with her? Do you plan to have children? If so, what kind of parent do you expect your spouse to be? Who stays home from work when a child is sick? The answers to these questions will help you to evaluate the degree to which you and your partner agree on your respective marital roles. What you expect to do and what you expect your partner to do are less important than that you and your partner view your roles the same way.

Adaptability

Since you and your partner may differ in your marital role expectations, how important is it that you select a marital companion who is both flexible and empathic? Since you and your partner do have differences and will change in unpredictable ways throughout your relationship, it is highly desirable that you link yourself with someone who has the capacity to minimize the stress associated with differences and change. Just as adaptability and flexibility are positively correlated with marital happiness, the absence of these skills is associated with marital unhappiness (Buerkle et al., 1961; Crouse et al., 1968; Kieren & Tallman, 1972).

Communication

The happiest marriages are those in which the partners display good communication skills (Corrales, 1974). Being able to express what one feels is a prime requisite for good communication (Bienvenu, 1970). Expressing one's feelings involves using "I" and being specific. The statement, "I would like you to tell me that you love me," is preferable to the statement, "It would be nice if you would be the way you were when we first met." The former statement communicates clearly how the individual feels and what he or she wants.

Good communication also involves congruent messages. Every message has two parts—verbal and nonverbal (Satir, 1964). When the verbal does not match the nonverbal, or vice versa, a confused message is transmitted. "He told me that he loves me, but he hasn't called me in a week," remarked a bewildered woman. To assess the degree to which your partner displays good communication skills, begin to notice specific "I" statements, and the degree to which his or her words and behavior say the same thing.

Power Compatibility

Since each partner is continually trying to influence the other, good communication may involve an understanding of the power distribution in the relationship. Power in the marital relationship has been assessed by observing who makes the decisions (Blood & Wolfe, 1960), who wins a disagreement (Heer, 1962) and by asking, "Who's the real boss in your family?" (Turk & Bell, 1972). Using these criteria, two researchers studied the power relationships in 211 families and concluded that, in general, husbands had more power than their wives (Turk & Bell, 1972, pp. 216–17).

The relationship between who has the power and how happy the spouses are is unclear. One study concluded that mates are happiest when the husband has the most power (Kolb & Straus, 1974). But other studies conclude that equal or shared power is associated with marital happiness (Blood & Wolfe, 1960; Centers, Raven, & Rodrigues, 1971). In your relationship, it may be less important who has the power and more important that you and your partner are aware of who has how much power in what areas and that you feel comfortable with the power distribution in your relationship.

PREDICTING MARITAL HAPPINESS

Does carefully considering compatibility issues before making your commitment choice ensure that you will be happily married ten years from now? No. It is not even possible to predict what your degree of marital satisfaction will be three days after your wedding. There are several reasons why.

Illusion of the Perfect Mate

You will not find the perfect mate—a partner who satisfies all of your expectations. And the one quality that is lacking may become the only quality that is important to you (Sammons, 1978). Because it is lacking, you may become willing to consider a divorce. When columnist Ann Landers asked her readers, "If you had it to do all over again, would you marry the same person?" she received fifty thousand responses. Fifty-two percent replied "No" and 48 percent said "Yes" (Landers, 1977).

Deception During Premarital Period

The premarital period for many is a time of deception. Each partner is reluctant to criticize the other (Haun & Stinnett, 1974, p. 17) and tries to present only those facets of himself or herself which the other will perceive favorably. To illustrate this deception, 170 university students who dated steadily or were engaged kept a record of everything they did for one week and exchanged their daily logs for each other's evaluation. Throughout the evaluations were phrases like "I have discovered," "I didn't realize," and "I found out." Specific revelations included:

> "I didn't realize that Frank drank so frequently and heavily. He does not indulge so heavily when with me."
>
> "Though aware of a female's tendency to curse when among other females, I did not realize it was to such an extent and quite often as vile as a male's language."
>
> "He persuades me not to cut any of my classes and to keep up with my studies while he ignores all of his own obligations." (Knox & Patrick, 1971, p. 110)

A major reason for withholding undesirable aspects of one's self is the desire to maintain the relationship. If heavy drinking or cursing will be disapproved by one's partner, it is "safest" to exhibit these behaviors only around those other than the potential mate. This allows for the expression of the behaviors without threatening the upcoming marriage.

Confinement of Marriage

Another factor that makes it impossible to predict your continued happiness is the difference between the premarital period and marriage. While premarital norms permit relative freedom to move in and out of relationships, marriage involves a legal contract. One recently married person described marriage as an iron gate that clangs shut behind you, and "getting it open is almost impossible." One's freedom to leave a premarital relationship is transformed by the wedding ceremony. Thereafter there is social pressure to "work things out" and a feeling of obligation to do so that was not previously present. The new sense of confinement often brings out the worst in partners who seemed very cooperative before marriage.

Balancing Work and Relationship Demands

Predicting marital happiness is also difficult because the partners must necessarily shift their focus from each other to the business of life. Careers and children emerge as concerns which often take precedence over seeing movies and having fun together. Time and energy spent on jobs and childrearing often leave marriage partners too tired to interact with each other. And the more abrasive communication encouraged by conditions of stress has negative consequences for the way the partners feel about each other.

Most newlyweds expect their marriages to be happy, but in reality it is impossible to know whether or not a marriage will last. Change is inevitable, and it may just as well weaken as strengthen a marital relationship.

Inevitability of Change

Change is inevitable. Just as you are not the same person you were ten years ago, you will continue to change again and again. The nature, direction, and intensity of the ways in which you will change is predictable neither for you nor for your partner. You, your partner, and your relationship will never be the same two years (or two months) in a row.

Reflecting on change in her marriage, one woman recalled, "When we were married we were very active in politics. Now I have my law degree and I'm working for legal aid, but Jerry is totally immersed in meditating. I never imagined that we'd have nothing to say to each other after only three years of marriage."

Hence, whether you will be happily married ten years after your wedding cannot be predicted. While selecting a compatible companion is basic, giving up any illusions of finding a perfect mate, minimizing premarital deception, accepting the confinement of marriage, balancing work and relationship demands, and adapting to whatever changes occur are equally crucial.

COMMITMENT TIMING

Launching an exploratory satellite to a distant planet involves precise timing. If lift-off occurs at other than the right time, the satellite will miss its orbit and be lost in space. Getting into a successful marital orbit also involves timing. (Staying in such an orbit is a separate problem.) Two matters to consider in timing your commitment to marriage are age and education.

Age

Your age and that of your partner at the time of marriage are highly predictive of future marital happiness and stability (Lee, 1977; Bahr, 1977). Individuals who get married in their teens report greater marital unhappiness and have higher divorce rates than those who delay marriage (Lasswell, 1974; DeLissovoy, 1973; Glick & Norton, 1971). While age itself does not increase marital happiness and stability, increased age at marriage is associated with greater personal maturity, higher education, better income, and parental approval of the wedding. Those who are older are more likely to have prepared for marriage by clarifying their values and goals, establishing an economic base, and working out good relationships with parents and in-laws.

But how old is "older"? How long does a couple need to wait in order to maximize their potential for a good marriage? Women who marry when they are twenty-five and men who marry when they are twenty-eight report greater marital satisfaction and have lower divorce rates than those who marry earlier (Lasswell, 1974, pp. 241–42). Supporting the positive consequences of delaying marriage, a researcher who analyzed the divorce rates in California by age at first marriage concluded that "A marriage begun at age eighteen was 2.2 times as likely to end in divorce as a marriage begun when the male was twenty-nine" (Schoen, 1975, p. 554). For women getting married at age sixteen rather than waiting until age twenty-seven increased the chances of divorce 2.4 times (p. 554). After hearing these statistics in a marriage and family class, one student responded, "Getting married at my age [eighteen] would be like being operated on by a surgeon with one arm. I'd have half the chance of coming out of the thing alive."

Education

The amount of education you get and whether you or your partner has more education may also affect your marital happiness and the stability of your relationship. Men who complete college have a lower probability of divorce than men who complete only high school or who leave college without graduating (Glick & Norton, 1971, p. 315). The reason for greater marital stability among college-educated men is not the education itself but the economic potential associated with increased education.[3] Well-educated men with low incomes are more likely to divorce than men with little schooling but high incomes (Cutright, 1971). The availability of money determines what a couple can have and do. "Consumption is a daily activity, and it provides the wife with a constant empirical monitoring of how well her husband is doing in his role as breadwinner. A satisfactory level of consumption should help the wife to maintain her own feelings of competence in her role of wife . . . and should act to reinforce her positive view of her husband" (Cutright, 1971, p. 296). One despondent wife mused, "It's hard to love a man who can't afford to take you to the movies."

While the variable most influencing the marital stability of women is age rather than economic potential, the college-educated woman is more likely to be happily married than the non-college woman (Bumpass & Sweet, 1972). In addition, better educated women are more satisfied with the love and affection in their marriages (Blood & Wolfe, 1960, p. 229) and are more sexually responsive (Kinsey et al., 1953). In view of the benefits associated with a college education, one researcher flatly stated, "Don't marry until you are out of school" (Stephens, 1970, p. 195).

But does it make a difference if the wife stays in school longer than her husband? Yes. When the wife has more education than her husband, when she is a college graduate and he isn't, there is a greater risk of divorce than if the husband has more education (Bumpass & Sweet, 1972; Scanzoni, 1968).

Timing the commitment to marriage is important, then. The more age and education you and your partner have, the greater your chances of achieving marital stability and happiness. If there are differences in your age and education at the time of marriage, the educational differences seem to be more important if they are great or if the wife's education is superior to the husband's.

TERMINATION BEFORE ENGAGEMENT

What about breaking up before a marital commitment is made? Why and how do relationships end? To find out, a team of researchers studied 103 couples who had terminated their relationships (Hill et al., 1976). The couples were part of a larger group of 220[4] dating couples who had completed a questionnaire two years earlier.

Reasons

By comparing the data from those couples who broke up and those who were still together, it is possible to identify causes of the terminations.

Minimal involvement. When completing the initial questionnaire, the couples who eventually broke up had the following characteristics: (1) They had been dating each other for a short period of time; (2) They were not dating each other exclusively; (3) They were reluctant to define themselves as being "in love" or to predict that they would eventually marry; (4) They did not feel close to their partners (Hill, Rubin, & Peplau, 1976, p. 151).

While these characteristics suggest that the couples who eventually broke up never felt very strongly about each other, over half of them reported that they were "in love" at the time of the initial survey. Hence, the idea that "love will keep us together" was not true for these couples.

Being too different.   Being dissimilar was also related to breaking up. Specifically, those partners who were different in age, educational plans, intelligence, and physical attractiveness were more likely to break up than those who were alike in these respects (Hill, Rubin, & Peplau, 1976, p. 153). But differences in other background variables, including social class, religion, and desired family size, didn't seem to matter. The researchers suggested that before the time of their initial questionnaire most couples were already sufficiently matched on these issues (p. 154).

One partner more involved.   There was a greater likelihood that relationships would break up when one partner was more involved than the other. Fifty-four percent of such relationships were terminated by the end of the two-year period. In contrast, only 23 percent of the relationships had been terminated in which the partners were equally involved (Hill, Rubin, & Peplau, 1976, p. 153). And one partner's being more involved than another is not unusual. Of 150 romantically involved couples at UCLA, more than half saw themselves as more involved (20 percent) or less involved (30 percent) than their partners (White, 1977).

The explosive nature of an unequal relationship was suggested by Blau (1964): "Commitments must stay abreast for a love relationship to develop into a lasting mutual attachment. . . . Only when two lovers' affection for and commitment to one another expand at roughly the same pace do they tend mutually to reinforce their love" (p. 84). One partner who was the less involved in an eight-month relationship said, "I'm getting too much control of the relationship, and I don't like it. I don't want to hurt her, but I'm beginning to view her as the clinging vine type. I figure we won't be together next semester. I'm sure of it."

Timing of Terminations

For students, breakups tend to occur with the school calendar (Hill, Rubin, & Peplau, 1976, p. 156). June (when school is over), September (when summer vacation is over), and January (when the first semester is over) are the months in which couples are most likely to break up. As one marriage and family student said, "I told him that I wanted us to date others [translation: I wanted to date others] while we were separated during the summer. As it turned out, I didn't write after that, became involved with someone else, and didn't see him again."

Who Terminates the Relationship?

Relationships are rarely ended by mutual agreement. Eighty-five percent of the women and 87 percent of the men reported that one person wanted to end the relationship more than the other. That person is more often the woman (Hill, Rubin, & Peplau, p. 161). Fifty-one percent of the relationships were ended by women, 42 percent by men (p. 158). Two additional studies have observed the same phenomenon (Hill, 1974; Rubin, 1969).

One possible explanation why women are more likely to terminate a relationship is that women may be more sensitive to signs of eventual trouble. For example, women not only cited more problems in relationships than men did but pointed to different kinds of problems. While women expressed concern about "differences in interests" and "differences in intelligence," men were more likely to cite "living too far apart" as a reason to break up (Hill, Rubin, & Peplau, 1976, p. 147).

Recovery

Recovering from a relationship that the other partner has terminated is more difficult for men than for women. Men tend to feel more depressed and lonely than women who have been "dumped." In addition, men find it extremely difficult to accept the fact that they are no longer loved and that the relationship is over (Hill, Rubin, & Peplau, 1976, p. 147).

In summary, lack of deep involvement, one partner being more involved than the other, and being dissimilar in certain ways were significantly related to terminating a relationship. A woman is more likely to terminate a relationship, and a student breakup is most likely to occur in June, September, or January. Getting over a breakup is easier for the person who initiated it and generally easier for women than men.

ENGAGEMENT

What are the implications of becoming engaged and how can the engagement period be used to increase future marital happiness?

Implications of Engagement

The engagement period is usually regarded as serious, partner-exclusive, public, and as a time for attending to wedding preparations. Let's look more closely at some of the implications and consider several ways of assessing and strengthening relationships during engagement.

Serious.   An engagement is a specific commitment to marry. Once the words "Let's get married" have been spoken and agreed to, the relationship assumes a different status. The other person is no longer viewed as a casual partner but as a future spouse. While some regard engagement (and marriage) frivolously, there is a strong tendency to take it seriously.

Partner-exclusive.   Engagements are usually exclusive relationships with no outside dating. While each partner may have gone out with several people during the pre-engagement stage of their relationship, doing so after the engagement is usually considered "cheating" and often regarded as a potential threat to the impending marriage. "After I found out he had been seeing his old girlfriend," said one fiancée, "I figured he would also be unfaithful to me when we were married. I confronted him about it, and he said to mind my own business. We broke up."

Public.   Prior to the announcement of a future wedding, the love relationship belongs solely to the partners. Engagement makes it public. Parents and peers become involved and communicate their evaluations of each partner's marital choice. A senior recalled, "When I was just dating Laura, my best friend said nothing about her one way or the other. But when I told him we were getting married after graduation he told me that she had a 'for rent' sign in her head (vacant brains) and I would be crazy if I married her." One researcher observed that evaluations of this nature by significant others (parents and friends) are related to the breakup of relationships (Lewis, 1973).

The period of engagement is typically both exciting and exhausting. Choosing rings may be a personally satisfying task for the couple, but many aspects of wedding preparations (e.g., ordering and sending invitations, planning the service and reception) tax the patience and endurance of both the couple and their families.

Wedding preparations. Most first weddings take place in a traditional setting—a church or synagogue—with bridesmaids and ushers. The traditional wedding requires tremendous preparation. *Modern Bride* magazine lists forty-seven responsibilities for the bride and seventeen for the groom if they are to have the "perfect wedding" (1976, pp. 38, 92).

Using the Engagement Period

Productive use of your engagement period might include examining your relationship, recognizing danger signals, visiting your future in-laws, assessing your "comfort" level, prolonging the engagement under certain conditions, and clarifying your expectations.

Examine your relationship. In a commercial for an oil filter, a mechanic says that he has just completed a "ring job" on a car engine which will cost the owner over $300. He goes on to say that a $3.98 oil filter would have made the job unnecessary and ends his soliloquy with, "Pay me now, or pay me later." The same idea applies to the consequences of using or not using the engagement period to examine your relationship. At some point you will have to take a very close look at your partner and your relationship, but will you do it now or later? Doing so later may be more costly than doing so before the wedding.

In examining your relationship, consider the compatibility issues discussed earlier in this chapter. To what degree are you and your partner compatible, similar, or dissimilar on the issues that matter to you?

Recognize danger signals. As you examine your relationship, you may observe patterns that predict doom for your marital relationship. Two such danger signals are an on-and-off engagement and frequent arguments (Landis & Landis, 1977, pp. 52–53). A roller coaster engagement is predictive of a marital relationship with the same pattern. But the costs of separating during a marriage are higher. Peers say of an engaged couple who temporarily break their engagement, "They've split up." If the same couple splits up after they are married, their peers will say, "They're separated and headed for a divorce." The same is true of arguments. Lovers' quarrels become the married couple's fights. Use the engagement period to develop a pattern of resolving differences. And if this is not possible, consider the consequences of being married to someone with whom you can't resolve conflict.

Visit your future in-laws. Since engagements often involve increased interaction with each partner's parents, you might take the opportunity to assess more closely the type of family your partner came from and the implications for your marriage. When visiting your future in-laws, observe their standard of living, their emotional closeness, and the degree to which your partner is like the parent of the same sex. How does the standard of living of your partner's parents compare with the standard of living of your own family? And how does the emotional closeness of your partner's family compare with that of your own family? Such comparisons are significant because both you and your partner will reflect to some degree your respective home environments. And if you want to know what your partner may be like in twenty years, look at his or her parent of the same sex. There is some tendency for a male to become like his father, a female like her mother.

Assess your relationship comfort level.　As a final way of using your engagement period productively, ask yourself, "How comfortable do I feel with my partner in our relationship?" Two researchers (Haun & Stinnett, 1974) developed a scale to assess six basic elements of relationship comfort (Hindman, 1972):

1. Empathy—the ability to mentally place oneself in the position of another and see things from that person's viewpoint;
2. Spontaneity—the open and natural expression of feelings, and freedom from extreme guardedness;
3. Trust—the willingness to entrust oneself to the other person's care and to be honest and trustworthy in the relationship;
4. Interest-care—having a genuine interest in and concern for the other person's welfare;
5. Respect—a consideration and regard for the uniqueness of the other individual;
6. Criticalness-hostility—the tendency to criticize the other person and express hostility when the other's actions are different. (Haun & Stinnett, 1974, p. 14)

The Couple Comfortableness Orientation Scale based on these characteristics and a Marriage Prediction Scale (Burgess, Locke, & Thomes, 1963) were completed by 143 formally engaged couples. A comparison of the scores on both scales demonstrated that those who rated themselves high in comfort level also had high scores on the marriage prediction scale.

Prolong your engagement if . . .　Even though you and your partner may feel comfortable with each other, there are four conditions under which you might consider prolonging your engagement. In combination, these conditions argue against getting married.

1. Short Courtship. While you may know happily married people who married soon after they met, the probability of such marital success is low. In general, the longer a couple's involvement before marriage, the greater their chance of achieving a happy marital relationship. An extended courtship provides you with an opportunity to observe your mate in a variety of settings. But how long is long enough? A year is the minimum (Stephens, 1970).

2.   Lack of Money. A divorced woman listened intently as her lover explained the details of his finances: "Since I too am divorced, I pay alimony and child support. The money that's left barely pays for my food and rent. I'm writing a novel now and will be financially OK if it sells. If it doesn't sell, my money situation will be tight." The woman refused to see this man again and said, "I love him, but I loved my first husband, too. We literally ate soup, bologna, and peaches for most of our meals. I'm tired of being poor. People who say that love is all you need to make a marriage work must have money." And research demonstrates the significance of money on the marital relationship: the higher the husband's income the greater the chance that a couple will remain married (Cutright, 1971).

3.   Parental Disapproval. A parent recalled, "I knew when I met the boy it wouldn't work out. I told my daughter and pleaded that she not marry him. She did anyway and now they are divorced." Such parental predictions often come true. But parental predictions are also true when parents approve of the marriage and predict a happy marital relationship.

Even though parents who reject the commitment choice of their offspring are often regarded as unfair, their opinions should not be taken lightly. The parents' own experience in marriage and their intimate knowledge of their offspring combine to help them assess how their child might get along with a particular mate in marriage. Should your parents disapprove of your marital choice, try to evaluate their concerns objectively. Their insights may prove valuable.

4.   Premarital Pregnancy. About one fourth of all marriages occur while the bride is pregnant (Broderick & Hicks, 1970). The spouses of such marriages report more marital unhappiness and have a higher incidence of divorce than those who do not conceive children before marriage (Christensen & Meissner, 1953; Monohan, 1960). Combined with a short premarital relationship, lack of economic preparation, and parental/in-law hostility, premarital pregnancy represents an ominous beginning for newlyweds.

Although you *can* marry after knowing your partner for a brief time, with little money, while pregnant, and against your parents' wishes, consider the consequences of doing so. Even if you have a stable, enjoyable relationship, the odds are stacked against you. In contrast, you can begin marriage with the chances of success in your favor—a relationship of at least one year, a stable, adequate income, parents who approve, and no pregnancy.

Delaying marriage until all of the right conditions are met may be extremely difficult. Most couples assume that *their* marriage will be different, will not end in divorce, and that love is enough to compensate for factors such as a premarital pregnancy or lack of money. Of 1,300 couples who had applied for a marriage license and who were involved in premarital counseling, only 1 percent decided not to marry. Only thirteen couples broke their relationship even though over half the females were pregnant at the time of the counseling (Shonick, 1975, p. 322).

Although a premarital pregnancy by no means guarantees trouble for a marriage, it does increase the likelihood of it—as do parental disapproval, a short courtship, and lack of money.

PERSONAL MARRIAGE CONTRACTS

Some couples attempt to minimize misunderstandings by developing a private contract that reflects their understanding of the relationship in which they wish to be involved. (See *Antenuptial Agreement.*) One researcher reported on eight hundred personal marriage contracts including those of married, engaged, and cohabiting couples (Sussman, 1975). While the contracts varied widely they dealt with some or all of the following issues:

1. a division of household labor
2. use of living space
3. each partner's responsibility for childrearing and socialization
4. property, debts, living expenses

    5. career commitment and legal domicile

    6. rights of inheritance

    7. use of surnames

    8. range of permissible relationships with others

    9. obligations of the marital dyad in various life sectors such as work, . . . leisure, community, and social life

   10. grounds for . . . divorce

   11. initial and subsequent contract periods, and negotiability

   12. position regarding procreation or adoption of children (Sussman, Cogswell, & Ross, 1973)

The legality of marriage contracts often depends on whether or not the partners have a marriage license. If they are legally married, their private agreement will not take precedence over the laws of the state governing their marriage (Wells, 1976). For example, although the partners may agree in writing that the husband will not pay alimony to the wife if they divorce, the wife may still collect alimony if the state awards alimony because she is his legal wife. On the other hand, if the partners are not married, their agreement has legal force like any other private contract.[5]

Although you may choose not to develop a written document specifying your understanding of the marriage relationship, discussing issues you regard as relevant is likely to have positive consequences.[6]

TRENDS

The forecast for commitment patterns includes new criteria for selecting a mate, greater caution in entering marriage, and the development of alternatives to formal engagement. "Increasingly individuals are seeking a relationship that will provide growth for them as individuals and as a couple. More than a companionship marriage as defined by Burgess, there is a search for an authentic and mutually actualizing relationship" (Olson, 1972, p. 390).

With the continuing increase in divorce, couples will become more cautious about entering marriage. The growing possibility that "divorce may happen to me, too" should reduce the number of hasty, ill-conceived marital commitments. The fact that the age at marriage is inching upward may reflect a greater determination to marry when the conditions are right, not when the emotions are ready. And the use of personal marriage contracts reflects a concern that each partner be aware of the other's expectations so as to help prevent misunderstandings.

In addition to new criteria for selecting a mate and increased caution in entering marriage, alternatives to the traditional formal engagement will become more acceptable. While the engagement ring and announcement of the impending wedding will probably be the script for most people, a growing number, particularly those who cohabit, will bypass the formality of an engagement period.

Antenuptial Agreement

WILLIAM K. O'CONNELL and MARIJEAN SUELZLE, in contemplating their marriage this day, have entered into an agreement with respect to such marriage for the following reasons and with reference to the following facts:

I PURPOSE

A. Purpose of Agreement. We intend by this Agreement to recognize each other as equal partners in our marriage and to overcome the inequalities and unequal burdens thrust upon married persons by custom and tradition and by California's laws.

B. Intent to Define Property Rights. The parties to this Agreement intend and desire to define their respective rights in the property of the other, and to avoid such interests which, except for the operation of this Agreement, they might acquire in the property of the other as incidents of their marriage relationship.

C. Agreement Conditioned Upon Marriage. This Agreement is entered into in consideration of marriage, and its effectiveness is expressly conditioned upon such marriage between the parties actually taking place; and if, for any reason, the marriage is not consummated, the Agreement will be of no force or effect.

D. Respective Contributions to Household. The parties to this Agreement desire to define the respective contributions each will make to the expansion and maintenance of the household from their separate property and the community property in order to maintain the standard of living desired by both.

II RECITAL

A. Disclosure of Property. Both parties to this Agreement have made to each other, and in the future will make to each other, a full and complete disclosure of the nature, extent and probable value of all their property, estate and expectancies.

III AGREEMENTS

A. Property of Each Spouse to Be Separate Property; Exceptions.

1. MARIJEAN SUELZLE covenants and agrees that all property now owned by WILLIAM K. O'CONNELL, of whatsoever nature and wheresoever located and any property which he may hereafter acquire, whether real, personal, or mixed, including but not limited to any earnings, salaries, commissions, or income resulting from his personal services, skills, and efforts shall be and remain his sole and separate property, subject to his control and management, to use and dispose of as he sees fit and as if no marriage had been entered into, except as herein otherwise provided.

2. WILLIAM K. O'CONNELL covenants and agrees that all property now owned by MARIJEAN SUELZLE, of whatsoever nature and wheresoever located and any property which she may hereafter acquire, whether real, personal, or mixed, including but not limited to any earnings, salaries, commissions, or income resulting from her personal services, skills, and efforts shall be and remain her sole and separate property, subject to her control and management, to use and dispose of as she sees fit and as if no marriage had been entered into, except as herein otherwise provided.

3. Whenever any real or personal property, or any interest therein or encumbrance thereon, is acquired by either party by an instrument in writing, the presumption is that the same is his or her separate property, subject to his or her management and control.

4. The parties during the marriage may contract and agree from time to time to change certain items of property from separate property to community property and from community property to separate property, by a written contract duly acknowledged by the parties, or by oral contract if the contract is fully confirmed, ratified, and executed after the marriage.

5. In the event either party is involuntarily employed or voluntarily unemployed by agreement of the parties, or is unable to work during the period of injury, infirmity, maternity, or illness, then the earnings, salaries, commissions, or income of both parties during any of said periods shall be deemed to be community property subject to the joint control of the parties.

B. Control of Community Property.

1. The parties shall have joint control of the community personal property and community real property, and neither shall make a gift of, nor dispose of the same without valuable consideration, nor sell, nor convey, nor lease, nor encumber the real or personal property of the community without the voluntary, written consent of the other.

2. Either party may act as agent for the other.

C. Liability of Property for Debts and Torts of the Parties.

1. Property designated as community property of the parties herein in accordance with the terms hereof shall be liable for the contracts and debts of the parties after marriage, if said contracts and debts are connected with community business, but only after resort is had to the separate property of the party incurring such contract or debt.

2. Property designated as community property of the parties herein in accordance with the terms hereof shall be liable for the contracts, debts and tortious obligations of the parties incurred before marriage, but only after resort is first had to the separate property of the party incurring such contract, debt, or tortious obligation.

3. The separate property of neither party is liable for the debts or tortious liability of the other, but such separate property shall be liable for the payment of the debts heretofore or hereafter incurred by the parties for the necessities of life furnished to them or either of them while they are living together or for debts heretofore or hereafter contracted for goods, materials, money, or services not considered by the parties to be necessities of life, provided both parties contract in writing with the furnishers of said goods, materials, money, or services.

4. The separate property of the parties shall not be liable for any debts or obligations secured by a mortgage, deed of trust, or other hypothecation of the community property unless each party expressly assents in writing to the liability of his or her separate property for such debts or obligations.

D. Responsibilities of the Parties to Each Other.

1. Each party shall share the expenses of maintaining and expanding their household in the same proportion as their earnings shall bear to each other. Neither party shall expect to be reimbursed from community funds any amounts expended from their separate funds for the maintenance and expansion of their household.

2. Both parties shall be obligated to share the household duties, provide affection and companionship to the other, and to be available for sexual relations.

3. In the event the parties give birth to or adopt children, the parties shall share the responsibilities of and the privileges of the care of the children and shall provide for the support of the children in the same proportion as their earnings shall bear to each other.

E. Other.

1. It is the parties' present intention that each shall continue working outside the household and shall continue further their educations.

2. The parties shall jointly head the family, and both shall choose the family residence and mode of living. Each party shall have the right to maintain his or her own legal residence, notwithstanding the legal residence or domicile of the other.

3. Each party shall, after marriage, use the name he or she chooses.

4. Our children shall carry as their surname, "O'Connell."

IV RECORDATION

This Antenuptial Agreement, or a memorandum thereof, may be recorded in the Official Records of Alameda County, or in any County where we hold real property or reside, by either of us.

V SAVING CLAUSE

If any portion of this Antenuptial Agreement be unenforceable under the laws of California, it is the intention of the parties that the remaining portions thereof shall remain in full force and effect.

IN WITNESS WHEREOF, we have hereunto set our hands and entered into this Agreement at Angel Island, San Francisco Bay, the date first hereinabove written.

_____

William K. O'Connell

_____

Marijean Suelzle

SOURCE: Suelzle and O'Connell, 1972.

SUMMARY

For most, marriage implies a lifetime commitment. It is one of the most significant commitments you might make. Both the time when you make the marital commitment and the characteristics of the person you commit yourself to are important. The available research suggests that marriage in the mid-twenties after college is associated with greater marital happiness than teenage marriage.

Selecting someone who shares a similar philosophy of life is essential for creating and maintaining a compatible relationship. Consider the degree to which you and your partner are religious, introspective, and politically sensitive.

In addition to selecting one who shares your views, consider recreational compatibility. Such compatibility involves having similar needs for social life and enjoying similar leisure interests in which you can jointly participate. Consider also the degree to which you and your partner have similar desires for frequency of intercourse and experimentation. It is important that each be aware of the other's sexual expectations, as well as other marital role expectations.

Regardless of your initial compatibility, both you and your partner will change throughout your relationship. Such changes necessitate the skills of adaptability. Related to adaptability are good communications skills. These include expressing one's feelings and sending congruent verbal and body language messages. The person who makes specific statements that are prefaced by "I" displays good communication skills.

Although you may begin marriage with the most compatible companion imaginable, it is really impossible to predict your future marital happiness. Deception during courtship, the confinement of marriage, the "business" of marriage, and the inevitable changes that occur after marriage result in a different relationship which requires flexibility and adaptation. You will never be married to exactly the same person in the same relationship two months in a row.

The private commitment to marry usually leads to a public commitment— engagement. Not only are engagements more serious than casual relationships; they are frequently partner-exclusive and open to the scrutiny of peers and parents as the couple move toward their wedding day. The engagement period should be used to examine your relationship, recognize danger signals, visit your future in-laws, and assess your comfort level.

The future of marriage commitment patterns includes selecting a mate who will provide or permit growth for the partner, delaying commitment until favorable conditions prevail, and bypassing the traditional engagement period. While most couples will become formally engaged, not doing so will become more common.

STUDY QUESTIONS

1. Discuss the meaning of commitment from an individual, social, and legal perspective. In what four ways does state law control marriage?
2. Why is "Know yourself and marry yourself" a basic guideline for choosing a mate?
3. What are the essential elements of sociability and why are these important in marital choice?
4. In what way may recreational activities relate to marital happiness?
5. Define sexual compatibility and discuss its significance for marital happiness.
6. What is body-clock compatibility and what are its implications for marriage?
7. To what degree do you and your partner share similar marital-role expectations? Discuss the research on marital-role expectations.
8. Discuss the relationship between adaptability and happy marriages. Is adaptability important for each spouse?
9. What are the basic elements of good communication?
10. How can power be assessed in the marital relationship?
11. What is the relationship between marital power and marital happiness?
12. Even though you feel extremely confident that you have selected the most compatible partner for yourself, why is it impossible to predict that you will be happily married ten years from today?
13. Discuss the relationship between age and future marital happiness.
14. What is the "best" age for females and males to marry in terms of predicted marital happiness?

15. Why is higher education associated with future marital happiness?
16. Discuss the consequences of the wife's having more education than her husband.
17. Discuss why pre-engagement relationships are terminated, when, and by whom and the nature of the recovery of the parties involved.
18. Discuss four implications of the engagement period.
19. Discuss the ways in which you can use your engagement period to the greatest advantage.
20. Discuss potential benefits of personal marriage contracts.
21. Discuss three trends in marital commitment patterns.

NOTES

1. Early marriage particularly reduces the probability that the female will continue her formal education (Elder and Rockwell, 1976).

2. Early marriage particularly reduces the subsequent level of income for the male (Call and Otto, 1977).

3. Higher grade-point averages are also associated with higher incomes. In one study of business administration students, those with higher grade-point averages (for seven classes) were making $700 more per month ten years after graduation than those with low grade-point averages (Harrell & Harrell, 1974). This study supports the adage, "The more you learn, the more you earn."

4. Ninety percent were not engaged at the time the study was initiated.

5. The legal status of personal marriage contracts may be changing. See Sussman (1975).

6. Rolfe (1977) identified issues that are relevant to discuss (and perhaps treat in a contract) for the situation in which a couple marries and lives with either set of parents. Also, available from the Institute for Human Responsiveness, Inc. (Dept. J), 6200 Winchester Road, Lexington, Kentucky 40511, is *Equalog Contract*. This is a do-it-yourself guide which helps couples specify the nature of their relationship and encourages an open negotiation process in which both partners are equal.

BIBLIOGRAPHY

Adams, B. N., and Cromwell, R. E. Morning and night people in the family: A preliminary statement. *The Family Coordinator,* 1978, *27,* 1, 5–13.

Athanasiou, R., Shaver, P., and Tavris, C. Sex. *Psychology Today,* July 1970, 39–52.

Bahr, Stephen. The effects of income and age at marriage on marital stability. Paper presented at the meeting of the American Sociological Association, Chicago, 1977.

Bell, R. R. Some emerging sexual expectations among women. In *The social dimension of human sexuality,* R. R. Bell and M. Gordon (eds.). Boston: Little, Brown, 1972, 158–65.

_____. *Marriage and family interaction.* Homewood, Ill.: Dorsey Press, 1975.

Bell, R. R., and Lobsenz, N. M. Married sex. *Redbook,* September 1974, 75 et passim.

Benson, P. The interest of happily married couples. *Marriage and Family Living,* 1952, *14,* 276–80.

Bienvenu, M. J., Sr. Measurement of marital communication. *The Family Coordinator,* 1970, *19,* 1, 26–31.

Blau, P. M. *Exchange and power in social life.* New York: John Wiley and Sons, 1964.

Blood, R. O., Jr., and Wolfe, D. M. *Husbands and wives.* New York: Free Press, 1960.

Broderick, C., and Hicks, M. Toward a typology of behavior patterns exhibited during courtship in the United States. *Sociology of the Family,* 1970, *14,* 473–85.

Buerkle, J. V., Anderson, T., and Badgley, R. F. Altruism, role conflict, and marital adjustment: A factor analysis of marital interaction. *Marriage and Family Living,* 1961, *23,* 20–26.

Bumpass, L. L., and Sweet, J. A. Differentials in marital instability: 1970. *American Sociological Review,* 1972, *37,* 754–66.

Burgess, E. W., Locke, H. J., and Thomes, M. M. *The family* (3rd ed.). New York: American Book Company, 1963.

Call, V., and Otto, L. Age at marriage as a mobility contingency: Estimates for the Nye-Berardo model. *Journal of Marriage and the Family,* 1977, *39,* 1, 67–79.

CBS News Almanac 1978. M. A. Bacheller (ed.). Maplewood, N.J.: Hammond Almanac, Inc., 1977.

Centers, R., Raven, B. H., and Rodrigues, A. Conjugal power structure: A re-examination. *American Sociological Review,* 1971, *36,* 264–78.

Christensen, H. T., and Meissner, H. H. Studies in child spacing: Premarital pregnancy as a factor in divorce. *American Sociological Review,* 1953, *18,* 641–4.

Corrales, R. The influence of family life's cycle categories, marital power, spousal agreement, and communication styles upon marital satisfaction in the first six years of marriage. Unpublished doctoral dissertation, University of Minnesota, 1974.

Cromwell, R. E., Keeney, B. P., and Adams, B. N. Temporal patterning in the family. *Family Process,* 1976, *15,* 3, 343–8.

Crouse, B., Karlins, M., and Schroder, H. Conceptual complexity and marital happiness. *Journal of Marriage and the Family.* 1968, *30,* 4, 643–6.

Cutright, P. Income and family events: Marital stability. *Journal of Marriage and the Family,* 1971, *33,* 2, 291–306.

DeLissovoy, V. High school marriages: A longitudinal study. *Journal of Marriage and the Family,* 1973, *35,* 2, 245–55.

Elder, G., and Rockwell, R. Marital timing in women's life patterns. *Journal of Family History,* 1976, *1,* 1, 34–53.

Gerson, W. M. Leisure and marital satisfaction of college married couples. *Marriage and Family Living,* 1960, *22,* 360–61.

Glick, P., and Norton, A. J. Frequency, duration, and probability of marriage and divorce. *Journal of Marriage and the Family,* 1971, *33,* 2, 307–17.

Harrell, T. W., and Harrell, M. S. Relation of second year MBA grades to business earnings. *Personnel Psychology,* 1974, *27,* 3, 487–91.

Haun, D. L., and Stinnett, N. Does psychological comfortableness between engaged couples affect their probability of successful marriage adjustment? *Family Perspective,* 1974, *9,* 1, 11–18.

Hawkins, H., and Walters, J. Family recreation activities. *Journal of Home Economics,* 1952, *44,* 623–6.

Heer, D. Husband and wife perceptions of family power. *Marriage and Family Living,* 1962, *24,* 65–7.

Hill, C. T. The ending of successive opposite sex relationships. Doctoral dissertation, Harvard University, 1974.

Hill, C. T., Rubin, Z., and Peplau, L. A. Breakups before marriage: The end of 103 affairs. *Journal of Social Issues,* 1976, *32,* 1, 147–68.

Hindman, N. R. Interpersonal comfortableness orientation of college students. Unpublished master's thesis, Oklahoma State University, 1972.

Kieren, D., and Tallman, I. Spousal adaptability: An assessment of marital competence. *Journal of Marriage and Family Living,* 1972, *34,* 2, 247–56.

Kinsey, A. C. et al. *Sexual behavior in the human female.* Philadelphia: W. B. Saunders Co., 1953.

Knox, D., and Patrick, J. You are what you do: A new approach in preparation for marriage. *The Family Coordinator,* 1971, *20,* 109–14.

Kolb, T. M., and Straus, M. A. Marital power and marital happiness in relation to problem-solving ability. *Journal of Marriage and the Family,* 1974, *36,* 4, 756–66.

Landers, A. If you had it to do all over again, would you marry the same person? *Family Circle,* 26 July 1977, 2 et passim.

Landis, J. T., and Landis, M. *Building a successful marriage.* Englewood Cliffs, N.J.: Prentice-Hall, 1977.

Lasswell, M. E. Is there a best age to marry? An interpretation. *The Family Coordinator,* 1974, *23,* 237–42.

Lee, G. R. Age at marriage and marital satisfaction: A multivariate analysis with implications for marital stability. *Journal of Marriage and the Family,* 1977, *39,* 3, 493–504.

Lewis, R. A. Social reaction and the formation of dyads: An interactionist approach to mate selection. *Sociometry,* 1973, *36,* 3, 409–18.

Locke, H. J. *Predicting adjustment in marriage: A comparison of a divorced and a happily married group.* New York: Henry Holt and Co., 1951.

Miller, N. P., and Robinson, D. M. *The leisure age, its challenge to recreation.* Belmont, Calif.: Wadsworth, 1963.

Monohan, T. P. Premarital pregnancy in the United States: A critical review and some findings. *Eugenics Quarterly,* 1960, *7,* 145.

Olson, D. H. Marriage of the future: Revolutionary or evolutionary change? *The Family Coordinator,* 1972, *21,* 4, 383–93.

Orthner, D. K. Leisure activity patterns and marital satisfaction over the marital career. *Journal of Marriage and the Family,* 1975, *37,* 1, 91–102.

The Perfect Wedding. *Modern Bride,* April/May 1976, 38.

Reiser, C. The effect of television on perceived marital happiness. Unpublished paper, Department of Sociology, East Carolina University, 1977.

Rolfe, D. J. Pre-marriage contracts: An aid to couples living with parents. *The Family Coordinator,* 1977, *26,* 3, 281–5.

Root, E. M. For our sons—On how to choose a wife. In *Confronting the issues: Sex roles, marriage and the family,* K. W. Kammeyer (ed.). Boston: Allyn and Bacon, 1975, 133–47.

Rosenblatt, P. C. Needed research on commitment in marriage. In *Symposium on close social relationships,* G. Levinger and H. Raush (eds.). Amherst, Mass.: University of Massachusetts Press, 1975.

Rubin, Z. The social psychology of romantic love. Doctoral dissertation, University of Michigan, 1969.

Sammons, R. A. Sammons' first law of nature. Unpublished manuscript, Department of Psychology, East Carolina University, 1978.

Satir, V. *Conjoint family therapy.* Palo Alto, Calif.: Science and Behavior Books, 1964.

Scanzoni, J. A social system analysis of dissolved and existing marriages. *Journal of Marriage and the Family,* 1968, *30,* 3, 452–61.

Schoen, R. California divorce rates by age at first marriage and duration of first marriage. *Journal of Marriage and the Family,* 1975, *37,* 3, 548–55.

Shonick, H. Premarital counseling: Three years experience of a unique service. *The Family Coordinator,* 1975, *24,* 3, 321–4.

Stephens, W. Predictors of marital adjustment. In *A marriage reader,* L. Saxton. Belmont, Calif.: Wadsworth, 1970, 189–99.

Suelzle, M., and O'Connell, W. Antenuptial agreement. Marriage contract, 1972.

Sussman, M. B. Marriage contracts: Social and legal consequences. Paper presented at the meeting of the International Workshop on Changing Sex Roles in Family and Society, June 1975.

Sussman, M. B., Cogswell, B., and Ross, H. The personal contract—new form of marriage bond. Unpublished manuscript, 1973.

Trainer, J. B. Sexual incompatibilities. *Journal of Marriage and Family Counseling,* 1975, *1,* 2, 123–34.

Turk, J., and Bell, N. Measuring power in families. *Journal of Marriage and the Family,* 1972, *34,* 2, 215–22.

Wells, J. G. A critical look at personal marriage contracts. *The Family Coordinator,* 1976, *25,* 1, 33–7.

Whipple, C. M., Jr., and Whittle, D. *The compatibility test.* Englewood Cliffs, N.J.: Prentice-Hall, 1976.

White, G. L. Paper presented at the meeting of the American Psychological Association, San Francisco, 1977.

PART 3 Involvements

Chapter 10

Marriage Relationships

Dora and I are now married, but just as happy as we were before.
Bertrand Russell

Having made a decision and commitment to marry, couples move behind closed doors into a private and legal marital relationship. In this chapter, we explore the transition to and consequences of marriage in American society. In addition, since most marriages can be described according to the degree to which they are "traditional" or "open," we will explore these characteristics of marital relationships. And since marriage patterns vary from one group to another, we will look briefly at the differences in college, mixed, military, and group marriages.

TRANSITION TO MARRIAGE

People vary in the experiences they bring to their wedding. While some individuals have dated each other exclusively since high school and have not had intercourse (or have done so only with each other), other individuals have been involved in an array of love relationships or have lived together before their decision to marry. Because of such differences no couple experiences the transition to marriage in the same way.

Weddings

Regardless of the different experiences the respective partners bring to their wedding, the legal procedure for getting married remains the same. A couple must obtain a marriage license, signify their willingness to get married in a ceremony performed by someone legally permitted to do so, and have two witnesses of legal age verify the event. Following the ceremony, the couple, official, and witnesses must sign the marriage license. It is then sent, usually by the religious official or justice of the peace, to the state capital where it is recorded and filed.

When two people are under the influence of the most violent, most insane, most delusive, and most transient of passions, they are required to swear that they will remain in that excited, abnormal, and exhausting condition continuously until death do them part.
George Bernard Shaw

The wedding ceremony is like an initiation ceremony. It is a rite of passage which signifies the change from one social status to another. The solemnity of the ceremony is designed to impress upon the couple the seriousness of the responsibilities they are undertaking to each other, to subsequent children they have, and to the relatives of their respective families (Blood, 1972, p. 114).

Although a wedding may be performed by a justice of the peace in a civil ceremony, three fourths of weddings include religious ceremonies performed by a minister, priest, or rabbi (Benson, 1971, p. 173). While it is not known how many couples agree to a religious ceremony and perfunctorily participate because of their parents' wishes, traditional religious weddings emphasize that marriage is a sacred relationship ordained by God. The religious official, the setting, the music, and the words of the ceremony ("holy matrimony") take marriage from the secular realm into a spiritual one. Indeed, the ending of the traditional ceremony emphasizes God's presence and approval . . . "Therefore, whom God hath joined together, let no man put asunder."

But it is no longer unusual for couples to have weddings that are neither religious nor traditional. Only friends of the couple and members of the immediate families may gather in the backyard of the bride. Rather than the traditional white gown, the bride may wear her favorite dress. And while the groom may wear a suit (he just as well may not), everyone else wears anything they want.

In the exchange of vows, no one promises to obey anyone, and their relation-

"More or less."

An Exchange of Vows

I love you and want to be with you. I do not want to belong to you nor do I want you to belong to me, but rather I want us to have a relationship in which we will want to be with each other. I want this to be a relationship in which we will nurture each's growth while maintaining our own separateness and individuality. In that interest I express the following goals, promises, and commitments.

First of all, I accept the responsibility for myself. I will not depend on you for my fulfillment as a person. I will accept my ultimate aloneness in life and the responsibility for my own happiness. But out of my aloneness I desire to share time and space with you. I will be with you while intimately sharing past and present experiences along with hopes, dreams, and plans for the future.

I will be reliable and open to you so that we will maintain a basis of trust between us. I will love and trust myself in order to continually become a more trustworthy person to you and add fidelity, security and depth to our relationship. I will grow and change but through an honest dialogue I will maintain your trust in me.

I will respect you as an individual person and will cherish your uniqueness. I will strive to help you become more of yourself even though that may differ from what I would like for you to be. I will take pride in you and your differences from me. I will consistently remember those qualities and traits that are beautiful about you and consistently communicate my love by recognizing your inner beauty and your outer physical beauty through words and actions.

In times of need I will care for you and for me. I understand that there will be times of pain as well as joy in our relationship. In troubled times I will try to be considerate, compassionate, caring, nonjudgmental, and forgiving. I understand that you and I in our humanness will have limitations and will make mistakes. I will accept those limitations in myself and in you and will not expect either of us to be perfect. I understand that in your love you have exposed your human vulnerabilities. I will respond with consideration to cherish and invite you to feel protected from undue pain.

I will not take you for granted. I will consistently be aware and emotionally present to you. I will listen to you when you speak and I will encourage you whenever I possibly can.

In giving of myself to you I will give for my inner joy and not from duty. I will consistently enjoy sharing those parts of myself which you enjoy. I will enrich and preserve my body, my mind, and spirit for you and me. I will continue to change striving to become a more mature and stimulating person. I will accept changes in you as well as in myself. I will gracefully accept the limitations of aging in both of us. As I grow older I will try to develop wisdom and integrity of character, and I will encourage and appreciate similar growth in you.

I will consistently make time available

for being together, for communication, for work, for fun and for love. No matter how many demands or enticements I experience for success or childrearing I will set aside and give the highest priority to our time together.

I will share in the parenting experience of providing care, setting limits, and giving opportunities for Megan Carol and any other children born to us. I will share in helping them to grow as persons and achieve their own wishes, hopes, and dreams. With you I will give them roots and stability, but I will also let them go to develop their own wings.

I will share with you in the development of a community of friends and family. I will share with you in contributing to our larger community around us.

As much as possible, I will try to be aware of a sense of values, of eternal values. I will try to consider those things which are of real consequence as well as respond to the cares of the moment.

Most of all, I will try to be a real person to you. I will try to give you the kind of love that will encourage the realness in you. Let our lives be filled with effort, expectation and desire, and something evermore about to be.

Hal & Sherry
May 1, 1977

Source: Gillespie and LaPointe, 1977.

---

ship is spelled out by themselves rather than by tradition. Vows such as those which are said in less traditional ceremonies more often address issues of a psychological nature such as egalitarianism, individualism, humanism, and openness to change. (See *An Exchange of Vows.*)

Honeymoons

Couples who live together before their marriage are less likely to take a honeymoon following their wedding. After a brunch, dinner, or party, they may return to the apartment or house in which they have been living and finish the chest they were antiquing earlier that morning.

In contrast, the traditionally married couple are more likely to embark on a honeymoon. Their first week or ten days as a married couple are often spent in one resort location (e.g., near the mountains or the beach), traveling each day to a new place (Disneyworld to Miami), or loafing for several days with no schedule of places to be or things to do (Rapoport and Rapoport, 1964). Some couples go camping.

Regardless of where the couple go, the honeymoon serves various social, personal, and interpersonal functions. The social function of the honeymoon is to make it normative for the couple to isolate themselves from others (Van Gennep, 1960). Aside from pranks such as tampering with the couple's car or hiding their luggage just after the wedding, our society socializes us to regard honeymooners as deserving privacy.

The period of undisturbed privacy relates to another personal function of the honeymoon—recuperation. Since traditional weddings involve tremendous preparation, bridal showers, a rehearsal, a rehearsal dinner, and a long reception, the bride and groom often feel exhausted by the time they reach their first night's destination. The bride is usually more fatigued since she has assumed greater responsibility for the wedding than her partner. "I was sick when we got to the motel room," recalled an exhausted bride. "I hadn't slept soundly in three days and had eaten only peanuts and cookies. I was a wreck." But the honeymoon dictates no responsibilities, plenty of sleep, and good food. It's the physician's prescription for fatigue.

In addition to privacy and recuperation, the honeymoon has an interpersonal function. For the couple who have not had intercourse, the sexual aspect of their relationship begins. And the honeymooning couple will begin to spend "their" money (rather than his or hers), share a common bathroom, dress and undress around each other, and engage in various other behaviors associated with married life.

In making a decision to take a honeymoon or not a basic issue might be considered: There is only one honeymoon in a marriage. While a couple may take subsequent trips together, their first days following the wedding (particularly if they have not lived together) are unique.

Resorts such as this one in the Pocono mountains cater to honeymooners seeking relaxation, glamour, and romance. Although not all couples choose to take honeymoons, most do retreat for at least a brief period of privacy, recuperation, and adjustment to their new post-wedding roles.

CONSEQUENCES OF MARRIAGE

Whether a couple go on a honeymoon or not, they will become aware of various changes which occur as a result of getting married. These changes will have implications not only for them as individuals but will involve social relationships and the transfer of property.

Individual Consequences of Marriage

An initial enhanced self-concept is a predictable consequence of getting married. Since over 90 percent of all adults get married, a newly married person may feel relieved in having escaped the stigma of being single. One bride said, "I've made it. I am twenty-eight, and Mom has been hounding me since I graduated to get married."

Notice that your parents and closest friends will actually arrange their schedules to participate in your marriage and will even give you wedding gifts to express their approval. But if you are remaining single, there is no ceremony, no fussing and excited parents or friends, no gifts—only the question, "Is something wrong with you?" As a married person, you are assumed to be normal and to have made the right decision. The strong evidence that your spouse approves of you and is willing to spend a lifetime with you also tells you that you're OK.

In addition to an improved self-concept, the married person tends to begin adopting new values and behaviors consistent with the marital role (Waller and Hill, 1951, p. 262). Although new spouses often vow and believe that "marriage won't change me," it does. For example, rather than stay out all night at a party, which is not uncommon for singles, the married couples tend to go home by 1:00 A.M.[1] They develop a preference for more regular hours and getting a good night's sleep. Although there is an initial resistance to "becoming like old married folks," just as the couple was socialized by their single peers to exhibit courtship behaviors, they will be socialized by their married peers to display marital role behaviors.

Another consequence of marriage for the individual spouses is disillusionment. While it may not happen the first few weeks or months after the wedding, it is almost inevitable that the respective spouses will at some time become disillusioned about their relationship. While courtship is the anticipation of a life together, marriage is the day-to-day reality of life together. And reality does not always fit the dream. Daily marital interaction exposes both partners as they really are—human beings who get tired and irritable.[2] "Burt never snapped at me about anything when we were dating, but I never acted like a mean bitch (his term) before we were married either," expressed a wife of six months. Emphasizing the positive aspects of coming to know the mate, one psychotherapist observed, "When the couple find themselves in a rage, that is the time not for divorce but for celebration" (Jourard, 1975, p. 204). In essence, the couple must recognize that they are no longer in the love bubble of courtship and come to terms with the differences which divide them.

But such disillusionment is often tempered by more positive aspects of the new relationship. Married people of both sexes report greater personal happiness than never-married, divorced, separated, or widowed people (Glenn, 1975, p. 599). And a euphoric state is particularly common among newlyweds and women (Campbell, Converse, and Rodgers, 1975). After analyzing the "quality of life" of a random sample of 2,164 adults, one researcher concluded, "The best of all possible worlds, for most Americans, is to be newly married and not have children. If single people in their twenties feel that something is lacking in their lives, married couples of that age are the happiest of all groups—especially young wives, who are more satisfied than anyone else, anywhere, any age. They are positively euphoric" (Campbell, 1975, p. 38).

Changes in Social Relationships

In addition to individual consequences, marriage affects relationships with the parents, in-laws, and friends of both partners. Regarding parents, they are likely to be more accepting of the partner following the wedding. "I encouraged her not to marry him," expressed the father of a recent bride, "but once they were married, he was her husband and my son-in-law, so I did my best to get along with him."

Just as the acceptance of the mate by one's parents is likely to increase, the interaction with one's parents is likely to decrease. This is particularly true when the newly married couple moves to a distant town. "I still love my parents a great deal," said a new husband, "but I just don't get to see them very often." Parents whose lives have revolved around their children may feel particularly saddened at the marriage of their last child and may be reluctant to accept the reduced contacts. Frequent phone calls, visits, invitations, and gifts may be their way of trying to ensure a meaningful place in the life of their married son or daughter. And such insistence by the parents and in-laws may be the basis of the first major conflict between the spouses. There is no problem if both spouses agree on which set of in-laws or parents they enjoy visiting and on the frequency of such get-togethers. But when one spouse wants his or her parents around more frequently than the partner does, frustrations will be felt not only by the spouses but by the parents and/or in-laws.

Most marriage counselors recommend that when the spouses must choose between their partner and parents, there are more long-term negative consequences associated with choosing the parents than vice versa. Ideally, of course, such "choices" should be avoided. For either partner to try to deny his or her mate access to his or her parents is unwise. When an individual marries, he or she marries into an already existing family. And the parental/in-law relationships come with marriage.

In addition to parental/in-law concerns, traditional marriage affects relationships with friends of the same and opposite sex. Less time will be spent with friends of the same sex because the friends assume that "their old buddy" now has a built-in companion and is not interested in (or would be punished by the spouse for) continuing the life-style of the single person.

Opposite-sex relationships change, too. A single person is free to interact with someone of the opposite sex in a flirtatious way. The consequence of doing so may be very positive for both persons. But the traditionally married person has taken the vow, "hold myself only unto you as long as we both should live," and is expected to be "faithful." While a married person will still be attracted to people of the opposite sex, and may think about potential sexual relationships, acting on those thoughts usually has negative consequences for the marital relationship (Hunt, 1974, p. 278).

Less time with single friends of the same or opposite sex is replaced by more time together with other married couples. Spending time with other married couples is less threatening to the marriage since the spouses see friends together. And married couples have more in common with each other than with singles. "Drinking, staying out late, and hustling somebody are the primary social interests of our single friends," remarked a young bride. "We enjoy partying with our friends, but we're no longer into the other trips. We still care about our single friends; we just don't go out with them much anymore."

Transfer of Property

While marriage has implications for the individual's self-concept, happiness, and social relationships, it also involves the exchange of property. Once the words, "I do," are spoken during the wedding ceremony, each spouse is automatically entitled to inherit between one half to one third of the other's estate. Generally speaking a husband or wife cannot, even by will, cut off a surviving spouse (Weisberg, 1975, p. 549).

MARRIAGE RELATIONSHIPS—PLURAL

Having reviewed the personal, social, and property consequences of marriage, we will now explore several types of marriage relationships. A basic theme of this section is that there is no one marriage relationship. Each is different.

Table 10.1 reflects a partial list of types of marriage relationships that may be categorized according to freedom, intimacy, differences and similarities, social class, number, roles, and sexual relationship. While it is not possible here to discuss each of these marital relationships, we will focus on traditional, open, college, mixed, and military marriages. Such an array will provide an analysis of some of the more and less familiar marriage relationships.

TABLE 10.1   Types of Marriage Relationships.*

Classified according to:	Variations:
Degree of freedom	Traditional Modified traditional (certain activities separate but only by mutual approval) Open marriage Marriage with privacy (budgeted time away when neither partner has the obligation to play "show-and-tell" afterwards)
Degree of intimacy	Very intimate, almost no significant satisfactions outside marriage Moderately intimate, can enjoy separate activities Somewhat intimate, significant amount of satisfaction from separate activities Very little intimacy with major source of satisfaction outside marriage; marriage of convenience No intimacy (marriage perceived as financially or socially necessary or too many obstacles to separation)
Differences/similarities	Interracial Interfaith Intercultural Age (young, old, discrepancy in years) Handicapped (one or both) Previously divorced (one or both) Previously widowed (one or both) Parent (one or both) Living together experience (one or both) Education (high school, bachelor's, master's, doctorate—one or both) Athletic (one or both) Military (one or both)
Social class	High/medium/low income (one or both) Student (one or both) Welfare (one or both) Significant status in community (one or both) Close ties with family (one or both)
Number involved	Two Three More than three

*This list is not intended to be complete, but rather to stimulate thinking and discussion about all the variations in marriage relationships.

Continued on next page

TABLE 10.1   Cont.

Classified according to:	Variations:
Roles	Rigid traditional roles
	Modified traditional roles (wife working but responsible for domestic chores)
	Equalitarian roles (wife's career equal to husband's career; husband's domestic and parenting equal to wife's)
	Loose arrangement according to convenience, deciding each day, week, or month who does what, depending on health and other responsibilities at the time
Sexual relationship	Heterosexual
	Homosexual
	Bisexual
	Exclusive/non-exclusive
	Intense/frequent
	Low key/infrequent
	No genital sex

SOURCE: Adapted from Myers, 1978.

TRADITIONAL VERSUS OPEN MARRIAGES

Marriages vary in the degree to which they are considered traditional or open. Let's look at the extremes of this continuum.

Traditional Marriages

While not all traditional marriages share the following characteristics, many do. They include (O'Neill & O'Neill, 1972, pp. 52–53): (1) Possession or ownership of the mate. This implies that the time, body, and mind of the mate belong to the partner. Spending time away from one's mate, having intercourse with someone other than one's spouse, or making significant decisions without consulting the partner are taboo; (2) Denial of self. What a spouse must do to keep the marriage together usually takes precedence over what the spouse wants to do; (3) Maintenance of the couple front. The traditional spouse rarely feels comfortable attending a movie without the partner on Saturday night if the mate is in town; (4) Rigid role behavior. Chores and responsibilities are clearly separated into what is considered appropriate for men and women. In general, he takes out the garbage and she cooks dinner and takes care of the children.

Open Marriages

As an alternative to traditional marriage, Nena and George O'Neill have suggested open marriage.[3]

> Often misinterpreted, their description of open marriage emphasized role equality and flexibility—a peer relationship—and the potential for each spouse to grow separately. . . . While the O'Neills did not recommend outside sex, they did not advise people to avoid it either, maintaining a noncommittal, neutral position that extramarital relationships are not integral to open marriage but *may* be included if the couple has the necessary trust, identity, and open communication. Thus, actualized outside sexual relationships are not necessary for the marriage to be *open.* (Knapp & Whitehurst, 1977, pp. 147–48)

And, five years after the publication of *Open Marriage,* Nena O'Neill emphasized that while sexually open marriage may be suitable for a small minority, it hasn't proved practical for the majority (O'Neill, 1977).

While we will examine sexually open marriages in Chapter 14, our concern here is with open marriage in the broader sense. Typical characteristics of open marriages described by the O'Neills (1972, pp. 72–73) include:

1. Living for now. For the couple in an open marriage, the past and future are less important than the present. They are concerned less about traditional practices (a white wedding dress, church every week, returning a dinner invitation) or the acquisition of material goods (a cottage by the sea) than couples in a traditional marriage. Rather, spouses in an open marriage focus on their own personal growth, that of their partner, and their emotional and intellectual exchange. If parents invite them for Thanksgiving dinner, rather than ask each other, "*Should* we be with our parents for Thanksgiving?" they are more likely to ask, "Do we *want* to be with our parents for Thanksgiving?"

2. Privacy. "The granting of privacy is essential for examination of self and psychic regeneration" (O'Neill & O'Neill, 1972, p. 451).[4] Neither partner in an open marriage regards the desire to be alone as an indication of lack of love for the partner. Rather, the wish for solitude is interpreted as not only realistic but desirable for collecting one's own thoughts and getting in touch with one's own feelings.

3. Flexibility in roles. "It's your job to take out the garbage" is not likely to be spoken in an open marriage. Both spouses are concerned not about "his" work or "her" work, but rather what needs to be done and who is there to do it. The spouse who cooks is more likely to do so because of preference than from a feeling of "that's what I'm supposed to do." If neither wants to cook, the couple will either share the meal preparation or eat out. Either way, neither spouse feels locked into specific role responsibilities.

4. Equality. Since no one person can ever be exactly equal to another in terms of capacities, abilities, talents, needs, or desires, equality in reference to open marriage means "personhood." This term means that each partner has the

right to his or her individuality and to pursue the goals necessary for personal fulfillment. For example, personhood might mean that the wife has the right to pursue a career (in contrast to a job) or that the husband has the right to have a job (in contrast to a career).

    5.   Trust. While trust in the traditional marriage often refers to predictability such as, "I trust you to be faithful to me, to call me when you are to be late, etc.," trust in the open marriage refers to the feeling that you can share your inner thoughts with your partner without fear of the information being used against you. Trust for the open couple also means they respect one another's differences and yet become closer for having done so.

Of course, couples in a traditional marriage may share some of the characteristics of those in an open marriage and vice versa. For example, "trust" as defined above is not necessarily unique to the traditional or open marriage. In essence, all relationships are highly individual.

Marriage is still basically two people trying to love each other and answer each other's needs. It may not be forever, it may have changed, but it still gives us opportunities no other relationship can give us.

Nena O'Neill

And preference for involvement in a relationship that tends to be traditional or open is also individual. When three hundred university students were asked to comment on marriages in their parents' generation, only 12 percent felt that they were too "tradition bound"; only 7 percent described these marriages as "dull" (Whitehurst, 1977, p. 295).

In contrast, the overwhelming majority of 104 individuals who were involved in open marriages (which included sex outside the primary relationship) reported that these relationships permitted them to "live their personal philosophies or beliefs" and to "meet unfulfilled emotional, physical, intellectual, and social needs," which the traditional marriage relationship could not satisfy (Knapp & Whitehurst, 1977, pp. 154–55).

COLLEGE MARRIAGES *are stupid!*

In addition to the traditional/open continuum, marriage relationships differ in the degree to which the partners have similar or different characteristics. One of these characteristics is education. Let's examine more closely young college marriages. Twenty-one percent of undergraduates enrolled in colleges and universities in the United States are married (Busselen & Busselen, 1975, p. 281). This proportion of undergraduate married students is radically different from those of earlier years. Prior to 1940, it was not uncommon for a college or university to require students to drop out if they married. It was believed that married students would have an undesirable influence on other students. After World War II, the return of married veterans to college established the acceptance of the college marriage.

Characteristics of Students Who Marry During College

One researcher compared the background characteristics of over two thousand married and two thousand single college students in a national representative sample (Bayer, 1972). Students likely to marry before they graduated were more popular with the opposite sex, came from lower socioeconomic backgrounds (measured by family income and father's education), were less academically able, and had lower academic aspirations than students who remained single (pp. 602–3). Another study found that women were more likely than men to marry during college. One of every three women who dropped out of college said that getting married was a factor in her decision; only one in ten male dropouts cited this reason (Astin & Panos, 1969).

The motivations for marrying during college do not appear to be unique. A language major asked, "Why not marry? We're tired of waiting, don't believe in living together, and we're miserable living in separate dorms." And her fiancé said, "It's simple. I'm happiest with her and she feels the same way about me. We talked to our parents during semester break, and while they would prefer that we wait until we graduate, they will support us if we decide to marry now. We've decided."

Effect on Grades

Some students assume that marriage will "settle" them down and improve their grades. At least sixteen studies have been conducted to test this assumption. The results of the studies differ and suggest that marriage neither improves nor hurts student's grades in a consistent way (Busselen & Busselen, 1975, p. 283). One student's grades may improve, another's stay the same, and another's get worse after marriage. An engineering major mused, "I had always heard that marriage helps your grades. I've been married two years now and I'm still waiting for it to help."

Role Changes

While it is not possible to predict the effect of marriage on grades, role changes are predictable. In addition to the basic change from the role of single student to that of spouse, the additional roles of employee and parent may be taken on after marriage.

Employee. When two college students marry, unless their parents continue to pay for tuition, books, etc., one of them (traditionally the wife) drops out to get a job. The implications of the wife's trading her student role for the employee role may be significant for the couple's marriage:

> The wife, by virtue of her youth, is usually forced to work at a fairly mundane job such as file clerk or salesgirl. She must leave the tiny apartment each day before 8:00 a.m. and does not return until after 6:00 p.m., usually thoroughly fatigued. He is burdened with homework . . . and the evening passes with little if any opportunity for interaction. If she is a bright girl, much of her fatigue will be the result of boredom on the job and lack of self-fulfillment and achievement feelings. Meanwhile her husband is being stimulated by his studies . . . . He finds her to be less interesting with each passing day . . . . How stimulating can a person be after eight hours as a file clerk? As the gap widens, she begins to feel wronged. After all, she is making his academic career possible. (Cox, 1974, pp. 86–87)

Getting married during college also decreases the chances that the wife will complete her college degree. If a female student marries in her freshman year, there is a 5 percent chance that she will graduate. If she marries in her sophomore year, there is a 20 percent chance that she will complete her degree; if a junior, 75 percent; if a senior, 99 percent (Womble, 1966, p. 194). Even if both spouses get part-time jobs and stay in school, the employee role involves strain unlike the student role. "As a student, you can miss a class or 'study later' if you need to. But when you're working for somebody, they expect you to do exactly what they want, when they want it, or you're fired," reflected a student working in a fast-food chain near campus. "And if you've got a test that day, your boss doesn't care. Those hamburgers still have to be wrapped."

Parent. Although most couples who marry in college plan to delay any children until after graduation, unwanted pregnancies may occur. And an unplanned pregnancy after marriage is often handled differently from a premarital one. After marriage, there is an increased chance the couple will have the baby. "I might have had an abortion had I gotten pregnant when we were living together," recalled a wife who had been married three months. "But now it's different. We're going to have the baby, and I will finish school later."

While role strain is not unique to the college marriage, one role may be stacked on another without sufficient time to adjust to the previous role. Stacking the roles of student, spouse, employee, and, possibly, parent requires a greater degree of adaptation than is required of the single college student with fewer responsibilities.

Money—The Proverbial Problem

Implicit in the role changes married college students experience is an unexpected confrontation with money problems. Some couples glide into marriage with the belief that "love will keep us together" and are shocked when faced with stark economic realities. A sophomore who had married in his freshman year wrote:

Many married students experience role strain—difficulty in being a good student, good spouse, good employee, and in some cases good parent—all at the same time. For these people, graduation day is not only a day of celebration, but also one of relief at having one less role to juggle.

We made a decision at the time of our marriage to go it alone financially, without any help from our parents. The result was a tremendous strain on our once happy relationship. Not having enough money put us both under tensions that neither of us had known before. We struggled to make rent, utilities, tuition, and other payments. We squeezed our budget for money to buy food with. Our recreational life-style had changed drastically because we rarely had money to eat out or to see a movie. We bought no new clothes—birthdays were the only times we got new ones. The result was unhappiness which we would not let others know about because of our pride. We were both from middle-class families, but we were poor.

Even when parents continue to subsidize their children who marry during college, money may still be a problem because "strings" are attached. Many parents expect frequent visits or feel they have a right to visit their offspring as long as they, the parents, are paying the bills. However, due to increased mobility and voluntary childlessness, visits by and with parents may become less frequent (Johnson, 1977).

In spite of the role changes and potential money problems associated with college marriage, over three fourths of the students who marry during college regard the experience in positive terms and say that they would do it over again (Eshleman & Hunt, 1967). As one married student commented, "I was unhappy when I was single. Marriage is the only way to go—it's sharing your life with someone you love. Even though we've had the usual problems, I'm glad we married when we were freshmen."

But another student who married during her freshman year said, "It was a mistake. We've both changed a lot since then, and the strains we've been through haven't been worth it. We both feel stifled and want the life of single college students. We're separated now and will be divorced next month."

The Older College Marriage

The marriages just described reflect those in which the partners married during the typical college years at age seventeen to twenty-one. But a look around any college classroom reveals a number of older students, many of whom are married. In contrast to the young college married set, many of these spouses have been or are employed in full-time jobs, have children, and regard education as something they (rather than their parents) want for themselves.

But how does returning to school affect the marriage relationship? In a study of 361 women (age twenty-six and over who were married and had at least one child), half of those who dropped out before completing their degree and one third of those who did complete their degree reported that their return to school had resulted in some strain on the marriage (Berkove, 1976). Examples of the strain included the husband's jealousy in competing with his wife's new interest, his annoyance over occasional late meals, and a cluttered house. Some husbands expressed their anger by withholding financial support.

But benefits also resulted from the wife's return to school. While most of the wives reported increased personal and intellectual development, half reported that their husbands showed greater appreciation of, satisfaction with, and pride that their wife had returned to school (Berkove, 1976, p. 4).

MIXED MARRIAGES

Interracial and interfaith marriages are also unique. Let's examine more closely these types of mixed marriages.

Interracial

Although interracial marriages may involve an array of combinations including American whites, American blacks, Indians, Chinese, Japanese, Mexican, Malaysian, and Hindu mates, this section will focus on black-white marriages in America.[5] At one time, as many as thirty states, primarily southern and western, prohibited intermarriage between blacks and whites. But on June 12, 1967, the United States Supreme Court stated that "under our Constitution, the freedom to marry a person of another race resides with the individual and cannot be infringed by the state" (Stuart & Edwin, 1973).

In 1970, there were 64,789 black-white marriages in America (U.S. Bureau of the Census, 1972). These marriages represented less than one percent of all marriages in the United States at that time. While the number of black-white marriages is likely to increase, the relative proportion of black-white marriages to homogamous marriages (black-black or white-white) will remain relatively low. One researcher suggests that there are more than two thousand such marriages each year, or about one in every 1,200 marriages (Porterfield, 1978, p. 24).

Who marries outside their race?   But what are the characteristics of those who cross racial lines to marry? In seven out of ten cases, it is a black man and a white woman who marry (Monahan, 1976, p. 229). And those who cross racial lines to marry also tend to be older, to have been married before (Stuart & Edwin, 1973), and to have fewer ties with their families (Burma et al., 1970). Each of these characteristics is associated with being less concerned about what those outside and inside their respective families think.

Problems.   Disapproval from parents, employers, and landlords is a problem for most black-white couples, and it varies with the degree to which those people have been socialized to perceive interracial unions as appropriate or inappropriate. Rural, conservative, dogmatic individuals are likely to stare at such couples with hostile eyes. Liberal people who live in large metropolitan centers are more likely to have a "live and let live" philosophy and to regard such couples neutrally or with admiration.

Given the range of alternative reactions, how are black-white couples actually treated by their parents, employers, and landlords? In general, both sets of parents reject the interracial marriage of their son or daughter. Such rejection springs from their concern about how the marriage will affect the parents' own status and their fear for the couple and the problems they must face. Such hostility often disappears when the couple has a baby (the parents want access to their grandchild) or tragedy strikes (cancer is discovered in one partner) (Black, 1973). Difficulties with employers and landlords are less predictable. Some employers and landlords discriminate against an individual if they know of the interracial marriage. Others, particularly those in larger cities, are indifferent to the marital status or choice of marriage partner of their employee.

A black-white couple is also concerned about the effect of the interracial marriage on their children. Some, fearing potential problems, decide not to have children. After analyzing 1970 census data, one researcher observed that wives in black-white marriages are more likely to be childless than those in homogamous marriages (Heer, 1974). Regardless of the color of their skin, the children of a black-white marriage are regarded by both the black and white community as black. While the children may experience discrimination because they are black, it has not been demonstrated that they are further discriminated against because of their parents' interracial marriage. To the contrary, having children has often had distinctly beneficial effects on interracial marriages. Not only do the spouses report being reunited with their parents, they report greater acceptance in the neighborhood because the children play with other children in the neighborhood (Seattle Urban League Special Report, 1967).

Stability. In view of the difficulties experienced by some black-white couples, are they more likely to get divorced? There is no clear-cut answer. Some researchers say yes (e.g., Heer, 1974), but other researchers say no (e.g., Monahan, 1970). The best answer seems to be that due to the lack of social support (and sometimes overt hostility), black-white marriages have a slightly higher probability of ending in divorce than homogamous marriages. But this probability can be offset if the partners have particularly strong personalities and an accepting set of social relationships into which they may immerse themselves.

Interracial couples commonly face disapproval from their parents as well as others, but having a child in many cases eases the situation. The couple's parents become more accepting because of their interest in their grandchild, and neighbors become friendlier as a result of their children playing together and making friends.

Interfaith

Marriages between people of different faiths represent another type of mixed marriage. Although most people do marry those within their own faith, 22 percent of Catholics marry non-Catholics, 8 percent of Protestants marry non-Protestants, and 7 percent of Jews marry non-Jews (Carter & Glick, 1970). Characteristics of those who marry outside their faith include having nonreligious parents, feeling less close to parents when young, and feeling emancipated from parental influence at the time of marriage (Heiss, 1960).

All of the major faiths oppose the marriage of one of their members to someone of a different faith. Their opposition is based on the belief that marriage within the faith is more likely to ensure lifelong membership as well as participation in the faith. Prior to 1970, the Catholic church required the non-Catholic spouse to sign an Ante-Nuptial Agreement whereby he or she promised that all children born of the marriage would be reared in the Roman Catholic Church. Under current practice, only the Catholic partner must promise to rear them in the Catholic church.

But what about the stability of interfaith marriages? Analyzing data from the 1970 National Fertility Study, the authors concluded that mixed-faith marriages were associated with more separation and divorce than same-faith marriages. While the most stable marriages were those between individuals of the same faith, the least stable marriages were those in which the wife was Protestant and the husband regarded himself as "other"—neither Protestant, Catholic, nor Jewish (Bumpass & Sweet, 1972). Several studies support this basic finding—that interfaith marriages are more likely to have negative consequences for personal and marital happiness (Gordon, 1964; Burchinal & Chancellor, 1963; Christensen & Barber, 1967).

But other studies disagree. When a happily married group was compared with a divorced group, the researcher found that the differences in religion were just as frequent for both groups (Locke, 1951). And, although Catholic-Jewish marriages were associated with marital maladjustment, interfaith marriages involving Protestants did not demonstrate this effect (Heiss, 1960).

Why the different conclusions in the various studies? Devoutness is probably the issue. When religion is an important part of an individual's philosophy of life, that individual is unlikely to consider as a mate one who does not share his or her religious perspective. An active member of the Student Campus Methodist Center recalled, "We were becoming ambivalent about whether or not we should continue dating. So I suggested that we pray about it and ask God's will for shaping our lives. He laughed at the suggestion, and that was our last date." Hence, religious affiliation is less significant than the strength of the person's beliefs.

MILITARY MARRIAGES

Having considered traditional/open marriages, college marriages, and mixed marriages, we now turn to another variation—military marriages. In such marriages at least one spouse (usually the husband) is regarded as military personnel. In

1976, 2,089,000 people were on active duty for the Army, Air Force, Navy, and Marines (The U.S. Fact Book, 1977, p. 335). Military marriages are different in regard to the expectations imposed on them, frequent moves, and subsequent separations.

Expectations of Married Couples in the Military

Married couples in the military live in a fishbowl. They live and work in a tightly organized and observant community that demands conformity to conservative and relatively inflexible behavioral standards. And the actions of the wife can significantly influence her husband's promotion (Allen & Gale, 1973, p. 173).

Among the values held by the military community and typically imposed on those for whom the military is a career are the following (Hatch, 1976, p. 3).

Traditional sex roles. The husband is expected to regard his career above his marriage and the "good" military wife understands his military obligations, supports his performance of them, and is submissive. One wife mused, "We've moved five times in four years and when he tells me we're moving to the desert, I'm supposed to like it. The military expects the wives to be like their officers— obedient."

Double standard. During forced separations, the husband may have intercourse, but his wife is expected to remain faithful to him. The wife of a career officer was asked if she ever worried about her husband's having sex while he was stationed overseas. Her answer: "Yes! Because there is peer pressure to do so, and the women are available." In general, both husbands and wives accept the double standard.

Social involvement. As the husband advances in rank, there is increased pressure for the couple to "entertain" in their home and for the wife to become involved in community activities. One husband explained, "We're not party-type people, but you don't have a choice in the military. When the colonel tells me that he is having a get together at his house Saturday night at nine, I am expected to be there with my wife. And when I get to be a colonel, I'll be expected to have the same silly parties."

Frequent Moves

Military couples also move frequently and are rarely allowed to "settle down" in one place (Allen & Gale, 1973, p. 171). A study of twenty-nine Army wives who had been married an average of five years reported that they had moved six times during their marriage (McKain, 1973, p. 207). Although moves become less frequent as the rank increases and during peacetime, the military couple can expect to move approximately every two and a half to three years with a maximum of four years at one duty station (Hatch, 1976, p. 3).

In addition to moving difficulties (selling the old home, preparing for the movers, staying in a motel while looking for new quarters, waiting for delivery of belongings, unpacking, etc.), and moving anxieties (what will the next place be like?), the consequences of frequent moves may include the following.

Loss of friendships. "We've been stationed here almost four years and have become very close with another couple," remarked the wife of a career officer. "In June, we will be transferred eight states away and that will probably be the end of the friendship. That's sad because close friends are hard to develop. Mac and I are beginning to wonder if making new friends every time we move is worth the effort."

Separation from extended family. The ties that bind are often blood ties, and even these may be strained by military life. While many couples do not choose to live in the same house or community with their parents, few choose to live on the other side of the world from them, either. "I see my mom once a year," reflected a young wife, "and that's just not enough. I'm hoping we'll be stationed closer to home on our next tour. Being away from your family is the worst part of military life."

Alienation. The loss of friendships and separation from the extended family often contribute to a sense of alienation. McKain (1973, p. 205) explained the alienation problem as not being well identified with or integrated into either the military or the civilian community. The degree of alienation experienced is related to the frequency of moves, the location of the move, and the discrimination against military personnel which exists in the new area (Hatch, 1976, p. 8). Regarding the latter, the wife of a career officer recalled, "When we were transferred to Norfolk, Virginia, we saw a sign which read, 'Dogs and Sailors Keep Off the Grass.' Most girls in the community were not allowed to date young military men because they were 'wild' and 'no good.' It's hard to feel friendly in a place that isn't friendly to military people."

Children. Although military career couples are often concerned about the effects of moving on their children, the available data suggest that their children are not adversely affected by such moves. Parents of 318 children who had moved a great distance from their previous location reported that their children made friends easily (80 percent) and that changing schools had not been difficult (75 percent) (Barrett & Noble, 1973, p. 181). While these were not military parents, the effects of moving on their children were negligible.[6]

Not all families regard moving in negative terms. One wife recalled, "We've moved seven times in ten years, but how else would we have seen Japan, Taiwan, or California? We also know through experience that people in different places live different ways. We have given our children a sense of tolerance and understanding of others that they might only get from having lived in the different countries and states."

Separations

In some situations a military spouse is transferred overseas without his family.[7] Adjustment in these cases is likely to be more difficult than when the entire family moves (Peck & Schroeder, 1976). "Periodic separation of the husband-father is almost universally considered to be one of the most troublesome and difficult aspects of military life" (Hatch, 1976, p. 11). Adjustment for the wife involves assuming responsibility for family financial matters and acting as disciplinarian for any children the couple may have. The wife functioning in these roles often becomes very independent. A career officer who returns from a two-year tour of duty is likely to find a wife who is self-sufficient to the point that he no longer feels needed.

Although the wife may fulfill both her role and that of her husband while he is away, her social situation is more problematic. Because she is married but has no husband, she "fits in" with neither singles nor married couples. And, as noted earlier, the military has a double standard of sexual morality. While the husband may have intercourse while overseas, the wife is expected to remain faithful to her husband. One military wife noted, "Any contacts with men are viewed by others as infidelity. . . . It is impossible to have male friends" (Bey & Lange, 1974, p. 284).

In summary, military marriages, which are characterized by frequent moves and separations, follow a unique pattern. The partners are expected to live their marriage in a closed community that exercises considerable influence over them. While requests to be stationed at specific places are sometimes granted, the needs of an individual do not take precedence if they conflict with those of the military. Military personnel are socialized to value their military obligations above their families.

But there are also rewards which are unique to military life. Service personnel are provided housing and medical benefits and a secure income. Those who stay in the military for twenty years become eligible for good retirement benefits. In addition there are other less obvious benefits. A sociologist married to a military career officer has observed:

> Many people find "social security" in a well-defined social structure. There is no uncertainty about what behavior is expected of them or who their peers are. This "social security," along with the financial security is very comfortable and attractive to many people. They not only "belong" but know "who they are" socially. The values and standards of the military society are largely traditional American middle-class values. People who hold these values find it comfortable to live in a society where the traditional values are dominant, and are not being challenged to the degree that they are in society at large. If one is willing to accept most of the norms of military society and be an active member, one becomes a member of a close-knit, supportive community which can quite effectively replace the extended family and mitigate the hardships associated with military life. (Hatch, 1976, p. 10)

GROUP MARRIAGES

An uncommon but distinct marital pattern is group marriage. A group marriage consists of a minimum of three people each of whom considers himself or herself to be married to at least two other members of the group (Ramey, 1972). Any person in a group marriage must have at least two mates. Although the average group consists of four adult partners and three children—usually the children of the couples' preexisting conventional marriages (Constantine & Constantine, 1977)—the number may range from three to seven adults (Ramey, 1972).

Regarding the number of group marriages that exist, Rimmer (1973) states, ". . . the true statistics of what is happening in alternate marriage forms (including long-lasting bigamous relationships) will never be revealed until society provides either a social or legal structure that condones group relationships" (pp. 236–37). Although group marriage is illegal and in some states a felony, one estimate suggests that there are at least one thousand such marriages (Constantine & Constantine, 1973, p. 32).

Interest in group marriage was stimulated by the publication of Robert Rimmer's *The Harrad Experiment* in early 1967. Twenty thousand readers of *Psychology Today* expressed their views on group marriage three years later. One fourth were either in favor of group marriage or thought they might be interested (Athanasiou et al., 1970). Prior to the publication of Rimmer's book, there is no evidence of group marriage in existence in its current form (Constantine & Constantine, 1973, p. 31).

Motivations Toward Group Marriage

The motivations for becoming involved in group marriage are similar to those for becoming involved in sexually open relationships. Eighty percent of the respondents in one study on group marriage noted variety of sexual partners was among

Group marriage is not widespread, but the minority who do choose it see in it possibilities for greater personal fulfillment, growth, and sexual variety.

their reasons for seeking a group marriage. However only 18 percent regarded this as an important motivation (Constantine & Constantine, 1977). Most of the respondents were primarily concerned about their own personal growth and fulfillment, both as individuals and as marriage partners. They felt that such growth could be maximized through intimate living with others with whom they would share an additional pair bond. Those who become involved in group marriages are generally not rebelling against society, protesting the establishment, acting on religious convictions, or trying to improve an unsatisfactory marriage (Constantine & Constantine, 1973, p. 109).

Of the 104 participants in the group marriage study referred to above, most tended to be in their late twenties, to have been married six to eight years, and to have two or three children. Most lived in urban or suburban areas, with only a few living in rural areas (Constantine & Constantine, 1973, p. 67). Most were middle-class people employed as college professors, carpenters, engineers, social workers, nurses, ministers, and physicians. One gets the impression that most members of group marriages have done a lot of thinking about their life-style choice.

Problems in Group Marriage

Communication is the most frequent problem reported by members involved in group marriages. This is not surprising in view of the number of interaction patterns inherent in this arrangement. Interaction between three people involves triple the number of interpersonal relationships of a couple. Among four partners, there are twelve relationships which must be dealt with and maintained.

To help facilitate open communication, most group marriages have family meetings in which they discuss issues relevant to the group's functioning and try to smooth any eroding relationships before a spreading effect occurs. For example, relationships between same-sex members may become strained over feelings of jealousy. If this issue is not dealt with immediately, misunderstandings may increase, feelings may be hurt, and the task of resolving one relationship problem increases to six.

Effective communication skills may improve the group's ability to handle an array of other problems common to group marriages. Issues to work out include:

> . . . group goals, ground rules, "no-no's," privacy, division of labor, role relationships, careers, relationships with outsiders, degree of visibility, legal jeopardy, dissolution of the group, personal responsibilities outside the group (e.g., parent support), urban or rural setting, type of shelter, child-rearing practices, taxes, pooling assets, income, legal structure, education, etc. (Ramey, 1972, p. 451)

Sex is not an overwhelming problem among participants in group marriages. Each member has heterosexual intercourse with other members in the group (some groups have a rotating policy, while others are more flexible) and tends to regard the experience in very positive terms. "The participants report that both their frequency of sexual relations and their enjoyment of them remained at a higher level after than before they entered the group relationship" (Constantine & Constantine, 1977, p. 190).

Stability of Group Marriage

It is clear that the benefits derived from sexual exchange are not sufficient to induce permanence in group marriage relationships. Of the twenty-six groups studied, over half had dissolved after one year, over 80 percent by the third year, and by the fifth year, only 7 percent remained intact. The median length of time before dissolution was sixteen months. The basic reason for breaking up was the incompatibility between some of the members (Constantine & Constantine, 1973, p. 69).

Most couples return to their previous dyadic relationship; some divorce. Whether they stay married or split, almost two thirds remain friends with other members of their group marriage.

TRENDS

Marriage relationships of the future will less often begin with a traditional wedding and honeymoon. Weddings will occur in a variety of settings and will be more for the spouses than for their parents. And, because more couples are living together, fewer will take the traditional honeymoon. But regardless of the ceremony or the absence of a honeymoon, because of the changing roles of the sexes, traditional marriages which have been characterized by male dominance will become less frequent. The trend toward equalitarian relationships will continue.

The future of marriage relationships will also include the continuation of a wide range of variation in such relationships. And because of such diversity it will be difficult to categorize a specific relationship. Even within certain categories (e.g., college, mixed, or military marriage), the individual spouses in the respective relationships will develop their own relationship so as to be different from other relationships in the same category.

SUMMARY

Marriage relationships legally begin with the witnessed signing of the marriage license following a ceremony in which the bride and groom have made a commitment to each other before an approved official. Although most weddings occur in a church or synagogue, an increasing number are occurring in less traditional settings.

The individual consequences of marriage include an enhanced self-concept, new behaviors, disillusionment, and more personal happiness. Social relationships with parents, in-laws, and friends of both sexes are also likely to change. And, marriage involves the legal transfer of property.

But most spouses are more concerned about their relationship than their inheritance rights. And most relationships can be described in terms of the degree to which they are traditional or open. The traditional marriage has been criticized as permitting little individual growth. Individuals are said to wilt and choke in the confines of traditional marriage. But open marriage assumes an entirely different socialization which most people have not experienced. While an open marriage may be intellectually appealing, it is often emotionally difficult to achieve.

Whether involved in an open or traditional marriage, about one fourth of all college students are married. The primary effect of marriage on the college student is to increase the number of roles in rapid succession—spouse, employee, and, perhaps, parent. The wife's education is often threatened. Dropping out for a semester to increase the family income sometimes means dropping out forever. But most married students regard marriage during college in positive terms and say they would do it again.

While interracial marriages account for only a small percentage of marriage relationships, they most often involve a black man and a white woman. Those who cross racial lines to marry are often older, have been married before, and have fewer ties with their own families. Interfaith marriages occur more frequently but also involve social disapproval from parents. The stability of interracial and interfaith marriages is slightly less than the stability of homogamous marriages.

Military marriages are yet another variation in marriage relationships. The role relationship between the military husband and wife is traditional. Such traditional role relationships are functional for the service, which must move its personnel frequently and needs the wife's compliance. Such moves are problematic, though, because they involve separations from family and friends and tend to encourage a sense of alienation. Separations also take a toll on the marriage relationship and require a major adjustment by the military couple.

Group marriages account for only a small proportion of marriage relationships. Although motivation for involvement in a group marriage appears to be more the desire to expand the range of interpersonal relationships than for increased sexual access, group marriages are notoriously unstable.

Trends for the future of marriage relationships include fewer traditional weddings, honeymoons, and marriages. In addition, there will continue to be a wide range of marriage relationships. Referring to *the* marriage relationship will become almost meaningless as the variety of patterns expands still further.

STUDY QUESTIONS

1. What are some ways in which two individuals who marry may differ radically in the experience that preceded their wedding?
2. In order to be married, what events must take place?
3. How frequent are religious weddings in contrast to civil ceremonies? What are the implications of a church wedding?
4. What are some typical aspects of a nontraditional wedding?
5. Discuss the social, personal, and interpersonal functions of the honeymoon.
6. Discuss some personal consequences for the individual who gets married.
7. In general, what effect does marriage have on the newlywed's self-concept?
8. Discuss how marriage changes a person's relationships with parents, in-laws, and friends of both sexes.

9. How does marriage affect the inheritance of property belonging to either spouse?
10. All marriage relationships are not alike. What are some ways in which marriages may differ from one another?
11. Compare the characteristics of traditional and open marriage relationships.
12. How was the married college student regarded before 1940? Why? What event changed attitudes toward married students?
13. What are the background characteristics of students who marry during college?
14. How are grades and roles affected by marriage for the college student?
15. Discuss the frequency, characteristics, problems, and stability of black-white marriages.
16. How common are interfaith marriages between Protestants, Jews, and Catholics?
17. Why do most major religions discourage marriage outside their faith?
18. What factor may account for the conflicting data on interfaith marriage stability?
19. What are the military's expectations for its married couples?
20. In what ways are frequent moves problematic for the military couple?
21. What is the consequence of forced separations on the marital relationship of military couples?
22. What are some of the advantages of a military marriage?
23. Describe the typical composition of a group marriage.
24. When will accurate data on group marriage be available?
25. Comment on the background characteristics of those who become involved in group marriage, their motivations for doing so, and the problems they experience.
26. How stable are group marriages?
27. Discuss trends in marriage relationships.

NOTES

1. Part of the tendency among married couples to leave a party early is the result of not being available to seek a new sex partner for the night. Any exclusive pairing, including living-together relationships, may result in a tendency to "leave early."

2. Individuals who have lived together before marriage have already experienced some of the results of day-to-day reality.

3. Terms similar to open marriage include open-ended relationships, intimate friendships, commitment with freedom, self-fulfillment within marriage, and opening-up marriage (Knapp & Whitehurst, 1977, p. 147).

4. In general, what couples do on their "private time" is reportable to their spouse. While each partner may not choose to report all the details, the implicit understanding is that each spouse is not to do anything of which the other would disapprove. In contrast to the O'Neills' position, other authors have suggested that each partner should have private time and experiences that are not necessarily related to the partner (Myers & Leggitt, 1975).

5. The popular concept of race is based on pigmentation—skin color which may appear red, yellow, white, brown, and black. The scientific conception of race is broader and more diffuse. In addition to pigmentation, hair, facial features, bone structure, teeth, and blood type are also considered.

6. However, the researchers noted that ". . . children eleven and older might have more difficulty making new friends than would younger children. This may be due to the increased role of peers for adolescents and the greater cohesiveness of groups that the older child must enter" (Barrett & Noble, 1973, p. 187).

7. The frequency and duration of family separations varies greatly among branches of military service, as well as among occupational groups within each service. Navy submariners and aviators and Marine helicopter pilots are among the groups facing the most separation (Hatch, 1976, p. 12).

BIBLIOGRAPHY

Allen, F., and Gale, L., Family structure and treatment in the military. *Family Process,* 1973, *12,* 171–8.

Astin, A. W., and Panos, R. J. *The educational and vocational development of college students.* Washington, D.C.: American Council on Education, 1969.

Athanasiou, R., Shaver, P., and Tavris, C. Sex. *Psychology Today,* July 1970, 39–52.

Barrett, C. L., and Noble, H. Mothers' anxieties versus the effects of long distant moves on children. *Journal of Marriage and the Family,* 1973, *35, 2,* 181–8.

Bayer, A. E. College impact on marriage. *Journal of Marriage and the Family,* 1972, *34, 4,* 600–609.

Benson, L. *The family bond: Marriage, love and sex in America.* New York: Random House, 1971.

Berkove, G. Effects on the marriage when wives return to school. Paper presented at the meeting of the National Council on Family Relations, New York, 1976.

Bey, D., and Lange, J. Waiting wives: Women under stress. *American Journal of Psychiatry,* 1974, *3,* 131.

Black, A. D. Expectations and realities of interracial marriage. In *Interracial Marriage: Expectations and Realities.* New York: Grossman, 1973, 9–16.

Blood, R. O. *The family.* New York: Free Press, 1972.

Bumpass, L. L., and Sweet, J. A. Differentials in marital instability: 1970. *American Sociological Review,* 1972, *37,* 754–66.

Burchinal, L. G., and Chancellor, L. E. Survival rates among religiously homogamous and interreligious marriages. *Social Forces,* 1963, *41, 4,* 353–62.

Burma, J. H., Cretser, G. A., and Seacrest, T. A comparison of the occupational status in intramarrying and intermarrying couples: A research note. *Sociology and Social Research,* 1970, *54,* 508–19.

Busselen, H. J., and Busselen, C. K. Adjustment differences between married and single undergraduate university students: A historical perspective. *The Family Coordinator,* 1975, *24, 3,* 281–7.

Campbell, A. The American way of mating: Marriage si, children only maybe. *Psychology Today,* May 1975, 37–43.

Campbell, A., Converse, P. E., and Rodgers, W. L. *The perceived quality of life.* New York: Russell Sage Foundation, 1975.

Carter, H., and Glick, P. *Marriage and divorce: A social and economic study.* Cambridge, Mass.: Harvard University Press, 1970.

Christensen, H., and Barber, K. E. Interfaith versus intrafaith marriage in Indiana. *Journal of Marriage and the Family,* 1967, *29, 3,* 461–9.

Constantine, L. L., and Constantine, J. *Group marriage: A study of multilateral marriage.* New York: Macmillan, 1973.

————. Sexual aspects of group marriage. In *Marriage and alternatives: Exploring intimate relationships,* R. Libby and R. Whitehurst (eds.). Glenview, Ill.: Scott, Foresman, 1977, 186–94.

Cox, F. *Youth, marriage, and the seductive society.* Dubuque, Iowa: Brown, 1974.

Eshleman, J. R., and Hunt, C. Social class influences on family adjustment patterns of married college students. *Journal of Marriage and the Family,* 1967, *29,* 485–91.

Gillespie, H., and LaPointe, C. Personal communication, 1977.

Glenn, N. D. The contribution of marriage to the psychological well-being of males and females. *Journal of Marriage and the Family,* 1975, *37, 3,* 594–600.

Gordon, A. I. *Intermarriage.* Boston: Beacon Press, 1964.

Hatch, S. Military service and marriage. Department of Sociology, East Carolina University, Greenville, N.C. Unpublished paper, 1976.

Heer, D. M. The prevalence of black-white marriage in the United States, 1960 and 1970. *Journal of Marriage and the Family,* 1974, *36,* 246–58.

Heiss, J. S. Premarital characteristics of the religiously intermarried in an urban area. *American Sociological Review,* 1960, *25,* 47–55.

Hunt, M. *Sexual behavior in the 1970's.* New York: Dell, 1974.

Johnson, D. J. In-law relations: A research note. Paper presented at the meeting of the National Council on Family Relations, San Diego, 1977.

Jourard, S. M. Marriage is for life. *Journal of Marriage and Family Counseling,* 1975, *1,* 3, 199–208.

Knapp, J. J., and Whitehurst, R. N. Sexually open marriage and relationships: Issues and prospects. In *Marriage and alternatives: Exploring intimate relationships,* R. W. Libby and R. N. Whitehurst (eds.). Glenview, Ill.: Scott, Foresman, 1977, 147–60.

Locke, H. J. *Predicting adjustment in marriage: A comparison of a divorced and a happily married group.* New York: Henry Holt, 1951.

Mack, D. E. The power relationship in black families and white families. *Journal of Personality and Social Psychology,* 1974, *30,* 409–13.

McCubbin, H. I., Dahl, B. B., and Hunter, E. J. (eds.). *Families in the military system.* Beverly Hills, Calif.: Sage, 1976.

McKain, J. L. Relocation in the military: Alienation and family problems. *Journal of Marriage and the Family,* 1973, *35,* 2, 205–9.

Monohan, T. P. Are interracial marriages really less stable? *Social Forces,* 1970, *48,* 461–73.

_____. An overview of statistics on interracial marriage in the United States, with data on its extent from 1963–1970. *Journal of Marriage and the Family,* 1976, *38,* 223–31.

Myers, L. Personal communication, 1978.

Myers, L., and Leggitt, H. *Adultery and other private matters: Your right to personal freedom in marriage.* Chicago: Nelson-Hall, 1975.

O'Neill, N. In "Open Marriage" Modified-Sex Policy Flops, by Georgia Dullea. *Kansas City Star,* 16 October, 1977.

O'Neill, N., and O'Neill, G. *Open marriage: A new life style for couples.* New York: Avon Books, 1972.

Peck, B. B., and Schroeder, D. Psychotherapy with the father-absent military family. *Journal of Marriage and Family Counseling,* 1976, *2,* 1, 23–30.

Porterfield, E. *Black and white mixed marriages: An ethnographic study of black-white families.* Chicago: Nelson-Hall, 1978.

Ramey, J. W. Emerging patterns of innovative behavior in marriage. *The Family Coordinator,* 1972, *21,* 4, 435–56.

Rapoport, R., and Rapoport, R. N. New light on the honeymoon. *Human Relations,* 1964, *17,* 33–56.

Rimmer, R. Comment on "Can group marriage work?" In *Communes: Creating and managing the collective life,* R. M. Kanter (ed.). New York: Harper and Row, 1973, 233–9.

Seattle Urban League Special Report. People who intermarry: Pioneers or protestors? Seattle, Washington, April, 1967.

Stuart, I. R., and Edwin, L. *Interracial marriage: Expectations and realities.* New York: Grossman Publishers, 1973.

U.S., Bureau of the Census. Census of Population: 1971 Marital Status, Final Report. PC (2)—4C. Washington, D.C.: U.S. Government Printing Office, 1972.

The U.S. fact book: The American almanac. New York: Grosset and Dunlap, 1977.

Van Gennep, A. *The rites of passage.* Chicago: University of Chicago Press, 1960.

Waller, W., and Hill, R. *The family: A dynamic interpretation.* New York: Holt, Rinehart and Winston, 1951.

Weisberg, D. K. Alternate family structures and the law. *The Family Coordinator,* 1975, *24,* 4, 549–59.

Whitehurst, R. N. Youth views marriage: Awareness of present and future potentials in relationships. In *Marriage and alternatives: Exploring intimate relationships,* R. Libby and R. Whitehurst (eds.). Glenview, Ill.: Scott, Foresman, 1977, 294–301.

Womble, D. *Foundations for marriage and family relations.* New York: Macmillan, 1966.

Chapter 11

Dual-Career Marriage

EMPLOYED WIVES: PAST AND PRESENT

Historical Overview • Today's Employed Wives • Motivations for Employment

JOB VERSUS CAREER: SOME DIFFERENCES

Criteria for a Career • Obstacles to Pursuing a Career

DUAL-CAREER MARRIAGES

Dual-Career Patterns • Consequences of Two Careers in One Marriage

TWO CAREERS IN YOUR MARRIAGE?

Considerations for the Wife • Considerations for the Husband

TRENDS

SUMMARY

"Hectic" is the best way to describe our dual-career marriage.
A lawyer's husband

In the past, the typical American family consisted of a husband who earned the income and a wife who stayed home and took care of their children. But an increasing number of women and men are rejecting this tradition. In a national random sample of over two thousand American youth (ages fourteen through twenty-five), 56 percent of the young women and 46 percent of the young men disagreed with the statement, "While there are some exceptions, the idea that 'Woman's place is in the home' still makes sense" (American Council of Life Insurance, 1976, p. 53). Since nine out of ten couples will, at some time during their marriage, be earning two incomes, this chapter focuses on this increasingly common pattern.

EMPLOYED WIVES: PAST AND PRESENT

Before examining a profile of today's employed wives, let's explore the historical context of female labor force participation.

Historical Overview

A dominant theme throughout American history has been that women could find happiness only through fulfilling their roles as wives and mothers. A woman's place was in the home. But this expectation was most often in reference to the married, white, middle-class woman. Prior to 1940, working women were primarily single, poor, black, immigrant, or a combination of these variables (Chafe, 1976, p. 9).

World War II marked the point at which female employment became more acceptable for all classes of women. Their participation in the labor force became "a national necessity instead of a social aberration" (Chafe, 1976, p. 15). And while most of the middle-class wartime employed women were expected to return to the role of wife/mother after the war was over, a Women's Bureau survey conducted in 1944 and 1945 revealed that between 75 and 80 percent of all women war workers wanted to remain on the job after the fighting had stopped (Chafe, 1976, p. 16). Although demobilization resulted in the loss of jobs for many women (and men), the trend toward increased participation of women in the labor force had been established. The proportion of employed married women in the labor force[1] increased from 15 percent in 1940 to 30 percent in 1960 and to 40 percent by 1970. By 1977, employed wives made up almost 47 percent of the labor force (Department of Labor, 1977).

Two factors continue to influence the trend toward increased employment among women—the women's movement and a decreased birth rate. Spearheaded by the National Organization for Women (NOW), the women's movement seeks concrete legislation and judiciary action to end economic discrimination against women. Regarding the relationship between the decreased birth rate and employment of married women, it has been found that as responsibilities at home decrease, labor force participation by wives usually increases.

If we have come to think that the nursery and the kitchen are the natural sphere of a woman, we have done so exactly as English children come to think that a cage is the natural sphere of a parrot—because they have never seen one anywhere else.

George Bernard Shaw

Today's Employed Wives

In March 1977, 46.6 percent of all wives living with their husbands were employed (Department of Labor, 1977). The most typical roles for employed wives are typist, teacher (elementary or secondary), nurse, cashier, sales-person, or maid (Kreps & Leaper, 1976, p. 70). Women tend to work in a narrow range of occupations. One half of all working women are employed in only 21 of the 250 occupations listed by the Bureau of the Census, while half of all working men are employed in 65 of these occupations (Whitehurst, 1977, p. 56).

Among all married women, those more likely to be employed have completed college, do not have preschool children, and have fewer children (Burke & Weir, 1976; Taeuber & Sweet, 1976). One explanation for the relationship between education and employment is the greater appeal of jobs that are available to college-educated women. A forty-three-year-old mother who dropped out of high school to get married said, "It's hard for a person like me to get a job—even as a file clerk; and, when you get a job, the pay is lousy."

While education is a factor in female employment, the presence or absence of children has the greatest effect. Just as the married woman with no children is more likely to be employed, women with children, and particularly preschool children, are more likely to be at home. While about 47 percent of married women are employed, only about 39 percent of those with children under six years of age work outside the home (Department of Labor, 1977). In general, a wife/mother's employment follows the development of her children. Times of peak employment are before children are born and after they leave home. One mother of three grown children remarked, "While my children were small and needed me, I stayed home. But it never occurred to me not to work after that."

Motivations for Employment

Why do 22 million married women work outside the home? An advertisement in *Ms.* magazine reads, "Women like being Merrill Lynch account executives for a deep, psychological reason—money." Most women work for the same reason men do. In general, the lower the husband's salary, the greater the likelihood that the wife will work (Waite, 1977). A saleswoman for Kodak observed, "Money tends to dribble in but pour out. When you've got bills like we do, you've got to do everything possible to get more money dribbling in."

Aside from being economically motivated, many married women work for the personal satisfaction they derive from employment. A recently married college-educated woman said, "Housework bores me and so does staying home alone all day. I'm beginning my new job on Monday. It doesn't pay much, but it will sure beat this."

Other women seek employment because of their need for adult interaction. A mother of two-year-old twins caught herself talking "baby talk" to her husband one afternoon. She remarked, "I guess it's time for me to go back to work if I don't want my brain to become like that of a two-year-old."

JOB VERSUS CAREER: SOME DIFFERENCES

Regardless of the motivations for involvement in the labor market, work doesn't mean the same thing to all employed wives. Some married women (particularly those without children) pursue a career in the same sense that many men do. But more often, wives have jobs and their husbands have careers.

Almost half of married women work at jobs outside the home, but only a small proportion of these pursue long-range, full-time careers. Although the trend is for more women to have careers, family responsibilities still prevent many women from devoting the time and personal commitment to a career that are necessary.

Criteria for a Career

A career, in the fullest sense, differs from a job in its demand for training, commitment, continuity, and mobility. A clinical psychologist who is employed in a mental health center said, "I didn't get where I am just because I like to work with people. I went to school for twenty years, read myself blind, and wrote a 230-page dissertation to get the Ph.D."

In addition to formal training, a career implies commitment in time and energy to pursue the goals of an organization or profession. An executive for an appliance manufacturer observed, "The corporation wants your soul. If you are not willing to make phones calls in the evenings to your branch managers or to work on Saturday morning—in general, work when the corporation needs you—you'll never be an executive or make $60,000 a year."

Related to career commitment is continuity. This involves moving up the ladder and remaining "full time." Careers within large organizations are often thought of in terms of a progression of posts leading upwards in some kind of hierarchy. Careers in professions are thought of as proceeding through stages of cultivation and experience, accumulating expertise (Rapoport & Rapoport, 1971). A middle-aged woman said, "I am now the hospital administrator because I didn't want to be a nurse all my life. I wanted this position when I first came here twenty years ago, and I've made a lot of sacrifices to get it. But it's been worth it. I earn good money and make this hospital run like a well-oiled machine."

Mobility is a final element which helps to define *career*. The trained, committed, full-time professional must be willing to move to another city as his or her career demands it. An army career officer observed, "Once you decide the army is your career, you better decide to put up with the moving. We've moved eleven times in the last twenty years."

Not all husbands have or want careers as just defined. Many have jobs which require less training, commitment, continuity, and mobility. And when asked to move their families across country, some turn down a promotion (Renwick et al., 1978). Nevertheless, husbands are more likely than wives to have careers.

Obstacles to Pursuing a Career

What are the obstacles to a wife who wants to pursue a career? There are at least three.

Responsibility for children. Over 90 percent of all wives express a desire for children. And, while there are exceptions, both wives and husbands tend to expect that the wife will be primarily responsible for childrearing—an expectation that blocks the wife's career advancement (Bryson et al., 1976). The demands of home and family make it difficult for women to compete with male colleagues who are not encumbered with the daily responsibilities of homemaking and child rearing (Hudis, 1976; Renwick et al., 1978).

In a study of two hundred dual-career couples, the researchers observed of the wives that, "Because of the demands and role conflicts, women often fit their careers around children and husbands" (Heckman et al., 1977, p. 328). An elementary school teacher said, "There is tremendous social pressure on me to be responsible for my children. I don't have to be with them personally to take care of them, but I end up being responsible for arranging that someone takes Sandy from school to piano lessons, that Sam starts his homework after baseball practice, and that Melody is picked up at the nursery. My husband is very willing to help with the kids, but he's trying to build his practice as an attorney, and I can't see bothering him with the details. If I did, it would soon cut into his career and neither of us wants that. Of course, my career suffers, but I see no alternative."

Some executives are reluctant to hire or promote women for fear that they will give primary concern to their families rather than to their work. In a nationwide sample of over fifteen hundred managers and executives, a team of researchers revealed that women were *perceived* as giving their family top priority and that this perception would influence their being discriminated against when competing with men for career opportunities (Rosen et al., 1975).

Any woman who has a career and a family automatically develops something in the way of two personalities, like two sides of a dollar bill, each different in design. But one can complement the other to make a valuable whole. Her problem is to keep one from draining the life from the other. She can achieve happiness only as long as she keeps the two in balance.

Ivy Baker Priest

No "wife" at home.   Relative to a married man, an employed married woman is further handicapped in that she rarely has someone at home to do those things the traditional wife typically does. Keeping milk in the refrigerator, the meals prepared, the clothes clean, the social arrangements made, and the children cared for are chores for which someone must be responsible. In most families, a wife who has a full-time job is still expected to do most of the domestic work when she gets home.

> In spite of . . . [my husband's] enthusiasm for my professional development, I have been completely responsible for child care and regular domestic-type things. I consider this to have been a major detriment to my career—I do not object strongly to having these responsibilities, but in viewing my husband's attitude toward my professional life I find it difficult to live up to his expectations in both areas. (Heckman et al., 1977, p. 328)

In general husbands of employed wives aren't much help at home. Most spend only a few hours on household tasks each week (in contrast to twenty-six hours for the employed wife), and most of what they do is shopping (Vanek, 1974). As for help with the kids, the average American father spends twelve minutes per day with them (Stone, 1972). Overall, though, women seem more alarmed at inequality in the marketplace than at home. In a national sample of American households, only 19 percent of the wives said that they wanted more help from their husbands (Robinson & Robinson, 1975).

Lack of assertive skills. Being responsible for children and having no "wife" at home are primary obstacles to pursuing a career. But even though a woman may share the child-rearing and domestic chores with her husband, she may lack the assertiveness to compete in the business world.

A woman executive editor of a major book company said, "The business world is no place for the meek. I have had to make decisions and stick by them to get where I am. That means confronting colleagues and challenging their ideas and behavior. If you've got a weak stomach or want everyone to always like you, a career isn't for you." As indicated in Chapter 2, women are socialized to be less assertive than men. This lack of assertiveness may result in not getting salary increases and promotions.

While an increasing number of American women are demonstrating that it is possible to manage a job and a family, there is evidence to suggest that combining a *career* and a family is more difficult. Despite these obstacles, though, more women are pursuing careers. Graduate school enrollment for women is up and increasing numbers of women are earning law, medical, and Ph.D. degrees.

DUAL-CAREER MARRIAGES

When a wife does pursue a career, what is the marriage like? Let's review the patterns and consequences of dual-career marriages.

Dual-Career Patterns

In a study of fifty-three marriages in which the wife was a physician, lawyer, or university professor, one researcher observed the degree to which both spouses pursued their careers. The patterns he observed follow (Garland, 1972).

Traditional. In this arrangement, the husband was the primary breadwinner while the wife's occupational involvement was seen by both spouses as secondary to the husband's career and to the wife's domestic duties. This pattern was characteristic of 40 percent of the couples.

Neotraditional. In 50 percent of the marriages, the wife's career was viewed by both spouses as a significant factor to consider in making any career-related decision. A New York Shell Oil executive was to be promoted and transferred to

California. Because his wife, a university professor, could not find a position in the area to which her husband was assigned, he declined the promotion. In the neo-traditional dual-career marriage, the wife's employment is seen more in reference to the income she earns (that is necessary to maintain the family's standard of living) than in terms of her commitment to her career.

Matriarchal. Although the two patterns described above suggest the dominance of the husband's career, in the matriarchal pattern the wife has outdistanced her husband through educational achievement, career success, and/or income. This pattern accounted for 10 percent of the couples.

Egalitarian. In the egalitarian marriage, the career spouses shared the housework and took equal responsibility for rearing their children. This pattern was true for only 1 percent of the couples. Apparently, for 99 percent of the couples sharing the "breadwinning" did not necessarily mean sharing the domestic work.

The above patterns should be viewed in perspective. First, because the respondents in this study were not randomly selected, it cannot be assumed that the types of marital relationships they reflected provide an accurate picture of other dual-career couples. Second, dual-career couples of today may be different from

In egalitarian dual-career marriages, the husband and wife share the income-earning and domestic and child-rearing roles equally. Probably because of the influence of long-standing sex-role expectations, the fully egalitarian pattern remains very rare.

those in 1970, the year these interviews were conducted. Third, the criteria we have used for a career may be unrealistic. Perhaps what is needed is a new definition of career which does not require that all other activities be subordinate to it. For example, although dual-career wives more often make special arrangements with their employer or school regarding time schedules because of family responsibilities (Holmstrom, 1972), they may still feel a strong sense of commitment to their careers. A dean at a large university said, "I am as committed to my work as my husband is to his. I don't write a book every year or attend all the professional meetings in my field, but a lot of 'career men' don't either. While they leave work early to play golf, I leave early to spend time with my children. To say that you don't have a career unless you devote every minute to your work is nonsense."

Consequences of Two Careers in One Marriage

Regardless of the type of dual-career pattern couples have, there are various consequences for the spouses and their marriages that are different from those in which only one spouse has a career. Let's examine these consequences more closely.

Personal consequences.   Employment for a married woman involves personal consequences for both herself and her husband. It is unmistakably clear that most wives who have careers are personally happy (Rapoport & Rapoport, 1971; Holmstrom, 1972; and Poloma & Garland, 1971). One researcher compared housewives with wives who were university teachers or physicians in terms of self-esteem, mental health, and similar variables (Birnbaum, 1975). The results are given in Table 11.1—the career wives were more satisfied with themselves and their lives than housewives. Other researchers have reported a similar pattern (Gove & Geerken, 1977). Among the benefits wives derive from a career include increased interaction with a variety of individuals, a broader base for recognition, enhanced self-esteem, improved economic conditions for self and family, and greater equality between self and spouse.

But working wives "also pay for these benefits in reduced free time for themselves, a more hectic pace, and a more complicated life" (Wright, 1978, p. 312). Additional problems include ambivalence regarding the wife/mother/worker roles, job discrimination, and having little in common with neighborhood nonemployed wives. Regarding the latter problem, one wife said:

> Social and personal problems include the problem of relating to the women in the neighborhood, to whom I have trouble talking. From feeling like a wishy-washy liberal in graduate school, I have come to feel like a flaming radical in suburbia! . . . I always turn out to have more in common with the two men than with the other woman, and feel something of a role conflict . . . yet I am bored stiff with conversation which centers on detergents, car pools, and the best way to clean an oven (Heckman et al., 1977, p. 325).

TABLE 11.1   A Health and Happiness Comparison of 29 Housewives and 25 Career Wives.

	Percentage of Housewives	Percentage of Career Wives
Self-esteem score (competence in five areas: domestic, social, child-care, cultural, intellectual)		
Good to very good	14	54
Average to good	55	42
Poor to average	31	4
Mental-emotional health		
Good to very good	61	88
Poor to average	39	12
Feelings of uncertainty about who you are and what you want		
Hardly ever	34	64
Fairly often	66	36
Feeling lonely		
Hardly ever	28	72
Sometimes to often	72	28
Would like to have more friends	40	12
Misses challenge and creativity	42	4
Feels "not very" attractive to men	61	12
Very happily married	52	68

SOURCE: Birnbaum, 1975.

But how do husbands feel about the career involvement of their wives? After interviewing the husbands of the fifty-three professional women referred to earlier, Garland observed, "Most husbands of professional wives reported that they wanted to marry a woman who would either have a career of her own or be intellectually active and stimulating" (Garland, 1972, p. 207). Most reported that they got what they wanted. A physician said, "I married Anne because she was devoted to the practice of medicine. This has provided a basis for understanding each other that would not be possible if she had a job and I had a career."

Husbands of career women also enjoy the economic benefits of a two-income marriage (Heckman et al., 1977). "Together we make about $50,000 annually, which allows us to afford the luxuries we enjoy," remarked a hotel manager.

"Don't let anybody fool you," he continued. "When you've got two people pouring money into the kitty, it fills up faster and you can buy what you want *now.*" Some couples adjust to a standard of living that is based on two incomes so that it is difficult for them to drop back to a one income life-style.

But more income doesn't always make the husband feel better—particularly if his wife makes more money than he does (Garland, 1972). "I know it doesn't make sense, but the fact that I make $15,000 and my wife make $20,000 bothers me *and* her. We don't talk about it," remarked one husband. On the other hand, another husband who made less money than his wife observed, "It's not the dollar amount of difference that counts. It's how the couple interpret the wife's higher salary. If a husband gets depressed because she makes more money, that's his problem. I am proud of my wife's accomplishments and earnings. We use her income and mine for us. Who makes more really doesn't matter."

A free-lance writer summarized the ambivalence many husbands feel about their employed wives:

> A man may be proud of his wife's accomplishments, yet resent having to help out at home. He may welcome the money she earns, yet feel his masculine role as the breadwinner is being downgraded. He may be pleased that his wife has become a more interesting person, yet fearful that she is becoming too independent. He may be grateful that she shares the financial burdens, yet reluctant to share major family decisions with her. (Lobsenz, 1976, p. 8)

Marital consequences.[2]   In addition to the consequences experienced by the respective spouses when the wife works, what are the consequences for their marriage? Findings from early studies on this issue were inconsistent (Locke & Mackeprang, 1949; Williamson, 1954; Axelson, 1963; and Grover, 1963). While some of these studies reported improved marital satisfaction when the wife was employed, others reported a decrease in marital satisfaction.[3]

More recently, two researchers studied 189 married couples, comparing those which included an employed wife and those which did not (Burke & Weir, 1976). The spouses in each group differed on how they sized up their marriages. The employed wives reported happier marriages than did their husbands. In contrast, husbands of the nonemployed wives reported happier marriages than did their wives (Burke & Weir, 1976). Possible reasons for the husband experiencing less marital satisfaction when his wife works includes his wife's performing fewer traditional services (meal preparation, house cleaning, etc.) and the husband feeling more obligated to help with such chores. (We have already noted that his feeling obligated to perform more domestic duties does not necessarily translate into his doing so.)

Regardless of how marital happiness is affected, employment of the wife alters the traditional pattern of their relationship. The money she earns increases her power in the marriage (Moore & Sawhill, 1976). An interior designer said, "Now that I make a good income, my preferences are given equal weight by my husband. Whether we eat out or not, where we eat, and where we vacation are

TABLE 11.2   How Parents Feel the Mother's Employment Affects Their Children.

"Mothers with small children should go to work only if the money is really needed."

	Percent Who Agree or Partially Agree
Total parents	82
Fathers	81
Mothers	83
Working mothers	75

"Sometimes mothers must work, but children are better off when mothers don't."

	Percent Who Agree or Partially Agree
Total parents	69
Fathers whose wives work full time	68
Fathers whose wives do not work full time	75
Mothers who work full time	48
Mothers who do not work full time	73

SOURCE: General Mills, 1977.

now joint decisions. Before, he would say, 'We can't afford it . . .' and I would acquiesce." The adage, "He who pays the piper calls the tune," summarizes the relationship between money and power. In the dual-career marriage, there are two pipers and two potential tunes. In their classic work, *Husbands and Wives,* Blood and Wolfe (1960) wrote, "A working wife's husband listens to her more and she listens to herself more."

Consequences for children.   While most husbands and wives feel that the wife's employment has more positive than negative personal and marital consequences, they are more ambivalent about the consequences for their children. To assess how parents feel on this issue, General Mills supported a nationwide study of 23 million American families with children under thirteen years of age. A random sample of these families resulted in 1,230 interviews with the parents. Table 11.2 reflects their feelings about the mother working.

Most of the respondents, including the employed wives, feel that the mother should not work when her children are small. And, about half of the working mothers feel that their children would be better off if they did not work. Less participation in the labor force by mothers with small children reflects this value. Sixty percent do not work outside the home (Department of Labor, 1977).

However, no negative effects of a mother's employment on her children have been verified. Academic performance, psychosomatic symptoms, I.Q. scores, school conduct, and the affectional relationship with the mother are not significantly affected by the mother's working (Nye & Hoffman, 1963). Indeed, white adolescent girls sixteen to eighteen have fewer personal problems if the mother is employed (Whitemarsh, 1972) and appear to have a greater admiration for their mothers (Nye & Hoffman, 1963) than those daughters whose mothers stay home.

The only relationship that has been found between the mother's working and the child's adjustment concerns the mother's work satisfaction. If the mother is unhappy with her work, she tends to be demanding and neglectful of her children. If she enjoys her work too much, and is too involved in her career, she may feel guilty and try to compensate by overindulgence (Nye & Hoffman, 1963).

Working mothers may have another influence on their children, particularly on their daughters. In essence, by their own career involvement they teach their daughters not to view life's satisfactions primarily or exclusively in reference to marriage and children (Bruce, 1974). The daughter of a physician said, "Mom has always had her medical practice. I admire that and want a life-style like hers. She and my dad are very happy so I know a meaningful career doesn't necessarily cancel out a good marriage."

Other consequences. Couples in dual-career families note that household chores, child-rearing responsibilities, and time priorities become potential problems (Garland, 1972). Since each spouse's occupational role makes considerable demands, each needs a "back up." In the traditional marriage, the nonworking wife serves as the support for her husband by preparing meals, cleaning the house, making social arrangements, and so forth. The dual-career marriage has no full-time "wife" to back up either spouse.

Patterns of response to the "no wife at home" problem vary. Some spouses spend a portion of their joint income to hire "wife" substitutes—someone to prepare the meals, clean the house, etc. "It's spend the money, or do it yourself. Our careers are too demanding to consider doing the 'wife work' when we get home," observed an architect.

Other couples extend themselves after they get home to perform the necessary chores. "Hired help in this town is nonexistent. We do it ourselves or it doesn't get done," remarked a fashion merchandiser. Still other couples neither hire help nor do it themselves—they simply lower their standards. "We eat a lot of meals from the deli . . . beds go unmade, and we've put off remodeling the kitchen for years," a university professor explained.

As already noted, the wife in the two-income family usually ends up doing more of the domestic work (Holmstrom, 1972; Poloma & Garland, 1971; Rapoport & Rapoport, 1971). One third of the dual-career wives in Holmstrom's (1972) sample felt "bitter and resentful" that their husbands did not help as much around the house as they expected. "I have to ask him to do his share of the housework. He drags around and does it after I remind him, but slips back to his old pattern after a couple of days. It annoys me terribly, but it's not important enough to divorce him over it. I guess he knows that."

Regardless of how the work gets done, dual-career couples complain that they have little time for each other. "We have to schedule Saturday from three till midnight for ourselves. If it weren't for the Saturday nights alone together, we would be divorced. If you don't spend time with each other, you grow away from your partner," remarked a real estate broker.

A final problem for the dual-career marriage is where to live. "Although the husbands in two-career families were supportive of their wives' careers, the wives were, generally, expected to follow their husbands when they changed jobs and to live where his career demanded" (Holmstrom, 1972). But, studies of dual-career marriages only report the relationships of those couples who have stayed together. We do not know how often a career woman says, "My office is moving to Atlanta and I am going. If you don't want to come, that's your decision."

TWO CAREERS IN YOUR MARRIAGE?

The considerations in deciding whether to have a dual-career marriage are different for the wife and the husband. Let's examine the relevant issues for each partner.

When both spouses have careers that drain much of their time and energy, getting household chores done can be a problem. Some couples hire help, some cut into precious leisure time to get the housework done, some lower their housekeeping standards, and many adopt a pattern combining all of these solutions.

Considerations for the Wife

Personal needs, husband's support, desire for children, and the amount and timing of training required are issues the wife should consider in making a decision to pursue a career during her marriage. It is clear that some women are miserable in the sole roles of wife and mother. A newswoman for a major television network said, "My career offers me the chance to stay alive. When my children leave home or if my husband dies first and leaves me alone, I will still be a journalist. Otherwise I'd be nothing."

The husband's emotional support for his wife's career is another consideration. A "job" may be preferable to a "career" if the woman's husband has a passive attitude toward her pursuing a career. A university biology professor remarked,

"I might say that my present husband has the best attitude toward my working that a husband possibly could . . . if you're going to combine work with marriage, you've got to have a husband who not only tolerates your career, but actively wants you to work. Because, you know, the toleration will go just so far. But when you're up

Key factors in a dual-career marriage are the husband's support for the wife's career and his willingness to share child-rearing responsibilities. Few wives can pursue their careers successfully, rear their children to their satisfaction, **and** care for their homes effectively without the active cooperation and full backing of their husbands.

against it and you need help and support, then you've got to have this from a husband who wants you to do what you're doing, rather than putting up with it." (Holmstrom, 1972)

In addition to personal needs and husband's support, the desire for children is another important consideration. Unless a woman's husband is willing to share the responsibility of rearing children fully (he takes the children to piano lessons or sees that someone else does), her career will suffer. And, she may experience personal strain in managing the roles of mother and worker (Johnson & Johnson, 1977). As noted earlier, it is common for women to handle the conflict between children and career by reducing career commitment to meet family needs.

Since a career usually involves specialized training, the timing of the training becomes important. "Get your training over with before you get married," said a young female attorney. "I earned my law degree while we were married. The strain of preparing for my exams, caring for our son, and making time for my husband was almost unbearable."

Summarizing these various considerations, a college professor observed:

I think it is perfectly possible to combine a profession and marriage—as long as you have these basic premises: as long as the man is not threatened by the woman's capabilities and achievements; as long as he sees it as adding to his stature and not diminishing it; as long as a woman has worked out her own role as a mother; and as long as she is not ambivalent about her roles. (Poloma, 1972)

Considerations for the Husband

A husband should also weigh the pros and cons of his wife's having a career before urging her to pursue or not pursue a career. As already noted, husbands point to the intellectual/companionship aspects, more money, and the knowledge that their wives are happier working than being at home as primary benefits of the wife's being involved in a career. The potential disadvantages seem to focus on missing the services of the domestic wife, feeling obligated to help more with household chores, and feeling threatened by the wife's own income, increased power, and independence.

In evaluating these advantages and disadvantages, questions the husband might ask include: "Is the loss of domestic services counterbalanced by more income?" "Is my wife's absence from home made up for by her greater fulfillment?" and "Am I truly willing to share the responsibility for parenting?"

TRENDS

An increasing number of married women will continue to be employed in the labor force. While most of these women will have jobs rather than careers, an increasing number will become involved in careers (Hopkins & White, 1978). Indeed, for some brides, the understanding that they will pursue a career during their marriage is a nonnegotiable issue. "I want to be married," said one woman, "but I won't let it interfere with my career as a musician."

An increased commitment by wives to paid employment will mean fewer mothers with small children will remain at home. To encourage young mothers to continue working, more companies will offer "flexitime." This system permits a worker to select the eight hours he or she will work between 7:30 a.m. and 6:30 p.m. By 1976, over 300,000 Americans were enjoying flexitime in over one thousand companies and government agencies (Stein et al., 1976). Spouses who share child-rearing responsibilities are particularly attracted to flexitime.

In addition to more couples in the work force enjoying flexitime schedules, there will be an increase in commuter marriages. Also referred to as "weekend" or "long distance" marriages, commuter marriages refer to spouses who live apart because the demands of their respective careers require that they live in different cities[4] (New York Times News Service, 1977). Such an arrangement reflects the difficulty some couples experience in maintaining two careers in one marriage.

SUMMARY

Employed wives are becoming increasingly common, particularly in the middle class. Prior to 1940, female workers were primarily single, poor, black, and/or immigrant, but with World War II middle-class wives flooded the labor force. In 1940, only 15 percent of married women were employed, but by 1977 that figure had jumped to almost 47 percent. In addition to World War II, the women's movement and a lower birth rate have contributed to this trend.

In general, while wives are motivated by money and the desire for adult interaction, their labor force participation is related to the development of their families. While wives with no children are the most likely to be employed, those with preschool children are the least likely to work outside the home. Sixty percent of mothers with children under six are at home with them.

When a career is defined in terms of training, commitment, continuity, and mobility, most wives have a job rather than a career. The responsibility for children and having no "wife" at home are among the obstacles married women must overcome in pursuing a career.

Dual-career marriages may be described as being traditional, neotraditional, matriarchal, or egalitarian. While research is limited, only a small percentage of dual-career marriages appear to be those in which the spouses are equally pursuing their careers and sharing the housework and child-rearing responsibilities.

When wives are asked to evaluate the effect of their employment on themselves, their marriages, and their children, most report being happier individuals and happier in their marriages. About their children, they differ. Some wives feel that their children derive positive benefits from their working but other wives feel guilty about working outside the home.

Husbands report mixed feelings about their wives' employment. While many are delighted that their wives are happier and enjoy the economic benefits of a dual-career marriage, they may also feel threatened by the wives' increased independence and feel frustrated when wives do not perform the traditional domestic chores.

Trends for dual-career marriages include more such marriages, more mothers of small children working outside the home, more companies offering flexitime, and more commuter marriages. Evidence for the general trend toward more employed wives is reflected in Department of Labor figures. The proportion of employed married women in the labor force has increased from 15 percent in 1940 to almost 47 percent in 1977.

STUDY QUESTIONS

1. How do American youth feel about the statement, "A woman's place is in the home"?
2. What were the typical characteristics of employed women before 1940?
3. What began the trend toward greater participation in the labor force by middle-class married women?
4. What proportion of the labor force are employed wives?
5. Which married women are most likely to be employed and which are least likely to be employed?
6. Discuss the motivations for wives seeking employment.
7. How does a career differ from a job?
8. Evaluate the statement, "Most married woman have a job rather than a career."
9. Discuss several obstacles a wife and mother must overcome if she is to pursue a career.
10. Discuss the personal benefits wives derive from participation in the labor market.
11. What do wives consider to be the disadvantages of being involved in a dual-career marriage?
12. Discuss the impact of the wife's employment on the marriage relationship as viewed by the respective spouses.
13. What is the effect of a mother's employment on academic performance, psychosomatic symptoms, I.Q. scores, and school conduct of her children?
14. Under what conditions does a mother's employment have a negative effect on her children?
15. What does the career mother teach her children about marriage and employment?
16. How do dual-career couples solve the problem of "no wife at home"?
17. Comment on the problems of time and domestic work experienced by dual-career couples.
18. What issues should be considered before becoming involved in a dual-career relationship
19. Discuss several trends in dual-career marriages.

NOTES

1. The term *labor force* includes people who are working and those who are looking for work. As of March 1977, almost half (49 percent) of all women sixteen years or older (including never married, divorced, separated, widowed, married, etc.) were in the labor force (Department of Labor, 1977).

2. While this section focuses on the impact of the wife's work involvement on the marriage, one study focused on the impact of the husband's work involvement on the marriage. The authors concluded, "Husbands' work time did not significantly reduce their participation in the housekeeper and therapeutic roles, nor their competence in the housekeeper, therapeutic, sexual, and recreation roles" (Clark et al., 1978).

3. In addition to the contradictory conclusions, it is still debated whether a cause-and-effect relationship is involved, and if so, what kind. If a career for the wife and marital unhappiness are correlated, is it that the wife's employment causes a marriage to go sour, or that an unhappy marriage causes women to seek employment?

4. Couples in commuter marriages rarely have children.

BIBLIOGRAPHY

American Council of Life Insurance. Youth—1976. New York: American Council of Life Insurance (277 Park Avenue, 10017).

Axelson, L. J. The marital adjustment and marital role definitions of husbands of working and non-working wives. *Marriage and Family Living,* 1963, *25,* 189–95.

Birnbaum, J. A. Life patterns and self-esteem in gifted family-oriented and career-oriented women. In *Women and achievement: Social and motivational analyses,* M. T. S. Mednick, S. S. Tangri, and L. W. Hoffman (eds.). New York: Halstead Press, 1975, 396–419.

Blood, R. O., and Wolfe, D. M. *Husbands and wives.* New York: Free Press, 1960.

Bruce, J. A. The role of mothers in the social placement of daughters: Marriage or work? *Journal of Marriage and the Family,* 1974, *35,* 4, 492–7.

Bryson, R., et al. The professional pair: Husband and wife psychologists. *American Psychologist,* 1976, *31,* 10–16.

Burke, R. J., and Weir, T. Some personality differences between members of one-career and two-career families. *Journal of Marriage and the Family,* 1976, *38,* 3, 453–9.

Chafe, W. H. Looking backward in order to look forward: Women, work, and social values in America. In *Women and the American economy: A look to the 1980s,* J. M. Kreps (ed.). Englewood Cliffs, N.J.: Prentice-Hall, 1976, 6–30.

Clark, R. A., Nye, I. F., and Gecas, V. Husbands' work involvement and marital role performance. *Journal of Marriage and the Family,* 1978, *40,* 1, 9–21.

Garland, N. T. The better half? The male in the dual-profession family. In *Toward a sociology of women,* C. Safilios-Rothschild (ed.). Lexington, Mass.: Xerox College Publishing, 1972.

General Mills, Inc. *Raising children in a changing society.* Minneapolis, Minn.: General Mills, Inc., 1977.

Gove, W. R., and Geerken, M. The effect of children and employment on the marital health of married men and women. *Social Forces,* 1977, *56,* 1, 66–76.

Grover, D. A. Socio-economic differential in the relationship between marital adjustment and wife's employment status. *Marriage and Family Living,* 1963, *25,* 452–58.

Heckman, N. A., Bryson, R., and Bryson, J. B. Problems of professional couples: A content analysis. *Journal of Marriage and the Family,* 1977, *39,* 2, 323–30.

Henning, M., and Jardim, A. *The managerial woman.* New York: Doubleday, 1976.

Holmstrom, L. L. *The two-career family.* Cambridge, Mass.: Schenkman, 1972.

Hopkins, J., and White, P. The dual-career couple: Constraints and supports. *The Family Coordinator,* 1978, *27,* 3, 245–9.

Hudis, P. M. Commitment to work and to family: Marital-status differences in women's earnings. *Journal of Marriage and the Family,* 1976, *38,* 2, 267–78.

Hunt, J. G., and Hunt, L. L. Dilemmas and contradictions of status: The case of the dual-career family. *Social Problems*, 1977, *24*, 407–16.

Johnson, C. L., and Johnson, F. A. Attitudes toward parenting in dual-career families. *American Journal of Psychiatry*, 1977, 134, *4*, 391–5.

Kreps, J. M., and Leaper, R. J. Home work, market work, and the allocation of time. In *Women and the American economy: A look to the 1980s*, J. M. Kreps (ed.). Englewood Cliffs, N.J.: Prentice-Hall, 1976, 61–81.

Lobsenz, N. M. How husbands really feel about working wives. *Woman's Day*, July 1976, 8 et passim.

Locke, H. J., and Mackeprang, M. Marital adjustment and the employed wife. *American Journal of Sociology*, 1949, *54*, 536–8.

Moore, K. A., and Sawhill, I. V. Implications of women's employment for home and family life. In *Women and the American economy: A look to the 1980s*, J. M. Kreps (ed.). Englewood Cliffs, N.J.: Prentice-Hall, 1976, 102–22.

New York Times News Service. Commuter marriages on rise. *Raleigh News and Observer*, 31 October 1977, 6.

Nye, I. F., and Hoffman, L. W. (eds.). *The employed mother in America*. Chicago: Rand McNally, 1963.

Poloma, M. M. Role conflict and the married professional woman. In *Toward a sociology of women*, C. Safilios-Rothschild. Lexington, Mass.: Xerox College Publishing, 1972.

Poloma, M. M., and Garland, T. N. The married professional woman: A study in the tolerance of domestication. *Journal of Marriage and the Family*, 1971, *33*, 531–40.

Rapoport, R., and Rapoport, R. *Dual-career families*. Baltimore: Penguin Books, 1971.

Renwick, P. A., Lawler, E. E., and the *Psychology Today* staff. What you really want from your job. *Psychology Today*, May 1978, 53 et passim.

Robinson, N. H., and Robinson, J. P. Sex roles and the territoriality of everyday behavior. Unpublished manuscript, Survey Research Center, University of Michigan, 1975.

Rosen, B., Jerdee, T., and Prestwich, T. Dual-career adjustment: Potential effects of discriminatory managerial attitudes. *Journal of Marriage and the Family*, 1975, *37*, 3, 565–72.

Stein, B., Cohen, A., and Gadon, H. Flexitime: Work when you want to. *Psychology Today*, July 1976, 40–44.

Stone, P. J. Child care in twelve countries. In *The use of time*, A. Szalai (ed.). The Hague, The Netherlands: Mouton, 1972, 249–64.

Taeuber, K. E., and Sweet, J. A. Family and work: The social life cycle of women. In *Women and the American economy: A look to the 1980s*, J. M. Kreps (ed.). Englewood Cliffs, N.J.: Prentice-Hall, 1976, 31–60.

U.S., Department of Labor. Single men and married women show unusually large labor force gains. Washington, D.C.: GPO News Release 77–792, 14 September 1977.

Vanek, J. Time spent in housework. *Scientific American*, 1974, *231*, 14, 116–20.

Waite, L. J. Social and economic determinants of employment of wives over the family life cycle. Paper presented at the meeting of the American Sociological Association, Chicago, 1977.

Whitehurst, C. A. *Women in America: The oppressed majority*. Santa Monica, Calif.: Goodyear Publishing, 1977.

Whitemarsh, R. E. Adjustment problems of adolescent daughters of employed mothers. *Journal of Home Economics*, 1972, *57*, 201–4.

Williamson, R. C. Socio-economic factors and marital adjustment in an urban setting. *American Sociological Review*, 1954, *19*, 213–16.

Wright, J. D. Are working women really more satisfied? Evidence from several national surveys. *Journal of Marriage and the Family*, 1978, 40, *2*, 301–13.

Chapter **12**

Conflict in Marriage

MYTHS ABOUT MARRIAGE

"Our Marriage Will Be Different" • "Love Will Keep Us Together" • "We Will Make Each Other Happy" • "Children Will Make Our Marriage Even Happier" • "My Spouse Is All I Need"

ASSESSING MARITAL HAPPINESS AND ADJUSTMENT

What Affects Happiness? • Measuring Marital Adjustment • Marital Happiness and the Family Life Cycle • Stages of the Family Life Cycle

CONFLICT

Inevitability of Conflict • Desirability of Conflict • Sources of Conflict • Types of Conflict • Areas of Conflict • Motivations to Manage Conflict

CONSTRUCTIVE CONFLICT MANAGEMENT

Listen • Give Feedback • Pinpoint Behaviors to Change

OBSTACLES TO CONFLICT MANAGEMENT—DEFENSE MECHANISMS

Escapism • Rationalization • Projection • Displacement • Emotional Insulation

MARRIAGE COUNSELING

Styles of Marriage Counseling • Cost and Number of Sessions • Effectiveness of Marriage Counseling • Reluctance to Contact a Marriage Counselor • Locating a Counselor

MARRIAGE ENRICHMENT

TRENDS

SUMMARY

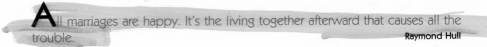

All marriages are happy. It's the living together afterward that causes all the trouble.

Raymond Hull

Many people whose roles change from lover to spouse experience a rude awakening. Disillusioned, they sometimes feel marriage has turned an exciting love relationship into a deadening routine. Part of their disillusionment may be due to having had unrealistic expectations about marriage. More important, though, their inability to manage conflict effectively in the new relationship may create despondency. In this chapter we examine several myths about marriage and explore a systematic way to manage conflict. In addition, we offer an overview of the larger issue of marital adjustment and explore opportunities for marriage counseling and marriage enrichment.

MYTHS ABOUT MARRIAGE

The authors of *The Mirages of Marriage* wrote that marriage is "like taking an airplane to Florida for a relaxing vacation in January, and when you get off the plane you find you're in the Swiss Alps. There is cold and snow instead of swimming and sunshine. . . . After you buy winter clothes and learn how to talk a new foreign language, you can have just as good a vacation in the Swiss Alps as you can in Florida. But . . . it's one hell of a surprise when you get off that marital airplane. . . ." (Lederer & Jackson, 1968).

One of the reasons for being surprised by the actual experience of marriage is that the day-to-day living together in marriage occurs behind closed doors. And our assumptions about what actually happens behind those doors are often distortions of reality. Some of the more unrealistic beliefs our society perpetuates about marriage include the following.

"Our Marriage Will Be Different"

Everyone has known married people who were bored, fought often, or who eventually divorced. Despite this, every bride and groom assume that their marriage will be different. "I feel sad when I look at other marriages," said a new bride. "Spouses seem so callous toward each other — like they don't care for each other at all. I'm certain that such indifference will not happen to Kirk and me." Four years later this same bride and her husband were in marriage counseling. "I don't know what happened," she said. "We've been drifting apart for a long time. It worries me."

The feeling prior to marriage that "it won't happen to me" reflects the deceptive nature of courtship. If you are determined that your marriage will be different, what steps will you take to ensure that it is? This question is relevant because many of those couples who enter marriage believing that theirs will be different blindly imitate the marriage patterns of others instead of making a conscious effort to manage their own relationship so as to make it as fulfilling as they desire.

"Love Will Keep Us Together"

"If people knew how we felt about each other, they would know that our relationship could weather anything," said an engaged man. Notice that the motivation for working things out with the partner is love. But little attention is ever given to where feelings of love come from or what makes them continue.

The good feelings between two people in an interpersonal relationship—love, affection, intimacy—are based on "an exchange of behaviors at a rate and of a kind that is mutually satisfying" (Turner, 1977). In essence, love will keep you and your partner together only as long as the behaviors that engender love continue at the desired frequency. If they do not continue, you (and your partner) may seek someone else who offers the desired behaviors at the desired rate. "Although that's really a mechanical explanation of love," said one student in a marriage and family class, "I think it's true. I used to love a girl who told me how great I was, studied with me, and slept with me. We did everything together. But when she stopped those three behaviors and told me I was a bore, I quickly fell out of love with her."

"We Will Make Each Other Happy"

Many spouses believe that they alone are responsible for each other's happiness. "When my husband committed suicide," one woman recalled, "I couldn't help but think that if I had been the right kind of wife he would still be alive. But I've come to believe that there was more to his depression than just me. He wasn't happy with his work and had taken a real beating in the stock market."

While you and your partner will be a tremendous influence on each other's happiness, each of you has roles (employee, parent, sibling, friend, son, or daughter) beyond the role of spouse. And these other role relationships will color the interaction with your mate. If you've lost your job or flunked out of school, and your brother has cancer, and your closest friend moves away, and your mother, who can no longer look after herself, resists going into a nursing home, it will be almost impossible for your spouse to "make you happy." In other words, while you may make every effort to ensure your spouse's happiness, circumstances can defeat you.

Although many couples acknowledge that they will have disagreements, they assume that theirs will be minor and "just part of being married." Unresolved conflict that can threaten the marriage is rarely considered, and both partners are shocked when such conflict surfaces. "All I wanted was for him to spend more time with me," recalled a divorced woman. "But he said he had to run the business because he couldn't trust anyone else. I got tired of spending my evenings alone and got involved with someone else."

Every unresolved issue has the potential to threaten the marriage. It is helpful to think of the bride and groom as getting a little red wagon on their wedding day. And into their wagon go stones—the problems of their relationship. If they do not unload the wagon—that is, face up to and resolve the problems—the wagon becomes heavy and difficult to pull. Finally the weight becomes unbearable, and the partners stop pulling. The marriage ends in divorce. Then the former partners enter into new marriages and get new wagons which begin to fill up with new stones.

"Children Will Make Our Marriage Even Happier"

Just as we have been socialized to believe that getting married is part of being an adult, we also tend to believe that having children is part of being married. We have been taught that children are a sign of the love between a woman and a man and that children make them happier. But some research suggests the opposite is true. While having children may increase personal happiness (particularly the wife's), children tend to bring a decrease in marital happiness (Renee, 1970; Feldman & Feldman, 1977). Marriages are happiest before children come and

"We were relying on you to hold our marriage together."

after they leave home. Married couples with children spend less time looking into each other's eyes, holding hands, laughing together, having calm discussions, and working on joint projects than couples without children do (Rollins & Feldman, 1970; Ryder, 1973; Rosenblatt, 1974).

"My Spouse Is All I Need"

Every individual has certain needs. These range from needing someone to see movies with to needing someone to talk to about personal problems. And while it is encouraging to believe that your partner can satisfy all your intellectual, physical, and emotional needs, it is not realistic. You now have an array of friendships and acquaintances who help meet your different needs, and the pattern of having your needs met by a variety of people is likely to continue after marriage.

> The need for intimacy is met by a combination of intimate relationships rather than by one individual. This is not to deny the importance of a central relationship in one's life; however, for an increasing number of individuals a combination of intimate relationships is the mechanism that enables them to meet or to approximate the meeting of their needs for close human contact and for intimate involvement. (Keiffer, 1977, p. 277)

In summary, it is unrealistic to believe that your marriage will be different, that love will keep you and your spouse together, that the happiness of each of you can be guaranteed by the other, that your disagreements will be minor, that children will increase your marital happiness, and that you can satisfy all your partner's needs. A more realistic appraisal of marriage suggests that your marriage *may* be different, that love *may* keep you together, that you will be *one* important influence on your partner's happiness, that your disagreements *need not* be major, that children *may* increase your marital happiness, and that you will be able to satisfy *some* of your partner's needs. As this appraisal indicates, it is possible to be both realistic and positive about one's future marriage.

ASSESSING MARITAL HAPPINESS AND ADJUSTMENT

With or without a belief in various myths, most couples enter marriage expecting to be happy. But what does "being happy" mean? Let's explore the subjective and dynamic nature of marital happiness and the many factors that influence it.

What Affects Happiness?

Happiness is a subjective term. The nature of happiness depends on one's point of view. One husband remarked that he had a fantastic relationship with his wife because each was free to have sex with others. But another said that their relationship was the best because they did not allow other relationships to interfere.

For their marriages to be happy, husbands and wives often want different behaviors from each other. For example, traditional husbands tend to want their wives to engage in *instrumental behaviors* —behaviors that are considered necessary for the marriage to survive as an economic and social unit. Shopping, preparing meals, taking care of the children, and making social arrangements are examples (Willis, Weiss, & Patterson, 1974). But not every husband is concerned about his wife performing domestic duties. "I want a wife who makes money so that we can use her income to travel every summer," said a school teacher.

In addition to being subjective and highly individual, marital happiness is constantly changing. Marriage is a process, not a static entity. When one spouse was asked, "How happily married are you?" he replied, "It depends on when you ask me. If you ask me when the kids are raising hell in the living room and when it's been ten days since my wife and I had some good dialogue and sex, I'll tell you, 'Not too happy.' But if you ask me when the kids are with their grandmother and my wife and I have had a chance to be alone, I'll tell you, 'Fantastic.' " Every marriage has its good and bad periods.

Other factors which affect how spouses will rate marriages at any given time include their relationships with other people, their fantasies about the happiness of other marriages, and their comparisons of their marriage now with their marriage in happier times (Farson, 1974). One twenty-three-year-old career woman explained how an outside friendship affected her feelings about her marriage: "I guess I was happily married until I met Max. Since we worked together we spent a lot of time together. I felt I could talk to him, and I began to compare the time with him with the time I spent with my husband. Within a few months I defined my marriage as a failure, and I wanted out."

Even without a rewarding alternative relationship, imagining that other spouses are very happy can decrease one's own marital happiness. "I feel like I'm caught in a bum marriage," observed one husband. "My best friend and his wife have the kind of marriage I want. They are both professionals, they like the same things, and they don't get hassled by their in-laws. They've got it made."

And comparing one's own marriage as it now is to the way it once was may be even more devastating. "Before the twins came," recalled a young mother, "Roger and I used to spend all our time together. Now we never get to eat out, to see movies, or to sleep late on weekends."

To summarize, marital happiness depends on one's personal point of view, is subject to constant change, and is appraised in varying contexts. The degree to which spouses regard themselves as happy depends on how happy they once were, how happy they assume others are, and how happy they are in other relationships.

Measuring Marital Adjustment

While the concept of marital happiness is somewhat elusive, one way of measuring it is to ask the respective partners to complete a form similar to the Dyadic Adjustment Scale *(See Box)*. This scale measures four aspects of the marital or cohabiting relationship: consensus (agreement in philosophy of life, decision making, etc.), affection (demonstrations of affection, sex relations), satisfaction (feeling good about the relationship, not regretting the marriage), and cohesion (working on projects together, etc.) (Spanier, 1976).

Measuring Happiness: The Dyadic Adjustment Scale

The following scale was developed to measure adjustment in couple relationships. To measure your relationship, circle a number for each of the thirty-two items and compare

your total score with those of 218 married and 94 divorced individuals.[1] The average score for the married was 114.8, and for the divorced, 70.7.[2]

1. The 218 spouses had an average age of 35.1 years and had been married an average of 13.2 years. They had an average of 13 years of education and 2 children. The 94 divorced individuals had an average age of 30.4 years and had been married for an average of 8.5 years. They had an average of 14 years of education and 1.6 children.

2. The standard deviation for the marrieds was 17.8. This means that scoring 114.8 plus or minus 17.8 points is about the same as scoring exactly 114.8. The standard deviation for the divorced individuals was 23.8. This means that scoring 70.7 plus or minuse 23.8 points is about the same as scoring exactly 70.7. SOURCE: Spanier, 1976, pp. 23 and 27–28.

Most persons have disagreements in their relationships. Please indicate below the approximate extent of agreement or disagreement between you and your partner for each item on the following list.

	Always Agree	Almost Always Agree	Occasionally Disagree	Frequently Disagree	Almost Always Disagree	Always Disagree
1. Handling family finances	5	4	3	2	1	0
2. Matters of recreation	5	4	3	2	1	0
3. Religious matters	5	4	3	2	1	0
4. Demonstrations of affection	5	4	3	2	1	0
5. Friends	5	4	3	2	1	0
6. Sex relations	5	4	3	2	1	0
7. Conventionality (correct or proper behavior	5	4	3	2	1	0
8. Philosophy of life	5	4	3	2	1	0
9. Ways of dealing with parents or in-laws	5	4	3	2	1	0
10. Aims, goals, and things believed important	5	4	3	2	1	0
11. Amount of time spent together	5	4	3	2	1	0
12. Making major decisions	5	4	3	2	1	0
13. Household tasks	5	4	3	2	1	0
14. Leisure time interests and activities	5	4	3	2	1	0
15. Career decisions	5	4	3	2	1	0

	All the time	Most of the time	More often than not	Occasionally	Rarely	Never
16. How often do you discuss or have you considered divorce, separation, or terminating your relationship?	0	1	2	3	4	5
17. How often do you or your mate leave the house after a fight?	0	1	2	3	4	5
18. In general, how often do you think that things between you and your partner are going well?	5	4	3	2	1	0
19. Do you confide in your mate?	5	4	3	2	1	0

		Almost			
20. Do you ever regret that you married? (or lived together)	0	1	2	3	4	5
21. How often do you and your partner quarrel?	0	1	2	3	4	5
22. How often do you and your mate "get on each other's nerves"?	0	1	2	3	4	5

	Every Day	Almost Every Day	Occasionally	Rarely	Never
23. Do you kiss your mate?	4	3	2	1	0

	All of them	Most of them	Some of them	Very few of them	None of them
24. Do you and your mate engage in outside interests together?	4	3	2	1	0

How often would you say the following events occur between you and your mate?

	Never	Less than once a month	Once or twice a month	Once or twice a week	Once a day	More often
25. Have a stimulating exchange of ideas	0	1	2	3	4	5
26. Laugh together	0	1	2	3	4	5
27. Calmly discuss something	0	1	2	3	4	5
28. Work together on a project	0	1	2	3	4	5

These are some things about which couples sometimes agree and sometimes disagree. Indicate if either item below caused differences of opinions or were problems in your relationship during the past few weeks. (Check yes or no)

Yes No

29. 0 1 Being too tired for sex.
30. 0 1 Not showing love.
31. The dots on the following line represent different degrees of happiness in your relationship. The middle point, "happy," represents the degree of happiness of most relationships. Please circle the dot which best describes the degree of happiness, all things considered, of your relationship.

0	1	2	3	4	5	6
Extremely Unhappy	Fairly Unhappy	A Little Unhappy	Happy	Very Happy	Extremely Happy	Perfect

32. Which of the following statements best describes how you feel about the future of your relationship?

___5___ I want desperately for my relationship to succeed, and **would go to almost any length** to see that it does.

___4___ I want very much for my relationship to succeed, and **will do all I can** to see that it does.

___3___ I want very much for my relationship to succeed, and **will do my fair share** to see that it does.

___2___ It would be nice if my relationship succeeded, but **I can't do much more than I am doing** now to help it succeed.

___1___ It would be nice if it succeeded, but **I refuse to do any more than I am doing** now to keep the relationship going.

___0___ My relationship can never succeed, and **there is no more that I can do** to keep the relationship going.

Scores on marital adjustment scales are in some ways deceptive, and it can't be assumed that any one score is "good" or "bad." Disagreements on a variety of fronts does not necessarily imply poor relationship adjustment. "We don't agree on a lot of issues, but we agree on important matters," one spouse said. Conversely, total agreement does not imply a fantastic relationship. One partner said that she and her husband agreed "on everything" but that she was bored silly.

In addition to the deceptive nature of scores on marital adjustment scales, another problem is that people tend to answer the way they think they should rather than the way things actually are (Edmonds, 1967; Riedell, 1976). This tendency to give socially desirable answers keeps the marriage experience hidden and makes it difficult to determine what type of relationship couples actually have. [1] "There is virtually no research in this area [marital adjustment] in which observation of behavior by trained observers provides the data or in which self report data were validated against such objective criteria [marital adjustment scales]" (Hicks & Platt, 1970, p. 555). In other words, we know only what people say they do in their marriage, not what they actually do.

Marital Happiness and the Family Life Cycle

Marriage is not the same in all its innings. An eminent psychologist who had been married over twenty-five years said, "I don't know how many marriages I have had by now, but I am married at the present time to a different woman of the same name in ways that are suited to our present stage of growth as human beings" (Jourard, 1975, p. 203). That your marriage will be different throughout the years is inevitable. And these changes can be described as occurring within different stages of the family life cycle.

Stages of the Family Life Cycle

Since most married couples have children, it is helpful to describe the various stages of the marriage in reference to the children. [2] Figure 12.1 divides the family life cycle into eight stages and gives the approximate length of each stage. The typical woman marries when she is twenty-one, gives birth to her last child at thirty, attends the wedding of her last child at fifty-two, and buries her husband when she is sixty-five (Glick, 1977, pp. 5–9). The corresponding stages for men are generally parallel except that men marry later and die earlier.

A couple's experience in the family life cycle will be affected by the number of years they are married before they have children, the number of children they have, and the health of their children. With several children, the couple will spend a longer time in the launching stage, and a handicapped child may prolong that stage indefinitely. The parent of an autistic child said, "My child is incapable of caring for himself, and we will never send him to an institution, so he'll be with us as long as he lives. He's now twenty-eight."

The most accurate way to find out how a wife and husband feel about their marriage over the years is to ask them at each stage of the family life cycle to

FIGURE 12.1   The Family Life Cycle by Length of Time in Each of
Eight Stages.

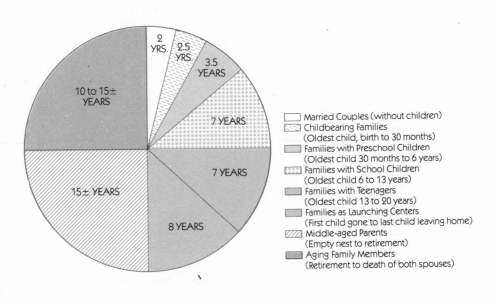

SOURCE: Adapted from Duvall, 1977, p. 148.

complete a marital adjustment inventory similar to the one already described. Such longitudinal research requires that a researcher wait until the couple gets to the next stage before asking them to complete the questionnaire again. But because researchers may die while waiting, they prefer to conduct cross-sectional research, which involves asking different couples in the various stages of the family life cycle to complete marriage adjustment inventories. Such research is imperfect because the groups compared cannot be identical. Couples in the later stages may be more likely to give socially desirable responses (Ahammer & Baltes, 1972) and may have a greater need to say they are happy since it is too late for them to get a divorce (Abelson et al., 1968). And those couples who have already gotten divorces have been eliminated from the later stages (Spanier, Lewis, & Cole, 1975).

With these cautions in mind, what can we conclude about marital happiness and adjustment over time? From the moment the bride and groom repeat "I do" until their first child is ready to enter grade school, there is a progressive decline in reported marital satisfaction (Blood & Wolfe, 1960; Rollins & Feldman, 1970; Rollins & Cannon, 1974; Spanier, Lewis, & Cole, 1975).

But what about the rest of the life cycle? What happens to marital satisfaction in stages four through eight? Researchers don't agree on the pattern. While some say that there is a steady decrease in reported satisfaction throughout the family life cycle (Blood & Wolfe, 1960; Pineo, 1961; Paris & Luckey, 1966), others find that couples reach a low point during their children's teen years but become happier during the launching and empty nest stage (Rollins & Feldman, 1970; Rollins & Cannon, 1974). And, still other researchers say that spouses with young children are the least likely to be happy (Glenn & Weaver, 1978).

Assuming that most couples experience maximum marital happiness before the children come and after they leave, how do husbands and wives differ in their evaluation of their marriage across the years? In general, they don't; they report similar degrees of satisfaction and dissatisfaction throughout the family life cycle (Rollins & Cannon, 1974, p. 280).[3]

CONFLICT

We turn our attention now to a major reason for marital dissatisfaction—conflict. As one professor in a marriage and family class said, "If you haven't had a disagreement with your spouse, you haven't been married long enough." In this section, we explore the inevitability, desirability, sources, types, and areas of conflict.

Inevitability of Conflict

If you are alone this Saturday evening from six until midnight, you are assured of six conflict-free hours. But if you plan to be with your partner or roommate during that time, each minute holds the potential for conflict. Where you eat, where you go after dinner, and how long you stay must be negotiated. While it is relatively easy for you and your companion to agree on one evening's agenda, marriage involves the meshing of desires on an array of issues for up to sixty or so years.

While most brides and grooms agree on a variety of subjects, new needs and preferences arise throughout the marriage. And changed circumstances sometimes call for the adjustment of old habits. "I can honestly say that before we got married, we never disagreed about anything," a wife of three years recalled. "But things were different then. Both my husband and I got money from our parents and never worried about how much we spent on anything. Now I'm pregnant and unemployed, and Jerome still acts like we've got millions. He buys expensive toys like a stereo, a ham radio, and a pool table. He thinks that because he uses Mastercharge we can pay the monthly minimum and still live high. We're getting over our heads in debt, and we're always fighting about it."

Although other married couples may not disagree on who spends how much on what, the probability that they will agree throughout the marriage on every issue related to sex, in-laws, recreation, religion, children, and division of labor is zero. Marital conflict is inevitable.

Desirability of Conflict

Not all conflict is bad. By expressing their dissatisfactions, spouses can negotiate for the changes they desire. Rather than brood because their partners are doing things they do not like, spouses may specify what they would like their mates to do differently. One wife with a full-time job said she was "sick and tired of picking up her husband's clothes and picking up wet towels from the bathroom floor." By asking her husband to put his clothes away and to hang up his wet towels and by agreeing to do something he wanted in return (make a cherry pie once a week), she got rid of the couple's negative feelings on these issues. Not to resolve a problem is to keep it alive. (Specific procedures for managing conflict are discussed later in this chapter.)

Seldom, or perhaps never, does a marriage develop into an individual relationship smoothly and without crises; there is no coming to consciousness without pain.

Carl Jung

Sources of Conflict

Conflict develops when one spouse's behavior does not match the other spouse's expectations or hopes (Patterson, Hops, & Weiss, 1975, p. 295). Table 12.1 illustrates that spouses feel upset when their mates engage in negative behavior. Only when the mates engage in the positive behavior do the spouses begin to feel better about each other.

Our *interpretation* of our partner's behavior is another major source of conflict. For example, two students who married in their senior year had planned to open a pet shop after they graduated. But the wife became interested in graduate school and was granted a fellowship. Her husband interpreted her desire to continue school as a way of avoiding working with him in the pet shop. Although his wife tried to assure him otherwise, he continued to think so, accused her of having lost her love for him, and became depressed. Had he taken pride in her scholarly aspirations, their marital happiness would have increased. In effect, it is not necessarily the way a spouse behaves but the interpretation of that behavior that results in happiness or unhappiness (Ellis, 1962; Lazarus, 1971).

Types of Conflict

Conflicts can be described as basic, nonbasic, or irrational (Scanzoni, 1972, pp. 72–73). Basic conflicts are those which threaten the marriage. In the traditional marriage, if the husband refuses to earn an income for his wife and children, a basic pillar of the marriage is threatened. "If he's not going to support me, what's he good for?" asked an unemployed wife whose husband wanted to resign his $20,000-a-year job, move to Oregon, and "rough it."

TABLE 12.1   Behavior as a Source of Conflict.

Spouse	Negative Feelings Based on Negative Behavior	Negative Behavior of Partner	Positive Behavioral Goal for Partner	Positive Feelings Based on Positive Behavior
Wife	"I don't like him."	He ignores me. He drinks too much. He yells at me. He provides no foreplay.	Pay attention to me. Be sober. Talk softly to me. Provide one hour of foreplay before intercourse.	"He is an attentive, sober companion and a great lover."
Husband	"She's a bad wife."	She avoids intercourse. She nags me. She neglects our child. She's too fat.	Approach me for intercourse. Compliment me. Change baby's diapers. Reduce weight to 115 pounds.	"She is a good lover, conversationalist, and mother who is concerned about her appearance."

SOURCE: Adapted from Knox, 1975, pp. 12–13.

Nonbasic conflict is irritating to both partners but does not put the marriage on the line. The wife's working, the husband's changing jobs, and frequency of intercourse are examples of issues that can cause such conflict. Regarding the latter, one researcher observed, "One spouse may consider unjust his/her spouse's definition of the proper frequency of coitus (too frequent or not frequent enough), or the propriety of certain techniques of sexual gratification. These are serious kinds of conflicts, but since they are presumably less basic than the desire and willingness per se to engage in sexual activity, they may therefore be considered relatively less central to the bonds of marital consensus" (Scanzoni, 1972, p. 74).

Both basic and nonbasic conflicts are caused by situations that one or both partners want changed. These conflicts are rational in that the partners differ about an issue. When irrational conflict exists, one partner enjoys arguing with the other and may choose anything to argue about. "When my spouse gets angry with me, I know she loves me," said one husband. "Otherwise, she would be indifferent."

Areas of Conflict

What do spouses argue about? For a list of possible causes of conflict in nine areas of marital interaction, see the box on "Common Issues of Marital Conflict."

Studies disagree as to which problems cause the most marital conflict. In one

Common Issues of Marital Conflict

MONEY (Too little; who earns it; who spends how much and on what; who manages the money; what type of bank accounts; borrowing money; investing money.)

SEX (How much; what kind; where; what time of day; use of contraceptives; overcoming sexual dysfunctions, e.g., impotence, premature ejaculation, frigidity; who initiates; how much affection to be shown in front of children.)

IN-LAWS (Which ones to visit or have visit, and how often, for how long; coping with aloofness or rejection by in-laws; coping with dislike of in-laws or with in-laws who dislike each other; avoiding meddling by deciding whether to seek or give financial help/advice from [or to] in-laws.)

RECREATION (Amount of time spent in various activities; solitary or family recreation; when to work and when to enjoy recreation [after work or before, on Sunday morning or Saturday]; where to spend vacations; how much money to spend on recreation.)

FRIENDS (Having different friends; not liking each other's friends; resentment of time with and closeness to friends; inequities or disagreement on number of friends.)

ALCOHOL, MARIJUANA, TOBACCO (Who drinks or smokes and when, where, how much; what to teach children about alcohol/marijuana/ tobacco; embarrassment or violence because of drinking/smoking; assessment of and concern over health hazards; concern over money spent on these substances.)

RELIGION (Having different religions; teaching religion to children; whether or how often to attend services; one spouse more religious than the other; how to celebrate holidays; disagreement over religious rituals [baptism, circumcision, saying prayers]; changing religions; amount of money donated to religious organizations.)

CHILDREN (How many to have and when; type of discipline; activities children should become involved in; emphasis on family closeness or on independence; rivalry for children's love; caring for handicapped or emotionally disturbed child; spending time with children; relationship with stepchildren; providing sex education to children.)

SOURCE: Adapted from Knox, 1971, pp. 140–43.

TABLE 12.2   List of Resources Potentially Exchanged Between Spouses.

1. Socioeconomic	{ Money Social Mobility Prestige	4. Companionship	{ Social Leisure Intellectual
2. Affective	{ Affection Love (loving — being loved) Feeling Needed — needing the other	5. Sex	
3. Expressive	{ Understanding Emotional Support Special Attention	6. Services	{ Housekeeping Services Child Care Personal Services "Linkage"* Services
		7. Power in the relationship	

*Linkage refers to services which link a family to other social systems. For instance, the wife's helping with voter registration links the family to the political system.

SOURCE: Safilios-Rothschild, 1976, p. 356.

study, over three thousand spouses reported that money, children, and sex were subjects they fought over most (Scanzoni, 1975). But in another study, 1,550 husbands and wives reported that they disagreed most over who was to do what around the house and about recreational issues (Chadwick et al., 1976). Individual circumstances and temperaments will dictate the degree and kind of conflicts experienced by different couples at different times in their relationship.

Motivations to Manage Conflict

The basic reason spouses try to get along with each other is that doing so is rewarding and not doing so is unpleasant. But the particular reasons for managing conflict include the desire to get what the partner has, the desire to reciprocate, the desire to avoid discord, the desire to avoid divorce, and the desire to avoid physical injury to the spouse.

Desire to get what the partner has.   Spouses negotiate the differences in their relationship because doing so helps to ensure that each will continue to get what the other has to exchange. Table 12.2 lists the resources that spouses may exchange.

Wives have traditionally exchanged resources two through six for their husbands' money and status. The exchange has been unequal and is likely to remain so. One sociologist observed,

> In sexist societies in which women have little or no access to desirable socioeconomic resources, husbands most often have exclusive access to these resources and can exchange them in return for all of the other resources listed in Table [12.2]. Unless,

therefore, the sex structure changes so as to allow men and women equal access to income, status, and power, husbands will have a great advantage over their wives in the marital exchanges and the determination of family power.[4] (Safilios-Rothschild, 1976, p. 357)

But wives expect more from their husbands than money, and husbands expect more from their wives than clean laundry. The essential point is that each wants things from the other, and gives in order to get. As already mentioned, a happy marriage may be defined as an exchange of behavior at a rate and of a kind that is mutually satisfactory to both spouses. In order for each partner to feel happy about giving what the spouse wants as often as the spouse wants it, the spouse must reciprocate. But there are exceptions. Some people do things for others because it feels good to do so. And in this sense, they are altruistic.

Marriage has a great deal to offer, but it is not a magic kingdom where the usual principles don't apply and where you get something for nothing.

David and Vera Mace

Moral obligation.   In addition to the desire to continue the exchange of specific benefits, most spouses feel a sense of moral obligation to reciprocate. "When one party benefits another, an obligation is generated. The recipient (Y) is now indebted to the donor (X) and remains so until he/she repays" (Gouldner, 1960, p. 173). As one husband remarked, "We spent Thanksgiving with my parents so there wasn't much I could say when she suggested that we spend Christmas with her parents." And such exchanges may go on indefinitely out of each partner's sense of fair play. As soon as Y repays X, the cycle commences all over again (Scanzoni, 1972, p. 46). Where the couple spend their Easter weekend may be the husband's choice, since they spent Christmas with the wife's parents.

Exchanges need not be as explicit or calculated as the above example suggests. Spouses do not keep ledgers. Rather most have an awareness of whether or not they are being treated fairly and whether or not they are responding in kind. Their sense of moral obligation encourages them to be fair in the everyday exchanges with their partner.

Disgust with discord.   If there are rewards for managing conflict and reciprocating, there are also costs for failing to do so. "When we're not getting along, I can't stand it," said one husband. "I'm irritable all day, don't eat well, and watch late movies until I fall asleep." Many spouses express similar feelings. Conflict is like a storm in a marriage, and the sooner it passes, the better.

Individual reasons for trying to cope with and reduce conflict vary greatly. This couple may have turned to a marriage counselor because they feared they were headed for divorce.

Fear of divorce.   As unresolved conflict mounts, some spouses feel as though they are on a conveyer belt carrying them toward divorce. The closer they come to calling a lawyer, the more clearly they can picture the consequences of separation. And so they try, once more, to resolve their conflicts. "When we saw that our problems were going to split us up, we got our relationship under control," recalled one wife.

Fear of spouse.   While fear of divorce sometimes motivates spouses to reduce conflict, fear of their partner may also do so. Such fear results in many cases from having been beaten by the spouse. Of the approximately 50 million couples in America, it is estimated that 3.3 million wives and over a quarter million husbands have experienced severe beatings from their spouses (Steinmetz, 1977).

CONSTRUCTIVE CONFLICT MANAGEMENT

The mere fact that the partners are motivated to try to manage a conflict is not enough to resolve the problem. Rather, constructive conflict management results from engaging in specific behaviors. These include the following behaviors.

Listen

The first step in conflict management is for each partner to understand the other's point of view. As a beginning, ask your partner, "Just how do you see the problem? Talk about how you feel."

Give Feedback

After your partner describes how he or she sees the conflict, say back to your partner what he or she said to you (Rogers, 1951). By giving direct feedback, you accomplish two goals. Not only do you assure your partner that you are really listening; you also check out what your partner said with what you heard. For example, a wife told her husband, "I get upset when you go out with Ben." Her husband's feedback (what he heard) was, "You don't want me to see Ben anymore." And the wife replied, "No, I didn't say that. I like to be with him, too, but Saturday night is our time, and I would like you two to play handball sometime other than Saturday night." Continual nondefensive dialogue will narrow your discussion to the issues that are relevant to your partner's dissatisfaction.

The manner in which you reflect back to your partner what he or she said to you is equally important. Assume that it is your job to understand your partner's viewpoint, not to evaluate the perception. In the example given above, the appropriate reflective statement would be, "You got angry when I went out with Ben on Saturday night." Such feedback reflects the content of the partner's statement

A constructive response to conflict in marriage is for the partners to listen carefully to what each has to say, to give nondefensive feedback to be sure of understanding one another, and to plan together specific behavioral changes.

("I get upset when you go out with Ben") and does not include an evaluation. An example of a reflective statement which does evaluate what the partner said would be, "You always get upset when I go anywhere because you're jealous of all my friends." Such a remark would stop the wife from expressing how she feels because her husband's evaluation would indicate to her that "he will use whatever I say against me."

Pinpoint Behaviors to Change

After each partner has listened to the other's point of view and given appropriate feedback, define the problem in terms of specific behaviors that each would like the other to engage in or specific behaviors each would like the other to stop. Refer again to Table 12.1 and notice that feeling unhappy is often a result of the partner's engaging in undesired and unanticipated behavior. When your partner criticizes you, keeps you waiting for hours, or lies to you, you probably feel unhappy and upset. But when your partner compliments you, is on time, and is honest with you, you are likely to have good feelings toward your partner.

The importance of being specific about what you want your partner to do cannot be overemphasized. Asking your partner to "be like you used to be," "be

---

T he greatest thing in family life is to take a hint when a hint is intended—and not to take a hint when a hint isn't intended.

Robert Frost

---

nice," or "show me you care" is too vague. One wife asked her husband to "be considerate." He thought that meant providing a lot of foreplay before intercourse. But for her "being considerate" meant asking her if she wanted a snack when he fixed one for himself in the evening.

Some spouses feel, "If I tell him what I want and he does it, it will be only because I asked him to do it, not because he loves me." Such a perspective puts the partner in a double bind. For example, if the husband does not ask his wife if he can bring her something from the kitchen when he goes to prepare a snack for himself, his wife will be angry. But if he asks her if she wants a snack, his wife may feel he is doing so for the wrong reason—not out of love or thoughtfulness but because she asked him to. Either way, he loses. To avoid this unnecessary predicament, the wife should recognize that her husband has a choice: He can change or not change his behavior in response to her request. And the fact that he chooses to ask her if she wants a snack before he goes to the kitchen indicates that he wants to please her and improve their relationship. What better evidence of love is there than trying to do what pleases the partner?

OBSTACLES TO CONFLICT MANAGEMENT— DEFENSE MECHANISMS

The bulk of conflict can be managed through listening, providing feedback, and pinpointing behaviors to change. And such behavior change usually has a positive effect on each partner's attitudes and feelings. But resolving conflict can be blocked by defense mechanisms. Their purpose is to minimize anxiety, lessen emotional hurt, and avoid self-devaluation (Coleman & Hammen, 1974, p. 137). They usually operate below the level of awareness of the individual, who often denies that he or she is using one of these mechanisms to avoid managing conflict and resents the suggestion. The more frequently used defense mechanisms include the following.

Escapism

When a problem is too difficult or painful to face, a spouse may deny that it exists and try to escape from dealing with it. The usual form of escape is avoidance. The spouse becomes "busy" and "doesn't have time" to think about or deal with the problem. Marriage counselors often refer to it as "keeping the drift alive." You keep your relationship drifting aimlessly without any direction and with no intent to sort problems out. And the longer an unresolved conflict continues, the less time the spouses spend talking with each other, sharing sex (Stuart, 1969), and going places together (Birchler et al., 1972).

Some channels of escape include recreation, sleep, alcohol, marijuana, or work. And some people escape family tension by watching televison (Rosenblatt & Cunningham, 1976). Regardless of the avenue of escape, the problem in the relationship remains unconfronted. And because the source of the dissatisfaction is avoided, the problem often continues, increasing the need to escape. "I can't go on," one wife said. "There is nothing for me to live for." Suicide is the ultimate escape that may result from a failure to deal with problems as they arise.

Rationalization

When avoiding or escaping the problem does not work, a spouse may try to rationalize it away. For example, the husband who is having an affair may justify his sexual involvement with another woman on the grounds that his wife is unwilling to have sex as often as he desires. "I'm tired of begging my wife to have intercourse with me," one husband said. "The woman I'm involved with makes it clear to me that she wants me. And that makes the cheating worthwhile."

It is sometimes difficult to know what is rationalization and what is truth. Hunting for reasons to justify our behavior, being unable to recognize inconsistencies that others see, and becoming emotional when others question our reasoning are good indications that we are rationalizing (Coleman & Hammen, 1974, p. 142).

And rationalization, like other defense mechanisms, is unproductive. It shifts the focus from the problem the spouses wish to eventually resolve to a temporary solution that may compound the problem.

Projection

In addition to escapism and rationalization, projection may interfere with conflict management. Projection occurs when one spouse who is guilty of a particular behavior accuses the other spouse of the same behavior. For example, the wandering husband referred to above may accuse his wife of being involved in an affair and of being unfaithful to him. Such blaming helps shift the focus from his affair and puts his wife on the defensive.

Other examples of projection are illustrated in such statements as "You spend too much money" (projection for "I spend too much money"), and "You think I'm neurotic as hell" (projection for "I'm afraid I am neurotic"). Projection cancels conflict resolution by creating a mood of hostility and defensiveness in both partners. And attack creates counterattack while the issues to be resolved in the relationship remain unchanged and become more difficult to discuss.

Displacement

Displacement shifts the frustration one spouse may be experiencing in other role relationships to the other spouse. The wife who is turned down for a promotion and the husband who is driven to exhaustion by his boss may direct their hostilities (displace them) against each other rather than against their respective employers. "I hate to say it, but our marital happiness is usually a reflection of how happy I am in my work," expressed the manager of a fast-food chain. "At the end of the month when the regional manager drops in to check the books, I get nervous. I am under pressure to increase profits, and I feel on edge by the time I get home. Last night my wife asked me to pass her the TV guide and I blurted, 'Get it yourself.' My real problem is the regional manager, but there is no way I can vent my anger on him." Partners should be aware that in some cases, the source of marital dissatisfaction is outside the marriage and attempt to resolve such dissatisfaction. Or, they can at least make a conscious effort to avoid allowing it to spill over into the marriage.

But displacement may be dysfunctional for yet another reason. Spouses who lack assertive skills may be unable to express their dissatisfactions to their partners and may displace their hostilities through scapegoating.[5] A spouse who resents the amount of time his or her partner is spending with someone else may develop intense hatred for that person and blast that person in a bitter verbal attack. The fact that the *spouse* has chosen to spend the "excessive" amount of time with the friend or relative may be ignored.

Emotional Insulation

While escapism, rationalization, projection, and displacement are obstacles to direct management of conflict, emotional insulation prevents conflict by reducing the commitment of the spouse to the relationship. One remarried person said, "I was devastated emotionally by my first marriage because I let myself be vulnerable. I hid nothing and loved as fully as possible. But my partner took advantage of my love and did not reciprocate. I don't want it to happen again so I am very guarded in my current marriage."

This spouse developed a protective guard to avoid being hurt. But the price of such protection may be high. "Getting hurt is part of growing up," observed a divorced person. "And if you take your resentments with you into the next relationship, you've had it. You can't make your new partner responsible for something your previous partner did. I did, and it cost me my second marriage."

By knowing about these defense mechanisms—escapism, rationalization, projection, displacement, and emotional insulation—and their consequences, you can be alert to their appearance in your own relationship. The essential characteristics of all defense mechanisms are the same: They are unconscious and they distort reality. Where a conflict continues without resolution, one or more defense mechanisms may be operating.

MARRIAGE COUNSELING

An alternative to attempting to resolve one's own problems is to look for help through marriage counseling. In this section we explore several styles of marriage counseling; what to expect in terms of cost, number of sessions, and outcome; and how to locate a marriage counselor.

Styles of Marriage Counseling

All marriage counselors are not alike. Primary differences are the ways they identify the causes of marital problems and the ways they attempt to solve them. The various approaches to marriage counseling include the following.

Transactional analysis. The "T.A." counselor believes that spouses are unhappy because one spouse is interacting with the other as though the mate were someone else. For example, a wife may relate to her husband as though he were her father; or a husband may relate to his wife as though she were his mother. The T.A. counselor encourages spouses to examine the ways in which their role relationships with others have been problematic and how they may have introduced these unresolved conflicts into their marriages (Berne, 1961; Warren, 1972).

Adlerian therapy.   Applying the theories of the Austrian psychiatrist Alfred Adler, the Adlerian marriage counselor views marital discord as a result of power struggles. The individual is seen as trying to compensate for feelings of inferiority from the moment of birth. The therapists seek to improve the marital relationship by helping couples to feel secure and to regard their power struggles as unnecessary (Dreikurs et al., 1959).

Behavioral counseling.   The behavioral marriage counselor believes that spouses are unhappy because each is engaging in behavior that upsets the other. The counselor encourages each spouse to engage in positive behaviors at a rate desired by the partner and may suggest behavior contracts to help ensure that new behavior occurs (Patterson, Hops, & Weiss, 1975; Knox, 1971).

Rational-emotive therapy.   Working from the theories of Albert Ellis, the executive director of the Institute for the Advanced Study of Rational Psychotherapy, the rational-emotive counselor believes that spouses are unhappy because of irrational beliefs they have about themselves and each other. Partners are encouraged to examine their beliefs and to change them if they have a negative impact on the marriage. For example, the belief that "My spouse should care more about me than anything else" would be examined for its potential negative consequences on the relationship (Ellis, 1962).

Transactional analysis, Adlerian therapy, behavioral counseling, and rational-emotive therapy are only a few of the different approaches used in marriage counseling (Hardy & Cull, 1974; Olson, 1976; Ard & Ard, 1976). Gestalt, psychodynamic therapy, humanistic psychotherapy, and reality therapy are others. And "no single theoretical viewpoint has gained ascendancy over all others . . ." (Nichols, 1973, p. 9). But all forms of counseling can be lumped into two basic categories—directive versus nondirective. In reality therapy, rational-emotive therapy, and behavior therapy counselors are directive. They suggest specific ways in which the spouses can improve their marriage. Counselors of the transactional analytic, Adlerian, Gestalt, psychoanalytic, and humanistic persuasions may or may not make specific recommendations. While some clients want specific direction, others want to explore their relationships and develop insight into the dynamics of their marital interaction. Clients should seek the therapist who will provide the style and form of counseling they want. But regardless of particular orientation, the trained marriage counselor can be expected to express a genuine concern for clients, to be nonjudgmental, and to regard all information as confidential.

Cost and Number of Sessions

Marriage counseling is expensive. Table 12.3 illustrates the range of fees and the average fees per session charged by 166 psychologists and 110 social workers in Washington, D.C. (Adams & Orgel, 1975, p. 27). The lower fees are usually paid by clients with low incomes who are receiving counseling in mental health clinics.

TABLE 12.3   Hourly Fees for Individual Therapy (1975 Figures).

	Psychologist	Social Worker
Lowest common fee	$10.00	$ 5.00
Average fee	$33.77	$26.07
Highest common fee	$50.00	$45.00

SOURCE: Adapted from Adams and Orgel, 1975, p. 27.

Such clinics usually make services available on an ability-to-pay or sliding scale basis. The higher fees would be paid to marriage counselors in private practice. And of course, fees have gone up at least 10–20 percent in the inflationary period since the data in Table 12.3 were collected.

Most counseling sessions last about fifty minutes during which the spouses most often will be seen together in what is referred to as conjoint marriage counseling. As to the number of sessions that will be necessary, counselors "are sometimes reluctant to tell consumers how long they expect therapy to last" (Adams & Orgel, 1975, p. 31). How long it will take a couple to achieve their goals is difficult to predict. Some exceptional spouses need only one session. Others may stay in counseling for years. Most spouses can anticipate seeing the counselor a minimum of six sessions.

Effectiveness of Marriage Counseling

Is marriage counseling worth the time and money? Dorothy Beck, Director of Research of the Family Service Association of America, reviewed the results of a variety of counseling approaches as reported in studies made from 1949 through 1974. In general, based on assessments of clients and counselors and on pre- and post-treatment measurements (Locke-Wallace Marital Adjustment Test, Taylor-Johnson Temperament Analysis, etc.), the results were positive. More specifically, "statistically significant positive gains were reported in all but one of the thirty-two controlled studies" (Beck, 1975, p. 166).

In another review of sixty-seven studies on marriage counseling, positive effects occurred in 65 percent of the cases. The percentage showing improvement was about the same regardless of the approach of the marriage counselor (Gurman & Kniskern, in press). However, when the spouses were seen alone rather than together by the therapist, improvement rates were only 48 percent (Gurman & Kniskern, in press). This suggests that the orientation of the therapist may be less important than whether the therapist counsels the partners together or separately.

Reluctance to Contact a Marriage Counselor

Even when a couple's marriage is dissatisfying and drifting toward divorce, our society promotes a number of attitudes that create obstacles to their consulting a marriage counselor. The idea, that "some couples have it and some couples don't," reflects the belief that when two people love each other, they will naturally get along in marriage. Unless couples recognize that this myth of naturalism is only a myth (Vincent, 1977), they may assume that there is something "unnatural" about their relationship if they have to give it the time and energy after marriage that they gave it during courtship. And becoming involved in marriage counseling takes both time and energy.

In addition to accepting the myth of naturalism, many married couples believe that their marriage is "nobody else's business." Such privatism prevents couples from seeking the help they need at the time they need it (Mace, 1975). Related to both naturalism and privatism is the belief that those who seek marriage counseling are "weak." "I can handle my own life with my wife," said one male in a marriage and family class. "My parents never needed a marriage counselor, and neither will we."

And some couples feel that if they need a marriage counselor, they have already failed. One marriage counselor observed,

> Couples seem to think they should be able to solve all their problems on their own. Yet these same spouses do not feel inadequate if they go to a dentist for a problem tooth or a mechanic for a stalled car. A marriage counselor is a professional . . . who has been trained to help couples fix the aching in their marriage and get it to run smoothly again. The only failure comes from allowing a problem to continue so long that no solution is possible. If the decaying tooth is not filled or the spark plugs changed, the tooth must come out and the car will stop. In marriage, it's called a divorce." (Quick, 1975, p. 51)

Many couples who become unhappy in marriage hope that something magical will happen to make things better. It rarely does. Marriage counseling can help by encouraging husbands and wives to sort out values, make decisions, and begin new behaviors to provide the basis for renewed happiness. It takes courage, commitment, and work.

Locating a Counselor

The American Association of Marriage and Family Counselors (225 Yale Avenue, Claremont, California 91711) is the foremost organization in the nation for accrediting and certifying marriage counselors. You can call the Association at 714-621-4749 (toll free) for a list of three qualified marriage counselors in your area. Members of AAMFC have at least a master's degree in one of the behavioral sciences (sociology, psychology, education, social work) plus two years of clinical experience in marriage counseling under the supervision of an approved agency or a member of AAMFC. It may be important to call AAMFC since only five states (California, Michigan, New Jersey, Utah, and Nevada) regulate marriage counselors. If you live in a state without such legislation, the marriage counselors in

"Now just be firm! Don't let him talk you into any reconciliation!"

your area who are not members of AAMFC may have neither training nor experience.

　　While many clergymen, psychologists, psychiatrists, sociologists, and social workers are excellent marriage counselors, do not assume that they all are. Rather, ask about your counselor's training, fields of special interest or competence, and experience. Since you will be placing your marriage in the counselor's care, consider it your obligation to ask such questions. Once you are involved in counseling, you and your partner are the best judges of whether the sessions are worthwhile (Adams & Orgel, 1975, p. 4).

MARRIAGE ENRICHMENT

Marriage counselors are often looked upon as the last resort, the final chance before a divorce is sought. They are thought of as an emergency medical team at the bottom of a cliff who minister to those who have already crashed in the hope of reviving them. But why not a guard rail at the top to prevent couples from slipping off the edge? Such preventive intervention is the goal of marriage enrichment programs, which are for couples who have a good marriage and who want to keep it that way. "What we are trying to do," write David and Vera Mace, cofounders of the Association of Couples for Marriage Enrichment (ACME), "is to equip married couples with the insight and training that will keep their marriages in such good order that the danger of going on the rocks will be as far as possible avoided" (Mace & Mace, 1975, p. 133).

By 1975 approximately 180,000 couples had met in small marriage enrichment groups for weekend or weekly evening sessions. The cost ranged from $5 to $75 per couple, and the content included such areas as couple or family communication, sexual relationships, roles, contracting, problem solving, and myths of marriage (Otto, 1975, p. 139). One marriage enrichment program (there are over twenty such programs), Mardilab, deals with the following subjects during its five, weekly two-hour sessions: how to talk when it hurts; loving without devouring; expressing anger constructively; male/female roles in transition; achieving intimacy; expressing sexual needs; outgrowing marital games; dealing with differentness; changing without threat; parenting; fact and fantasy (Stein, 1975, pp. 167–77).

Marriage enrichment programs are most often sponsored by religious groups and community agencies. Each session may consist of some combination of teaching by a group leader, dialogues between a husband and wife, and group discussion (Smith et al., 1976, p. 36). Some programs emphasize one format over another.

Whereas most couples who go to a marriage counselor have specific problems they want help with, couples who participate in marriage enrichment programs do so as a preventive measure. Instead of focusing on immediate crises, marriage enrichment programs attempt to give couples the interpersonal skills they need to avoid major problems in the future.

The Pairing Enrichment Program is husband-wife oriented. "All the communication exercises and transactions are experienced privately by each couple. The objective is to open up new communication and feeling experiences between each couple and there is no emphasis on group problem solving" (Travis & Travis, 1975, p. 162).

But what are the effects of becoming involved in a marriage enrichment program? After reviewing the research on such programs, Dr. Rebecca Smith and her colleagues concluded: "It seems that most of the gains measured were better understanding of self and better use of some techniques of interaction; however, the ability to put this knowledge into practice during and after the enrichment experience seemed doubtful" (1976, p. 36). This conclusion should not be interpreted to mean that marriage enrichment programs are useless. Rather, they are very effective in increasing a couple's self-understanding and could be still more useful by providing more training in developing specific skills.

TRENDS

The most significant trend in the management of difficulties arising in marriage is the increased willingness of couples to "go public" with their problems. The realization that it is normal for couples to be faced with problems in their relationships is replacing the old idea that good marriages don't have problems. In an article about "The Urgent Drive to Make Good Marriages Better," the authors point out that chapters of the Association of Couples for Marriage Enrichment have been started in all fifty states and in eighteen other countries (Koch & Koch, 1976, p. 33).

Meanwhile, professional standards for marriage counselors are being raised. In July 1978, a master's degree in marriage and family counseling or its equivalent became the basic academic requirement for admission into the American Association of Marriage and Family Counselors (AAMFC). While only a few states currently have laws governing marriage counselors, AAMFC launched a nationwide campaign in 1978 to encourage such legislation in the future. The hoped-for result will be a supply of highly trained and experienced marriage counselors sufficient to meet the growing demand for such services.

SUMMARY

Our society perpetuates various myths about marriage. These include the notions that love will keep a couple together, that children increase marital happiness, and that each spouse can fulfill all the other's needs. A more realistic perception is that love *may* help to keep spouses together, that children *may* improve a marriage, and that spouses will fulfill *some* of each other's needs.

Although being happily married is a major goal of most Americans, there is little agreement on what constitutes happiness. The definition is subjective and always changing, and marital happiness is subject to multiple influences. Although marriage adjustment may be assessed through the use of various scales, the results are often distorted by the desire of respondents to report a happy marriage whether they have one or not.

The family life cycle is often useful in estimating marital happiness and satisfaction over time. In general, spouses report being happiest in the early and late stages of the cycle, with the years when their children are teenagers among the most difficult.

But marital conflict may erupt at any time. It is both inevitable and, under certain conditions, desirable. While the usual cause for conflict is the behavior of one or both spouses, interpretation of behavior may also create problems.

Regardless of the source of marital conflict, most spouses are motivated to manage it. By doing so, they continue the high rate of positive exchanges and avoid the trauma of discord and divorce.

Some couples consult a marriage counselor. Since these counselors are not regulated by law in all states, care should be exercised in selecting one. Since theoretical approaches may range from humanism to behavior modification, it is important to select a counselor who offers the style and form of counseling you want. Marriage counseling is effective for most couples who become involved in it. But it is most effective when used early in the relationship rather than as the last resort before divorce.

Marriage enrichment programs are for couples who have good marriages and who want to keep them that way. The marriage enrichment movement, spearheaded by ACME, is gaining increased attention and attracting many spouses who meet together to share common problems and solutions.

Trends in managing marital conflict include growing participation in marriage enrichment programs. In addition, more states can be expected to pass legislation to ensure that those offering their services as marriage counselors are qualified by training and experience to do so.

STUDY QUESTIONS

1. Criticize five common beliefs about marriage.
2. What three factors does the perception of marital happiness depend on?
3. How is marital adjustment measured? Comment on the problems of such measurement.
4. Describe the various stages of the family life cycle and the pattern of marital satisfaction throughout the cycle.
5. How do husbands and wives differ in their evaluation of marital satisfaction across the years?
6. Why is marital conflict inevitable and often desirable?
7. Describe two sources of conflict and three types of conflict.
8. Discuss the reasons spouses are motivated to manage conflict.
9. Using as an example a conflict in an interpersonal relationship you have experienced, specify how you could have used the three steps outlined in this chapter for effective conflict management.
10. Give examples of reflective versus evaluative feedback.
11. Why is "Be nice" a difficult request to comply with?

12. Criticize the statement, "I want my partner to do as I ask because he/she loves me, not because I asked him/her to."

13. What are defense mechanisms and how do they inhibit conflict management? Give examples of how five defense mechanisms may operate within the marital relationship.

14. Describe at least four different approaches to marriage counseling. Into what two categories may all forms of marriage counseling be divided?

15. How effective is marriage counseling?

16. Discuss three attitudes that discourage spouses from seeking professional help for their marriage problems.

17. To what extent are marriage counselors regulated?

18. Discuss marriage enrichment. Who is involved, why, and what are the benefits?

19. Discuss future trends in conflict management.

NOTES

1. Regardless of the tendency to distort answers, whites, husbands, and nonparents usually score higher on marital adjustment inventories than blacks, wives, and parents (Scanzoni, 1975; Shaver & Freedman, 1976; Renee, 1970).

2. A major criticism of the family life cycle model is that it does not account for the couple who choose to remain childfree. It is also ineffective in accounting for families with children who are widely spaced (oldest is a teenager; youngest is an infant).

3. All researchers do not agree. Shaver and Freedman (1976) found that husbands report higher marital satisfaction than wives.

4. An exception to this exchange is when the husband is in love with his wife. The more he needs and values her loving him, the more willing he is to do anything to get her to continue to love him (Safilios-Rothschild, 1976).

5. Among the ancient Israelites, the priest symbolically heaped all the sins of the people upon an unblemished goat—the scapegoat—which was then driven into the wilderness to die.

BIBLIOGRAPHY

Abelson, R. P., et al. *Theories of cognitive consistency: A sourcebook.* Chicago: Rand McNally, 1968.

Adams, S., and Orgel, M. *Through the mental health maze: A consumer's guide to finding a psychotherapist.* Washington, D.C.: Health Research Group, 1975.

Ahammer, I. M., and Baltes, P. B. Objectivity versus perceived age differences in personality: How do adolescents, adults, and older people view themselves and each other? *Journal of Gerontology,* 1972, *27,* 1, 46–51.

Ard, B. N., Jr., and Ard, C. C. *Handbook of marriage counseling* (2nd ed.). Palo Alto, Calif.: Science and Behavior Books, 1976.

Beck, D. F. Research findings on the outcomes of marital counseling. *Social Casework,* 1975, *56,* 3, 153–81.

Berne, E. *Transactional analysis in psychotherapy.* New York: Grove Press, 1961.

Birchler, G. R., Weiss, R. L., and Wampler, L. D. Differential patterns of social reinforcement as a function of degree of marital distress and level of intimacy. Paper presented at the meeting of the Western Psychological Association, Portland, Ore., April, 1972.

Blood, R. O., and Wolfe, D. M. *Husbands and wives: The dynamics of married living.* Glencoe, Ill.: Free Press, 1960.

Chadwick, B. A., Albrecht, S., and Kunz, P. Marital and family role satisfaction. *Journal of Marriage and the Family,* 1976, *38,* 3, 431–40.

Coleman, J. C., and Hammen, C. *Contemporary psychology and effective behavior.* Glenview, Ill.: Scott, Foresman, 1974.

Dreikurs, R., et al. (eds.) *Adlerian family counseling.* Eugene, Ore.: University of Oregon Press, 1959.

Duvall, E. M. *Family development* (4th ed.). Philadelphia: J. B. Lippincott, 1971.

Edmonds, V. H. Marital conventionalization: Definition and measurement. *Journal of Marriage and the Family,* 1967, *29,* 681–8.

Ellis, A. *Reason and emotion in psychotherapy.* New York: Lyle Stuart, 1962.

Farson, R. Why good marriages fail. In *Choice and challenge,* C. Williams and J. Crosby (eds.). Dubuque: Brown, 1974, 103–11.

Feldman, H., and Feldman, M. Effect of parenthood at three points in marriage. Unpublished manuscript, Cornell University, 1977.

Glenn, N., and Weaver, C. N. A multivariate, multisurvey study of marital happiness. *Journal of Marriage and the Family,* 1978, *40,* 2, 269–82.

Glick, P. C. Updating the life cycle of the family. *Journal of Marriage and the Family,* 1977, *39,* 1, 5–13.

Gouldner, A. W. The norm of reciprocity: A preliminary statement. *American Sociological Review,* 1960, *25,* 161–78.

Gurman, A. S., and Kniskern, D. P. Research on marital and family therapy: Progress, perspective, and prospect. In *Handbook of psychotherapy and behavior change: An empirical analysis* (2nd ed.), S. L. Garfield and A. E. Bergin (eds.). New York: John Wiley and Sons, in press.

Hardy, R. and Cull, J. G. (eds.) *Techniques and approaches in marital and family counseling.* Springfield, Ill.: Charles C. Thomas, 1974.

Hicks, M. W., and Platt, M. Marital happiness and stability: A review of the research in the sixties. *Journal of Marriage and the Family,* 1970, *32,* 553–74.

Jourard, S. M. Marriage is for life. *Journal of Marriage and Family Counseling,* 1975, *1,* 3, 199–208.

Keiffer, C. New depths in intimacy. In *Marriage and Alternatives,* R. W. Libby and R. N. Whitehurst (eds.). Glenview, Ill.: Scott, Foresman, 1977, 267–93.

Knox, D. *Marriage happiness: A behavioral approach to counseling.* Champaign, Ill.: Research Press, 1971.

_____. *Marital exercise book.* New York: David McKay, 1975.

Koch, J., and Koch, L. The urgent drive to make good marriages better. *Psychology Today,* September 1976, 33 et passim.

Lazarus, A. *Behavior therapy and beyond.* New York: McGraw-Hill, 1971.

Lederer, W. J., and Jackson, D. D. *The mirages of marriage.* New York: W. W. Norton, 1968.

Mace, D. Marriage enrichment concepts for research. *The Family Coordinator,* 1975, *24,* 2, 171–3.

Mace, D., and Mace, V. C. *We can have better marriages if we really want them.* Nashville: Abingdon Press, 1974.

_____. Marriage enrichment—Wave of the future? *The Family Coordinator,* 1975, *24,* 2, 131–5.

_____. *How to have a happy marriage.* Nashville: Abingdon Press, 1977.

Nichols, W. C., Jr. The field of marriage counseling: A brief overview. *The Family Coordinator,* 1973, *22,* 3–13.

Olson, D. H. (ed.) *Treating relationships: Bridging research, theory, and practice.* Lake Mills, Iowa: Graphic Press, 1976.

Otto, H. A. Marriage and family enrichment programs in North America—Report and analysis. *The Family Coordinator,* 1975, *24,* 2, 137–42.

_____. *Marriage and family enrichment: New perspectives and programs.* Nashville: Abingdon Press, 1976.

Paris, B. L., and Luckey, E. B. A longitudinal study of marital satisfaction. *Sociology and Social Research,* 1966, *50,* 212–23.

Patterson, G. R., Hops, H., and Weiss, R. Interpersonal skills training for couples in early stages of conflict. *Journal of Marriage and the Family,* 1975, *37,* 2, 295–302.

Pineo, P. C. Disenchantment in the later years of marriage. *Marriage and Family Living,* 1961, *23,* 3–11.

Quick, S. Marriage counseling at East Carolina University. *The New East,* May–June 1975, 51–2.

Renee, K. Correlates of dissatisfaction in marriage. *Journal of Marriage and the Family,* 1970, *32,* 54–66.

Riedell, W. F. Marital adjustment and conservatism: A re-examination. Unpublished master's thesis, East Carolina University, 1976.

Rogers, C. *Client centered therapy.* Boston: Houghton Mifflin, 1951.

Rollins, B. C., and Cannon, K. L. Marital adjustment over the family life cycle: A re-evaluation. *Journal of Marriage and the Family,* 1974, *36,* 2, 271–83.

Rollins, B. C., and Feldman, H. Marital satisfaction over the family life cycle. *Journal of Marriage and the Family,* 1970, *32,* 20–28.

Rosenblatt, P. C. Behavior in public places: Comparison of couples accompanied and unaccompanied by children. *Journal of Marriage and the Family,* 1974, *36,* 4, 750–55.

Rosenblatt, P. C., and Cunningham, M. R. Television watching and family tensions. *Journal of Marriage and the Family,* 1976, *38,* 1, 105–11.

Ryder, R. G. Longitudinal data relating marriage satisfaction and having a child. *Journal of Marriage and the Family,* 1973, *35,* 4, 604–606.

Safilios-Rothschild, C. A macro and micro examination of family power and love: An exchange model. *Journal of Marriage and the Family,* 1976, *38,* 2, 355–63.

Scanzoni, J. *Sexual bargaining.* Englewood Cliffs, N.J.: Prentice-Hall, 1972.

_____. Sex roles, economic factors, and marital solidarity in black and white marriages. *Journal of Marriage and the Family,* 1975, *37,* 1, 130–44.

Shaver, P., and Freedman, J. Your pursuit of happiness. *Psychology Today,* August 1976, 26 et passim.

Smith, R. M., Scott, J. P., and Shoffner, S. M. *Marriage and family enrichment.* The North Carolina Family Life Council, Inc. and Department of Child Development and Family Relations, Center for Research Monographs, Number 1, The University of North Carolina at Greensboro, 1976.

Spanier, G. B. Measuring dyadic adjustment: New scales for assessing the quality of marriage and similar dyads. *Journal of Marriage and the Family,* 1976, *38* (February), 15–28.

Spanier, G. B., Lewis, R. A., and Cole, C. L. Marital adjustment over the family life cycle: The issue of curvilinearity. *Journal of Marriage and the Family,* 1975, *37,* 2, 263–76.

Stein, E. V. Mardilab: An experiment in marriage enrichment. *The Family Coordinator,* 1975, *2,* 167–77.

Steinmetz, S. K. *The cycle of violence: Assertive, aggressive, and abusive family interaction.* New York: Praeger, 1977.

Stuart, R. B. Operant interpersonal treatment for marital discord. *Journal of Consulting and Clinical Psychology,* 1969, *33,* 675–82.

Travis, R. P., and Travis, P. Y. The pairing enrichment program: Actualizing the marriage. *The Family Coordinator,* 1975, *24,* 2, 161–65.

Turner, J. Associate Director for Evaluation and Training, Huntsville-Madison County Mental Health Center, Huntsville, Alabama. Personal communication, 1977.

Vincent, C. E. Barriers to the development of marital health as a health field. *Journal of Marriage and Family Counseling,* 1977, *3,* 3, 3–11.

Warren, D. How to use transactional analysis in counseling. In *Techniques of marriage and family counseling,* P. Popenoe (ed.) Los Angeles: The American Institute of Family Relations, 1972, 101–103.

Willis, T. A., Weiss, R. L., and Patterson, G. R. A behavioral analysis of the determinants of marital satisfaction. *Journal of Consulting and Clinical Psychology,* 1974, *42,* 6, 802–10.

Chapter 13

Economic Fulfillment

SIGNIFICANCE OF MONEY

Self-Respect • Power • Security • Freedom • Social Relationships • Love

ECONOMIC PROBLEMS IN MARRIAGE

Life Cycle Needs • Getting Money • Spending Money

PLANNING AND INVESTING

Developing a Budget • Saving and Investing • Life Insurance and Disability Insurance

CONSUMER, BE WISE

How to Use Credit • Buying a Car • Buying a House

TRENDS

SUMMARY

Money is like a sixth sense without which you cannot make the most of the other five.

Somerset Maugham

While people may marry for love, it is money that buys food for meals, electricity for lighting a home, and gasoline for the car. Because our very survival depends on it, money is a powerful and often explosive issue in marriage. In this chapter we explore the meanings of money, its effects on each spouse, and its impact on the marital relationship. We also examine various elements in financial planning, including budgets, credit, insurance, investments, and purchases for young married couples.

SIGNIFICANCE OF MONEY

Economists regard money as the medium of exchange that makes possible the distribution of goods and services in our society. But money has more personal meanings. These include self-respect, power, security, freedom, social relationships, and even love.

Self-Respect

Money affects one's self-concept because, in our society, human worth is often equated with financial achievement (Feldman, 1976, p. xi). "I've been working for seven years," mused a young husband and father, "and I've got nothing to show for it. I can't even pay the bills we've got, let alone think about buying the things we want. My two closest friends are making good money in their own businesses. It makes me feel bad when I know that I can't provide for my family the way they provide for theirs. I'm a failure."

Power

Those who have money—lots of it—feel a sense of power and control over things, events, and people. While the average shopper may say to himself or herself, "I can't afford that," the person with unlimited means needn't ask the price of anything but can buy as desires dictate. It is this ability to purchase goods and services at will that results in a feeling of power, since power means getting what we want when we want it.

Money can mean many things, including self-respect. This ad for career training courses attests to the fact that economic success and high self-esteem tend to go hand in hand in American society.

Money provides not only the power to possess things but the power to control events. For the poor, a combination of sub-zero temperatures and high fuel prices is almost certain to mean discomfort and may mean death by freezing. For the wealthy, the high prices caused by a shortage of fuel are not even an inconvenience. No matter how high the prices or how low the temperature, the rich will be snug and warm.

Money also means power over people—employers over employees, parents over offspring, and employed husbands over unemployed wives. Anyone who has worked for another knows the power of employers. Unless the employee complies with the wishes of the employer, the employer will cut off the paycheck. Parental power extends to their offsprings' private lives. The parents of one student threatened to withdraw their financial support of their daughter if she continued to live with her boyfriend. Since she was committed to pursuing an art career and would be unable to pay her tuition without her parents' help, she moved out. Money gave her parents power, and they used it.

Money as power may also be exercised in the marriage relationship (Safilios-Rothschild, 1970). "My husband gives me only enough money for groceries," said one housewife, "and if I try to buy a little something for myself once in a while, he becomes furious. He says he makes the money, and he'll decide how it's spent."

Security

Money represents security. People without money often feel that they live on the verge of something unpleasant happening to them. "My car has four slick tires," said a senior who was putting herself through school, "and when one of those pops, I've had it. I don't have enough money to buy new tires, and I can't walk to work."

Buying life insurance, as nine out of ten American families do (Porter, 1976, p. 789), expresses the desire to provide a secure future for loved ones. "If something happens to me," said a young husband, "my wife and two children will need more than the sympathy they'll get at my funeral. They'll need money." Without money there is no security, either present or future. And money also provides a type of security from ill health. Because medical care is often dependent on the ability to pay for such care, health is directly related to one's financial resources. Money buys health insurance and is an essential part of preventive medicine. It provides for a balanced diet,[1] a well-heated home in winter and regular medical checkups which can help to catch small problems before they escalate into major ones.

Freedom

Money also means freedom and independence. The end of slavery in America did not mean freedom for blacks. Without money they were still tied to the will of white landowners (Haley, 1976). And so it is with offspring and wives without jobs. College students who are economically dependent must abide by the wishes of their parents or face being cut off. Wives who have no source of income of their own are in a more vulnerable position than wives who can support themselves. "Everybody tells me I'm a fool to stay with my husband," one wife admitted. "He criticizes everything I do, never demonstrates any love or affection, and sometimes gets violent. But I'm stuck. My parents are dead, and I don't have a job. I'm about as free as a prisoner of war."

Money provides the freedom to do things one likes to do. "When we were in school," recalled one husband, "we didn't have money to eat out or see a movie. It was a terrible feeling being cooped up all the time with no money to do anything. Now we've graduated, and we both have good jobs. We've got money in the bank and in our pockets. We're free to do what we want when we want to. It's a nice feeling—very nice."

Social Relationships

Money affects the relationships of couples with parents and peers. A married couple who are financially dependent on their parents often discover that their use of parents' money is not "free." In exchange for parental support, the couple is expected to visit frequently and, in some cases, to consult the parents before making major decisions. "You bet," said one parent. "After sending them $400 a month I expect them to appreciate what I'm doing. And that means before buying a new car or taking a job out of state, they should consult me."

Money also affects relationships with peers. "Our neighbors eat out every Saturday night at an expensive restaurant and have asked us to join them," recalled one wife. "But we're on a tight budget and simply can't afford to spend $25 on a meal. We wave at them when we get the afternoon newspaper, but we haven't socialized with them in three months. If we had more money it would be different."

Love

Money may also mean love. While admiring the diamond ring of her newly engaged roommate, a woman said, "Look how big this rock is! He must really love you a lot." Notice the assumption: Big diamond equals high price equals lots of love.

Similar assumptions are often made when gifts are given or received. People tend to spend more money on presents for people they love, assuming that the value of the gift symbolizes the depth of their emotion. And when getting presents, many people tend to assume that the cost of the gift reflects the feelings of the giver. "She must love me more than I thought," mused one man. "I gave her a record album for Christmas, but she gave me a digital watch. I felt embarrassed." His feeling of embarrassment is based on the assumption that the woman loves him more than he loves her because she paid more for her gift to him than he paid for his gift to her.

Similarly, the withdrawal of money may mean absence of love. A husband who tells his wife that he is no longer going to support her is giving her a clear message: he no longer loves her. When a couple get divorced, it is assumed that their economic sharing is over.

ECONOMIC PROBLEMS IN MARRIAGE

It is commonly acknowledged that money is a major source of problems in marriage. Let's review the role of money throughout the family life cycle and look at how it becomes a problem in marriage.

FIGURE 13.1   Economic Needs Throughout the Family Life Cycle.

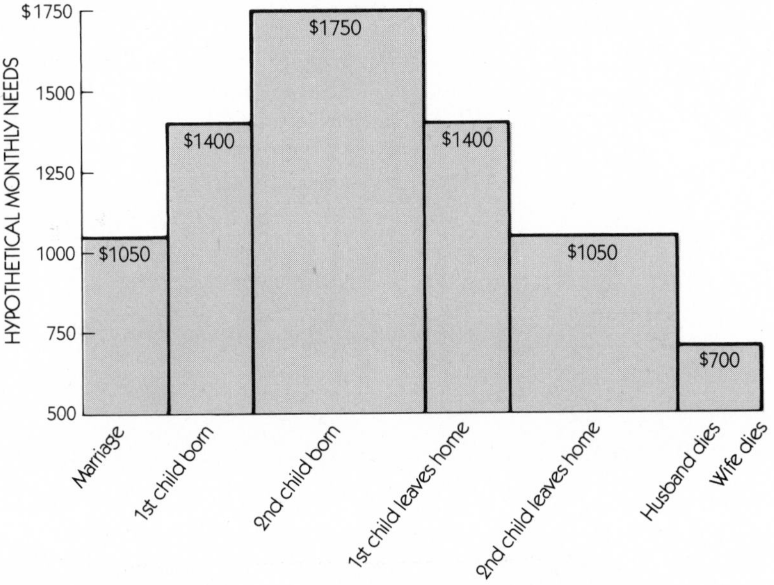

SOURCE: Adapted from Bailard et al., 1973, p. 129. Figures updated to reflect projected costs for 1979.

Life Cycle Needs

Money is a potential problem in every marriage because there is never a time when it is not necessary. Even if childfree or retired, couples continue to need food, shelter, clothing, and medical care. Figure 13.1 shows the need for money throughout the family life cycle.

Getting Money

Aside from an occasional birthday check from parents, married couples get money from wages or salaries.[2] In 1976 where the husband was the sole provider the median family income[3] was $13,931. When both husband and wife worked, the median income was $18,731 (U.S. Bureau of the Census, 1977, p. 443). By the end of 1976, family income[4] was distributed as indicated in Table 13.1.

Couples who don't have enough money to meet their needs may increase their family income in several ways: (1) by moonlighting, or holding two jobs at

TABLE 13.1   Distribution of U.S. Annual Family Income, 1976.

Annual family income	Percent of all families	Percent of all white families	Percent of all black & other nonwhite families
Under $3,000	3.9	3.1	9.6
$3,000–4,999	6.5	5.3	14.9
$5,000–6,999	7.8	7.3	11.8
$7,000–9,999	11.8	11.5	14.4
$10,000–14,999	20.2	20.5	19.2
$15,000–24,999	32.0	33.4	21.8
$25,000 & over	17.8	19.1	8.3

SOURCE: Adapted from U.S. Bureau of the Census, 1977, p. 440.

once, (2) by having both spouses employed, (3) by reducing expenditures, and (4) by producing goods within the household. Moonlighting may be necessary to reduce debts (birth of a child, automobile repair, new car), but if prolonged it may eventually damage the marital relationship. A husband and father who is anxious over bills may put in long hours of overtime or moonlight. One result is that he spends less time with his family and his wife feels that his work is more important to him than she is.

"Just call me Alan's widow," said Nancy, who had been married four years. "He leaves early in the morning, and except for the twenty minutes he's home for supper, I don't see him. He is a comanager of an interior design firm, and I'm

A married man with a family will do anything for money.
Charles de Talleyrand

proud of him, but I resent his spending all his time at work or sleeping on the couch recuperating. I don't want a color television—I want him."

Employment of the second spouse will immediately increase income. In 1976, white women contributed an average of $4,000 to $5,000 to annual family income, and black women, from $3,200 to $6,000 (Feldman, 1976, p. 11). While the wife's employment usually has positive consequences for reducing debt, improving her personal satisfaction, and improving the couple's marital happiness, there may be several negative consequences. For example, if her husband is opposed to her employment, or if she works a different shift from her husband or child care provisions are lacking, her employment may not be worth the money.

Instead of generating more income, some couples reduce expenses by eliminating some of them. These may include high insurance premiums, entertainment expenses, second car payments, and so on.

Growing one's own food also can be a major contribution to the family budget. A home garden measuring one sixth of an acre can produce $561.25 worth of fresh vegetables annually (Hughes, 1977, p. 15). Planning, planting watering, fertilizing, weeding, and harvesting a garden also offer the opportunity for family members to share an enjoyable experience.

Spending Money

Regardless of where the money comes from, where does it go? Table 13.2 illustrates how money is spent by families of four with three different standards of living—low, intermediate, and high. As the "personal income taxes" line reveals, a larger overall budget must take into account a considerably higher annual income tax assessment. The amount of your full salary is not the amount you will have to spend in a year.

Who decides where the money goes? Are the decisions joint, or are they made by the wife or the husband? Since innumerable conditions determine who decides how much money is spent on what, it is only possible to say which alternatives tend to occur under particular conditions. Joint financial decision making is characteristic of young middle-class families, wife-dominated financial decisions are characteristic of lower-income families and older families, and husband-dominated financial decisions are characteristic of higher-income families (Ferber, 1973, p. 27).

Conflict threatens the marriage relationship whenever one spouse wants to buy something that would prevent the other spouse from making a desired purchase. For example, a husband wanted to purchase stereo equipment that cost around $600. His wife, on the other hand, wanted to buy a piano for their three-year-old son. While a used piano could be bought for $600, the one she wanted cost $1,000. The husband thought the child was too young for a piano and the wife thought that $600 for a record player and radio was "crazy." While money conflicts in most marriages may not be over radios and pianos, the issue remains the same—money spent for X can't be spent for Y.

Spending money may also become a problem at the beginning of every month when a decision must be made concerning which bills are to be paid and how much is to be paid on each bill. Some spouses are relatively unconcerned about unpaid bills. Other spouses are extremely anxious about them and feel guilty until all bills are paid. Considerable strife may occur when these value systems collide.

TABLE 13.2   Annual Budget for a Four-Person Family[1] at Three Levels of Living (Urban United States, Autumn 1976).

Item	Lower Budget[2] (In Dollars)	Intermediate Budget (In Dollars)	Higher Budget (In Dollars)
TOTAL COST	**10,041**	**16,236**	**23,759**
Cost of Consumption, Total	8,162	12,370	17,048
Food	3,003	3,859	4,856
Housing[3]	1,964	3,843	5,821
Transportation	767	1,403	1,824
Clothing and Personal Care	1,064	1,496	2,173
Medical Care	896	900	939
Other Family Consumption	468	869	1,434
Other Costs[4]	451	731	1,234
Social Security and Disability Insurance Payments	604	898	911
Personal Income Taxes	825	2,236	4,565

1. Four-person family refers to annual living costs for a family comprising a 38-year-old employed husband, a wife not employed outside the home, an 8-year-old girl, and a 13-year-old boy.

2. Not intended to represent a minimum or subsistence level.

3. Includes the weighted average cost of renter and homeowner shelter, house furnishings, and household operations. Four-person families in the lower budget are assumed to be renters. A small allowance for lodging away from home city is included in the higher budget.

4. Includes gifts, contributions, life insurance, and occupational expenses.

SOURCE: U.S. Bureau of Labor Statistics, Autumn 1976 Urban Family Budgets and Geographical Comparative Indexes. (Reprinted in **Statistical Abstract of the United States: 1977,** 98th edition. Washington, D.C., 1977, p. 482.

PLANNING AND INVESTING

Becoming overwhelmed with debts can happen before couples are aware of it. A Gallup opinion poll sought to learn whether respondents lived within, somewhat beyond, or far beyond their means. While the national response disclosed that 80 percent lived within their means, respondents under thirty years of age were more likely to live beyond their means. And more than a fourth of this group were classified as living far beyond their means (Gallup Opinion Index, 1974). One reason for this overextension is that "large numbers of young couples, at the beginning of their marriage, want the comfort and luxuries their parents obtained only after a lifetime of work, thrift, and self-denial" (Feldman, 1976, p. 77).

Developing a Budget

Working out a budget is a method of planning your spending. Since money spent on X cannot be spent on Y, budgeting requires conscious value choices as to which bills should be paid, what items should be bought, and what expenditures should be delayed. Couples need to develop a budget if they are out of money soon after cashing their paychecks, if they can't pay off their existing bills and keep incurring new debts, or if they cannot save money. The dividends earned by developing a budget include having money available when you most need it, avoiding unnecessary debt, saving money, and knowing how your money is spent.

To develop a budget (see Table 13.3), list and add up all your monthly take-home (after taxes) income from whatever source. This figure should represent the amount of money your family will actually have to spend each month. Next, list and add up all of your fixed monthly expenses—rent, utilities, telephone, and those items you are buying on installment—car, stereo, etc. Other fixed expenses include life insurance, health insurance, and automobile insurance. Since you don't receive a bill for each of these expenses every month, divide the yearly cost by twelve so that you can budget each item on a monthly basis. For example,

Developing a family budget can be beneficial in several ways. By keeping track of money and planning expenditures, a couple can reduce the likelihood that money problems will be a major source of conflict or crisis in their marriage.

TABLE 13.3 Monthly Budget for a Young Couple.

Sources of Income		
Husband's take-home pay		$ 730
Wife's take-home pay		600
Interest earned on savings		15
	TOTAL	$1,345
Fixed Expenses		
Rent		$300
Utilities		70
Telephone		30
Insurance		70
Car payment and expenses		220
Furniture payments		75
Savings		100
	TOTAL	$865
	DIFFERENCE	$480
	(Amount available for day-to-day expenses)	
Day-to-Day and Discretionary Expenses		
Food		$250
Clothes		130
Personal Care		40
Recreation and Miscellaneous		60
	TOTAL	$480

Monthly income equals the total fixed expenses plus the total day-to-day and discretionary expenses if the couple live within their means. If income is greater than their expenses, they will be able to spend, save, or invest additional money. If income is less than their expenses, they are living beyond their means.

if your annual life insurance premium is $240, you should budget $20 per month for that expense.

Earmark a minimum of 5 percent of your monthly income, and more if possible, for savings, and include this sum in your fixed expenses. By putting a fixed amount in a savings account each month, you will not only have money available for major purchases such as a car or major appliances, you will also have an emergency fund to cover the unforeseen expenses such as those caused by an extended illness or a long-distance move. The size of an emergency fund should be about twice your monthly income. While you yourself can set aside some of your monthly income for savings, you may instead instruct your bank to transfer a certain sum each month from your checking account to your savings account, or you can join a payroll savings plan. Under the latter arrangement, a portion of your monthly salary is automatically deposited in your savings account without ever passing through your hands.

After adding together all your fixed monthly expenses, including savings, subtract this amount from your monthly take-home income. What remains can be used for such day-to-day expenses as food (groceries and restaurant meals), clothes (including laundry, dry cleaning, alterations, and new clothes), personal care (barber and hairdresser, toilet articles, cosmetics), and recreation (theater, movie, concerts, books, magazines). If you come out even at the end of the month, you are living within your means. If you have money left over, you are living below your means. If you had to tap your savings or borrow money, you are living beyond your means. And, of course, knowing whether you are living within, below, or above your means is dependent on keeping accurate records.

> **N**owadays, two can live as cheaply as one large family used to!
> Joey Adams

Saving and Investing

As mentioned above, saving should be part of every budget. By allocating a specific amount of your monthly income to savings, having your employer do it through the payroll savings plan, or putting your change every evening in a container on your dresser,[5] you can accumulate money for both short-term goals (vacation trip, down payment on a house) and long-term goals (college education for children, retirement income).

But loose change in a container on your dresser is not earning you the money it could. By investing, you use money to make more money. All investments must be considered in terms of their risk and potential yield. In general, the higher the rate of return on an investment, the greater the risk. For example, putting your money in a bank or savings and loan institution is risk-free, since your deposit is insured up to $40,000. By saving $50 per month for one year, you would earn $30. In slightly over fourteen years, your $600 investment, compounded annually, would grow to $1200.

Another way to invest money for a fairly stable return is to buy a blue chip stock such as American Telephone and Telegraph or Eastman Kodak. Stocks pay dividends as do banks and savings and loan institutions. But while there is greater potential return from these investment stocks than money put in the bank, there is also more risk.

But the greatest risk is in speculative stocks. Suppose you could afford to lose the $600 and were willing to take a gamble on a high return. You could buy one hundred shares of stock selling slightly below $6.00 per share. If the stock sold for $12.00 a share one year later, your original $600 investment would be worth $1,200 and you would have doubled your money in one year (in contrast to over fourteen years with the bank). But the stock might also be selling for $1.00 per share one year later. One person invested in a company specializing in bananas and looked forward to tripling her investment. But less than a week after she had purchased the stock, a hurricane in Puerto Rico wiped out the banana crop, and the value of her stock plummeted.

Fortunately, investment opportunities are not limited to banks and stocks.[6] Table 13.4 illustrates several alternatives and provides information on other factors which should be considered in deciding on an investment. In addition to risk and return on investment (average and compound yield), the liquidity, or the ease with which your investment can be converted into cash, is an important consideration. Stocks and bonds can be sold quickly to provide cash in hand. But it may take months to convert real estate (house, land, office building, etc.) to cash by selling it.

The amount of your time that is required to make your investment grow is also important. A real estate investment can provide a considerable return on your money, but it may also demand a lot of time perusing the newspaper for hours, arranging loans, placing ads, and showing houses, not to mention fixing leaky faucets, mowing grass, and painting rooms.

And consider the maturity date of your investment. For example, suppose you invest in a six-year certificate at a savings bank. Although the bank will pay you 7.5 percent interest and guarantee your investment, you can't get your principal (the money you deposited) or the interest until the six years is up unless you are willing to pay a substantial penalty.[8] Since regular savings accounts have no maturity date, you can withdraw whatever amount you want whenever you want it (but you earn only about 5 percent interest).

A final investment consideration is taxation. The issue to keep in mind when investing is not how much money you will make, but how much you can keep. Tax angles should be considered as carefully as risk and yield issues (see Table 13.4).

Life Insurance and Disability Insurance

In addition to saving and investing it is important to be knowledgeable about life insurance. In 1975, $2.1 trillion worth of life insurance was bought by Americans. Two out of three people were insured (Life Insurance Fact Book, 1976, p. 17). The major purpose of life insurance is to provide income for dependents when the primary wage earner dies. A wife who is not employed and has no private income is dependent on her husband for money to buy food, pay the rent, and so forth. When he dies, his paycheck stops, but the survival needs of the wife and any chil-

TABLE 13.4   Selecting an Investment

Investment Type	Degree of Risk	Average Annual Compound Yield*	Liquidity (average time before conversion to cash)	Personal Investment Management Required	Maturity	Protection Against Inflation	Tax Aspects
Savings (time deposits)	None, if insured	2–6%	1 day (up to 90 days for some accounts)	None	90 days to 10 years, depending upon specific media	Almost none	Income taxes on interest (some are tax deferred)
Life Insurance and Annuities	None, if company is financially sound	2–4%	2 to 3 weeks	None	10 years to life, depending on specific media	None	Income taxes deferred to maturity
Common Stocks	Moderate to substantial	5–16%	1 week or more	Generally moderate to substantial	May be sold at any time	Variable, but generally good	Income taxes on dividends over $100 a year; capital gains taxes on sale
Corporate Bonds	Low to moderate	3–10%	1 week or more	Very little	Up to 30 years	None	Income taxes on interest; capital gains taxes on sale
Mutual Funds	Generally moderate (substantial in some funds)	5–14%	1 to 2 weeks	Very little	May be sold at any time	Variable, but generally good	Income taxes on dividends; capital gains taxes on sale
Real Estate (other than residence)	Moderate to substantial	5–20%	2 months to 2 years	Generally moderate to substantial	Depends on specific investment	Generally good	Some income sheltered by depreciation; capital gains taxes on sale
Syndicate Shares	Moderate to substantial	5–20%	Depends on specific investment	Very little	Depends on specific investment	Generally good	Same as above

* Range over last twenty years.

SOURCE: Bailard et al., 1973, p. 287.†

dren continue. "My husband kept putting off buying life insurance," said a widow of two months. "Without any regular income, my two small children and I will barely be able to manage."

Life insurance is essential when there are children or other dependents in addition to the spouse. If a husband's mother is dependent on him, for instance, he needs life insurance to prevent this economic responsibility from being shifted to his widow. Or if a husband borrows $40,000 to buy a house, he needs insurance so that his widow can pay off the debt instead of being forced to move from her home by the bank that holds the mortgage. But unless there are dependents or other economic responsibilities, the need for life insurance is questionable. A young, childless widow can usually earn enough to support herself. Regarding the insurance needs of the unmarried, childfree college student, *Consumer Reports* concluded, "Insurance is the last thing most college students need" (*Consumer Reports,* 1977a, p. 171).

When considering income protection for dependents, there are two basic types of life insurance policies: (1) term insurance and (2) insurance-plus-investment. As the name implies, term insurance provides protection for a specific time period, usually one, five, ten, or twenty years. At the end of the time period, the protection stops. Although a term insurance policy offers the greatest amount of protection for the least cost, it does not build up cash value (money the insured would get if he or she surrendered the policy for cash).

Insurance-plus-investment policies are sold under various names: (1) Straight life, ordinary life, or whole life, in which the individual pays a stated premium (based on age and health) as long as he or she lives. When the insured dies, the beneficiary is paid the face value of the policy, the amount of insurance that was bought. But during the life of the insured, the policy also builds up a cash value which permits the insured to borrow money from the insurance company at a low rate of interest. (2) Limited-payment policy, in which the premiums are paid up after a certain number of years (usually twenty) or when the insured reaches a certain age (usually sixty or sixty-five). As with straight, ordinary life, or whole life policies, limited-payment policies build up a cash value, and the face value of the policy is not paid until the insured dies. (3) Endowment insurance, in which the premiums are paid up after a stated number of years and can be cashed in at a stated age.

Regardless of how they are sold, insurance-plus-investment policies divide the premium paid by the insured. Part pays for the actual life insurance, and part is invested for the insured, giving the policy a cash value. Unlike term insurance, insurance-plus-investment policies are not cancelled at age sixty-five.

Which type, term or insurance-plus-investment, should you buy? An insurance agent is likely to suggest the latter and point out the advantages of cash value, continued protection beyond age sixty-five, and level premiums. But the agent has a personal incentive for your buying an insurance-plus-investment policy. The commission he or she gets on this type of policy is much higher than if you buy term insurance. [9]

A cogent argument can be made for buying term insurance and investing the additional money that would have been needed to pay for the more expensive insurance-plus-investment policy. The annual premium for $50,000 worth of renewable term insurance at age twenty-five is $175. [10] The same coverage offered in an ordinary life policy, the most common of the insurance-plus-investment types, would cost $668 annually so the difference is $493 per year. If you put this money in the bank at a modest interest rate of 5 percent at the end of five years you would have $2,860.32. In contrast, the cash value of an ordinary life policy after five years would be $2350. But in order to get this money you would have to pay the insurance company interest to borrow it. If you didn't want to pay the interest, the company would give you this amount but cancel your policy. In effect, you would lose your insurance protection if you got the cash value of your policy. With term insurance, you have the $2,860.32 in the bank earning interest, and you can withdraw it at any time without affecting your insurance protection.

It should be made clear that in order for term insurance to be cheaper you must invest the money you would otherwise be paying for an ordinary life insurance policy. If you can't discipline yourself to save, buy an insurance-plus-investment policy, which will ensure savings.

But what of the fact that term insurance stops when you are sixty-five, just as you are moving closer to death and needing the protection more? Again, by investing the money that you would otherwise have spent on a straight life policy, you will have as much or more money for your beneficiary.

Whether you buy term or an insurance-plus-investment policy or both, there are three options to consider—guaranteed insurability, waiver of premiums, and double or triple indemnity. All are inexpensive and generally should be included.

Guaranteed insurability means that the company will sell you more insurance in the future regardless of your medical condition. For example, suppose you develop cancer after you have bought a policy for $10,000. If the guaranteed insurability provision is in your contract, you can buy additional insurance. If not, the company can refuse you more insurance.

Waiver of premiums provides that your premiums will be paid by the company if you become disabled for six months or longer and are unable to earn an income. Such an option ensures that your policy will stay in force because the premiums will be paid. Otherwise, the company could cancel your policy.

Double or triple indemnity means that if you die as the result of an accident, the company will pay your beneficiary twice or three times the face value of your policy.

An additional item you might consider adding to your life insurance policy is a disability income rider.[11] If the primary wage earner is disabled and cannot work, the financial consequences for the family are the same as though he or she were dead. With disability insurance, the wage earner can continue to provide for the family up to a maximum of $3,500 per month, or two thirds of his or her salary, whichever is smaller. If the wage earner is disabled by accidental injury, payments are made for life. If illness is the cause, payments may be made only to age sixty-five[12] (Bailard et al., 1973, p. 112). Said a twenty-five-year-old husband and father who was paralyzed in an automobile accident, "It was the biggest mistake of my life to think I needed only life insurance to protect my family. Disability insurance turned out to be more important."[13]

There are four basic rules in buying life insurance (Consumer Survival Kit, 1975, p. 12): (1) Shop for insurance. There are price variations of from 60 to 324 percent on all important policies.[14] (2) Look for group coverage. The savings in premiums can be substantial. (3) Select your insurance agent with care. Be wary of buying an insurance policy from someone who is new to the business. Well-established agents are more likely to be available when you need them. (4) Update your insurance program every year. Having a child (or additional children), buying a home, or borrowing a large sum will mean you need additional insurance. It will take only a short while to update your policies, but it may take a lifetime to recover completely from not doing so.

CONSUMER, BE WISE

While developing a budget, saving money, investing money, and buying life insurance are essential elements of a positive financial management program, consumer awareness of credit, car, and home ownership are equally important. Let's examine how to use credit, and how to buy a car and a home.

"Your seeming indifference to the matter of your past-due account is difficult to understand. We have every confidence in you and believe that you intend to pay, but your account has now reached the stage where we can no longer simply continue making requests for payment . . ."

TABLE 13.5   Calculating the Cost of Installment Credit.

1. The amount to be financed

Cash price	$ 600.00
Minus down payment (if any)	− 50.00
Amount to be financed	550.00

2. The amount that will be repaid

Monthly payments	$ 35.00
Times number of payments	× 18
Total amount repaid	630.00

3. The cost of the credit

Total amount repaid	$ 630.00
Minus amount financed	−550.00
Cost of credit	$ 80.00

4. The total cost of the color TV

Total amount repaid	$ 630.00
Plus down payment (if any)	+ 50.00
Total cost of TV	$ 680.00

How to Use Credit

You use credit when you take an item home with you today and pay for it later. The amount you pay later will depend on the arrangement you make with the seller.

Types of credit accounts.   Suppose you want to buy a color television set that costs $600. Unless you pay cash, the seller will set up one of three types of credit accounts with you—installment, revolving charge, or open charge.

Under the installment plan, you make a down payment and sign a contract to pay the rest of the money in monthly installments. You and the seller negotiate the period of time over which payments will be spread and the amount you will pay each month. The seller adds a finance charge[15] to the cash price of the television set and remains the legal owner until you have made your last payment.[16] Most department stores and appliance and furniture stores, as well as automobile dealers, offer installment credit. The cost of buying the $600 color television set can be calculated as illustrated in Table 13.5.

Instead of buying your $600 color television on the installment plan, you might want to buy it on the revolving charge plan. Most credit cards (Master-Charge, Visa, etc.) represent revolving charge accounts that permit you to buy on credit up to a stated amount during each month. At the end of the month you may pay the total amount you owe or any amount over the stated "minimum payment due" amount. If you were to pay $600 at the end of the first month, there would be no charge for the credit. But if you chose to pay less than the full amount, the cost of the credit on the unpaid amount would be 1.5 percent per month or 18 percent per year. For instance, if you paid $100 per month for six months, you would still owe $31.62 to be paid the next month for a total cost (television plus finance charges) of $631.62.

You can also purchase items on an open charge (thirty-day) account. Under this system you agree to pay in full within thirty days. Since there is no direct service charge or interest for this type of account, the television set would cost only the purchase price. Sears and J. C. Penny's offer open charge (thirty-day) accounts. If you do not pay the full amount in thirty days, a finance charge is placed on the remaining balance. Both the use of revolving charge and open charge accounts are wise if you pay off the bill before finance charges begin. In deciding which type of credit account to use, remember that credit usually costs money, and the longer you take to pay for an item, the more the item will cost you.

Whether or not you can get credit will depend on the rating you receive on the "Three C's": character, capacity, and capital. *Character* refers to your honesty, sense of responsibility, soundness of judgment, and trustworthiness, and *capacity* refers to your ability to pay the bill when it is due. Such issues as the amount of money you earn and the length of time you have held a job will be considered in evaluating your capacity to pay. *Capital* refers to such assets as bank accounts, stocks, bonds, a car, etc.

It is particularly important that a married woman establish a credit rating in her own name in case she is eventually widowed or divorced. Otherwise, her credit will depend on her husband, and when he goes her credit does too. While the law now provides some protection against financial discrimination by lenders, it remains the responsibility of the individual to establish his or her own credit rating.[17]

Avoid credit snags.   When you buy an item on the installment plan, you should be aware of several potential problems. One is the "add-on" clause, in which the seller keeps title to a whole list of items you are buying until all payments have been made on all items. For example, suppose you bought a stereo system from the same dealer who sold you the television set. If you fail to make any one payment, the seller may repossess both the stereo and the television set, even though you had paid all but a few dollars for both. The "add-on" clause permits the seller to add purchase after purchase to your original installment contract. In theory, a dealer who furnished your entire apartment under such an arrangement could collect all but fifty cents of the total amount you owed and then strip your apartment because you forgot the final payment. Don't sign an agreement that has an "add-on" clause.

Also, watch out for the "balloon" contract, which provides for a final payment considerably larger than the preceding monthly payments. For example, you might pay $50 down and $10 for twenty-four months for your television set and then face a final payment of $210. If you didn't have the $210, the seller could repossess the set before you could produce the money. "Balloon" contracts are illegal in some states.

An "acceleration" clause may also be part of an installment contract. It not only permits the seller to repossess your television if you miss a payment but requires you to make all remaining payments immediately if you lose your major source of income. If you lost your job after making payments on the television set for a couple of years, you would lose the set as well unless you could pay the balance owed at once.

If possible, try to buy items on a revolving or open charge account and avoid installment accounts. Sellers of major items on an installment plan often charge as high as 4 percent per month on the unpaid balance. This means a true annual interest rate of 48 percent. Hence, the worst place to get credit for the purchase of expensive items is from the store or dealer that sells them. To get a lower interest rate, borrow the money from a commerical bank, savings bank, or credit union, and pay cash to the dealer.[18]

Buying a Car

An automobile is the first major purchase a person is likely to make. A basic issue to consider is whether to buy a new car or a used one. While the desire to buy a new car is often compelling, it is not economical to do so. Depreciation—the difference between what you pay for a car and what you can sell it for later—is the major cost of buying a new car. After one year, the value has dropped about 30 percent; after two years, another 18 percent; after three years, another 14 percent.

On the other hand, it may cost a lot to keep a used car running. But how used does a car need to be before it begins to give trouble? In general, repair costs begin to escalate significantly after the fifth year. Hence, by purchasing a two-year-old car and driving it about three years before trading it in for another two-year-old car, the astronomical depreciation of the first two years and the repair costs beyond the fifth year can often be avoided.

In buying a used car, there are fundamental rules to follow:

1. Deal only with a respected, reliable dealer.
2. Or shop newspaper ads by private owners for low mileage, one-owner cars, other pluses. . . .
3. Resist the temptation of questionable "bargains."
4. Have a qualified mechanic or automotive clinic inspect any used car you are considering buying.
5. Read and understand any contract before you sign it.

Car payments are one of the first economic responsibilities that many young couples take on. Before buying any car—new or used—a couple should determine what size payments they can comfortably handle.

6. Shop among several sources of used cars to find the best deal for you.

7. Try to get at least a 30-day warranty with the dealer responsible for paying in full for all needed repairs.

8. Be sure, if reconditioning has been done, that the warranty spells out the details—and whether the car is guaranteed to pass state inspection. (Porter, 1976, pp. 310–11)

If you decide to buy a new car, you can find out the actual cost of the car to the dealer from Car-Puter International Corp., 1603 Bushwick Avenue, New York, New York 11207. Knowing what the car actually costs the dealer is a starting point for your negotiations with the dealer.

Buying a House

The first issue to consider before buying a house is to compare the advantages of doing so with those of renting. One financial adviser outlined the following advantages of renting:

> Renting gives you much more financial flexibility than home ownership. If your income slumps or your job involves frequent transfers, your commitment lasts only as long as your lease.
> It is probably the best initial course for a young couple with limited financial means.

You shouldn't rush long-term decisions until you have children and a definite idea of where and how you want to live permanently.

Renting holds distinct advantages if you are moving into a new neighborhood, particularly in a fast-growing suburb. If possible, rent for a year or so, and become thoroughly acquainted with the area before making a final decision to invest and settle.

Renting means that taxes, insurance, major repairs, and often costs of utilities too are the landlord's responsibility. In some places it may be simpler for you to find suitable quarters by renting. (Porter, 1976, p. 545).

But home ownership has its advantages. The principal advantages are in terms of investment return and tax deductions. Buying a home is a good investment in that the value of a house increases every year. Between 1970 and 1977, the price of the average home almost doubled. Many couples buy a house, hold it for several years, sell it and buy another house that is closer to their "dream house."

Regarding tax deductions, when a couple buy a house they usually borrow money from the bank to pay for it and make arrangements with the bank to pay the money back plus interest. The money paid in interest is not taxable. The result is that a couple can buy a house now, and while they may be paying for it thirty years, the money they pay as interest during this period is not taxed.

In addition to the investment potential and tax benefits, homeowners may do as they wish (within limits) with their own home. A home represents a geographical commitment and provides the opportunity for a strong tie with the community.

While a "home of our own" has been part of the American dream, double-digit inflation and high interest rates have priced three out of four Americans out of the new house market. In 1977 the median cost for a new home was $47,000. Economists advise that one should not buy a home which costs more than two to

Owning a home has long been a standard feature of the American dream. But as the cost of homes goes up, young couples will probably end up having to rent longer and settle for less when they do buy a home.

two-and-a-half times one's gross annual income. The monthly payments (including mortgage payment, utilities, taxes, and insurance) should be no more than one week's gross salary. Though many couples are willing to sacrifice to buy a home of their own—both spouses work, both cut back on other luxuries—housing expectations are dropping. Instead of a bright new home in a sparkling suburb, more couples are buying older homes which they "fix up."

TRENDS

Economic fulfillment in the marriage relationship of the future is likely to involve more budget-conscious expenditures, conservation of energy resources, and fewer children. Spiraling inflation, if it continues, will result in spouses being more cost conscious in purchasing anything from apples to houses. For some, the purchase of their "dream home" will become virtually impossible. As a result, new definitions of the meaning of adequate shelter will emerge. Rather than referring to a new single-unit house with four bedrooms and two baths on a wooded two-acre lot, "home" for an increasing number of couples will mean an apartment, a townhouse, a condominium, or mobile home.

And energy conservation will become a reality. The prices of electricity, natural gas, gasoline, and oil will reach the point where people turn down their thermostats, drive less, and in general restrict their use of energy so that they will have money to spend on other priority items. Initially such decisions to conserve will be erratic, but as the prices of energy resources escalate, only the very affluent will continue to use them indiscriminately. Many Americans have already begun to conserve energy. In a random sample of 302,602 readers of *Better Homes and Gardens,* 82 percent reported that they had lowered their thermostats, 71 percent had reduced their use of electricity, 46 percent had reduced the use of air conditioning, and 42 percent had improved home insulation (*Better Homes and Gardens,* 1978, p. 172).

As will be discussed in greater detail in the chapter on "Planning a Family," one reaction to living in a world of increasing prices and diminishing energy resources will be the decision to have fewer children. Since children represent the greatest expense for most couples, an increasing number will decide to have no children or fewer children than in previous generations in order to achieve and maintain their desired standard of living.

SUMMARY

It is said that although money isn't everything, it's way ahead of whatever is in second place. Money may represent power, self-respect, security, freedom, social position, and love. Although economic responsibilities for young married couples are minimal, the need for money escalates as children are born. Expenses become highest during the child-rearing years, though maximum family income is usually not achieved until the primary wage earner is between forty-five and fifty-four years old (U.S. Bureau of the Census, 1977, p. 451) and the children are leaving home.

Unless couples plan their spending, they risk drifting deep into debt. Although McDonald's claims "We do it all for you," and Texaco says, "We're working to keep your trust," the primary motivation of corporations is making a profit. Similarly, merchants are eager to sell items on credit so they can obligate customers to pay them money every month, and, in the process, increase their own profit margin. Without positive financial planning, economic fulfillment in a marriage is left to chance.

By developing a budget, using credit wisely, buying life and disability insurance, saving, and investing, spouses can protect themselves and their dependents from economic disaster and have more money available to buy what they want.

Trends in the economics of marriage relationships include spouses who are more budget conscious in their expenditures, spouses who are more concerned about conserving energy, and spouses who choose to have fewer children. The latter decision will be based on recognition of the fact that rearing children is a major expense and that it may not be possible to afford as large a family as one might wish.

STUDY QUESTIONS

1. Explain the significance of money in terms of six personal meanings it may have.
2. Trace the need for money throughout the family life cycle.
3. Discuss four different ways to increase or stretch one's family income.
4. Under what conditions do the wife, husband, or both spouses typically have the decision-making power to spend money?
5. How successful are most Americans in living within their means? What age group is most likely to live beyond their means? Why?
6. Under what conditions do couples need to keep a budget?
7. What are the rewards for keeping a budget?
8. Describe three methods of saving.
9. Describe several ways you could invest your money.
10. Discuss risk, yield, liquidity, maturity, time investment, and taxation as issues to consider before deciding to make an investment.
11. What is the purpose of life insurance? Under what conditions do you need life insurance? Do most unmarried college students need life insurance?
12. What are the two major types of life insurance? What are the advantages and disadvantages of the two types?
13. What are three options you should consider including in your insurance policy?
14. What is disability insurance? What is the consequence of becoming disabled and having no disability insurance?
15. Discuss three types of credit accounts. Which is most and least expensive?
16. Under what conditions does a person receive a good credit rating?
17. Why should wives be concerned about establishing credit in their own names? How can they do this?
18. What three clauses should you be alert to before signing a credit contract?

19. Discuss the advantages of buying a used car.
20. What issues should be considered in deciding whether to buy or rent?
21. Why is buying a home a good investment?
22. What are two basic guidelines in deciding how much you can afford to pay for a home?
23. What are three trends in family economic patterns?

NOTES

1. About twenty-five cents of every family dollar is spent on food (Community Council of Greater New York, 1975, p. 16; Porter, 1976, p. 23).

2. Other sources of income may include rent, interest, dividends, and public assistance (Feldman, 1976, p. 6).

3. ·Half of all incomes are higher than the median income, and half are lower.

4. Family income represents the income of all the people living in one household, related by blood, marriage, or adoption, and spending their income as a unit.

5. Under this method you decide in advance to spend only paper money and to use all change as savings.

6. All stocks do not involve the same risk. Over-the-counter stocks, those listed on neither the New York nor the American exchanges, are usually issued by smaller companies and represent considerable risk.

7. While savings, life insurance, real estate, and stock investments are probably familiar to you, the other types of investments listed in this table may be less familiar. (1) Annuities provide monthly income after age sixty-five (or earlier if desired) in exchange for your investing monthly premiums during your working years. For example, a sixty-five-year-old man may receive $100 per month as long as he lives (or a lump sum) if he has paid the insurance company $283 annually since age thirty. (2) Bonds are issued by corporations and federal, state, or local governments that need money. In exchange for your money, you get a piece of paper that entitles you to the return of the sum you lend at a specified date (up to thirty years) plus interest on that money. While bonds are safer than stocks, you could lose all your money if the corporation you lend money to goes bankrupt. United States Savings Bonds are safe but pay a comparatively low rate of interest. (3) Mutual funds provide a way of investing in a number of common stocks, corporate bonds, or government bonds at the same time. You invest your money in shares of the mutual fund, whose directors invest the fund's capital in various securities. If the securities they select increase in price, so does the value of your shares in the mutual fund, and vice versa. (4) Syndicates are formed when a group of investors pool their money to buy real estate or a business. For example, you might want to begin a record store in your college community. If you don't have the money to rent space, purchase albums, etc., you might pool your money with several friends who would share in the profits (and debts).

8. Three months' interest is forfeited, and the interest on the amount withdrawn is reduced to the passbook rate (usually 5 percent).

9. In 1975, 90 percent of all life insurance policies sold to individuals were the insurance-plus-investment variety. Ten percent were term policies (Life Insurance Fact Book, 1976, p. 14).

10. The figures in this paragraph reflect 1977 rates (*Consumer Reports,* 1977b).

11. Only one third of the insurance companies offer the disability income option. If your life insurance policy does not offer such an option, you should strongly consider buying the protection in a separate policy.

12. In many policies, there is a clause which states that payments may not begin until up to a year after the disability occurs.

13. Persons covered by the Social Security Act are eligible for disability income if they will be disabled for one year or more. The amount they receive depends on their age and previous earnings. It is possible to receive a maximum of $466 per month.

14. This variation includes those for health, auto, and homeowner's insurance.

15. Finance charges are all the charges you are asked to pay to get the item on credit.

16. Under the provision of the Truth-in-Lending Law, the installment contract must state the annual percentage rate; the total of all finance charges, including all add-on charges such as loan fees, investigation fees, and required insurance; the purchase price, and any down payment or trade-in allowance; the net amount being financed with credit; the size of weekly or monthly payments; the due dates of payments; and the total number of installments before the debt is entirely paid (Consumer Credit Protection Act of 1968).

17. Purchase a major item such as a stereo on the installment plan and make regular monthly payments. By doing so you establish that you can meet your financial obligations. Meeting regular payments on a student loan is another good way to establish credit-worthiness.

18. Avoid borrowing money from small loan companies. Also known as consumer finance or personal loan companies, these companies tend to charge a high rate of interest.

BIBLIOGRAPHY

Bailard, T. E., Biehl, D., and Kaiser, R. *Personal money management.* Chicago: Science Research Associates, 1973.

Better Homes and Gardens. A report on the American family from the editors of *Better Homes and Gardens.* Des Moines, Iowa: Meredith Corporation, April 1978.

Community Council of Greater New York. *Annual price survey: Family budget costs.* New York: Research and Program Planning Information Department, 1975.

Consumer Reports. Campus life insurance: At best a delusion, at worst a snare. *Consumer Reports,* 1977, *42,* 3.(a)

———. *The consumer's union report on life insurance.* Orangeburg, N.Y.: Consumer's Union, 1977.(b)

Consumer Survival Kit. *Life insurance.* Owings Mills, Md.: Maryland Center for Public Broadcasting, 1975.

Economic Report of the President, 1975. Washington, D.C.: U.S. Government Printing Office, February 1975.

Feldman, L. *The family in today's money world* (2nd ed.). New York: Family Service Association of America, 1976.

Ferber, R. Family decision making and economic behavior. In *Family economic behavior: Problems and prospects,* E. B. Sheldon (ed.). Philadelphia: J. B. Lippincott, 1973.

Gallup Opinion Index. Report No. 112, October 1974, 9–13.

George, R. *The new consumer survival kit.* Boston: Little, Brown, 1978.

Haley, A. *Roots.* New York: Doubleday, 1976.

Hughes, G. R. *How much is a garden worth? FCX vegetable garden guide.* Raleigh, N.C.: Farmers' Cooperative Exchange, 1977, 15.

Life Insurance Fact Book. New York: American Council of Life Insurance, 1976.

Porter, S. *Sylvia Porter's money book.* New York: Doubleday, 1975; Avon, 1976.

Safilios-Rothschild, C. The study of family power structure; A review 1960–1969. *Journal of Marriage and the Family,* 1970, *32,* 4, 539–52.

Trooboff, B. M., and Boyd, F. L. *Personal finance for consumers.* Morristown, N.J.: General Learning Press, 1976.

U.S. Bureau of the Census. *Statistical abstract of the United States: 1977 (98th ed.).* Washington, D.C.: U.S. Government Printing Office, 1977.

U.S., Bureau of Labor Statistics. *Autumn 1976 urban family budgets and geographical comparative indexes.* Washington, D.C.: U.S. Government Printing Office, 1977.

Chapter **14**

Sexual Fulfillment

THE NATURE OF SEX IN MARRIAGE

Legitimacy • Declining Frequency • Importance

MEANINGS OF MARITAL INTERCOURSE

Communication • Power • Good and Evil

SEXUAL FULFILLMENT: SOME PREREQUISITES

A Good Relationship • Demonstration of Sexual Interest in the Partner •
Open Communication • Self-Knowledge • Realistic Expectations

SEXUAL FULFILLMENT: SOME FACTS

Sexual Fulfillment Is Couple-Defined • The Effects of "Spectatoring" •
Male and Female Sexual Response Cycles • The Effects of Drugs •
Sexual Attitudes and Behaviors Are Mostly the Result of Learning

SEXUAL FULFILLMENT: SOME MYTHS

Myth 1: Simultaneous Orgasm Is the Ultimate Sexual Experience • Myth 2:
Intercourse During Menstruation Is Harmful • Myth 3: Intercourse During
Pregnancy Should Be Avoided • Myth 4: Masturbation Ends with Marriage •
Myth 5: Extramarital Sex Strengthens Marriage Relationships • Myth 6:
Extramarital Sex Destroys Marriage Relationships

SEXUAL FULFILLMENT: MANAGING DIFFERENCES

Frequency of Intercourse • Variety

SEXUAL DYSFUNCTIONS

Masters and Johnson • Female Sexual Dysfunctions • Male Sexual Dysfunctions

TRENDS

SUMMARY

Marriage is popular because it combines the maximum of temptation with the maximum of opportunity.

George Bernard Shaw

In this chapter we are concerned with identifying factors which contribute to sexual fulfillment in marriage. In addition, we will explore the nature of sex in marriage, the facts and myths about sexual fulfillment, and the sexual dysfunctions of both sexes.

THE NATURE OF SEX IN MARRIAGE

The sexual relationship of a couple after marriage is different from their sexual relationship before marriage. The differences are in terms of legitimacy, declining frequency, and varying importance. Let's examine each of these in more detail.

Legitimacy

A unique aspect of marital sex is its legitimacy or social acceptability. "Regardless of recent changes in sexual values, sex with spouse remains the most legitimate and approved form of sex available in U.S. culture" (Gagnon, 1977, p. 191). All forms of nonmarital sex, whether they involve an unmarried man and woman, a couple of the same sex, or a man and woman who are married but not to each other must occur without our society's official sanction.

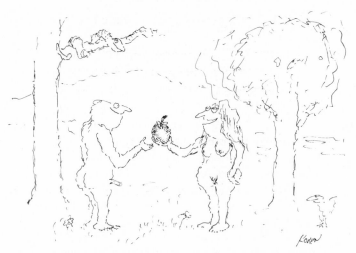

"Of course, you realize that this offer is void where prohibited by law."

Declining Frequency

Marital sexual relations are also characterized by declining frequency. The longer most couples are married, the less often they will have intercourse. While married couples in their twenties have intercourse almost three times per week (more specifically, about ten times every twenty-eight days), couples at forty have intercourse a little over once per week (more specifically, about five times every twenty-eight days) (James, 1974, p. 212).

A traditional wedding prank is based on awareness of this decline in frequency. Someone gives the bride and groom a half-gallon jar on their wedding day with the following instructions taped on it: "Every time you have intercourse during your first year of marriage, put a penny in this jar. Then, beginning with your second year, take a penny out every time you have intercourse. It will take you five years to empty this jar, which you will fill in one."

The birth of children also reduces the frequency of marital intercourse. In general, couples with children have intercourse less frequently than couples without children (James, 1974, p. 212). Taking care of children, particularly young children, is an exhausting chore. A spouse, more often the wife, who is up all night with a colicky infant and then spends much of the day in the pediatrician's waiting room may not feel "up" for sex that evening.

The career or careers of the respective partners may also take their toll on a couple's sex life. One sociologist observed, "If a man spends sixteen hours a day, and many do, at his career and career-related activities, he not only isn't home much for 'family life' but isn't the most scintillating husband, father, and lover when he is there" (Cuber, 1974, p. 20). The wife of such a career-oriented husband said, "He's their top designer and everybody knows it. Next year he's sure to be a vice president. But when he gets home at night, he is tired. . . . We don't have much sex—but I don't expect it under the circumstances" (Cuber, 1974, p. 24). Of course, the career demands of the wife may have an equally negative effect on the couple's sex life.

Psychological and sociological factors may also account for the gradual decline of sex in marriage. Such factors involve loss of peer interest, loss of reproductive capacity, and boredom. Prior to marriage, peers often exchange information about their sexual conquests. Particularly among males, the sexual self-image may depend on peer group approval, based on the number of sexual conquests. But married men can only "count their wives once. The wedding night is it as far as peer group approval is concerned" (Gagnon, 1977, p. 210).

For spouses who feel that conceiving children is the major justification for intercourse, loss of reproductive capacity may end all interest in sex. "What good is sex to me now? My children are grown, and all I want now is to have grandchildren." And because marital sex happens with the same partner, usually in the same way, year after year, both spouses may simply become bored. The popularity of sex manuals and of columns in women's and men's magazines that offer advice on sexual relations suggests that a yearning to recapture the sexual excitement of earlier years is widespread.

Importance

How important is sex to married couples? The range is very wide. Whether for physiological or psychological reasons, some couples have "sexless marriages" (Cuber, 1969). For them, sex is not a meaningful event. Yet they may love each other deeply and delight in the companionship they share.

Other couples regard sex as the only positive aspect of their relationship. One husband said that he and his wife had decided to separate, "and since we both knew that I would be moving out on Friday we had intercourse twice a day that week." A year after the separation, he said, "Sex with us was the best there is. I don't miss the fights we had, but I do miss the sex."

Between the extremes of "sex is nothing" and "sex is everything" is "sex is good but not everything." Gagnon has observed that if the average couple spends about fifty hours having intercourse per year, they will also spend about one thousand hours in front of the television and two thousand hours at work (forty

Sex is extremely important in some marriages and less so in others. If sex is the most important part of a couple's relationship, sexual boredom could be disastrous despite an otherwise satisfactory relationship.

hours a week for fifty weeks) (Gagnon, 1977, p. 194). While sexual involvement may have been a dominant theme before marriage, it diminishes in importance after marriage.

> We have assumed an important role for sexuality in the maintenance of marital bonds because we have assumed that sex itself is an important part of most people's lives. This may not be true. Particularly after the formation of the marital unit, it is quite possible that sex—both as a psychological reward and a physical outlet—declines in salience. It may become less important than alternative modes of gratification (work, children, security, constant affection—any or all may become more significant), or the weight of these alternative gratifications may minimize the effects of any sexual dissatisfaction. (Gagnon & Simon, 1973, pp. 82–83).

MEANINGS OF MARITAL INTERCOURSE

While intercourse may have a relatively low priority in marriage, the meanings married couples give to the experience vary. In general, these meanings go beyond physical satisfaction to include communication, power, and some feeling about the inherent value of sex.

Communication

Intercourse communicates how the partners are feeling and serves as a barometer for the relationship. Each partner brings to intercourse (sometimes unconsciously) a motive (pleasure, reconciliation, procreation, duty); a psychological state (love, hostility, boredom, excitement); and a physical state (tense, exhausted, relaxed, turned-on). The combination of these variables will change from one encounter to another. Tonight the wife may feel aroused and loving and seek pleasure. But her husband may feel exhausted and hostile and only have intercourse out of a sense of duty. But tomorrow night each may feel like the other did the previous night. And on the third night both may feel relaxed and have intercourse as a means of expressing their love for each other.

The verbal and nonverbal communication preceding, during, and after intercourse also may serve as a barometer for the relationship. "I can tell how we're doing," said one wife, "by whether or not we have intercourse and how he approaches me when we do. Sometimes he just rolls over when the lights are out and starts to rub my back. Other times he plays with my face while we talk and kisses me and waits till I reach for him. And still other times we each stay on our side of the bed so that our legs don't even touch."

Power

Intercourse may also imply power, in terms of which partner initiates it and what positions the respective spouses prefer. "I like my partner to seduce me, to be on top and take control when we have intercourse," said one spouse. "I like it when I feel dominated."

And intercourse may reflect power in that one spouse uses it to manipulate the other. A wife in her thirties said, "I can get anything I want from my husband because he loves sex and I know how to do what he likes. I've tried asking him for things without sex being involved, but it doesn't work." Withholding sex in order to punish the spouse or to express anger is another common power game.

Good and Evil
Intercourse is value laden. Some regard the experience as potentially uplifting. In the bestseller, *The Total Woman,* Marabel Morgan discusses the spiritual aspect of intercourse:

> For sexual intercourse to be the ultimate satisfaction, both partners need a personal relationship with their God. When this is so their union is sacred and beautiful, and mysteriously the two blend perfectly into one. Intercourse becomes the place where man and woman discover each other in a new dimension." (1975, p. 128).

But others view sex as dirty and shameful. Talking with Dr. Masters of Masters and Johnson, a husband disclosed his feelings about intercourse:

> For a long time I believed that the act of intercourse was dirty. My whole experience with it—not being married—meant being reminded that it was all dirty. And since I couldn't understand how it could be dirty only if it was out of marriage, I thought it was more or less dirty even when you were married." (Masters & Johnson, 1976, p. 67)

The consequences of viewing sex as dirty and shameful can be devastating. Since guilt is expressed in terms of anxiety, someone who feels guilty about sex may become so anxious that he or she will not be able to perform. Anxiety can create impotence in the man and make achieving an orgasm almost impossible for the woman. When sex is viewed as a positive, desirable experience, the performance in and enjoyment of sex are greatly enhanced.

SEXUAL FULFILLMENT: SOME PREREQUISITES

Having explored the nature of sex in marriage and the meanings couples associate with intercourse, let's examine several prerequisites for sexual fulfillment. While these will vary from couple to couple, they often include the following.

A Good Relationship
A rule among counselors who work with married couples who have sexual problems is "Treat the relationship before focusing on the sexual problem." The rule is based on the premise that the sexual relationship is embedded in the context of the larger relationship between the spouses. What happens outside the bedroom in day-to-day interaction has a tremendous influence on what happens inside the bedroom. The frequently expressed feeling that "I can't fight with you all day and want to have sex with you at night" illustrates the social context of the sexual experience. A wife expressed this context very clearly:

I don't understand him. He's ready to go any time. It's always been a big problem with us right from the beginning. If we've hardly seen each other for two or three days and hardly talked to each other, I can't just jump into bed. If we have a fight, I can't just turn it off. He has a hard time understanding that. I have to know I'm needed and wanted for more than just jumping into bed." (Rubin, 1976, p. 50)

Demonstration of Sexual Interest in the Partner

In addition to a caring and loving relationship, another prerequisite for sexual fulfillment is for each spouse to convey to the other a desire to interact sexually in the relationship. The importance of such a demonstration of sexual interest was illustrated in a nationwide survey of over four thousand men. Sixty percent reported that the most irritating aspect of sexual intercourse was "when the woman seems cold or disinterested" (Pietropinto & Simenauer, 1977). And the need to feel wanted is not unique to males. A happily married wife in her middle thirties said, "I like to know that I'm still sexually appealing to him."

As I remarked to my husband the other night . . . [sex] is the most exciting thing to do, the most interesting thing to do, the most enjoyable thing to do, and just generally the thing to do.

From **The Hite Report**

Open Communication

Sexually fulfilled spouses not only love each other and communicate a sexual desire for each other, they are comfortable expressing what they enjoy and don't enjoy in the sexual experience. Unless both spouses communicate their needs, preferences, and expectations to each other, neither is ever sure what the other wants. The classic example is the husband who picks up a copy of *The Erotic Man* at the drugstore and leafs through the pages until a section on breast manipulation catches his eye. He may read that "women" enjoy having their breasts stimulated by their partner's tongue and teeth. Later that night in bed, he may roll over and begin to nibble on his wife's breast. Meanwhile, she wonders what has possessed her husband and is unsure what to make of this new (possibly unpleasant) behavior. Sexually fulfilled spouses take the trauma and guesswork out of their relationship by communicating preferences and giving feedback.

Self-Knowledge

Spouses must know what they like before they can ask for it. This fact emphasizes the importance of self-knowledge. Being in touch with one's own feelings and one's own sexuality involves feeling comfortable and good about being female or male. To be in touch with your own body is to know how you can experience sexual pleasure. "I've read all the books on how to get the most out of sex," said one husband. "I've concluded that the experts know a lot about what some people like sexually, but nothing about what *I* like. I don't like the idea that I'm supposed to be able to pick up a book and become a super sex machine. Good sex for me is more related to the context than to the technique. And I'm sure that for the next person it's something else."

Realistic Expectations

To achieve sexual fulfillment, expectations must be realistic. A couple's sexual needs, preferences, and expectations may not coincide. Women and men not only have different biological makeups; they have been socialized differently. It is unrealistic to assume that your partner will want to have sex with the same frequency and in the same way that you do on all occasions. Sexual fulfillment necessitates not requiring things of the marriage relationship that it can't deliver.

SEXUAL FULFILLMENT: SOME FACTS

Sexual fulfillment also requires an awareness of basic facts about human sexuality. Here are some of the important ones.

Sexual Fulfillment Is Couple-Defined

The meaning of sexual fulfillment varies tremendously, and the conditions under which different couples achieve it vary also. Indeed, there is no one definition or set of behaviors which make up "sexual fulfillment." It exists, or doesn't, in the

Self-knowledge and good communication are important for a satisfying sexual relationship. If spouses fail to understand and communicate their preferences, they may find themselves "au naturel" in the wilderness when they would have been happier spending a romantic weekend together at a hotel.

FIGURE 14.1 The Female Sexual Response Cycle.

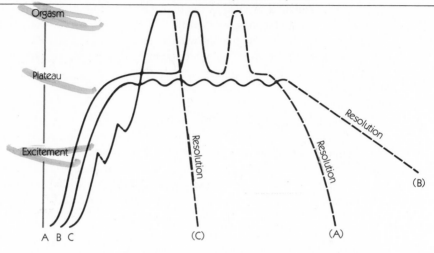

SOURCE: Masters and Johnson, 1966.

couple's own perceptions. A couple who never have sexual intercourse may be as sexually fulfilled as a couple who have intercourse three times a day. Frequency of intercourse and occurrence of orgasm may have everything or nothing to do with it. Rather, it is the couple's agreement that is the essence of sexual fulfillment.

The Effect of "Spectatoring"

In their early studies of how individuals actually behave during sexual intercourse, Masters and Johnson (1966) observed a tendency for sexually dysfunctional partners to act as spectators during intercourse. In essence, these partners would mentally observe their own and their partners' sexual performance (or lack of it). For example, the man would focus on whether or not he was having an erection, how complete it was, and whether or not it would last. He might also "watch" to see whether or not his partner was having an orgasm. Meanwhile his partner would be asking herself similar questions about herself and him.

"Spectatoring" as Masters and Johnson conceived it interferes with each partner's enjoyment in the sexual experience because it creates anxiety about performance, and anxiety blocks performance. A man who worries about getting an erection reduces his chances of doing so. A woman who is anxious about achieving an orgasm probably won't. A more desirable alternative to spectatoring is to relax, focus on and enjoy one's own pleasure, and permit the body's natural sexual responsiveness to take over.

FIGURE 14.2   The Male Sexual Response Cycle.

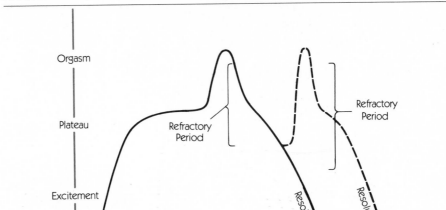

SOURCE: Masters and Johnson, 1966.

Male and Female Sexual Response Cycles

As the spectatoring problem reveals, human sexuality has a psychosocial component. The other major component is the biophysical, which includes the sexual response cycle. Masters and Johnson observed over ten thousand complete sexual response cycles and reported that women and men do not necessarily progress through the cycle the same way (1966).

The four phases of the sexual response cycle are excitement, plateau, orgasm, and resolution. These phases represent what people report they experience when they have sexual intercourse. First, there is the period when sexual activity is about to begin (excitement phase); then the partners give pleasure to each other for some time but not to the point of orgasm (plateau phase); then one or both have a climax (orgasm phase); and this is followed by a period of relaxation and a return to the state that preceded sexual excitement (resolution phase).

The female sexual response cycle is illustrated in Figure 14.1. Once sexual excitement begins, there may be three outcomes: progression from excitement to plateau, to orgasm, to resolution (see line C); or progression from excitement to plateau to orgasm, to plateau, to orgasm (or a number of additional orgasms), to resolution (see line A); or progression from excitement to plateau, to resolution without experiencing an intense orgasm (see line B).

The male sexual response cycle is illustrated in Figure 14.2. Once sexual response begins, there is essentially only one outcome—progressing through plateau to orgasm to resolution. While males may have additional orgasms, there is usually a considerable refractory (or recovery) period before doing so.

Observation of the sexual cycles of the two sexes reveals two essential differences: (1) While the male usually climaxes once during sexual intercourse, the female may do so not at all or several times, and (2) When the female does experience several climaxes, she is capable of doing so with only a brief time (seconds) between climaxes. In contrast, the male needs a considerably refractory period (minutes to hours) before he is capable of additional orgasms.

The Effects of Drugs

Progression through the sexual response cycle may be affected by drugs, particularly for the male. While alcohol may provide a feeling of relaxation, it depresses the central nervous system. Too much alcohol is a major cause of impotence. In a typical situation, the husband has been to a holiday party with his wife and returns home a little tipsy. If the couple decide to have intercourse, he may discover that he cannot get an erection. He may panic and feel that his masculinity is threatened. Later, even when he has not been drinking, he may be so anxious about achieving an erection (if he is a spectator of his own performance) that he cannot do so. Thus while alcohol may cause the initial failure, anxiety can be responsible for continued impotence.

Other drugs can also cause impotence. The effects of barbituates and some medications for hypertension (high blood pressure) on male sexual performance may create panic in the unsuspecting user.

Regarding marijuana, Kaplan wrote:

> Many persons report that smoking a few "joints" significantly enhances their sexual experience. They claim to feel more sensuous, more receptive to and more interested in erotic activity and to more easily lose themselves in the sexual experience while they are under the influence of a mild "high." Some also claim that orgasm is more prolonged and pleasurable. (Kaplan, 1974b, p. 90)

Sexual Attitudes and Behaviors Are Mostly the Result of Learning

From the belief "Sex is sinful" to "If it feels good, do it," sexual attitudes are learned. While parents and peers have a major impact on generating a "conservative" or "liberal" attitude toward sex, other sources such as school, church or synagogue, and the media have their input. Whatever an individual's attitude about sex, it would have been different if the influences had been different.

And the same is true of sexual behavior. What spouses do behind closed doors has largely been learned. The words they say (or don't say), the sequence of events (talking softly, touching, kissing), the behaviors they engage in (intercourse, cunnilingus, fellatio), and the positions they adopt ("missionary," female superior, etc.) during intercourse are a product of their individual and joint learning histories.

SEXUAL FULFILLMENT: SOME MYTHS

Just as sexual fulfillment involves basic prerequisites and a knowledge of the facts of human sexuality, it also involves recognition that some of the information that passes for fact in our society is actually myth. Let's examine some of the more prevalent myths.

Myth 1: Simultaneous Orgasm is the Ultimate Sexual Experience

While having orgasm at the same time one's partner does may be an enjoyable and pleasurable experience, there are two problems in achieving such a goal. First, it is difficult to fully enjoy one's own orgasm while trying to do what is necessary to assist the partner in achieving an orgasm. Since the male usually has only one orgasm, many couples plan for the husband to delay his climax until his wife has climaxed (one or several times). In this way the wife can focus on the sexual sensations that are being produced in her body without worrying about whether her husband is climaxing. After she has achieved sexual satisfaction, she can devote her attention to her husband, and he can focus on enjoying his own climax.

In addition to making it hard to concentrate on one's own climax, simultaneous orgasm may have another drawback:

> Men and women react quite differently in their respective bodily movements at the time of orgasm. The man's tendency is to plunge into the vagina as deeply as possible at the moment of his orgasm, to hold this position for a length of time, and to follow, perhaps, with one or two deep deliberate thrusts. The woman's tendency, on the other hand, is to have the same stroking, plunging movements of the earlier stages of intercourse continued during the orgasmic reaction, with perhaps an acceleration of the thrusts and an increase of pressure in the vulva area. These two highly pleasurable patterns of movement are obviously incompatible. Since they cannot both be executed at the same time, whichever pattern is carried out during simultaneous orgasm must perforce detract from the full pleasure of one of the partners. (McCary, 1976, p. 287)

Myth 2: Intercourse During Menstruation Is Harmful

Although a woman may prefer not to have intercourse during her period because of an unusually heavy flow or because of cramps (Paige, 1976), there is no harmful effect on her or on her partner if they do so. Some women report that intercourse helps to relieve menstrual cramps. The hesitancies a couple might have for engaging in intercourse during this time are usually associated with their feelings about blood. Most have been taught that blood is "bad" and should be avoided.

The taboo against intercourse during menstruation is culturally pervasive and has a long history. Many women are socialized to regard menstruation as "the curse," "doom's day," or "being unwell." The Old Testament warns that anyone lying with a woman within seven days of the onset of her period "shall be unclean seven days and every bed whereon he lieth shall be unclean" (Lev. 15:24). For many, breaking this taboo is difficult.

Myth 3: Intercourse During Pregnancy Should Be Avoided

Unlike the other myths, this one has some basis in truth. The woman who has had a miscarriage during the first three months of a previous pregnancy should be cautious about having an orgasm (through intercourse or masturbation) in the first trimester. An orgasm during this time may stimulate uterine contractions and initiate another miscarriage. In addition, an orgasm during late pregnancy can initiate labor, though this occurrence is extremely rare (Masters & Johnson, 1976).

In a study of forty-three women in their first pregnancies, thirty-three reported losing interest in sex during the first three months. Chronic fatigue, sleepiness, and contending with nausea were the primary causes for such loss of interest (Masters & Johnson, 1976, p. 157). Reduced interest also characterized the third trimester but not the second trimester. During these middle three months, "their sex drive is unlimited, regardless of how many episodes they may have. One of the explanations is the increased blood supply to the female reproductive organs as pregnancy progresses. This may cause many women to remain in a relatively constant state of sexual excitation" (Masters & Johnson, 1976, p. 86).

Keeping in mind the above precautions, intercourse may continue up to the moment of labor under three conditions—that there are no vaginal bleeding, no pain during intercourse, and no broken membranes.

Myth 4: Masturbation Ends with Marriage

In a study of over fourteen hundred spouses, 72 percent of the husbands and 68 percent of the wives in their late twenties and early thirties reported masturbating in the preceding year (Hunt, 1974, p. 86). The median rate for husbands was twenty-four times a year; for wives, ten times a year. Although unavailability of the spouse (absence, illness, disinclination) was the primary motivation for masturbating, some spouses preferred it as a variation. "I can climax best when I masturbate," said one wife, "and while I enjoy my husband's penis inside me, I also enjoy turning myself on."

Just as masturbation before marriage occurs in private, the same pattern continues in marriage. Some spouses are shocked to learn that their partners occasionally masturbate and regard their doing so as a personal affront (Gadpaille, 1974). Such a reaction reflects the ingrained nature of the belief that masturbation "should" end with marriage.

Myth 5: Extramarital Sex Strengthens Marriage Relationships

Among the most controversial myths are those that relate to extramarital sex. Having sexual intercourse with someone other than one's spouse may involve a one-night encounter or a full-blown affair with considerable emotional involvement over a long period of time. Relatively few extramarital relationships are of the involved affair variety because most spouses do not have the time and energy to manage them.

What percent of spouses engage in sex outside their marriages? Although no satisfactory studies exist to provide an accurate answer, it appears that about 45 percent of husbands and about 35 percent of wives have at least one extramarital sexual encounter (Kinsey, 1948, 1953; Hunt, 1974; Levin, 1975; Pietropinto & Simenauer, 1977). Such encounters vary with age (older more likely), length of marriage (longer more likely), social class (lower more likely), employment pattern (employed more likely), and religion (devout less likely).

When 831 respondents (both men and women) were asked, "Overall, how do you rate your marriage?" those who had been involved in an extramarital encounter reported lower marital satisfaction than those who had not been involved (Glass & Wright, 1977). In another study of over 75,000 wives, 83 percent of those who had not been involved in an extramarital encounter reported higher marital satisfaction in contrast to 61 percent of those who had been involved (Levin, 1975). One researcher suggested that extramarital sex contributes to the divorce rate "because it is viewed as a violation of the marriage contract and because it is part of the process of next-mate selection" (Gagnon, 1977, p. 220). In addition, extramarital sex "is often experienced as a deep personal shock by the spouse who has been faithful to the contract. The offended partner often experiences a deep sense of rejection and inadequacy, and if the events become public, both men and women are profoundly ashamed in front of their friends" (p. 226).

Myth 6: Extramarital Sex Destroys Marriage Relationships

If it is a myth that extramarital sex always improves a marriage relationship, it is also a myth that extramarital sex always has negative consequences for the spouses and their marriage. To begin with, different kinds of marriage relationships permit different degrees of sexual freedom for the spouses. While the term *extramarital sex* is typically associated with adultery or unfaithfulness and implies that one spouse neither knows nor would approve of the partner's sexual relationships with others, *comarital sex* has a different connotation. Comarital sex applies to

> . . . married couples who are either actually involved together in establishing relationships beyond that of the marital dyad for sexual purposes, or to couples in which there is both knowledge of and consent to such relationships regardless of whether the sexual activity includes both partners or is independent to some degree. (Smith & Smith, 1970, p. 134)

In Knapp's study of seventeen couples who had sexually open marriages, twenty-two of the thirty-four respondents (65 percent) reported increased satisfaction with their marriage (Knapp, 1976). One woman in her late forties said that she and her husband "live more or less like single people—when something interesting comes along, for either of us, we pursue it. . . . And this doesn't mean we have separate rooms at home or even beds. Far from it! . . . I'd say my husband and I love each other—we just don't own each other" (Cuber & Harroff, 1965, p. 156).

Even when only one spouse has an extramarital affair, the marriage may not only survive but improve. An Ann Landers reader wrote:

To look at me, you'd never guess I have two teenage children. I have no gray hairs, no wrinkles, and no excess baggage.

A few months ago, I became fascinated by an art dealer whose studio is near our apartment. I am not the type to sneak around, so I told my husband everything. I didn't want a divorce or separation, only his patience and understanding until the tornado blew itself out.

Being broadminded and intelligent, he treated me beautifully and he put up the usual front of the happily married couple.

In less than three months, the affair was over. I love my husband more than ever for his maturity and wisdom. He is thrilled to have me back on a full-time basis. No one was hurt and I learned, in the best way possible, there's no place like home. We are closer than ever and I'll never look at another man again. Everyone profited. Please agree in print. I'll feel better. (Landers, 1977)

SEXUAL FULFILLMENT: MANAGING DIFFERENCES

For a couple to realize sexual fulfillment, they must have not only a good "out of bed" relationship but also the ability to manage differences in sexual preferences. Two common sources of disagreement are how often sex will occur and what sexual behaviors are considered appropriate.

Few couples are in perfect agreement as to the ideal timing and frequency of intercourse. Where there is disagreement, the couple must arrive at a compromise or one spouse must adapt to the other's needs.

Frequency of Intercourse

Given different body clocks, different work schedules, and different psychological attitudes toward the marital sexual relationship, it is not uncommon for spouses to differ in their desire for frequency of intercourse. In a study of 196 college-educated wives, one fourth reported that intercourse did not occur frequently enough (Bell, 1967). In another study of 210 spouses, 78 percent of the husbands said that they wanted intercourse more frequently than their wives did, and 71 percent of the wives agreed (Nye & Berardo, 1973, p. 323). Differences are managed by compromise or by one spouse adapting to the needs of the other. A spouse who wants more frequent intercourse may masturbate or encourage the partner to manipulate him or her to orgasm. Open communication and a concern for each partner's feelings about frequency of intercourse are essential keys to managing the differences.

Variety

Spouses may also disagree over what sexual behaviors are appropriate before and during intercourse. Some behaviors to include or not are manual manipulation, oral-genital relations, and a range of coital positions.

In general, willingness to include a variety of sexual behaviors in lovemaking is related to age, education, social class, and religious orientation. The younger, better educated, higher social class individual who does not have a fundamentalist religious orientation is more likely to include manual and oral stimulation prior to intercourse and to experiment with a range of positions during intercourse.

Managing differences regarding sexual variety must be handled like the mating of two porcupines—with great care. Forcing one's desires on the mate is never wise. Rather, through reading and attending lectures on human sexuality and through discussing their differences, spouses can explore together the basis of their feelings and consider ways in which they might arrive at a compromise acceptable to both. In general, any sexual behaviors *both* spouses consider appropriate for their relationship are appropriate. And, getting one's partner to engage in a new sexual behavior takes time. Patience is the key. For example, if getting the spouse to engage in a variety of different intercourse positions is the goal, the reluctant spouse may begin by reading books on the subject. Such reading should be viewed by the other spouse as progress toward the eventual goal.

SEXUAL DYSFUNCTIONS

Specific sexual dysfunctions are a concern in many marriages. In essence, sexually dysfunctional spouses want to engage in sexual behaviors they can't achieve (e.g., orgasm) or to stop engaging in sexual behaviors they currently engage in (e.g., ejaculating prematurely). In this section we explore the major sexual dysfunctions of both sexes. But before doing so, let's review the contributions of Masters and Johnson, who pioneered major breakthroughs in the understanding and treatment of sexual dysfunctions.

Masters and Johnson

Codirectors of the Reproductive Biology Research Foundation in St. Louis, Missouri, William Masters and Virginia Johnson are regarded as the founders of what has become known as direct sexual therapy. Such therapy involves educating the couple about the intricacies of their sexual relationship, providing information about human sexuality, and making specific recommendations about what the couple can do during several sexual practice sessions to overcome sexual dysfunctions. The details of their treatment procedures were published in *Human Sexual Inadequacy* (1970) for professionals and in *Understanding Human Sexual Inadequacy* (Belliveau & Richter, 1970) for nonprofessionals.

Although other therapists and counselors (Hartman & Fithian, 1972; Kaplan, 1974b; Annon, 1975) now model their treatment of sexual dysfunction on that of Masters and Johnson, the primary alternative prior to the breakthrough was traditional psychoanalysis. Therapists of this orientation regard sexual dysfunctions (lack of orgasm, premature ejaculation) as symptomatic of an underlying conflict in one's interpersonal relationships—usually with a parent or spouse. And the resolution of such conflicts becomes the focus of therapy. But the results of psychoanalysis have been disappointing.

> Traditional psychoanalysis has had very little success in the treatment of most sexual problems. The successes it has had appear to be related to the emotional attachment between patient and therapist, a dependency that helps the patient reshape behavior in a direction that the therapist approves. However, because the rule in psychoanalysis is that the therapist not give advice or be a direct guide, discovery by patients of how to cure themselves is rare. (Gagnon, 1977, p. 369)

Because Masters and Johnson have provided sufficient data to justify the use of their procedures, the following discussion of sexual dysfunctions will rely heavily on their work. We now explore the major sexual dysfunctions of women and men and how they are resolved.

Female Sexual Dysfunctions

Lacking sexual responsiveness, failure to achieve orgasm, experiencing pain during intercourse (dyspareunia), and being unable to control constrictions of the vagina (vaginismus) are four main female sexual dysfunctions. Let's examine the causes and treatment of each of these.

Lacking sexual responsiveness. "The sexually unresponsive woman is essentially devoid of erotic feelings and responses. She does not usually desire sex, and upon stimulation of her erotic areas she feels no sexual pleasure, only the sensation of touch. Sometimes she is virtually anesthetic on the clitoris and vaginal entrance, the two areas of greatest erotic sensibility" (Kaplan, 1974a, p. 128). Although a sexually unresponsive woman does not experience sexual pleasure during intercourse, she may enjoy the bodily contact and cuddling aspects of intercourse.

Causes for the lack of sexual responsiveness include:

1. Restrictive child rearing. The unresponsive woman usually was told as a child that genitals, sexual stimulation, and sexual pleasure were sinful and dirty. As a result, she has learned to associate guilt and shame with sexual feelings.

2. Passive sexual role. In addition, the woman who is devoid of sexual feelings has often been taught to be a passive and dependent sexual partner. In a sense, she has been told that it is "unladylike" to lose herself in sexual ecstasy. Since such abandonment is incompatible with the traditional feminine role of passivity, she does not permit herself to become sexually excited.

3. Fear of rejection. In addition to being taught that sex is bad and that passivity is good, the sexually unresponsive woman may fear rejection by her husband: "How can a woman abandon herself when she fears he does not like her odor, is not pleased by her body, or is interested in other women?" (Kaplan, 1974a, p. 132)

Treatment for sexual unresponsiveness in a woman involves reeducation, the creation of a safe emotional environment, and the use of sensate focus. Reeducation includes a systematic examination (ideally with a female therapist) of the thoughts, feelings, and attitudes the woman was taught as a child and a reevaluation of them. The goal is to redefine sex so that it is viewed as a positive, desirable, pleasurable experience.

Regarding the creation of a safe emotional environment, the woman's relationship with her husband becomes a central issue. Does she love him? Does she trust him? Does she feel emotionally close to him? And, most important, does she feel comfortable "letting herself go" in sexual abandonment with him? Unless the interpersonal relationship with her partner is loving and emotionally comfortable, gains in increasing sexual responsiveness may be minimal.

In addition to the cognitive and relationship issues which often block sexual responsiveness, the wife and her husband are encouraged to participate in sensate focus exercises. Introduced over twenty years ago by Masters and Johnson, the procedure involves the spouses discovering each other through touch, massage, fondling, or tracing. Specific guidelines for the exercise include the following: (1) Both partners are nude. (2) The partners are not to have intercourse or touch each other's genitals, and the husband is not to touch his wife's breasts. (3) One partner is to give pleasure by touching and gently massaging the spouse. (4) The other partner is to pay attention to the pleasurable feelings of being touched and gently massaged and to let the mate know when the mate does something that is or is not pleasurable. (5) The partners are to switch roles so that each gives and gets sensual pleasure each session.

The result of practicing sensate focus twice a day for a period of weeks is that "the woman, free of the pressure to perform and to 'service' her husband, learns to begin to assume responsibility for her own sexual fulfillment. She learns to be less passive and more active in her own behalf. She learns that she will not be rejected if she asks her husband to caress and stimulate her" (Kaplan, 1974a, p. 135).

Inability to achieve orgasm. A woman may be sexually responsive and still not be able to experience an orgasm. Masters and Johnson characterized women who have never had an orgasm as having *primary* orgasmic dysfunction. Those who have had an orgasm by any means at any time in the past they regarded as having *situational* orgasmic dysfunction. Whether primary or situational, the result is the same—the wife is not currently capable of experiencing orgasm.

Some of the causes for not being able to achieve an orgasm are similar to those for being sexully unresponsive (restrictive rearing, passive sexual role, fear of rejection). Others include the following.

1. Focusing on partner. Many women have been socialized to feel it is their duty to satisfy their husbands sexually. But "if she accepts this idea and tries only to accommodate the man, she inhibits her own response" (Belliveau & Richter, 1970, p. 160). Having an orgasm requires focusing on the sexual sensations one is experiencing. If a woman is overly intent on pleasing her partner, she does so at the expense of her own orgasm.

2. Feelings about the mate. While the wife may feel it is her duty to "service" her husband, she may not like him. Masters and Johnson suggest that negative feelings about the mate are a major explanation for the wife's being inorgasmic. "Does he meet the woman's requirements of character, intelligence, ego strength, drive, physical characteristics, etc?" (1970, p. 241). If he does not measure up to her criteria of what a man and husband "should be," she may be incapable of becoming sexually excited about him or with him.

3. Sexually inadequate mate. Though the woman may feel very positive about her mate and focus on her own sexual feelings during intercourse, her partner may ejaculate before she has had a chance to respond. After repeated episodes of being left unsatisfied, she may want to avoid intercourse altogether.

Since the causal factors for primary and situational orgasmic dysfunction are extremely variable, the treatment must be individually tailored to meet the couple's needs. While insistence that the wife focus on her own sexual pleasure may be the "key" to orgasmic behavior in one woman, recreating love feelings for her partner may be the key for another. And where the husband routinely ejaculates prematurely, his sexual inadequacy may become the focal point of therapy.

More often than not assisting the woman in becoming orgasmic involves addressing a number of issues and using a number of procedures. Regarding the latter, Masters and Johnson again recommend the technique of sensate focus. In addition to the behaviors indicated for sensate focus in the discussion of the treatment of sexual unresponsiveness, additional stages include genital touching and intercourse. The wife is encouraged to guide her husband's hand over her genitals and breasts and indicate where she enjoys being touched and what pressure (soft or heavy) feels best. Masters and Johnson even recommend a position for experiencing genital play—the man is to sit "leaning against pillows at the head of the bed with the woman seated between his legs leaning with her back against his chest and resting her head on one of his shoulders. She separates her legs and extends them across her husband's legs" (Belliveau & Richter, 1970, p. 176).

The goal of genital play is not orgasm. Rather, the exercise is to provide a chance for the woman "to focus on her own sexual feelings, to discover what her preferences are and to communicate this information to her husband" (Belliveau & Richter, 1970, p. 179). As a result of not feeling pressured to have an orgasm yet getting the kind of stimulation she enjoys, the woman often experiences an orgasm.

The next stage is for the woman to insert her husband's penis inside her vagina while she is in the superior position. The object is for her to experience the same pleasurable sexual sensations she did in genital play. But, again, there is no demand for orgasm. The woman is instructed to be aware of her sexual feelings but not to force them. And the results are encouraging. Of 193 women being treated for primary orgasmic dysfunction, 83 percent experienced an orgasm during the two-week program. For women being treated for situational orgasmic dysfunction, 77 percent experienced an orgasm (Masters & Johnson, 1970, p. 314).

An alternative to the Masters and Johnson treatment package is one which uses masturbation as the primary means for becoming orgasmic:

> The use of self-stimulation as opposed to partner stimulation as the method of becoming familiar with orgasm is central; having the orgasm under the woman's own control allows her to go at her own pace while eliminating outside distractions provided by the presence of another person. In this manner, the woman can take gradual steps and learn to become familiar with the feelings that accompany sexual excitation rather than having to guard against them for fear they will overwhelm her. She can stop the stimulation if she feels afraid, or continue on as she grows more secure. As the result of growing familiarity and confidence, the woman becomes capable of experiencing an orgasm on her own. (Barbach, 1974, p. 143)

A detailed discussion of using masturbation to encourage orgasm can be found in *Becoming Orgasmic: A Sexual Growth Program for Women* (Heiman et al., 1976). The book deals with all aspects of masturbation, including the feelings of shame and guilt often associated with it.

Dyspareunia. While being sexually unresponsive and inorgasmic are the most frequent female sexual dysfunctions, dyspareunia, or painful intercourse sometimes occurs. Complaints of pain at the vaginal opening, on or around the clitoris, and inside the vagina are the most common. Since the usual cause of dyspareunia is physical rather than psychological, problems of this nature should be treated by a physician. "The best approach to understand female dyspareunia is anatomically" (Wabrek & Wabrek, 1975, p. 238).

Vaginismus. While a woman may not experience pain during intercourse, the outer portion of her vagina may constrict so as to make penetration impossible (Fertel, 1977). Masters and Johnson noted two background characteristics of women who experienced vaginismus: They tended to have impotent husbands, and they had strong religious feelings that sex was dirty and shameful. Masters and Johnson recommend the following procedure only after relationship and psychological issues have been dealt with.

In order to teach the spouses that vaginismus is an involuntary spasm, the wife lies on an examining table in the physician's office with the husband and physician present. The physician notes for the husband that as soon as he (the physician) attempts to insert a finger in the woman's vagina, it involuntarily constricts. The husband also puts on examining gloves and feels the constrictions.

"Once the clinical existence of vaginismus has been demonstrated to the satisfaction of both marital partners, resolution of this form of sexual inadequacy becomes relatively easy" (Masters & Johnson, 1970, p. 263). The remaining procedure is for the husband, with his wife's guidance, to insert increasingly larger dilators (cone-shaped objects) into the vagina in the privacy of their bedroom. Masters and Johnson reported successful treatment of twenty-nine out of twenty-nine women who experienced vaginismus—an impressive record (1970, p. 264).

Male Sexual Dysfunctions

Sexual dysfunctions among wives are only one side of the marriage bed. Husbands may be troubled by an inability to create and maintain an erection (impotence), inability to delay ejaculation as long as they or their wives would like (premature ejaculation), or inability to ejaculate at all (ejaculatory incompetence).

Impotence. There are two kinds of impotence. Primary impotence exists when the man has never been able to have intercourse. Secondary impotence exists when the man has had intercourse in the past but is not able to currently. Possible causes for impotence vary with the type of impotence being experienced. Background characteristics for some men with primary impotence include a seductive mother, religious indoctrination that sex is sinful, homosexual attachments as a teenager, and a traumatic first attempt at intercourse (Masters & Johnson, 1970). An example of the latter may have involved a negative experience with a prostitute: "The squalid quarters, repelling physical appearance of the women and their degrading approach made sexual arousal for the young men impossible" (Belliveau & Richter, 1970, p. 133).

While causal factors for secondary impotence may include those for primary impotence, more often the man has stopped getting erections good enough to complete intercourse because of premature ejaculation or excessive use of alcohol (Masters & Johnson, 1970). Of 213 secondarily impotent men seen by Masters and Johnson, sixty-three had a long-term pattern of ejaculating prematurely (p. 161). In essence, they became discouraged at their inability to delay their ejaculation and the sexual frustration of their wives that resulted. In an attempt to avoid premature ejaculation, they adopted the spectator role during intercourse. This focused their attention on the impending ejaculation and created more anxiety, which caused erectile failure. Once they were fearful of becoming impotent, their anxiety mounted so that impotence occurred again—and again.

Alcohol is another cause of secondary impotence. After more than the usual number of drinks, the husband initiates sex but fails to achieve an erection. By becoming anxious and struggling to get an erection he ensures that he won't do so. Thus while alcohol may be responsible for his initial failure, his impotence continues because of his anxiety over nonperformance.

Although anxiety is the main culprit for both primary and secondary impotence, the cause may, in some cases, be physiological. Before any sexual therapy is begun for either type of impotence, physiological causes should be ruled out by a physician. Once this has been done, the treatment involves a number of directives to the couple.

As a beginning, they are instructed not to have intercourse. This is done to remove the anxiety over nonperformance. If there is no expectation of intercourse, the anxiety associated with an erection is minimized.

In addition to eliminating any demand for intercourse, the therapists and couple may discuss religious taboos, alcohol, and premature ejaculation if these issues seem related to the man's impotence. In essence, the spouses develop a way of understanding the husband's impotence rather than continuing to feel mystified by its occurrence.

The husband is also instructed to give up the spectator role and to stop focusing on whether or not he is getting an erection. Rather, he is told to give pleasure to his wife through means other than intercourse. After several sensate focus sessions during which there is no pressure to perform and the husband focuses on his wife's pleasure, an erection becomes more likely. Sixty percent of 32 primarily impotent males and 73 percent of 213 secondarily impotent males were treated successfully by Masters and Johnson using these procedures (1970, p. 213).

Premature ejaculation. More common than impotence, premature ejaculation is the man's inability to delay ejaculation as long as he or his partner wishes. "I get so aroused," explained one husband, "that the moment I insert my penis inside her, and sometimes before, I ejaculate."

Most authorities agree that the cause of premature ejaculation is psychological rather than physical (Fink, 1972; Kaplan, 1974b). In this context, psychological means anxiety, which triggers the ejaculatory reflex. Masters and Johnson report that all men experiencing premature ejaculation have the same history. Early heterosexual attempts were hurried. They always felt pressure to ejaculate as soon as they could.

Developed by Masters and Johnson (1970), use of the "squeeze technique" is the most effective procedure for treating premature ejaculation. The wife stimulates her husband's penis manually until he signals her that he feels the urge to ejaculate. At his signal she places her thumb on the underside of his penis, and her first and second fingers on either side of the ridge formed by the head of his penis and squeezes hard, for three to four seconds. Her husband will lose his urge to ejaculate. After thirty seconds, she should resume stimulation, applying the squeeze technique again when her husband signals. The important rule for the couple to remember is that the wife should apply the squeeze technique whenever the husband gives the slightest hint of readiness to ejaculate.

In a variation of the Masters and Johnson procedure, the wife stimulates her husband's erect penis until he feels he is about to ejaculate (Semans, 1956). At that point, he signals her to stop. When he loses his urge to ejaculate, he signals his wife to resume stimulation. After practicing this stop-start method for several weeks, the husband can tolerate stimulation longer without ejaculating.

Ejaculatory incompetence. While the man who experiences premature ejaculation complains of ejaculating too soon, the man who suffers from *ejaculatory incompetence* can't ejaculate at all during intercourse. Even after prolonged intercourse, ejaculation does not occur.

The causes for ejaculatory incompetence are psychological. For example, a thirty-three-year-old husband revealed that he considered his wife's vagina contaminated because she had confessed on their wedding night that she had had intercourse before she met him. "How such a good woman, represented by his wife, could possibly have permitted such a transgression was inexplicable to him" (Masters & Johnson, 1970, 120).

In another case, a thirty-six-year-old husband, at age thirteen, had been

> . . . surprised in masturbation by his dismayed mother, severely punished by his father, and immediately sent to religious authority for consultation. Subsequent to his lengthy discussion with the religious adviser, the semi-hysterical, terrified boy carried away the concept that to masturbate to ejaculation was indeed an act of personal desecration, totally destructive of any future marital happiness and an open gate to mental illness. He was assured that the worst thing a teenage boy could do was to ejaculate at any time. This youngster never masturbated nor experienced a nocturnal emission again after the shocking experience of being surprised in autostimulation." (Masters & Johnson, 1970, p. 118)

What does or does not happen in bed often has important implications for an entire marriage relationship. Because sexual problems do not occur in a vacuum, most marriage counselors usually treat them within the context of the whole relationship.

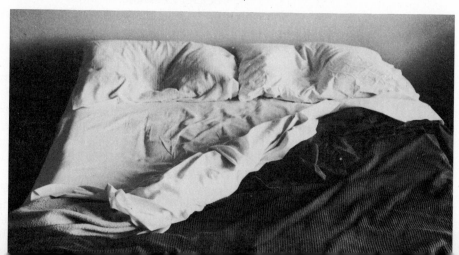

Fear of a pregnancy, lack of sexual excitement, and efforts to ejaculate too often in too short a time are other causes of ejaculatory incompetence.

Treatment for ejaculatory incompetence involves the wife manually stimulating her husband to a high level of sexual excitement and, at the moment of orgasm, inserting his penis into her vagina so that he ejaculates inside her. After several sessions of hand-to-vagina stimulation, the wife gradually reduces the amount of time she manually manipulates her husband and increases the amount of time she stimulates him with her vagina. Using this procedure, Masters and Johnson (1970) report a success rate of 82 percent (p. 134). Their lack of complete success in reversing ejaculatory incompetence is related to the psychological nature of this dysfunction. Of the husband who could not forget his wife's intercourse in a previous relationship, they wrote, "His haunting fear of vaginal-menstrual contamination . . . could not be neutralized" (p. 134).

The resolution of all sexual dysfunctions, both female and male should occur within the context of the interpersonal relationship. No set of tricks or procedures will be effective unless the partners have positive feelings about each other. As a matter of course, marriage counselors usually focus on the marital relationship before attempting to treat a specific dysfunction.

Instead of a marriage counselor, some couples consult a sex therapist for assistance in resolving a sexual dysfunction. Extreme care should be taken when selecting a counselor who presents himself or herself as a sex therapist. It is estimated that of the 3,500 to 5,000 sex clinics in America, only about one hundred are operated by trained professionals (Holden, 1976, p. 98).

TRENDS

Greater access to information about achieving sexual fulfillment, increased willingness to seek help for sexual dysfunctions, and a larger supply of trained professionals in marital counseling are among the current trends that promise more widespread sexual fulfillment in the future. Magazines such as *Redbook, Ladies Home Journal, McCall's* and *Family Circle* regularly feature articles on sexual aspects of the woman-man relationship. Masters and Johnson are names no longer known by professionals alone since their research is available to every person who stands in the line to pay for groceries.

Reading about sex therapy alerts individuals to the causes and potential cures of sexual dysfunctions they may be experiencing in their own relationships. Becoming aware that others have consulted professionals to assist them in achieving various sexual goals increases the chance that they will do likewise.

To meet the increasing demand for sex therapy, more professionals are being trained. A beginning point is to provide physicians with more training in sexuality. In the early 1960s, only three schools offered any instruction in sexuality. In the mid–1970s, 106 of the country's 112 medical schools offered sex courses (Holden, 1976, p. 99). In addition, the American Association of Sex Educators accredits trained experts in sex education. As standards for sex therapists are raised, more will seek the appropriate training that will ensure better service to couples. In essence, Americans will become more sophisticated about sexual matters and will expect more help with their sexual problems from professionals.

SUMMARY

In contrast to sex before marriage, marital sex is characterized by its legitimacy and its declining frequency. For some spouses, intercourse has no importance, but for the majority it is the barometer of their relationship. It is a means of communicating and a way by which they may express their love for each other.

Prerequisites for sexual fulfillment include a good relationship, demonstration of sexual interest in the partner, open communication, self-knowledge, and realistic expectations. And there must be basic information that separates facts about human sexuality from myths. Some basic facts are that sexual fulfillment is defined by the couple, that being a "spectator" interferes with sexual enjoyment, that the sexual response cycles of women and men differ, that drugs may affect sexual performance, and that sexual attitudes and beliefs are mostly learned. Common myths about sex include the notions that simultaneous orgasm is the ultimate sexual experience, that intercourse during menstruation and pregnancy has negative consequences, that marriage puts an end to masturbation, and that extramarital affairs necessarily strengthen or necessarily destroy the marriage relationship.

Differing attitudes toward frequency of intercourse and appropriate sexual variety may interfere with sexual fulfillment. Managing such differences calls for open communication, concern for each other's feelings, and compromise.

Among women, sexual dysfunctions include lack of sexual responsiveness, lack of orgasm, dyspareunia, and vaginismus. Among men, impotence, premature ejaculation, and ejaculatory incompetence are most common. Masters and Johnson have developed relatively effective treatment procedures for each of these dysfunctions.

Trends in sexual fulfillment include greater public awareness of sexual dysfunctions and treatment procedures, an increased willingness for couples to seek professional help, and a growing supply of trained professionals to meet the need.

STUDY QUESTIONS

1. Explain the statement, "Marital sex is legitimate."
2. How do age, length of marriage, children, and careers affect the frequency of marital intercourse? What other psychological and sociological factors contribute to the gradual decline of intercourse in marriage?
3. Comment on the importance of sex in marriage.
4. How does intercourse serve as a communication channel and barometer for a couple's relationship?
5. Give examples of how some spouses use sex to manipulate each other.
6. Discuss two opposing value perceptions of intercourse.
7. Explain why sexual fulfillment depends on a good relationship, demonstration of interest, open communication, self-knowledge, and realistic expectations.

8. What is sexual fulfillment?
9. Define spectatoring. How does it affect sexual enjoyment?
10. How do the sexual response cycles of women and men differ?
11. How do alcohol and marijuana affect sexual functioning?
12. Why is simultaneous orgasm with one's partner difficult to achieve?
13. How may intercourse during menstruation be beneficial?
14. How does a woman's interest in sex vary with her stage of pregnancy?
15. What is the main reason given for masturbation in marriage?
16. About what percentage of husbands and wives are estimated as having intercourse with someone other than their spouses?
17. How may engaging in extramarital sex contribute to divorce?
18. Distinguish between extramarital and comarital sex. Give examples of how some marriages may be strengthened by extramarital and comarital sex.
19. Why are different desires for frequency of intercourse somewhat inevitable? To what degree do spouses report differences over desired frequency of intercourse?
20. How do some spouses manage their differences over frequency of intercourse?
21. How is a willingness to explore sexual variety in one's marriage related to various background characteristics? How do some spouses resolve different feelings about sexual variety?
22. Comment on the significance of the work by Masters and Johnson for helping couples achieve sexual fulfillment.
23. Prior to the research by Masters and Johnson, what was the primary mode of therapy? Evaluate it.
24. What could cause a woman neither to desire sex nor to feel pleasure in it? Discuss the treatment procedures.
25. Why are some women unable to experience an orgasm? What procedures did Masters and Johnson develop to increase women's ability to have orgasms?
26. Discuss the causes and treatment of dyspareunia and vaginismus.
27. What are the types, causes, and treatment procedures for impotence?
28. What are the typical background characteristics of men who ejaculate prematurely? What procedures did Masters and Johnson recommend to treat this dysfunction?
29. What are some causes of ejaculatory incompetence and how is it treated?
30. What are three trends related to sexual fulfillment?

NOTE

1. See Gecas and Libby (1976) and Neubeck (1972) for an expanded discussion of sex as communication.

BIBLIOGRAPHY

Annon, J. S. *The behavioral treatment of sexual problems: Intensive therapy* (Vol. 2). Honolulu, Hawaii: Enabling Systems, 1975.

Barbach, L. G. *Journal of Sex and Marital Therapy,* 1974, 2, 1, 139–45.

Bell, R. Some emerging sexual expectations among women. *Medical Aspects of Human Sexuality,* 1967, 65–7, 72.

Belliveau, F., and Richter, L. *Understanding human sexual inadequacy.* New York: Bantam Books, 1970.

Cuber, J. F. The sexless marriage. *Medical Aspects of Human Sexuality.* November 1969.

_____. Sex in the upper middle class. *Medical Aspects of Human Sexuality,* July 1974, 8 et passim.

Cuber, J. F., and Harroff, P. *Sex and the significant Americans.* Baltimore: Penguin Books, 1965.

Fertel, N. S. Vaginismus: A review. *Journal of Sex and Marital Therapy,* 1977, *3,* 2, 113–21.

Fink, P. J. Premature ejaculation. *Medical Aspects of Human Sexuality,* 1972, *6,* 8, 93.

Gadpaille, W. J. Masturbation by married individuals. *Medical Aspects of Human Sexuality,* 1974, 63–4.

Gagnon, J. H. *Human sexualities.* Glenview, Ill.: Scott, Foresman, 1977.

Gagnon, J. H., and Simon, W. *Sexual conduct: The social sources of human sexuality.* Chicago: Aldine, 1973.

Gecas, V., and Libby, R. Sexual behavior as symbolic interaction. *The Journal of Sex Research,* 1976, *12,* 1, 33–49.

Glass, S. P., and Wright, T. L. The relationship of extramarital sex, length of marriage, and sex differences on marital satisfaction and romanticism: Athanasiou's data reanalyzed. *Journal of Marriage and the Family,* 1977, *39,* 4, 691–704.

Hartman, W., and Fithian, M. *Treatment of sexual dysfunction.* Long Beach, Calif.: Center for Marital and Sexual Studies, 1972.

Heiman, J., LoPiccolo, L., and LoPiccolo, J. *Becoming orgasmic: A sexual growth program for women.* Englewood Cliffs, N.J.: Prentice-Hall, 1976.

Holden, C. Sex therapy. Making it as a science and an industry. In *Focus: Human sexuality,* A. Kilbride (ed.). Guilford, Conn.: Dushkin Publishing Group, 1976, 98–101.

Hunt, M. *Sexual behavior in the 1970's.* New York: Dell, 1974.

James, W. H. Marital coital rates, spouses' ages, family size, and social class. *Journal of Sex Research,* 1974, *10,* 3, 205–18.

Kaplan, H. The classification of the female sexual dysfunctions. *Journal of Sex and Marital Therapy,* 1974, *1,* 2, 124–38.(a)

—————. *The new sex therapy: Active treatment of sexual dysfunctions.* New York: Brunner/Mazel, 1974.(b)

Kinsey, A. C., et al. *Sexual behavior in the human male.* Philadelphia: W. B. Saunders, 1948.

—————. *Sexual behavior in the human female.* Philadelphia: W. B. Saunders, 1953.

Knapp, J. J. An exploratory study of seventeen sexually open marriages. *The Journal of Sex Research,* 1976, *12,* 3, 206–19.

Landers, A. She says affair helped marriage. *Raleigh News and Observer,* 27 June 1977, 9.

Levin, R. J. The Redbook report on premarital and extramarital sex. *Redbook,* October 1975, 38 et passim.

Masters, W. H., and Johnson, V. E. *Human sexual response.* Boston: Little, Brown, 1966.

—————. *Human sexual inadequacy.* Boston: Little, Brown, 1970.

—————. *The pleasure bond.* New York: Bantam Books, 1976.

McCary, J. L. Sexual myths and fallacies. In *Modern views of human sexual behavior,* J. L. McCary and D. Copeland (eds.). Palo Alto: Science Research Associates, 1976, 286–312.

Morgan, M. *The total woman.* Old Tappan, N.J.: Revell, 1975.

Neubeck, G. The myriad motives for sex. *Sexual Behavior,* 1972, *2,* 50–6.

Nye, I. F., and Berardo, F. M. Unpublished study on which spouse desires sexual intercourse more frequently. Referred to in Nye and Berardo, *The family: Its structure and interaction.* New York: Macmillan, 1973.

Paige, K. E. Women learn to sing the menstrual blues. In *Modern views of human sexual behavior,* J. L. McCary and D. R. Copeland (eds.). Palo Alto: Science Research Associates, 1976, 109–15.

Pietropinto, A., and Simenauer, J. *Beyond the male myth.* New York: Quadrangle, 1977.

Rubin, L. B. The marriage bed. *Psychology Today,* August 1976, 44 et passim.

Semans, J. H. Premature ejaculation: A new approach. *Southern Medical Journal,* 1956, *49,* 353–62.

Smith, J., and Smith, L. Co-marital sex and the sexual movement. *Journal of Sex Research,* 1970, *6,* 131–42.

Wabrek, A. J., and Wabrek, C. J. Dyspareunia. *Journal of Sex and Marital Therapy,* 1975, *1,* 3, 234–41.

Chapter **15**

Planning a Family

DO YOU WANT TO BE A PARENT?

Social Influences Toward Parenthood (Pronatalism) • Personal Reasons for Having Children • The Childfree Alternative

HOW MANY CHILDREN DO YOU WANT?

An Only Child? • Two Children? • Three Children? • Four or More Children?

TIMING YOUR CHILDREN

The First Child • Timing Subsequent Births

CONTRACEPTION

Oral Contraceptive (The Pill) • Intrauterine Device (IUD) • Condom • Diaphragm • Spermicidal Agents • Withdrawal • Rhythm • Douche • Contraception: A Personal Decision • Effective Use of Contraception

STERILIZATION

Female Sterilization • Male Sterilization • Sterilization: A Personal Decision

ABORTION

The Law on Abortion • Methods of Abortion

TRENDS

SUMMARY

Love is a fourteen letter word—family planning.
Planned Parenthood Poster

As a university student, before each academic term you decide how many courses you want to take and when you want to take them. You probably try to avoid an overload and feel pleased when you get the schedule you want. Successful family planning means having the number of children you want (if any) at the times you want to have them. Although having a family in this way seems very sensible and practical, many couples leave having a family to chance. Between 1966 and 1970, 44 percent of all births to married women were unplanned (Commission on Population Growth, 1972, p. 163).

Family planning has benefits for the mother and child. Since having several children at short birth intervals increases the chance of premature birth, infectious diseases, and death for the mother or baby, parents can minimize such risks by planning fewer children at longer birth intervals.

Conscientious family planning may also reduce the number of children born to parents who don't want them. Although most unplanned births are failures in timing and not unwanted births, one unwanted child is too many. The child reared by cold, rejecting parents may be emotionally scarred for life.

Society also benefits from family planning by enabling the poor to avoid having children they lack the money to feed and clothe adequately—children who may be abandoned or whose rearing must be subsidized by the state.

In this chapter, you are encouraged to consider four basic questions: Do you want to be a parent? If so, how many children do you want? When is the best time to begin your family? And which method of contraception is best for you?

DO YOU WANT TO BE A PARENT?

In the next chapter we will explore in detail the personal and marital consequences for the wife and husband when they become parents. In this section, we examine the pressures on couples to have children, the reasons people give for wanting children, and the childfree alternative to parenthood. Although the decision to become a parent is "not a fully rational act" according to psychoanalyst Donald Kaplan (Whelan, 1976, p. 59), over 90 percent of young adults in America say they want to have children (Institute of Life Insurance, 1975, p. 61).

Social Influences Toward Parenthood (Pronatalism)

Unless the members of a society have children, the society will cease to exist. In general, our society favors and encourages childbearing, an attitude known as *pronatalism.* The ways in which we are encouraged to become parents include the following.

Family. The fact that we were reared in families encourages us to have families of our own. Our parents are our models. They married, we marry; they had children, we have children. Some parents exert a much more active influence. "I'm sixty-seven and don't have much time. Will I ever see a grandchild?" asked the mother of an only child. Other remarks parents make to induce their children to provide them with grandchildren include: "If you don't hurry up, your younger sister is going to have a baby before you do." "We're setting up a trust fund for your brother's child, and we'll do the same for yours." "Did you know that Nash and Marilyn [the child's contemporaries] just had a daughter?" "I think you'll regret not having children when you're old." "Don't you want a son to carry on your name and be like you?"

Friends. In addition to our parents, our friends who have children influence us to do likewise. After sharing an enjoyable weekend with friends who had a little girl, one husband wrote to the host and hostess, "Lucy and I are always affected by Roxie—she is such a good child to be around. We haven't made up our minds yet, but our desire to have a child of our own always increases after we leave your home." This couple became parents sixteen months later.

Religion. Some religious denominations exert pressure toward parenthood. Catholics are taught that having children is the basic purpose of marriage and gives meaning to the union. A Catholic graduating senior said, "My body was made by God and I should use it to produce children for Him. Other people may not understand it, but that's how I feel." Judaism also has a strong family orientation. Couples who choose to be childfree are less likely than couples with children to adhere to any set of religious beliefs.

Government. Taxes imposed by our federal and state governments encourage parenthood. Married couples without children pay higher taxes than couples with children. A newly married couple with an annual income of $12,000 will pay about $1,820 in federal income taxes (taking the standard deduction). With one child, their taxes drop to $1,755; with two children their taxes would be $1,590. Clearly, our tax system favors the couple with dependents.

Mother's Day and Father's Day. Society reaffirms its approval of parents every year by allocating a day for Mom and Dad. Parents receive gifts and embraces from their offspring with delight. On these two days each year parenthood is celebrated across the nation. Family, friends, religion, government, and special observances all emphasize that parenthood is an experience worth having. "The most effective controls on fertility are those which operate at the informal level and which, in our society, constitute 'coercive pronatalism' "(Blake, 1973).

Personal Reasons for Having Children

Because they have absorbed the social bias toward parenthood ever since their own early childhood, few couples know precisely why they want to have children. But the reasons parents give for their decision to have children include the following.

Social expectations ("It's the thing to do").   A sociologist and father of two daughters said, "Having children was never a conscious decision. It was more of a feeling that one *ought* to have a family." A mother of two expressed a similar feeling: "All my friends were having babies, and I never questioned whether I would, too." Our society expects its members to conform to certain conventions, not the least important of which is having children. Conforming to society's expectations has many rewards. It assures a degree of acceptance from peers and places us in the mainstream of American life.

Personal fulfillment ("I've always wanted to have children").   As part of the socialization that prepares her for the female role, a young girl is encouraged to play with dolls and to anticipate having children of her own. In some cases the socialization is so strong that womanhood is equated with motherhood. "I suppose I felt I had to get pregnant to verify that I was a real woman," a young mother said.

Men also derive personal fulfillment from children. Having children permits men to be affectionate as fathers and to affirm their masculinity by proving that they can conceive children. A son will also carry on the family name, an important issue for some men. After his fourth daughter was born, one father said, "I always wanted a son to carry on the family name, but it looks like I'll fill up the back yard with girls before I get one."

Personal identity ("I know who I am now").   Related to the quest for personal fulfillment is the feeling that a baby provides a specific identity for the parent. As one woman explained, "Before my son, Benny, I was nothing. I was bored, I hated my job, and I didn't have any goals or focus to my life. Now I know who I am—a mother—and I feel that I am needed." And some fathers express the same feeling. "Having my child is the meaning of life," remarked the father of a newborn. "I am a lousy employee, but I'm a great father. For the first time in my life, I really feel like somebody."

Marital fulfillment ("A baby will make our marriage happier").   In general, the longer a couple have been married, the less happy they are likely to be. And for some spouses, the waning of marital happiness is frightening. "I knew it happened to my parents, and I saw it happen to my sister and her husband, but I didn't think it would happen to Tom and me," explained Brenda, married three

THE MATERNAL INSTINCT

years. Many couples decide to have children in the belief that a baby will revitalize their marriage. It is an old folk remedy for a bad marriage that a tiny baby's chubby little hands are going to take two quarreling hearts and pull them together. This is an awesome responsibility to place on a new baby (Wright et al., 1978, p. 25). (The effect of children on the marital relationship is reviewed in Chapter 16.)

Influence of spouse ("I want us to have a baby"). Some spouses have children primarily to please their mates. "I wasn't wild about the idea of having children but decided to go along with it because my husband wanted one. As it turns out, I'm glad we did," one parent said. When husband and wife feel differently about having children, the disagreement is not always resolved in favor of having them. But most couples decide to have children.

Accident ("It just happened"). A good many couples have children without intending to. "I was out of pills and we didn't have any condoms," recalled a young wife, "but we wanted to have intercourse and decided to take a chance. An eight-pound baby was the result."

Such accidents are not unusual. In a study of 102 first-time fathers, almost one third reported that their child was not planned (Knox & Gilman, 1974, p. 32). And, as already noted, of all births to married women between 1966 and 1970, 44 percent were unplanned.

Generativity ("We just like kids"). *Generativity* implies an interest in establishing and guiding the next generation (Erikson, 1963, p. 10). According to one view, a child's mind is originally like an empty house, and it is the delight of some parents to fill that house with useful, truthful, and accurate information. One mother of three children said, "I guess one of the reasons we had kids was because we like to teach them. We are both teachers by profession, we have enormous patience, and we really like children. We particularly enjoy taking them to historical and cultural events."

Whatever the reasons parents give for having children, the rewards of parenthood are basically intangible. Parents often speak of (1) the delight of seeing children discover their world for the first time, (2) the joy of holding a baby in your arms and realizing that it is part of you and your partner, and (3) the pleasure of following the development of children through the years and of relating to them as adults. One clinical psychologist, the father of three children, said, "The real problem with children is not their coming but their going. My first daughter will soon be married and move six states away. I used to feel that babies were not worth the trouble, but now I know the joy of a fantastic parent-child relationship."

The Childfree Alternative

For all the happiness they may provide, children also cause problems. They tend to interfere with the marriage relationship, disrupt careers (particularly the mother's), cost money, and make noise. In addition, parenthood is a demanding role that not all people feel qualified to assume. For these and other reasons, couples who choose the option of remaining childfree are gaining increased acceptance. The National Organization for Non-Parents (NON) has been working since 1972 to make the childfree life-style a fully approved option for those who choose it and a viable alternative for those who are not sure they want to be parents. Making the facts about children available and attacking the stigma associated with the childfree marriage are specific objectives of NON (NON Annual Report, 1978).

There are no reliable data concerning the benefits of parenthood (Veevers, 1974a). To claim that every spouse and couple will benefit either from having children or from a childfree marriage is nonsense. Those who choose the childfree alternative often become victims of negative stereotyping. They are sometimes regarded as selfish, irresponsible, unnatural, immature, emotionally unstable, unhappy in their marriage, divorce-prone, and psychologically maladjusted. NON attacks the stereotypes as false, dehumanizing, and tragic, particularly when they force couples who don't want children to have them simply to avoid the continued social pressure.

Members of NON also question the reasons couples give for having children and ask, "What's wrong with these reasons for non-parenthood?"

1. There are too many people in the country and the world already.
2. The planet has finite resources.
3. One can like children but not enjoy parenting.
4. Being childfree allows room for more spontaneity in daily living.
5. A career can be more rewarding for some women than motherhood.
6. Relationships can be satisfying and fulfilling without children. In fact, university studies have concluded that childfree marriages are often happier.
7. Non-parenthood allows for human creativity beyond bio-reproduction; non-parenthood allows for time to concentrate on the wider "family" of community and society and can ultimately be far less "selfish" than a narrower "family" concern. (NON, 1978)

But what are the reasons couples actually give for remaining childfree? When 55 couples who chose not to have children were asked about their reasons, the wives gave as the most important reasons their desire for more personal freedom, greater time and intimacy with their spouses, and career demands. The most important reasons for husbands included the desire for more personal freedom, disinterest in being a parent, and the desire to take on fewer responsibilities. Less

Many couples who remain childfree do so in order to have more time with their spouses and more freedom to relax and pursue their personal interests.

TABLE 15.1   Number of Children Expected by Young Adults (Ages 14–25).

	Female (N = 1,198) Percent	Male (N = 1,312) Percent
None	4	5
One	10	10
Two	47	45
Three	23	19
Four	8	9
Five or more	4	4
Don't know or no answer	4	8

SOURCE: Institute of Life Insurance, 1975, p. 61.

common or less important reasons given by the 55 childfree couples included financial reasons, concern with overpopulation, and dislike of children (Cooper et al., 1978, p. 78).

In another study of fifty-two married women who were childfree by choice only a third had decided on the childfree alternative before marriage. The other two thirds kept putting off getting pregnant ("I'll wait until I'm out of school . . . until we get a house . . . until we get more money," etc.) until they became satisfied with the childfree life-style and decided to continue it (Veevers, 1974b).

Is the childfree life-style for you? If you get your primary satisfactions from your career and your spouse and if you require an atmosphere of freedom and privacy, perhaps the answer is "yes." But if no career or adult relationship or amount of freedom can match your desire to have your own child, the answer is probably "no." For some people the childfree life-style is a viable alternative to having children.

HOW MANY CHILDREN DO YOU WANT?

If you decide to have children, how many do you want? Table 15.1 shows the number of children American youth (ages 14 through 25) expect to have. In this section, we explore the various issues that need to be considered in deciding to have one, two, three, or more children.

TABLE 15.2   Advantages and Disadvantages of a One-Child Family as Reported by Only Children and Their Parents.

| Only Children (N = 105) | | Parents of Only Children (N = 168) | |
Advantages	Percent	Advantages	Percent
More possessions, opportunities	34	Financial	35
More parental attention	30	Child gets more attention, experience, time	28
Better for personal development	16	Less demanding for parents	13
No sibling problems	20	Closer parent-child relationship	8
		Freedom of career for mother	5
		Other (no estate problems, no sibling comparisons, parents have more time for each other)	11
Disadvantages	**Percent**	**Disadvantages**	**Percent**
Lack of companionship	58	Too much attention, protection, focus, etc.	28
Parents over-focus, protect, expect, etc.	27	Child lonely	24
Personal development retarded	10	Child misses sibling experience	22
Other (no motherhood preparation, holidays lonely, no excitement, etc.)	5	Parents have to entertain child	5
		Other (parent criticized, feel we've deprived child, etc.)	21

SOURCE: Hawke and Knox, 1977, pp. 188–89 and 198–99.

An Only Child?

Most people decide to have children, and most want more than one. In a national sample, only 10 percent of young adult Americans expressed the desire to have an only child (See Table 15.1).[1] Asked why they are reluctant to have just one child, individuals often answer, "It's not fair to the child." And they go on to say that "only children are lonely," "only children are spoiled," and "one child doesn't make a *real* family."

Are these beliefs justified? Is the one-child family bad for the child and the parents? To find out, 105 only children and 168 parents of only children were surveyed (Hawke & Knox, 1977). Table 15.2 indicates what these only children and their parents saw as the advantages and disadvantages to the one-child family pattern.

When the same parents of only children were asked how many children would they have if they were starting over, 23 percent said that they would wish to have an only child, 40 percent would like to have two, and another 21 percent would like to have two or more (Hawke & Knox, 1977, p. 205).

For those who regard the one-child family as a desirable life-style, the Association for the One-Child Family (AOCF), a national nonprofit organization, was established in 1977 by Sharryl Hawke. The purpose of AOCF is to "stimulate public interest in and support of the one-child family as a desirable life-style for today's society and as an important dimension in world population control" (AOCF Brochure, 1978).

Two Children?

The most preferred family size in America is the two-child family (see Table 15.1). But how does having two children differ from having one? One hundred and forty-four mothers[2] who had two children and whose second child was less than five years old revealed their motivations for having a second child and the consequences of doing so (Knox & Wilson, 1978). About half of the mothers gave as their reason for having a second child that they enjoyed the first child and wanted to repeat the experience. Another important reason (for 28 percent) was that they wanted a companion for the first child. Other reasons included that the husband wanted another child, that they had a second child for reasons of personal fulfillment, or that they wanted a child of the other sex (Knox & Wilson, 1978, pp. 23–24).

In addition to giving their motivations, these mothers commented on the consequences of having a second child. Almost half (49 percent) said that the first child had made a greater personal impact than the second child. Specific comments included: (1) "I lost my freedom to truly enjoy life and do what I wanted with the first child. Once I began forgetting self, my second child had little effect"; (2) "Childbirth and responsibility for a baby were new experiences with the first child. I felt more confident with the second child"; (3) "I got used to never being alone after my first child was born" (Wilson & Knox, 1978, p. 24).

While the second child had a minimal personal impact relative to the first, the mothers reported that their marriages were more affected by their second child than by their first. Specific statements included: "The main difference I noticed with the second child was that I was more tired more of the time since I had to relate emotionally to two children throughout the day." Another woman said, "After I had listened to incessant pleadings such as 'I need a fork' 'Can I have some more grape juice?' and 'I don't like oatmeal,' there was little left of me for my husband. And when the children were finally in bed, I needed to use the rest of the evening to catch up on the housework I was unable to do during the day because of the constant interruptions" (p. 25).

Three Children?

About 21 percent of young adult Americans express a preference for the three-child family (see Table 15.1). Wanting to have a third child is related to the perceived consequences of doing so. For example, fifty-nine married women with two children were asked whether they intended to have another. Those who wanted a third child felt that the child would further their self-development, help fulfill them as wives and mothers,[3] and strengthen the relationship with their husbands. Those not desiring another child felt that the opposite consequences would occur (Werner et al., 1975, p. 354).

Couples who decide to have three children should be alert to the difficulties that may arise with the second child when the third is born. The middle child may grow up feeling neglected (Forer & Still, 1976, p. 79).

A reader of Ann Landers wrote:

> Dear Ann: I could kiss you for your advice to "Mother of Two Pluses and One Minus." I am a middle child. My older sister (according to my parents) was "brilliant, sensitive, and creative." My younger sister was "honest, sweet, kind and good." I was "moody, belligerent, willful and unmanageable." Mother called me "stupid" so often I thought it was my given name. My school work and my social life were a disaster because of the emotional turmoil at home.
>
>   We are all grown now and here's the picture: My younger sister weighs nearly 300 pounds. My older sister dislikes my parents so intensely that when they come to visit, I'm the only one who will meet them at the plane and give them a place to stay. Neither of my sisters will have them over for a meal.
>
>   Do I like my parents: No. Do I forgive them? Yes. But it took many years of costly therapy. It's obvious who the losers are. And also quite sad. —THE MIDDLE ONE. (Landers, 1977)

As a result of such frustration, some research suggests that middle children are verbally more aggressive than other children (McGurk & Lewis, 1972, p. 366), and that they may develop excitable, demanding, attention-getting, undependable personalities (Forer & Still, 1976, pp. 57–60).

Four or More Children?

About 9 percent of young adult Americans expect to have four children, and 4 percent expect to have five or more children (see Table 15.1). These larger families involve complex interactional patterns and different values. The addition of each subsequent child dramatically increases the possible relationships in the family. For example, in the one-child family, four interpersonal relationships are possible—mother-father, mother-child, father-child, and father-mother-child. In a family of four, eleven interrelationships are possible; in a family of five, twenty-six; and in a family of six, fifty-seven (Henry & Warson, 1951, p. 60).

In addition to interrelationships, values change as families get larger. While members of a small family tend to value independence and personal development, large-family members necessarily value cooperation, harmony, and sharing (Bossard & Boll, 1956, pp. 311–12). A parent of nine children said, "Meals around our house are a cooperative endeavor. One child prepares the drinks, another the bread, and still another sets the table. You have to develop cooperation or nobody gets fed."

Before deciding on the number of children you and your spouse want, keep two issues in mind. First, each child will be different. One couple had decided to have an only child but because their daughter was beautiful, cooperative, and happy they decided to have another. Their second child had an ugly birthmark on his face, and was demanding and withdrawn. "We should have stopped while we were ahead," the mother said. Genetic differences, birth order, and parental experience (parents of the third child are more experienced at parenting than with the first child) ensure that each child will be different—often radically different.

A second consideration is that every family size has inherent advantages and disadvantages. While only children tend to have ample possessions, opportunities, and parental attention, they may be lonely. Two children provide companionship for each other, but such interaction may become intense sibling rivalry. Three children also provide companionship for each other, but the middle child may be neglected. Four or more children provide still more companionship, but the parental resources of time and money usually must be spread thin. In a large family each child is more likely to get "lost in the shuffle." And, while family size may have both positive and negative consequences on an array of issues, for other issues it may make no difference. For example, a child's intelligence and the amount of

In large families such as this one, cooperation, harmony, and sharing tend to become extremely important. Intense individualism is sometimes counterproductive in a large family.

education he or she expects to get are unrelated to family size (Bahr & Leigh, 1978).

Married women preferring smaller families tend to be from a small family (Johnson & Stokes, 1976, p. 175); from a higher social class (Groat & Neal, 1973, p. 85); currently employed (Cochrane & Bean, 1976); earning a good income (Defronzo, 1976; Ewer & Crimmins-Gardner, 1978); career oriented (Scanzoni & McMurry, 1972); and they perceive their status with their husbands as that of equal partners (Scanzoni, 1976). Those preferring larger families tend to have the opposite characteristics.

Although American women have a total of about three million babies each year, the number of babies born per 1,000 population in a given year has been declining since 1957. In 1972, the American birthrate dropped below the replacement level[4] for the first time. Whether or not the birthrate will stay below replacement level is not known. Two researchers examined recent birth data from five states and concluded, "The decline in the nation's birthrate is coming to a halt and an upturn is in the making" (Sklar & Berkov, 1975, p. 694). They suggested that the reduced birthrate was caused by women's decision to postpone having children, not to remain childfree. "Within the next few years, many will have to begin 'making up' the births they delayed in previous years" (p. 698).

But other researchers do not agree. They say that the longer a couple waits to have children, the fewer they will have. "Couples who delay having children until relatively late in life are subject to fewer pressures to have children (or more children) even as the reasons not to begin (or increase) their families become more salient" (Rindfuss & Bumpass, 1976, p. 226).

TIMING YOUR CHILDREN

Having decided how many children you want to have (if any), when is the best time to have them? Let's consider the various issues.

The First Child

Since most couples (85 percent) are fertile (Menning, 1977), few are concerned about their capacity to have children. Rather, the timing of the pregnancy becomes the central issue. There are at least five considerations in planning the first pregnancy.

Wife's age. Medically, the best time for a woman to have her family is in the prime of her reproductive life—between ages twenty and thirty-five. While the chance of dying during childbirth is extremely low,[5] the risks increase with advancing age. Maternal deaths are three times more likely to occur to women aged thirty-five through thirty-nine, and four and a half times more likely to occur to women over forty, than to those aged twenty through twenty-four (Siegel & Morris, 1974, p. 995).

Risk to the baby's life is also associated with the mother's age. The chance of the baby's dying is almost one third higher among women thirty-five years of age and older than among women aged twenty through twenty-four (Commission on Population Growth, 1972, p. 166). The chances that the baby will be born a mongoloid[6] increase from 1 in 1,500 for mothers under age thirty to 1 in 130 for mothers between forty and forty-four (Whelan, 1976, p. 173).

Risks to the baby are also great if the mother is too young. Studies have shown that mothers seventeen or younger are more likely to give birth to premature babies and babies with birth defects and to babies that will die before they are a year old (Nye, 1976, p. 5). Hence, the wife should avoid having her first child in her teens.

In 1975, the average age of American wives when their first child was born was 23.5 (Gibson, 1976, p. 251). This age has positive consequences for the mother and child and permits ample time for subsequent births. "A woman who waits until she is thirty-five or so to seek a first pregnancy is going to have less time to work out fertility problems with her physician if they do come up" (Rosenfield, quoted in Whelan, 1976, p. 171).

Husband's age. The wife's age is not the only consideration in timing the first child. Mongolism can come from the father as well as from the mother, and such a genetic mutation seems to occur more frequently with increasing age. Other abnormalities that may be related to the age of the father include achondroplasia (a type of dwarfism), Marfan syndrome (height, vision, and heart abnormalities), Apert syndrome (facial and limb deformities) and fibrodysplasia ossificans progressiva (bony growths). While the probability of a male having the genetic mutation to create one of these abnormalities is very small, it increases with age (Evans & Hall, 1976, p. 49). In addition, the ability of a man to impregnate a woman steadily declines after the age of forty (Menning, 1977, p. 51).

Number of years married. While most spouses are confident in their decision to have children when in their twenties or early thirties, they are somewhat ambivalent about how long it is best to be married before having a baby. One viewpoint suggests that newlyweds need time to adjust to each other as spouses before becoming parents. Spouses who cannot adjust would avoid custody disputes when divorcing, child-support payments, and the single-parent status.

But if spouses wait several years to have a baby, they may become so adjusted and so content with their life-style that parenthood is an unwelcome change. "We were married for seven wonderful years before Helen was born," recalled one mother. "The adjustment hasn't been easy. We resented her intrusion into our relationship."

Career commitment. In addition to age and number of years married, how committed you are to your career is an issue to consider in timing your first child. The career-minded woman is more likely to delay having children than the woman who is less serious about her work. For example, over 33 percent of 323 women who were earning their doctorates in 1968 waited until they had received their degrees before having their first child (Centra, 1974, p. 111). At the time they received their degrees, their average age was thirty-six (p. 22). The career of the man is less likely to affect when he has children. Only 22 percent of 552 males who earned their doctorates in 1968 waited until after they had received their degrees to have their first child (p. 111).

Cost of first birth.   Although you and your partner will "make" your own baby, getting it into the bassinet will cost you money—lots of it. In 1975 the cost of a baby in the first year (prenatal, delivery, and postnatal care) ranged from $1,600 to $2,800° (Porter, 1976, p. 705; Whelan, 1976, p. 181). In general, the yearly cost of rearing *one* child is approximately 15 to 17 percent of the parents' income (Porter, 1976, p. 704). Costs of rearing a second child are only about $500 less (Commission on Population and the American Future, 1972, p. 81).

Timing Subsequent Births

Assuming that you decide to have more than one child, what is the best interval between children? Most couples space their children two to two-and-a-half years apart. Such an interval lets parents avoid being overwhelmed with the care of two small infants yet is close enough for the children to become playmates (Westoff et

Couples who plan to have a seond child most often space the births about two years apart. In one study, the reason about half the women gave for wanting a second child was that they enjoyed having the first one.

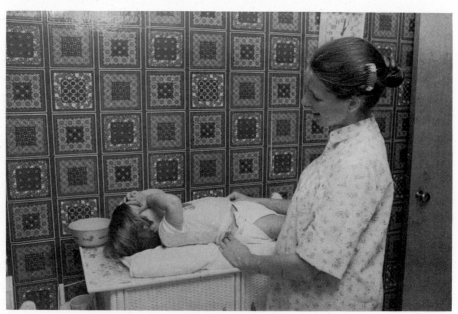

al., 1961, p. 134). In general, the smaller the family, the larger the interval between the children and vice versa.

While a family's economic situation may influence the spacing of children, the economic situation of the family may also be influenced by child-spacing. In one study, the slower the rate of family growth, the better the financial position of the family, the less likely the head was unemployed, the higher the wage, and the greater the likelihood of home ownership (Reimer & Maiolo, 1977).

Child-spacing may also have implications for the marriage relationship. Two researchers assumed that because of the economic, psychological, and physical demands of parenthood, "the higher the ratio of children per years of marriage, the less generally satisfactory the marital experience would be" (Hurley & Palonen, 1967). Their study of forty married student couples confirmed their hypothesis, but another study (Figley, 1973) failed to do so. In view of these conflicting studies, it is probably not the child-spacing pattern per se that has the crucial impact on the marriage but the success of parents in controlling the interval they want between their children (Christensen, 1968).

CONTRACEPTION

To help ensure that you have the number of children you want at the intervals you want them (and to avoid having children you don't want or having children at inconvenient intervals), the effective use of one or more contraceptive techniques is essential. These techniques have a common goal—to prevent the male sperm from fertilizing the female egg or to keep the egg from implanting in the uterus. In performing these functions, contraception permits couples to make love without making babies. A married woman between the ages of twenty and twenty-four has intercourse an average of ten times per month (Westoff, 1974, p. 137). If no method of contraception is used for one year, there is an 80 percent probability that she will become pregnant (Trussell & Chandler, 1971, p. 19). With contraception, the risk of becoming pregnant can be reduced to practically zero depending on the method and how systematically it is used.

Here are the major methods of contraception in use in America today, in the order of their effectiveness.[8]

Oral Contraceptive (The Pill)

The pill is the contraceptive preferred by 36 percent of American married women and by two thirds of young married women (Westoff, 1976, p. 55).[9] Although there are more than twenty brands available in North America, each brand uses some combination of artificial estrogen and progesterone. These female hormones prevent ovulation (inhibit the development of an egg in the ovary) and affect the lining of the uterus so as to make implantation of a fertilized egg difficult.

TABLE 15.3 Approximate Failure Rate of Contraceptive Methods (Pregnancies per 100 Woman Years).

	Theoretical Failure Rate	Actual Use Failure Rate
Abortion	0	0+
Abstinence	0	?
Hysterectomy	0.0001	0.0001
Tubal Ligation	0.04	0.04
Vasectomy	0.15	0.15+
Oral Contraceptives (combined)	0.34	4–10
I.M. Long Acting Progestin	0.25	5–10
Condom + Spermicidal Agent	Less than 1.0	5
Low-Dose Oral Progestin	1–1.5	5–10
IUD	1–3	5
Condom	3	10
Diaphragm (with spermicide)	3	17
Spermicidal Foam	3	22
Coitus Interruptus	9	20–25
Rhythm (calendar)	13	21
Lactation for 12 months	25	40
Chance (sexually active)	90	90
Douche	?	40

SOURCE: Emory University Family Planning Program, CONTRACEPTIVE TECHNOLOGY 1976–1977.

The pill currently prescribed by most physicians is known as the combination pill.[10] It is taken daily for twenty-one days, beginning on the fifth day after the start of the menstrual flow. Three or four days after the last pill is taken, menstruation occurs and the twenty-eight-day cycle begins again. To eliminate the problem of remembering when to begin taking the pill every month, some physicians prescribe a low-dose combination pill for the first twenty-one days and a placebo (sugar pill) or iron pill for the next seven days. In this way, the woman takes a pill every day (Connell, 1975).

The pill should be taken only when prescribed by a physician who has detailed information about the woman's previous medical history. Contraindications, or reasons for not prescribing the pill, include a personal history of breast cancer or some history in the woman's immediate family, impaired liver function, known or suspected tumors that are estrogen-dependent, undiagnosed abnormal genital bleeding, being pregnant at the time of the examination, and a past history of poor blood circulation (varicose veins or blood clotting). The major complication associated with taking the pill is the increase risk of having a heart attack, particularly if the woman is forty years of age or older and smokes. Such women are advised to use some other method of contraception.

While the long-term negative consequences of taking the pill are still the subject of research, short-term negative effects are experienced by 25 percent of women who begin taking it. These mild side effects include nausea, slight weight gain, breakthrough bleeding (vaginal bleeding between periods), tender breasts, mild headaches, and minor mood changes. Only about 4 percent of new pill users are unable to adjust to the pill (Trussell & Chandler, 1971, p. 26).

There are also immediate health benefits. Aside from providing a very effective protection against pregnancy, the pill tends to protect the woman from ovarian cysts, regularizes her menstrual cycles, reduces premenstrual tension, and reduces blood loss during menstruation (Connell, 1975, p. 62).

Intrauterine Device (IUD)

Used by 10 percent of American married women, the IUD, or intrauterine device, is a small object that a physician inserts into the woman's uterus (Westoff, 1976, p. 57). Two threads attached to the IUD usually hang down into the vagina so the woman can feel them and check regularly that the device is in place. The IUD stays inside the uterus until it is removed by the physician. While used most frequently by women who have had a child, some women who have never been pregnant may also use the IUD.

Just how the IUD works is not known. One theory suggests that it stimulates the entry of white blood cells into the uterus. Since white blood cells attack and destroy "invading" cells, it is thought that they attack the fertilized egg. Another theory suggests that the IUD irritates the lining of the uterus and makes it impossible for the fertilized egg to become implanted.

Side effects of the IUD include cramps, excessive menstrual bleeding, and irregular bleeding between menstrual periods (spotting). These effects usually disappear after the first two months of use. Severe cramps and heavy or irregular bleeding cause 8 to 10 percent of the women who use the IUD to have it removed (Cherniak & Feingold, 1973, p. 29). Infection is another potential side effect.

The most serious problem associated with the IUD is its expulsion. In some women, the presence of the IUD irritates the muscles of the uterus and stimulates them to push out the IUD. Between 10 and 12 percent of all women who receive the IUD expel the device in the first year of use. Once a woman expels an IUD, there is only a 50 percent chance that she will be able to retain another one.

Condom

Also referred to as "rubber," "safe," and "prophylactic," the condom is the most widely used mechanical form of contraception in the world. It is a thin sheath, usually made of rubber or lamb intestine, which is rolled over and down the shaft of the erect penis prior to intercourse. When the man ejaculates, the sperm are caught inside the condom. When used with a spermicidal agent (see below), the condom is a highly effective contraceptive. It is the only contraceptive that provides some protection against venereal disease.

Like any contraceptive, the condom is effective only when properly used. A space should be left at the tip of the condom (some condoms already have a recessed tip) when it is rolled on the penis so as to provide room for the ejaculate to flow. Otherwise the condom may break. In addition, the penis should be withdrawn from the vagina soon after ejaculation; otherwise, as the erection subsides, the ejaculate will leak from the base of the condom into the vaginal lips. The sperm can then "swim" up the vagina into the uterus and fertilize an egg. As an added protection, (to increase the effectiveness rate in general) many women insert a spermicidal, or sperm-killing, agent prior to intercourse.

The lubrication spermicides provide permits easy entrance of the condom-covered penis into the vagina. If no spermicide is used and the condom is not of the pre-lubricated variety, K-Y Jelly, a sterile lubricant, may be needed. Vaseline or any other kind of petroleum jelly should never be applied to rubber condoms since these lubricants destroy rubber.

Condoms can be purchased at drugstores and most convenience stores. In general, only established brands should be used. These include Trojan, Ramses, Sheik, Naturalamb, and Fourex.

Diaphragm

The diaphragm is a shallow rubber dome built around a circular steel spring. Varying in diameter from two to four inches, the diaphragm covers the cervix and prevents sperm from moving beyond the vagina into the uterus. It should always be used with a spermicidal jelly or cream.

To obtain a diaphragm, the woman must have an internal pelvic examination by a physician, who will select the appropriate size of diaphragm and instruct the woman on how to insert it. She will be told to apply the spermicidal cream or jelly and insert the diaphragm within two hours before intercourse and to leave the diaphragm in place six to eight hours after intercourse to permit the spermicidal cream to kill any lingering sperm.

After the birth of a child, a miscarriage, any surgical operation, or the gain or loss of ten pounds, a woman who uses a diaphragm should consult her physician to ensure a continued good fit. In any case, the fit should be checked every two years.

Use of the diaphragm has been declining since 1965 for the same reason the use of the condom has declined—the introduction of the pill. In 1973 less than 4 percent of all married women and less than 2 percent of married women aged fifteen through twenty-four were using the diaphragm (Westoff, 1976, p. 55).

Spermicidal Agents

Foams, jellies, creams, and vaginal suppositories are chemical compounds that kill sperm. They must be applied near the cervix (appropriate applicators are included when the product is purchased) no more than twenty minutes prior to intercourse.

And each time intercourse is repeated, more of the spermicidal agent must be applied. When used alone, these chemicals are not very effective. But when combined with a condom or diaphragm, they are extremely effective.

Withdrawal

In the withdrawal technique, also known as coitus interruptus, the man takes his penis out of the vagina before ejaculating. Not only does this procedure interrupt sexual pleasure, but it is not reliable. Sperm may leak from the penis before ejaculation. However, 2 percent of married women report that their husbands use withdrawal as their method of contraception (Westoff, 1976, p. 57). Although not a reliable method of contraception, withdrawal is more effective than the rhythm method.

Rhythm

About 4 percent of all married women use the rhythm method of birth control (Westoff, 1976, p. 55). It is the only method of contraception approved by the Catholic Church. The rhythm method is based on the premise that conception cannot occur unless live sperm are present when the live egg is in the fallopian tubes. Sperm usually live 4 to 5 days while an egg lives 12 hours (Boston Women's Health Book Collective, 1973, p. 132). Women who use the rhythm method must know their time of ovulation and avoid intercourse just before and after that time. There are two ways of predicting the "safe" period, the calendar and basal body temperature methods.

When using the calendar method to predict when the egg is ready to be fertilized, the woman keeps a record of the length of her menstrual cycles for eight months. Counting the length of her shortest cycle as the earliest likely menstruation and the length of her longest cycle as the latest likely menstruation, she can calculate her fertile period by subtracting eighteen days from the earliest and eleven days from the latest. The resulting figures indicate the range for her fertility period. It is during this time that she must avoid intercourse.

For example, suppose that during an eight-month period, a woman had cycle lengths of 26, 32, 27, 30, 28, 27, 28, and 29 days. Subtracting eighteen from her shortest cycle (26) and eleven from her longest cycle (32), she knows the days the egg is likely to be in the fallopian tubes. To avoid getting pregnant, she must avoid intercourse on days eight through twenty-one of her cycle when she counts the first day of her menstrual flow as day one.

The calendar method of predicting the "safe" period is unreliable for two reasons. First, the next month the woman may ovulate at a different time from any of the previous eight months and invalidate her calculations. Second, it is not known how long a specific set of sperm will live; they may live long enough to catch the next egg in the fallopian tubes.

A second method of predicting when the woman is least likely to become pregnant involves the calculation of basal body temperature. Theoretically, the woman's temperature stays at a constant level during the first part of her menstrual cycle, drops slightly just before ovulation, and rises slightly immediately after ovulation. By recording the average time when her temperature rises, the woman can predict when the egg is in the fallopian tubes and avoid intercourse for three days preceding the predicted rise and three days following the actual rise in temperature.

Unfortunately, there are also problems with this method. The woman's temperature may rise for reasons unrelated to ovulation (staying out late the night before, infection, etc.). In addition, to get an accurate baseline, she must take her temperature—immediately upon awaking and before getting out of bed—for several cycles. Except for the person who is unwilling to use other more reliable and less troublesome forms of contraception, the rhythm method has little to recommend it (Mastroianni, 1974).

Douche

Even less effective than the rhythm method is the vaginal douche. After intercourse the woman fills a syringe with water and/or a spermicidal agent and flushes the sperm from her vagina. But since a large number of sperm may already have passed through the cervix to the uterus, the douche may do little good. In 1973 less than 1 percent of married women reported using the douche as their method of contraception (Westoff, 1976, p. 57).

Contraception: A Personal Decision

With the array of contraceptive methods available (and more being developed), the question becomes, "Which one is best for me?" Notice that this question implies a willingness to use some form of contraception until you are ready to begin your family. For a young adult in the most fertile period of life, pregnancy is the price to be paid for not using contraception during intercourse.

The choice of a contraceptive depends on a variety of individual matters, including age, health, and whether or not the couple has children already. Family planning clinics and private physicians can help a couple choose a contraceptive method that suits their needs.

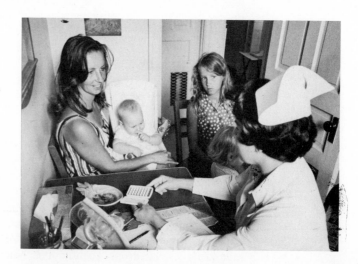

TABLE 15.4   Annual and Lifetime Costs of Various Contraceptives.

Method	First Year Cost	Lifetime Cost
Pill	$45.00 to $90.00	$1,350 to $2,700*
IUD	$20.00 to $65.00	$600 to $1,950*
Condom	$25.00 to $150.00	$750 to $4,500
Foam	$25.00 to $35.00	$750 to $1,050
Diaphragm	$20.00 to $60.00	$600 to $1,800*

*Includes annual checkups after first year.

SOURCE: Porter, 1976, p. 706.

Issues to consider include personal values, health, the reliability and cost of contraceptive procedures (see Tables 15.3 and 15.4), sexual fulfillment, and psychological contentment. Do your personal values permit you to use any form of contraception? "It's a sin to use anything but the rhythm method," one woman said. "I would feel immoral putting any of those devices in my body or contaminating my system with the pill." But others feel it is immoral *not* to use some form of contraception. Follow your own values in making this decision.

Another major concern is one's health. It is dangerous for some women to use the pill or IUD and the potential for pregnancy resulting from less effective forms of contraception may be even more hazardous. Using appropriate contraception under the care of a physician is essential.

We all worry about the population explosion but we don't worry about it at the right time.

Arthur Hoppe

Choice of a contraceptive also depends on a couple's relationship and past experiences. "Circumstances change with the development of trust, with increasing or decreasing frequency of intercourse, with illness, with the number of pregnancies, etc." (Pierson, 1973, p. 16). The contraceptive you select this year may be different from the one you will select in your later reproductive life. One pattern is to use the pill or IUD until the desired family size is achieved and then for either the husband or the wife to be sterilized (Westoff, 1976, p. 55).

Effective Use of Contraception

There are wide differences in the degree to which contraception is used effectively to control family size. Unwanted children are born more often into those homes where education and income are low. In 1970, women with no high-school education reported that 31 percent of their births in the preceding five years had been unwanted, in contrast to 7 percent of the births of college-educated women (Commission on Population Growth, 1972, p. 163). Unwanted births were twice as great among couples whose annual incomes were below $4,000 as among those with incomes of $10,000 or higher (p. 165).

The fact that the poor, both black and white, have bigger families than the well-to-do is easily explained: Lower-status couples do not have more children than higher-status couples simply because they want more. They have more children because some of them do not use contraception regularly and effectively. If couples in all education and income groups were to use contraception equally well, there would be only small differences in average family size (Whelpton et al., 1966, p. 234).

STERILIZATION

Unlike the temporary and reversible methods of contraception already discussed, sterilization is a surgical procedure that prevents pregnancy. Sterilization is losing its stigma as an extreme and undesirable method of birth control. Health, convenience, economics (can't afford more children), and political commitments (zero population growth) are some reasons for its increased approval. Married women over thirty-five prefer sterilization over any other form of contraception.[11] In 1973, 19 percent in that age category had been sterilized in contrast to 18 percent who were using the pill (Westoff, 1976, p. 57).

Female Sterilization

Although a woman may be sterilized by removal of her ovaries and/or uterus (hysterectomy), these operations are not normally undertaken for the sole purpose of sterilization. The ovaries produce important hormones as well as eggs. And while a hysterectomy may be necessary because of disease, it is major surgery which involves significant risks not associated with the usual procedures of female sterilization—salpingectomy and laparoscopy.

Salpingectomy, also known as *tubal ligation* or "tying the tubes," is performed while the woman is under a general anesthetic. An incision is made in the lower abdomen, just above the pubic hair, and the fallopian tubes are brought into view one at a time. A part of each tube is cut out, and the cut ends are tied, clamped, or cauterized (burned). The cost for the twenty- to thirty-minute operation is about $500. This does not include the charge for the operating room or the four to five days (at $100 per day) recuperating time in the hospital (Porter, 1976, p. 708).

A less expensive, quicker form of salpingectomy (fifteen minutes) that permits the woman to go home the same day is the *laparoscopy*. While the woman is under a general anesthetic, the surgeon inserts a small telescope-like instrument (laparoscope) through the abdominal wall just below the navel. Looking through the laparoscope, he can see the uterus and the fallopian tubes. He then makes another small incision in the lower abdomen and inserts a special pair of forceps that carry electricity to burn the tubes closed. The laparoscope and forceps are then withdrawn, the small wounds are closed with a single stitch, and small bandages are put on (the laparoscopy is known as "the Band-Aid operation").

Both these procedures for female sterilization are highly effective. About one tube in a thousand grows back and makes pregnancy possible (Hulka, 1973, p. 98). But there may be complications. In 1 to 2 percent of the cases a blood vessel in the abdomen is torn open during the sterilization and bleeds into the abdominal cavity. When this happens another operation is necessary to find the bleeding vessel and tie it closed. Another occasional complication involves injury to the small or large intestine, which may cause nausea, vomiting, and loss of appetite (Cherniak & Feingold, 1973, p. 40). The fact that death—though rare—may result is a reminder that female sterilization is surgery and, like all surgery, involves some risks (as does pregnancy itself).

In a follow-up study of 168 women one to five years after they had been sterilized, 96 percent reported improvement in their social and mental well-being. Slightly under 4 percent felt guilty or regretful about the sterilization (Black & Sclare, 1973, p. 168). In another follow-up study of 519 sterilized women, the researchers concluded, "Psychological findings reported indicate that sexual relations are substantially not affected by sterilization, while the sterilized patients experienced a marked improvement in their expressed level of happiness (Paniagua et al., 1973, p. 183).

Male Sterilization:

The most frequent form of male sterilization is vasectomy. Among husbands in the thirty-five to forty-four age category, 17 percent had been sterilized.[12] A vasectomy is usually performed in the physician's office and involves making two small cuts in the scrotum so that a small portion of each vas deferens (the ducts which carry sperm) can be cut out and the ends tied closed. Sperm are still produced in the testicles, but since there is no vas deferens to take the sperm to the penis, the sperm remain in the testicles and eventually dissolve. The operation takes about fifteen minutes and costs about $150, and the man can leave the physician's office within a short time. Most vasectomies are performed Friday afternoon so that an employed man will not have to miss any work.

Sperm do not disappear from the ejaculate immediately after a vasectomy. Another method of contraception should be used until the man has had about twenty ejaculations. He is then asked to bring a sample of his ejaculate to the physician's office so that it can be examined under a microscope to see if sperm are present. In about 1 percent of vasectomy cases the vas deferens grows back and the man becomes fertile again.

A vasectomy does not affect the man's desire for sex, his ability to have an erection, or his orgasm. In a follow-up study of 1,012 men who had had vasectomies, 98 percent reported that their sex life had improved or was unchanged. Two percent said that their sex life had become worse (Simon Population Trust, 1973, p. 135). In another study, the respondents reported an increase in intercourse of 2.5 times per month following their vasectomies (Maschoff et al., 1976). And when 330 American couples in which the husband had had a vasectomy were asked if they could recommend the vasectomy to a friend, all but 1 percent reported that they would do so and would have the operation again if they were given the choice (Landis & Poffenberger, 1966).

Although men report that they are not very concerned about the effect of a vasectomy on their masculinity or sexual desire, they are concerned about its irreversibility (Mullen et al., 1973, p. 335). The probability of a man's impregnating a woman after he has had an operation to reverse the vasectomy is between 20 and 30 percent (Davis, 1973, p. 196). But some men don't count on a successful reversal and deposit some of their sperm in a sperm vault.

Summarizing this new form of "fertility insurance," one physician wrote,

> The ability to freeze human semen and subsequently defrost it and still preserve the normal fertilizing capacity of the sperm has been available since 1960. Over three hundred children have been born by artificial insemination of the female, using previously frozen semen which has been stored for periods of one to ten years. No abnormalities in fetal growth or in the development of the children have been reported. (Davis, 1973, pp. 196–97)

Although the reversibility of a vasectomy and the use of sperm banks are possibilities, neither should be considered completely reliable. There may be difficulty in reversing a vasectomy, and the sperm bank in which the sperm has been deposited may go out of business.[13]

Sterilization: A Personal Decision

Since sterilization should be regarded as permanent, you might consider four issues before making a decision to be sterilized.

Self-image. How will you feel about yourself following sterilization? As a woman, will you feel "less feminine" knowing that you are no longer capable of conceiving a child? As a man, will you feel "less masculine" because you can no longer make a woman pregnant?

Effect on marriage. How do you think sterilization will affect your marriage? Are you considering sterilization as a means of improving your marriage? In one study, following the vasectomy both husbands and wives reported slight decreases in the amounts of affection they received from their spouse. But there were reported increases in the amount of communication and a marked decrease in the number of men who considered separation or divorce (Maschoff et al., 1976).

The future.   In addition to considering the effect of sterilization on you, your partner, and your marriage, what about the future? Are you sure you won't want another child under any conditions? If you are childfree, do you think it is possible that you will change your mind and decide you want to have a baby? If you have children, suppose they are killed by disease or an accident? Would you then want the capacity to have another child?

Suppose you were to get divorced. Might you want to be fertile in order to have children with a new spouse?

There is also a possibility that your present spouse will die while you are still young enough to have children. In 1975 there were 200,000 widowed women under thirty-five years of age (U.S. Bureau of Census, 1975, Table 1). One woman said, "I was twenty-nine and had my tubes tied after my second child was born. Brock and I had the boy and girl we wanted and saw no more reason for me to continue taking the pill. But only a month after that, Brock had a heart attack. I'm now in a second marriage and my new husband and I want a child of our own."

In deciding about sterilization, you must balance considerations of its effect upon you, your marriage, and the future against the risks and inconvenience associated with less permanent forms of contraception. Most couples complete their intended childbearing in their late twenties or early thirties. This leaves over fifteen years of continued risk of unwanted pregnancy. In conjunction with the risk of pill use at older ages and the lower reliability of alternative methods, sterilization is being chosen by many as a primary method of fertility control.

ABORTION

What if an unwanted pregnancy occurs? One alternative is abortion—the removal of the fetus from the woman's uterus early in pregnancy, before it can survive on its own. Other alternatives are to keep the baby whether single or married, or to allow the baby to be adopted by other parents.

The Law on Abortion

In 1973 the U.S. Supreme Court ruled that during the first three months of pregnancy, a woman has the right to obtain an abortion from a licensed physician (usually in the physician's office) without interference by the state. From the fourth through the sixth month, the decision to have an abortion is still completely up to the woman and her physician,[14] but because an abortion at this later stage of pregnancy is more dangerous, the state may require that the abortion be performed in a hospital. During the last three months of pregnancy, the state may prohibit abortion except in those cases where the life or health of the mother is in danger. Since the Supreme Court ruling, the number of legal abortions obtained in the United States has increased every year. In 1975 there were over one million abortions, an increase of 11 percent over 1974 (Weinstock et al., 1976, p. 58).

Methods of Abortion

Excluding hysterectomy, there are four ways of aborting an unwanted fetus. The method chosen depends mainly on the length of the pregnancy to be interrupted.

Morning-after pill.   For the woman who fears that she might be pregnant and who does not want to wait for confirmation, the "morning-after pill" (known as diethylstilbestrol, or DES, and containing high doses of estrogen) is highly effective in protecting against pregnancy if taken within seventy-two hours after intercourse, preferably within twelve to twenty-four hours. Usually given in twenty-five milligram doses twice a day for five days following an unprotected midcycle coitus, DES is an emergency treatment only, not a routine method of birth control (FDA, 1975). Nausea, vomiting, bleeding abnormalities, and risks associated with blood clots make routine use of this drug undesirable.

Suction.   The most frequently used method of abortion is suction, also called vacuum aspiration. It is used when the woman is less than 3 months pregnant. This technique involves sucking out the contents of the uterus through a tube inserted into the uterus through the cervix. This operation can be performed while the woman is awake in five to ten minutes with little blood loss and a low risk of complications.

Dilation and curettage (D and C).   Before the development of suction abortion, dilation and curettage was the standard method of abortion in early pregnancy (less than three months). This procedure involves increasing the size of the cervical canal by inserting a series of gradually-widening metal dilators. When the opening is wide enough the physician uses a curette (small metal surgical instrument) to scrape the embryo and placenta from the walls of the uterus. Since the D and C operation takes longer and is more dangerous than the suction method, the woman is put to sleep.

Saline.   After twelve weeks, the fetus is too large to be removed safely by the suction or D and C methods. Pregnancies after the twelfth or thirteenth week are aborted by inserting a long needle through the abdominal and uterine walls into the cavity of the uterus. A concentrated salt solution is inserted into the amniotic sac, destroying the fetus. In from six to forty-eight hours after the fetus is destroyed, the uterus will contract until the fetus is pushed out into the vagina. Because saline abortion is a major surgical procedure, earlier termination of pregnancy by the suction method or D and C is much more desirable.

TRENDS

The future of family planning will involve increased tolerance for the childfree alternative. College students no longer regard children as essential for a happy marriage (Peterson, 1975), and research suggests that childfree couples are similar to couples who have children in life satisfaction, maturity, and self-esteem (Silka & Kiesler, 1977). Whether the number of couples who choose the childfree life-style will increase significantly is unknown. The key seems to be the availability of rewarding career opportunities for young women. If low-status, low-paying jobs remain the predominant employment opportunity, motherhood will continue to be viewed as the more rewarding alternative (Silka & Kiesler, 1977).

It is likely that the one-child family will also become more acceptable. Current concerns about inflation, population growth, and the wife's career will influence young couples to question whether the two-child family is indeed "ideal." And as more parents examine the myths about only children, fewer will have a second child "to save the first."

It is also likely that new methods of contraception will continue to be developed. Recent developments include a time-release capsule that is implanted under the woman's skin which inhibits the possibility of conception. When the capsule is removed, the woman becomes fertile again. Another method involves a procedure in which the testes are painlessly heated by low-level ultrasonic radiation to stop the production of sperm. Depending on the amount of heat, the male is

Abortion has been a hotly debated political issue throughout the 1970s. Both pro- and anti-abortion groups have lobbied intensively on the local, state, and national levels.

rendered infertile for months. But the most encouraging new contraceptive is a vaccine against pregnancy. Already tested in lower animals and on women volunteers, the immunity lasts about one year but can be prolonged by an additional injection (Talwar, et al., 1976). However, these contraceptive alternatives are still being tested and have not yet been approved by the Federal Drug Administration for public use.

While there is general agreement that safer and more effective contraceptive procedures are desirable, the debate over abortion will continue. Pope Paul VI called abortion a threat to world peace and accused women who have abortions of "murdering the fruit of their wombs" (Stafford, 1977). The right-to-life movement continues to lobby for more restrictive abortion laws and to reflect the antiabortion views of many Catholics and non-Catholics. Commenting on opinions on abortion, two researchers said, "The debate is marked by honest and deeply felt differences of opinion, and public policy with regard to abortion is still subject to shifts in either direction" (Tietze & Lewit, 1977).

A final trend in family planning is the increased use of test-tube conception. In the summer of 1978 the world's first "test-tube" baby was born to Lesley Brown, a thirty-year-old British woman. The procedure of uniting a sperm and egg in the laboratory and implanting the fertilized egg in the uterus was developed by Dr. Patrick Steptoe and Dr. Robert Edwards. Both predicted an increase in the use of this procedure among women whose fallopian tubes are blocked or damaged.

SUMMARY

The decision to become or not to become a parent is one of the most important you will ever make. Unlike marriage, parenthood is a role from which there is no easy withdrawal. "We can have ex-spouses and ex-jobs but not ex-children" (Rossi, 1968, p. 32). Spouses, children, and society all benefit from family planning.

But your decision to become a parent or not is less than "free." You are probably encouraged by your parents and peers to have children. And religion, government, and special observances (Mother's Day and Father's Day) all tend to encourage parenthood. Among the few external influences toward childfree marriage are childfree peers and the National Organization for Non-Parents.

Once a couple decide to have children, they usually want two. It is a "double or nothing" decision. Less than 10 percent of young unmarried adults express a preference for one child. Yet the one-child family has advantages for both parents and child.

Mothers of two children say that they had their second child because they enjoyed their first child and wanted to repeat the experience. In addition, they wanted a companion for their first child because they felt that it was unfair for the first child to be left alone. Few regretted their decision to have a second child.

While two children is currently the preferred family size in America, about 20 percent of young adult Americans express a preference for a three-child family. A potential difficulty is the middle child, often referred to as the "forgotten" child.

Multi-child families (four or more) are preferred by about 10 percent of young adult Americans. These larger families involve complex interactional patterns, different values, and fewer advantages for each child. The point to keep in mind in deciding how many children to have is that every family size has inherent advantages and disadvantages. One child may be lonely, but two may be competitive, and three may result in the middle child's being relatively overlooked.

The timing of the birth of the first child and the interval between children are important. Issues to consider in beginning a family include the ages of both spouses, the number of years you've been married, your career commitments, and your financial situation. Issues related to subsequent children include spacing the children far enough apart to ease the burden of infant care but close enough together to ensure that the children can become playmates. Typical American couples have their first child within eighteen months of their marriage and their second child a little over two years after the first.

To ensure that the desired and achieved family size are the same, an effective method of contraception is essential. Personal values, health, failure rates, cost, level of sexual fulfillment, and psychological contentment are among the factors to consider in selecting a contraceptive technique. While the pill remains the preferred method of birth control for young married women, sterilization is becoming increasingly popular after age thirty-five.

About one million legal abortions are performed each year. While the morning-after pill, if taken within seventy-two hours after exposure, will terminate pregnancy, the suction method of abortion is most frequently used.

Family planning in the future is likely to lead to greater tolerance for the childfree marriage and the one-child family. The future will also include a continued search for improved methods of contraception, continued debate over abortion, and more test-tube conceptions.

STUDY QUESTIONS

1. What percent of all births to married women between 1966 and 1970 were unplanned?
2. How might parents, children, and society benefit from family planning?
3. Discuss various pronatalist influences in our society.
4. Discuss the reasons parents report for having children.
5. In what way are the rewards of parenthood basically intangible?
6. What percent of young adults in America say they do not want children?
7. What organizations have developed to encourage and support the childfree life-style and the one-child family?
8. Describe the reasons spouses report for wanting to be childfree.
9. Discuss the advantages and disadvantages of the one-child family from the perspective of the child and the parents.
10. List several reasons why mothers of two children had a second child? When did they decide to do so?
11. How does having one child differ from having two from the viewpoint of the mother? Include in your answer both personal and marital considerations.

12. What positive consequences are expected by mothers who elect to have a third child?
13. What is a potential hazard in the three-child family?
14. What are the consequences (positive and negative) of having a large family?
15. What are two central considerations in deciding the number of children you want?
16. What are the characteristics of those desiring small families?
17. Discuss the current American birthrate and the predictions of different researchers for the future.
18. When is the best time for a woman to have children? What are the risks associated with having children while in the teens or after the mid-thirties?
19. Why is the man's age a factor to consider in family planning?
20. Discuss two viewpoints as to when children should be born into the marriage relationship.
21. How is a woman's career related to the timing of the birth of her first child?
22. At what intervals do most couples want their children?
23. How is the rate of family growth related to the financial position of the family?
24. How likely is pregnancy when no contraceptive is used?
25. Under what conditions should a woman not take the pill?
26. What is the most serious problem associated with the intrauterine device?
27. Why should the condom be used with a spermicidal agent?
28. What are two methods of predicting the time a woman is least likely to get pregnant? Why is each of these unreliable?
29. Discuss the various considerations involved in selecting a contraceptive.
30. What are the characteristics of those who use contraception effectively to ensure that the number of children they want is the number they actually have?
31. Discuss methods of sterilization for women and men.
32. What three issues should be considered before deciding whether to become sterilized?
33. What was the Supreme Court's 1973 decision regarding abortion?
34. Describe the various methods of abortion.
35. Discuss trends in family planning.

NOTES

1. In another study based on a random sample of 1,490 adults (eighteen and over) in the United States, 10 percent of the married respondents had or expected to have one child. This percentage included those who had no children and wanted one child and those who had one child and did not want more (General Social Science Survey, National Opinion Research Center, Chicago, July, 1975). Appreciation is expressed to Dr. Ken Wilson, Department of Sociology, East Carolina University, for analyzing all the NORC data referred to in this chapter.

2. No comparable research on fathers is available.

3. Definitions of fulfillment as wife and mother may vary. One mother of two children (not a respondent in the Werner study) explained her motivation for having a third child this way: "I'm having a third child because if I don't I'll have to go back to work or school. I feel that I ought to do more than stay home when my two kids are in school, but if I have another baby, I will have a good excuse to stay home and can delay the employment or school decision for five more years."

4. Calculated at 2.1 children per family, replacement level is defined as the birthrate which, if continued, would lead eventually to zero population growth.

5. Twenty-four women die for every 100,000 live births in the U.S. (Commission on Population Growth, 1972, p. 165).

6. Mongolism is a genetic defect also known as Down's syndrome and caused by an extra chromosome. A mongoloid child is physically deformed and mentally retarded and will have a shorter life span.

7. The costs of supporting an eighteen-year-old are 30 to 45 percent higher than the costs of supporting a one-year-old (Porter, 1976, p. 704).

8. Appreciation is expressed to Dr. Paul Tschetter, Department of Sociology, East Carolina University, for providing appropriate material for the development of this section.

9. Percentages reflect use in 1973.

10. With sequential pills, a pill containing estrogen only is taken for the first fifteen days and a pill containing both estrogen and progesterone is taken the following five days. Since they are less effective than the combination pill and have more serious side effects, they should not be used (Cherniak & Feingold, 1973, p. 18).

11. This percentage refers to all races. Data indicate that black wives are much more likely to be sterilized than white wives. In the thirty-five to forty-four age category, 47 percent of black wives in 1973 were sterilized in contrast to 18 percent of white wives (Westoff, 1976, p. 57).

12. This percentage refers to all races. White husbands are much more likely to be sterilized than black husbands. In the thirty-five to forty-four age category, 18 percent of white husbands in 1973 were sterilized in contrast to 2 percent of black husbands (Westoff, 1976, p. 57).

13. Because the consumer demand for commercial sperm banks is declining, the two largest sperm banks in America, Idant of New York and Genetics Laboratories, Inc., in St. Paul-Minneapolis, have closed their branch offices.

14. In effect the Supreme Court ruled that the fetus is a potential life and not a "person." The abortion decision rests with the woman and her physician. Neither a woman's husband nor parents may veto her decision.

BIBLIOGRAPHY

Association for the One-Child Family. *The one-child family . . . a life-style for today* (a brochure). Boulder, Colorado: Educational Resources Center, 1978.

Bahr, S. J., and Leigh, G. K. Family size, intelligence, and expected education. *Journal of Marriage and the Family*, 1978, *40*, 2, 331–5.

Black, W. P., and Sclare, A. B. Sterilization by tubal ligation—A follow-up study. In *Foolproof birth control: Male and female sterilization*, L. Lader (ed.). Boston: Beacon Press, 1973.

Blake, J. Coercive pronatalism and American population policy. In *Aspects of population growth policy*, R. Parke, Jr. and C. F. West (eds.). Washington, D.C.: Commission on Population Growth and the American Future, 1973, 85–109.

Bossard, J. H., and Boll, E. S. *The large family system: An original study in the sociology of family behavior*. Philadelphia: University of Pennsylvania Press, 1956.

Boston Women's Health Book Collective. *Our bodies, ourselves*. New York: Simon and Schuster, 1973, 132.

Centra, J. A. *Women, men and the doctorate*. Princeton: Educational Testing Service, 1974.

Cherniak, D., and Feingold, A. *Birth control handbook* (11th ed.). Montreal: Montreal Press, 1973.

Christensen, H. T. Children in the family: Relationship of number and spacing for marital success. *Journal of Marriage and the Family*, 1968, *30*, 2, 283–9.

Cochrane, S. H., and Bean, F. Husband-wife differences in the demand for children. *Journal of Marriage and the Family*, 1976, *38*, 2, 297–307.

Connell, E. B. The pill revisited. *Family Panning Perspectives*, 1975, *7*, 2, 62–71.

Cooper, P. E., Cumber, B., and Hartner, R. Decision-making patterns and post-decision adjustment of childfree husbands and wives. *Alternative Lifestyles*, 1978, *1*, 1, 71–94.

Davis, J. E. The reversibility of male sterilization. In *Foolproof birth control: Male and female sterilization*, L. Lader (ed.). Boston: Beacon Press, 1973.

Defronzo, J. Cross-sectional areal analysis of factors affecting marital fertility: Actual versus relative income. *Journal of Marriage and the Family*, 1976, *38*, 4, 669–76.

Erikson, E. *Childhood and society.* New York: W. W. Norton, 1963.

Evans, G., and Hall, J. The older the sperm. *Ms.,* January 1976, 49.

Ewer, P. A., and Crimmins-Gardner, E. Income in the income and fertility relationship. *Journal of Marriage and the Family,* 1978, *40,* 2, 291–9.

Figley, C. R. Child density and the marital relationship. *Journal of Marriage and the Family,* 1973, *35,* 2, 272–82.

Forer, L. K., and Still, H. *The birth order factor: How your personality is influenced by your place in the family.* New York: David McKay, 1976.

General Social Science Survey, National Opinion Research Center, Chicago, July 1975.

Gibson, C. The U.S. fertility decline, 1961–1975: The contributions of changes in marital status and marital fertility. *Family Planning Perspectives,* 1976, *8,* 5, 249–52.

Groat, H. T., and Neal, A. G. Social class and alienation correlates of Protestant fertility. *Journal of Marriage and the Family,* 1973, *35,* 1, 83–88.

Hawke, S., and Knox, D. *One child by choice.* Englewood Cliffs, N.J.: Prentice-Hall, 1977.

_____. The one-child family: A new life-style. *The Family Coordinator,* 1978, *27,* 3, 215–19.

Henry, J., and Warson, S. Family structure and psychic development. *American Journal of Orthopsychiatry,* 1951, *21,* 60.

Hulka, J. F. Tying the tubes with laparoscopy. In *Foolproof birth control: Male and female sterilization.* Lader (ed.). Boston: Beacon Press, 1973.

Hurley, J. R., and Palone, D. P. Marital satisfaction and child density. *Journal of Marriage and the Family,* 1967, *29,* 483–4.

Institute of Life Insurance. *Youth—1974.* New York: Institute of Life Insurance, 1975.

Johnson, N. E., and Stokes, C. S. Family size in successive generations: The effects of birth order, intergenerational change in lifestyle, and familial satisfaction. *Demography,* 1976, *13,* 2, 175–87.

Knox, D., and Gilman, R. C. The first year of fatherhood. *Family Perspective,* 1974, *9,* 31–34.

Knox, D., and Wilson, K. The differences between having one and two children. *The Family Coordinator,* 1978, *27,* 1, 23–5.

Landers, A. *Raleigh News & Observer,* 13 January, 1977.

Landis, J. T., and Poffenberger, T. Hesitations and worries of 330 couples choosing vasectomy for birth control. *Family Life Coordinator,* 1966, *15,* 143–7.

Maschoff, T., Fashier, H., Hansen, D. Vasectomy: Effect upon marital stability. *The Journal of Sex Research,* 1976, *12,* 4, 295–314.

Mastroianni, L., Jr. Rhythm: Systematized chance-taking. *Family Planning Perspectives,* 1974, *6,* 209–12.

McGurk, H., and Lewis, M. Birth order: A phenomenon in search of an explanation. *Developmental Psychology,* 1972, *7,* 3, 366.

Menning, B. E. *Infertility: A Guide for the Childless Couple.* Englewood Cliffs, N.J.: Prentice-Hall, 1977.

Mullen, P. et al. A vasectomy education program: Implications from survey data. *The Family Coordinator,* 1973, *22,* 3, 331–8.

National Organization for Non-Parents. *Motherhood is optional, or is it?* Baltimore, Md.: National Organization for Non-Parents, 1978.

Nye, F. I. School-age parenthood. *Extension Bulletin 667.* Cooperative Extension Service, Washington State University, Pullman, Washington, 1976.

Paniagua, M. E. Medical and psychological sequelae of surgical sterilization of women. In *Foolproof birth control: Male and female sterilization,* L. Lader (ed.). Boston: Beacon Press, 1973.

Peck, E. *The baby trap.* New York: Bernard Geis, 1971.

Peterson, R. A. Change in college students' attitude toward childrearing from 1971 to 1973. *Journal of Personality Assessment,* 1975, *39,* 3, 225–27.

Pierson, E. C. *Sex is never an emergency.* Philadelphia: J. B. Lippincott, 1973.

Porter, S. *Sylvia Porter's money book.* New York: Avon Books, 1976.

Reimer, R. J., and Maiolo, J. Family growth and socioeconomic status among poor blacks. Unpublished manuscript, 1977.

Report of the Commission on Population Growth and the American Future. New York: New American Library, Inc., 1972.

Rindfuss, R. R., and Bumpass, L. L. How old is too old? Age and the sociology of fertility. *Family Planning Perspectives*, 1976, *8,* 5, 226–30.

Rindfuss, R. R., and Sweet, J. A. *Postwar fertility trends and differentials in the United States*. New York: Academic Press, 1977.

Rossi, A. S. Transition to parenthood. *Journal of Marriage and the Family*, 1968, *30,* 1, 26–39.

Scanzoni, J. Gender roles and the process of fertility control. *Journal of Marriage and the Family*, 1976, *35,* 4, 677–91.

Scanzoni, J., and McMurry, M. Continuities in the explanation of fertility control. *Journal of Marriage and the Family*, 1972, *34,* 2, 315–32.

Siegel, E., and Morris, N. M. Family planning: Its health rationale. *American Journal of Obstetrics and Gynecology*, 1974, *118,* 995.

Silka, L., and Kiesler, S. Couples who choose to remain childless. *Family Planning Perspectives*, 1977, *9,* 1, 16–25.

Simon Population Trust, Vasectomy: Follow-up of a thousand cases. In *Foolproof birth control: Male and female sterilization*. L. Lader (ed.). Boston: Beacon Press, 1973.

Sklar, J., and Berkov, B. The American birth rate: Evidence of a coming rise. *Science*, 1975, *189,* 693–700.

Stafford, R. Pope terms abortion threat to world peace. Greenville (N.C.) *Daily Reflector*, 2 January 1977, A6.

Talwar, G. P., et al. Various articles. *Contraception*, 1976, *13,* 129–268.

Tietze, C., and Lewit, S. Legal abortion. *Scientific American*, January 1977.

Trussell, J., and Chandler, S. *The loving book*. Charlotte, N.C.: Red Clay Publishers, 1971.

U.S., Bureau of the Census. *Current Population Reports*, Series P-20, No. 287. Washington, D.C.: Government Printing Office, March 1975.

Veevers, J. E. Voluntary childlessness and social policy: An alternative view. *The Family Coordinator*, 1974, *23,* 4, 397–406.(a)

—————. The life style of voluntarily childless couples. Paper presented at the meetings of the National Council on Family Relations, St. Louis, 1974.(b)

Weinstock, E. et al. Abortion need and services in the United States, 1974–1975. *Family Planning Perspectives*, 1976, *8,* 2, 58–69.

Werner, P. D., Middlestadt-Carter, S. E., and Crawford, T. J. Having a third child: Predicting behavioral intentions. *Journal of Marriage and the Family*, 1975, *37,* 2, 348–58.

Westoff, C. F. Coital frequency and contraception. *Family Planning Perspectives*, 1976, *6,* 3, 136–41.

—————. Trends in contraceptive practice: 1965–1973. *Family Planning Perspectives*, 1976, *8,* 2, 54–7.

Westoff, C. F. et al. *Family growth in metropolitan America*. Princeton: Princeton University Press, 1961.

Whelan, E. M. *A baby . . . maybe?* New York: Bobbs-Merrill, 1976.

Whelpton, P. K., Campbell, A. A., and Patterson, J. E. *Fertility and family planning in the United States*. Princeton: Princeton University Press, 1966.

Wright, J., and Knox, D. Couplehood vs. parenthood: Should you have children? *Modern Bride*, March 1978.

Chapter 16

Having a Family

The value of marriage is not that adults produce children, but that children produce adults.

Peter De Vries

Ask parents how they feel about their children and you are likely to hear, "They are the meaning of life. . . . Nothing, and I mean nothing, is more important to me than my kids." In this chapter, we explore the positive and negative aspects of parenthood, the reactions of wives and husbands to a new baby, and the impact of children on the marriage relationship. Our basic theme suggests that the best preparation for having children is a realistic analysis of the consequences. One specialist on parenthood noted that, "In some ways the romantic complex surrounding parenthood is even deeper and more unrealistic than that relating to marriage" (LeMasters, 1977).

PARENTHOOD

There are advantages and disadvantages in becoming a parent. Let's examine both.

Positive Aspects of Parenthood

The love parents have for their children, the satisfactions they derive from interacting with them, and the delight they experience in fostering their development are sometimes difficult for nonparents to understand. Ask parents to name some positive aspects of having children, and they are likely to mention the following.

Spontaneity. Children are spontaneous. They have no internal schedule which tells them what they should do next. Picking daisies, playing hide and seek, and flying a kite always have the potential for the next moment. Unlike adults, children feel free to follow their desires where they may lead.

Honesty. Children are also honest. Unburdened by years of social programming, children express exactly what they feel. A family therapist knows that one of the quickest ways to assess the relationship between the husband and wife is to ask one of the children, "How do Mommy and Daddy get along?" One child's answer to this question was, "Mommy and Daddy yell a lot when they drink and Mom takes us to Granny's house when she's real mad at Dad." And their honesty also reflects their positive feelings. "When your five-year-old wraps his arms around your neck and says, 'I love you,' you know the feelings are real," one father said.

Companionship. A mother of three children said, "After you finish school, your friends all scatter. The only relationships that really last are family relationships. Having children builds in meaningful companionship across the years." A father said, "My wife travels a great deal because she's a sales representative. The children provide me with companionship during her absence. It's really nice not to be alone." A young wife whose husband is in the Navy remarked, "At night I'm all alone. I wish I'd gotten pregnant before he went overseas. My neighbor whose husband is also away has two children. I envy her and the life she shares with her children."

Parental pride. "I can't describe the pleasure it gave me to see my son write his name for the first time. He is my son and he can write now! It makes me swell with pride to watch him," remarked one father. Parental satisfaction and pride in children is a major reward of parenthood. And it is not dependent on the child's being elected President. Parents feel pride when their children first sit up, ride a bike, or learn to swim.

Spouses also delight in sharing this pride with each other. It is they who conceived and nurtured these children. A father said, "My wife and I generally enjoy

A well-documented and easily recognized response to parenthood is pride. Parents take pride not only in having produced a healthy and happy child, but also in their child's daily accomplishments.

different things. But we both really enjoy taking our children skiing and watching them develop their skills. It's magic."

Spouse-child relationship.   An additional delight of parents is to observe the interaction between their child and their spouse. A young mother said, "Amy asks when she awakens from her nap, 'When's Daddy coming home?' When he gets home, he lifts her into the air, and they begin laughing with each other. As a result of watching them play together, I've developed a special love for my husband." "The care and concern Julia shows for our son is outstanding," said the father of a four-year-old. "I never thought much about what kind of mother she would be, but she is fantastic. I wish I'd had her as a mother."

Negative Aspects of Parenthood

But these positive aspects of parenthood have a flip side. The spontaneity children exhibit may erupt at the wrong time—when the parents are making love, reading, or watching the evening news, talking on the telephone or to each other. And the honesty of children may also include telling a neighbor that Mommy said Daddy was a pompous ass or telling Grandma that the oil painting she gave the family is only hauled out on the occasion of her annual visit.

Parent-child companionship may also leave one spouse feeling excluded. And parental pride can become parental grief—when the child fails a grade, steals candy from the neighborhood grocery, or becomes involved in a premarital pregnancy at fifteen. Parenthood also involves loss of sleep, restricted social life, increased expenses, noise, and new routines. These complaints have been reported by parents in various studies (Wente & Crockenberg, 1976; Hobbs & Cole, 1976; Russell, 1974). Let's examine these latter negative aspects in more detail.

People who say they sleep like a baby usually don't have one.

Leo J. Burke

Loss of sleep.   "The best preparation for parenthood," reflected the mother of a three-month-old son, "is to set your alarm clock to go off at 2:00 a.m. Then get up, go into the kitchen, and fix yourself a glass of orange juice and take it to the guest bedroom in your apartment or house (the future nursery), sit in a chair, and talk to yourself for twenty minutes. Go back to your room, but set the alarm for 4:00 a.m. before getting into bed. Repeat the procedure again at 6:00 a.m. Do this for at least four consecutive nights while maintaining your regular work schedule. You'll get a dose of what parenthood really is by the fifth day."

A father said, "For those husbands whose wives do all the getting up at night, or for those fathers whose baby sleeps all night, or for those guys who have flexible schedules, infancy might be a delight. As for me, I've been in a daze since my daughter was born. I'll be glad when this stage is over."

Chronic exhaustion takes its toll not only in individual feelings but in job relationships as well. "My boss asked me for the first time in four years, 'What's the matter with you?' " said a sales manager. "I told him I hadn't had much sleep the past few weeks and he replied, 'You better get some—sales in your division are dropping.' "

Restricted social life.   In a study of 102 first-time fathers, the respondents were asked how often on the average they went out with their wives to eat, see a movie, or take a drive before and after the baby was born. Half of the fathers reported that their social lives were cut after the baby came, while the other half reported little change (Gilman & Knox, 1976).

Among those reporting a decline in social life, some bitterly resented having their life-style changed. "Before you have a baby you assume that you can always get a baby-sitter when you want to go out and that your social life really won't change," said a high-school football coach. "What a joke. The truth is that when you decide to go someplace it is usually too late to find a baby-sitter. You have to plan every social event at least three days ahead. The result—you go out less often or you go alone."

Some fathers who share a number of recreational interests with their wives are likely to feel the social restraints imposed by a baby most severely. A father who had been married ten years before his first child arrived expressed bitter resentment about the baby's interference with the sailing weekends he and his wife had enjoyed from April through late fall. "You can't take a baby on a sailboat, and being with Carol was part of the fun. We fought it for three months but finally sold the boat. If I had known that a baby equals no more sailing with my wife, I would have reconsidered having a baby."

Increased expenses.   Go into any infant's room and you will see Pampers, Q-Tips, baby oil, baby lotion, baby powder, cotton balls, and Vaseline. In the bathroom, where the dirty diapers may soak in the toilet, you will see medicines for colds, congestion, cough, and diarrhea. On your way to the bathroom you are likely to stumble over toys including a stuffed cat, Snoopy, and a chatter telephone. With the exception of Q-Tips and Vaseline, it is unlikely that any of these items was present before the baby arrived. These initial expenses are followed by a car seat ($50), a little red wagon, and a plastic pool. And the expenses will continue.

Although parents usually don't begrudge spending money on their children, that same money is no longer available for other items. "Sharon has no teeth under her baby teeth," said one father. "I would rather her mouth have teeth in it than buy a Winnebago. But, as a result, the kind of travel I want for the family will have to wait for several more years. Once you have children, their needs come first." And having a baby may mean a couple's income is cut in half, since the wife

may drop out of the work force when she becomes a mother. It also means that expenses increase about a third. The cost of prenatal care, delivery, and aftercare services range between $1,600, and $2,880 the first year (Porter, 1976, p. 705; Whelan, 1975, p. 181).

Noise. Stretching across the living room in a suburban home is a gray spiral cord. One end is attached to the television set; the other, to earphones. The father, showing guests through the home, says, "Listening to the evening news is almost impossible with a baby in the room. And when one of us can't take any more crying, we plug in to the TV or tape player for a short reprieve."

New routines. While some parents are not affected by the additional noise a baby creates, all parents must adapt to changes brought about by the baby's needs. These include more frequent visits by parents and in-laws, less sleep on Saturday and Sunday mornings, and not seeing movies on the spur of the moment. Although none of these changes is dramatic, they do require some flexibility.

The positive and negative aspects of parenthood are experienced in different degrees by different spouses at different times throughout the family life cycle. The essential point is that parenthood is neither positive nor negative all the time but involves a mixture of these experiences across the years.

WHEN A WIFE BECOMES A MOTHER

"I had been married several years when my baby was born," recalled one mother. "Prior to her birth I had an interesting job and a good marriage and had seriously considered remaining a childfree wife. But despite my hesitations, I think down deep I always expected that someday I'd become a mother."

Such feelings are not uncommon. While many women are aware of the problems associated with motherhood, over 90 percent want to have a baby of their own (Institute of Life Insurance, 1975, p. 6). Whether instinctive or learned, the desire to become a mother cuts across races, social classes, and religious preferences.

Because having children is such a common experience, society tends to overlook the profound effect that becoming a mother has on the individual woman. In this section, we explore what that effect is and how it changes the life of a woman from the time she conceives until her death.[1]

Being Pregnant

Motherhood begins not with childbirth but with conception, which occurs when the female egg is fertilized by the male sperm. Following this process, which occurs in the fallopian tubes, the fertilized egg floats down the fallopian tube into the uterus and attaches itself to the inner wall of the uterus. Furnished with a rich supply of blood and nutrients, the fertilized egg becomes an embryo and subsequently a fetus.

While a missed period, morning sickness, enlarged breasts, and more frequent urination are indications of pregnancy, it is best confirmed by laboratory tests and a physical examination. Lab tests involve examination of the woman's urine or blood to determine whether hormones indicative of pregnancy are present. The urine test can be accurate 42 days from the first day of the woman's last menstrual period whereas the blood test can verify a pregnancy eight days after conception.[2] In addition to one or more laboratory tests, the physician usually conducts a pelvic examination to find out if the woman's uterus has enlarged. Confirmation of the pregnancy is dependent on hearing and counting the fetal heart pulsations.

Excitement. The woman frequently reacts to knowledge of her pregnancy with excitement. Eighty-six percent of sixty-six first-time mothers reported a feeling of "happiness" when they became aware that they were pregnant (Cobliner, 1965). The wife's protruding abdomen announces to the world that her role in life is soon to change. Her husband, parents, and friends help to define her movement toward motherhood in positive terms. Brick says of Maggie in *Cat on a Hot Tin Roof,* "There's life in that body." Parents often smile in silent delight, and friends remark, "That's wonderful."

Much of a woman's attention during pregnancy is focused on her changing body. Unable to see the baby itself, a pregnant woman views her growing belly and breasts as confirmation that she is capable of creation, that there is a baby, and that the pregnancy is on course. While some women are distressed at the loss of a shapely figure or the appearance of stretch marks, most accept these bodily alterations as a natural aspect of becoming a mother.

Fears. Pregnancy may also involve anxiety. One concern is the gnawing fear that the developing fetus will not be a "perfect baby." "My closest friend was born with a birthmark that covered her right leg below the knee. I always avoid looking at her leg and hope it won't happen to my baby," remarked a wife in her seventh month.

Pregnant women also worry about the health of their babies. One remarked, "Diabetes is present in both my husband's family and mine. I hope that our child will not have to inject insulin into its veins throughout life. I would hate that."

Still other women are anxious about the sex of their baby—boys are still preferred (Westoff & Rindfuss, 1974). "Both of us want a boy," said one wife. "We tried the recommended procedure for having a boy[3] and hope that it works. Although I know it's unfair to think this way, I'll be disappointed if it's a girl."

Near the end of pregnancy, a more serious concern may arise—fear of childbirth. Sixty-three percent of pregnant women in one study reported a fear of the delivery (Poffenberger et al., 1952). Common were fears of pain, of the un-

Understandably, many women are fearful about the potential pain and danger involved in giving birth. Childbirth techniques such as the Lamaze method attempt to minimize these fears by educating and preparing both parents for the delivery of their child.

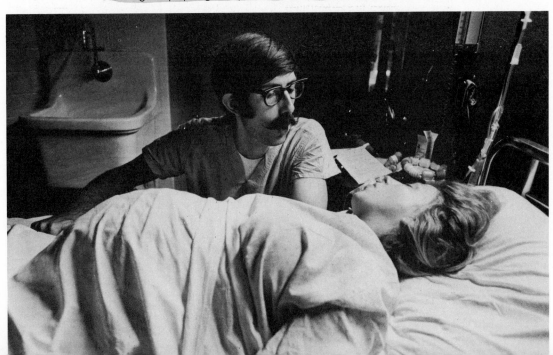

known, and of losing one's "cool" during the delivery. Some feared death. While these fears may still be common in the 1970s and 1980s, many current childbirth techniques (Lamaze, LeBoyer, etc.) are designed to calm these fears, help the woman work through them, and give her the moral support she needs.

Compounding the anxiety over childbirth are the physical problems of nausea and vomiting which half or more of all pregnant women experience (Hern, 1971). Some pregnant women also complain of severe fatigue, lassitude, irritability, and a tendency to burst into tears easily (Jessner et al., 1970, p. 209).

When the Baby Is Born

Once her baby has been delivered, a woman feels an enormous sense of pride. She has participated in the miracle of life. Out of almost nothing she has created a unique human being.

This pride is heightened as husband, parents, and friends come to the hospital to view the baby, give gifts, and assure the new mother that she has accomplished a miracle. A mother of three days explained, "I love to hear people tell me how beautiful my baby is. I immediately project into the future and count them lucky to have seen a baby who is destined for greatness."

Not all mothers respond to their new baby with feelings of ecstasy. About 50 percent experience a mild depression characterized by irritability, crying, loss of appetite, and difficulty in sleeping. Known as postpartum blues (also "the blues," postpartum depression, maternity blues, and fifth-day blues), the feeling is thought to be the result of the numerous physiological and psychological changes that occur as a result of late pregnancy, labor, and delivery. While the depression may take place in the hospital, it usually occurs when the woman returns home with her baby. Most women recover within a few days. About 5 percent require some form of counseling (Newton, 1976).

A similar reaction to postpartum depression may occur two, three, or even four weeks after the mother is home. A study by Richard and Katherine Gordon at the Englewood Hospital in New Jersey revealed that adopting the following behavior patterns before and during pregnancy helped women avoid the blues: (1) getting advice about parenthood, (2) making friends with couples who had young children, (3) continuing outside interests, (4) having the husband rearrange his schedule to be home more, and (5) having a relative or private nurse help with the baby soon after the arrival from the hospital (Newton, 1976).

Since, at one time or another, a sizable proportion of mothers have negative feelings about their children, we might ask, "Is mother love instinctive or learned?" Animal studies suggest that human mothers who care for their children have been taught to do so. They are surrounded by a physician, a husband, parents, in-laws, siblings, and friends, all of whom expect fairly specific positive behavior (and feelings) in reference to the baby. Without adequate socialization into the role of the loving, protective parent, it is possible that a new mother might drift toward other interests.

A female rhesus monkey, if raised in isolation, does not treat her infant in a "normal" way when she becomes a mother. She may ignore, reject, or even beat her offspring. This suggests that monkeys learn how to rear their young from living in a social group and watching other monkeys handle their young (Harlow, Harlow, & Hanson, 1963).

The fact that some mothers choose not to nurse their infants may also illustrate that maternal care and protection are learned rather than instinctive responses. Not only do some mothers have insufficient milk for their infants (nature does not ensure the survival of all offspring), but some prefer to bottle-feed their babies. One researcher observed, "The running war between the mother who does not want to nurse and the philosopher-psychologist who insists that she must stretches over two thousand years" (Kessen, 1965).

That 14 percent of 582 mothers in one study reported "unpleasant feelings for their baby" suggests that "mother love" is not instinctive (Miller & Swanson, 1958). In another study, of all births to currently married women during the five years 1966–1970, 15 percent were reported by the parents as having never been wanted (Commission on Population Growth and the American Future, 1972). Although an unwanted birth does not necessarily mean an unwanted child, the initial negative reaction may suggest that the "maternal instinct" is a questionable concept. But even though a mother's love for her child may be learned rather than instinctive, in most cases it is a strong, compelling emotion that new mothers can expect as one of the changes accompanying parenthood.

Adjusting to Motherhood

Whether maternal instincts guide mothers or the mother role is learned, the role implies that certain changes are likely to occur in the woman's life. "You can read about motherhood, watch your friends as they become mothers, and fantasize about having your own baby, but until you've done it, you can't really evaluate how you will take to motherhood." This statement by a reflective young mother points up an essential fact of motherhood: there is no way for a woman to know just how she will feel about being a mother until she is one. While trial marriage is "in," there is no trial motherhood.

Since every woman goes into motherhood naively, it is not surprising that women have widely differing experiences in managing the role. For some women, motherhood is the ultimate fulfillment; for others, the ultimate frustration. In reality, most women experience mixed emotions during their mothering experience. Whatever a woman's attitude prior to her baby she is not likely to take her role lightly. From the point of knowing she is pregnant (or about to become an adoptive mother), no woman's life is ever the same.

Motherhood brings with it change in a woman's daily work, responsibility, worry, isolation, and career. While the extent of these changes will be influenced by her husband's participation in child rearing, let's explore each of these changes in more detail.

Work. The new mother finds herself with a new set of tasks. And while she may typically spend much of her day feeding and diapering her infant, the work of motherhood does not end when the baby can feed itself and eliminate unattended. Brushing teeth, scrubbing knees, tying shoes, and washing baby clothes continue. While these tasks may be boring to some mothers, others take a great deal of pride in presenting to the world a clean, neatly dressed child. One mother said, "I feel good when my daughter has on her green dress and has white ribbons in her ponytails. She is what everybody thinks about when they think of a beautiful child."

Responsibility. But most mothers contend that the actual day-to-day (and night-to-night) work involved in child care is not the variable that makes motherhood a difficult role. The critical factor is the incessant and unrelenting responsibility. "The new mother starts out immediately on twenty-four-hour duty, with responsibility for a fragile and mysterious infant totally dependent on her care. It is as if the woman shifted from a graduate student to a full professor with little intervening apprenticeship experience of slowly increasing responsibility" (Rossi, 1968, p. 35).

Even in those relationships where the husband and wife say that they share the responsibility for child care, the final responsibility tends to fall to the wife. A university teacher married to a physician said,

> True, my wife has always worked at her profession, even when our sons were only some weeks old. . . . True, I help in many ways and feel responsible for her having time to work at her professional interests. But I do partial, limited things to free her to do her work. I don't do the basic thinking about the planning of meals and housekeeping or the situation of the children. Sure, I will wash dishes and "spend time" with the children; I will often do the shopping, cook, make beds, "share" the burden of most household tasks; but that is not the same thing as direct and primary responsibility for planning and managing a household and meeting day-to-day needs of children. (Miller, 1971)

Thus, with little or no preparation and with limited help from her husband, the new mother is faced with almost total responsibility for her child. She spends more time with her child than anyone else and becomes the governing parent (Clifford, 1959; Aldous, 1961). The responsibility of motherhood causes some women to feel trapped. Shirley Radl, former director of the National Organization for Non-Parents, commented on the discrepancy between what a woman "hears" about motherhood and what she actually experiences.

> The TV says all mothers are pretty and happy and have nice hairdos and wear fashionable pantsuits when they're scrubbing the floor. When Junior comes in and sloshes up the floor, she says, "It's okay," because she's got this new Zippy cleaner and will fix it in a snap. Actually, she's usually wearing jeans or some old shift and tennis shoes, her hair is up in rollers and it's been a bad day, and when Junior messes up the floor she says it's not okay and what she says isn't printable. . . . Furthermore, in the commercials, children are all well-behaved and clean except when showing how they get

their clothes dirty; they don't cry, and when they do misbehave slightly, Mom is able to have a nice chat with them and straighten things out. (Radl, 1973, p. 24)

Radl compares her own experience to this Johnson and Johnson image:

It was five o'clock, the mother's witching hour, the kids were yelling and I suddenly wondered if a person could die from irritation. I love my children (Adam, seven and Lisa, eight) but I don't like doing all the things I have to do: give them enriching experiences; interact with their school; do it all with a smile on my face and never get bored. (Radl, 1973, p. 24)

Overwhelmed with the responsibility of child care, another mother remarked, "After we had our first child, I developed a complete understanding of child abuse. There have been times that I felt like choking my son's throat and I felt this way even though our son was planned, wanted, and loved."

And the responsibility of motherhood does not disappear quickly. A middle-class woman with two children observed, "People tend to think of having children only in terms of the baby period. While it may seem like an eternity, the baby-toddler stage of a child is short compared to the twelve or sixteen years of the school-age child. Parents may not be legally responsible for a child beyond age twenty-one but morally and emotionally, once a parent, always a parent."

Worry. "You can lock them in their room but not out of your mind," said the mother of three daughters. Her observation reflects that children are an emotional as well as a physical drain. For example, a child's safety becomes primary to the mother. "I look at the clock at three and know that my child will soon be crossing the street from school," one mother said, "and although there is a policewoman there, I don't relax until I hear, 'I'm home, Mom.' " When mothers don't worry about busy streets, it's money (Will there be enough for them to complete college?), or peer persecution (Will they make fun of her because she has one crossed eye?), or health (Does a scratchy throat warrant a trip to see the doctor?), or her own employment (Will my children become delinquents because I am too involved in my career?).

Isolation. A side effect of the mobility of young American parents has been the mother's feeling of being restricted and isolated. In most societies, a young couple lives near the husband's or wife's parents and relatives (Stephens, 1963). In our society, the nuclear family most often lives away from both sets of parents, with the result that grandparents, aunts, and sisters aren't readily available to help with infant care. The American mother is essentially isolated and alone, with full-time responsibility for feeding, cleaning, protecting, and comforting her baby, while mothers in other societies are surrounded by female relatives who share the work of motherhood.

In *Occupation: Housewife,* Lopata reported on interviews with over five hundred full-time homemakers with children. One theme expressed by the house-bound mothers was restriction. "With young children you're tied down more than you can imagine," one mother said. The concept of "being tied down" seems to relate not only to spatial restrictions, but also to limitations on time and activity. It's not just being kept at home by the needs of an infant that "ties" the mother. It's also the constant presence of the child, the unremitting demand for attention, and the time providing such attention required (Lopata, 1971).

The career woman as mother.   For the traditional housewife, adding the role of mother may be relatively easy. She will have the time and resources (with her husband's economic support) to cope with the basic demands of her new infant. Indeed, having her own baby at home with her is her dream come true.

But some housewives are shocked to find that the incessant demands of an infant make it impossible for them to continue the life-style they had established before the baby arrived. One housewife said, "Before Jill came I could do a lot of reading in addition to cleaning the house. Now I just take care of Jill. I resent being able to read only when she is asleep."

The career woman is even more likely to experience stress in accommodating her life to a child. To her demanding roles of employee and wife, she must add that of mother. Even with her husband's verbal and behavioral support, the career woman must find ways to fit the demands of motherhood into her busy schedule. And priorities must be established. When forced to chooose between career and family responsibilities (the baby-sitter does not show up, the child is sick or hurt, etc.), the professional woman and mother generally responds to the latter role first (Poloma, 1972, p. 190). "Sarah, my two-year-old, fell and cut her lip as I was about to leave for the office," remarked a young lawyer. "Instead of dropping her at the day-care center, I took her to the doctor, who stitched her up. I didn't have to think about whether I was going to be late to the office. My child is more important to me."

But other career women decide on their priorities at the time of a crisis. The managing editor for a national magazine said, "My work comes first. I will see that my child is taken care of, but I'm not playing the role of the resident nurse. Last week, my son got sick, but I took him to the sitter anyway. Of course, there are occasions I will let my job go, but they are rare."

When no crisis is involved, some career women use "compartmentalization" to increase their effectiveness in their respective roles. This means keeping the career and family separate. "I can honestly tell you that before I leave this house, I try to prepare for everyone here," a career-woman mother said. "When I leave, I don't give them a thought, not a thought" (Poloma, 1972, p. 191).

But for the career-woman mother the rewards are high: "They have the best of all worlds" (Bernard, 1974, p. 171). In a study of the life patterns of career women, a researcher concluded:

> These married professional women, while relatively unswerving in their occupational commitment, do make it clear that they have chosen a difficult albeit an extremely rewarding life for themselves. They seem intensely involved with and gratified by both work and family commitments, although they are sometimes assailed by doubts about

their competence on both fronts. Finally, they are quite open about how hard it sometimes seems and how pressed for time they feel. While they do not seem overwhelmed and by no means seem willing to give up their role, one senses their fervent wish that things would somehow change to make life more manageable for women who refuse to forego either achievement striving or the joys and the tribulations of womanhood complete with marriage and children. (Birnbaum, 1971)

WHEN A HUSBAND BECOMES A FATHER

While the wife may have dreamed of being a mother since early childhood and nourished her dream during pregnancy, her husband often has not fully considered the implications of fatherhood. One researcher suggested that the impact of becoming a parent is usually more profound for the husband than for the wife (LeMasters, 1977). In this section, we explore how men view parenthood, their transition from husband to father, and their reactions to their new role.

How Men View Fatherhood

Most fathers are guided by certain impressions they have of what a father is and does. They tend to view the father as provider, teacher, authority, and companion[4] (Tasch, 1952; Broderick, 1977).

Provider. When eighty-five fathers were asked to explain their concept of parenthood, sixty-five listed "economic provider" as their primary role (Tasch, 1952). Other studies agree that the breadwinner function is central to the father's role (Fein, 1976; Maxwell, 1976).

Males are socialized to compete with other males, not to spend time with children. In our society the successful man is the executive who makes $50,000 per year, not the father who spends afternoons in the park with his children.

Earning money to support a family makes it necessary to be responsible to an employer (Benson, 1968). A salesman must face his field manager periodically with a report on the number of items sold. If there are too many consecutive bad reports he loses his job. The employer is not interested in knowing if his employee goes camping with his children or eats lunch with them or picks them up after school. "How many did you sell?" is the only question. The conflict between family and career is particularly acute if the father chooses to climb the executive ladder in a large company. This requires taking work home at night, traveling extensively, and working more than the standard forty-hour week—all of which may interfere with spending time with kids and relaxing as a family together. For the men whose career comes first, the Research Institute of America, Inc., offers the periodical *Personal Report* which provides executives with "novel ways to get understanding from family members when you must spend long hours at the office . . . or miss an occasional family function" (Bernard, 1974, p. 175). For the man whose family comes first, there will be fewer promotions, smaller raises, and generally less in the way of career rewards of all types.

Because men are rewarded for putting their career above their family, they often justify their minimal parenthood contribution in economic terms. "I've given them everything they ever wanted," said one father. But fathers are often criticized because making money is all they do. One college senior said, "My dad put me through school and bought me a car, but he is a stranger to me. I'll never get over his not spending time with me when I was younger.

Teacher.   Some fathers never go back to the office at night, never work on weekends, and always spend their leisure time with their families. "Regardless of how busy my dad was, he always spent some time with me in the evening and on weekends. We would talk about everything from the Mets to what really matters in life. I've always felt my dad cared about me, and I've tried to be the same kind of father to my children," said the father of two youngsters.

Fathers like this one hold the view that a child "can't just grow" and that it is the father's responsibility to make his child "ready for life." These fathers want their children to be independent, self-sufficient, and self-reliant, and feel they must influence them in this direction.

Authority.   Fathers also see their role as one of authority (Tasch, 1952, p. 350). In general, fathers consider exercising authority through discussion and guidance preferable to either an autocratic or overly indulgent approach (p. 350). One father spoke of "treating children as individuals." Another referred to "guiding my child's development." Still another said, "You should give children reasons why you do things."

A father may fill many roles, including teacher, companion, and friend to his children. At moments such as this one, it is clear that a father's relationship to his children runs much deeper than simply being an economic provider.

But not all fathers share these democratic perceptions of authority. The autocratic father demands obedience from his children and does not consult them about decisions which affect them. One authoritarian father insisted that his sons go to the same college he had attended and study law. "If you want to be anything but a lawyer," he told them, "find somewhere else than my table to eat."

Some fathers reject the role of authority. "My dad left us alone to make our own decisions," recalled one son. "And he never criticized our decisions. He expected us to use our best judgment, so we did."

Companion. A father often likes to think of himself as a friend and companion to his offspring, though the relationship varies with the age and sex of the children. For example, a father may relate quite differently to his son and daughter during their childhood and adolescence. "I've always been closer to my son, even when he was kid," observed one father. "We just had more in common. When he was an adolescent, we worked on cars together and did some hunting. Now we're in business together. I love my daughter but have never had much in common with her."

But a father of two daughters said, "I can't imagine what it would be like to have a son because I've always related to my two children as people, not girls. I have enjoyed them since they were babies, and while we had our differences when they were teenagers, we are friends. It's really nice."

In summary, fathers tend to view themselves as economic providers, teachers, authority figures, and companions. But these are all subdivisions of the fundamental role of father. Let's look at the transition to this new role.

Transition to Fatherhood

The husband's role as father begins with his relating to his wife as mother-to-be. This involves sharing her excitement about the pregnancy with parents and close friends. "It was like telling people that we were getting married," said one father. "We delighted in breaking the news to people who were as excited as we were."

Beyond sharing the excitement of telling others about the impending baby, husbands do very little to prepare for fatherhood. In a study of 102 first-time fathers, only one third attended parenthood classes offered by a local university, while one fourth attended Lamaze (natural childbirth) classes (Knox & Gilman, 1974, p. 32). It would be inaccurate to assume that the fathers-to-be already knew what to expect from the fatherhood role. In fact, only 25 percent of them had discussed fatherhood with another male on several occasions and over 40 percent had never fed a baby or changed a baby's diapers.[5]

Since most fathers know little about the details of fatherhood, what goes on in their heads when their wives are pregnant? One physician divided fathers into three general categories on the basis of their reactions to and behavior during their wives' pregnancies:

1. The "solid" fathers who show a reasonable amount of concern and understanding toward pregnant wives and are cooperative and supportive of the prenatal program without trying to run it.

2. The "selfish dolt," who has the instincts and sensibilities of a herd bull. This type believes he has done his proud duty by inseminating his female, and the consequences are her problem, not his. He has a minimal interest in the progress of his wife's pregnancy and is resentful when it interferes with his regular routine or her household duties.

3. The "nervous itch" who overidentifies with his wife. He is just the opposite of the "selfish dolt." He worries excessively, listens to Old Wives' Tales, tries to interpret the meaning of every new symptom, and wants to know why the obstetrician is not using the new "systems" he hears and reads about.

(Anonymous M.D., 1972)

Thirty men whose wives were in their last month of pregnancy said that while they were mostly concerned about what labor and delivery would be like, they were also worried about how to care for a baby and how to parent. Some men mentioned that their fathers had been emotionally distant from them when they had been growing up and that they (the fathers-to-be) did not want to repeat that pattern (Fein, 1976, p. 345).

For the couple who have decided to have their baby Lamaze-style (natural childbirth), the husband is literally by his wife's side throughout her labor and delivery. "What you see on television about the guy pacing in the waiting room until the nurse tells him his child is born isn't the way it happened for me. I was able to help my wife relax, give her ice when she needed it, and call the nurse when necessary," recalled one Lamaze father. Lamaze fathers describe the birth experience with their wives as "one of the most important events of their lives" (Wente & Crockenberg, 1976, p. 356).

Participation in Child Care

After the mother and baby are home from the hospital, one of the discoveries of the new father is that a baby requires an enormous amount of physical care. To assess the degree to which fathers actually participate in child care, the 102 first-time fathers who had been parents for an average of slightly over six months were asked, "How many times have you fed your baby in the last week?" Five was the average number reported by those fathers whose babies were bottle fed.[6] When asked how often they had changed their babies' diapers during the last week, the fathers reported an average of six times (Knox & Gilman, 1974, p. 32). A six-month-old baby requires feeding and changing about four and six times per day respectively.

Although today's father may help with the day-to-day care of the infant, his wife does most of the work. But there are exceptions. One father of an eleven-month-old toddler remarked, "I do everything for my boy that my wife does. If he needs a new diaper, I change him. If he needs a slice of cheese or a bath, I deliver. He is as much my responsibility as hers." Women who advocate equal sharing in child-care responsibilities suggest that as men become increasingly involved in parenting, they will experience more of the rewards of parenthood.

In several studies of the degree to which fathers participate in child care, two researchers concluded that (a) fathers are interested in newborns and, if provided with the opportunity, do become involved; (b) fathers are just as nurturant as mothers in their interactions with newborns; (c) fathers do apparently engage in less caretaking; but, (d) fathers can be capable and competent in the execution of caretaking activities (Parke & Sawin, 1976, p. 369).

In practice, then, fathers can, but generally don't, participate equally with their wives in the physical care of their infants. Rather, they tend to spend their time watching and playing with their babies (Rendina & Dickerscheid, 1976, p. 375).

Reactions to Fatherhood

Since there is tremendous social pressure to make only positive remarks about one's own baby, it is difficult to find out how fathers really feel about their new role. One researcher suggested that parents who do not return questionnaires on their reaction to parenthood are more likely to have had a negative reaction than parents who do return their questionnaires (Russell, 1974). However, 25 percent of the 102 first-time fathers referred to earlier agreed with the statement, "Sometimes I wish my wife and I could return to the time before my baby was born" (Knox & Gilman, 1974, p. 32). And in a study of eighty-five fathers, one third agreed that children were "work, worry, and bother" (Tasch, 1952, p. 341).

Men differ in the degree to which they are bothered by the irritations of early fatherhood. These differential reactions are related to the wife's feelings about motherhood, the effect of the baby on the marriage, and various characteristics of the father, and the baby.

Effect of wife's attitude.   A wife who responds favorably to her role as parent influences her husband to react in the same way (Knox & Gilman, 1974, p. 33). "To be honest, I could have gone either way," one father said. "After several nights of lost sleep, the sound of a crying baby during meals, and a drawer full of baby bills, I was ready to admit that we had made a big mistake. But Connie was excited about Pam and encouraged me to bathe her, feed her, and get involved. As a result, I began to see the potential delights of fatherhood. Had it not been for Connie, my attitude would have been pretty negative."

Effect of baby on marriage.   Related to the wife's reaction is the way the husband perceives the effect of the baby on his marriage. In the study of 102 first-time fathers, if the marriage improved after the baby was born, the father reported a very favorable reaction to the baby (Knox & Gilman, 1974, p. 33). "Our baby gave us a common goal, a purpose," said the manager of a grocery store. "Since she was born, we have been much closer. She's the best thing that ever happened to our marriage."

In contrast, husbands who perceived the baby as having had a disrupting effect on the relationship with their wives reported more difficulty in adjusting to fatherhood (Wente & Crockenberg, 1976). "No baby is worth my marriage," grumbled a computer programmer for IBM. "I wish the baby had never been born. My wife feels differently and it has cost us our relationship. We are getting together with our lawyers on Thursday to sign separation papers."

Other factors. Fathers who are in their twenties are more likely to report a favorable reaction to parenthood than fathers who are in their thirties when their first child is born (Russell, 1974). In addition, fathers report a more favorable adjustment if the baby is healthy (Hobbs & Cole, 1976) and quiet (Russell, 1974).

It is not clear whether taking classes in preparation for parenthood is effective in easing the transition to fatherhood. For example, two studies have found that fathers who attended parenthood classes reported more satisfaction with their infants than those fathers who did not attend such classes (Russell, 1974; Beebe, 1978). But another study which compared fathers who attended Lamaze classes with those who did not found that adjustment was unrelated to Lamaze preparation (Wente & Crockenberg, 1976).

WHEN A COUPLE BECOMES A FAMILY

Having explored how children affect the mother and father, let's examine their effect on the marriage relationship.

The Couple During Pregnancy

When the woman becomes aware that she is pregnant, the developing embryo begins its influence on the marriage relationship. In anticipating the baby, the couple will deal with matters that are entirely new to them—telling parents and friends about the pregnancy, allocating existing space for the baby (or getting a larger house or apartment), furnishing a nursery, choosing names for the child, deciding on whether or not to attend parenthood classes, and having intercourse with a fetus in the middle.

In addition, pregnancy may affect the division of labor. In a study of married couples during the wife's first pregnancy, one wife said, "I love being pregnant. I've never gotten so much attention in my life, from Alan and everybody else. . . . [For example] I don't think Alan would have considered doing it [cleaning the tiles in the bathtub] if I weren't pregnant." And when the husband was asked if he would consider cleaning the tiles after the birth, he replied, "No, she'll have no excuse [for not doing it] then" (LaRossa, 1976).

The Baby Comes Home

While the husband and wife continue to make adjustments during the wife's pregnancy, the fetus continues to develop, and soon the baby is born. After the initial excitement of watching and holding their creation and sharing this experience with parents and friends, the couple bring their infant home. While parents may help during the first few weeks, soon the spouses are alone with their baby. Theirs is now a different marriage. The pre-baby days are gone forever.

"You've been neglecting me, Beatrice. Is there someone else?"

One mother reflected, "My son was a little over three weeks old when my husband came home from work one evening with the news that he would be going to San Francisco on business in a couple of days. My immediate reaction was, 'Great! I'll go with you,' since we'd always arranged to accompany each other on business trips. Then the reality hit me. I had a baby—a nursing baby at that. I could no longer just pack my bag and take off. Either I had to take our baby along, or I stayed home. Neither option appealed to me. It was then I began to realize how our baby would affect our marriage."

A baby alters the marriage relationship in very specific ways. While some of these changes may lead to dissatisfaction in the marriage, other changes seem to strengthen the relationship. Common changes which result when the couple become a family include the following.

Less talking. A baby shatters the privacy of a couple's world and slices their communication time in half (Rollins & Feldman, 1970). Only the parents of a newborn understand how this happens. "We were on our way to the post office to mail a letter and had begun to talk about a phone call we had received from a college friend," recalled a new father. "During the third sentence the baby started crying, and he didn't stop until we got home. By then, we were both frustrated so that we dropped the subject. After a while, you learn not to talk—that way you're not interrupted."

Not only does the baby's crying make talking difficult, but his or her needs may also result in the spouses spending less time together. Before the baby arrives, the couple tend to spend their evenings together sharing their experiences and thoughts. After the baby's arrival, one spouse usually devotes most of these evening hours to feeding, bathing, and diapering the baby and putting it to bed.

Even after the baby is tucked into its crib, the couple does not engage in much marital communication. The wife may use the remainder of the evening to catch up on the housework she wasn't able to complete during the day, finish an interrupted phone conversation with another new mother, or fall into bed exhausted. Or she may want to just sit and read a book or newspaper in the luxury of silence.

Less touching and looking.   Go to a restaurant that is frequented by teenagers or college students. Glance around the room and focus on the interaction occurring in boy-girl couples. Notice the hand-holding and eye contact. The entire attention of each partner is focused on the other.

Then go to a "family" restaurant. Sit near a table where a husband, wife, and one or more children are eating. Notice the amount of touching and talking these spouses engage in. Also see how frequently they gaze into each other's eyes. One researcher observed 440 couples, some with and some without children, in public places. He concluded that those couples with children were much less likely to touch, smile, and talk with each other than those couples without children (Rosenblatt, 1974).

Less shared recreation.   In addition to reducing conversation and touching between spouses, babies make shared recreation difficult (Gilman & Knox, 1976). "We used to play tennis together every weekend," said one father, "but with a baby, it's neither practical nor fun. We tried it, but it doesn't work. The result— one of us goes with a friend and the other baby-sits. It's not as much fun."

As children grow older, there are more opportunities to include them in recreational activities. Even so, parents find that they are sharing a Walt Disney movie, or playing putt-putt golf, or sliding down a slide with their children—not with each other. Of course, sharing the fun of being with children is a form of recreation, but it is not the same as adult recreation without children.

Effect of Children on the Marriage Relationship

What have researchers concluded about the effect of children on the marriage relationship?[7] In an early study, the researcher interviewed forty-six couples who were parents. Eighty-three percent reported that the coming of their first child represented a "crisis" for their marriage (LeMasters, 1957). Several years later, another researcher reported that 53 percent of the thirty-two couples in his study experienced an "extensive or severe" crisis with their first baby. Thirty-eight percent reported a "moderate crisis" (Dyer, 1963). Further confirmation for the negative effect of children on marital satisfaction was found by the Feldmans of Cornell University. Using a sample of 850 married couples, they compared those who had an infant with those who had been married the same length of time but were childfree. The result—lower marital satisfaction was characteristic of the couples with children. This remained true even in the middle and later years of marriage (Feldman & Feldman, 1977).

But other researchers disagree. When Russell (1974) defined *crisis* as "a change in self, spouse, or relationships with significant others which are 'bothersome,' " 75 percent of the 272 husbands and 58 percent of the 296 wives in her sample stated that their baby was a "slight" crisis. Only 6 percent of the husbands and 8 percent of the wives said that their marriages had deteriorated since the baby's birth. Supporting the idea that a baby is not an overwhelming crisis, 86 percent of the fifty-three couples in Hobbs' 1965 study reported that their baby represented only a "slight" crisis (Hobbs, 1965). Not one of these couples would use the terms "extensive" or "severe" in describing the impact of their child. Ten years later Hobbs replicated his study and arrived at similar conclusions (Hobbs & Cole, 1976). In a study of first-time fathers, 75 percent reported that their baby had no effect on their marriage, and 20 percent indicated that their marital relationship had improved since their baby's birth (Gilman & Knox, 1976).

One explanation for the different conclusions of studies on the impact children have on marriage is the degree to which spouses use various means to cope with a new baby. Fantasy (thinking back to pre-baby times when things were less hectic) and actually going out together without the baby are two means some couples use to help adapt to the new strains of parenthood. In a study focusing on how fathers coped with a new baby, only the second coping mechanism worked. Just staying at home thinking about how things used to be not only was not helpful but made things worse. However, getting a baby-sitter and going out together was associated with greater personal and marital happiness (Gilman & Knox, 1976). A car salesman said, "If you don't get out of the house and get alone with your spouse, you've had it. I know. We've got three kids and trying to communicate around them is like talking on a merry-go-round—you can't do it. We get a baby-sitter once a week and enjoy an evening out together—alone. It makes a difference."

And going out has implications for the spouses' sexual relationship. In one study, married couples who had gone out together in the preceding twenty-four hours were more likely to have also had sexual intercourse in the preceding twenty-four hours (Rosenblatt et al., 1976).

The differential use by parents of the practice of going out together alone as a means of coping with their new baby is only one explanation of why studies on the effect of children on marital satisfaction disagree. The differential ability to reduce role strain may also be a factor (Russell, 1975, p. 6). When the husband expects his wife, who is now a new mother, to give him the same time and attention that she did prior to the baby, it is unlikely that she will be able to meet his expectations. And the strain of managing the wife and mother role without a drop in the expectations of the former may be particularly difficult.

Analyzing the dilemma of such role strain, Russell continued, "The practical implication, then, becomes one of regulating role strain and 'role discrepancy' during the child-dependent years, not necessarily avoiding parenthood altogether.

The problem is not the child, but what the parents expect of one another as they take on the additional role of parent" (p. 6). Indeed, it is not children *per se* who decrease or increase marital satisfaction. Rather, it is the response spouses make to their role as parents. Using data from the 1970 National Fertility Study, one researcher observed that divorce rates were highest among women with large families and those with no children. Those women least likely to be divorced had a moderate number of children (Thornton, 1977).

TRENDS

The future of parenthood will include a greater awareness of what the role involves, increased sharing by both spouses of the birth of their child or children, new techniques of delivery, and more emphasis on fatherhood. Proponents of the childfree alternative, including authors of such books as *The Baby Trap* (Peck, 1971) and *A Baby? . . . Maybe* (Whelan, 1975), sensitize would-be parents to the realities of parenthood. As a result, although most couples opt for having children, they are likely to enter parenthood with a more realistic awareness of the positive and negative aspects of that role. And the increased availability of and enrollment in preparation-for-parenthood classes suggest that spouses will be better informed about parenthood when their children are born.

Having a baby usually brings on at least a slight marital crisis, but if the couple agree as to their expectations for each other and balance their parent and spouse roles to their mutual satisfaction, the marital relationship need not suffer.

Among the preparation-for-parenthood classes available to potential parents are Lamaze classes. Synonymous with natural childbirth, the Lamaze method emphasizes active involvement of the father in the delivery process (Phillips & Anzalone, 1978). Some hospitals are adapting to this trend toward couple participation in childbirth and permit the father to observe and participate (cut the umbilical cord) during the delivery. At Family Hospital in Milwaukee, fathers are not considered visitors but can spend as much time as they like with the mother and baby (Timberlake, 1975).

Some hospitals also are beginning to encourage the use of a delivery technique developed by Frederick LeBoyer, a French physician who emphasized the importance of bringing the baby into a quiet atmosphere. The lights in the delivery room are dimmed and the baby is handled gently rather than given the traditional slap on the bottom.

Indications are that the role of the father will become increasingly emphasized. "Far from being irrelevant or insignificant, fathers are salient figures in the lives of their infants from early life" (Lamb & Lamb, 1976, p. 383). Books such as *How to Father* (Dodson, 1974), *Father Power* (Biller & Meredith, 1975), and *Fathering* (Green, 1977) provide a guide to fathering in much the same way the Spock books have been a guide for millions of mothers.

One author observed the emergence of a more human father as a result of increased involvement in parenting: "Many fathers are more genuinely motivated to meet the needs of their children, are less likely to impose their own ambitions and hopes on their children, are less authoritarian and arbitrary, and are much less austere and unapproachable than fathers of the recent past" (Lynn, 1974, p. 12).

SUMMARY

Just as most single adults eventually marry, most married couples have (and enjoy) children. Observing their spontaneity, delighting in their honesty, sharing companionship with them, and experiencing a sense of pride in watching them develop are among the joys parents experience in rearing children. But there are drawbacks. Loss of sleep, restricted social life, increased expenses, noise, and new routines are also part of parenthood.

Although the wife and husband both become parents, the roles of mother and father are different. The wife is buoyed up by excitement about a baby growing in her body, but she may also experience nausea, fatigue, and irritability during pregnancy. Delivery itself is often a concern; 63 percent of the women in one study reported a fear of delivery. And after the delivery, 50 percent of new mothers experience postpartum depression or "the blues."

Since women react differently to their infants, it has been suggested that maternal love is a learned rather than an instinctive reaction. The new mother is surrounded by people (physician, husband, mother, friends) who expect her to develop positive ways of relating to her infant. Such expectations are important since the role of the mother involves not only joy but work, worry, and twenty-four-hour responsibility. While roles are changing, the wife's greater responsibility for the infant remains the primary difference between the roles of mother and father. Fathers see their roles as provider, teacher, authority, and companion; of these, the first is viewed as the most important.

Children are likely to affect the marriage relationship by reducing communication between the spouses and the amount of time they spend together. Couples who report a relatively smooth transition to parenthood make frequent use of baby-sitters and work to reduce the demands on each other that cause role strain.

Trends for the future include greater preparation for parenthood, more Lamaze births, and more emphasis on fatherhood. Perhaps the most significant trend is the more mutual involvement of both spouses in the parenting experience.

STUDY QUESTIONS

1. What are some positive and negative aspects of parenthood?
2. What physical signs suggest pregnancy?
3. What laboratory tests help confirm pregnancy?
4. Discuss the joys and fears women typically experience during pregnancy.
5. What is postpartum depression?
6. Discuss whether a mother's love is instinctive or learned.
7. Motherhood brings with it changes in a woman's daily work, responsibility, worry, isolation, and career. Discuss each of these.
8. Describe two ways career women may order their priorities of career and family.
9. How do men tend to view their role as father?
10. How does the provider role often interfere with the roles of teacher and companion?
11. Describe three general categories of men's reactions to their wives' pregnancy.
12. How do Lamaze fathers usually feel about being with their wives during labor and delivery?
13. To what degree do husbands actively participate in child care with their wives?
14. How does the wife's reaction to motherhood affect the husband's reaction to fatherhood?
15. How do the effect of the baby on the marriage, the father's age, and the baby's health affect the husband's adjustment to fatherhood?
16. What do research studies show about the effect of attending preparation-for-parenthood classes on adjustment to fatherhood?
17. How does pregnancy affect the division of labor for many couples?
18. Discuss three ways children affect the marriage relationship.
19. How do some couples cope successfully with the frustrations of parenthood?
20. Discuss emerging trends in parenthood.

NOTES

1. Appreciation is expressed to Sharryl Hawke for her assistance in the development of this and the following two sections.

2. The blood test for pregnancy is a recent innovation and may not yet be available in your physician's office.

3. See *Boy or Girl? The Sex Selection Technique That Makes All Others Obsolete* (Whelan, 1977) for a review of new procedures for preselecting the sex of your child.

4. Although men learn to engage in these social roles commonly associated with fatherhood, Rympa (1976) has suggested a biological basis for paternal responses.

5. These previously unpublished data are drawn from the same study of 102 first-time fathers reported on in Knox and Gilman, 1974, and Gilman and Knox, 1976.

6. These data are from the study referred to in note 5.

7. Most studies of the effects of parenthood on the marriage relationship are done as retrospective reviews. In other words, spouses are asked to remember how satisfied they were before the baby was born and compare that to their satisfaction after the baby was born. Such remembering may be biased by how the present is perceived. If the period after the baby is "bad," the pre-baby period may be remembered as "very good" and vice versa. The Feldmans' study is an exception. They studied their couples both before and after they had a child.

BIBLIOGRAPHY

Aldous, J. A study of parental role functions. *Family Life Coordinator,* 1961, *10,* 43–4.

Anonymous M.D. *Confessions of a gynecologist.* New York: Doubleday, 1972.

Beebe, E. R. Expectant parent classes: A case study. *The Family Coordinator,* 1978, *27,* 1, 55–8.

Benson, L. *Fatherhood: A sociological perspective.* New York: Random House, 1968.

Bernard, J. *The future of motherhood.* New York: Dial Press, 1974.

Biller, H., and Meredith, D. *Father power.* New York: Doubleday, 1975.

Birnbaum, J. L. A. Life patterns, personality style, and self-esteem in gifted family-oriented and career-committed women. Doctoral dissertation, University of Michigan, 1971.

Broderick, C. B. Fathers. *The Family Coordinator,* 1977, *26,* 3, 269–75.

Clifford, E. Discipline in the home: A controlled observational study of parental practices. *Journal of Genetic Psychology,* 1959, *95,* 45–82.

Cobliner, W. G. Some maternal attitudes toward conception. *Mental Hygiene,* 1965, *49,* 550–57.

Commission on Population Growth and the American Future. *Population and the American future.* New York: New American Library, 1972.

Dodson, F. *How to father.* New York: New American Library, 1974.

Dyer, E. D. Parenthood as crisis: A re-study. *Marriage and Family Living,* 1963, *25,* 196–201.

Fein, R. A. Men's entrance into parenthood. *The Family Coordinator,* 1976, *25,* 4, 341–8.

Feldman, H., and Feldman, M. Effect of parenthood at three points in marriage. Unpublished manuscript, Cornell University, 1977.

Gilman, R. C., and Knox, D. Coping with fatherhood: The first year. *Child Psychiatry and Human Development,* 1976, *6,* 3, 134–48.

Green, M. *Fathering.* New York: McGraw-Hill, 1977.

Harlow, H. F., Harlow, M. F., and Hanson, E. W. The maternal affectional system in infant monkeys. In *Maternal behavior in mammals,* H. J. Rheingold (ed.). New York: John Wiley and Sons, 1963.

Hern, W. M. Is pregnancy really normal? *Family Planning Perspectives,* 1971, *3,* 1.

Hobbs, D. F., Jr. Parenthood as crisis: A third study. *Journal of Marriage and the Family,* 1965, *27,* 367–72.

Hobbs, D. F., Jr., and Cole, S. P. Transition to parenthood: A decade replication. *Journal of Marriage and the Family,* 1976, *38,* 4, 723–31.

Jessner, L., Weigert, E., and Foy, J. L. The development of parental attitudes during pregnancy. In *Parenthood: Its psychology and psychopathology,* E. J. Anthony and T. Benedek (eds.). Boston: Little, Brown, 1970, 209.

Kessen, W. *The child.* New York: John Wiley and Sons, 1965.

Knox, D., and Gilman, R. C. The first year of fatherhood. *Family Perspective,* 1974, *9,* 1, 31–4.

Lamb, M., and Lamb, J. E. The nature and importance of the father-infant relationship. *The Family Coordinator,* 1976, *25,* 4, 379–85.

LaRossa, R. Conflict and power in marriage: Expecting the first child. In *Sage Library of Social Research* (50). Beverly Hills, Calif.: Sage Publications, 1977.

LeMasters, E. E. Parenthood as crisis. *Marriage and Family Living,* 1957, *19,* 352–5.

_____. *Parents in modern America*, 3rd ed. Homewood, Ill.: Dorsey Press, 1977.

Lopata, H. Z. *Occupation: Housewife*. New York: Oxford University Press, 1971.

Lynn, D. *The Father: His role in child development*. Monterey, Calif.: Brooks/Cole, 1974.

Maxwell, J. W. The keeping fathers of America. *The Family Coordinator*, 1976, *25*, 4, 387–92.

Miller, D. R., and Swanson, G. E. *The changing American parent*. New York: John Wiley and Sons, 1958.

Miller, S. M. On men: The making of a confused middle-class husband. *Social Policy*, 1971, *2*, 2, 33–9.

Newton, M. New baby! Why so sad? *Family Health*, 1976, *8*, 5.

Parke, R. D., and Sawin, D. B. The father's role in infancy: A re-evaluation. *The Family Coordinator*, 1976, *25*, 4, 365–71.

Peck, E. *The baby trap*. New York: Bernard Geis Associates, 1971.

Poffenberger, S., Poffenberger, T., and Landis, J. T. Intent toward conception and the pregnancy experience. *American Sociological Review*, 1952, *17*, 616–20.

Poloma, M. M. Role conflict and the married professional woman. In *Toward a sociology of women*, C. Safilios-Rothschild (ed.). Lexington, Mass.: Xerox College Publishing, 1972, 187–98.

Porter, S. *Sylvia Porter's money book*. New York: Avon Books, 1976.

Radl, S. Motherhood takes special skills. *Daily Camera*, 8 November 1973, 24.

Rendina, I., and Dickerschied, J. D. Father involvement with the first born infants. *The Family Coordinator*, 1976, *25*, 4, 373–8.

Rollins, B. C., and Feldman, H. Marital satisfaction over the family life cycle. *Journal of Marriage and the Family*, 1970, *32*, 20–28.

Rosenblatt, P. C. Behavior in public places: Comparison of couples accompanied and unaccompanied by children. *Journal of Marriage and Family Living*, 1974, *35*, 4, 750–55.

Rosenblatt, P. C., Titus, S. L., and Cunningham, M. R. The relationship between spousal recreation and sexual intercourse. Unpublished study, Family Social Science, University of Minnesota, 1976.

Rossi, A. S. Transition to parenthood. *Journal of Marriage and the Family*, 1968, *30*, 26–39.

Russell, C. S. Transition to parenthood: Problems and gratifications. *Journal of Marriage and the Family*, 1974, *36*, 2, 294–303.

_____. The transition to parenthood and beyond. Comments at symposium at the annual meeting of the National Council on Family Relations, 1975.

Rympa, C. B. Biological basis for the paternal response. *The Family Coordinator*, 1976, *25*, 4, 335–9.

Stephens, W. N. *The family in cross-cultural perspective*. New York: Holt, Rinehart and Winston, 1963.

Tasch, R. J. The role of father in the family. *Journal of Experimental Education*, 1952, *20*, 4, 319–61.

Thornton, A. Children and marital stability. *Journal of Marriage and the Family*, 1977, *39*, 3, 531–40.

Timberlake, B. The new life center. *American Journal of Nursing*, 1975, *75*, 9, 1456–61.

Wente, A. S., and Crockenberg, S. B. Transition to fatherhood: Lamaze preparation, adjustment difficulty and the husband-wife relationship. *The Family Coordinator*, 1976, *25*, 4, 351–7.

Westoff, C. F., and Rindfuss, R. Sex preselection in the United States: Some implications. *Science*, 1974, *184*, 4127, 633–6.

Whelan, E. *A baby . . . maybe?* Indianapolis, Ind.: Bobbs-Merrill, 1975.

_____. *Boy or girl? The sex selection technique that makes all others obsolete*. Indianapolis, Ind.: Bobbs-Merrill, 1977.

Youth—1974: A survey of Americans ages 14 through 25. New York: Institute of Life Insurance, 1975.

Chapter 17

Rearing a Family

Before I got married I had six theories about bringing up children; now I have six children and no theories.

John Wilmot, Earl of Rochester (1647–1680)

In the preface to his book, *Between Parent and Child,* Haim Ginott wrote:

> All parents want their children to be secure and happy. No one deliberately tries to make his child fearful, shy, inconsiderate, or obnoxious. Yet in the process of growing up, many children acquire undesirable characteristics and fail to achieve a sense of security and an attitude of respect for themselves and for others. (Ginott, 1965, p. 11)

We have already considered the planning and having of children. Now we turn to the difficult question of how to rear them to be productive and happy members of society. Relevant issues in rearing a family include keeping parenthood in perspective, developing the prerequisites for effective parenting, and being aware of the needs of children and ways of meeting them. In addition, we will explore some skills in responding to basic child-rearing problems. In the final section of this chapter we will examine the unique concerns of single-parent families.

CHILD REARING IN PERSPECTIVE

Although rearing children is a major undertaking, it is helpful to keep it in perspective. In this section we view parenthood through a wide-angle lens.

Parenthood Is Only One Stage in Life

A phrase common among middle-aged parents is, "Before you know it, your children are grown and gone." While parents of infants sometimes feel that the sleepless nights will never end, they do end. Unlike the marriage relationship, the parent-child relationship moves toward separation. Just as the couple were alone before their children came, they will be alone again after the children leave. Except for occasional visits with their children and possibly grandchildren, the couple will return to a childfree life-style. Their income and evenings will once again be their own.

Typical parents are in their early fifties when their last child leaves home (Glick, 1977). Since the average woman can expect to live until she is eighty-one and the man until he is seventy-two, at a minimum the spouses whose marriages last will have about twenty years together after their children leave home. Hence, parenthood might be perceived for what it is—one stage in marriage and in life. Children will live with their parents for about 60 percent of the parents' marriage and about 40 percent of the parents' lives.

Parents Are Only One Influence in the Development of Their Children

While parents often take the credit and the blame for the way their children "turn out," they are only one among many influences. Peers, siblings, teachers, relatives, and the mass media are also influential. While parental influence is initially significant, peer influence becomes more important and remains so into the college years. For example, having a favorable attitude toward premarital sexual intercourse and having engaged in it are positively related to perceiving one's peers as having permissive sexual attitudes and behaviors (Walsh et al., 1976).

While siblings are not necessarily peers, they, too, have an important and sometimes lasting effect on each other's development (Sutton-Smith & Rosenberg, 1970). For example, an older sibling may sometimes be required to take care of a younger sibling. He or she may resent such responsibility and may not take adequate care of the younger sibling. One researcher suggested that siblings who act as parent surrogates are the least likely to demonstrate the essential qualities of good parenting (Essman, 1977). And, siblings who compete for the family's resources (parental attention, money, rooms), sometimes carry the rivalry into later life. However, sibling influence may also be positive. "I've always been close to my sister," remarked a middle-aged teacher. "She's the best friend I have."

Relatives may also be significant child-rearing agents. About 25 percent of children between the ages of three and six whose mothers are employed full time are cared for by a relative. Between the ages of seven and thirteen, relatives account for 18 percent of day-care supervision (U.S. Bureau of the Census, 1976, Table 6). The child's grandmothers and aunts are the most frequent caretakers.

Teachers become influential once a child begins school, and they remain so until at least age sixteen when school attendance is no longer compulsory. Since most teachers are middle class, they tend to stress the values of achievement, striving, and discipline. But teachers may have another effect on their students. In his classic article on parent-youth conflict, Kingsley Davis (1940) observed that teachers were competing authorities who were sometimes instrumental in widening the intellectual gap between parents and their children.

In addition to being influenced by peers, siblings, relatives, and teachers, children are affected by different environmental contexts. An only daughter adopted into an urban, Catholic, upper-class family in 1980 will be exposed to a different environmental context than a girl born into a rural, Protestant, working-class family with three boys during the Depression. Some of the potentially important variables in the family and environmental context include: geographic location; family size; whether a child is born or adopted into the family; whether a child is the oldest, youngest, or a middle sibling; what sex the children are; how many and which adults are in the household; how authoritarian or permissive the family is; what the family's social class, religion, and racial or ethnic background are; and whether the children and parents are mentally and physically healthy.

Table 17.1   Two Views of the Family and Parenting.

The New Breed—43%	The Traditionalists—57%
Not Important Values:	Very Important Values:
Marriage as an institution	Marriage as an institution
Religion	Religion
Saving money	Saving money
Patriotism	Hard work
Success	Financial security
Characteristics and Beliefs:	Characteristics and Beliefs:
Parents are self-oriented—not ready to sacrifice for their children	Parents are child-oriented—ready to sacrifice for their children
Parents don't push their children	Parents want their children to be outstanding
Parents have a laissez-faire attitude—children should be free to make their own decisions	Parents want to be in charge—believe parents should make decisions for their children
Parents question authority	Parents respect authority
Parent are permissive with their children	Parents are not permissive with their children
Parents believe boys and girls should be raised alike	Parents believe boys and girls should be raised differently
Parents believe their children have no future obligation to them	Parents believe old-fashioned upbringing is best
Parents see having children as an option, not a social responsibility	Parents see having children as a very important value

SOURCE: Adapted from General Mills, 1977, p. 28.

Parents View Parenting Differently

In addition to viewing parenthood in perspective and being aware of multiple influences, another point to keep in mind is that there is no consensus among parents about the "best" way to parent. Because parents are different ages, have been reared differently themselves, and have been exposed to different people and environments, they view the parent role differently. Using a national probability sample of 23 million American families with children under thirteen years of age, a team of researchers interviewed 1,230 adults and classified them according to their views about parenting and family values (General Mills, 1977). As Table 17.1 indicates, 43 percent of the parents (both fathers and mothers) could be classified as the "New Breed." These parents tended to be better educated and more affluent than the "Traditionalists" who represented 57 percent of those interviewed.

PREREQUISITES FOR EFFECTIVE PARENTING

Having stepped back to consider child rearing from a broader perspective than just wiping runny noses, let's explore several qualities which are essential for effective parenting—patience, balance, support, and knowledge.

You can learn many things from children. How much patience you have, for instance.

Franklin P. Jones

Patience

Babies see the world from one point of view—their own. And from their point of view, there is only one set of needs to be met—their own. When a baby wants milk, he or she wants it immediately and needs the compliance of parents to get it. No matter that one parent is on the phone and the other is taking a nap or busy with another child. Although babies can and eventually do learn to "take the role of the other" (Mead, 1934) or to see a situation from another's point of view, it takes time. Parents needs to be patient while their children learn.

Balance

While patience is essential for effective parenting, so is a balance of interests. Parents need to balance their own needs and concerns with those of their children. The Group for the Advancement of Psychiatry advises:

> Parents are not only vehicles for the care of their children. They were persons before the child arrived; are persons while they are parents; and will be after the children leave. . . . They were once told to listen to their parents. They are now told to listen to their children. Both directives are valuable. They must, in addition, listen to themselves. (GAP, 1973, pp. 131–2)

Other researchers agree:

> We assume that parents who are more satisfied people are better influences on their children. The mother who does not give up completely her outside interests—in sport, drama, music or whatever—when her children arrive is less likely to press

them into doing what she had to renounce; less likely to resent (even if unconsciously) the sacrifice she has had to make on their behalf; less likely to arouse their guilt at the sacrifices she has had to make for them and so on. (Rapoport et al., 1977, p. 26)

Support

Parents also need the support of their spouse, relatives, friends, and/or day-care personnel. Transforming a helpless infant into an independent adult is one of the most difficult jobs in the world. And it is an awesome job to do alone. Western society is somewhat unusual in insisting that children be reared solely by their parents. In most other societies, the extended kin are available and expected to regularly participate in child care. To the degree that a parent is surrounded by a stable support system, that parent can restore his or her own energy and continue to be an effective parent.

Knowledge

Knowledge of child development, child rearing, and child management procedures can also increase parental effectiveness. Physicians, psychologists, electricians, etc., are required to have extensive training and certification before they are allowed to set a broken leg, treat a depressed person, or wire a house. But our

The daily pressures of family life often call for extreme patience. But parents should not lose sight of their own needs, even when family demands seem more urgent.

Children need love—and their self-acceptance and interpersonal relationships throughout life will depend on this one thing above all others.

society encourages spouses to have children with little preparation or training. It is assumed that everyone has the temperament and resources to be an effective parent. In reality, some people are considerably more effective than others at rearing and managing children (Bush, 1978).

WHAT CHILDREN NEED

Knowledge of the needs of children might be considered a basic prerequisite to effective parenting. Although the needs vary at different ages and from child to child, the following discussion focuses on some of the more pervasive psychological needs. Such needs become significant after those for food and protection from disease and physical discomfort have been satisfied.

Love

A family life specialist wrote,

> This need [love] is met by the child experiencing from birth onwards a stable, continuous, dependable and loving relationship with his/her parents [or permanent parent-substitutes]. . . . Through this relationship—first with his/her mother, then his/her father and gradually an ever-widening circle of other people—the child comes to a realization of personal identity and worthwhileness. (Pringle, 1975, pp. 34–35)

In essence, a child with a positive self-concept has been surrounded by social mirrors (parents) who confirm their love, affection, and concern for him or her. In the absence of such positive feedback, the child is thrown to the wind to work out his or her own identity and to wonder if anyone cares. If a child concludes that no one does care, the feeling that he or she is not worth caring about is predictable. Children need a clear message that they are important, that they are loved, and that they belong. Such a feeling provides the basis for all later relationships (Kernberg, 1978). To be loved provides the capacity to love. To feel rejected and unwanted is to feel skeptical of everyone.

Security

Closely related to the need for love is security. In the "Peanuts" comic strip, Linus and his blanket have come to symbolize the need for security, order, and stability in a child's life. Predictable and consistent responses from parents, a familiar bedroom or playroom, and an established routine encourage a feeling of security in children. Such a feeling provides them with the needed self-assurance to venture beyond the family. If the outside world becomes too frightening or difficult, a child can return to the safety of the family for support. Knowing that it is always possible to return to an accepting environment enables a child to become more involved gradually with the world beyond the family.

Exposure To New Experiences

Given a stable love relationship and a feeling of security, children develop delight in exploring their environment. And, they should be encouraged to do so. "If denied the opportunity of new experiences, no learning can take place" (Pringle, 1975, p. 43). Banging mobiles, shaking rattles, and crawling involve experience with sight, touch, sound, and muscle coordination. But with exposure must come help from the parents in labeling the environment. This means language. By their talking with infants about what they are experiencing (Hear the phone ring?), parents enable their children to name and organize their environment.

Praise

In addition to encouraging children to explore their environment, parents can give praise and recognition for positive accomplishments. Praise can be used to develop a range of desirable behaviors. The boy who is told that he is polite for not interrupting grandma when she is talking is likely to think of himself as a polite person and to avoid interrupting in the future. Children (as well as adults) need praise to develop a sense of accomplishment and to learn which behaviors are desirable.

Discipline

The other side of praise is disapproval. The parents of eight observed:

> The most difficult aspect of being a loving parent is to develop the ability to sometimes withhold overt acts of love (ignore or disapprove) to help the child learn appropriate ways to behave. When love responses between parent and child have been previously established, we can then respond in similar kind to the child's behavior. Thus, if a child misbehaves and we actively withhold our overt responses of love, we then teach the child that his behavior does not deserve to be followed by love responses from us. The most tragic mistakes of the parent occur when the courage to act in this way is absent, and the parent succumbs to "giving in." (Madsen & Madsen, 1975)

Since our society does not approve of various behaviors (stealing, talking loudly in a restaurant or movie, throwing a tantrum), it is important that children be disciplined so as to learn the socially approved behaviors. It is equally important that children learn that disapproval of specific behavior does not imply personal rejection. Parents must make clear that while they may disapprove of their child's behavior and withhold privileges as a means of discipline, they love their child.

Responsibility

While disciplining children helps them to learn appropriate behaviors for acceptance and survival in society, giving them increased responsibility encourages the autonomy and independence necessary to stand on their own. As children grow older, giving them more responsibility means permitting increased freedom "of taste in food, play, and clothes; and perhaps most important of all, of choice of friends, studies, hobbies, career, and eventually marriage partner" (Pringle, 1975, p. 55). Children who are not given more control and responsibility for their own lives remain dependent. Successful parents are defined in terms of their ability to rear children who can function as independent adults. One way to ensure such success is to give children increasing responsibility as they grow up.

In summary, the needs of children include love, security, exposure, praise, discipline, and responsibility. But parents should not become frantic in their own need to satisfy the needs of their children. As one psychologist pointed out:

> Children do not require any specific actions from adults in order to develop optimally. There is no good evidence to indicate that children must have a certain amount or schedule of cuddling, kissing, spanking, holding or deprivation of privileges in order to become gratified and productive adults. The child does have some psychological needs, but there is no fixed list of parental behaviors that can be counted on to fill these critical requirements. (Kagan, 1976, p. 88)

Parents should also be aware that they do not have total control over how their child turns out—many factors and other people play a part in it.

APPROACHES TO CHILD REARING

Given the needs of children and the limitations of parents in supplying those needs, we now explore five alternate approaches to child rearing.[1] In essence, parents are responsible for socializing their offspring. While socializing may be defined as "transforming infants from helpless newborns into adults helpful to themselves and others" (Koller, 1974, p. 264), there is no one or best theory for accomplishing this. As a Harvard team concluded after measuring the maturity levels achieved by some young adults who had been reared by various child-rearing methods, "most of what people do and think and believe as adults is not determined by specific techniques of child rearing in the first five years" (McClelland et al., 1978, p. 45). In addition, what works with one child may not work with another. It may not even work with the same child at two different times.

Gesell's Developmental-Maturational Approach

For the past fifty years, Dr. Arnold Gesell and his colleagues at the Yale Clinic of Child Development have been known for their ages-and-stages approach to child rearing. Their developmental-maturational approach has been one of the most widely used in the United States. Let's examine the basic perspective of this approach, its implications for child rearing, and some criticisms of the approach.

Basic perspective.[2]   Gesell theorizes that what a child does, thinks, and feels is the result of genetic inheritance. Although genes dictate the gradual unfolding of a unique personality, every individual passes through the same basic pattern of growth. This pattern involves four aspects of development—motor behavior (sitting, crawling, walking), adaptive behavior (picking up objects, walking around objects), language behavior (words and gestures), and personal-social behavior (cooperativeness, helpfulness). Through observation of hundreds of normal infants and children, Gesell and his co-workers identified norms of development. While there may be tremendous variations, these norms suggest the ages at which an average child displays various behaviors. For example, most infants begin to walk between the ninth and fifteenth month and to talk between the eighteenth and thirtieth month.

Implications for parents.   Gesell suggests that if parents are aware of the developmental clock in their children they will avoid unreasonable expectations. A child cannot walk or talk until the neurological structures necessary for those behaviors have matured. In addition, the hunger of a four-week-old can only be cured by food. But at sixteen to twenty-eight weeks the child has some capacity to wait because the hunger pangs are less intense.

In view of the biological/genetic clock of the infant, Gesell suggests that the infant's needs be cared for on a demand schedule. Instead of having to submit to a schedule imposed by parents, infants on a demand schedule are fed, changed, put to bed, and allowed to play when they want. Parents are admonished that they are "likely to find that difficulties increase when they impose a hard-and-fast schedule without responding to the maturational level of the child" (Mead, 1976, p. 44).

In addition to focusing on the ages-and-stages of child development and the need for a demand schedule of child care, Gesell alerts parents to the importance of the first years of the child's life. In Gesell's view, these early years assume the greatest significance since this is when the child's first learning experiences with the environment occur.

Criticisms of the developmental-maturational approach.   Gesell's work has been criticized because of: (1) its overemphasis on a genetic/biological clock; (2) the merits of the sample he used to develop maturational norms; and (3) his insistence on the merits of a demand schedule. Regarding his assumption that all human behavior may be traced to growth and development, it "seems to hold very well as long as one confines his attention to physical growth and maturation. However, when Gesell and his coauthors turn to the vast array of adaptive behavior acquired through interaction with the environment, the focus upon genetic influences to the almost total exclusion of the control exerted by environmental factors seems unjustified" (Mead, 1976, p. 45).

In addition, the children he studied to establish the developmental norms were mostly from the upper-middle class (Stolz, 1958). Children in different classes are exposed to different environments which influence their personalities. Norms established on upper-middle-class children may not adequately reflect those of children from other social classes.

While parents may not be too concerned about the developmental norms in reference to social class, they may be quite concerned about the suggestion that they do everything for the infant when the infant wants. Rearing an infant on the demand schedule can drastically interfere with the parents' personal and marital interests. As a result, most American parents feed their infants on a demand schedule but put them to bed to fit the parents' schedule (Shea, 1978).

Piaget's Cognitive-Developmental Approach

Jean Piaget, a Swiss psychologist, is the name most frequently associated with the cognitive-developmental approach to child rearing. Until recently, his work was largely ignored by the larger scientific community (Mead, 1976, p. 66). Let's examine Piaget's perspective, the implications for parents, and criticisms of the approach.

Basic perspective.[3]   Like Gesell, Piaget believes that development progresses in an orderly way through predictable stages. But Piaget is primarily concerned about the development of intelligence. And, rather than viewing such cognitive development as basically a function of genetic inheritance, Piaget believes that interaction with the environment is the key. The child's best teacher is experience.

Piaget stresses that experience is necessary at each of the cognitive-developmental stages. These include the sensorimotor, preoperational thought, concrete operations, and formal operational periods of development. During the sensorimotor period, which lasts from birth to approximately two years, the child learns "what he can do to and with the environment" (Mead, 1976, p. 86). Developing the skill to locate an object in space and coordinate the hands to pick it up is an example.

During the preoperational thought stage, which lasts from age two to seven, the child develops the capacity think about the external world internally. For example, he or she will develop an internal symbolic map of the rooms in the house rather than be dependent on going into each room to know where thay are or how they look.

The concrete operations period extends from seven to eleven and involves learning about the physical world and the nature of the environment—for example, learning to tell time, judging distances, and verifying cause and effect (glass will break if dropped on a solid surface). The final period, formal operations, extends from eleven to fifteen and involves more abstract thought such as predicting the probability of a given event.

Implications for parents.   Piaget did not give specific child-rearing advice. "The efforts of American educators to speed up the rate of cognitive development are a futile exercise in technology according to Piaget(Zimbardo & Ruch, 1975, p. 194). He believed that children should be allowed to develop their own cognitive skills naturally. Nevertheless, educators impressed with Piaget's work have extrapolated from his theory and suggested guidelines for child rearing.

For example, one child development specialist and father of three suggested one hundred Piaget-based activities for the first two years of life (Lehane, 1976). "Playing cars" is one such activity:

> Get a hard cover book and some little cars and trucks. Rest a car on the book. Does your baby press down and grind the toy? Now open the cover a bit so the toy is resting on top of a slight incline. Just a slight touch on the car by your baby should cause it to roll forward. Does this happen? What is his reaction? Play with this incline a few more times. Then close the cover. Does your baby still just give the car a little tap? If he starts using the incline, this means he's truly grasped the idea of momentum. (Lehane, 1976, p. 149)

Criticisms of the cognitive-developmental approach.   A basic criticism of Piaget's work comes more from professionals than lay parents. This criticism is in reference to the existence of stages. Although Piaget outlined discrete stages of cognitive development, some researchers question whether they exist or whether they are arbitrary divisions (Zeigler & Child, 1973).

Skinner's Behavior Modification Approach

Based on the work of B. F. Skinner, a relatively new behavioral approach to child rearing has evolved. Only within the last fifteen years have parents begun to use its principles in a systematic way. Let's look at the basic perspective, implications, and criticisms of this approach to child rearing.

Basic perspective.[4]   Aside from genetic and biochemical influences, behavior is learned through classical and operant conditioning. Classical conditioning involves presenting a stimulus with a reinforcer. For example, an infant comes to associate the face of his or her parents with food, warmth, and comfort. While initially only the food and feeling of being held will satisfy the infant, later, just the approach of the parent will soothe the infant. This occurrence may be observed when a mother hands her infant to a stranger. The infant may cry because the stranger is not associated with pleasant events. But when the stranger hands the infant back to the parent, the crying may subside because the parent represents positive events and is a stimulus associated with them.

Other behaviors are learned through operant conditioning which focuses on the consequences of behavior. Two rules of learning are basic to the operant explanation of behavior—reward and punishment. The reward rule says that behaviors which are followed by a positive consequence will increase. If the goal is to teach a child to say "please," doing what the child requests only after he or she says "please" will increase the use of "please" by the child. Rewards may be in the form of attention, praise, activities (let's go to the pool), toys, or candy. Whatever consequence (e.g., attention) increases the chance of something happening (saying please) is, by definition, a reward.

The punishment rule is the opposite of the reward rule. A behavior that is followed by a negative consequence will decrease that behavior. Putting the child in isolation (called "time out") for ten minutes following an undesirable behavior will decrease that behavior. If the goal is to stop a girl from sticking out her tongue, putting her in "time out" for ten minutes after each occurrence will decrease the behavior. The most effective way to change behavior is to use the reward and punishment rules together to influence a specific behavior. When the child does not stick out her tongue, she is rewarded, and every time she does stick out her tongue, she is punished.

Implications for parents.   A common question among parents is, "Why does my child act this way and what can I do to change it?" The behavioral approach to child rearing suggests the answer to both—the child's behavior has been learned in that the child has been rewarded for the behavior; the child's behavior can be changed by eliminating the reward for the undesirable behavior and rewarding the desirable behavior. The child who cries when his or her parents are about to leave for a movie is often reinforced for crying by the parents' staying longer. To teach the child not to cry when the parents leave, the parents should reward the child for not crying when they are gone for progressively longer periods of time. For example, they should initially tell the child that they are going around the house and that they will give the child a treat when they get back if he or she plays until they return. The parents might then walk around the house and reward the child for not crying. If the child cries, they should be out of sight for only a few seconds and gradually increase the amount of time they are away (Madsen & Madsen, 1975, p. 113). The essential point is that children learn to cry or not depending on the consequences of crying. Since children will learn what they are taught, parents might systematically structure learning experiences to achieve the behavioral goals they want. Recent books which explain how parents can use the principles of learning in rearing their children include those by Madsen and Madsen (1975), Patterson (1976), and Rinn and Markle (1977).

Criticisms of the behavior modification approach.   Professionals and parents have attacked the behavioral approach to child rearing on the basis that it is deceptively simple, manipulative, and does not take into account cognitive issues. Often presented as an easy-to-use set of procedures for child management, many parents do not have the background or skill to use the procedures correctly. What constitutes an effective reward or punishment, presented in what way, in what situation, with what child, to influence what behavior are decisions which need to be made before attempting to increase or decrease the frequency of a behavior. But parents sometimes do not know the questions to ask or lack the training to make wise decisions in the use of behavioral procedures. One parent locked her son in the closet for an hour to punish him for lying to her a week earlier—a gross misuse of learning principles.

Skinner and his colleagues have also been criticized because their procedures are viewed as manipulative and controlling (Nye, 1975). Such deliberate control of human behavior has been denounced as devaluing human individuality.

Finally, the behavioral approach has been criticized because it does not adequately allow for thought processes as they influence behavior. One researcher argues that thoughts intervene and affect the individual's behavior in ways which are not explained by strict conditioning principles (Mahoney, 1974). For example, two children may perceive the same situation differently based on their respective learning histories. One child may become upset when he sees a little white mouse (if his past experience included being bitten), while another child may be delighted by the same mouse (if the mouse resembles a pet gerbil).

Gordon's Parent Effectiveness Training Approach

As B. F. Skinner is to behavior modification, so Thomas Gordon is to Parent Effectiveness Training. It is the largest of parent training programs with over 8,000 instructors and 250,000 trained parents (Brown, 1976).

Basic perspective.[5] Parent effectiveness training is based on Carl Rogers' existential-phenomenological theory. Rogers' theory focuses on what the individual is feeling and experiencing in the here and now—how he or she "sees" the world (Rogers, 1951). The theory also focuses on the development of one's self-concept and the development of each person's potential, of self-actualization. A positive self-concept is the result of other people reflecting positive images to that individual—letting the person know they like, admire, or approve of him or her. Rogers and his colleagues view how parents respond to children as critical to the development of the children's positive self-concept and self-love.

The term *self-actualization* refers to the individual's constant striving, at cognitive, emotional, social, and physical levels, to develop his or her full potential (Maslow, 1962). "Actualization is a state of being or becoming. The person is not static or stationary, but is always shifting to and from a state of more or less actualization. To be more fully actualized is the universal goal" (Mead, 1976, p. 94).

Implications for parents.   To assist in the development of a positive self-concept and in the self-actualization of both children and parents, Gordon makes a number of specific recommendations. These include managing the environment, engaging in active listening, using "I messages," and resolving conflicts through mutual negotiation. Environmental management by parents includes putting breakables out of reach, but towel racks and toy boxes within reach. It is sometimes easier and safer to manage the environment and not just the child.

The use of active listening becomes important when the child is much older. When Molly is upset with her teacher, it's better for the parent to reflect Molly's thoughts back to her than to take sides with her. By saying, "You're angry because Mrs. Jones made the whole class miss play period because Rebecca was

Active listening is a central component of the parent effectiveness training approach, and it plays an important part in resolving family problems in mutually acceptable ways.

chewing gum," rather than saying, "Mrs. Jones is unfair and shouldn't have made the whole class miss play period," shows empathy with the child without blaming the teacher.

In addition to managing the environment and listening actively, Gordon suggests using, "I" rather than "you" messages. Parents are encouraged to say, "I get upset when you're late and don't call," rather than, "You're an insensitive, irresponsible person for not calling me when you said you would." The former avoids damaging the child's self-concept while still encouraging the desired behavior.

Gordon's fourth and most controversial suggestion for parenting is the no-lose method of resolving conflicts. He rejects the use of power by parent or child. In the authoritarian home, the parent dictates what the child is to do and the child is expected to obey. In this system, the parent wins and the child loses. On the other extreme is the permissive home in which the child wins and the parent loses. The alternative, Gordon suggests, is for the parent and child to seek a solution that is acceptable to both and to keep trying until they find one. In this way, neither parent nor child loses and both win.

Criticisms of the parent effectiveness training approach.   While much is commendable about Gordon's approach to child rearing, parents may have problems with two of his suggestions. First, he suggests that, because older children have a right to their own values, parents should not interfere with their hairstyle, dress, career plans, and sexual behavior. Some parents may feel they do have a right to "interfere."

Second, Gordon's no-lose method of resolving conflict is sometimes unrealis-

"Father would be much happier if you wouldn't."

tic. Suppose a sixteen-year-old wants to spend the weekend at the beach with her boyfriend and her parents do not want her to do so. Gordon says to negotiate until a decision is reached that is acceptable to both. But how are the parents and a sixteen-year-old to negotiate? What if neither the parents nor the daughter can suggest a compromise or shift their position? To encourage parents to find a mutually agreeable solution is commendable, but the mechanics are unclear.

Adler's and Dreikurs' Socio-Teleological Approach

Alfred Adler, a physician and former student of Sigmund Freud, saw a parallel between psychological development and physical development. When a person loses his or her sight, the other senses (hearing, touch, taste) become more sensitive—they compensate for the loss. According to Adler, the same occurs in the psychological realm. When an individual feels inferior in one area, he or she will strive to compensate and become superior in another. Rudolph Dreikurs, a student of Adler, developed an approach to child rearing designed to alert parents to how their children might be trying to compensate for feelings of inferiority. Dreikurs' suggestions are based on Adler's theory.

Basic perspective.[6] According to Adler, it is easy for most children to feel that they are inferior and weak. "The small child, unable to control many events in his environment, stands in awe of the magical, powerful adults who so easily open doors or get drinks from taps far above the child's head" (Mead, 1976, p.47). Because children feel powerless in a sea of adult superiority, they try to compensate by gaining attention (making noise, becoming disruptive), exerting power (becoming aggressive, hostile), seeking revenge (becoming violent, hurting others), and acting inadequate (giving up, not trying). Adler suggested that such misbehavior is evidence that the child is discouraged or feels insecure about his or her place in the family. The term *socio-teleological* literally refers to social striving or seeking a social goal. In this case, the child is viewed as seeking a secure place within the family.

Implications for parents. When parents observe such misbehavior in their children, they should recognize it not as an attempt to be mean but as an attempt to gain a feeling of security in the family. According to Dreikurs, parents should not fall into playing the child's game, but should encourage the child, hold regular family councils, and let natural consequences occur. To encourage the child, the parents should be willing to let the child make mistakes. If Johnny wants to help Dad carry logs for the fireplace, rather than Dad's saying "You're too small to carry the logs," Johnny should be allowed to try. And Dad should give Johnny a small log that he can carry and praise him for his strength and cooperativeness.

Along with constant encouragement, the child should be included in a weekly family council. During this meeting, family problems such as bedtime, the appropriateness of snacks, and assignment of chores are discussed. Since the meeting is democratic, each family member has a vote. Such participation in family decision making is designed to enhance the self-concept of each child.

In addition to encouragement and family councils, Dreikurs suggests that the parents let natural consequences occur for their child's behavior. If a daughter misses the school bus, she walks or is charged "taxi fare" out of her allowance. If she won't wear a coat and boots, she gets cold and wet. If a son won't clean his room, he eventually lives in filth. If he won't bathe, he hears from the other kids that he's dirty and smells (Brown, 1976, p. 111). Of course, parents are to arrange suitable consequences where natural consequences either will not occur or would be dangerous. For example, a child who draws on the walls will have the crayons taken away.

Criticisms of the socio-teleological approach. This approach to child rearing has been criticized because of its lack of empirical research and its occasional impracticality. Regarding research, "The approach has been used and 'tested' clinically, but such research does not impress the empirical-minded. Science tends to pass over theories which fail to demonstrate their usefulness in predicting specific outcomes which can be demonstrated in nature" (Mead, 1976, p. 63). It is fair to say that some of the other child-rearing approaches already discussed also lack solid empirical support.

The impracticality of the socio-teleological approach is illustrated in letting the child take natural consequences. While this is an effective child-rearing procedure for most behaviors, it can backfire. Letting the child catch cold to teach the importance of a raincoat is questionable.

CHILD-REARING PROBLEMS

Having reviewed five of the major child-rearing theories, we now identify major problems parents report having with their children and suggest how these might be resolved using some of these approaches. Table 17.2 lists some "nagging problems in raising children who are twelve years or under" which a national random sample of parents identified.

Between Meal Snacks

Listed as the number one problem of all parents, between-meal snacks tend to interfere with eating a nourishing lunch or supper. The child who eats cookies or candy at four o'clock will rarely be hungry at six. Some potential solutions follow.

Skinner's behavioral approach. Assuming that a six-year-old child had lunch at noon, a behaviorist might suggest that he or she be allowed to eat half a banana or a comparable snack around three o'clock so as to prevent the child

TABLE 17.2   Ten Major Nagging Problems in Raising Children Who Are 12 Years or Under.

	Percent of All Parents	Percent of Parents Having Only Children Under 6 Years
Children filling up on snacks between meals	32	28
Children crying and whining	30	42
Children not eating what they should	27	27
Children always asking for things they see advertised	26	23
Children being irresponsible—not doing their chores	26	6
Children talking back and being disrespectful	26	20
Children having temper tantrums	24	35
Children watching too much television	23	9
Children not going to bed on time	23	21
Children not telling the truth	16	12

SOURCE: General Mills, 1977, p. 96

from becoming ravenous by six. The child would not be allowed to eat cookies or candy as a snack, and he or she would be punished (perhaps with "time out") for doing so. And, on subsequent days, the privilege of playing with peers would be contingent on not eating cookies or candy between meals. A behaviorist would suggest that if the parents want their child to eat at regular mealtimes, consequences must be used to control for eating unlimited snack foods between meals. Children should also be rewarded for eating properly.

Gordon's parent effectiveness training approach.   A parent who has had parent effectiveness training might say something to the child like, "It upsets me when you eat cookies and candy in the late afternoon and don't eat a good supper," and try to elicit the child's cooperation in limiting snacks and eating a good supper. At all costs, even if the child continued to eat cookies at four, Gordon would suggest that the parent not force the child to discontinue snacks or to eat a good supper. If the issue became too much of a conflict, Gordon might suggest that the child had a right to choose what to eat and for the parent to stop interfering.

Crying and Whining

Crying and whining is the second most frequently mentioned problem of all parents with children under twelve and the number one problem for parents with children under six.

Gesell's developmental-maturational approach. Suppose an infant begins to cry when his parents put him to bed. Gesell might suggest that the infant should determine his own schedule and that the crying indicates he is not sleepy. Only an older child has the maturity to conform to a predetermined schedule.

Piaget's cognitive-developmental approach. Piaget would view a certain amount of crying and noise-making as necessary prevocal activity. By exercising the vocal cords, the child "practices" and gets ready to use speech when the other neurological structures are ready.

Adler's and Dreikurs' socio-teleological approach. Dreikurs would view the child's crying as an attempt to control the parents and suggest that they let the child cry until he or she naturally stopped. The natural consequence of crying is to get tired of doing so.

Request for Advertised Items

Over a quarter of the parents reported that their children were always asking them for items they had seen advertised.

Gordon's parent effectiveness training approach. Gordon would probably suggest that parents communicate empathy with their child's request for certain advertised items. "You really would like to have a plastic robot, wouldn't you?" And if the child insists, the parents might negotiate a way for the child to get the robot. On the other hand, the parents might be annoyed by the insistent requests and say, "It makes me angry that you ask me to buy you things you see on television. The plastic robot would not be a good toy because it would break easily."

Skinner's behavioral approach. In contrast to Gordon, Skinner might view the child's constant requests for advertised items as a learned undesirable behavior and set up contingencies (rewards and punishments) to change that behavior. For example, the parent might say to the child, "If you make no requests for an advertised item for one week, I'll take you to the movie of your choice on Saturday. If you do make a request before the week is over, we will not go to the movie this weekend and you must rake leaves."

A messy room might be the natural consequence of this girl's living habits. If her parents follow the socio-teleological approach, they'll overlook the disarray and let their daughter alter the situation when she feels a need to do so.

Being Irresponsible (Not Doing Chores)

While irresponsibility is not a major issue for parents with children under six, it eventually becomes an issue for a quarter of all parents.

Skinner's behavioral approach. For Skinner, getting children to do their chores is simple—reward them by letting them do what they want to do (watch television, play, or whatever) only after they have done their chores. After Elizabeth makes her bed she can watch television.

Adler's and Dreikurs' socio-teleological approach. At a family council meeting, the parents would discuss the necessity of certain chores being performed in order for the household to function smoothly. The children would then have an opportunity to select certain chores they would do as a gesture toward helping other family members. If they did not wish to cooperate, the natural consequence might be that other family members would stop cooperating with them.

FIGURE 17.1 Three Disciplinary Patterns.

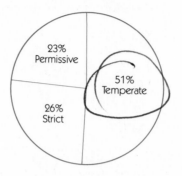

*Index is based on responses to three questions including self-appraisal, attitude toward old-fashioned discipline, and physical punishment.

SOURCE: General Mills, 1977, p. 101.

The Question of Discipline

In resolving any of the child-rearing problems mentioned above, parents will have a particular attitude toward discipline. But parents do not agree on what is an appropriate amount and form of discipline. Figure 17.1 reflects the three patterns of discipline which parents in a national random sample said they favored.

Parents who regard themselves as strict (26 percent) make no apologies for their "old-fashioned" disciplinary procedures. They believe that to spare the rod is to spoil the child. This attitude was particularly prevalent around the turn of the century (Osborn & Osborn, 1978). The 23 percent of the parents who regard themselves as permissive "recognize themselves as being less strict than most parents, reject the idea that old-fashioned discipline is the best way to raise children and question whether a good spanking is the best way to teach a child the difference between right and wrong" (General Mills, 1977, p. 101). Between the strict and permissive are the temperate parents. They represent over half the parents and feel that both extremes are undesirable. "You've got to be middle of the road with how you rear kids," expressed one parent. "If you're too strict, they'll rebel and leave home as soon as they can. If you're too lenient, they won't respect you and will run over you. It's a fine line for every parent."

Some disciplinary actions parents report taking are given in Table 17.3. While both parents together do 40 percent of the disciplining, mothers do more alone than do fathers (35 compared to 24 percent) (General Mills, 1977, p. 104). And, just as parents punish their children when they do something bad, they reward them when they do something good. Examples of such rewards include taking the children somewhere special, buying them something special, giving them something special to eat, giving them money, and letting them watch television (p. 107).

TABLE 17.3 Percentage of Parents Reporting Use of Various Disciplinary Measures.

Disciplinary Measures	Percentage Using
Yelling at or scolding the children	52
Spanking them	50
Making them stay in their rooms	38
Not allowing them to go out to play	32
Not letting them watch television	25
Making them go to bed	23
Threatening them	15
Giving them extra chores	12
Taking away their allowances	9

SOURCE: Adapted from General Mills, 1977, p. 104.

ISSUES CONCERNING PARENTS

Beyond dealing with specific child-rearing problems, parents are concerned about the effect on child rearing of the society at large, day care, public education, television, and nutrition.

Most parents view troubles in the society at large as the biggest problem they have in child rearing. Seventy-two percent of the parents in the national sample already referred to were dissatisfied with the standards of our society (General Mills, 1977, p. 35). Specifically, they expressed concern about the use of illegal drugs,[7] street crime, inflation, and broken marriages.

Parents are also concerned about the care their children receive in day-care centers. Over half (51 percent) feel that they can never be sure how their children will be treated (General Mills, 1977, p. 38). Perhaps this feeling is reflected in the fact that only 6 percent of children ages three to six whose mothers are employed full-time are enrolled in day-care centers (U.S. Bureau of the Census, 1976, p. 9).

Parental concern continues when their children move beyond the day-care center into public education. Forty percent believe that they cannot count on the schools to teach their children how to read and write (General Mills, 1977, p. 111). Other parents feel frustrated by forced busing, crowded schools, and the general disarray of our public education system.

While children spend about twelve thousand hours in school by the time they graduate from high school, they also devote an average of about fifteen thousand hours to watching television during the same years. This time is roughly equivalent to spending two full years, twenty-four hours a day, sitting in front of the television screen (Lesser, 1976, p. 320). While 23 percent of parents feel that television is a bad influence on their children, 73 percent believe that their children have learned a lot of good things by watching television (General Mills, 1977, p. 116). "It can show children things they have never seen, sounds they have never heard, people and ideas they have not yet imagined. It can show them how things work, how other people use them, what goes on in the world . . ." (Lesser, 1976, p. 325). Family life educators have also noted the potential uses and positive effects of television (Lieberman & Lieberman, 1977).

Parents are also extremely concerned about their children being overweight. Sixty-two percent expressed such a concern in the General Mills survey (p. 111). Parents who are college graduates are especially concerned. Seventy-four percent felt that something should be done to ensure that children do not become overweight.

In spite of the problems parents experience in rearing their children or the issues they are concerned about, most feel that they are doing a good job. Sixty-three percent report feeling good about the job they are doing in raising their children while 36 percent worry about the job they are doing (General Mills, 1977, p. 63).

SINGLE-PARENT FAMILIES

The problems and issues discussed above are common to most parents, but they may be especially troublesome to a single parent caring for children alone. Single parents must economically support their families, provide supervision and child care, and meet their children's emotional needs without the help of another adult in the home. About 20 percent of all families are headed by a single parent (15 percent of white families and 50 percent of black families) (U.S. Bureau of the Census, 1977, p. 6). And while the number of single fathers is increasing, most single parents (over 85 percent) are women.

Types

The typical single-parent family consists of a divorced mother and her two children. However, divorce is not the only mechanism for becoming a single parent. Single parents may be separated, widowed, or never-married men or women. They may have had their children naturally or through adoption. And, of course, a single-parent family could have from one to many children.

Problems

Single parents report feeling less adequate than dual husband-wife parents in rearing their children (General Mills, 1977, p. 40). Some specific problems are related to money, child care and supervision, the stigma of an "incomplete" family, social

Working single parents face quite a challenge—earning a good family income, keeping up a home, and still sharing time and emotional closeness with their children.

isolation, and satisfaction of the children's emotional needs. Although the number of divorced fathers who have custody of their children is increasing, it remains true that most children (90 percent) live with their mothers after a divorce (Hetherington et al., 1976). For this reason, our discussion of single-parent problems will focus on those of single mothers.

Money.   In general, when either parent leaves, the family's standard of living drops. The traditional housewife and mother who previously depended on her husband for money must now find employment to earn the money he formerly supplied. Even though the father may pay alimony and child support, such payments are rarely enough. And since enforcement of child support rulings is difficult, many women must cope with late or missed payments and face the possibility that the father might quit sending money at any time. "The family broken by death, desertion, separation, or divorce characteristically is headed by a woman and falls into the lower-income groups" (Feldman, 1976, p. 154). In 1976, the median income of families headed by women was $7,211; for families headed by men the median income was $16,095 (U.S. Bureau of the Census, 1977, p. 443). While employment is one way to get income, some women are supported by their relatives and others rely on welfare payments (Brandwein et al., 1974).

Child care and supervision.   For the divorced woman who is employed full time, supervision of her children (particularly preschool) must continue. This is often performed by a relative or hired sitter in the sitter's or relative's home (U.S. Bureau of the Census, 1976, p. 9). When such child-care services must be paid for, it may take a large slice out of the woman's already modest income.

Stigmatization.   In addition to decreased income and the arranging for child care and supervision, single-parent families must often contend with disapproval from society. Such families are often described as "broken," "disorganized" or "disintegrated." The terms "motherless" and "fatherless" clearly imply that "something" is missing and abnormal.

> Stigmatization is multifaceted. Stigma is ascribed to divorced and separated women for their presumed inability to keep their men. The societal myth of the gay divorcee out to seduce other women's husbands leads to social ostracism of the divorced woman and her family (Brandwein et al., 1974, p. 499).

Social isolation.   As just noted, stigmatization often results in social isolation and loneliness among single parents (Schlesinger, 1977, p. 140). Because they are considered deviant, they may be treated as though they don't exist. Dinner invitations may not be issued and efforts by neighbors to get to know them may not be great. Organizations such as Parents Without Partners[8] have emerged to provide a sense of community and support for single parents.

Satisfaction of emotional needs of children.   Perhaps the greatest challenge for single parents is to satisfy the emotional needs of their children—alone. When one parent leaves, the other must make a convincing demonstration of his or her own love and reliability. In the case of the father who has custody of his children, he must communicate that "Daddy is here, and Daddy is staying. Daddy will not leave" (Despert, 1953, p. 48).

TRENDS

Trends in child rearing include more single-parent families, more fathers being single parents, greater involvement by families in family enrichment programs, and less authoritative child-rearing discipline procedures. In addition to single-parent families created out of divorce, more never-married individuals are seeking to adopt children (Kopecky, 1977) or to have them even though they are not married. For example, a computer programmer and analyst expressed the desire to have and rear a child of her own without the "hassle" of a spouse (Whiteside, 1974).

While there will be an overall increase in the number of single-parent families (and less stigmatization), more fathers will seek custody of their children in divorce settlements (Mendes, 1976). Dr. Ken Lewis, a divorced father of two daughters, won custody of his children on the grounds that the word "mother" is a verb and that he had demonstrated better "mothering skills" than the biological mother. He also noted that the "tender years" doctrine which automatically gives custody to the mother during the child's "tender years" is an insidious example of sex discrimination (Lewis, 1977). Single men are also adopting children with increasing frequency (Levine, 1978).

In addition to an increase in single-parent families, including single fathers, there will be an increase in the number of families who become involved in family enrichment programs. Defined as "three to five families who meet together regularly and frequently for mutual care and support and for the development of family potential" (Anderson, 1974, p. 7), family growth groups may involve a weekend (Wilson & Wilson, 1976) or an extended camping experience (Branch, 1976). Such experiences reflect an increasing willingness of families to "go public" with their mutual concerns.

Finally, a new trend in child discipline may be in the offing. One psychologist observed that regular spankings and phrases like "Because I said so!" will be replaced by positive rewards, parent-child contracts, and family councils (Dodson, 1978).

SUMMARY

While parenthood is a major role in life, it should be kept in perspective. It is only one of several stages in the life of an individual and in a marriage. Furthermore, parents are only one among several influences in the lives of their children. Peers, siblings, teachers, and relatives may also have significant input. In addition, how parents view their role may vary from being very child-oriented to very self-oriented.

Spouses are frequently not well prepared to fill the parent role. Effective parenting requires abundant patience, balanced interests, support from the spouse and others, and knowledge. Such knowledge includes an awareness of what children need—love, security, exposure to new experiences, praise, discipline, and responsibility. The most important of these needs is love. Children who feel that they are important, that they belong, and that they are loved have a positive basis for all other relationships.

To assist parents in providing for their children's needs, a number of researchers have suggested ways of viewing child development and resolving some of the problems. Gesell is known for his ages-and-stages approach in which he developed maturational norms for children. By referring to these norms, parents can develop reasonable expectations for their children. In essence, the child cannot be expected to walk or talk before the neurological structures necessary for those behaviors have developed.

Piaget also focused on development occurring through predictable stages. But his concern was with intelligence and cognitive development and the child's ability to think in various ways at various maturational levels.

Unlike Gesell and Piaget, Skinner and other behaviorists have emphasized that children learn the various behaviors they engage in as a result of classical and operant conditioning. In essence, parents can teach their children what they want them to learn by systematically applying learning principles.

Gordon's approach represents the largest parent training program in the United States. Parents are encouraged to be concerned about their child's self-concept and self-actualization needs. Gordon's parent effectiveness program includes parental management of the environment, engaging in active listening, using "I" messages, and resolving conflicts.

Adler and Dreikurs emphasized that children's feelings of inferiority are the basis of their misbehavior (being aggressive, noisy, disruptive). By encouraging a child, holding family councils, and letting the child face the natural consequences of actions, parents can enhance the child's security about his or her place in the family.

While parents are concerned about resolving various specific child-rearing problems (eating snacks, crying and whining, etc.), they are also concerned about day-care facilities, public education, and television. In addition to these concerns, single-parent families often face extra economic difficulties, stigmatization, and social isolation.

Trends in child rearing include an increase in the number of single-parent families, more single fathers, and greater involvement of families in family enrichment programs. The latter may occur with neighborhood families or in workshops where families from the community congregate.

STUDY QUESTIONS

1. What percent of an individual's life and marriage is usually spent in the role of parent? What is the implication of these percentages?
2. Other than parent, discuss four categories of people who are influential in a child's socialization.
3. Identify several environmental contexts which will have an influence on childhood experiences.
4. Parents may be described as being "traditionalists" or "the new breed." Comment on the values and characteristics of these two types.
5. Why is patience an essential quality for effective parenting?
6. "Parents need to listen to themselves as well as to their children." Discuss the implications of this statement.

7. How is Western society somewhat unusual in its child-care support system?
8. How do the consequences of rearing a child in an atmosphere of love and security differ from those of rearing a child in an atmosphere of hostility and unpredictable change?
9. Why is exposure—both sensory and verbal—essential to a child's development?
10. How is responsibility related to teaching independence?
11. What four aspects of behavior is Gesell concerned with and what does he see as the basis for each?
12. How can Gesell's research help parents?
13. Criticize Gesell's developmental-maturational approach.
14. Piaget is concerned with the development of intelligence. Discuss the periods of cognitive development he outlined and suggest ways in which parents might enhance such development.
15. Distinguish between classical and operant learning.
16. What are two basic rules of operant learning and how can parents use them?
17. Criticize the behavioral approach to child rearing.
18. Discuss the use of Gordon's environmental management, active listening, "I" messages, and no-lose method of resolving conflict.
19. What two aspects of Gordon's parent effectiveness training program may be difficult for parents?
20. What is the "cause" of a child's misbehavior according to Adler and Dreikurs? What suggestions did they make to increase the child's security?
21. Criticize the socio-teleological approach.
22. Discuss at least three perspectives and solutions for dealing with child-rearing problems such as between-meal snacks, crying and whining, requests for advertised items, and not doing chores.
23. How might most parents in America be categorized in terms of how strongly they discipline their children?
24. What types of disciplinary actions do parents take when their children misbehave and in what ways do they reward their children?
25. Discuss parental concerns regarding society, day care, public education, television, and nutrition.
26. Discuss five problems the single-parent family faces beyond the usual child-rearing concerns.

NOTES

1. This section relies heavily on Eugene Mead's *Six Approaches To Child Rearing* (1976).
2. The information presented in this section is discussed in greater detail in Gesell's co-authored texts—*Infant and Child in the Culture of Today* (1943), *The Child from Five to Ten* (1946), and *Youth: The Years from Ten to Sixteen* (1956).
3. The information presented in this section is discussed in greater detail in several of Piaget's books, including *The Construction of Reality in the Child* (1954), *Science of Education and the Psychology of the Child* (1970), and *The Psychology of the Child* (1969). The latter book was co-authored with B. Inhelder.
4. The information presented in this section is discussed in greater detail in each of the following: *Parents and Children, Love and Discipline* (Madsen & Madsen, 1975); *Living with Children* (Patterson, 1976); and *Parenting* (Norton, 1977).

5. The information presented in this section is discussed in greater detail in Gordon's *Parent Effectiveness Training: The Tested New Way To Raise Responsible Children* (1975).

6. The information presented in this section is discussed in greater detail in *Social Interest* (Adler, 1964); *The Challenge of Parenthood* (Dreikurs & Solz, 1958); and *A Parent's Guide to Child Discipline* (Dreikurs & Grey, 1970).

7. Parents are particularly concerned about the use of marijuana, and use among teenagers is edging upwards. Based on a sample of 17,000 seniors in 125 high schools in the U.S. in 1976, 53 percent had tried marijuana and 8 percent used it daily (Johnston et al., 1977).

8. Parents Without Partners, Inc., 7910 Woodmont Avenue, Washington, D.C. 20014, has chapters throughout the world. In most communities they have weekly meetings with professional people to speak on issues of special concern to the single parent. They also have an array of programs including family night, babysitting, and weekend retreats (Blumberg & Paul, 1975, p. 75).

BIBLIOGRAPHY

Adler, A. *Social interest.* New York: Capricorn Books, 1964.

Anderson, D. The growth group: Guidelines for an emerging means of strengthening families. *The Family Coordinator,* 1974, *23,* 1, 7–14.

Blumberg, P. M., and Paul, P. W. Continuities and discontinuities in upper-class marriages. *Journal of Marriage and the Family,* 1975, *37,* 1, 63–77.

Branch, E. The family camp: An extended family enrichment experience. In *Marriage and family enrichment: New perspectives and programs,* H. A. Otto (ed.). Nashville, Tenn.: Abingdon Press, 1976, 50–57.

Brandwein, R. A., Brown, C. A., and Fox, E. Women and children last: The social situation of divorced mothers and their families. *Journal of Marriage and the Family,* 1974, *36,* 3, 498–514.

Brown, C. C. It changed my life: Parent training courses. *Psychology Today,* November 1976, 47 et passim.

Bush, S. Predicting and preventing child abuse. *Psychology Today,* January 1978, 99.

Davis, K. The sociology of parent-youth conflict. *American Sociological Review,* August 1940, 423–35.

Despert, L. *Children of divorce.* New York: Doubleday, 1953.

Dodson, F. *How to discipline with love, from crib to college.* New York: Rawson Associates, 1978.

Dreikurs, R., and Grey, L. *A parent's guide to child discipline.* New York: Hawthorn Books, 1970.

Dreikurs, R., and Solz, V. *The challenge of parenthood.* New York: Duell, Sloan, and Pearce, 1958.

Essman, C. S. Sibling relations as socialization for parenthood. *The Family Coordinator,* 1977, *26,* 3, 259–62.

Feldman, F. L. *The family in today's money world.* New York: Family Service Association of America, 1976.

General Mills. *Raising children in a changing society* (The General Mills American family report 1976–77). Minneapolis: General Mills, 1977.

Gesell, A., and Ilg, F. L. *Infant and child in the culture of today.* New York: Harper, 1943.
————. *The child from five to ten.* New York: Harper, 1946.

Gesell, A., Ilg, F. L., and Ames, L. B. *Youth: The years from ten to sixteen.* New York: Harper, 1956.

Ginott, H. G. *Between parent and child: New solutions to old problems.* New York: Macmillan, 1965.

Glick, P. C. Updating the life cycle of the family. *Journal of Marriage and the Family,* 1977, *39,* 1, 5–13.

Gordon, T. *Parent effectiveness training: The tested new way to raise responsible children.* New York: New American Library, 1975.

Group for the Advancement of Psychiatry. *Joys and sorrows of parenthood.* New York: Charles Scribner's Sons, 1973.

Hetherington, M. E., Cox, M., and Cox, R. Divorced fathers. *The Family Coordinator,* 1976, *25,* 4, 417–28.

Hollingshead, A. B. *Elmtown's youth.* New York: John Wiley and Sons, 1949.

Johnson, L., Backman, J., and O'Malley, P. Monitoring the future. *Institute for Social Research Newsletter,* 1977, *5,* 2, 5.

Kagan, J. The psychological requirements for human development. In *Raising children in modern America,* N. B. Talbot (ed.). Boston: Little, Brown, 1976, 86–97.

Kernberg, O. Why some people can't love. *Psychology Today,* June 1978, 55 et passim.

Koller, M. R. *Families: A multigenerational approach.* New York: McGraw-Hill, 1974.

Kopecky, G. What it is like for singles who adopt: Four family stories. *Ms.,* June 1977, 45 et passim.

Lehane, S. *Help your baby learn.* Englewood Cliffs, N.J.: Prentice-Hall, 1976.

Lesser, G. S. Education and the mass media. In *Raising children in modern America,* N. B. Talbot (ed.). Boston: Little, Brown, 1976, 319–31.

Levine, J. Real kids versus the average family. *Psychology Today,* June 1978, 14–15.

Lewis, K. *The tender years doctrine.* Norfolk, Va.: Glossary on Custody, 1978.

Lieberman, L., and Lieberman, L. The family in the tube: Potential uses of television. *The Family Coordinator,* 1977, *26,* 3, 235–42.

Madsen, C., and Madsen, C. *Parents and children, love and discipline.* Northbrook, Ill.: AHM Publishing, 1975.

Mahoney, M. J. *Cognition and behavior modification.* Cambridge, Mass.: Ballinger, 1974.

Maslow, A. H. *Toward a psychology of being.* Princeton, N.J.: D. Van Nostrand, 1962.

McClelland, D., Constantiou, C., Regalado, D., and Stone, C. Making it to maturity. *Psychology Today,* June 1978, 42 et passim.

Mead, D. E. *Six approaches to child rearing.* Provo, Utah: Brigham Young University Press, 1976.

Mead, G. H. *Mind, self, and society.* Chicago: University of Chicago Press, 1934.

Mendes, H. A. Single fatherhood. *Social Work,* 1976, *21,* 4, 308–12.

Norton, G. R. *Parenting.* Englewood Cliffs, N.J.: Prentice-Hall, 1977.

Nye, R. D. *Three views of man.* Monterey, Calif.: Brooks/Cole, 1975.

Osborn, D. K. and Osborn, J. D. Childhood at the turn of the century. *The Family Coordinator,* 1978, *27,* 1, 27–32.

Patterson, G. R. *Living with children* (rev. ed.). Champaign, Ill.: Research Press, 1976.

Piaget, J. *The construction of reality in the child.* New York: Basic Books, 1954.

————. *Science of education and the psychology of the child.* New York: Orion Press, 1970.

Piaget, J. and Inhelder, B. *The psychology of the child.* New York: Basic Books, 1969.

Pringle, M. K. *The needs of children.* New York: Schocken Books, 1975.

Rapoport, R., Rapoport, R., and Strelitz, Z. *Fathers, mothers, and society.* New York: Basic Books, 1977.

Reiser, C. The effect of television on perceived marital happiness. Unpublished paper, Department of Sociology, East Carolina University, Greenville, N.C., 1977.

Rinn, R. C., and Markle, A. *Positive parenting.* Cambridge, Mass.: Research Media, 1977.

Rogers, C. *Client centered therapy.* Boston: Houghton-Mifflin, 1951.

Schlesinger, B. One parent families in Great Britain. *The Family Coordinator,* 1977, *26,* 2, 139–42.

Shea, J. Department of Child Development and Family Relations, East Carolina University, Greenville, N.C., Personal communication, 1978.

Skinner, B. F. *About behaviorism.* New York: Alfred A. Knopf, 1974.

Stolz, L. M. Youth: The Gesell Institute and its latest study. *Contemporary Psychology,* 1958, *3,* 10–15.

Sutton-Smith, B., and Rosenberg, B. *The sibling.* New York: Holt, Rinehart and Winston, 1970.

U.S., Bureau of the Census. Daytime Care of Children: October 1974 and February 1975. *Current Population Reports,* Series P-20, No. 298. Washington, D.C.: U.S. Government Printing Office, 1976.

————. *Statistical Abstract of the United States 1977* (98th ed.). Washington, D.C.: U.S. Government Printing Office, 1977.

U.S. fact book, The American almanac for 1976. New York: Grosset and Dunlap, 1976.

U.S. fact book, The American almanac for 1977. New York: Grosset and Dunlap, 1977.

Walsh, R. H., Ferrell, M. Z., and Tolone, W. L. Selection of reference group, perceived reference group permissiveness, and personal permissiveness attitudes and behavior: A study of two consecutive panels (1967–1971; 1970–1974). *Journal of Marriage and the Family,* 1976, *38,* 495–507.

Whiteside, C. The communal alternative for single parents. Paper presented at the meeting of the American Psychological Association, New Orleans, 1974.

Wilson, R. L., and Wilson, J. N. The family enrichment weekend. In *Marriage and family enrichment: New perspective and programs,* H. A. Otto (ed.). Nashville, Tenn.: Abingdon Press, 1976, 38–49.

Zeigler, E., and Child, I. L. *Socialization and personality development.* Reading, Mass.: Addison-Wesley, 1973.

Zimbardo, P. G., and Ruch, F. L. *Psychology and life* (9th ed.). Glenview, Ill.: Scott, Foresman, 1975.

Middle Age and Beyond

All would live long but none would be old.
Benjamin Franklin

"Grow old along with me!" wrote Robert Browning. "The best is yet to be,/The last of life, for which the first was made." But most young people spend little time considering what the last of life will be like. And when they do consider the later years, they are plagued with negative stereotypes of old people sitting on park benches feeding pigeons or in nursing homes spilling soup on themselves.

In this chapter we look beyond the stereotypes at the reality of the middle and later years of life. These are the periods which your parents are now experiencing, or soon will be. And these are the periods through which you will also pass.

MIDDLE AGE

When does a person become middle-aged? The U.S. census bureau regards you as middle-aged when you reach forty-five. One researcher has suggested that you are middle-aged when you begin to think about how many years you have left rather than how many years you have already lived (Neugarten, 1968). If the family life cycle is used to define middle age—often referred to as the "empty nest" or "postparental" stage—it begins when the last child leaves home[1] and continues until the husband retires or either spouse dies[2] (Duvall, 1977, p. 355).

When your friends begin to flatter you on how young you look, it's a sure sign you're getting old.

Mark Twain

Regardless of how middle age is defined, it is a time of transition (Sheehy, 1976). Let's explore what happens to the wife, the husband, their marriage, and their sexual relationship during this period. While families naturally vary according to individual circumstances, certain events seem to be characteristic of middle age for many.

Wives in Middle Age

A major event for most women during the middle years is the departure of their children from the home. For a period of about twenty to thirty years, the traditional wife and mother has been primarily concerned with cooking meals, washing clothes, and nurturing children. Now the children are gone. For some mothers, their departure causes depression. "I've always been good at taking care of children," a middle-aged wife said. "When my last one leaves for college on Thursday, I don't know what I'll do. I know it's time—and it's best for her to go—but I'll miss her desperately. I almost feel like my life is over."[3]

But to other women their children's leaving means freedom from the restrictions of the parental role and the beginning of a second life (McClard, 1976). "I've enjoyed my children, and I love all of them," expressed one middle-aged mother, "but I'm very glad it's over. My husband and I are free at last to enjoy ourselves. It's almost like courtship again."

Some of these freed mothers seek employment,[4] others return to school, and still others become active in civic affairs. Those who find jobs soon become aware that the demands of employment and homemaking are different: "Competitiveness directed toward promotion replaces family cooperativeness, and individualism is sharpened, for each worker must look out for herself, whereas in the family unity gives protection and security" (Cavan, 1953, p. 573). Whether or not the middle-aged wife derives satisfaction from her employment will depend "on the extent to which she successfully accommodates to the different value system of the occupational world" (Nye & Berardo, 1973, p. 548). She may also be disappointed to discover that the skills she has developed as wife and mother have little market value and that most of the jobs available to her offer low pay for long hours.

Other middle-aged women return to school (Klass & Redfern 1977). "I've always wanted to complete my training," recalled a practical nurse, "and now I have the opportunity to do so. It's a nice feeling to know that, even at my age, I can still learn and compete with the younger students." Like women who reenter the job market, however, those who return to school may find it difficult to turn back the clock in some respects while rushing to catch up in others.

Still other women become actively involved in voluntary associations. Some sociologists have questioned whether or not such participation is an adequate substitute for the role of mother. "Hardly a day goes by but what the doorbell rings and some bored housewife demands money for a so-called philanthropy that offers her fund-raising as a way to improve her leisure. These angels of mercy with their tickets and pledge cards hardly strike us as having found the solution to their problem" (Foote, 1961, pp. 326–29).

In contrast to the traditional homemaker who gets a job, returns to school, or becomes involved in civic affairs when her children leave home, the career woman with children has always lived an active life outside the home. And because her career is firmly established, she is less likely to feel a void when her children move out. While she may miss them, she will be less likely to grieve over their absence.

But whether traditional homemakers or career women, how do middle-aged women whose children have left home regard their situation? A national survey was conducted in which postparental women were asked, "Taken all together, how would you say things are these days—would you say that you are very happy, pretty happy, or not too happy?" Almost half (48.2 percent) reported that they were "very happy." When the responses of these women were compared with those of women of similar age who still had children in the home, the postparental women were happier (Glenn, 1975).

Reported satisfaction during the "empty nest" period is often related to the woman's perception of her success as a mother. If she perceives her children as failing to progress, she feels threatened and unhappy. But if she perceives her children as progressing in a way that is congruent with her expectations, she is likely to enjoy her postparental years (Spence & Lonner, 1971).

Husbands in Middle Age

While major adjustment for middle-aged wives is often made necessary by the departure of their children, for husbands it may be brought about by change—or lack of change—on the job. Most men reach the top level of their earning power during middle age (Feldman, 1976, p. 120). And some find themselves well short of the peak they had hoped to reach. "A man of forty may be looking anxiously over his shoulder at the wolf pack yapping and slobbering at his heels as he slips along over competitive business ice. At forty, the status of many a man, whether in business or on the assembly line, is frozen, so he feels stuck and fearful" (Henry, 1974, p. 440). One researcher suggested that a principal task for men in the mid-life transition is *deillusionment*—realistically asking if the goals they have set for themselves are reasonable and attainable (Levinson, 1977).

For many, there is the feeling of having reached a dead end. "Had I known that this firm was never going to promote me," one man said, "I would have left fifteen years ago. But now it's too late. Who wants to hire a fifty-year-old when thirty-year-olds are a dime a dozen?" Still others reach the top only to find that "success" is meaningless for them. "I've been with the government since I left school and now I'm the head of my division. But so what? I move papers around on my desk and have conferences that are supposed to mean something but don't. I've always wanted to be a psychologist so I could work with people about something that matters, but now it's too late."

Whether they feel they have failed in the right career or succeeded in the wrong one, many middle-aged men see their jobs as a treadmill that is costing them their health. As Figure 18.1 shows, a man is more likely to develop a heart condition or cancer or to have a stroke between the ages of forty-five and sixty-four than at any other time in his working life.

This period in middle age when many men ask themselves "What's the point of it all?" has been referred to as "middle-escence." It provides an "opportunity for going on with the identity crisis of the first adolescence . . . a second chance to find out what it really means to 'do your own thing,' to sing your own song, to be deeply and truly yourself" (LeShan, 1973).

For some middle-aged husbands, pursuing their "own thing" may mean having an affair. Of 25,000 marriage counseling cases in which the spouses had been married over eighteen years, infidelity was the second most frequent problem (ill health was first) (Brayshaw, 1962).

FIGURE 18.1   Accidents and Other Major Causes of Death Among Men at the
Working Ages (United States, 1972–73).

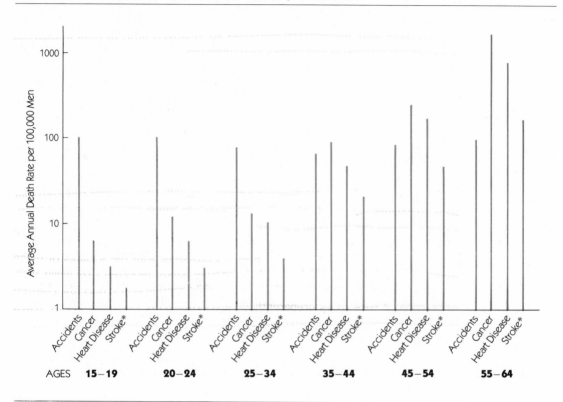

*Cerebrovascular disease.

SOURCE: Statistical Bulletin, 1975, p. 2.

For the man who does not find satisfaction in his work, who has done what he had to
do, rather than what he wanted to do, or whose life work has turned out to be not
quite what he thought it was . . . the cure to his lifelong disorder may seem to be the
young and beautiful woman. . . . She gives him a feeling that he is not lost after all,
he is not as weak as he thinks. She will, he feels, give him new creative powers,
because her sex interest proves that he is not dead wood." (Henry, 1974, pp. 440–41)

While some husbands in middle age are worried about their jobs and health
and some become involved in affairs, others are delighted with their careers, take
pride in their physical health, and regard affairs as foolish. Many of these husbands
perceive the last of life as the most fulfilling.

Marriages in Middle Age

While middle-aged wives are adapting to the departure of their children and their husbands are trying to cope with their careers, how are their marriages functioning? To begin with, postparental marriages are relatively new. In 1890 women (on the average) married at age twenty-two, bore their last child at thirty-two, buried their husband at age fifty-three, and attended their last child's wedding at fifty-five (Glick, 1955, pp. 3–9). Few spouses shared any postparental years because the husband died before the fifth child left home. Today, the typical woman marries when she is twenty-one, gives birth to her last child at thirty, attends the wedding of her last child at fifty-two, and buries her husband when she is sixty-five (Glick, 1977, pp. 5–9). As a result of having longer lives and fewer children, spouses now live together about thirteen years after the children are gone.

But what are these years like? How do spouses feel about their marriage during the postparental period?[5] Wives in a random middle-class sample reported that their marriages improved when the children left home (Feldman & Feldman, 1976).[6] "When our last child left," recalled one wife, "my husband and I had time for each other that was not disrupted by our parental roles. I love my kids, but it's nice to be alone with my husband again." Consistent with the feelings of these wives, the majority of 799 husbands in another study reported that while their marital satisfaction had decreased during the child-rearing years, once the children were gone, it rose to its preparenthood level (Rollins & Feldman, 1970). When middle-aged husbands and wives were asked to identify the most rewarding as-

Many couples find that the empty-nest period after their children have left home is one of the happiest periods of their marriage. It is a time of reduced responsibilities and increased companionship.

pect of their marriage, 62 percent said "companionship" (Hayes & Stinnett, 1971, p. 672).

And while it is often assumed that "being in love" is reserved for the young, ninety-nine out of one hundred middle-aged spouses reported that they were in love with their mates (Knox, 1970a). The attitude toward love held by these middle-aged people was romantic (Knox, 1970b). They tended to believe in "love at first sight," that "love comes but once in a lifetime," and that "a loveless marriage is tragic."

Sexuality in Middle Age

As the marriage improves and attitudes toward love become more romantic, what sexual changes do middle-aged spouses experience? For the woman, menopause occurs around age fifty.[7] This is when her monthly menstrual periods gradually stop as a result of diminished estrogen.

Although it is often assumed that menopause is an overwhelming trauma for a woman, the respondents in one study attached little significance to it. Rather, they were glad to be relieved of the monthly menstrual nuisance (Neugarten et al., 1963). (Similarly, a 1977 study by Meikle et al. found that women who have had a hysterectomy are no more likely to feel upset than those who have had a gall bladder removed.) But about 10 percent of women experience psychological disturbances during menopause. These include irritability, insomnia, "hot flashes," headaches, and depression (Katchadourian & Lunde, 1975, p. 102). These symptoms can usually be relieved by supplemental hormones prescribed by a physician[8] (Rubin, 1965, pp. 130–35).

While few women experience severe psychological disturbances during menopause, there are predictable physiological and behavioral changes as a result of decreasing levels of estrogen: (a) a delay in the reaction of her clitoris to direct stimulation, (b) less lubrication during sexual excitement, (c) a less intense orgasm (perhaps), (d) a smaller vaginal opening, and (e) (perhaps) increased sexual interest. The latter change may be a result of her freedom from pregnancy or the new ratio of androgen to estrogen in her body (Kaplan, 1974; Kaplan & Sager, 1971).

In men, production of testosterone begins to decline around age forty and continues to decrease gradually until age sixty.[9] At this time a man's testosterone level stabilizes for the remainder of his life (Huyck, 1974; Kaplan, 1974). Lowered testosterone results in: (a) more difficulty in creating and maintaining a firm erection; (b) the production of less ejaculatory fluid, which results in a less frequent need to ejaculate; (c) the need for a longer period of stimulation of the penis before ejaculation will occur; (d) fewer genital spasms during orgasm; (e) a lowered intensity of orgasm; (f) a qualitative change from an intense, genitally focused sensation to a more diffused and generalized feeling of pleasure; and (g) an increase in the length of the refractory period, during which time the male is unable to ejaculate or have another erection (Kaplan, 1974; Masters & Johnson, 1968).

One researcher summarized the effect of the physiological changes in both husband and wife on their intercourse experience:

> Excitement building is slower than in the past and involves more direct tactile stimulation. Intromission is physiologically more difficult—a less rigid penis, a smaller vaginal opening with less vaginal lubrication. There is less vaginal muscle tone to help maintain the erection. Both husband and wife will take longer to come to the point of orgasm/ejaculation and the orgasmic experience may be less intense than previously. (Cleveland, 1976, p. 235)

Do middle-aged men experience psychological symptoms similar to those reported by menopausal women? Some do. But their anxiety and depression seem to be more in response to their life situation than to hormonal changes. A middle-aged man who is not successful in his career is often forced to recognize that he will never achieve what he had hoped but carry his unfulfilled dreams to the grave. Coupled with this knowledge is the possible awareness of a more flaccid penis. If the man has been socialized to believe that his masculinity is dependent on success in his career and continued sexual prowess, middle age may be particularly traumatic.

We have explored the changes in spouses, marriage, and sexuality in middle age. But middle age means different things to different people. It may be either the best or the worst of times. On the positive side, a character in a novel by Hervey Allen says, "Grow up as soon as you can. It pays. The only time you really live fully is from thirty to sixty. . . . The young are slaves to dreams; the old, servants of regrets. Only the middle-aged have all their five senses in the keeping of their wits" (Allen, 1933, p. 447).

But some middle-aged spouses see themselves as members of the "caught generation." Addressing middle-aged spouses, Vincent wrote,

> The respect you were taught to give your parents may have been denied you by your children. . . . For the younger generation, your children in their late teens and early twenties, you may continue to provide at least the necessities of life, while they criticize your work ethos that makes it possible for them to do their thing. . . . As a child, you were to be seen and not heard, now as a parent you may feel you are to be neither seen nor heard. (Vincent, 1972, p. 143)

BEYOND MIDDLE AGE—THE AGED

In 1976, there were 22.9 million people in the U.S. over the age of sixty-five—10.7 percent of our population. The proportion of women to men was 144 to 100 (U.S. Bureau of the Census, 1977, p. 27). Figure 18.2 shows where they lived. Florida and Arkansas had the highest percentages of elderly citizens—16.1 and 12.8 percent respectively (U.S. Office of Human Development, 1976).

FIGURE 18.2   Proportion of U.S. Population Aged 65 and Over (1975).

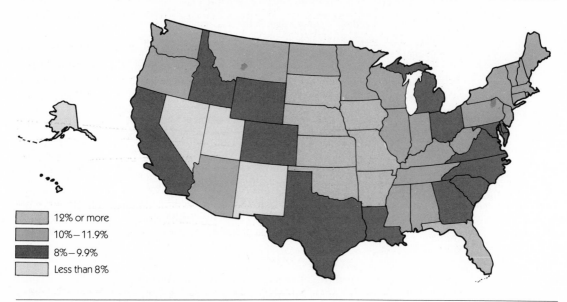

	12% or more
	10%–11.9%
	8%–9.9%
	Less than 8%

SOURCE: Adapted from U.S. Office of Human Development, 1976.

Definition of Aging

Aging may be defined chronologically, physiologically, sexually, psychologically, sociologically, or culturally. Chronologically, an "old" person is defined as one who has lived a certain number of years. How many years it takes to be "old" varies with the perspective. A child of twelve may regard a sibling of eighteen as "old"—and his or her parents as "ancient." But the teenagers and the parents may regard themselves as "young" and reserve the label "old" for the grandparents' generation.

Physiologically, the auditory, visual, and respiratory capabilities of an individual decline with age. The per capita cost of health care for a person over sixty-

Y ou know you're getting old when the candles cost more than the cake.

Bob Hope

five is three times that for a younger adult (U.S. Office of Human Development, 1976). "Sometimes I feel like a young person trapped in an old body," observed one eighty-six-year-old woman. "My wits are as sharp as ever, but my hands tremble and I can't get around like I used to."

Sexually, certain attitudinal and behavioral changes accompany advancing age.[10] Older couples report a decline in sexual feelings with advancing years. Table 18.1 indicates the responses of one hundred spouses married to each other for fifty years. As the percentages reveal, most of the spouses perceive their present sexual feelings as less intense than in previous years. And a study by Verwoerdt et al. (1970) also found that interest in sex decreases with age. Table 18.2 illustrates the frequency with which married men between the ages of forty-six and seventy-one reported having intercourse. As those percentages indicate, there is a gradual reduction in sexual intercourse with advancing age. By the late sixties, about half these husbands were having intercourse about once a month, about 25 percent once a week, and about 25 percent none at all. Books have begun to appear which emphasize that while the elderly should be free not to have sex, they should also feel free to enjoy it (Butler & Lewis, 1976).

While older couples tend to report a decline in sexual feelings, they also tend to agree as to what sexual activity is desirable in their marriage and to report high levels of marital satisfaction.

TABLE 18.1   Sexual Feelings of 100 Spouses in Marriages
Lasting for Over Fifty Years.

	Number of Subjects	
Intensity of Sexual Feelings	In Younger Years	At Present Time
None at all	1	29
Weak	6	30
Moderate	54	34
Strong	35	3
No response	4	4

SOURCE: Adapted from Roberts and Roberts, 1975, p. 5.

In another study of 149 spouses whose ages ranged from sixty to ninety-three, 54 percent reported that they were still sexually active. (Spouses who had intercourse with any degree of regularity were defined as "active." Their frequency of intercourse ranged from once a month to three times a week.) Those who reported the most interest in sex and the highest frequencies of intercourse were black, male, younger, and from a lower socioeconomic class (Newman & Nichols, 1970; Pfeiffer & Davis, 1972).[11] In general, older married spouses agree with each other about whether or not to have intercourse and how often (Pfeiffer et al., 1970).

Psychologically, a person's self-concept is important in defining how "old" that person is. In one study, half the people over eighty viewed themselves as middle-aged (Eisdorfer & Lawton, 1973). "The way I see it," said one eighty-seven-year-old woman, "you're not old until you feel that way."

Sociologically, people age as they assume roles that have traditionally been defined as those occupied by old people—grandparent, widow, retiree. "After our daughter had her first child, it occurred to me that I would be sleeping with a grandmother," recalled a retired dentist. "I kidded my wife about that, and she said, 'Yes, grandpa, that's right, and I'll be sleeping with a grandfather.' It made us feel old just to know that the word grandparents now meant us."

Culturally, the society in which an individual lives defines when and if a person becomes "old" and what it means to do so. An anthropologist commented on the variation in cultural definitions of old age:

Old age has been said to begin quite early or rather late in life, and it may last a very long or a short time. By conventional norms, its coming may be resented and discounted or welcomed and treasured. It may be considered an idle and useless period in life or an active and fruitful one. It may bring promotions in position and homage or demotions in both. It may be expected to drag itself out in dull, tedious boredom or go

TABLE 18.2   Frequency of Sexual Intercourse Reported by Men, Ages 46–71.*

Age Group	Number of Respondents in Group	None	Percent of Respondents Reporting Each Frequency			
			Once a Month	Once a Week	2–3 Times a Week	More than 3 Times a Week
46–50	N = 43	0	5	62	26	7
51–55	N = 41	5	29	49	17	0
56–60	N = 61	7	38	44	11	0
61–65	N = 54	20	43	30	7	0
66–71	N = 62	24	48	26	2	0
Total	N = 261	12	34	41	12	1

*Two percent of the 261 men represented in these data were not married. No comparable data are available for married women in this age category.

SOURCE: Adapted from Pfeiffer et al., 1974, p. 247.

by quickly with interest and zest. Thus, the onset of aging may be viewed as a curse on the one hand or as a challenge on the other. (Simmons, 1952)

In many cultures, age brings with it prestige and status. The older Navajo tribesman, for example, is a revered leader commanding the respect of less experienced members of the tribe (Huyck, 1974).

One researcher has suggested that members of some societies act old—that is, give up practically all productive work—because their society expects them to (Keller, 1977b). And in societies where the old are expected to be productive, they are. In three cultures in Ecuador, Pakistan, and Russia, for instance, the elderly are expected to weed the fields, milk the cows, do the laundry, and take care of the children on a daily basis (Leaf & Launois, 1973). Kept so busy, they have little time to "act old."

Attitudes Toward Aging

Regardless of how aging is defined, most Americans grow old reluctantly.[12] A woman identified as "Wrinkled in New York," wrote to Dear Abby: "I am a fifty-nine-year-old woman, and believe me I look every day of it—and then some. . . . I'm sure a facelift would not only improve my appearance, but do wonders for my morale, so I've decided to get one." She went on to ask if Abby had ever had a facelift. Abby replied, "No, I never have, but when I think I need one, I'll certainly give it serious consideration" (Van Buren, 1977).

Most Americans of both sexes want to keep a youthful appearance, but it seems more critical for women. As Huyck (1974) notes, men are considered "desirable if potent, and potency is equated with power and control. Generally, men increase in power (social, not physical) at least through middle age. Thus, women lose femininity and value as they age while men enhance their masculinity as they grow older" (p. 15).

Concern over wrinkled skin and physical deterioration is not the only basis for reluctance about growing older. A fear of becoming useless is also involved in the negative attitude toward aging. With no children to look after and no jobs to go to, the elderly are not expected to contribute to our society. "Their declining physical capacities have been regarded as synonymous with their potential. As a result, our society has the attitude of 'do for' for the elderly" (Keller, 1977b). And they soon learn the message implied in such an attitude: You can't do anything for yourself—you are useless.

In addition to looking old and feeling useless, reluctance about growing older is fed by the dread of being lonely. "It is one of the most painful problems during the later years" (Stinnett & Walters, 1977, p. 328). "I could die in my sleep," said an elderly widow, "and rigor mortis would set in before anybody would know or care that I was gone. Being lonely is the hardest part of growing old." And some individuals are unable to cope with the depression that comes with loneliness. Twenty-five percent of all suicides are committed by those over sixty-five (Butler, 1976).

As might be expected, not everyone "grows old" in the same way. In a study of fifty-nine men and women between the ages of seventy and seventy-nine, the researcher concluded:

> As men and women move beyond age seventy in a modern, industrialized community, they regret the drop in role activity that occurs in their lives; at the same time, most older persons accept this drop as an inevitable accompaniment of growing old; and they succeed in maintaining a sense of self-worth and a sense of satisfaction with past and present life as a whole. (Havighurst, 1976, pp. 198–99)[13]

Some elderly Americans not only maintain a sense of self-worth but have organized to combat attitudes that would deny them such pride. The Gray Liberation Movement denounces ageism in the same way that blacks denounce racism and women denounce sexism. *Ageism* may be defined as the systematic persecution and degradation of people because they are old. Being forced into retirement is one issue around which the elderly have rallied, and legislation was passed in early 1978 moving the age of retirement from sixty-five to seventy.

RETIREMENT

What is retirement really like? Sylvia Porter says, "There are *few* real-life counterparts of the contented older couples you see pictured in newspaper and magazine ads and TV commercials—basking in the sun, indulging in leisure activities, comfortably and independently enjoying family and friends . . . " (1976, p. 763). The realities are sometimes more grim. Let's explore them.

Lower Income

Living out one's life in luxury requires money—lots of it. And the person accustomed to living off a regular earned income will feel its loss. Social Security and pension benefits, when they exist, are rarely equal to the income a retired person formerly earned. In a study of retirees of the 1970s, the authors concluded,

> Incomes may be most important in accounting for the objective quality of retirees' lives. . . . One's financial status directs the type of leisure activities he or she can undertake, the amount of diagnostic and preventive medical care he or she can seek, the amount of traveling he or she can do, the quality of housing, the quality of diet, and so on. (Irelan & Bond, 1976, p. 235)

For most retirees, retirement means reducing their incomes by half. Eighty-two percent of those who live alone or with nonrelatives have annual incomes of less than $6,000, and 43 percent of retired married couples have less than that amount to live on each year (U.S. Office of Human Development, 1976). The average income of elderly married couples (including income from Social Security and private pension benefits) is about $5,500 (Porter, 1976, p. 763). Were the typical retired couple to take a European summer tour, they would hardly have enough money to buy an apple upon their return to the States. Retirement for most couples means doing without most of the things they have always wanted that money can buy. And many elderly people without savings and investments to draw on are helpless to improve their economic situation. While their income is fixed, the cost of rent, food, clothes, and medical care continues to escalate. The elderly often have no defense against inflation.

Declining Health

While the majority of elderly people are in good health, almost 40 percent of those over sixty-five have long-term chronic conditions such as arthritis, rheumatism, heart disease, and high blood pressure that interfere somewhat with their daily activities. In contrast, only 7 percent of younger people are hampered by such health problems (U.S. Office of Human Development, 1976).

The healthiest among the elderly are those who exercise, control their weight, and avoid cigarettes (Palmore, 1974). Of one hundred elderly people (average age, seventy-nine) who reported good health habits, 71 percent perceived their health as better than or unchanged from previous years (Roberts & Roberts, 1975, p. 4). "In retirement, health can either enable or prevent the activities which are essential to many people's contentment. It is also, for many older people, a deciding factor in the extent of their contact and interaction with other people" (Irelan & Bond, 1976, p. 239).

Isolation and Loneliness

In addition to lower incomes and poorer health, the elderly are sometimes plagued with feelings of isolation and loneliness. The view that a person is what he or she does means that the roles of working person and homemaker/mother are key elements in most people's self-concepts. Retirement shatters that self-concept by separating the teacher from students, the lawyer from clients, the physician from patients. "Without my research laboratory to go to," said a retired chemist, "I don't know who I am or what to do with myself."[14] And the retired manager of an A&P grocery store said, "Every time I drive by the store, I can't help wondering if the meat freezers have been serviced lately."

But the role of productive worker does more than define one's identity. It provides a sense of status and an opportunity to interact with colleagues. "For the past twenty years," growled one retired army colonel, "what I thought and said meant something. People looked to me for answers. Now I'm regarded as a bumbling old fool who is ready for the grave."

These feelings are not unique to retired men. Career women also miss the income and the social contacts generated by employment (Fox, 1977). Some evidence suggests that retirement is more difficult for them. In a study comparing men and women who were retired schoolteachers and telephone company employees, women reported taking longer to adjust to retirement and feeling lonelier and more depressed than men (Atchley, 1976).

For many retired people, interaction with family quells feelings of loneliness. About 70 percent of those over sixty-five have one or more children or grandchildren (Stewart, 1977). Eighty-seven percent of retired spouses in a national sample reported seeing or talking with at least one of their children at least once a month (Irelan & Bond, 1976, p. 246).

Other methods of reducing feelings of isolation include cohabitation, polygyny, communal living, and, for some, homosexuality (Dressel & Avant, 1978). Regarding cohabitation, in 1977 about 85,000 couples aged sixty-five and over[15] were living together unmarried (Glick & Norton, 1977).

While most of the elderly do not live with their children—and both the elderly and their children prefer it that way (Stewart, 1977)—the issue of where to live is a concern for the elderly. Choosing between keeping a large home, paying ever increasing rent for an apartment, or moving to a retirement village or nursing home can be a difficult decision (Silverstone & Hyman, 1976).

Types of Retirement

Some individuals never retire. Margaret Mead was writing books at seventy-five and George Burns was making movies at eighty-one. But for the majority who do retire, there seem to be four basic patterns (Sheldon, McEwan, & Ryser, 1975).

1. Maintenance. The retiree tries to maintain his or her old role by continuing to work in one way or another. An example is the carpenter who retires from a large construction firm but opens his own shop to continue in the same role.

2. Withdrawal. This is the opposite of the maintenance pattern. The retiree, perceiving retirement as a time to relax, gives up former interests without adopting new ones. A retired employee said, "I wake up every morning and think I'm in heaven. I enjoyed working for forty-two years, but I enjoy doing 'nothing' more."

3. Changed activities. The retiree attempts to satisfy the old needs in new ways. A retired schoolteacher who enjoyed contact with young people became a scout leader and led his troop to top honors.

4. New needs. The retiree views retirement as a chance to satisfy an entirely different set of needs. "I've always had the desire to paint," said a retired librarian. "Now I've got the time. I've already enrolled in a painting course at the local technical institute."

The retired person must learn to make new use of the time once devoted to his occupation, or must learn to value and enjoy leisure (Frank, 1977). For some the latter is particularly difficult, in view of the prevailing Protestant work ethic: To work is good and responsible, to do nothing is bad and irresponsible.

Marital Satisfaction During Retirement

Almost 80 percent of men and 50 percent of women over age sixty-five are married (U.S. Office of Human Development, 1976). For many of these spouses, it is the first time since courtship (twenty-five or more years earlier), that they have been together without jobs or children interfering with their relationship. The respondents in two studies reported that they were enjoying their last years together. In a study of fifty couples whose average age was seventy-nine and whose

Whether retirement is enjoyed or just tolerated depends in large part on a person's ability to shift gears. Time given over to work must be reallocated to leisure pursuits, which in turn must be felt to be valuable and rewarding.

TABLE 18.3   Older People's Ratings of Their Marriages.

Ratings	Percentages
Marital Happiness	
Very Happy	45
Happy	49
Unhappy	3
Undecided	3
Marriage Improved or Worsened Over Time	
Better	53
Worse	4
About the Same	41
Undecided	2
Happiest Period in Marriage	
Present Time	55
Middle Years	27
Young Adult Years	18

SOURCE: Adapted from Stinnett, Carter, and Montgomery, 1972, p. 667.

years of marriage were over fifty, not one described their marriage as "unhappy," and 93 percent said that they would marry the same person if they were to live their lives over again (Roberts & Roberts, 1975, pp. 6–7).

Table 18.3 gives the results of a second study, showing how 408 husbands and wives (most of whom were between sixty-five and sixty-nine) felt about their marriages. They described their relationships in very favorable terms.

GRANDPARENTHOOD

While grandparenthood begins in middle age, it continues into the retirement years. When you were a child someone probably read you the story of Little Red Riding Hood. And the first sentence you heard was, "Once upon a time there was a little girl who was dearly loved by all—most of all by her grandmother" (Jones, 1969, p. 33). You learned about Little Red Riding Hood's encounter with the big bad wolf, but you also learned that Little Red Riding Hood's grandmother loved her, and that grandparents traditionally love their grandchildren. In later years, the role of grandparent may await you. Over 70 percent of all elderly Americans are grandparents and 40 percent are great-grandparents (Atchley, 1972).

Unique Aspects of the Grandparent Role

Unlike parents, grandparents have neither legal authority over, nor primary responsibility for their grandchildren.[16] If a twelve-year-old is caught shoplifting, the police call the parents, not the grandparents. And, as a result of not having to reprimand and "be a parent" to their grandchildren, grandparents may interact with them in an atmosphere that is relatively tension-free[17] (Radcliffe-Brown, 1952).

Grandparents worry less about their grandchildren than parents do about their children. While parents worry about whether their children will need braces or learn to drive a car without killing themselves, the grandparents, who went through these experiences decades earlier, regard such worrying as unnecessary. "You've got to teach them what you can," said a grandfather of six, "and let them

Being a grandparent can be a very enjoyable role. Grandparents may establish a close and loving relationship with their grandchildren without taking on the full-time and primary responsibility for children in the way that parents must.

learn the rest themselves. It's a waste of time to worry about the bad experiences they will have. A 'hard knock' can teach them more than you can in a month."

Grandparenthood differs from parenthood in yet another way: Grandparents have been taught to expect that their contact with their grandchildren will be limited. After she became a grandparent, Margaret Mead said, "I think we do not allow sufficiently for the obligation we lay on grandparents to keep themselves out of the picture—not to interfere, not to spoil, not to insist, not to intrude" (Mead, 1972). About 30 percent of grandparents in one study reported feeling distant from their grandchildren (Neugarten & Weinstein, 1964).

Grandmotherhood

While grandmothers represent only half of grandparenthood, researchers have focused more on their role than on that of grandfathers. Traditionally, grandmothers have been stereotyped as "jolly, white-thatched bespectacled old ladies who lavish goodies and attention on their grandchildren" (Robertson, 1977, p. 165). But what are grandmothers really like? To find out, Robertson and her colleagues interviewed 125 women who had an average of three grandchildren. Over half of the respondents (55 percent)[18] were primarily concerned about doing what was expected of them as grandmothers—setting a good example, teaching their grandchildren how to live decent, upright lives, indulging them, and so on. "We want our grandchildren to get a good education, to be good, clean people, good workers as they grow up. . . . A good grandparent is to be a real Christian, set examples, practice what you preach" (Robertson, 1977, p. 170). Women who felt this way about their role as grandmother tended to be younger, presently married, employed, involved with their own friends, and very satisfied with their own life in contrast to the "individualized" or "remote" types of grandmother.

The "individualized" grandmothers were the opposite of those just described. They tended to be older, widowed, unemployed, and without friends of their own. They were lonely. Grandmotherhood was seen in more personal "individualized" terms. Grandchildren were viewed as curbing loneliness, keeping the grandparent youthful, and carrying on the family bloodline. "They've helped me forget I'm getting older—they keep me from getting lonesome. . . . They help me forget my problems" (Robertson, 1977, p. 170). Seventeen percent of the sample were grandmothers of this type.

The "remote" grandmothers, who comprised 28 percent of the sample, were, as the label implies, "not very involved with, or concerned about, the elements of any relationship with their grandchildren. . . . They responded to grandparenting in a distant, impersonal, and ritualistic manner" (Robertson, 1977, p. 170). And their lack of involvement with their grandchildren seemed to mirror the rest of their lives. When compared with the other two groups, they scored the lowest on a scale of life satisfaction.

When the 125 grandmothers were asked if they preferred grandparenting or parenting, 37 percent chose grandparenting, 32 percent chose parenting, and 25 percent said that they have enjoyed both roles equally. But 79 percent agreed that "as a grandmother you are free from upbringing responsibilities . . . you have more time to spend with and enjoy grandchildren than when your children were young . . . and you can see and enjoy grandchildren, then send them home" (Robertson, 1977, p. 171). In essence, grandparenthood is regarded by most grandparents as one of the delights of the later years.

TRENDS

Gerontology (the study of aging) will continue to be an expanding field, not only because there is an interest in discovering causes of the aging process (with the hope of slowing it), but because there will be an increasing number of older people in our society. The number of elderly will double in the next fifty years. Such a rapid growth is due to the "graying" of those born in the post–World War II baby boom.

Governmental interest in the elderly will also continue. The raising of the mandatory retirement age, the growth of Social Security benefits, and the plans for a White House Conference on Aging in 1981 all reflect the growing political power of the elderly. Further gains can be expected.

Attitudes toward aging in our society will also become more positive as the elderly increase in number and visibility and become more normative and politically powerful. Increased political clout can be used to ensure benefits for them. The "Gray Revolution" has begun.

Although the political, economic, and social status of the elderly as a group has in some ways been low, the picture seems to be changing. As their numbers grow, the elderly are likely to increase their political power, make gains in social and economic programs, and generally improve their "quality of life."

SUMMARY

Middle age is a time most spouses look forward to without enthusiasm. For the woman who has devoted almost a quarter century to child rearing, the postparental stage may be difficult. Many return to work or school for alternative sources of fulfillment. Others become involved in community activities. Most report a successful adjustment.

Because of commitment to a career, most men have had less involvement in parenthood than their wives. A man's children leaving home may be overshadowed by anxiety about his career: Did he choose the wrong one? Has he been a success? Has success proved meaningless? Feelings of inadequacy may push the middle-aged man into an affair with a younger woman who tells him he is "great" in spite of his self-doubt or career deficiencies.

While both the wife and husband are making personal adjustments during middle age, their marriage is in the empty nest stage. Without the children to interfere with their relationship, most couples regard this as one of the happiest times in their marriage.

The elderly represent the one minority we will all join if we live long enough. And unless we are luckier than most, the "golden years" of retirement will mean not basking in the sun but struggling with an inadequate income, poor health, and feelings of loneliness and isolation.

One source of delight for some elderly couples is grandchildren. While many grandparents don't see their grandchildren as often as they would like to, they enjoy interacting with them (with the freedom to let parents take over when the old folks grow tired).

Trends for the elderly include doubling their numbers in the next fifty years, increased Social Security benefits, and continued governmental interest. Attitudes toward the elderly will also improve as their numbers increase and they become more politically powerful.

STUDY QUESTIONS

1. What are the various ways of defining middle age?
2. What is the major event in the life of a middle-aged mother?
3. What new roles do women seek when their children leave home? Compare each of these roles to the role of motherhood.
4. How happy are women whose children have left home? Under what conditions is a woman likely to regard the postparental stage as happy or sad?
5. Explain the doubts many middle-aged men entertain about their careers.
6. What do middle age and adolescence have in common?
7. Why may the middle-aged husband be particularly vulnerable to an affair during this period?
8. Compare the average life cycle of a marriage today with that of 1890.
9. What do spouses report about their marriages during the postparental period? How do these reports vary by social class?
10. Discuss the attitude of middle-aged spouses toward love.

11. What is the average age for menopause? What percentage of women experience what type of psychological disturbances?
12. How do most women regard menopause?
13. What are the physiological and behavioral consequences of lowered testosterone production in men? Summarize the effect of physiological changes on intercourse experienced by middle-aged husbands and wives.
14. Discuss six ways the concept of aging can be defined.
15. What are the attitudinal and behavioral changes in the sex lives of older couples?
16. Discuss American attitudes toward aging.
17. Compare the cultural stereotype and the reality of retirement.
18. Discuss four patterns of retirement.
19. How happy are marriages among the retired?
20. What are some unique aspects of the grandparent role?
21. Compare the cultural stereotype of grandmothers with those in the study conducted by Robertson.
22. What is gerontology?
23. When is the current population of the elderly expected to double?
24. Discuss trends regarding the elderly in our society.

NOTES

1. Some researchers view this stage as beginning when the first child leaves home (Nye & Berardo, 1973, p. 543).
2. A major criticism of the concept of the family life cycle is that it does not include those individuals who neither marry nor have children.
3. One author observed, "To avoid forty-year-old jitters, middle-class women must be trained for later life—for the time when their children no longer need them; and they must not be permitted to forget that, as children grow to puberty in contemporary America, the maternal function has little reward and that guidance is resented by the children they have liberated by their permissiveness" (Henry, 1974, pp. 447–48).
4. About half of America's middle-aged women are employed (Duvall, 1977, p. 359).
5. Some evidence suggests that evaluation of the postparental period varies by social class. In a study by Saunders (1974), working-class spouses reported more satisfaction with this period than did middle-class spouses. In explaining this finding, the author said, "When the children leave home, the freedom from the . . . financial burdens of children would be more pronounced for the working-class . . . husband and wife than for their peers in the middle class" (p. 27).
6. Those wives whose last child had left home some time ago reported more marital satisfaction than those wives whose last child had left home recently.
7. However, menopause (also known as climacteric) may occur at any time between the mid-thirties and early sixties (American Medical Association, 1972, p. 81). The process usually does not exceed two years (McCary, 1973, p. 98).
8. Some physicians feel the risks of supplemental hormones outweigh their benefits.
9. For 85 percent of men, the hormonal change is slow and gradual; 15 percent experience a rapid, sharp decline (Sheehy, 1976, p. 315).
10. When a group of college students were asked to complete the sentence, "Sex for older people is . . . ," the words they chose most frequently were "unimportant," "negligible," and "past" (Lear, 1974, p. 40). Their description accurately reflects the larger society's view that sex is reserved for the young and attractive. Notice that when you think of a couple engaging in sexual intercourse, your image probably does not include gray hair, wrinkled skin, and frail bodies.
11. One researcher has suggested that, in view of the limitations imposed by age, older couples should adopt a new perspective of sexuality consistent with the reality of the aging process

(Cleveland, 1976). Such a new framework would imply that "sexuality is not 'performance' oriented—not oriented toward orgasm. Instead, the objective is to gain intimacy, joy, and fulfillment through a broad spectrum of sensual/sexual interactions. Genital intercourse resulting in orgasm is just one form of such interaction" (Cleveland, 1976, p. 236). Without adopting a new perspective on sexuality, the older person may become depressed when trying to cope with physiological limitations (Sviland, 1975).

12. Social class affects how a person perceives the aging process. While members of the middle class tend to view old age in terms of leisure, relaxation, and security, lower-class people regard old age as a period of progressive physical decline, senility, and full retirement (Huyck, 1974, p. 11).

13. Appreciation is expressed to Dr. Jeffrey Rosenfeld for sharing this and other references on aging.

14. Young people sometimes experience the feeling of role loss during the summer when they long for a reactivation of the role of student.

15. This figure refers to households in which the head of the household is sixty-five or older.

16. This discussion focuses on the unique aspects of the grandparent role, not on the specific role behaviors. These have been reviewed by Robertson (1977) who points out that grandparents function as babysitters, parental surrogates, interveners in times of crisis, bearers of family history, supplementers of family income, and household caretakers when parents are ill, giving birth, or on vacation.

17. In a study of seventy-five societies, Apple (1956) concluded that the tendency of grandparents and grandchildren to be close is not universal.

18. This percentage represents a combination of the "apportioned" and "symbolic" grandmother types as described by Robertson (1977).

BIBLIOGRAPHY

Allen, H. *Anthony Adverse*. New York: Farrar and Rinehart, 1933.

American Medical Association Committee on Human Sexuality. *Human sexuality*. Chicago: American Medical Association, 1972.

Apple, D. The social structure of grandparenthood. *American Anthropologist*, August 1956, *58*, 656–63.

Atchley, R. *The social forces in later life: An introduction to social gerontology*. Belmont, Calif.: Wadsworth, 1972.

———. Selected social and psychological differences between men and women in later life. *Journal of Gerontology*, 1976, *31*, 204–11.

Brayshaw, A. J. Middle-aged marriages: Idealism, realism, and a search for meaning. *Marriage and Family Living*, 1962, *24*, 358–64.

Butler, R., and Lewis, M. *Sex after sixty*. New York: Harper and Row, 1976.

Cavan, R. S. *The American family*. New York: Thomas Y. Crowell, 1953.

Cleveland, M. Sex in marriage: At 40 and beyond. *The Family Coordinator*, 1976, *25*, 3, 233–40.

Dressel, P. L., and Avant, W. R. Neogamy and older persons: An examination of alternatives for intimacy in the later years. *Alternative Life Styles*, 1978, *1*, 1, 13–36.

Duvall, E. *Marriage and family development*. Philadelphia: J. B. Lippincott, 1977.

Eisdorfer, C., and Lawton, M. P. (eds.). *The psychology of adult development and aging*. Washington, D.C.: American Psychological Association, 1973.

Feldman, F. L. *The family in today's money world*. New York: Family Service Association of America, 1976.

Feldman, H., and Feldman, M. Marriage in the later years: Cohort and parental effects. Unpublished paper, Department of Human Development and Family Studies, Cornell University, 1976.

Foote, N. N. New roles for men and women. *Marriage and Family Living*, 1961, *23*, 325–29.

Fox, J. H. Effects of retirement and former work life on women's adaptation in old age. *Journal of Gerontology,* 1977, *32,* 3, 196–202.

Frank, H. Retirement: An ego alien view. *International Journal of Family Counseling,* 1977, *5,* 1, 44–7.

Fuchs, E. *The second season: Life, love, and sex–Women in the middle years.* New York: Doubleday, 1977.

Glenn, N. D. Psychological well-being in the postparental stage: Some evidence from national surveys. *Journal of Marriage and the Family,* 1975, *35,* 1, 105–10.

Glick, P. C. The life cycle of the family. *Marriage and Family Living,* 1955, *17,* 1, 3–9.

_____. Updating the life cycle of the family. *Journal of Marriage and the Family,* 1977, *39,* 1, 5–13.

Glick, P. C., and Norton, A. J. Marrying, divorcing, and living together in the United States today. *Population Bulletin,* 1977, *32,* 5.

Havighurst, R. J. Personality and patterns of aging. In *Aging in America: Readings in social gerontology.* C. S. Kart and B. B. Manard (eds.). New York: Alfred Publishing, 1976, 192–99.

Hayes, M. P., and Stinnett, N. Life satisfaction of middle-aged husbands and wives. *Journal of Home Economics,* 1971, *63,* 9, 669–74.

Henry, J. Forty-year-old jitters in married urban women. In *Marriage and the family,* C. Perrucci and D. Tary (eds.). New York: David McKay, 1974, 440–48.

Huyck, M. H. *Growing older.* Englewood Cliffs, N.J.: Prentice-Hall, 1974.

Irelan, L. M., and Bond, K. Retirees of the 1970s. In *Aging in America: Readings in social gerontology,* C. S. Kart and B. B. Manard. New York: Alfred Publishing, 1976, 231–51.

Jones, E. (ed.). Little red riding hood. In *Fairy tales and rhymes.* New York: Golden Press, 1969, 31–52.

Kaplan, H. *The new sex therapy.* New York: Quadrangle, 1974.

Kaplan, H., and Sager, C. J. Sexual patterns at different ages. *Medical Aspects of Human Sexuality,* 1971, *5,* 10–23.

Katchadourian, H. A., and Lunde, D. *Fundamentals of human sexuality* (2nd ed.). New York: Holt, Rinehart and Winston, 1975.

Keller, J. *Freedom for elders.* San Francisco: Canfield Press, 1977. (a)

_____. The gray revolution: The life and times of the elderly. Paper presented at the seventeenth annual Family Life Conference, East Carolina University, Greenville, N.C., April 1977. (b)

Klass, S. B., and Redfern, M. A. A social work response to the middle-aged housewife. *Social Casework,* 1977, *58,* 2, 101–10.

Knox, D. Love in middle age. Unpublished paper, Department of Sociology, East Carolina University, 1970. (a)

_____. Conceptions of love at three developmental levels. *The Family Coordinator,* 1970, *19,* 151–7. (b)

Leaf, A., and Launois, J. Search for the oldest people. *National Geographic,* 1973, *143,* 93–118.

Lear, M. W. Is there a male menopause? In *Growing older,* M. H. Huyck (ed.). Englewood Cliffs, N.J.: Prentice-Hall, 1974, 37–49.

LeShan, E. J. *The wonderful crisis of middle age.* New York: David McKay, 1973.

Levinson, D. J. The Mid-life transition: A period in adult psycho-social development. *Psychiatry,* 1977, *40,* 2, 99–112.

Masters, W., and Johnson, V. Human sexual response: The aging female and the aging male. In *Middle age and aging,* B. Neugarten (ed.). Chicago: University of Chicago Press, 1968.

McCary, J. L. *Human sexuality.* New York: D. Van Nostrand, 1973.

McClard, M. Middle age. In *Scenes from life,* J. Blankenship (ed.). Boston: Little, Brown, 1976, 447–50.

Mead, M. *Blackberry winter.* New York: William Morrow, 1972.

Meikle, S., Brody, H., and Pysh, F. An investigation into the psychological effects of hysterectomy. *The Journal of Nervous and Mental Disease,* 1977, *164,* 1, 36–41.

Neugarten, B. The awareness of middle age. In *Middle age and aging,* B. Neugarten (ed.). Chicago: University of Chicago Press, 1968.

Neugarten, B., and Weinstein, K. The changing American grandparent. *Journal of Marriage and the Family,* 1964, *26,* 199–204.

Neugarten, B., et al. Women's attitudes toward the menopause. *Vita Humana,* 1963, *6,* 140–51.

Newman, G., and Nichols, C. R. Sexual activities and attitudes in older persons. In *Studies in human sexual behavior: The American scene,* A. Shiloh (ed.). Springfield, Ill.: Charles C. Thomas, 1970.

Nye, I., and Berardo, F. *The family: Its structure and interaction.* New York: Macmillan, 1973.

Palmore, E. Health practices and illness. In *Normal aging II,* E. Palmore (ed.). Durham, N.C.: Duke University Press, 1974, 49–55.

Pfeiffer, E., and Davis, G. Determinants of sexual behavior in middle and old age. *Journal of the American Geriatrics Society,* 1972, *20,* 4, 151–8.

Pfeiffer, E., Verwoerdt, A., and Davis, G. Sexual behavior in middle life. In *Normal aging II,* E. Palmore (ed.). Durham, N.C.: Duke University Press, 1974, 243–51.

Pfeiffer, E., Verwoerdt, A., and Wang, H. S. Sexual behavior in aged men and women. In *Normal aging* (Vol. 1), E. Palmore (ed.). Durham, N.C.: Duke University Press, 1970, 299–310.

Porter, S. *Sylvia Porter's money book.* New York: Doubleday, 1976.

Radcliffe-Brown, A. R. *Structure and function in primitive society.* London: Cohen and West, 1952.

Roberts, A. E., and Roberts, W. L. Factors in lifestyles of couples married over 50 years. Paper presented at annual meeting of National Council on Family Relations, Salt Lake City, August 1975.

Robertson, J. F. Grandmotherhood: A study of role conceptions. *Journal of Marriage and the Family,* 1977, *39,* 1, 165–74.

Rollins, B. C., and Feldman, H. Marital satisfaction over the family life cycle. *Journal of Marriage and the Family,* 1970, *32,* 1, 20–28.

Rubin, I. *Sexual life after sixty.* New York: Basic Books, 1965.

Saunders, L. E. Empathy, communication, and the definition of life satisfaction in the post parental period. *Family Perspective,* 1974, *8,* 2, 21–35.

Sheehy, G. *Passages: Predictable crises of adult life.* New York: E. P. Dutton, 1976.

Sheldon, A., McEwan, P., and Ryser, C. P. *Retirement patterns and predictions.* Washington, D.C.: U.S. Government Printing Office, 1975.

Silverstone, B., and Hyman, H. K. *You and your aging parent.* New York: Pantheon Books, 1976.

Simmons, L. W. Social participation of the aged in different cultures. *The Annals of the American Academy of Political and Social Science,* 1952, *279,* 43–51.

Spence, D., and Lonner, T. The "empty nest": A transition within motherhood. *The Family Coordinator,* 1971, *20,* 4, 369–75.

Statistical Bulletin. New York: Metropolitan Life, September 1975.

Stewart, D. Department of Sociology, East Carolina University, Personal communication, 1977.

Stinnett, N., Carter, L. and Montgomery, J. Older persons' perceptions of their marriages. *Journal of Marriage and the Family,* 1972, *34,* 665–70.

Stinnett, N., and Walters, J. *Relationships in marriage and family.* New York: Macmillan, 1977.

Sviland, M. A. P. Helping elderly people become sexually liberated: Psycho-social issues. *Counseling Psychologist,* 1975, *5,* 1, 67–72.

U.S., Bureau of the Census. *Statistical abstract of the United States: 1977* (98th ed.). Washington, D.C.: U.S. Government Printing Office, 1977.

U.S., Office of Human Development, Administration on Aging. Publication No. (OHD) 77-2006, 1976.

Van Buren, A. Face lifts can be deducted. *The Greenville (N.C.) Daily Reflector,* 1 May 1977.

Verwoerdt, A., Pfeiffer, E., and Wang, H. S. Sexual behavior in senescence. In *Normal aging* (Vol. 1), E. Palmore (ed.). Durham, N.C.: Duke University Press, 1970, 282–99.

Vincent, C. E. An open letter to the "caught generation." *The Family Coordinator,* 1972, *21,* 2, 143–50.

Chapter 19

Endings and New Beginnings

DIVORCE

History of Divorce • Frequency of Divorce • Causes of Divorce •
Characteristics of Divorced People • The Marriage Relationship from
First Meeting to Divorce • Alternatives to Divorce • Consequences of Divorce

WIDOWHOOD

The Bereavement Process • Adjustment for Widows • Adjustment for
Widowers • Preparation for Widowhood

REMARRIAGE

Remarriage for the Divorced • Remarriage for the Widowed

TRENDS

SUMMARY

If the quality of family life deteriorates, there is no "quality of life."
Michael Novak

Divorce and death are the principal means by which marriages end. (Others are desertion and annulment.) From such endings emerge an array of human emotions—frustration, disappointment, grief, relief, hope, and growth. In this chapter we explore the process of, and adjustment to, marital dissolution by divorce and death. We also look at the option of remarriage.

DIVORCE

Each year there are over a million divorces in the United States (U.S. Vital and Health Statistics, 1978). Preceding them, spouses express feelings like these to each other:

> "I'm tired of waiting for things to get better. I'm afraid that twenty years from now we'll be in the same stale relationship. Let's separate."
> "I feel trapped and want out."
> "It's not that I think bad things about you; it's just that I don't think about you at all anymore."
> "I am involved in a new relationship and want a divorce."

What began at a wedding ceremony, usually complete with minister, parents, and friends, ends in a courtroom with a judge and lawyers. The reality of day-to-day living failed to meet the hopeful expectations the parties shared during courtship.

In this section we are concerned about marriage relationships that end in divorce. After reviewing the history of divorce, we examine who gets divorced, why, how, and with what consequences. We will also explore several alternatives to divorce.

History of Divorce

For the ancient Greeks, Romans, and Hebrews, divorce (like marriage) was a private affair. Marital dissolutions were arranged by the spouses and their relatives (Fullerton, 1977, p. 393). Particularly in the Mediterranean societies from which our Judeo-Christian traditions spring, customs ruled that only the husband could initiate a divorce. The ancient Hebrew husband could say "I divorce thee" to his wife, and their marriage would end. Not until the days of the Roman Empire did wives acquire the right to divorce their husbands (Fullerton, 1977).

Under Christianity, marriage was regarded as a sacrament, a religious act that only the Church could validate. The relationship could be dissolved only by death. But in time the Church fathers recognized that, under conditions of extreme cruelty, married life might become intolerable. To deal with these unusual circumstances, ecclesiastical courts would sometimes issue a limited divorce that allowed the spouses to live separately, though neither could remarry.

After the Protestant Reformation, marriage came to be viewed in other than sacramental terms. Some Christian denominations abandoned the concept of marriage as an insoluble bond, and with the growth of secular power responsibility for the regulation of marriage was transferred from Church to state. Among non-Catholics a recognition of absolute divorce ensued. In general, divorce was granted only for reasons of adultery, cruelty, and desertion, where one spouse had clearly "wronged" the other.

Traditionally, the United States has had an adversary system of divorce in which one party is found innocent and the other guilty. Under the "fault doctrine," it was (and in many states still is) necessary to prove that one spouse had performed some specific act detrimental to the other spouse or to the marriage. For example, the wife might say (and prove), "He beat me" (physical cruelty), or "He won't give me money for groceries" (nonsupport). Likewise, the husband might accuse his wife of having an affair (adultery). The "innocent party" would then be granted a divorce.

As an alternative to the fault system of divorce, the California legislature in 1970 initiated the no-fault system so that spouses could dissolve their marriage if either partner felt there were "irreconcilable differences" in their relationship. Such differences are "those grounds which are determined by the court to be substantial reasons for not continuing the marriage and which make it appear that the marriage should be dissolved" (Wheeler, 1974, p. 21). Under the no-fault doctrine, spouses who don't want to live with each other because they are not happy, have grown apart, or don't care for each other as they once did can get a divorce with relative ease.

By 1978 almost all of the states had adopted similar no-fault provisions. Other labels for "irreconcilable differences" included "irretrievable breakdown," "irremediable breakdown," and "no reasonable likelihood of preserving the marriage." Some states have also adopted separation as a ground for divorce. Under this provision, the couple need only prove that they have been living apart for one year.

Frequency of Divorce

Historically, the collection and interpretation of divorce statistics has been far from perfect. It was only during the 1930s that even birth and death statistics became available in accurate form for the entire country. Before that time, estimates from limited existing data had to be made. And divorce data are quite a bit behind birth and death statistics. The National Office of Vital Statistics began improving the marriage and divorce statistics in 1946. At the present time, slightly over half

TABLE 19.1   Crude and Refined Divorce Rates in the United States.

Year	Number of Divorces	Divorces per 1000 population (Crude divorce rate)	Divorces per 1000 married women over fifteen (Refined divorce rate)
1960	393,000	2.2	9
1965	479,000	2.5	11
1970	708,000	3.5	15
1975	1,036,000	4.9	20.3
1976	1,077,000	5.0	na*

*Not available.
SOURCE: U.S. National Center for Health Statistics, 1978, 23.

the fifty states report full information to the federal government on the number and characteristics of the divorces granted. The total figures for the other states are estimated from what information they do send in and from comparisons with reporting states that are similar in overall characteristics of life-style. Although these statistics are improving, all we can do is present the best available information and hope the estimations involved are accurate. Figures on divorce from other countries are also often lacking. Nevertheless, of all the modern industrial societies, the United States has the least reliable marriage and divorce statistics.

Not only are the data on divorce limited, but there are also three ways of describing the frequency of divorce: the crude divorce rate, the refined divorce rate, and the ratio of current marriages to current divorces. The crude divorce rate is the number of divorces per 1000 population. In general, this index of divorce rate is the least useful since not all members of our society are married. The refined divorce rate is the number of divorces per 1000 married women who are over age fifteen. Table 19.1 reflects the crude and refined divorce rates at five-year intervals beginning in 1960. Whether the crude or the refined divorce rate is used as an index of the frequency of divorce, divorce is clearly increasing.

But what about the statements we hear concerning the high and alarming divorce rates? "Over half of the marriages in some California and Florida counties end in divorce." "Almost half of all marriages everywhere in the United States go on the rocks." "Most marriages end up in the courts." We tend to apply such statistics to our own lives and wonder, "If *my* marriage would stand only a fifty-fifty chance, why bother?" Such thinking is erroneous.

Most of the divorce statistics we hear are grossly misleading. The figures most often cited are based on the ratio of marriages to divorces in a particular year. For example, if one hundred marriage licenses and fifty divorce decrees are granted in your county this year, one interpretation might be that half of the marriages in your county end in divorce. Such a conclusion is misleading because the fifty divorces granted this year represent not just marriages that began this year but marriages that began long ago. People married three, five, eighteen, and forty years ago are included in the fifty divorces. One researcher observed that the ratio of current marriages to current divorces is "how *not* to measure the incidence of divorce" (Scanzoni, 1972, p. 10).

The basic question remains: If one hundred couples marry today, what percent of these couples will eventually divorce? The only way to answer this question conclusively is to follow the marriages of all one hundred couples until they are ended by death, divorce, desertion, or annulment. While this is not possible, current estimates suggest that about one third of recent marriages will probably end in divorce (U.S. Bureau of the Census, 1976, p. 4).

Высокие divorce rates do not indicate that marriage is no longer considered important by Americans. Rather . . . marriage has become so important a source of emotional satisfaction that few people can endure a relationship which does not provide this. If only one out of three first marriages ends in divorce Americans are either phenomenally successful at marriage or phenomenally tolerant of poor marriages.

Richard Udry

Causes of Divorce

Finding the causes of divorce is not simple. The reasons are embedded in the makeup of the individuals involved and in the makeup of the society in which the divorce occurs. Let's explore the possible societal and personal reasons for divorce.

Societal factors. A number of factors have combined to make divorce increasingly common in America. They include the following:

1. Changing family functions. Many of the protective, religious, educational, and recreational functions of the family have largely been taken over by outside agencies. Family members may now look to the police, the church or synagogue, the school, and public recreational facilities rather than to each other for fulfilling these needs. The result is that beyond meeting emotional needs, which remains a primary function of the family, there is less reason to keep the family together.

2. Employed wives. In the past, the unemployed wife was dependent on her husband for food, clothes, and shelter. No matter how unhappy her marital

situation, she could think about divorce, but that was about all she could do. Her husband literally represented her lifeline. But finding gainful employment outside the home made it possible for her to "afford" to withdraw from an unhappy situation. Now that over 50 percent of wives are employed (and this number is escalating), fewer and fewer wives are economically trapped in an unhappy marriage relationship.

3. Fewer moral and religious sanctions. Although the Catholic church remains reluctant to recognize divorce, most Protestant denominations have taken a more permissive view. Many clergymen recognize that divorce may be the only alternative in a particular marital relationship and attempt to minimize the guilt a member of their congregation may feel at the failure of his or her marriage. In essence, marriage is often viewed in secular rather than sacred terms.

4. Increasing divorce rate. As more and more Americans are divorced each year, the probability increases that a person's friends, parents, or siblings will be divorced. And the more divorced people a person knows, the more "normal" divorce will seem to that person. The less deviant the person perceives divorce to be, the greater the probability that person will divorce if his or her own marriage becomes strained.

5. Personal mate selection. As noted in Chapter 7 on "Pairing Off," American parents have, in the past, had more control over whom their son or daughter married. In some cases, if the parents did not approve of a particular partner, elopement was the only alternative. The result of parentally controlled mate selection was that marriages were not entered into on a wave of emotion. If the parents had to approve before the wedding could occur, other factors than love— money, property, family background, etc.—were considered. But today love may be the primary consideration in the decision to marry, and feelings of love are sometimes not enough to weather fifty years together.

6. Goal of happiness. To achieve and maintain personal happiness is a primary goal of most people who marry. Few are concerned about the functional and institutional aspects of marriage. When spouses become unhappy, the typical question they ask themselves is, "Why should I stay married to someone if I'm not happy?" While the current answer of many Americans tends to be, "You shouldn't," until fairly recently the answer of the great majority was "It's not unusual to be unhappy in marriage. Work it out. You've taken vows and owe it to yourselves, to your children, and to your parents to keep your marriage together." While couples were expected to "stick it out" in an unhappy marriage in years past (and still are to some degree), increasingly the question is asked, "Why?"

7. Liberal divorce laws. In their study of divorce laws and divorce rates, two researchers concluded that as laws make divorce easier, divorce rates climb (Stetson & Wright, 1975, p. 545). In 1970, the first year under California's no-fault divorce law, the number of divorces jumped 46 percent (Wheeler, 1974, p. 27). While this increase can't be attributed entirely to the new legislation, states that adopt more liberal divorce laws can expect an increase in the divorce rate.

Individual factors. While various societal factors may make divorce a viable alternative to marital unhappiness, they are not sufficient to "cause," a divorce. One spouse must actually initiate divorce proceedings. What encourages him or her to do so? Here are some of the possibilities:

1. Negative behavior. People marry because they anticipate greater rewards from being married than from being single. During courtship, the positive behavior of the partner (compliments, eye contact, physical affection) influences the individual to make the relationship and its reinforcing qualities permanent. Marriage helps ensure that the person you spend time with today will "be around" to share the same experiences tomorrow.

Just as love feelings are based on positive behavior from the partner, hostile feelings are created when the partner engages in negative behavior. In one study of the sources of marital dissatisfaction among six hundred couples who applied for divorce (Levinger, 1966), wives complained that their husbands drank too much, only touched them when they wanted intercourse, yelled obscenities at them, beat them, and were sexually unfaithful. The husbands complained that their wives did not approach them for intercourse, sided with their mothers against their husbands, and nagged too much.

When the positive behavior on the part of one or both spouses diminishes to such a point that continuing the relationship involves more costs than rewards, either partner may begin to seek a more reinforcing situation. Divorce (being single again) or remarriage may appear to be an attractive alternative to being married to the present spouse.

2. Boredom. A twenty-six-year-old who had been married for four years said, "It's not that my wife is terrible. I'm just tired of the same thing all the time. I dated a lot before I was married, and I miss the excitement of new people."

A variety of individual factors may lead a person to file for divorce—for instance, boredom, an extramarital relationship, or a buildup of hostility between the two partners.

"Satiated" best describes his feelings. As though he had been watching the third rerun of a TV movie, he is bored. He views divorce as a means of freeing himself from the stale relationship with his wife.

3. Extramarital relationship. Spouses who feel mistreated by their partners, bored, and trapped sometimes consider the alternative of being in a relationship with someone who is good to them, is exciting, is new, and who offers an escape from the role of spouse to the role of lover. Extramarital involvements sometimes speed a decaying marriage to divorce because the partner begins to contrast the new lover with the spouse. Since the spouse is often associated with negative feelings and the lover almost exclusively with positive feelings, the choice is stacked in favor of the lover. But some spouses who are involved in an extramarital relationship would like to stay married. In such cases, the spouse may feel "left out" and threaten divorce if the mate does not terminate the affair. While society does not encourage divorce, it often accepts a divorce more readily than an affair.

4. Spouse. Sometimes a spouse who is happy with the marriage accepts divorce because the partner wants a divorce. Four of every ten couples who get a divorce include one member who does not want it (Glick, 1975, p. 22).

Characteristics of Divorced People

Divorce occurs more frequently among some categories of people than among others. Groups that tend to be overrepresented among the divorced include: those who marry early (U.S. Bureau of the Census, 1976; Schoen, 1975); are pregnant when they marry (Christensen & Meissner, 1953); drop out of high school or college (Glick & Norton, 1971; Glick, 1975); are from a low socioeconomic background (Scanzoni, 1972; Renne, 1970); are black (Cutright, 1971; Udry, 1974); or have been previously divorced (U.S. Bureau of the Census, 1976).[1]

Marry'd in haste, we may repent at leisure.
William Congreve

The Marriage Relationship from First Meeting to Divorce

For most couples, the divorce process involves six predictable stages. One researcher identified the stages as: (1) the emotional divorce, which centers around the problem of the deteriorating marriage; (2) the legal divorce, based on official grounds or justification for filing; (3) the economic divorce, which deals with money and property; (4) the coparental divorce, which deals with custody, single-parent homes, and visitation; (5) the community divorce, that is, the

Are You a Candidate for Divorce?

Reviewing the various categories of those who divorce often leaves the impression that divorce is something that happens to someone else. We tend to feel, particularly at the beginning of a marriage, that "this is it—this is for life." But the reality is quite different. Advice columnist Ann Landers wrote of her divorce:

DEAR READERS: In my 20 years as Ann Landers this is the most difficult column I have ever tried to put together.

I do so after many hours of soul-searching. Should it be written at all? Would it be appropriate? Would it be fair? I have decided yes—because, you, my readers, are also my friends. I owe it to you to say something. There should be some word directly from me.

The sad, incredible fact is that after 36 years of marriage Jules and I are being divorced. As I write these words, it is as if I am referring to a letter from a reader. It seems unreal that I am writing about my own marriage.

Many of you may remember the column that appeared in 1969. It was in honor of our 30th wedding anniversary. You may also recall the column I wrote when my beloved mother-in-law, Gustie Lederer, passed away. On both occasions I gave you some intimate glimpses of our life together. Thousands of readers were kind enough to write and say they considered those columns best.

Every word that appeared in those columns was true when I wrote them, and very little that was said then could not be said today—in complete honesty.

Jules is an extraordinary man. His nickname for me was "The Queen." He was loving, supportive and generous. He is still all those things—and I will always cherish our wonderful years together.

That we are going our separate ways is one of life's strangest ironies. How did it happen that something so good for so long didn't last forever? The lady with all the answers does not know the answer to this one.

Perhaps there is a lesson there for all of us. At least, it is there for me. "Never say, 'It couldn't happen to us.' "

Please, don't write or call and ask for details. The response would be, "Sorry, this is a personal matter. . . ." Time will not alter my position. I shall continue to say, "No comment." There will be no compromising . . . no exceptions. Just wish us both well.

Not only has this been the most difficult column I ever have written, but also it is the shortest. I apologize to my editors for not giving you your money's worth today. I ask that you not fill this space with other letters. Please leave it blank—as a memorial to one of the world's best marriages that didn't make it to the finish line.

ANN LANDERS

Are you a candidate for divorce? We all are.

SOURCE: Landers, 1975.

FIGURE 19.1 A Marital Relationship—From Beginning to End.

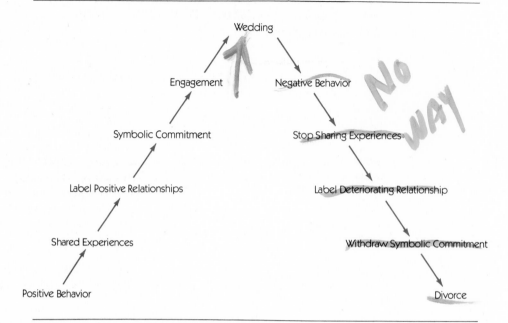

changed interaction with friends and community that every divorced person experiences; and (6) the psychic divorce, involving the problem of regaining individual autonomy (Bohannan, 1971, p. 34). Figure 19.1 depicts the buildup and disintegration of a marital relationship visually. Since the emotional divorce is the first step in the divorce experience, let's back up and examine precisely how it comes about.

The beginning.   A relationship begins when two people exchange positive behaviors in the form of compliments, attention, and actual or promised physical contact. "I like you," "You are fun to be with," and "You're beautiful" are examples of the positive phrases partners exchange which communicate that each regards the other in a very favorable way. These words are often exchanged while the partners are looking directly into each other's eyes and holding hands. All such behaviors indicate unconditional positive regard of each toward the other (Rogers, 1951).

The relationship gathers momentum when the partners begin to share activities and time. Eating together, seeing movies together, dancing together, sailing together, and attending sporting events or concerts together provide a positive base of common experience. And all these behaviors occur along with increased physical intimacy.

If the positive shared experiences continue, the partners are likely to interpret the feelings they experience as love feelings. Labeling the relationship as a love relationship gives the pair's interaction a special quality. Each begins to see the other with a degree of commitment that may result in both disengaging themselves from other involvements.

As other heterosexual relationships are minimized, the unspoken commitment is verbalized and symbols are used to signify the new level of the relationship. The partners are now seen exclusively with each other, and property lines of what belongs to whom disappear. She may set up his stereo in her apartment, and he may use her car. Either may pay for food or entertainment.

Formal engagement makes the personal commitment public. The wedding is one of the crowning events of the developing relationship which began with the exchange of positive behaviors. After the honeymoon, the marriage relationship may continue to fulfill the needs of the respective spouses. That is, an acceptable level of positive behavior may continue, the marriage relationship may be defined as creative rather than stifling, and extramarital relationships may not be permitted to interfere.

The end.[2] Causes of the beginning of the end of a marital relationship may include any number of problems. Twelve hundred spouses who applied for a divorce specified the following reasons:

1. Neglect of home or children: frequent absence, irregular hours, emotional distance.
2. Financial problems: either inadequate support (by husband) or poor handling of family's money.
3. Physical abuse: committing overt physical hurt or injury to other partner.
4. Verbal abuse: profanity, name-calling, shouting.
5. Infidelity: attachment to an alternate partner, frequently sexual in nature, which excludes spouse; adultery.
6. Sexual incompatibility: reluctance [about] or refusal of coitus, inconsiderateness and other sources of dissatisfaction.
7. Drinking: drunkenness or excessive drinking.
8. In-law trouble: interference or pressure by in-laws, spouse's excessive loyalty to parental kin.
9. Mental cruelty: suspicion, jealousy, untruthfulness, and vague subjective complaints.
10. Lack of love: insufficient affection, communication, companionship.
11. Excessive demands: impatience, intolerance, strictness, possessiveness.
12. Other: miscellaneous category.

(Levinger, 1966)

In general, unless the behaviors which prompt complaints of this type in a marriage are modified, the negative feelings the behaviors cause will be likely to continue, and the possibility that the marriage will drift toward divorce will increase (Christiansen & Robinson, 1975). As a result, the partners will stop spending time together. One thirty-two-year-old fashion merchandiser said,

"Since my husband criticizes me every time I'm around him, I've started avoiding him. I go to bed late and try to leave in the morning before he gets up. We rarely see each other any more." Failure to spend time together makes it impossible for spouses to re-create the positive feelings necessary to motivate them to stay married.

As feelings grow more distant, the deteriorating relationship is negatively labeled. One partner comes out and says, "I think we should get a divorce." This labeling is significant and seems to carry the couple to the lawyer. A husband and father of two children said, "After she told me she wanted a divorce, things haven't been the same. I feel dead inside."

The "dead" feeling inside results in public demonstration that the marriage is ending. The spouses take off their rings, go alone (or with someone new) to events they would normally attend together, and tell their closest friends that "we aren't getting along." Once the symbols of marriage are withdrawn and friends begin to ask, "What's the latest?" the momentum toward divorce is strong enough to sweep the couple into the courtroom.

But this progression toward divorce can stop at any point. It is not unusual for spouses to become unhappy, discuss divorce, and even separate, yet still resolve their differences (alone or through counseling) so that the relationship stays intact and an acceptable level of happiness is recaptured.

If negative behaviors such as loud arguing and criticizing go unchecked in a marriage, the partners are likely to label their relationship negatively and see divorce as a positive alternative to remaining in the relationship.

Alternatives to Divorce

Divorce is not the inevitable response to marital unhappiness. Spouses unable to reconcile their differences may terminate their relationship by annulment, separation (formal or informal), or desertion.

Annulment. An annulment differs from a divorce, which presupposes that a valid marriage did exist but is terminated because of certain "grounds" that arose subsequent to the marriage. The concept of annulment had its origin in the Roman Catholic Church, which takes the position that marriage is insoluble except by death. An annulment states that no valid marriage ever existed and returns both parties to their premarital status. Any property that has been exchanged as part of the marriage arrangement is returned to its original owner. Neither partner has obligations to the other for economic support.

Common reasons for annulments are fraud, bigamy, age, impotence, and insanity or lack of understanding. A university professor became involved with one of his students. During courtship he promised her that they would rear a "house full of babies." After the marriage, she discovered that he had had a vasectomy before their marriage and had no intention of having his own or adopting children. The marriage was annulled on the basis of fraud—his misrepresenting himself to her.

Another annulment suit (Frances B. *vs.* Mark B.) was initated by Frances B. She asserted that her "husband" had fraudulently represented himself to be a man named Mark B. and that she (the wife) had entered into marriage with Mark B. believing that he was a male. But Mark B. was anatomically a woman. An annulment was granted on the premise that marriage is and always has been a contract between a man and woman *(Family Law Newsletter, 1974)*. Half of all annulments are for fraud of one kind or another.

Bigamy accounts for another 35 percent of annulments (Landis & Landis, 1977). An unhappy soldier became emotionally involved with a barmaid during his basic training. They married. The bride was unaware of her husband's previous marriage until she read the return address on a letter in their mailbox. The marriage was annulled.

Most states have age requirements for marriage. When individuals are younger than the minimum age and marry without parental consent, the marriage may be annulled if either set of parents does not approve. However, if neither set of parents or guardians disapproves of the marriage and if the state recognizes common-law marriage, the marriage is not automatically annulled and may be regarded as legal.

Intercourse is a legal right of marriage. In some states, if the male is impotent (cannot create and maintain an erection), his wife can have the marriage annulled. Likewise, if the wife refuses to have intercourse or is unable to do so for physical (vaginismus or dyspareunia) or psychological reasons, annulment is a possibility.

Insanity and lack of understanding are also reasons for annulment. A man was shot in a hunting accident shortly after marriage. The bullet struck his head, affecting his memory, speech, and muscle coordination. Saying, "He's not the man I married," the wife sought an annulment. In this case the annulment was not granted because the hunting accident occurred after the wedding. Where insanity before the marriage or lack of understanding of the marriage agreement can be shown, an annulment is often granted.

Annulments account for a small proportion—about 3.5 percent—of broken marriages (U.S. National Center for Health Statistics, 1973). When spouses decide to terminate their marital relationship, they look for the legal reasons that will permit them to do so. Where a state specifies several grounds for divorce, annulments are rare. Where divorces are difficult to get, annulments are more numerous.

Separation—Formal.   An equally small proportion of emotionally dead relationships end in separation. Separations, or limited divorces, are sought by couples who, for religious or personal reasons, do not want a divorce and who do not have grounds for an annulment. The consequences of a legal separation agreement are these: (1) The husband and wife live separately; (2) the right to sexual intercourse with each other is ended; (3) the economic responsibility of the spouses to each other is limited to the separation agreement (usually the husband will pay the wife a fixed amount for alimony and child support); and (4) custody of the children is specified in the agreement, with visitation privileges granted the other parent (Pilpel & Zavin, 1964). A separation implies that the separated spouses are legally free to become involved with others, but neither party has the legal right to remarry. While some couples live under this agreement until the death of one spouse, others draw up a separation agreement as a prelude to divorce. For example, in some states, the fact that spouses have been legally separated for one year is a ground for divorce.

Separation—Informal.   An informal separation is similar to legal separation except that no lawyer is involved in the agreement, which may not even be written down. The husband and wife settle between themselves the issues of child custody and alimony. Since no legal papers are drawn up, from the state's point of view, they remain married. Attorneys advise against an informal separation (unless it is strictly temporary) to avoid subsequent legal problems. For example, after three years of an informal separation, a mother decided that she wanted custody of her son. Although the father would have been willing earlier to sign a separation agreement that would have given her legal custody of her son, he was now unwilling to do so. They hired lawyers and had a bitter and expensive court fight.

Desertion.   Desertion differs from informal separation in that the deserter walks out and breaks off all contact. Although either spouse may desert, it is the husband who usually disappears. A major reason for deserting is to escape the increasing financial responsibility of a family (Eshleman, 1978). A husband may also desert because he can't afford the cost of a divorce. The sudden withdrawal that desertion involves often has more severe negative consequences than divorce. For example, unlike the divorced woman, the deserted woman is not free to remarry for several years. In addition, no child-support payments are received, and the children are deprived of husband and wife role models.

But desertion is not unique to husbands. In 1973, there were close to one million (971,000) motherless families (those situations where the mother had died are excluded from this figure) (U.S. Bureau of the Census, 1974). A Canadian study of thirty-eight runaway wives revealed that while women who desert their families feel a sense of relief from leaving an intolerable marriage, they feel guilty about leaving their children behind (Todres, 1978).

Consequences of Divorce

While annulment, separation, and desertion are alternatives to divorce, most marriages not terminated by death are terminated by divorce. The granting of the formal decree has certain consequences for the spouses and their children.

Personal reaction. A marriage and family counselor who divorced after twenty-five years of marriage said, "I knew all about divorce, except what it felt like." Divorce is for most an emotionally devastating experience. In a random sample study of over two thousand adults, the authors concluded, "In spite of all the cheerful books on creative divorce, no-fault divorce, and better living through divorce, people whose marriages fail are miserable. Most of them, more men than women, marry again, but while they are divorced they face problems that their single and married friends do not" (Campbell, 1975).

In a study of seventy-two middle-class couples at two-month, one-year, and two-year intervals following their divorces, the authors concluded, "We didn't find a single victimless divorce among the families we studied. At least one member of each family reported distress or showed a negative change in behavior, particularly during the first year. Most of them were ultimately able to cope with their problems, but the adjustment was often unexpectedly painful" (Hetherington et al., 1977, p. 46).

Wives may experience the impact of divorce more severely than husbands. In a study of 277 members of the organization "Parents Without Partners," women perceived themselves as having experienced greater stress than their husbands in the divorce process (Raschke, 1976). In another study of 180 divorced and remarried spouses, the ex-wives preferred greater social distance from their former husbands than vice versa (Goetting, 1978). Among white wives, being traditional (home and children as primary interests, strict division of labor in the home, etc.) was associated with more difficulty in adjusting to the divorce than being nontraditional (Brown et al., 1977).

Feelings of depression and hopelessness in both women and men occur in response to three basic changes in the divorced person's life: termination of a major source of intimacy, disruption of the daily routine, and awareness of a new status—divorced person.

Most Americans fall in love and share their lives with others, at least partly as a result of the need to experience feelings of intimacy in a world of secondary relationships. Most people don't care about the intimate details of your life, nor do they have the background information to understand you. One reason divorce hurts is that you lose one of the few who knew you and who, at least at one time, did care about you.

Divorce also shatters your daily routine and emphasizes your aloneness. Eating alone, sleeping alone, driving alone to a friend's house for companionship are role adaptations made necessary by the destruction of your marital habits. A divorced man said, "When you're married, things happen without your thinking about it. Eating, going out, visiting friends with your wife seem to occur with little effort. Once you're divorced it's different. You feel like you have to make everything happen since there is just you. It reminds me that I depended on her more than I thought."

Compounding the loss of intimacy (which may have disappeared before the divorce) and disruption of daily habits is acquisition of the negative label "divorced." Although divorce can be the wisest and most mature response to a failing marriage, society still does not completely accept the divorced person. Even from friends, one can expect an "I'm sorry" response. Since an individual's self-concept is a result of how other people see him or her, maintaining a positive evaluation of one's self under these circumstances is difficult. However, by socializing with other divorced people who also are or have been victims of the negative stereotyping, many people succeed in gaining a positive feeling about their experi-

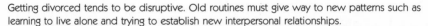

Getting divorced tends to be disruptive. Old routines must give way to new patterns such as learning to live alone and trying to establish new interpersonal relationships.

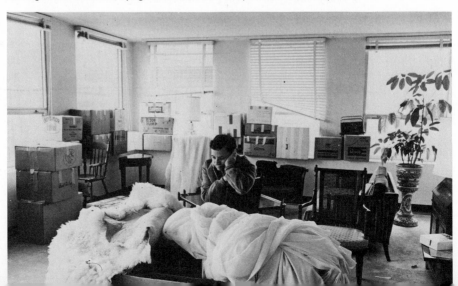

"To tell the truth, we're saving up for a divorce."

ence. One divorced woman said, "It's a pity that when you do the right thing [get out of an emotionally dead relationship], people look down on you."

Of course, divorce is not necessarily a negative experience. One wife and mother of two children said of her divorce, "It was, without a doubt, the happiest day of my life. I was finally free of him." The negative aspects of divorce may be particularly transitory for those who are already involved with a new partner. Enjoying a new relationship is often incompatible with feeling despondent about an old one.

A number of books are available which encourage the separated and divorced to view the ending of their marriage as an opportunity for personal growth. *Creative Divorce* (Krantzler, 1974), *The Courage to Divorce* (Gettleman & Markowitz, 1975), and *Growing Through Divorce* (Smoke, 1976) all have the same theme. The negative aspects of divorce are socially induced, and, rather than feeling sorry for one's self, one can use the divorce as a transition to a more rewarding, fulfilling life. Divorce counselors have also emerged to assist in this growth process (Fisher, 1974; Tubbs, 1973).

Money.   The divorced person pays for the divorce in yet another way—financially. Two can only hope to live as cheaply as one if they live together. A divorced civil service worker said, "I went from a four-bedroom home and a color television to a one-room studio apartment with a flickering black-and-white set. It's all I can afford." One lawyer said, "Marriage counselors probably save some marriages, but when spouses see the price tag of their divorce, they stop dreaming about the single and free life of the divorced."

What is the price tag? Alimony and child support payments (also referred to as the high cost of leaving) represent the largest expenses. While the actual payments depend on the family's standard of living, whether or not the wife is able to work, her independent income, and the number of children and their ages, the husband of a wife with two small children can expect to pay between one third and one half of his after-taxes income in alimony and child support (Porter, 1976, p. 715).[3] But payments depend on the state in which the divorce is granted. For example, in Texas there is no alimony.

Lawyers' fees are the second major expense. If a couple's income is between $10,000 and $20,000, the cost of drawing up a separation agreement is likely to run between $500 and $2,500 for each lawyer. While the house usually goes to the wife, the car goes to the person who most needs it. Stocks, bonds, cash, etc. are normally divided evenly (Porter, 1976, p. 717). For a wife with young children, a divorce usually means putting the children in a day-care center and finding a job. For the husband, it means reducing his standard of living and working harder and longer.

And the economic strain may be felt across the years. Not only may the husband be expected to pay alimony indefinitely, the unemployed divorced woman may be economically devastated by losing Social Security benefits that would normally be paid. If she lived with her husband less than twenty years before the divorce, she will receive no Social Security benefits at age sixty-five unless she has sufficient earnings *of her own* to qualify.

Children. "I'm caught between staying married for my children and going crazy. I don't want to hurt my children, but I can't stay with Floyd. I am bitterly unhappy." Since about 60 percent of couples considering divorce have children, the dilemma of this young mother is quite common. Over a million and a half children are affected every year (Davis, 1972). Table 19.2 shows that the larger the number of children, the smaller the percentage of divorces.

"How will divorce affect my children?" is a nagging concern of every unhappily married parent. The answer is unclear. Some studies suggest that children from "broken homes" are less well-adjusted and more likely to be juvenile offenders than children from intact homes (Kalter, 1977; Chilton & Markle, 1972; Bowerman & Irish, 1962; Koch, 1961; Glueck & Glueck, 1960; and Russell, 1957). In direct contradiction, Nye (1957) concluded in his study of ninth through twelfth graders that children with divorced parents showed "less psychosomatic illness, less delinquency, and better relationships with parents than children from intact homes." Other research confirms that divorce rarely has an indelible negative effect on children (Thomas, 1976; Burchinal, 1964; Perry & Erdwin, 1963; Landis, 1962; Thomes, 1968; and Goode, 1965).

TABLE 19.2   Divorce by Number of Children Under 18 Years Old, 1973.

Number of children	None	1	2	3	4	5 or more
Percent of divorces	38.7	24.4	18.1	8.6	3.5	2.2

SOURCE: U.S. National Center for Health Statistics, 1975.

These studies are confusing and their meaning is unclear because many couples who stay married for their children may be miserable. "We live in the same house physically, but we are worlds apart emotionally," sighed a middle-aged father. "We go on this way for Debbie and Kim." Spouses who are miserable with each other and who have already had an "emotional divorce" may do their children a disservice by staying married (Landis, 1962; Despert, 1953). One teenager said, "It's better to be from a broken home than to still be living in one."

Conditions under which divorce is likely to have the least negative effect on children include the following:

1.   The child understands that he or she is not personally responsible for the divorce.

2.   The parents continue to love their children even though they have stopped loving each other. The children should not feel that their parents wish to be free of them.

3.   The divorce occurs when the children are very young (under three years) or grown up (over eighteen) (Blaine, 1969; Bowerman & Irish, 1962). At these ages, the children either aren't old enough to understand the social meaning of divorce or are old enough to perceive it in an appropriate context.

4.   The parents maintain an air of friendship following the divorce (Westman et al., 1971). The most devastating effect divorce can have on children occurs when each parent makes charges against the other to the child.

5. Access to the "other parent" should not be forbidden (Westman et al., 1971). Children should be encouraged to keep caring about both of their own parents.

The belief that psychological damage occurs to children of divorced parents is based on the assumption that since divorce itself is a stressful situation and the separation of the parents causes disequilibrium in the family, the ongoing process of divorce is therefore a permanent condition of distress and disequilibrium. This argument ignores the time dimension (Brandwein et al., 1974). In reality, as time passes, the intensity of the stress subsides and the divorced persons and their children learn to cope with the new state.

FIGURE 19.2 Distribution of Older Persons by Marital Status, 1975.

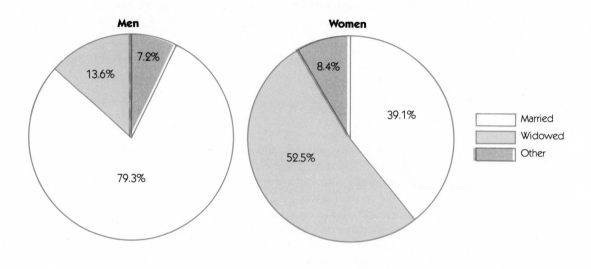

SOURCE: U.S. Office of Human Development, 1976.

WIDOWHOOD

A marriage relationship may also be ended by the death of one spouse. That spouse is usually the husband. Typically, men die in their late sixties or early seventies, leaving their wives in the role of widow for about ten years. Figure 19.2 shows that over half of women over the age of sixty-five are widows while only 13.6 percent of men in that age group are widowers. (U.S. Office of Human Development, 1976).

As Table 19.3 shows, the death of one's spouse requires greater social readjustment than any other crisis. "After my husband died," wrote a mother of two children, "I felt like one of those spiraled shells washed up on the beach. Poke a straw through the twisting tunnel, around and around, and there is nothing there. No flesh. No life. Whatever lived there is dried up and gone" (Caine, 1974, p. 11). Echoing these feelings, another widow said, "In the old romantic novels, a bereft lover frequently died of a broken heart. Don't count on it. It doesn't happen that way, and those of us who are widows have been left to cope with a life unlike anything we could ever have imagined" (Yates, 1976, p. 22).

TABLE 19.3 Ranking of Life Events Requiring Social Readjustment (from Most Adjustment Required to Least Adjustment).

Life Events

Death of spouse
Divorce
Marital separation
Death of a close family member
Sex difficulties
Major personal injury or illness
Fired from work
Jail term
Marriage
Marital reconciliation
Retirement
Death of a close friend
Pregnancy
Change in financial state
Business readjustment
Major change in health of family member
Gain of a new family member
Mortgage or loan over $10,000
Change in number of arguments with spouse
Change in responsibilities at work
Change to a different line of work
Trouble with in-laws
Foreclosure of mortgage or loan
Change in living conditions
Son or daughter leaving home
Begin or end school
Wife begins or stops work
Outstanding personal achievement
Change in work hours or conditions
Change in residence
Mortgage or loan less than $10,000
Change in social activities
Trouble with boss
Change in schools
Revision of personal habits
Change in recreation
Change in number of family get-togethers
Change in church activities
Vacation
Change in eating habits
Change in sleeping habits
Christmas
Minor violations of the law

SOURCE: Adapted from Ruch, 1977, p. 75.

The Bereavement Process

The general pattern of adjusting to the death of a spouse is similar for both widows and widowers (Glick et al., 1974). Upon learning that one's mate is dead, the initial reaction is shock and disbelief. "I had just seen my wife earlier that morning," recalled a widower, "and *knew* that she couldn't possibly be dead. I kept believing that she was alive until I reached into the casket and felt her cold stiff arm. Then I believed that she was dead." In the absence of a corpse, some spouses continue their disbelief. The wife of the famous bandleader, Glenn Miller, kept his clothes in his closet awaiting his return for twenty years following his disappearance in a small plane over the English Channel during World War II.

After accepting the reality of death, most widows and widowers move to the next stage of bereavement—deep sorrow and grief. "I can't tell you how lonely I am," said one widow. "I feel like there's a heavy weight inside me. It takes a huge effort just to get up and go through the daily routines. You won't understand what it's like until it happens to you." Coupled with these feelings is a profound disorientation. "Everything is up in the air now. I don't know who I am anymore," expressed a widower.

During this period of sorrow, grief, and disorientation, widows and widowers often have fears of mental and physical breakdown and become inordinately dependent upon others. "I guess I wanted someone with me all the time during those first weeks after Philip died," recalled one widow. "I was afraid of what I might do because I had no reason to go on living without him."

> **A** widow. A widow is different. It takes time to realize just how different. There was a transition period when every morning I had to grapple with the fact of Martin's death all over again. Every morning it was new. A raw wound that took a long time to heal.
>
> Lynn Caine

While relatives, friends, and business associates are initially quite willing to assist the bereaved in every way possible, after a few weeks or months their support dwindles as they redirect their energies to their own families and job responsibilities. When such support is withdrawn, the bereaved often enter a new stage of grief as they are confronted with the reality of living without their mate and without continued help from others.

Adjustment does not come easily. When compared with older people who still live with their mates, older widows and widowers are preoccupied with grief, express more unhappiness and worry, and have a lower degree of morale and a greater fear of death (McKain, 1969). In addition, the mortality and suicide rates are higher among widowed elderly people than among those still married (Atchley, 1972). But most do adjust. While few forget their dead spouses or the grief they have suffered, they develop confidence in their ability to manage alone and return to active social lives (Glick et al., 1974).

Adjustment for Widows

For a widow some aspects of adjustment are difficult while others are relatively easy. The difficult part is in reference to money and decisions. Since most wives depend on their husbands as the major source of income, the husband's death often means an end to the much-needed regular monthly check. "Aside from missing my husband terribly," recalled one widow, "it means that I need to get a job and support myself. But I'm old and have little work experience so my employment opportunities will be limited."[4]

Other widows complain about difficulty in making decisions. "Hunt and I always talked everything over and I depended on him to make the final decision. Now that he's gone I can hardly decide which salad dressing to buy." Decisions about selling property, moving into smaller living quarters, and buying health insurance may be particularly difficult for the woman who has always depended on her husband to make such decisions.

But for widows there are compensating factors. For example, the widow is more likely than a widower to derive emotional satisfaction from her children and

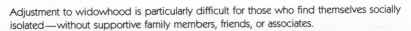

Adjustment to widowhood is particularly difficult for those who find themselves socially isolated—without supportive family members, friends, or associates.

grandchildren and is more likely to be welcome in the home of her son or daughter because she can help with the household responsibilities. Widows also have more widows with whom they share a similar role than widowers have other widowers. Large churches often have Sunday school classes for widows, and community centers offer special programs for them (Hiltz, 1975). And between interactions with other widows and with children and grandchildren, the widow is likely to continue the daily tasks of cooking, cleaning, and doing the laundry. These traditional domestic activities often serve to provide order and stability in her life (Cosneck, 1970). Although her companion is gone, what she does each day doesn't change much.

Adjustment for Widowers

Loss of a spouse is probably more difficult for men. This is particularly true among older widowers, who become victims of social isolation (Berardo, 1967). When they get up in the morning, most have no job to go to that could provide meaning, order, and contact with friends. And because they may do little more than sit[5] at their children's or grandchildren's homes, they are less likely than widows to live with them or to see them very often. They also have fewer friends than widows, attend church less frequently, and are less likely to be members of any formal organizations or groups (Berardo, 1967).

In addition, since the widower has probably not been socialized to perform regular domestic activities, "he is more likely than the surviving wife to need someone to prepare his meals, to do the cleaning, and to provide him with other types of general care" (Nye & Berardo, 1973). "If it weren't for the corner restaurant," said one widower, "I'd be dead. I really don't know how to cook."

In addition to being socially isolated and minimally involved in daily domestic activities, the elderly widower may be acutely aware of the approach of death. The seventy-year-old man can expect to live about eight more years, in contrast to the woman of seventy, who can expect to live eleven more years (U.S. Office of Human Development, 1976). "All my brothers and close friends are dead," said a seventy-three-year-old widower. "It's hard not to wonder if I'm next."

Preparation for Widowhood

Planning ahead for eventual widowhood may be unpleasant to deal with because it forces us to confront our own and our spouse's mortality. But as one widow said, "It's not as hard as making the arrangements later." There are several key areas to consider in preparing for the death of either spouse. Such preparation includes giving careful attention early to wills, insurance, titles, and funeral expenses.

Wills.[6] A will ensures that your belongings will go to those you want to have them. If you die intestate (without leaving a will), the state in which you lived will decide who gets what and how much. For example, suppose a married man with no children dies intestate. While he may want his wife to have everything, she may get only half if the state law provides that his parents are entitled to half of his estate.[7]

Before drawing up a will, consult a lawyer. He or she will be familiar with the laws relating to the distribution of property and the guardianship of children in your state. If you move to another state, you might have a lawyer there check your will to make sure that it conforms to the laws in that state.

Under federal law, an estate tax (also known as an inheritance or transfer tax) return must be filed for every estate with gross assets of more than $60,000 and any tax due must be paid at the time the return is filed. In other words, when you die the government looks to your survivors for money.

By leaving a will, you are permitted to give to your surviving spouse up to 50 percent of your estate, tax free. This provision, allowed in every state by the Internal Revenue Service, is known as the "marital deduction."

Insurance. Having made a will, check your life insurance policy for amount, type of payment, and ownership of policy. Assuming that the insured feels that the face value of the policy is adequate, check to see if the payments are to be made monthly or in a lump sum.[8] One widow recalled her experience this way:

> I petitioned our insurance company to convert our family income policy, which made monthly payments, into a lump-sum payment but was refused because, in their words, "minor children are involved." Of course, the fact that I need the money to educate those minors boggled the company's corporate minds, so I'll still be receiving my little monthly check long after the children have all left home. (Yates, 1976, p. 17)

Also check your life insurance policy for ownership. If the husband owns the policy and names the beneficiary as his wife (which is the usual case), the face value of the policy will be included in his estate, and she will need to share the proceeds with the tax collector. If you are a man, you can keep your money out of the tax collector's net by having your wife take out an insurance policy on your life. Because she is the owner of the policy, it is not included in your estate and, hence, is not taxable.

Titles. Just as life insurance benefits can be saved from estate taxes, so can your house, car, and checking accounts. If these are listed in the wife's name, they are considered her property and consequently not part of the husband's estate. Of course, if the wife dies first, the husband will face the inheritance tax problems she was to have avoided. So some balance of ownership is desirable. Retitling property to achieve a balance is only advisable, however, in a stable relationship. The transfer of ownership of large items followed by a divorce may create havoc.

Funeral expenses. Preparing for your own funeral can also save money (Consumer Reports, 1977). Assuming that you will die before your partner, ask yourself if you would rather your spouse spend $1,500 to bury you[9] or use the money to help pay for a semester of your child's college education?

Expenses for a casket, vault, and burial plot can be avoided by contacting a medical school and asking them to arrange for donation of your body for research or teaching purposes. At the time of your death, your spouse would contact a local mortician and ask him to notify the medical school with whom you made arrangements. The mortician would then make the necessary arrangements with the medical school. Although you have donated your body to medicine, the traditional funeral service may still be held, with your body being transferred to the medical school rather than to a cemetery afterwards. Or your body may be removed to the medical school immediately after death, and a memorial sevice can be held. In either case, the medical school usually pays the embalming fee and the cost of transporting your body up to two hundred miles.

An alternative to donating your body to science is cremation. The cost usually is well under $100 since all costs associated with the traditional funeral service are avoided. However, crematorium rules and state laws may inflate this basic cost to almost $1,000 so check the rules in your state before selecting this alternative (Porter, 1976, p. 751).

But suppose you don't feel comfortable bequeathing your body to science or having your body cremated? What then? You can still have the traditional funeral but at a reasonable cost ($150 to $350) by joining a "memorial society" or similar organization which has arrangements with one or more funeral parlors to provide members with a predetermined package of funeral services at a fixed cost. Details on the 120 such societies in the United States can be obtained from the nonprofit Continental Association of Funeral and Memorial Societies, 1828 L Street, NW, Washington, D.C. 20036.

Or you can contact a mortician and make whatever arrangements you prefer in advance of the inevitable event. Making such decisions in advance can save your spouse considerable expense and difficulty later.

REMARRIAGE

Although the ending of a marriage is traumatic for most people, life does go on. And for both divorced people and widows and widowers, remarrying is an alternative which may soften the blow and ease recovery from the dissolution of the previous marriage. In roughly ten million marriages in this country, one or both of the spouses have been married before (Duberman, 1975).

Remarriage for the Divorced

Eighty percent of divorced persons eventually remarry. Divorced men are more likely to remarry and to do so sooner than divorced women, but the median interval overall between divorce and remarriage is three years (U.S. Bureau of the Census, 1976, p. 14). Remarriages are less likely than first marriages to involve an engagement announcement, a religious ceremony, or a traditional honeymoon trip (Bernard, 1956).

Although remarriage is a popular option, those who choose it must often face difficult adjustments. Particular problems reported by the remarried concern children and finances.

Children.   About 60 percent of the remarriages of divorced people involve children from a previous marriage. Such children represent a permanent link between the first marriage and the second. In a study of seventy couples who had been divorced and remarried, the researcher reported that children were the biggest source of difficulty in the second marriage (Messinger, 1976, p. 196).

The problems related to children in a second marriage include the following:

1. Competition. The new spouse often regards the partner's children as competition. "He cares more about his kids than me," said the new bride of a divorced father. "On weekends he wants them to visit us and he wants them with us for our vacation. I know he wants to see his kids, and I think he should, but I'm wondering where we can fit in time alone together."

The divorced father's attitude reflects a different perspective: "I've busted up my kids' home, and I want to do everything I can to make it up to them. Making myself available on weekends is the least I can do."

2. The "closed family." A variation of the competition problem is the feeling

"This is Arthur, son. He's going to be your new daddy."

of the man without children who marries a woman with children. Because the interdependence the mother and children may have developed may be intense, the new husband-father often experiences considerable difficulty penetrating the closed system (Bohannan & Erickson, 1978). "I felt like a stranger after I moved in with Cheryl and her children," said one such husband. "They already had their routines established and really didn't need me as a family member."

3. Step-parent. Assuming the role of the parent in the manner desired by the spouse may also be difficult. In the study of seventy couples who had divorced and remarried, the researcher observed, "Again and again respondents reported tensions which arose when the new mate was critical of the children's behavior. . . . Individuals reported being caught between loyalty to their biological children and their desire to please the new partner" (Messinger, 1976, p. 197). And the children often resent having to relate to a new adult as their "parent." In some remarriages, the children are "required to respond to the parent's new mate as though he or she were the child's 'real' parent" (Messinger, 1976, p. 196).

Finances. The second most significant difficulty reported by the seventy divorced couples who remarried was money (Messinger, 1976, p. 196). Alimony and child-support payments often threaten the harmony and sometimes even the economic survival of the second marriage. One wife said that her paycheck was endorsed and mailed to her husband's first wife to cover his alimony and child-support payments. "It irritates me beyond description to be working for a woman who lived with my husband for seven years," she said.

And a remarried woman receiving modest or inadequate child support payments may feel embarrassed that her new husband must bear much of the cost of rearing children who are not his own. "I hated to tell my husband that my son needed braces. It meant expensive dental bills that his paycheck couldn't handle."

The situation becomes still more complicated when the husband also has children and is paying child support to his former wife. Such husbands are very hesitant to provide for their new partner's children since they feel it is the responsibility of the biological father to foot the bill for them (Messinger, 1976, p. 193). "If your son wants to go to summer camp, then let his father come up with the money for it," one remarried man complained.

The woman with no children who is married to a divorced father may also feel that money is a problem. One such wife asked her husband why his former wife and children had a nice home in the suburbs when he couldn't provide her with the same. "How will we ever save the money for our own home when you send so much to them?" she asked.

In essence, the ghosts of the first marriage (former spouse, children, economic responsibilities) may haunt the second marriage. Even though many have had to contend with such problems, individuals who remarry and stay married are as likely to report that their marriages are happy as those who have married only once (Glenn & Weaver, 1977).

Remarriage for the Widowed

One answer to the loneliness and despair some widows and widowers experience is remarriage. Such marriages may be either "December" marriages—those in which both spouses are elderly—or "May-September" marriages—those in which one spouse is considerably younger than the other.

December marriages.   In a study of twenty-four elderly couples, the need to escape loneliness and live with a companion was the primary motivation for remarriage. And the men reported a greater need to remarry than the women (Vinick, 1977). Most of the spouses met through a mutual friend or relative (75 percent) and married in less than a year after their partner's death (63 percent). This and another study (McKain, 1969) indicated that the children of the elderly couple had mixed reactions to the remarriage. While most children were happy that their parents were happy, some disapproved. Contributing to the disapproval was a concern over their inheritance rights. "If that woman marries Dad," said a woman with two children, "she'll get everything when he dies. I love him and hope he lives forever, but when he's gone, I want the farm."

Friends of the December marriage couple usually support the marriage. In a study of one hundred remarriages of older couples, two thirds of their friends approved of their marriage (McKain, 1969). "I know what it's like to be lonely," said one widow. "I wish I were getting married, too."

What about the success of such remarriages? Seventy-four of the one hundred couples in McKain's study were regarded as having successful marriages. Criteria included expressing affection, respect, and consideration for each other, enjoying each other's company, taking pride in the marriage, and not complaining about each other (McKain, 1969). Those spouses who particularly enjoyed their remarriages, in contrast to those who were unhappy, had known each other for several years before they married, had children who approved of their remarriage, shared a number of common interests and activities, and had an income that was adequate to insulate them from perpetual worry (McKain, 1969). Summarizing the data on December marriages, two researchers said, "These marriages tend to be very successful. For many older persons who are alone, marriage offers a great potential for satisfying many emotional and social needs" (Stinnett & Walters, 1977, p. 349).

May-September marriages.   In the May-September marriage the husband is usually considerably older than the wife. Issues involved in these age-discrepant marriages include the following:

1.   Motives. Instead of marrying a middle-aged woman with three children, the man in the May-September marriage often marries a young woman with whom he can start life over. From his young wife's perspective, she is marrying a man who has already made his mark in the world. She begins her marriage with instant status and probably an ample bank account (Presser, 1975).

2.   Interests. Although partners of very different ages may develop mutual interests, there is a greater potential for their interests to be different. While the younger partner might enjoy hard rock, the older partner may delight in classical music. And the younger partner may feel that her mate is "showing his age" by such a preference.

3.   Children. The age-discrepant couple may experience several difficulties in reference to children: (a) The wife may want children, but he may feel too old to be a father and may fear his wife's transition from lover to mother. (b) Children from a husband's previous marriage may require child-support payments, limiting the money available for the couple. The wife may resent not being able to take a trip to Hawaii because money is sent to his children, in whom she has little emotional investment. (c) Visits by the husband's grandchildren may be unwelcome because the wife resents playing the role of mother—preparing extra meals, doing extra laundry, making extra beds, and performing other such tasks.

4.   Sex. A sixty-year-old man may not be able to meet the sexual demands of a much younger wife. As a consequence, she may seek a sexual companion outside the marriage. The husband might be threatened by such competition and the marriage relationship jeopardized.

5.   Early widow. Since men in America die approximately ten years earlier than women, the wife in the May-September marriage is likely to be a widow longer than the woman married to someone closer to her age. But reflecting on this concern, one woman said, "I'd rather have fifteen years with this man than fifty with anybody else I've ever known."

None of the above concerns is necessarily unique to the May-September marriage. Conflicts over sex, children, and recreation may occur in marriages in which the partners are the same age, and no newlywed is guaranteed that his or her spouse will be healthy and alive tomorrow.

Regarding the outcome of May-September marriages, one sociologist commented:

> Can any sensible kind of determination be made which might permit a judgment as to the advisability of this kind of marriage? My answer is "no." Not because we know so little but because we know enough not to generalize. All marriages work themselves out amidst an admixture of sunshine and shadow. Can one draw a balance sheet? Even if one is fully rational—and few of us in this aspect of life really are—one really cannot. (Cuber, 1975, p. 356)

Research confirms that it is best not to generalize about the likelihood of success or failure in May-September marriages. In a study comparing couples who stayed married with those who got divorced, researchers discovered that May-September couples were just as likely to stay together and just as likely to divorce as couples in which both partners were of similar age (Bumpass & Sweet, 1972).

TRENDS

Trends in marital dissolution include an increasing divorce rate, [10] new divorce laws, and the establishment of a National Center for the Study of Divorce. Regarding the frequency of divorce, "If the current trends continue, over one-half of America's populus will have been directly touched by divorce before the turn of the century" (Johnson, 1977, p. 263). And these divorces are not limited to those in the early years of marriage. Increasingly, spouses who have been married over twenty years are splitting up.

In addition to an escalating divorce rate, there are several trends in divorce legislation. These include an increasing number of states switching from fault grounds for divorce to no-fault divorce, the granting of alimony payments to either sex (e.g., Maryland), the granting of child custody to the husband (e.g., Arizona), and the inclusion in divorce settlements that grandparents will have visitation rights (e.g., Wisconsin).

One researcher has suggested the establishment of a National Center for the Study of Divorce (Johnson, 1977). Such a center would go "beyond the traditional legalistic approach to divorce, making use of that vast body of knowledge and resources[11] available with the social sciences to institute a comprehensive program directed at understanding marital breakdown" (p. 265).

SUMMARY

The most frequent forms of marital dissolution are divorce and death. Divorce has not always been controlled by the state, nor is the ceremony always performed under religious auspices. Throughout most of Western history, marriages and divorces have been arranged by the people involved and their kinship system.

Regardless of how the divorce rate is calculated (crude, refined, or ratio of marriages to divorces), it has been increasing in recent years. Societal factors contributing to such increases include the loss of family functions, more employed wives, and no-fault divorce legislation. Individual factors include a high frequency of negative verbal and nonverbal behavior, feeling trapped in an unrewarding relationship, and becoming involved in an extramarital relationship.

Certain categories of people have a higher probability than others of getting divorced. These include the young marrieds, the premarital pregnant, those with low incomes, blacks, and those previously divorced.

For most, divorce represents a difficult transition. Loss of self-esteem, lack of money, and concern over children are among the potential consequences of divorce. But divorce may also represent a bridge from an unhappy relationship and personal confinement to new relationships and personal growth. For some, divorce is the beginning of a new life.

Death terminates those marriages not ended by divorce, annulment, or separation. Adjusting to the death of one's spouse is the most difficult life crisis either spouse ever experiences. The emotionally draining bereavement is often more devastating for widowers than for widows. Attention to wills, insurance, titles, and funeral arrangements while both spouses are living may help avoid financial losses by minimizing estate taxes and funeral costs.

Many divorced and widowed people are merely in a stage of transition to another marriage. It is estimated that between 20 and 25 percent of all marriages in any year are remarriages (Leslie, 1976, p. 723). Those who remarry and stay married report comparable marital happiness to those in their first marriages.

STUDY QUESTIONS

1. Briefly discuss the history of divorce.
2. Contrast the "fault" and "no-fault" systems of divorce.
3. What are three measures of the frequency of divorce? How do they differ?
4. Discuss several societal factors that contribute to our increasing divorce rate.
5. Mention several factors that motivate the individual to get divorced.
6. Divorce occurs more frequently among certain categories of people than among others. What are several of these categories?
7. What is an annulment? Discuss the conditions under which a marriage may be annulled.
8. What are the consequences of a legal separation?
9. Why is it potentially unwise to have an informal separation?
10. For some, divorce engenders feelings of depression. What three changes in one's life does a divorce create?
11. Discuss how divorce may be a transition to a more creative and fulfilling life.
12. Discuss the financial cost of a divorce.
13. What percent of divorces involve children?
14. Identify the conditions under which divorce is likely to have the least negative impact on children.
15. What percent of women over sixty-five are widows?
16. What percent of men over sixty-five are widowers?
17. How significant is the death of one's spouse when compared with other life crises?
18. Trace the bereavement process.
19. Discuss the different adjustment concerns of widows and widowers.
20. Why might it be more difficult for widowers to adjust to the death of their spouses than vice versa?
21. In what ways can a person prepare for widowhood?
22. What percent of divorced individuals remarry?
23. What is the median interval between divorce and remarriage?
24. How successful are remarriages compared to first marriages?
25. Discuss two problems that may affect the second marriage.
26. Discuss December marriages. Why do the children of some widows and widowers disapprove of the remarriage of their aging parent?
27. Comment on the success of older marriages.
28. Discuss May-September marriages. How successful are they?
29. Discuss several trends in marital dissolution.

NOTES

1. Other research has failed to find evidence that one divorce increases the chances of further divorce. Following the life-time marriage and divorce patterns of 1,445 men and 520 women, Riley and Spreitzer (1974) noted that 25 percent of men in their third marriages became divorced, while 28 percent of men in their first marriages became divorced.

2. Waller and Hill (1951) discuss the ending of a relationship as "The Process of Alienation," in *The Family: A Dynamic Interpretation* (p. 513). This section includes elements of their discussion.

3. The husband usually pays less in no-fault divorce cases than if the divorce is granted on the basis of the husband's fault. Under the fault system, the husband is often willing to pay higher alimony and child-support payments if his wife will agree not to contest the divorce.

4. Only 8 percent of women over sixty-five are in the labor force.

5. Not all widowers "sit" when visiting their children and grandchildren. One retired man built a house, a backyard fence, and a sundeck for his daughter. For his granddaughter, he built a swing and a sandbox. And he regularly services the family car and changes the filter in the air conditioner.

6. To prepare for their own death, women with property or children also need a will to specify distribution of such property and to name a guardian for their children.

7. North Carolina is an example of a state that provides for relatives to share in the estate of an individual who dies without a will. Inheritance laws vary from state to state.

8. This will depend on what the other sources of income are, such as social security payments. To find out how social security payments will supplement your income, order *The Social Security Handbook* from the Superintendent of Documents, U.S. Government Printing Office, Washington, D.C. 20402. The cost is $2.25.

9. The average cost of a traditional adult funeral in the United States is $1,500 (Porter, 1976, p. 749). To help defray these expenses, Social Security pays a lump-sum death benefit of $255 to all widows covered by the system who are living in the same household with the worker at the time of his death (Porter, 1976, p. 809).

10. Researchers disagree on this trend. Dr. Lois N. Glasser at the University of Michigan expects the rate to stabilize and start to decline by 1980 (Lesem, 1977). And, data as of March 1978 indicate that the crude divorce rate for the preceding twelve months had changed very little when compared with the same period a year earlier (March 1976–March 1977) (U.S. National Center for Health Statistics, June 1978).

11. Sources on divorce information include (1) *Divorce in the 1970's,* a guide to books, articles, dissertations, government documents and films on divorce in the United States, 1970–1976, by Dr. Ken Sell, Department of Sociology, Catawba College, Salisbury, NC 28144; (2) *Current Divorce Research,* by Drs. Helen and Vern Raschke, 3308 Mapleton Crescent, Chesapeake, VA 23321.

BIBLIOGRAPHY

Atchley, R. *The social forces in later life: An introduction to social gerontology.* Belmont, Calif.: Wadsworth, 1972.

Berardo, F. *Social adaptation to widowhood among a rural-urban aged population.* Washington Agricultural Experiment Station Bulletin 689, College of Agriculture, Washington State University. Pullman, Wash., December 1967.

Bernard, J. *Remarriage: A study of marriage.* New York: Dryden Press, 1956.

Blaine, G. B., Jr. The effect of divorce upon the personality development of children and youth. In *Explaining divorce to children,* E. A. Grollman (ed.). Boston: Beacon Press, 1969, 76–86.

Bohannan, P. The six stations of divorce. In *Divorce and after,* P. Bohannan (ed.). Garden City, N.Y.: Doubleday, 1971, 33–62.

Bohannan, P., and Erickson, R. Stepping in. *Psychology Today,* January, 1978, 53 et passim.

Bowerman, C. E., and Irish, D. P. Some relationships of stepchildren to their parents. *Marriage and Family Living,* 1962, *24,* 113–28.

Brandwein, R. A., Brown, C. A., and Fox, E. M. Women and children last: The social situation of divorced mothers and their families. *Journal of Marriage and the Family,* 1974, *36,* 498–514.

Brown, P., Perry, L., and Harburg, E. Sex role attitudes and psychological outcomes for black and white women experiencing marital dissolution. *Journal of Marriage and the Family,* 1977, *39,* 3, 549–62.

Bumpass, L. L., and Sweet, J. A. Differentials in marital instability: 1970. *American Sociological Review,* 1972, *37,* 754–67.

Burchinal, L. Characteristics of adolescents from unbroken, broken, and reconstituted families. *Journal of Marriage and the Family,* 1964, *26,* 44–51.

Caine, L. *Widow.* New York: William Morrow, 1974.

Campbell, A. The American way of mating: Marriage si, children only maybe. *Psychology Today,* May 1975, 35–43.

Chilton, R. J., and Markle, G. E. Family disruption, delinquent conduct, and the effect of subclassification. *American Sociological Review,* 1972, *37,* 93–9.

Christensen, H. T. Childspacing analysis via record linkage: New data plus a summing up from earlier reports. *Marriage and Family Living,* 1963, *25,* 272–80.

Christensen, H. T., and Meissner, H. H. Studies in child spacing: Premarital preganacy as a factor in divorce. *American Sociological Review,* 1953, *18,* 641–4.

Christiansen, J. R., and Robinson, P. H. Fulfillment of marital expectations among married and divorced persons: A test of exchange theory. Paper presented at the meeting of the National Council on Family Relations, Salt Lake City, 1975.

Consumer Reports, Editors of. *Funerals: Consumers' last rights.* Orangeburg, N.Y.: Consumers Union, 1977.

Cosneck, B. J. Family patterns of older widowed Jewish people. *The Family Coordinator,* 1970, *19,* 368–73.

Cuber, J. Age-discrepant marriages. In *Sexual issues in marriage,* L. Gross (ed.). New York: Spectrum Publications, 1975, 245–58.

Cutright, P. Income and family events: Marital stability. *Journal of Marriage and the Family,* 1971, *33,* 291–308.

Davis, K. The American family in relation to demographic change. In *Research reports (Vol. 1, Demographic and social aspects of population growth),* C. F. Westoff and R. Parke (eds.). Washington, D.C.: U.S. Government Printing Office, 1972.

Despert, J. L. *Children of divorce.* Garden City, N.Y.: Doubleday, 1953.

Duberman, L. *Reconstituted families.* Chicago: Nelson-Hall, 1975.

Eshleman, R. *The family: An introduction.* Boston: Allyn and Bacon, 1978.

Family Law Newsletter, Summer 1974, *15,* 1, 14.

Fisher, E. O. *Divorce—The new freedom: A guide to divorcing and divorce counseling.* New York: Harper and Row, 1974.

Fullerton, G. P. *Survival in marriage.* New York: Holt, Rinehart and Winston, 1977.

Geismar, L. L., and LaSorte, M. A. Factors associated with family disorganization. *Marriage and Family Living,* 1963, *25,* 479–81.

Gettleman, S., and Markowitz, J. *The courage to divorce.* New York: Ballantine Books, 1975.

Glenn, N. D., and Weaver, C. N. The marital happiness of remarried divorced persons. *Journal of Marriage and the Family,* 1977, *39,* 2, 331–37.

Glick, I. O., Weiss, R. S., and Parkes, M. *The first year of bereavement.* New York: John Wiley and Sons, 1974.

Glick, P. C. A demographer looks at American families. *Journal of Marriage and the Family,* 1975, *37,* 1, 15–27.

Glick, P. C., and Norton, A. J. Frequency, duration and probability of marriage and divorce. *Journal of Marriage and the Family,* 1971, *33,* 307–17.

Glueck, S., and Glueck, E. *Unraveling juvenile delinquency.* Cambridge, Mass.: Harvard University Press, 1960.

Goetting, A. The normative integration of the former spouse relationship. Paper presented at the meeting of the American Sociological Association, 1978.

Goode, W. Marital satisfaction and instability: A cross-cultural class analysis of divorce rates. *International Social Science Journal,* 1962, *14,* 507–26.

——————. *Women in divorce.* New York: Free Press, 1965.

Gunter, B. G. Notes on divorce filing as role behavior. *Journal of Marriage and the Family,* 1977, *31,* 1, 95–8.

Hetherington, E. M., Cox, M., and Cox, R. Divorced fathers. *Psychology Today,* April 1977, 42–6.

Hiltz, S. R. Helping widows: Group discussions as a therapeutic technique. *The Family Coordinator,* 1975, *24,* 3, 331–6.

Johnson, W. D. Establishing a national center for the study of divorce. *The Family Coordinator,* 1977, *26,* 3, 263–8.

Kalter, N. Children of divorce in an out patient psychiatric population. *American Journal of Orthopsychiatry,* 1977, *47,* 1, 40–51.

Koch, M. B. Anxiety in preschool children. *Merrill-Palmer Quarterly,* 1961, *7,* 225–31.

Krantzler, M. *Creative divorce.* New York: M. Evans, 1974.

Landers, A. Queen, Jules going separate ways. *Raleigh (N.C.) News and Observer,* 2 July 1975.

Landis, J. T. A comparison of children from divorced and non-divorced unhappy marriages. *The Family Life Coordinator,* 1962, *11,* 61–5.

Landis, J. T., and Landis, M. G. *Building a successful marriage.* Englewood Cliffs, N.J.: Prentice-Hall, 1977.

Lesem, J. Some signs U.S. divorce rate now leveling off. *The Daily Reflector,* 26 October 1977, 12.

Leslie, G. R. *The family in social context* (3rd. ed.). New York: Oxford University Press, 1976.

Levinger, G. Sources of marital dissatisfaction among applicants for divorce. *American Journal of Orthopsychiatry,* 1966, *36,* 803–7.

McKain, W. C. *Retirement marriage.* Storrs, Conn.: University of Connecticut Press, 1969.

Messinger, L. Remarriage between divorced people with children from previous marriages: A proposal for preparation for remarriage. *Journal of Marriage and Family Counseling,* 1976, *2,* 2, 193–200.

Nye, I. Child adjustment in broken and in unhappy unbroken homes. *Marriage and Family Living,* 1957, *19,* 356–61.

Nye, I., and Berardo, F. *The family: Its structure and interaction.* New York: Macmillan, 1973.

Perry, J. B., Jr., and Erdwin, P. H., Jr. Adjustment of children in "solo" and "remarriage" homes. *Marriage and Family Living,* 1963, *25,* 221–3.

Pilpel, H. F., and Zavin, T. *Your marriage and the law.* New York: Macmillan, 1964.

Plateris, A. *Divorce: Analysis of changes in the United States, 1969.* U.S. Public Health Service Publication, No. 73-1900, Series 21, No. 22, March 1973.

Porter, S. *Sylvia Porter's money book.* New York: Avon Books, 1976.

Presser, H. B. Age differences between spouses: Trends, patterns and social implications. *American Behavioral Scientists,* 1975, *19,* 2, 190–205.

Raschke, H. J. Sex differences in voluntary post-marital dissolution adjustment. Paper presented at the meeting of the American Sociological Association, New York, 1976.

Renne, K. S. Correlates of dissatisfaction in marriage. *Journal of Marriage and the Family,* 1970, *32,* 54–67.

Riley, L. E., and Spreitzer, E. A. A model for the analysis of lifetime marriage partners. *Journal of Marriage and the Family,* 1974, *36,* 64–70.

Rogers, C. R. *Client-centered therapy.* Boston: Houghton Mifflin, 1951.

Ruch, L. O. A multidimensional analysis of the concept of life change. *Journal of Health and Social Behavior,* 1977, *18,* 1, 71–83.

Russell, I. L. Behavior problems of children from broken and intact homes. *Journal of Health and Social Behavior,* 1977, *18,* 1, 71–83.

Russell, I. L. Behavior problems of children from broken and intact homes. *Journal of Educational Sociology,* 1957, *31,* 124–9.

Scanzoni, J. *Sexual bargaining.* Englewood Cliffs, N.J.: Prentice-Hall, 1972.

Schoen, R. California divorce rates by age at first marriage and duration of first marriage. *Journal of Marriage and the Family,* 1975, *37,* 3, 548–55.

Smoke, J. *Growing through divorce.* Irvine, Calif.: Harvest House, 1976.

Stetson, D. M., and Wright, G. C., Jr. The effects of laws on divorce in American states. *Journal of Marriage and the Family,* 1975, *37,* 3, 537–47.

Stinnett, N., and Walters, J. *Relationships in marriage and family.* New York: Macmillan, 1977.

Thomas, C. How good is the one parent home? *The Single Parent,* 1976, *19,* 6, 5–6; 43.

Thomes, M. M. Children with absent fathers. *Journal of Marriage and the Family,* 1968, *30,* 89–96.

Todres, R. Runaway wives: An increasing North American phenomenon. *The Family Coordinator,* 1978, *27,* 1, 17–21.

Tubbs, A. L. *Divorce counseling: A workbook for the couple and their counselor.* Danville, Ill.: Interstate, 1973.

Udry, J. R. *The social context of marriage* (3rd ed.). Philadelphia: J. B. Lippincott, 1974.

U.S., Bureau of the Census. *Current Population Reports,* Series P–20, No. 223. Washington, D.C.: U.S. Government Printing Office, 1971.

———. Number, timing, and duration of marriages and divorces in the United States, June 1975. *Current Population Reports,* Series P–20, No. 297. Washington, D.C.: U.S. Government Printing Office, 1976.

———. *Statistical abstract of the United States: 1974* (95th ed.). Washington, D.C.: U.S. Government Printing Office, 1974, 43.

———. *Statistical abstract of the United States: 1977* (98th ed.). Washington, D.C.: U.S. Government Printing Office, 1977.

U.S., National Center for Health Statistics. Children of divorced couples: United States, selected years. *Vital and Health Statistics,* Series 21, No. 18. Washington, D.C.: U.S. Government Printing Office, 1970.

———. One hundred years of marriage and divorce statistics, United States 1867–1967. *Vital and Health Statistics,* Series 21, No. 24, December 1973. Washington, D.C.: U.S. Government Printing Office, 1973.

———. Divorce and divorce rates. *Vital and Health Statistics,* Series 21, No. 29, March 1978. Washington, D.C.: U.S. Government Printing Office, 1978.

———. *Monthly Vital Statistics Report,* Vol. 24. Washington, D.C.: U.S. Government Printing Office, 1975.

———. *Monthly Vital Statistics Report,* Vol. 27, No. 3, 16 June 1978, DHEW Publication No. (PHS) 78-1120. Washington, D.C.: U.S. Government Printing Office, 1978.

U.S., Office of Human Development, Administration on Aging, Publication No. (OHD) 77-20006, 1976. Washington, D.C.: U.S. Government Printing Office, 1976.

The U.S. fact book: The American almanac (97th ed.). New York: Grossett and Dunlap, 1977.

Vinick, B. Remarriage in old age. *The Family Coordinator,* 1978, *27,* in press.

Waller, W., and Hill, R. *The family: A dynamic interpretation.* New York: Holt, Rinehart and Winston, 1951.

Westman, J. D., Cline, D., Swift, W., and Kramer, D. The role of child psychiatry in divorce. *Archives of General Psychiatry,* 1971, *70,* 405.

Westoff, L. A. *The second time around.* New York: Viking Press, 1977.

Wheeler, M. *No-fault divorce.* Boston: Beacon Press, 1974.

Yates, M. *Coping: A survival manual for women alone.* Englewood Cliffs, N.J.: Prentice-Hall, 1976.

Appendix A: Sexual Anatomy, Physiology, and Reproduction

If we think of the human body as a special type of machine, *anatomy* refers to that machine's make-up and structure—what its parts are and how they are put together. *Physiology,* on the other hand, refers to the mechanics of the machine—how it works, and what each part does to contribute to the whole machine's functioning (Landau, 1976, p. 3). In this brief overview, we will review the sexual anatomy and physiology of humans and the human reproductive process. Figure 1 illustrates a cross-sectional view of the male and female reproductive organs referred to below.

Male Anatomy and Physiology

Testes. These oval glands are about one and a half inches long and hang from the base of the pelvis in a thin-walled, muscular sac known as the scrotum. Each of the two testes produces sperm and hormones—the main one being androgen. The temperature inside the scrotum is three to four degrees cooler than normal body temperature, providing the ideal environment for the sperm which can not survive long at a higher temperature.

Epididymis. After the sperm are produced in the testes, they collect in a coiled tube known as the epididymis. The epididymis is situated above each testis within the scrotum. The sperm mature in the epididymis and are stored here until they are ejaculated or they disintegrate.

Vas deferens. When ejaculated at orgasm, the sperm travel from the epididymis through a duct, the vas deferens, which is about eighteen inches long. The sperm are propelled through the vas deferens by its rhythmic contractions.

Seminal vesicle. The vas deferens leads to the seminal vesicle, a gland about two inches long, just below the bladder. The seminal vesicle secretes a viscous substance that makes up the largest part of the semen in which the sperm cells are suspended when ejaculated.

Prostate. The prostate is a gland that secretes another fluid which makes up part of the semen. The fluid is alkaline and serves to protect the sperm in the more acidic environments of the male urethra and female vagina.

Urethra. After passing through the seminal ves-

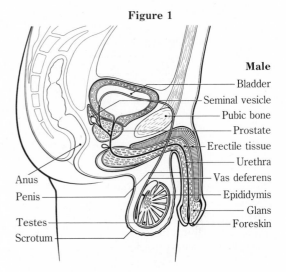

Figure 1

Male
- Bladder
- Seminal vesicle
- Pubic bone
- Prostate
- Erectile tissue
- Urethra
- Vas deferens
- Epididymis
- Glans
- Foreskin
- Anus
- Penis
- Testes
- Scrotum

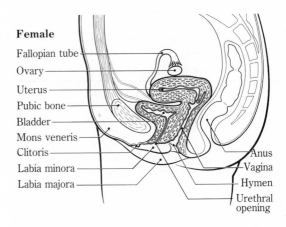

Female
- Fallopian tube
- Ovary
- Uterus
- Pubic bone
- Bladder
- Mons veneris
- Clitoris
- Labia minora
- Labia majora
- Anus
- Vagina
- Hymen
- Urethral opening

icle and prostate and mixing with the fluids from those glands, the sperm pass through the urethra of the penis. Another function of the urethra is the elimination of urine. Urine and semen very rarely pass through the urethra at the same time since a small, valvelike structure (the bladder sphincter) closes the tube leading from the bladder during ejaculation.

Penis. Ejaculation normally occurs when the penis is erect. Erection occurs, usually in response to sexual stimulation, when three columns of erectile tissue which run the length of the penis become engorged with blood. The glans, located at the tip of the penis, is richly supplied with nerve receptors. Overhanging the glans is the foreskin, which is often removed surgically shortly after birth (circumcision).

In sequence, the sperm produced in the testes collect in the epididymis and travel via the vas deferens to the seminal vesicle during ejaculation. Here and in the prostate they mix with additional fluids and then pass out the urethra of the erect penis.

Female Sexual Anatomy and Physiology
Ovaries. There are two ovaries, one situated on either side of the uterus. At birth, the two ovaries contain nearly half a million ova (egg cells), one of which matures and is expelled during ovulation about every twenty-eight days beginning at puberty. The ovaries also secrete hormones—primarily estrogen and progesterone.

Fallopian tubes. The fallopian tubes connect the two ovaries to the uterus. When an ovum matures, it is released into one of the fallopian tubes, where it may be fertilized by a sperm. Inside the fallopian tubes, small hairlike structures called cilia propel the fertilized egg down the tube and into the uterus.

Uterus. The uterus, which is also called the womb, is normally about three inches long, but stretches to over twelve inches during pregnancy. A fertilized egg becomes implanted in the wall of the uterus and continues to grow and develop there until delivery. At the lower end of the uterus is the cervix, an opening which leads into the vagina.

Vagina. The vagina is a thin-walled, elastic canal about four to six inches long that stretches between the cervix and the vaginal opening. The vaginal opening may be closed partially by a membrane known as the hymen. The vagina serves as the birth canal and, during intercourse, receives the penis and ejaculated sperm.

Mons veneris. This fatty cushion, which becomes covered with hair at puberty, is the most visible of the female genitalia. The labia majora extend out from it.

Labia. Just below and behind the mons veneris are two pairs of liplike structures surrounding the openings of the vagina and urethra. The labia majora, the larger lips which are covered with hair, are comparable to the male scrotum. Just inside these lips are the two smaller folds, the labia minora. Both sets of labia, but particularly the inner labia minora, have a rich supply of nerve endings which are sensitive to sexual stimulation.

Clitoris. At the top of the inner lips is the clitoris, which also has a rich supply of nerve endings. It is the primary site of sexual excitement in the female and, like the penis, becomes erect during sexual excitation.

Urethral opening. The urethral opening is below the clitoris. It connects to the bladder, and urine passes out of the body through this opening. The urethra is unrelated to the sexual organs except that the opening is sensitive to stimulation.

To summarize, eggs are stored in the ovaries until maturation and then released into one of the fallopian tubes. The egg travels down to the uterus, where it becomes implanted if it has been fertilized. During pregnancy, the uterus houses the fetus, and at childbirth the fetus passes through the vagina, or birth canal, on its way out of the mother's body. During intercourse, the vagina receives the sperm ejaculated by the male partner.

Reproduction
Creating a human being involves three basic stages—fertilization of an egg cell by a sperm cell, pregnancy, and childbirth. While many intricate factors enter into the process, about 85 percent of the couples who try to have a child succeed in doing so.

Intercourse is the usual prerequisite to fertilization. (The exception is test-tube conception.) During intercourse, the man ejaculates a grayish-white fluid called semen in which as many as 500 million sperm cells may be suspended. Once the semen is released at orgasm and deposited in or near the vagina, the sperm begin to travel from the vagina, through the opening of the cervix, up the uterus, and into the fallopian tubes of the woman's body. If the woman has ovulated (released a mature egg cell from the ovaries into the fallopian tubes) within three days, or if she ovulates during the four or five days the sperm may remain alive within her, a sperm cell that has reached the fallopian tube may penetrate and fertilize the egg there. This is called conception. Because conception depends on some rather precise timing (it usually occurs within one day of ovulation), and because a variety of contraceptive techniques may be employed to prevent conception, intercourse does not always result in conception.

Once the egg cell is fertilized, it begins to divide and to travel down the fallopian tube into the uterus, where it becomes implanted. (Occasionally, an unfertilized egg will have already reached the uterus and be fertilized by a sperm there.) The embryo, as it is called at this stage, continues to grow and develop in the uterus. By the third month, when it is referred to as a fetus, the basic organs and structures are almost completely formed. The remaining six months are devoted to growth and maturation.

The pregnant woman will experience a variety of changes, one of the first signs being that menstruation stops. Other common changes in the first three months of pregnancy include more frequent urination (because the enlarging uterus crowds the bladder), enlarged breasts, and feelings of nausea. Since this nausea occurs mostly in the morning, it is referred to as "morning sickness."

In the course of a pregnancy, some basic matters of concern include the mother's diet (an ample supply of protein, vitamins, and minerals is important), weight gain (twenty-five to thirty pounds over the nine-month period is acceptable), exercise, rest, exposure to disease, and use of drugs. Infectious diseases such as smallpox, chicken pox, measles, mumps, scarlet fever, and syphilis can have serious negative consequences for the developing fetus. Drug use also affects the fetus in that most drugs, including nicotine and alcohol, pass easily from the mother's blood through the placenta to the blood of the fetus. Alcohol may adversely affect the developing brain tissue of the fetus, and among women who smoke cigarettes during pregnancy the likelihood of spontaneous abortion or premature birth is greater.

Childbirth is the final event in bringing a new person into the world. The day of delivery can be estimated using "Naegle's rule"—by counting backward three months from the first day of the last menstrual period and adding seven days. But the actual delivery date may be from one to two weeks earlier or later than the expected date.

Labor, or the process by which the baby is expelled from the mother's body, has three phases. The first stage begins when oxytocin, a hormone secreted by the pituitary gland, triggers the muscular contractions of the uterus. In a contraction, the muscles of the uterus work involuntarily to pull open the muscles around the cervix. As the cervix dilates, a small plug of cervical mucus which has helped prevent infection during pregnancy is discharged. The amniotic sac in which the baby has been growing breaks, and the amniotic fluid spills out through the vagina. The first stage of labor, which lasts an average of twelve hours for the firstborn child, ends when the cervix is dilated enough for the baby to begin moving out (about ten centimeters).

The second stage of childbirth starts when the baby's head begins to push through the cervix and into the vagina. Contractions now occur every two or three minutes, and the baby moves further with each contraction. Gradually the baby emerges—head first, under normal circumstances, then shoulders, then body. After the baby is born, the umbilical cord connecting the baby and mother may be clamped and severed. This is the end of the second stage of childbirth, which usually lasts from about thirty to ninety minutes for the first child.

The third, and last, stage of childbirth involves the expulsion of the afterbirth, or placenta and amniotic sac, from the uterus. This may occur within a few minutes of delivery or up to about half an hour later.

*Portions of the discussion of anatomy, physiology, and reproduction are based on B. R. Landau, *Essential human anatomy and physiology*, Scott, Foresman and Company, 1976.

Appendix B: Sexually Transmissible Diseases

While the term venereal disease typically refers to gonorrhea and syphilis, sexually transmissible diseases (STD) refers to all those diseases which can be transmitted through sexual contact from one person to another. STD affects 10 to 15 million Americans every year and most (75 percent) are between the ages of fifteen and thirty. Anyone, regardless of sex, race, or social status, can get one or more of the STDs.

What Are They?

Although there are many types, some of the most common STDs are: gonorrhea (GC, clap), syphilis (syph, pox), herpes progenitalis (genital herpes), cytomegalovirus (CMV), group B streptococcus, nongonococcal urethritis (NCU, gleet), trichomonas vaginitis (trich, TV, vaginitis), monilial vaginitis (moniliasis, yeast, candidiasis), venereal warts (genital warts), pediculosis pubis (crabs, cooties, lice), and scabies (itch).

How Are the STDs Spread?

The STDs are caused by germs that are catching. In most instances they are transmitted from person to person by intimate sexual relations or other close bodily contact. It is possible to get an STD from an object (for instance, a bed sheet, toilet seat, hypodermic needle), but it is very rare. A number of factors (such as drugs, tension, other infections, pregnancy) can stimulate the development of a genital infection.

What Are the Signs of the STDs?

Early Signs: The first signs usually appear close to where the germ first enters the body—usually on or near the sex organs. These signs might be a sore, a discharge from the sex organ, a persistent itch, a burning sensation when urinating, or swollen glands.

Late Signs: Later signs may appear on any part of the body as a rash, a sore, abdominal pains, hair loss, or swollen glands.

Any changes in the sex organs of a sexually active person may indicate that he or she has an STD, although the signs may not be noticeable at first (especially in the female with gonorrhea) and may appear elsewhere on the body. The early signs always disappear without treatment; but, the person still has the disease and can give it to someone else.

How To Keep from Getting an STD

Avoiding sexual relations is the best way not to get an STD. Likewise, if you and your sexual partner have sex with each other only, you are not likely to get an STD. If you are sexually active, you can do things to reduce your chances of getting an STD such as carefully selecting your sexual partners (don't have sex with persons you suspect could have an STD or with persons you don't know very well), looking for sores or discharge, using a condom (rubber), washing sex parts after contact, douching after contact, using a contraceptive foam, cream, or jelly, and urinating after contact.

Can the STDs Be Cured?

If detected early enough, most STDs can be cured rather easily and quickly without any after-effects. Even the newer penicillin-resistant gonorrhea can be cured. Unfortunately, the STDs caused by viruses (e.g., genital herpes) cannot be cured. If you have an STD, it is important that you be treated as soon as possible before any permanent damage (e.g., blindness, insanity, sterility, heart disease, deformity) occurs. Only a doctor can conduct the proper examinations and prescribe the correct drugs to cure the STDs. You should not try to cure yourself.

Where To Go for Help

You can get treatment from a family physician or from a public health VD clinic. All fifty states now permit minors to be treated for STD infections without parental consent or knowledge, although in some states this applies to anyone over twelve years of age and in others it's fourteen years of age. To learn of the closest free and confidential VD clinic or about the age limits of your state, call toll-free the national VD Hotline (1-800-523-1885). A good way to stop the spread of the STDs is to name your sexual partners or take them to the VD clinic if you have an STD. You are not bad if you get an STD; you are sick and need medical care.

*This section relies heavily on the information contained in William L. Yarber's "New Directions in Venereal Disease Education," *The Family Coordinator,* 1978, 27, 2, 121–27.

Appendix C: Resources and Organizations

COUNSELING

American Association of Marriage and Family Counselors, 225 Yale Avenue, Claremont, California 91711. Telephone: (714) 621–4749 (toll-free). This is a professional organization which maintains a list of trained marriage counselors throughout the country.

American Association of Sex Educators, Counselors, and Therapists (AASECT), 5010 Wisconsin Avenue, N.W., Washington, D.C. 20016. This is a professional organization whose interest is in developing competency and standards for sex educators and sex counselors through training, education, and research.

American Institute of Family Relations (AIFR), 5287 Sunset Blvd., Los Angeles, California 90027. The professional staff provides counseling services, childbirth training, and other programs, and also trains counselors in the field of family relations.

Association of Couples for Marriage Enrichment (ACME), 459 S. Church Street, P.O. Box 10596, Winston-Salem, North Carolina 27101. Founded by David and Vera Mace, this international organization encourages married couples to join together in promoting better marriages.

Family Service Association of America (FSAA), 44 East 23rd Street, New York, New York 10010. This is a federation of three hundred local agencies providing casework, family counseling services, and other programs to help families in everyday problems of family living.

National Association for Mental Health (NAMH), 1880 N. Kent Street, Rosslyn, Vermont 22209. This citizens' voluntary organization devotes itself to the fight against mental illness and to the advancement of mental health.

National Council on Family Relations, 1219 University Avenue, S.E., Minneapolis, Minnesota 55414. This is an organization for interprofessionals working in the field of marriage and the family.

SEX INFORMATION

American Social Health Association, 260 Sheridan Road, Palo Alto, California 94306. This organization publishes a newsletter, *VD News,* and pamphlets that discuss the problem of sexually transmissible diseases and eradication approaches. Single copies of these pamphlets are free and are suited for both students and teachers.

Association for Voluntary Sterilization, 708 Third Avenue, New York, New York 10017. This association promotes the decision of sterilization and provides information about the various sterilization procedures.

Community Sex Information, Inc., 888 7th Avenue, New York, New York 10019. Telephone: (212) 765–2055. This is a "hot line" which provides sex information.

Institute for Sex Research, Inc., Room 416, Morrison Hall, Indiana University, Bloomington, Indiana 47401. This institute, founded by Alfred Kinsey, continues to do research in human sexuality and also maintains one of the most extensive bibliographies on sex research in the world.

National VD Hotline. Telephone: (800) 523–1885. To learn of the closest free and confidential VD clinic or about the age limits of your state for treatment without parental consent, call this toll-free number.

Operation Venus, 1213 Clover Street, Philadelphia, Pennsylvania 19107. Telephone: (800) 523–1885. This is a national "hot line" for information on venereal disease.

Sex Information and Education Council of the U.S. (SIECUS), 137 North Franklin Street, Hempstead, New York 11550. This national organization promotes public awareness of the need for sex education.

The VD Book: For People Who Care About Themselves and Others, by Joseph A. Chiappa and Joseph J. Forish (Holt, Rinehart and Winston, 1976). This is the official publication of the United States Alliance for Eradication of Venereal Diseases. It includes the latest information about sexually transmissible diseases in a nontechnical manner.

PARENTHOOD

Adoption Resource Exchange of North America (ARENA), 67 Irving Place, New York, New York 10003. Telephone: (212) 254–7410. This is a clearinghouse of information about adoption in North America.

American Fertility Society, 1608 13th Avenue South, Suite 101, Birmingham, Alabama 35205. Telephone: (205) 933–7222. The Society maintains a list of physicians throughout the country who specialize in fertility problems.

Association for the One-Child Family (AOCF), Educational Resources Center, 855 Broadway, Boulder, Colorado 80302. Founded by Sharryl Hawke, the Association encourages consideration of the one-child family and provides psychological support for those who choose it.

Family Synergy, P.O. Box 30103, Terminal Annex, Los Angeles, California 90030. This is an organization based on and dedicated to the implementation of the premise that people can live fuller and more rewarding lives, realizing more of their potential, by belonging to "family groups" larger than the nuclear family.

National Organization for Non-Parents (NON), 806 Reisterstown Road, Baltimore, Maryland 21208. Founded by Ellen Peck, the organization promotes and supports the childfree alternative in marriage.

Parents Without Partners, Inc., 7910 Woodmont Avenue, Washington, D.C. 20014. This is a national clearinghouse for the over 850 Parents Without Partners chapters which exist in all fifty states and most Canadian provinces.

Planned Parenthood Federation of America, 810 Seventh Avenue, New York, New York 10019. The Federation is a resource of information about family planning, health care, and physicians.

RESOLVE, Inc., P.O. Box 474, Belmont, Massachusetts 02178. This is a nonprofit organization to help with fertility problems.

World Family Adoptions Ltd., 5048 Fairy Chasm Road, West Bend, Wisconsin 53095. This is an international adoption agency.

CONSUMER RESOURCES

Bureau of Consumer Protection, Federal Trade Commission, Washington, D.C. 20580. The bureau investigates possible deceptive advertising, illegal sales tactics, violations of the Truth in Lending law, and a host of other categories of consumer frauds, misrepresentations, and unfair trade practices.

Consumers Union, 256 Washington Street, Mt. Vernon, New York 10550. This organization publishes *Consumer Reports* magazine, the classic shopper's guide, which includes results of Consumers Union tests of products ranging from cars to contraceptives —for safety, convenience, and effectiveness. It also participates in lawsuits on behalf of consumers.

Continental Association of Funeral and Memorial Societies, 1828 L Street, N.W., Washington, D.C. 20036. This is a nonprofit organization which supplies details on the 120 memorial societies in the United States.

Council of Better Business Bureaus, 1150 17th Street N.W., Washington, D.C. 20036. This is the headquarters of the well-known Better Business Bureaus which can put you in touch with the right local bureau.

A Guide to Budgeting for the Young Couple, by Agricultural Research Service, United States Department of Agriculture, Hyattsville, Maryland 20782. This is a short but detailed pamphlet on setting up a budget. It gives information on the types of credit available and the federal credit laws.

Office of Consumer Affairs, Washington, D.C.

20201. The consumer's "man in Washington" is a government agency concerned with all kinds of consumer problems, consumer education, and consumer legislation.

Social Security Administration, U.S. Department of Health, Education, and Welfare, Washington, D.C. 20201. This office distributes a number of publications, free, on social security, including *A Woman's Guide to Social Security* and *Your Social Security.*

Sylvia Porter's Money Book, by Sylvia Porter (Avon, 1976). This is a source book of general information on personal money management with pertinent details on buying a house and a car.

SPECIAL INTEREST GROUPS

Administration on Aging, Office of Human Development, U.S. Department of Health, Education, and Welfare, Washington, D.C. 20201. This is the national clearinghouse on aging which publishes a fact sheet supplying a summary of facts on current programs and telling also where application can be made for assistance or further information. It also distributes a directory of state agencies on aging and regional offices.

Gray Panthers, 3700 Chestnut Street, Philadelphia, Pennsylvania 19104. This is a consciousness-raising activist group whose aim is to combat ageism. It advises and organizes local groups of young and old together.

National Council of Senior Citizens, 1511 K Street, N.W., Washington, D.C. 20005. This is an education and action group which helps to organize and develop programs for state and local groups.

National Gay Task Force, 80 Fifth Avenue, New York, New York 10011. This organization promotes support for the homosexual life-style.

National Organization for Women (NOW), 425 13th Street, N.W., Suite 1001, Washington, D.C. 20004. NOW is a large organization of men and women whose aim is to end prejudice and discrimination against women—socially, politically, and personally. It is an action group, promoting its views through research, litigation, and political pressure.

National Right to Life Committee, 557 National Press Bldg., 529 14th Street, N.W., Washington, D.C. 20045. This is an anti-abortion organization whose purpose is to have Congress pass a human life amendment.

Widowed, Inc., 1406 Spring Rock, Houston, Texas 77055. Telephone: (713) 468–9849. This organization provides support and practical information about such issues as Social Security, insurance, etc.

Glossary

Abortion (p. 421) The removal of a fetus from a woman's uterus in early pregnancy, before it can survive its own.

Abstinence (p. 84) One of several premarital sexual values, it is based on the belief that sexual intercourse between unmarried men and women is wrong.

Acceleration clause (p. 361) In a contract for installment credit, an acceleration clause requires the buyer to make all remaining payments immediately if the buyer loses his or her major source of income. If the buyer cannot make immediate payment, the seller is authorized to repossess the items that the buyer purchased on credit. Consumers are usually advised not to sign a contract with an acceleration clause. *See also* Add-on clause.

Add-on clause (p. 360) In a contract for installment credit, an add-on clause authorizes the seller to keep title to all items that the buyer purchases until *all* items are paid for. Consumers are usually advised against signing a contract with an add-on clause. *See also* Acceleration clause.

Adlerian therapy (p. 332) A type of therapy, based on the work of Alfred Adler, which views marital problems as the result of power struggles between spouses. According to Adler, power struggles arise as individuals try to compensate for feelings of inferiority.

Ageism (p. 500) The systematic persecution and degradation of people because they are old.

Aging (p. 498) The process of growing old. It may be defined chronologically, physiologically, sexually, psychologically, sociologically, and culturally.

Alienation (p. 281) A feeling of not being a part of a society or group.

Androgen (p. 39) The dominant male hormone, which is thought to have an effect on aggression.

Androgynous (p. 51) The quality of having both masculine and feminine characteristics.

Annulment (p. 527) An official declaration that no valid marriage ever existed between the parties. An annulment returns both parties to their premarital status.

Ante-Nuptial agreement (p. 279) This agreement, a policy of the Roman Catholic Church, requires all Catholic spouses to promise to rear their children in the Roman Catholic Church. Non-Catholic spouses are not required to sign but are merely informed of the agreement. *See also* Personal marriage contract.

Apgar score (p. 37) A physician's rating of a newborn infant's color, muscle tonicity, reflex irritability, and heart and respiratory functioning.

Appetitional theory of sexual motivation (p. 122) The view that the first sexual experience in a relationship stimulates a desire for more varied and advanced forms of sexual involvement. The typical step-by-step progression is holding hands, kissing, breast manipulation, etc.

Arapesh (p. 34) A New Guinea tribe in which both males and females are taught to be feminine by Western standards.

Arranged marriage (p. 184) The practice of having the parents select the marriage partner for their son or daughter on the basis of criteria such as bride price, social status, and family custom.

Australopithecines (p. 32) Regarded as the first ancestors of modern humans, they lived in southeastern Africa about two million years ago.

Balloon clause (p. 361) In a contract for installment credit, a balloon clause requires the buyer to make a final payment that is considerably larger than the preceding monthly payments. Consumers are generally advised not to sign a contract with a balloon clause.

Banns (p. 12) In Puritan New England, a public notice of intent to wed that was required to be posted several days prior to the marriage.

Behavioral counseling (p. 332) A type of counseling, based on learning theories, which attempts to change behavior through reinforcement techniques. *See also* Child rearing, behavior modification approach.

Behavioral psychology (p. 34) The systematic application of learning principles to the understanding and management of human behavior. *See also* Behavioral counseling.

Bigamy (p. 527) Being married to two people at the same time.

Birthrate (p. 408) The number of babies born per 1000 population in a given year.

Bisexuality (p. 91) Having sexual relationships with partners of the same and opposite sex.

Blue chip stock (p. 353) A stock in a company which is an established leader in an industry. For example, Eastman Kodak and Polaroid are established leaders in the camera industry. Blue chip stocks have a long history of cash dividend payments, and the companies they represent have a history of good earnings in recessions as well as booms.

Bride price (p. 184) Money paid to the father for giving his daughter to another man to marry. The bride price is given to the father as compensation for the loss of his daughter's services.

Budget (p. 351) A method of planned spending. It involves identifying monthly income, fixed expenses, and discretionary expenses. Subtracting expenses from income provides information about whether one is living below, within, or beyond his or her means.

Bundling (p. 14) A courtship custom in colonial America whereby the boy and girl would spend the evening or whole night in bed together with their clothes on and with a board between them.

Career (p. 294) A life work, profession, or occupation. In contrast to a job, a career usually involves training and the desire to advance in a particular occupation. Such a desire usually involves staying employed full-time and being willing to move to another location when a promotion is offered.

Cash value (p. 356) The amount of money the insured gets for surrendering his or her life insurance policy. A policy with a cash value permits the insured to borrow money from the insurance company at a low rate of interest.

Child rearing, behavior modification approach (p. 469) Based on the work of B. F. Skinner, this approach views human behavior as learned and emphasizes the use of consequences to encourage desirable behavior. *See also* Behavioral counseling.

Child rearing, cognitive-developmental approach (p. 467) Based on the work of Jean Piaget, this approach focuses on the development of intelligence, which is viewed as a result of interaction with the environment.

Child rearing, developmental-maturational approach (p. 466) Developed by Arthur Gesell, this approach views child development as the result of genetic programming rather than environmental factors.

Child rearing, parent effectiveness training approach (p. 470) Developed by Thomas Gordon, the parent effectiveness approach encourages parents to manage the environment, engage in active listening, send "I" messages, and resolve conflicts through mutual negotiation.

Child rearing, socio-teleological approach (p. 473) Based on the theories of Alfred Adler, this approach emphasizes that the inferiority feelings inherent in the infant's attempt to function in an adult world are the basic cause of most parent-child conflicts. Rudolf Dreikurs, who developed the approach, encouraged parents to help their children develop mastery of their environment.

Classical conditioning (p. 469) Modifying behavior through stimulus-reinforcement techniques. By consistently presenting a stimulus with a reinforcer, the stimulus eventually takes on the same value as the reinforcer. *See also* Operant conditioning.

Cognitive-developmental theory of sex-role development (p. 35) According to this theory, the ability to acquire gender identity depends on mental maturity.

Cohabitation (p. 202) A heterosexual living arrangement in which two unrelated adults who are not legally married share the same bed for a number of consecutive nights (at least four). Also referred to as quasi-marriage, nonmarital living arrangement, consensual union, unmarried liaison, para marriage, and nonmarital unit.

Comarital sex (p. 381) Sexual relationships which include partners other than the spouse. Such relationships may be with or without the knowledge of the spouse. *See also* Open marriage.

Common-law marriage (p. 13) A marriage which becomes legally recognized after the woman and man have lived together for some time as though they were wife and husband. About one third of the states recognize common-law marriage.

Commune (p. 162) A group of people who live together by choice rather than because of blood or legal ties. Also referred to as an intentional community.

Commuter marriage (p. 306) Also referred to as a "weekend" or "long-distance" marriage, commuter marriage refers to spouses who live apart because the demands of their respective careers require that they live in different cities.

Complementary needs (p. 192) According to this theory of mate selection, people with opposite personality traits, such as a dominant and a submissive person, are attracted to each other. The theory, developed by Dr. Robert Winch, has been heavily criticized.

Condom (p. 413) Also known as a "rubber" or "prophylactic," the condom is a thin sheath, usually made of rubber, which is rolled over and down the shaft of the erect penis prior to intercourse. While used primarily as a method of contraception, it also protects against venereal disease. For maximum protection against conception, the condom should be used with a spermicidal agent.

Contraception (p. 411) Devices or chemical agents designed to prevent conception. *See also* Sterilization.

Contract cohabitation An eating, sleeping, and living arrangement between two adults who assume the roles of employer and employee. The understanding of the living-together relationship is defined by the employer and accepted in advance by the employee, who receives a salary for compliance.

Crude divorce rate (p. 518) The number of divorces per 1000 population.

Cunnilingus (p. 378) Oral contact with female genitalia.

December marriage (p. 543) A marriage in which both spouses are elderly, usually over the age of sixty-five.

Deillusionment (p. 493) Reassessing whether the goals that one has sought to achieve are reasonable and attainable. This process is regarded as a principal task for middle-aged men.

DES (p. 422) Abbreviation for diethylstilbestrol, known as the morning-after pill. It contains high doses of estrogen and terminates a pregnancy if taken within twenty-four hours of intercourse.

Desertion (p. 528) The act of leaving one's spouse without notice and breaking off all contact.

Diaphragm (p. 414) A shallow rubber dome built around a circular steel spring, which is placed over the cervix to prevent sperm from entering the uterus.

Dilation and curettage, abortion by (p. 422) A method of scraping the embryo and the placenta from the uterine walls. It can be used when the woman has been pregnant for less than three months.

Directive counseling (p. 332) A type of counseling in which the counselor gives spouses specific recommendations as to how they can achieve their goals.

Disability income rider (p. 357) A clause in a life insurance policy which guarantees that the insurance company will pay the insured two thirds of his or her salary up to a designated maximum per month if the insured becomes disabled and cannot earn an income.

Displacement (p. 330) Venting hostility on someone who is less threatening than the person who aroused the hostility.

Divorce (p. 516) The legal termination of a valid marriage contract, which gives each spouse the right to remarry. *See also* Separation.

Divorce, adversary system (p. 517) A legal system which allows divorce only if one spouse is guilty of certain acts (infidelity, cruelty). It is assumed that the other spouse is innocent.

Divorce, no-fault system (p. 517) A legal system which permits spouses to dissolve their relationship if either partner feels that there are "irreconcilable differences." The no-fault divorce system is an alternative to the adversary system of divorce.

Double or triple indemnity (p. 357) A clause in a life insurance policy which provides that the beneficiary will be paid two or three times the face value of the policy if the insured dies as a result of an accident.

Double standard (p. 85) Different standards of appropriate sexual behavior for men and women. It means that it is more acceptable for men to engage in all types of sexual behavior than for women to do so.

Douche (p. 416) Flushing the vagina with water or with a spermicidal agent after intercourse. A relatively unreliable method of contraception.

Dyspareunia (pp. 384, 387) Pain during intercourse. A sexual dysfunction among women.

Ego enhancement (p. 101) Acts performed to increase one's sense of worth. Ego enhancement usually occurs at the expense of someone else (exploitation).

Ejaculatory incompetence (p. 388) Inability to ejaculate during intercourse. *See* Premature ejaculation.

Embryo (p. 436) The name given to the human organism from the time of conception until the end of the eighth week. *See also* Fetus.

Emotional insulation (p. 331) Withdrawing from an active role in relationships with others to avoid being hurt.

Empathy (p. 238) The ability to understand another person's feelings and to view a situation from that person's point of view.

Empty nest (p. 491) Also known as the postparental stage of the family life cycle, this period begins when the last child leaves home and continues until the husband retires or either spouse dies. *See also* Middle age.

Endogamy (p. 185) Marriage within a particular group. For example, there is strong social pressure to marry within one's own racial group.

Escapism (p. 329)   Avoidance of a problem through such means as sleep, drugs, or work.

Estrogen (p. 39)   The dominant female hormone.

Exchange theory (p. 193)   A theory which, applied to mate selection, states that people select marriage partners who seem to offer the greatest rewards at the lowest costs (unpleasant consequences of association with a partner).

Existential-phenomenological theory (p. 470)   Developed by Carl Rogers, this theory focuses on the individual's current feelings and experiences and on the development of each person's self-concept and potential.

Exogamy (p. 185)   Marriage outside a particular group. In the U.S., one is legally required to marry outside the immediate family of one's parents, siblings, and first cousins.

Extended family (p. 9)   A nuclear or polygamous family and the parental generation. The typical extended family includes the husband, wife, their children, and the parents (or aunts/uncles) of the spouses.

Extended kinship system (p. 17)   Refers to those relatives beyond the nuclear family. Such relatives include parents, grandparents, siblings, uncles, aunts, cousins, etc.

Fallopian tubes (p. 436)   The two tubes in the female reproductive system which link the ovaries to the uterus. Eggs released from the ovaries move down these tubes to the uterus.

Family (p. 8)   A group of two or more persons who are related by blood, marriage, or adoption (U.S. Census definition). The term usually implies the presence of children, a common residence, and economic cooperation.

Family enrichment programs (p. 482)   Groups of three to five families who meet together regularly for mutual care and support and for the development of family potential (Anderson, 1974, p. 7).

Family life cycle (p. 318)   A model designed to explain the behavior patterns of married couples. It divides marriage into various stages according to the number, age, and health of a married couple's children.

Family of orientation (p. 9)   The family into which an individual is born or adopted.

Family planning (p. 397)   Controlling the number and spacing of children through systematic use of contraceptive methods.

Family of procreation (p. 9)   The family which one begins by marrying and having one's own children.

Fellatio (p. 378)   Oral contact with male genitalia.

Fetus (p. 436)   The name given to the developing human organism from eight weeks after conception until birth. *See also* Embryo.

Flexitime (p. 306)   A system being offered by some corporations which permits each employee to select the eight hours he or she will work between 7:30 A.M. and 6:30 P.M.

Freudian stages of sexual development (p. 99)   Freud believed that human sexuality evolves through predictable stages. Among these are the oral, anal, phallic, and latency stages.

Gender identity (p. 31)   The psychological state of viewing oneself as a girl or a boy. While one's gender identity and biological sex are usually the same, they may be different. *See also* Sex.

Gender role (p. 32)   *See* Sex role.

Generativity (p. 401)   An interest in establishing and guiding the next generation. People who have generativity enjoy teaching and working and playing with children.

Gerontology (p. 509)   The study of aging.

Gray liberation (p. 502)   An organization of elderly Americans which opposes ageism and attempts to encourage a more positive attitude toward the elderly.

Guaranteed insurability (p. 357)   A clause in a life insurance policy which permits the insured to purchase additional insurance regardless of his or her medical condition.

Homogamy (p. 187)   The tendency to marry someone who is similar in terms of such characteristics as age, education, and physical appearance.

Homosexuals (p. 159)   Individuals who have a preference for or engage in sexual behavior with members of their own sex.

Homosocial behavior (p. 127)   A common pattern among males that includes engaging in sexual behavior with females in order to make an impression on the male peer group.

Hysterectomy (p. 418)   A surgical procedure which removes a woman's uterus. While hysterectomies result in sterility for the woman, they are usually conducted because of a malignancy.

Impotence, primary (p. 388)   The state of never having been able to have intercourse. A dysfunction among men.

Impotence, secondary (p. 388)   The state of having been able to have intercourse in the past but being currently unable to do so.

***In loco parentis* (p. 206)**   A Latin phrase which means "in the place of parents." Until recently, university officials were expected to act as parents and to monitor the moral behavior of students.

Inorgasmic behavior (p. 386)   Inability to achieve an orgasm.

Installment charge account (p. 359)   A system of credit which allows a buyer to pay for an item by making a down payment and then making monthly payments until the item is paid for. It is considered an expensive form of credit because it involves finance charges. *See also* Revolving charge account.

Instrumental behaviors (p. 314)   Those which are considered necessary for the marriage to survive as an economic and social unit. Meal preparation, child care, and making social arrangements are examples.

Insurance-plus-investment (p. 356)   A type of life insurance which uses part of the premiums for investment, thus establishing a cash value for the policy. *See also* Term insurance.

Intestate (p. 538)   Having made no valid will.

Intrauterine device (p. 413)   Known as the IUD, it is a small object that a physician inserts into a woman's uterus to prevent conception from occurring.

Job (p. 304)   An assigned piece of work. In contrast to a career, a job may require little training or commitment.

Labor force (p. 291)   Those people who are working and those who are looking for work.

Lamaze method (p. 453)   A method of natural childbirth which involves the participation of the husband during labor and delivery.

Laparoscopy (p. 419)   A two-step sterilization procedure for women. A telescopelike instrument (laparoscope) inserted into the abdominal wall is used to locate the fallopian tubes. A special pair of forceps that carries electricity is then used to burn the tubes closed.

Levirate custom (p. 184) An arrangement whereby a male marries his brother's wife if his brother dies. In some cultures this custom is a privilege; in others, it is a duty. *See also* Sororate custom.

Love (pp. 58, 68) An emotion based on private individual experience. Love is said to exist when the concern for another is as great as the concern for oneself.

Marriage (p. 5) Regarded in America as a relationship in which two adults of the opposite sex make an emotional and legal commitment to live together. Any children of the couple are socially and legally recognized as a legitimate. *See also* Monogamy.

Marriage contract (p. 5) A legal agreement between the couple and the state designed to structure the rights and duties of spouses to each other. *See also* Personal marriage contract.

Marriage squeeze (p. 149) An excess of women at the most marriageable age. The result is that more women do not marry because of the relative unavailability of potential mates.

Masturbation (p. 119) Any voluntary erotic activity that involves self-stimulation.

Mating gradient (p. 188) The tendency for males to marry down and females to marry up in age, education, and social class.

May-September marriage (p. 543) A marriage in which one spouse is considerably younger than the other.

Memorial society (p. 540) An organization which has arrangements with one or more funeral parlors to provide members with a predetermined package of funeral services at a fixed cost.

Middle age (p. 491) The period in a person's life from about age forty-five to sixty-five. *See also* Empty nest.

Middle-escence (p. 493) A term used to refer to a second adolescence that many people experience in middle age. It usually involves a reevaluation of one's life.

Missionary position (p. 378) A position for sexual intercourse in which the male is on top of the female.

Modeling theory of sex-role development (p. 35) The proposition that an individual engages in appropriate sex-role behaviors as a result of imitating other males and females as they engage in the appropriate behaviors.

Monogamy (p. 7) The state of being married to one person at a time. *See also* Marriage.

Morning-after pill (p. 422) *See* DES.

Mundugumor (p. 34) A New Guinea tribe in which both males and females are taught to be masculine by Western standards.

Naturalism, myth of (p. 334) The belief that two people will naturally get along in marriage if they love each other.

Nondirective counseling (p. 332) A type of counseling in which the counselor assumes that the individual or spouses are best able to solve their own problems and that this can best be accomplished in the context of a warm and supportive therapeutic relationship.

Nuclear family (p. 9) A group of persons, consisting of a married couple and their children, who live by themselves. The children may be natural or adopted by the couple.

Open charge account (p. 360) A system of credit which allows buyers to pay for items thirty days after they purchase them.

Open marriage (p. 271) A relationship which emphasizes role equality and the freedom for each partner to maximize his or her own potential. While extramarital sexual relationships may be involved, they are not necessary for a marriage to be regarded as open. *See also* Comarital sex.

Operant conditioning (p. 469) Modifying behavior by controlling the consequences of behavior. Behaviors followed by a positive consequence (reward) will increase; behaviors followed by a negative consequence (punishment) will decrease. *See also* Classical conditioning.

Oral contraceptive (p. 411) Known as "the pill," it contains estrogen and progesterone (female hormones), which prevent ovulation and make implantation of a fertilized egg in the uterus difficult.

Orgasmic dysfunction, primary (p. 386) The state of never having experienced an orgasm. A dysfunction among women.

Orgasmic dysfunction, situational (p. 386) The state of having experienced an orgasm in the past but not being able to do so now. A sexual dysfunction among women.

Ovulation (p. 411) The release of a mature egg from the ovary.

Parental image theory (p. 194) A theory, based on Freud's ideas, which suggests that a man looks for a wife who is like his mother and that a woman looks for a husband who is like her father.

Payroll savings plan (p. 353) A plan for saving money whereby employers deposit a predetermined amount of money into employees' savings accounts before paying them their wages.

Permissiveness with affection (p. 87) The belief that increasing levels of sexual intimacy are appropriate with increasing levels of affection.

Permissiveness without affection (p. 89) The belief that sexual intimacy is appropriate regardless of the level of affection between the partners.

Personal marriage contract (p. 250) A private agreement (verbal or written) developed by a couple or with a lawyer which reflects the understanding of each partner about the nature of the relationship in which they are involved. Division of labor, rights of inheritance, and debts are among the issues which may be addressed in the contract. Also referred to as an antenuptial agreement when established prior to marriage.

Petting (p. 122) Heterosexual physical stimulation that does not involve intercourse. Common forms of petting include kissing, breast manipulation, and stimulation of the genitals.

Polyandry (p. 7) A form of plural marriage in which one female is married to several males.

Polygamy (p. 7) Plural marriage. The term most often refers to polygyny or polyandry. *See also* Bigamy.

Polygyny (p. 7) A form of plural marriage in which one male is married to several females.

Postparental stage (p. 491) *See* Empty nest.

Postpartum depression (p. 438) Also known as the blues, it is a feeling of depression, after giving birth, characterized by irritability, crying, loss of appetite, and difficulty in sleeping. Such feelings are thought to be a result of numerous physiological and psychological changes that occur as a result of pregnancy, labor, and delivery.

Premature ejaculation (p. 388) The inability to delay ejaculation as long as the male or his partner wishes. *See* Ejaculatory incompetence.

Primary group or primary relationship (p. 9) A group of people characterized by intimate face-to-face association and cooperation. Primary group members care for each other and have a durable relationship. A parent, spouse, and sibling are examples of primary group members. *See also* Secondary group.

Projection (p. 330) A defense mechanism that involves ascribing one's own faults or difficulties to someone else.

Pronatalism (p. 397) Any policy or attitude that encourages having children.

Propinquity (p. 186) Usually referred to as residential propinquity, the theory holds that the probability that *A* and *B* will marry each other decreases as the distance between their residences increases.

Psychosexual view of sexual behavior (p. 113) The theory that individuals learn sexual behavior patterns from their culture and society. *See also* Social script.

Random sample (p. 22) A sample in which each member of the larger population has an equal chance of being included in the sample.

Rational-emotive therapy (p. 332) A type of therapy, based on the work of Albert Ellis, which views irrational thoughts as a major determinant of unhappiness. By using a systematic set of procedures, the individual learns to change beliefs that have a negative impact on the marriage.

Rationalization (p. 329) A defense mechanism involving the attempt to justify one's behavior to oneself or others who question it.

Realistic love (p. 68) Most often discussed in contrast to romantic love, this view of love is based upon the belief that love takes time to develop and that there are many people an individual could fall in love with.

Refined divorce rate (p. 518) The number of divorces per 1000 married women who are over age fifteen.

Revolving charge account (p. 359) A system of credit which allows buyers to purchase items on credit up to a stated amount each month with no finance charge if the total amount is paid at the first billing. If the total amount is not paid at the first billing, however, the buyer is assessed a finance charge. MasterCharge and Visa are revolving charge accounts. *See also* Installment charge account.

Rhythm method (p. 415) A birth-control method involving avoidance of sexual intercourse when the egg is in the fallopian tubes. The "calendar method" (p. 415) and the "temperature method" (p. 415) are used to predict this time. The rhythm method is a relatively unreliable contraceptive technique.

Rite of passage (p. 262) An event which signals the transition of an individual from one position in society to another. The wedding ceremony is a rite of passage which changes the social position of an individual from an unmarried to a married state.

Romantic love (p. 68) A view of love based on the idea that there is love at first sight, that there is only one true love, and that love is the most important criterion for marriage.

Saline, abortion by (p. 422) Destruction of the fetus by insertion of a concentrated salt solution into the amniotic sac. In six to forty-eight hours after the fetus is dead, the uterus contracts, pushing the fetus out of the vagina. This method is used after the twelfth or thirteenth week of pregnancy.

Salpingectomy (p. 418) A sterilization procedure for women, also known as tubal ligation, which involves surgically cutting and clamping the fallopian tubes so that the egg cannot pass into the uterus.

Sample (p. 22) In social science, a group of somewhat representative respondents selected from a larger group for study.

Secondary group or secondary relationship (p. 27) In contrast to a primary group, a secondary group consists of individuals who are usually unrelated by blood, marriage, or adoption and who usually have no long-term interest in each other. *See also* Primary group.

Secondary sex characteristics (p. 31) Those characteristics typically associated with being a male or female. For example, a male typically has a low voice; a female, a high voice. These characteristics are in contrast to primary sex characteristics such as external genitalia.

Self-actualization (p. 470) The process of developing one's cognitive, emotional, social, and physical potential.

Sensate focus (p. 385) A treatment for sexual unresponsiveness developed by Masters and Johnson. It encourages sexual partners to enjoy physical contact without the pressure to perform sexually.

Separation (p. 528) Termination of the living-together arrangement between husband and wife by mutual consent or by legal agreement. Economic responsibility and custody of children are usually specified in a legal separation agreement. *See also* Divorce.

Sex (p. 31) Refers to biological classifications—male and female—which are based on physiological characteristics. These include external/internal reproductive systems, chromosomes, and hormones.

Sexism (p. 41) The systematic persecution, domination, and degradation of women based on the supposed inferiority of women and the supposed superiority of men.

Sex role (p. 32) Socially accepted characteristics and behaviors typically associated with one's identity as a male or female.

Sexual dysfunctions (p. 383) Those behaviors or responses which characterize sexual problems in women and men. Sexual dysfunctions of women include lack of sexual responsiveness, inorgasmic behavior, dyspareunia, and vaginismus. Sexual dysfunctions of men include impotence, premature ejaculation, and ejaculatory incompetence.

Sexual liberalism (p. 91) A willingness to engage in certain sexual behaviors that have previously been regarded as forbidden.

Sexual response cycle (p. 377) A sequence of responses through which a sexually functioning adult is capable of progressing. The cycle includes four basic phases: excitement, plateau, orgasm, and resolution.

Sexual values (p. 84) Standards of desirability which affect decisions about sexual behavior.

Singlehood (p. 147) An adult style of life which is characterized by neither cohabitation nor marriage. In essence, the person functions autonomously and is usually not emotionally, sexually, or financially dependent on one other person.

Socialization (pp. 9, 466) The process by which a human being acquires the values and knowledge of his or her society and learns the social roles appropriate to his or her position in it.

Social-learning theory of sex role development (p. 34) According to this theory, culturally appropriate sex roles are developed by rewarding sex-appropriate behaviors and punishing sex-inappropriate behaviors.

Social script (p. 114) Shared interpretations and expected behaviors of a social situation. Scripts define situations, name actors, and plot behaviors.

Sororate custom (p. 184) An arrangement whereby a woman replaces her sister as a wife when the sister dies. This custom is the father's way of ensuring that the man who pays him a good price for his daughter gets what he pays for.

Acknowledgments

If the first wife dies, he gets a replacement. *See also* Levirate custom.

Spectatoring (p. 376) The tendency for individuals who are having intercourse to become overly concerned about their own and their partner's sexual performance. Such spectatoring creates anxiety and interferes with sexual performance.

Spermicidal agents (p. 414) Chemical compounds that are inserted into the vagina near the cervix at least twenty minutes prior to intercourse in order to kill sperm. Foams, jellies, creams, and vaginal suppositories are all forms of spermicidal agents.

Squeeze technique (p. 389) Developed by Masters and Johnson, this procedure is used to prevent premature ejaculation.

Sterilization (p. 418) The use of surgery to prevent pregnancy by altering the person's reproductive organs. Common methods of sterilization for females are salpingectomy, laparoscopy, and hysterectomy. Vasectomy is the most common form of sterilization for males. *See also* Contraception.

Suction, abortion by (p. 422) A method of sucking the contents out of the uterus with a tube inserted into the uterus through the cervix. It can be used when the woman has been pregnant for less than three months.

Tchamuli (p. 34) A New Guinea tribe in which males are socialized to be submissive and females are socialized to be dominant.

Tender years doctrine (p. 483) A legal doctrine which automatically gives custody to the mother during the child's "tender years" in a divorce suit. This doctrine has recently been viewed as a form of sex discrimination.

Term insurance (p. 356) A type of life insurance which provides payments to the beneficiary if the insured dies within a specified period of time. After this time, the protection stops unless the policy is renewed. *See also* Insurance-plus-investment.

Transactional analysis (p. 331) A type of therapy, also known as T.A., which examines how a person may relate to others in ways other than those appropriate for a specific role relationship. For example, a spouse may relate to his or her partner as though he or she were a child or a parent.

Trial marriages (p. 203) Cohabitation between two people who intend to marry. *See also* Cohabitation.

Vaginismus (p. 384) Vaginal constriction that prevents penetration.

Value (p. 84) Standard of desirability from which behavioral choices are made.

Vas deferens (p. 419) Small duct which carries sperm to the penis.

Vasectomy (p. 419) A sterilization procedure for males. The vas deferens is cut and tied so that sperm cannot be carried to the penis.

Waiver of premiums (p. 357) A clause in a life insurance policy which provides that the premiums will be paid by the company if the insured becomes disabled for six months or longer and is unable to earn an income.

Will (p. 538) A legal document which specifies how an individual's belongings are to be distributed to others after his or her death.

Withdrawal (p. 415) Removing the penis from the vagina before ejaculation. A relatively unreliable method of contraception.

CHAPTER 1: 3/From "All Happy Clans Are Alike" by Jane Howard, from *The Atlantic* (May 1978). Copyright © 1978 by The Atlantic Monthly Company, Boston, Mass. Reprinted by permission of The Atlantic Monthly Company and Simon & Schuster. 5/Louis Kaufman Anspacher. Address given, December 30, 1934. Cited in *Familiar Quotations* by John Bartlett, edited by Emily Morison Beck. Boston: Little, Brown and Company, 1968, p. 943. 10/Table 1.1: Leland Axelson, Virginia Polytechnic Institute, Blacksburg, Virginia.

CHAPTER 2: 31/Henrik Ibsen. "A Doll's House" in *Anthology: An Introduction to Literature* edited by Lynn Altenbernd. New York: Macmillan Publishing Co., Inc., 1977, p. 1293. 35, 36/Juanita H. Williams. *Psychology of Women: Behavior in a Biosocial Context.* New York: W. W. Norton & Co., Inc., 1977. 38/Carol Tavris and Carole Offir. *The Longest War: Sex Differences in Perspective.* New York: Harcourt Brace Jovanovich, Inc., 1977, p. 181. 39/Shirley Weitz. *Sex Roles.* New York: Oxford University Press, 1977, p. 18. 41, 46, 48/Carol Whitehurst. *Women in America: The Oppressed Minority.* Santa Monica: Goodyear Publishing Company, 1977. 45/"The Boy Wolf Story" by Jack Wright. Unpublished paper, 1978. Reprinted by permission of the author. 45/From "Why I Want a Wife" by Judy Syfers, from *The First Ms. Reader* by the Editors of Ms. Magazine. Copyright © 1973 by Judy Syfers. Reprinted by permission of Warner Books, Inc. 50/Summary of personal communication, 1977. Reprinted by permission of Joan Huber. 50, 51/Tables 2.2 and 2.3: Reprinted from *Psychology Today* magazine. Copyright © 1976 Ziff-Davis Publishing Company.

CHAPTER 3: 58/Franklin P. Jones. Cited in *Peter's Quotations* by Laurence J. Peter. New York: William Morrow & Company, Inc., 1977, p. 308. 58/H. S. Sullivan. Cited in *Marriage: Who? When? Why?* by David Knox. Englewood Cliffs, N.J.: Prentice-Hall, Inc., 1975, p. 110. 58/Erich Fromm. *The Art of Loving.* New York: Harper & Row Publishers, 1956, p. 20–21. 58/F. A. Magoun. Cited in *Marriage: Who? When? Why?* by David Knox. Englewood Cliffs, N.J.: Prentice-Hall, Inc., 1975, p. 110. 58/E. L. Koos. Cited in *Marriage: Who? When? Why?* by David Knox. Englewood Cliffs, N.J.: Prentice-Hall, Inc., 1975, p. 110. 58–59/Morton M. Hunt. *The Natural History of Love.* New York: Alfred A. Knopf, 1959. 65/Figure 3.1: Reiss, Ira L., "Toward a Sociology of the Heterosexual Love Relationship," *Marriage and Family Living,* May 1960, Figure 1, p. 143. Copyrighted 1960 by the National Council on Family Relations. Reprinted by permission. 67/Figure 3.2: "An Alternative Model of the Wheel Theory" by Dolores M. Borland, Ph.D., Center for Studies in Aging, North Texas State University, Denton, Texas 76203. From *The Family Coordinator,* July 1975, Figure 2, p. 290. Copyrighted 1975 by the National Council on Family Relations. Reprinted by permission. 70–71/Table 3.2: Knox, David, "Discussion Guide to Cover a Love Attitude Inventory," Family Life Publications, Inc., © 1971. 73, 74, 75, 76, 77/From "Male/Female Similarities and Differences in Conceptualizing Love" by Terry S. Hatkoff and Thomas E. Lasswell. Paper presented at the Annual Meeting of the National Council on Family Relations, October 1976. Reprinted by permission of Terry S. Hatkoff. 73, 74, 75, 76/From "The Styles of Loving" by John A. Lee, from *Psychology Today* (October 1974). Reprinted from *Psychology Today* magazine. Copyright © 1974 Ziff-Davis Publishing Company. 74/Robert Frost. Comments by the Robert Frost cited in *Familiar Quotations* by John Bartlett, edited by Emily Morison Beck. Boston: Little, Brown and Company, 1968, p. 930. 76, 77, 78, 79/Constantina Safilios-Rothschild. *Love, Sex and Sex Roles.* Englewood Cliffs, N.J.: Prentice-Hall, Inc., 1977.

CHAPTER 4: 84/Excerpt from personal communication, 1978. Reprinted by permission of John Maiolo. 84, 87, 94/Ira L. Reiss. "The Effect of Changing Trends, Attitudes, and Values on Premarital Sexual Behavior in the United States." From *Sexuality Today and Tomorrow,* edited by Sol Gordon and Roger Libby. North Scituate, Mass.: Duxbury Press, 1976, p. 190–191. 85/From "Sexualization and Premarital Sexual Behavior" by Graham Spanier in *The Family Coordinator* (January 1975). Copyrighted 1975 by the National Council on Family Relations. Reprinted by permission of the National Council on Family Relations and the author. 85/Summary of "Sexual Conservatism and the College Student" by Mary Laner, Roy Laner, and C. Eddie Palmer. Paper presented at the National Council on Family Relations, 1977. Reprinted by permission of Mary Laner. 85, 93, 98/Summary of "Summary of a Longitudinal Study of Stanford Undergraduate Sexual Behavior" by Warren B. Miller and Carolyn Bowker. Unpublished paper, 1974. Reprinted by permission of Warren B. Miller. 87/Table 4.1: Simon, William; Berger, Alan; Gagnon, John, "Beyond Anxiety and Fantasy: The Coital Experiences of College Youth," *Journal of Youth and Adolescence,* Vol. 1, No. 3, p. 208, © 1972 Plenum Publishing Corporation. 88/Table 4.2: Collins, John K.; Kennedy, Judith; Francis, Ronald, "Insights Into a Dating Partner's Expectations of How Behavior Should Ensue During the Courtship Process," *Journal of Marriage and the Family,* May 1976, Table 1, p. 375. Copyright 1976 by the National Council on Family Relations. Reprinted by permission. 91/Woody Allen. Cited in *Peter's Quotations* by Laurence J. Peter. New York: William Morrow & Company, Inc., 1977, p. 440. 92, 96/John Gagnon and Bruce Henderson. *Human Sexuality: An Age of Ambiguity.* Boston: Little, Brown & Co., 1975, p. 45. 94/Lester A. Kirkendall and Roger W. Libby. "Interpersonal Relationships: Crux of the Sexual Revolution" in *Sexuality Today and Tomorrow* edited by Sol Gordon and Roger Libby. North Scituate, Mass.: Duxbury Press, 1966, pp. 290–291. 100/From *Understanding Human Sexual Inadequacy* by Fred Belliveau and Lin Richter. Copyright © 1970 by Fred Belliveau and Lin Richter. Reprinted by permission of Little, Brown and Company. 106/Summary of "The Sexual and Contraceptive Behavior of Never-Married College Students: Some Preliminary Remarks" by Judith J. Stephenson, David J. Kallen, Carol A. Darling, Raja S. Tanas, and Jo Dossey. Paper presented at National Council on Family Relations, San Diego, 1977. Reprinted by permission of Judith J. Stephenson. 106/Excerpt from "Sexual Behavior in the 1970s" by Morton Hunt. Copyright © 1973 by Morton Hunt. Originally appeared in *Playboy Magazine.* Reprinted by permission of Robert Lescher Literary Agency. 107/Summary of "Sexuality and Sex Roles" by Robert R. Bell. Paper presented at the Conference to Develop Teaching Materials on Family and Sex Roles, November 1975. Reprinted by permission of the author. 107/Constantina Safilios-Rothschild. *Love, Sex, and Sex Roles.* Englewood Cliffs, N.J.: Prentice-Hall, Inc., 1977.

CHAPTER 5: 113/Groucho Marx. Cited in *Peter's Quotations* by Laurence J. Peter. New York: William Morrow & Company, Inc., 1977, p. 440. 115/Summary of personal communication, 1971. Reprinted by permission of Roy Hedges. 116–17/From *Human Sexualities* by John Gagnon. Copyright © 1977 by Scott, Foresman and Company. 118, 121/Ira L. Reiss. *Family Systems in America.* Hinsdale, Ill.: Dryden Press, 1976. 118, 124, 125, 127/Morton Hunt. *Sexual Behavior in the 1970s.* New York: Dell Publishing Co., 1974. 122/From "Sexualization and Premarital Sexual Behavior" by Graham Spanier in *The Family Coordinator* (January 1975). Copyrighted 1975 by the National Council on Family Relations. Reprinted by permission of the National Council on Family Relations and the author. 123/Table

5.1: Curran, James B.; Neff, Steven; Lippold, Steven, "Correlates of Sexual Experience Among College Students," *Journal of Sex Research,* Vol. 9, No. 2, May 1973, p. 127. Copyright © 1973 by The Society for the Scientific Study of Sex, Inc. 127/Summary of "Female Masturbation in Sexual Development and Clinical Application" by Ruth Clifford. Unpublished doctoral dissertation, 1973. Used by permission of the author. 127/From "Sex Role Typing and Feminine Sexuality" by Mary L. Walshok. Paper presented at the American Sociological Association, 1973. Reprinted by permission of the author.

CHAPTER 6: 145/Richard Crashaw. "On Marriage." Cited in *Familiar Quotations* by John Bartlett, edited by Emily Morison Beck. Boston: Little, Brown and Company, 1968, p. 354. 148, 149/Peter J. Stein. *Single.* Englewood Cliffs, N.J.: Prentice-Hall, Inc., 1976, pp. 2–3. 150/Table 6.2: *Youth 1976,* Institute of Life Insurance, 1976, p. 49. 151/From "Creative Singlehood as a Sexual Lifestyle" by Roger W. Libby from *Marriage and Alternatives: Exploring Intimate Relationships* edited by R. W. Libby and R. N. Whitehurst. Copyright © 1977 Scott, Foresman and Company. 152/Table 6.3: Peter J. Stein, *Single,* © 1976, p. 65. Adapted by permission of Prentice-Hall, Inc., Englewood Cliffs, N.J. 155/Alvin Toffler. *Future Shock.* New York: Random House, Inc., 1970. 164/Margaret Mead. Cited in *Peter's Quotations* by Laurence J. Peter. New York: William Morrow & Company, Inc., 1977, p. 195. 166/From "Two Communal Houses and Why (I Think) They Failed" by Matthew L. Israel, from *Journal of Behavior Technology,* 1 (Summer 1971). Copyright © 1971 by the Behavior Research Institute, Inc. Reprinted by permission of the author.

CHAPTER 7: 173/Quote by Rose Kennedy from *Newsweek* magazine (January 1973). Copyright © 1973 by Newsweek, Inc. All Rights Reserved. Reprinted by permission. 177/Table 7.1: Melton, Willie; Thomas, Darwin, "Instrumental and Expressive Values in Mate Selection of Black and White College Students," *Journal of Marriage and the Family,* August 1976, Table 5, p. 516. Copyrighted 1976 by the National Council on Family Relations. Reprinted by permission. 189/Table 7.2: From *Men, Women, and Change: A Sociology of Marriage and Family* by Scanzoni and Scanzoni. Copyright © 1975 by McGraw-Hill, Inc. Used with permission of McGraw-Hill Book Company.

CHAPTER 8: 202/Excerpt from "Living Together" from *Newsweek* (August 1977). Copyright © 1977 by Newsweek, Inc. All Rights Reserved. Reprinted by permission. 202, 211, 215/From "Heterosexual Cohabitation Among Unmarried College Students" by Eleanor Macklin, from *The Family Coordinator* 4 (October 1972). Copyright © 1972 by The National Council of Family Relations. Reprinted by permission of The National Council of Family Relations. 203, 204, 207/From "Review of Research on Non-Marital Cohabitation in the United States" by Eleanor Macklin. Unpublished paper, 1975. Reprinted by permission of the author. 204/Excerpt from unpublished study in preparation for Master's Thesis in Individual and Family Studies by Brooke McCauley, 1975 (University of Delaware). Reprinted by permission of the author. 205/Table 8.1: Libby, Roger W.; Whitehurst, Robert N., *Marriage and Alternatives,* Copyright © 1977, Scott, Foresman and Company. 206/Summary of "University Student Cohabitation: A Regional Comparison of Selected Attitudes and Behavior" by Donald W. Bower and Victor A. Christopherson. Unpublished manuscript, 1975. Reprinted by permission of Donald W. Bower. 206/From "The Birth Control Revolution: Consequences for College Student Life-Styles" by James M. Makepeace. Unpublished dissertation, Washington State University, 1975. Reprinted by permission of the author. 208/Summary of "Correlates of Willingness Among College

Students to Participate in Prolonged Cohabitation" by Leslie Strong and Gilbert Nass. Unpublished paper, 1976. Reprinted by permission of Leslie Strong. 208/From "Deviance, Growth Motivation, and Attraction to Marital Alternatives" by Joan B. Mosher. Unpublished dissertation, University of Connecticut, 1975. Reprinted by permission of the author. 208, 210, 211, 212, 214–15, 218, 219, 225/Summary of "A Description and Analysis of a Cohabiting Sample in America" by Donald W. Bower. Unpublished master's thesis, University of Arizona, 1975. Reprinted by permission of the author. 208, 213, 214, 218/From "Unmarried Cohabitation on the University Campus" by Eleanor Macklin. Unpublished paper, 1974. Reprinted by permission of the author. 209, 210/From "Cohabitation Research Newsletter," Issue #4 (June 1974) by Eleanor Macklin. Reprinted by permission of the author. 209, 217/From "Cohabitation Research Newsletter," Issue #5 (April 1976) by Eleanor Macklin. Reprinted by permission of the author. 210, 218/Summary of "Cohabitation: A Preliminary Analysis" by Steven D. Keiser. Unpublished manuscript, 1975. Reprinted by permission of the author. 212/Summary of "Commitment in Married and Unmarried Cohabitation" by Robert A. Lewis et al. Paper presented at the American Sociological Association, 1975. Reprinted by permission of Robert A. Lewis. 213/Summary of "Nonmarital Cohabitation and Marriage: Questionnaire Responses of College Women and Their Mothers" by Dayle Steiner Sillerud. Unpublished Master's Thesis, 1975. Reprinted by permission of the author. 213/Summary of "Comparison of Parent and Student Attitudes Toward Non-Marital Cohabitation" by Eleanor Macklin. Unpublished paper, 1974. Reprinted by permission of the author. 215/Summary of "A Comparison of Marriage and Heterosexual Cohabitation with Respect to the Variables of Interpersonal Knowledge, Affective Support, and Satisfaction" by Jack K. Martin et al. Unpublished paper, 1975. Reprinted by permission of Jack K. Martin. 215, 216/Excerpt from "Cognitive and Behavioral Patterns in Cohabitive and Marital Dyads" by Collier Cole and John Vincent. Unpublished manuscript, 1975. Reprinted by permission of Collier Cole. 217/ Summary of unpublished study comparing persons who cohabited with present spouse before marriage with persons who did not by David E. Olday, 1976. Reprinted by permission of the author. 217/Excerpts from "Trial Marriage Follow-Up" by Miriam E. Berger. Reprinted by permission. Xerox copies of the unpublished manuscript are available from the author, at a cost of $5.00. 217/Excerpt from "A Comparison of Married Couples: Premarital Cohabitants With Non-premarital Cohabitants" by Nancy Moore Clatworthy and Linda Scheid. Unpublished paper, 1976. Reprinted by permission of Nancy Moore Clatworthy. 219/Table 8.2: Summary of "A Description and Analysis of a Cohabiting Sample in America" by Donald W. Bower. Unpublished master's thesis, University of Arizona, 1975. Reprinted by permission of the author. 219–20/ Summary of "Cohabitation: Does It Make for a Better Marriage" by Carl A. Ridley, Jan J. Peterman, A. W. Avery, from *The Family Coordinator* 27 (April 1978). Reprinted by permission of The National Council on Family Relations. 221–22/Table 8.3: Ridley, Carl A.; Peterman, Dan J.; Avery, Arthur, "Cohabitation: Does It Make For a Better Marriage?" from *The Family Coordinator*, April 1978, Table 1, pp. 135–36. Copyrighted 1978 by the National Council on Family Relations. Reprinted by permission.

CHAPTER 9: 229/Benjamin Franklin. "Poor Richard's Almanac." Cited in *Familiar Quotations* by John Bartlett, edited by Emily Morison Beck. Boston: Little, Brown and Company, 1968, p. 422. 231–32/Table 9.1: Table on United States Marriage Laws from *CBS News Almanac, 1978*. © 1977 Hammond Almanac, Inc. 237/Table 9.2: Adams, Bert N.; Cromwell,

Ronald E., "Morning and Night People in the Family: A Preliminary Statement," *The Family Coordinator,* January 1978, Table 1, p. 8. Copyrighted 1978 by the National Council on Family Relations. Reprinted by permission. 238/Summary of "The Influence of Family Life-Cycle Categories, Marital Power Spousal Agreement, and Communication Styles Upon Marital Satisfaction the First Six Years of Marriage" by Ramon Correales. Unpublished doctoral dissertation, 1974. Reprinted by permission of the author. 239/From "Robert A. Sammons' First Law of Nature" by Robert A. Sammons. Unpublished manuscript, 1978. Reprinted by permission of the author. 240, 248/Haun, David L. and Stinnet, Nick. *Family Perspective,* Vol. 9, No. 1, Provo, Utah: Brigham Young University Press, 1974. Reprinted by permission. 242/Summary of "The Effects of Income and Age at Marriage on Marital Stability" by Stephen Bahr. Paper presented at American Sociological Association, Chicago, 1977. Reprinted by permission of the author. 243–44, 245/Based on "Breakups Before Marriage: The End of 103 Affairs," by Charles T. Hill, Zick Rubin, and Letitia Anne Peplau, in *Divorce and Separation in America,* edited by George Levinger and Oliver C. Moles, to be published by Basic Books, Inc., Publishers, New York, in 1979. This article first appeared in the *Journal of Social Issues,* Volume 32, No. 1, 1976. Reprinted by permission of Charles T. Hill and Basic Books, Inc., Publishers. 250/Excerpt from "Marriage Contracts: Social and Legal Consequences" by Marvin B. Sussman. Paper presented at the International Workshop on Changing Sex Roles in Family and Society, June 1975. Reprinted by permission of Marvin B. Sussman. 250–51/Excerpt from "The Personal Contract— New Form of Marriage Bond" by Marvin B. Sussman, Betty Cogswell, and Hugh Ross. Unpublished manuscript, 1973. Reprinted by permission of Marvin B. Sussman. 252–54/ "Antenuptial Agreement" by Marijean Suelzle and William K. O'Connell. Marriage contract, 1972. Reprinted by permission of Marijean Suelzle.

CHAPTER 10: 261/Bertrand Russell. Cited in *Peter's Quotations* by Laurence J. Peter. New York: William Morrow & Company, Inc., 1977, p. 321. 261/George Bernard Shaw. "Getting Married." Cited in *Familiar Quotations* by John Bartlett, edited by Emily Morison Beck. Boston: Little, Brown and Company, 1968, p. 837. 263–64/Marriage Ceremony by Hal and Sherry Gillespie, 1977. Reprinted by permission of Hal G. Gillespie and Cheryl LaPointe Gillespie. 269–70/Table 10.1: Dr. Lonny Myers, Midwest Population Center, Chicago, Il. 270, 271–72/From *Open Marriage: A New Lifestyle for Couples* by Nena O'Neill and George O'Neill. Copyright © 1972 by Nena O'Neill and George O'Neill. Reprinted by permission of the publisher, M. Evans and Company, Inc., New York, N.Y. 10017 and Mary Yost Associates, Inc. 272/Nena O'Neill. "Sexuality Fidelity is Back." *Chicago Tribune,* 1978. 275/Summary of "In-law Relations: A Research Note" by Deborah J. Johnson. Unpublished paper presented at the National Council on Family Relations, San Diego, 1977. Reprinted by permission of the author. 276/ Summary of "Effects on the Marriage When Wives Return to School" by Gail Berkove. Paper presented at National Council on Family Relations meeting, 1976. Reprinted by permission of the author. 280, 281, 282, 287/Summary and excerpts of "Military Service and Marriage" by Sara Hatch. Unpublished paper, 1976. Reprinted by permission of the author.

CHAPTER 11: 292/George Bernard Shaw. Cited in *The Intimate Environment: Exploring Marriage and the Family* by Arlene Skolnick. Boston: Little, Brown and Company, 1973, p. 151. 293/Summary of "Social and Economic Determinants of Employment of Wives Over the Family Life Cycle" by Linda J. Waite, 1977. Reprinted by permission of the author. 295/From

Green Grows Ivy by Ivy Baker Priest. Copyright © 1958 by McGraw-Hill Book Company. Used with permission of McGraw-Hill Book Company. 295, 298, 299/From "Problems of Professional Couples: A Content Analysis" by Norma Heckman, Rebecca Bryson, and Jeff Bryson from *Journal of Marriage and the Family* (May 1977). Reprinted by permission of National Council on Family Relations and the authors. 296/ John P. Robinson. *How Americans Use Time: A Social Psychological Analysis of Everyday Behavior.* New York: Praeger Publishers, Inc., 1976, pp. 150, 153. 296–97, 299, 300, 302/ Summary of "The Better Half? The Male in the Dual Profession Family" by T. Neal Garland in *Toward a Sociology of Women* by Constantina Safilios-Rothschild, Copyright © 1972 by Xerox Corporation. Reprinted by permission of John Wiley & Sons, Inc. 298, 302–3, 304–5/Excerpts from *The Two Career Family* by Lynda L. Holstrom. Copyright © 1973 by General Learning Press. Reprinted by permission of Schenkman Publishing Company. 299/Table 11.1: *Women and Achievement*, Martha Mednick, Sandra Tangri, and Lois Hoffman, eds., Hemisphere Publishing Corp., a Halsted Press Book, John Wiley & Sons, 1975, p. 399. Copyright 1975 by Hemisphere Publishing Corporation. 301/Table 11.2: From *General Mills Report, 1976–77.* © 1977 General Mills, Inc.

CHAPTER 12: 311/Raymond Hull. Cited in *Peter's Quotations* by Laurence J. Peter. New York: William Morrow & Company, Inc., 1977, p. 321. 312/From personal communication, 1977. Reprinted by permission of Jack Turner. 313/ Summary of "Effect of Parenthood at Three Points in Marriage" by Harold and Margaret Feldman. Unpublished manuscript, 1977. Reprinted by permission of Harold Feldman. 316–17/ Spanier, Graham B., "Measuring Dyadic Adjustment: New Scales for Assessing the Quality of Marriage and Similar Dyads," *Journal of Marriage and the Family,* February 1976, Table 4, p. 23; Scale pp. 27–28. Copyrighted 1976 by the National Council on Family Relations. Reprinted by permission. 318/Summary of "Marital Adjustment and Conservatism: A Re-examination" by William F. Riedell. Unpublished master's thesis, 1976. Reprinted by permission of the author. 319/Figure 12.1: Duvall, Evelyn M., *Marriage and Family Development.* Copyright © 1977, J. B. Lippincott Company. 321/Carl Jung. "Contributions to Analytical Psychology." Cited in *Familiar Quotations* by John Bartlett, edited by Emily Morison Beck. Boston: Little, Brown and Company, 1968, p. 935. 322/Table 12.1: Knox, David, *Dr. Knox's Marital Exercise Book.* Copyright © 1975 by David Knox. 323/Knox, David, "Common Issues of Marital Conflict," *Marriage Happiness: A Behavioral Approach to Counseling.* Copyright © 1971 by Research Press. 324/Table 12.2: Safilios-Rothschild, Constantina, "A Macro- and Micro-Examination of Family Power and Love: An Exchange Model," *Journal of Marriage and the Family,* May 1976, Diagram 1, p. 356. Copyrighted 1976 by the National Council on Family Relations. Reprinted by permission. 325/From *We Can Have Better Marriages If We Really Want Them* by David and Vera Mace. Copyright © 1974 by Abingdon Press. Reprinted by permission of Abingdon Press. 328/Robert Frost. Comments by Robert Frost cited in *Familiar Quotations* by John Bartlett, edited by Emily Morison Beck. Boston: Little, Brown and Company, 1968, p. 930. 333/Table 12.3: Adams, Sallie; Orgel, Michael, *Through the Mental Health Maze.* Copyright © 1975 Public Citizen's Health Research Group.

CHAPTER 13: 343/Somerset Maugham. Cited in *The Individual, Marriage, and the Family,* 3rd edition by Lloyd Saxton. Belmont, Calif.: Wadsworth Publishing Company, Inc., 1977, p. 474. 347, 355/Figure 13.1 and Table 13.4: From *Personal Money Management* by Thomas E. Bailard, David L. Biehl, and

Ronald W. Kaiser © 1969, 1973, Science Research Associates, Inc. Reproduced by permission of the publisher. 348/Charles de Talleyrand. Cited in *Peter's Quotations* by Laurence J. Peter. New York: William Morrow & Company, Inc., 1977, p. 195. 353/Joey Adams. Cited in *Peter's Quotations* by Laurence J. Peter. New York: William Morrow & Company, Inc., 1977, p. 321. 359/Table 13.5: Trooboff, Benjamin M.; Boyd, Fannie Lee, *Personal Finance For Consumers.* Copyright 1976 Silver Burdett Company. 361–63 Excerpts from *Sylvia Porter's Money Book.* Copyright © 1975 by Sylvia Porter. Used by permission of Doubleday & Company, Inc. and Brandt & Brandt. 369/George Bernard Shaw. Cited in *Familiar Quotations* by John Bartlett, edited by Emily Morison Beck. Boston: Little, Brown and Company, 1968, p. 837.

CHAPTER 14: 374/Shere Hite. *Sexual Honesty: By Women For Women.* New York: Warner Books, Inc., 1974, p. 273. 376, 377/Figures 14.1 and 14.2: *Human Sexual Response* by W. H. Masters and Virginia E. Johnson, Co-directors, Reproductive Biology Research Foundation, St. Louis, Missouri. Published by Little, Brown & Co., 1966. 379/From *Sexual Myths and Fallacies* by J. L. McCary. Copyright © 1971 by J. L. and L. T. McCary. Published by Van Nostrand Reinhold Company. Reprinted by permission of the author. 382/From Ann Landers column in *News and Observer*, Raleigh, North Carolina (June 1977). Copyright © 1977 by the Field Newspaper Syndicate. Reprinted by permission of Ann Landers. 384–85, 386/Excerpt from "The Classification of the Female Sexual Dysfunctions" by Helen S. Kaplan, from *Journal of Sex and Marital Therapy,* Vol. 1, #2, Winter 1974. Copyright © 1974 by Human Sciences Press. Reprinted by permission of Human Sciences Press, 72 Fifth Ave., New York, New York 10011 and the author. 386–87, 388/From *Understanding Human Sexual Inadequacy* by Fred Belliveau and Lin Richter. Copyright © 1970 by Fred Belliveau and Lin Richter. Reprinted by permission of Little, Brown and Company. 386–91/Excerpts from *Human Sexual Inadequacy* by William H. Masters and Virginia E. Johnson. © 1970 by William H. Masters and Virginia E. Johnson. Reprinted by permission of the authors and Little, Brown and Company. 387/Excerpt from "Group Treatment of Preorgasmic Women" by Lonnie Garfield Barbach, from *Journal of Sex and Marital Therapy,* Vol. 1, #2, Winter 1974. Copyright © 1974 by Human Sciences Press. Reprinted by permission of Human Sciences Press, 72 Fifth Ave., New York, New York 10011 and the author. This material also appeared in *For Yourself: The Fulfillment of Female Sexuality* by Lonnie Garfield Barbach. Copyright © 1976 by Doubleday & Company, Inc.

CHAPTER 15: 397/From Planned Parenthood poster. Reprinted by permission of Planned Parenthood Federation of America. 401–2/Excerpt and summary from pamphlet and Annual Report (1978) of the National Organization for Non-Parents. Reprinted by permission of the National Organization for Non-Parents, 3 North Liberty Street, Baltimore, Maryland 21201. 403/Table 15.1: *Youth 1974,* Institute of Life Insurance, 1975, p. 61. 404/Table 15.2: Knox, David; Hawke, Sharryl, *One Child By Choice* © 1977 by Prentice-Hall, Inc., pp. 188–89, 198–99. 406/From Ann Landers column in *News and Observer,* Raleigh, North Carolina (January 1977). Copyright © 1977 by the Field Newspaper Syndicate. Reprinted by permission of Ann Landers. 411/Summary and excerpt of "Family Growth and Socioeconomic Status Among Poor Blacks" by R. J. Reimer and John Maiolo. Unpublished manuscript, 1977. Reprinted by permission of John Maiolo. 411–18/From "Trends in Contraceptive Practice: 1965–1975" by Charles F. Westoff. Copyright © 1976 by Planned Parenthood Federation of America, Inc. Reprinted with permission from *Family Planning*

Perspectives, Volume 8, Number 1, 1976. 412/Table 15.3: Hatcher, R. A.; Stewart, G. K. et al. Contraceptive Technology 1976–77, Emory University. 417/Arthur Hoppe. Cited in *Peter's Quotations* by Laurence J. Peter. New York: William Morrow & Company, Inc., 1977, p. 72. 417/Table 15.4: Excerpts from *Sylvia Porter's Money Book.* Copyright © 1975 by Sylvia Porter. Reprinted by permission of Doubleday & Company, Inc.

CHAPTER 16: 431/Peter De Vries. Cited in *Peter's Quotations* by Laurence J. Peter. New York: William Morrow & Company, Inc., 1977, p. 195. 433/Leo J. Burke. Cited in *Peter's Quotations* by Laurence J. Peter. New York: William Morrow & Company, Inc., 1977, p. 102. 440/From "The Making of a Confused Middle-Class Husband" by S. M. Miller, from *Social Policy* (July/August 1971). Copyright 1971 by Social Policy Corporation. Reprinted by permission of the publisher. 440–41/ Excerpt from interview with Shirley Radl as it appeared in the *Daily Camera,* Boulder, Colorado, November 8, 1973. Copyright © 1973 by The Associated Press. Reprinted by permission of The Associated Press. 442–43/From "Life Patterns, Personality Style, and Self-Esteem in Gifted Family-Oriented and Career-Committed Women" by Judith Birnbaum. Doctoral Dissertation, 1975. Reprinted by permission of the author. 446/ Excerpt from *Confessions of a Gynecologist* by Anonymous, M.D. Copyright © 1972 by Doubleday & Company, Inc. Used by permission of Doubleday & Company, Inc. and Knox Burger Associates, Ltd. 450–51/Summary of "Effect of Parenthood at Three Points in Marriage" by Harold and Margaret Feldman. Unpublished manuscript, 1977. Reprinted by permission of Harold Feldman. 451/Summary of unpublished, untitled study by Paul Rosenblatt, Sandra Titus, and Michael Cunningham, 1976. Reprinted by permission of Paul Rosenblatt. 451–52/ From "The Transition to Parenthood and Beyond" by Carolyn S. Russell. Paper presented at National Council on Family Relations, 1975. Reprinted by permission of the author.

CHAPTER 17: 458/John Wilmot, Earl of Rochester. Cited in *Peter's Quotations* by Laurence J. Peter. New York: William Morrow & Company, Inc., 1977, p. 102. 460, 475, 478, 479/ Tables 17.1, 17.2, 17.3, Figure 17.1: *General Mills Report, 1976–77.* © 1977 General Mills, Inc. 461/Franklin P. Jones. Cited in *Peter's Quotations* by Laurence J. Peter. New York: William Morrow & Company, Inc., 1977, p. 102. 466–67, 467–68, 471, 473, 474/D. Eugene Mead. *Six Approaches to Child Rearing.* Provo, Utah: Brigham Young University Press, 1976. 467/Summary of personal communication, 1978. Reprinted by permission of Jannis Shea. 483/Summary of "The Tender Years Doctrine" by Ken Lewis. Copyright © 1978 by Ken Lewis published by Glossary on Custody, P.O. Box 9356, Norfolk, Virginia 23505. Reprinted by permission of the publishers and the author.

CHAPTER 18: 491/Benjamin Franklin. Cited in *Scenes From Life* by Judy Blankenship. Boston: Little, Brown and Company, 1976, p. 443. 491/Mark Twain. Cited in *Peter's Quotations* by Laurence J. Peter. New York: William Morrow & Company, Inc., 1977, p. 356. 493, 494, 511/"Forty-year-old Jitters in Married Urban Women," by Jules Henry, in *The Challenge to Women,* edited by Seymour M. Farber and Roger H. L. Wilson, © 1966 by Basic Books, Inc., Publishers, New York. 494/ Figure 18.1: *Statistical Bulletin* of Metropolitan Life Insurance Company, New York, September 1975, p. 2. 495/Summary of "Marriage in the Later Years: Cohort and Parental Effects" by Harold and Margaret Feldman. Unpublished manuscript, 1976. Reprinted by permission of Harold Feldman. 498/Bob Hope. Cited in *Peter's Quotations* by Laurence J. Peter. New York: William Morrow & Company, Inc., 1977, p. 354. 500/Table 18.1: From "Factors in Lifestyles of Couples Married Over 50

Years" by Ann E. Roberts and William L. Roberts. Paper presented at National Council on Family Relations, 1975. Reprinted by permission of Ann E. Roberts. 501/Table 18.2: Pfeiffer, Eric; Verwoerdt, Adrian; Davis, Glenn C., *Sexual Behavior in Middle Life.* Copyright 1974 by Duke University Press. 501, 502/Summary and quote from "The Gray Evolution: The Life and Times of the Elderly" by James Keller. Paper given at 17th Annual Family Life Conference, 1977. Reprinted by permission of the author. 502, 503/Excerpts from *Sylvia Porter's Money Book.* Copyright © 1975 by Sylvia Porter. Used by permission of Doubleday & Company, Inc. and Brandt & Brandt. 503, 505–6/Summary of "Factors in Lifestyles of Couples Married Over 50 Years" by Ann E. Roberts and William L. Roberts. Paper presented at National Council on Family Relations, 1975. Reprinted by permission of Ann E. Roberts. 504/Excerpt from personal communication by Donald Stewart, 1977. Reprinted by permission of Mrs. Charlotte Stewart. 506/Table 18.3: Stinnett, Nick; Carter, Linda Mittelset; Montgomery, James E., "Older Persons' Perceptions of Their Marriages," from *Journal of Marriage and the Family,* November 1972, Table 1, p. 667. Copyrighted 1972 by the National Council on Family Relations. Reprinted by permission. 508–9/From "Grandmotherhood: A Study of Role Conceptions" by Joan F. Robertson from *Journal of Marriage and the Family* (February 1977). Reprinted by permission of National Council on Family Relations.

CHAPTER 19: 516/Michael Novak. "The Family Out of Favor." *Harper's* Magazine, 1976. 519/From *The Social Context of Marriage,* 3rd Edition, by Richard J. Udry. Copyright © 1974 by J. B. Lippincott Company. Reprinted by permission. 522/William Congreve. Cited in *Familiar Quotations* by John Bartlett, edited by Emily Morison Beck. Boston: Little, Brown and Company, 1968, p. 391. 523/From Ann Landers column in *News and Observer,* Raleigh, North Carolina (July 1975). Copyright © 1975 by the Field Newspaper Syndicate. Reprinted by permission of Ann Landers. 525/Summary of "Fulfillment of Marital Expectations Among Married and Divorced Persons: A Test of Exchange Theory" by John R. Christiansen and Peggy H. Robinson. Paper presented at National Council on Family Relations, 1975. Reprinted by permission of John R. Christiansen. 529/Summary of "The Normative Integration of the Former Spouse Relationship" by Ann Goetting. Paper presented at the American Sociological Association, 1978. Reprinted by permission of the author. 529/Summary of "Sex Differences in Voluntary Postmarital Dissolution Adjustment" by Helen J. Raschke. Paper presented at the American Sociological Association, 1976. Reprinted by permission of the author. 535/Table 19.3: Ruch, Libby O., "A Multi-dimensional Analysis of the Concept of Life Change," *Journal of Health and Social Behavior,* Vol. 18, March 1977, p. 75. Copyright 1977, American Sociological Association. 536/Lynn Caine. *Widow.* New York: William Morrow and Company, Inc., 1974, p. 79. 541, 542/Excerpts and summary of "Remarriage Between Divorced People With Children from Previous Marriages: A Proposal for Preparation for Remarriage" by Lillian Messinger, from *Journal of Marriage and Family Counseling* (April 1976). Copyright © 1976 by The American Association of Marriage and Family Counselors. Reprinted by permission of the publishers and the author. 543/Summary of "Remarriage in Old Age" by Barbara Vinick, from *The Family Coordinator* (October 1978). Copyright 1978 by the National Council on Family Relations. Reprinted by permission.

APPENDIX: 554–55/From "New Directions in Venereal Disease Education" by William L. Yarber, from *The Family Coordinator* (April 1978). Copyright © 1978 by The National Council of Family Relations. Reprinted by permission of The National Council of Family Relations.

ILLUSTRATION CREDITS

Cover: Gretchen Garner—Sculpture by Joseph J. O'Connell

1 Gretchen Garner—Sculpture by Egon Weiner
6 Library of Congress
8 David Strickler—Strix Pix
12 Photo, courtesy of *The Flowering of American Folk Art 1776–1876,* and the Whitney Museum of American Art and Viking Press (formerly in the collection of Mrs. Clarence C. Wells).
18 Burk Uzzle—Magnum
19 Bettmann
33 Betty Lane—Photo Researchers
36 Catherine Ursillo
41 Andy Mercado—Jeroboam
42 J. Berndt—Stock, Boston
48 © 1977 Johnny Hart, Field Newspaper Syndicate
52 © 1974 Jules Feiffer
60 By Chon Day
63 Jim Ritscher—Stock, Boston
66 Thomas England
69 Charles Gatewood
77 Steve Hansen—Stock, Boston
86 Robert Pacheco—Stockmarket
92 Charles Gatewood
97 Joan Lifton—Woodfin Camp
103 Shames—Black Star
114 Scott, Foresman
121 Charles Gatewood
130 IPA-Jeroboam
132 Pellegrino—Black Star
135 Drawing by B. Tobey; © The New Yorker Magazine, Inc.
143 Scott, Foresman
148 Dennis Brack—Black Star
154 Scott, Foresman
159 Lisa Ebright
165 Bob Fitch—Black Star
174 Culver
181 Esais Baitel—Rapho/Photo Researchers
187 Bill Owens
191 By Farris
195 Siteman—Stock, Boston
203 Drawing by William Hamilton; © 1971 The New Yorker Magazine, Inc.
207 Susan Meiselas—Magnum
211 Jean Claude Lejeune
214 Ellis Herwig—Stock, Boston
230 Drawing by Ed Fisher; © 1973 The New Yorker Magazine, Inc.
235 Eric Kroll—Taurus
241 James Edward Vaughan—Black Star
246 Jean Claude Lejeune
250 Bob Fitch—Black Star
259 Gretchen Garner—Sculpture by Armin Scheler
264 By William Hamilton
267 By courtesy of Pocono Gardens Lodge

277 Constantine Manos—Magnum
280 Bob Natkin
285 George Gardner
293 Peter Southwick—Stock, Boston
297 Jean Claude Lejeune
303 Charles Gatewood
304 Ken Heyman
313 © Punch—Rothco
326 Hanna W. Schreiber—Rapho/Photo Researchers
327 Ken Heyman
335 By Mel Scott—Rothco
336 Ellis Herwig—Stock, Boston
344 By courtesy of International Correspondence School
351 Doug Wilson—Black Star
358 By Booth
362 By courtesy of G.M.
363 Doug Wilson—Black Star
369 By Koren
371 Bill Aaron—E.P.A.
375 Karen Preuss—Jeroboam
382 Suzanne Szasz—Rapho/Photo Researchers
390 Christopher Johnson—Stock, Boston
395 Gretchen Garner—Sculpture by Joseph O'Connell
400 First published in National Lampoon Magazine. Reprinted from *National Lampoon Presents Claire Bretécher.* Translated by Valerie Marchant.
402 Richard Kalvar—Magnum
407 Roland Freeman—Magnum
410 Scott, Foresman
416 Ken Heyman
423 Daniel S. Brody—E.P.A.
432 Eric Kroll—Taurus
435 S. Trachtenberg—Rothco
437 Thomas England
444 Richard Stromberg
449 Punch—Rothco
452 Dorka Raynor
462 Paolo Koch/Photo Researchers
463 Dorka Raynor
471 Eric Kroll—Taurus
472 By James Thurber
477 From *Suburbia* by Bill Owens
481 Richard Stromberg
489 Courtesy of The Art Institute of Chicago, from the Edward B. Ayer Fund. Sculpture by Alberto Giacometti.
495 Jay Lurie—Tom Stack & Assoc.
499 Thomas Hopker—Woodfin Camp
505 Eric Kroll—Taurus
507 Thomas England
509 Martha Leonard
521 Enrico Natali—Rapho/Photo Researchers
526 David Powers—Jeroboam
530 Jean Claude Lejeune—Stockmarket
531 Serrano—Rothco
537 Ivan Massar—Black Star
541 Punch—Rothco
551 Drawing by Bernt Forsblad. From *Behold Man,* Little, Brown and Company, Boston.

Name Index

Subject Index